Encyclopedia
of Cultivated Plants

Encyclopedia of Cultivated Plants

FROM ACACIA TO ZINNIA

Volume 1: A–F

Christopher Cumo, Editor

 ABC-CLIO

Santa Barbara, California • Denver, Colorado • Oxford, England

Library of Congress Cataloging-in-Publication Data

Encyclopedia of cultivated plants : from acacia to zinnia / Christopher Cumo, editor.
    pages cm
Includes bibliographical references and index.
    ISBN 978–1–59884–774–1 (hardcopy : alk. paper) — ISBN 978–1–59884–775–8 (e-book)   1. Plants, Cultivated—Encyclopedias. I. Cumo, Christopher.
SB45.E47   2013
635.903—dc23   2012031374

ISBN: 978–1–59884–774–1
EISBN: 978–1–59884–775–8

17 16 15 14 13   1 2 3 4 5

This book is also available on the World Wide Web as an eBook.
Visit www.abc-clio.com for details.

ABC-CLIO, LLC
130 Cremona Drive, P.O. Box 1911
Santa Barbara, California 93116-1911

This book is printed on acid-free paper ∞

Manufactured in the United States of America

Contents

List of Entries

Guide to Related Topics

Alliums

Garlic

Leek

Onion

Beverages

Agave

Barley

Coffee

Grapes

Hops

Tea

Wheat

Carnivorous Plants

Bladderwort

Butterwort

Pitcher Plant

Sundew

Venus's Fly Trap

Dyes

Castor Bean

Indigo

Fiber Crops

Cannabis

Corchorus

Cotton

Flax

Raffia

Flavoring

Vanilla

Flower Buds

Broccoli

Cauliflower

Fruits

Almond

Apple

Apricot

Avocado

Banana

Blackberry

Blueberry

Boysenberry

Cacao

Cantaloupe

Cherry

Coconut

Coffee

Cranberry

Cucumber

Currant

Date Palm

Eggplant

Elderberry

Fig

Gooseberry

Gourd

Grapefruit

Grapes

Guava

Honeydew

Kumquat

Lemon

Lime

Mango

Nectarine

Olive

Orange

Papaya

Peach

Pear

Peppers

Pineapple

Pistachio

Plantain

Plum

Pomegranate

Pumpkin

Quince

Raspberry

Squash

Strawberry

Tomato

Walnut

Watermelon

Fungi

Mushrooms

Grasses and Seeds

Amaranth

Anise

Bamboo

Barley

Buckwheat

Caraway

Coriander

Corn

Flax

Millet

Oats

Quinoa

Rice

Rye

Sesame

Sorghum

Sugarcane

Sunflower

Teff

Timothy

Triticale

Wheat

Mangrove

Maple

Mulberry

Nectarine

Oak

Orange

Peach

Pear

Pine

Plum

Pomegranate

Quince

Rattan

Redwood

Rubber

Rue

Sage

Sagebrush

Sea Buckthorn

Shea Tree

Southernwood

Spruce

Sycamore (American Sycamore)

Teak

Walnut

Willow

Wintergreen

Vegetables

Artichoke

Asparagus

Brussels Sprouts

Cabbage

Caraway

Celery

Collard

Dandelion

Endive

Fennel

Garden Angelica

Good King Henry

Kale

Kohlrabi

Lettuce

Rhubarb

Spinach

Swiss Chard

Watercress

Vines

Squash

Tomato

White Bryony

Preface

The author of Genesis placed the first humans in a garden. The word "garden" evokes images of lush vegetation, as though the writer were telling the reader that from their origins, humans have had an intimate relationship with plants. Indeed, the association between humanity and plants may predate the emergence of anatomically modern humans. By one account *Homo erectus*, one of humankind's forbearers, might have been the first to brew tea. If this conjecture is true, the link between human-like animals and plants might be more than 1 million years old. The *Encyclopedia of Cultivated Plants: From Acacia to Zinnia*, a three-volume reference work, aims to document this long relationship between humans and plants. It also seeks to convey some of the enthusiasm and affection that humans have had for plants. There is seldom a home owner or apartment dweller who does not adorn his or her residence with at least one potted plant. The home owner typically has a lawn of turf grass, an area for ornamentals, several trees, and perhaps a vegetable garden. If one considers the sheer number of plants that the home owner has, he or she may seem to appreciate them more than the family dog or cat. At its core, this encyclopedia seeks to communicate something of the magnitude of humans' dependence on plants. Even as hunter-gatherers, humans relied on plants for sustenance. This dependence only grew with the rise of agriculture. According to one tale, a poor man survived the Great Depression on a diet of only peanuts. Whether true or not, this story underscores the potent role food plants play in human existence. Without them, the human population would crash.

High school, undergraduate, and graduate students should benefit from the entries in this encyclopedia. The interdisciplinary nature of this work should attract students of botany, agronomy, plant pathology, plant breeding, genetics, taxonomy, entomology, chemistry, soil science, history, folklore, religion, anthropology, and geography. Because the study of plants is tied to the migration of humans, the student or professional who reads any of these entries will enrich his or her knowledge of geography and the interconnectedness among different groups of people and the plants that they exchanged. The most celebrated transfer of plants occurred during the Columbian Exchange, after the discovery of the New World in 1492, when people from Africa, Asia, Europe, Australia, and the Americas carried plants between the Old and New Worlds. A classic case of this transfer involved the potato, an American native plant that by the 19th century had become the staple of the Irish tenant and laborer. The late blight of potato disease that occurred between 1845 and 1849 destroyed the crop. The scientists who study late blight of potato customarily capitalize it. One million Irish perished and 1.5 million more, among them the ancestors of President John F. Kennedy, immigrated to North America. Similar plant transfers occurred countless times in innumerable places. The reader of this encyclopedia will appreciate the enormous extent to which plants have shaped history. In this sense, the *Encyclopedia of Cultivated Plants* is more than a work of science. The social sciences and humanities loom large.

Scope

Perhaps the most notable features of the encyclopedia are its globalism, its vast time span, and its interdisciplinary content. Beginning with the first appearance of *Homo erectus* about 1.5 million years ago, this reference work spans more than 1 million years to reach the present. Geographically, the *Encyclopedia of Cultivated Plants: From Acacia to Zinnia* touches upon every locale where humans have cultivated plants. The tropics, subtropics, and temperate zone all receive treatment. There are plenty of scientific treatises on plants. Far fewer are as interdisciplinary as this study.

The 282 entries in this work include crops, ornamentals, and trees harvested for timber. Plants are listed under their common names because it is by these forms that the nonspecialist knows them. One does not speak of "a delicious *Lycopersicon esculentum*" but simply of "a delicious tomato." Wherever possible, this encyclopedia also furnishes the names of the plant family, genus, and species, which not only are widespread in the scientific literature but also permit more precise description. Many entries will discuss cultivars, shorthand for cultivated varieties. Because all the plants in this encyclopedia are cultivated, there is no distinction between a cultivar and a variety. Because of this work's focus on the importance of plants to humans, the major crops—corn, rice, potatoes, soybeans, sugarcane, wheat, and many others—receive extended treatment. The 26 contributors who wrote the entries in this work include professional botanists and plant pathologists, some who hold a terminal degree. Others are historians, folklorists, gardeners, and writers, and many who have made plants their avocation. Each entry concludes with at least two references for further reading or research.

The encyclopedia also includes an introduction to the topic of cultivated plants, providing background and a historical overview of plants and human civilization, including their economic, nutritional, social, cosmetic, and religious uses, and plant scientists may be discussed. The end of the third volume of the *Encyclopedia of Cultivated Plants* provides a selected bibliography of recommended print resources and a list of organizations and their Web sites. Many of these groups, botanical gardens, and agencies provide additional authoritative information about cultivated plants in their online offerings. The encyclopedia concludes with a comprehensive index.

Acknowledgments

A work of this kind requires the talents of many people. I thank the contributors. Their efforts were essential in completing a project of this scope. Without them, this encyclopedia would have been a lonely undertaking. I also wish to thank my acquisitions editor, David Paige, who responded enthusiastically when I proposed this three-volume work. Alexander Mikaberidze deserves thanks for shepherding me through the first one-quarter of the writing process, and Senior Development Editor Anne Thompson deserves thanks for helping me negotiate the last three-quarters of the journey. My daughters, Francesca and Alexandra, deserve special mention. They are adolescents now, and every day brings forth fresh confirmation of their many gifts. No father could be prouder of his children than I am of mine. Lastly, I thank my wife, Gerianne. Although she does not share my interest in plants, she did not protest too loudly the countless hours of research and writing that went into this project.

Please Note

Many of the entries in this book refer to health properties of the plants discussed. The information presented here is not intended to diagnose or suggest treatment, or substitute for consultation with a qualified medical or mental health professional. Information presented here is not intended to endorse or recommend any treatment, medication, product, or service. Especially in the case of diagnosis and treatment of health disorders, this book is intended only to provide information and resources for the reader to access other valid sources of information.

"Without Plants We Would Not Be Here": An Introduction to Cultivated Plants

Because plants have an evolutionary history, their definition has evolved over time. This encyclopedia, concerning cultivated plants, spans only the last 10,000 years and so is concerned with the definition of the modern plant. As used in this text, the word "plant" means a multicellular organism with two parts: root and shoot. The root is the part or parts of a plant underground: roots and underground stems (if it has any). The underground stem may be swollen, as in the case of the potato. The roots too may be swollen, as in the case of the sweet potato. Although both are called potatoes, they are not closely related. The shoot is the part of a plant above ground and includes stem, leaves, buds, and flowers, fruit, and seeds, if it has any of the last three. Along with algae and some types of bacteria, plants photosynthesize, converting sunlight, carbon dioxide, water, and elements from the soil, the most important being nitrogen, into sugar and oxygen. Because plants absorb carbon dioxide and release oxygen, they have over time altered the atmosphere, giving it enough oxygen to support the myriad animals that inhabit Earth. Without plants, we would not be here.

Classification and Nomenclature

All plants are members of the plant kingdom, the kingdom being the largest division of organisms. Below the kingdom in descending order of size are phylum, class, order, family, tribe, genus, and species. Wherever possible, this encyclopedia furnishes the names of the family, genus, and species. All grasses, for example, are members of the Gramineae or Poaceae family. The grass corn is a member of the genus *Zea* and the species *mays*. The scientific name for corn is thus *Zea mays*. The name of the genus and species are italicized. The names of all the taxa above the genus are not italicized. Further, the generic or genus name is capitalized and the specific or species name is all lowercase letters. The 18th-century

Swedish naturalist Carl Linnaeus was the first scientist consistently to use this system of naming plants and animals, the binomial nomenclature. Although scientists admit the existence of common names for plants, they prefer the binomial system because its names are precise. No two plants share the same scientific name. The parlance of ordinary names, however, does not permit this precision. In the United States, for example, corn is *Zea mays*, whereas in Europe corn is a generic term for grain. This encyclopedia uses corn in the American sense to mean only *Zea mays*. In the *Encyclopedia of Cultivated Plants: Acacia to Zinnia*, plants are listed first by their common name, which is the most familiar name for most nonspecialists. The scientific name for plants may include the name of the discoverer of a new plant or the name of someone being honored, such as the plants known as *Rudbeckia* (familiarly known in the United States as black-eyed Susan or coneflower plants). *Rudbeckia* was named by Carl Linneaus in honor of his Uppsala University professor Olof Rudbeck the younger (1660–1740) and his father, Olof Rudbeck the elder (1630–1702), who were botanists.

Scientists divide all plants into nonvascular plants or the bryophytes and vascular plants or tracheophytes. The nonvascular plants are the more primitive and include mosses, liverworts, and hornworts. The vascular plants may be seedless, as are the ferns, whisk ferns, horsetails, and club mosses. The vascular plants that produce seeds are either gymnosperms or angiosperms. The gymnosperms include conifers, cycads, ginkgo, and gnetophytes. The angiosperms or flowering plants are either monocots, germinating a single leaf, or dicots, germinating a stem with two leaves. The monocots include palms, grasses, orchids, and lilies. The dicots include a large number of plants, among them legumes, roots and tubers, vegetables, and fruit trees. The angiosperms include all the crops on which humans depend.

The Origin and Evolution of Plants

Algae arose 1.2 billion years ago, marking a milestone in the history of life because they were capable of manufacturing their own food by photosynthesis. From algae, the first plants evolved between 630 and 500 million years ago. Algae may have given rise to nonvascular plants, which in turn evolved into vascular plants. It is also possible that nonvascular and vascular plants, taking separate pathways, evolved from algae. Scientists favor the first hypothesis. The first plant may have originated from a type of algae that had filaments and lived in fresh water. These ponds may have dried up during periods bereft of rain. This protoplant must have evolved tolerance for aridity that made it possible to dwell on land. The evolution of vascular plants tied the fate of plants to terrestrial conditions. They had an outer layer that was waterproof to conserve water, and stomata that could close during periods of water stress. The vascular system of these plants, able to transmit water and nutrients over distances, allowed plants to grow tall. Height gave vascular plants an advantage because they were not shaded by neighboring flora and so could make full use of sunlight. Roots may have arisen early during the evolution of plants. Fossilized soil from the Late Silurian Period (about 420 million years ago) may bear the imprint of roots, but fossilized plants from this time do not appear to have roots. Leaves arose about 360 million years ago and may have first been spikes to deter herbivores. Over time they expanded and flattened to provide a large surface area to capture sunlight. In the Late Devonian Period (about 360 million years ago) arose the first plants with seeds. The first conifers, arising about 310 million years ago, were adapted to arid conditions and radiated across the land between 248 and 206 million years ago. The angiosperms, evolving about 140 million years ago, spread rapidly in the mid-Cretaceous Period, about 100 million years ago. By 65 million years ago, angiosperms totaled 70 percent of the world's flora. Today, angiosperms tally 300 to 400 families and 250,000 to 300,000 species. Evolving between 65 and 50 million years ago, the grasses total 10,000 species today, among them the grains and sugarcane on which humans erected civilization.

The Origin and Development of Plant Cultivation

Humans have always depended on plants. Even as hunter-gatherers, they must have obtained a large portion of their calories and nutrients from edible roots, tubers, grasses, nuts, and berries. Between 10,000 and 4,500 years ago, people in at least seven regions of the world began to cultivate plants. They planted seeds and portions of a root or tuber, weeded the soil to keep other plants from competing with theirs, irrigated their plants, and harvested them. This change in the relationship between plants and people occurred gradually, over millennia, though the process is called the Neolithic or Agricultural Revolution. The deliberate cultivation of plants marked a watershed in human existence. As a rule, agricultural societies produced more food than did hunter-gatherers, making possible large populations. Migration was no longer necessary to follow game. Farmers became sedentary and founded civilization. All of the subsequent inventions—writing, the wheel, the plow, the monotheistic religions, the automobile, the airplane, the computer, and so much else—were the product of plant cultivators.

The first people to cultivate plants appear to have lived in western Asia, in a region known as the Fertile Crescent, bound by the Mediterranean Sea in the west and Mesopotamia in the east. The first cultivated plants were barley, wheat, lentils, and the pea. About 10,000 years ago, the inhabitants of Jericho in the Jordan Valley, and Jarmo, Iraq, may have been the first to cultivate plants, emmer wheat (a type no longer cultivated) being possibly the earliest domesticate. The pea and lentil may have been domesticated about this time. Eikorn wheat (another type no longer cultivated), native to Turkey, may have been domesticated near Damascus, Syria, about 9,700 years ago and along the Euphrates River about

9,500 years ago. At the same time, barley became an important domesticate. Farmers grew barley with two rows of seeds near Damascus about 9,700 years ago and barley with six rows of seeds approximately 9,500 years ago. The domestication of wheat and barley over the 300 years between 10,000 and 9,700 years ago appears to have been a rapid event. From these early beginnings, the cultivation of wheat and barley spread throughout the Fertile Crescent and Turkey by 6000 BCE.

From western Asia, agriculture spread to Mediterranean Europe, Egypt, and North Africa between 6000 and 4500 BCE. Trade between the Levant and the rest of the Mediterranean brought hunter-gatherers in contact with the farmers of the Near East. This intercourse between farmers and hunter-gatherers brought the idea of agriculture and the seeds of cultigens to the latter. Italy and Greece were early adopters of plant cultivation, and agriculture in Mediterranean Europe may have predated its rise in Egypt about 4500 BCE. Sub-Saharan Africa depended on a different suite of crops: millet, sorghum, and rice. Millet and sorghum must have been prized for their drought tolerance. Farmers may have domesticated sorghum about 4000 BCE in the central Sahara Desert and millet about 3000 BCE in the southwestern Sahara. Africans domesticated rice, a different subspecies than Asian rice, about 200 CE along the Niger River.

In East Asia, the valleys of the Yellow and Yangtze Rivers may have been the regions of the earliest plant cultivation. The earliest cultivation of rice in East Asia is not settled. One thesis holds that farmers domesticated rice along the Yangtze River about 6500 BCE and later spread it to Southeast Asia and India by 4000 BCE. At first farmers grew rice in paddies and only later adopted cultivars suitable for dry-land cultivation and others suitable for cultivation in deep ponds. A cultivar is shorthand for cultivated variety. Because all plants in this encyclopedia are cultivated, there is no real distinction between a cultivar and a variety. Millet appears to have been first cultivated about 5500 BCE along the Yellow River. Southeast Asia arose as a separate site of plant cultivation. Farmers there may have domesticated taro, yam, arrowroot, coconut, sago palm, citrus, banana, and breadfruit. To this suite of crops, most scholars believe rice to be a latecomer, though Southeast Asia is today a land of rice farmers.

In the New World corn, beans, and squash dominated agriculture from Argentina to southern Ontario. In South America, farmers grew manioc and sweet potato and in the Andean highlands potato and quinoa. Farmers in Mesoamerica were the first to cultivate corn, beans, and squash more than 5,000 years ago. Of the three, corn was probably the earliest domesticate, being grown in the Tehuacan Valley of Mexico as early as 5000 BCE. The people of Mexico and the Andes independently domesticated beans, including the lima bean. In Mexico, corn and beans may have been domesticated around the same time. The people of the Andes domesticated four tubers: oca, moshua, ullua, and potato, the last being a world staple. In the central Andes, the potato may have been domesticated between 3000 and 2000 BCE. From its center in southern Mexico, corn migrated both south and north, reaching the American Southwest by 1200 BCE and the eastern woodlands by the time of Christ. In Mexico, South America, and the eastern United States, farmers domesticated goosefoot about 2000 BCE. In addition to goosefeet, the woodlands Native Americans added march elder and sunflower about 2000 BCE. They also grew squash, an import from Mexico. About 1000 BCE, farmers grew corn and squash in the Southwest, though only by the time of Christ was corn important in this region. Only about 1000 CE was corn dominant in the eastern woodlands.

The Major Groups of Plants in this Encyclopedia

Grasses are arguably the most important group of plants for sustaining civilization. The great civilizations of Mesoamerica laid a foundation on corn culture. China depended on rice and millet, the Near East and Egypt on wheat and barley, Europe on wheat, barley, oats, and rye, and sub-Saharan Africa on millet and sorghum. Humans rely on a precariously small number of grasses for sustenance: corn, wheat, rice, barley, oats, rye, millet, and sorghum. All grasses are monocots and account for 25 percent of the world's flora. The cereals are annuals whereas turf grass and sugarcane are perennial. The flowers are plain and may lack petals and sepals. Some grass flowers are perfect, bearing both male and female parts in each flower, but corn bears separate male and female flowers, an attribute that made it suitable for the spectacular success of 20th-century plant breeding. Wheat, rice, and corn account for half the calories consumed worldwide. The grass sugarcane is the world's principal source of sugar, being rivaled only by sugar from sugar beet and high-fructose corn syrup from corn.

Legumes include several world crops: soybeans, beans, peas, and peanuts. The soybean is the principal legume of Chinese civilization. The peanut has nourished the civilizations of South America and Africa. Farmers have long grown beans throughout the Americas. The pea has long been a staple of the Near East and Europe. The Romans prized peas, lentils, and chickpeas. They knew that legumes enriched the soil, though they were not aware of the science of nitrogen fixation. In the nodules of legume roots live bacteria that combine nitrogen and oxygen into nitrate ions and nitrogen and hydrogen into ammonium ions, both of which plant roots readily absorb. It is in this sense that scientist say that legumes fix nitrogen in the soil. Because legumes enrich the soil, a soybean-corn rotation is ubiquitous in the Corn Belt. In some states of the Corn Belt, Ohio for example, soybeans occupy more acreage than corn. All legumes are in the Fabaceae or Leguminosae family. In addition to food legumes, alfalfa and clover are also legumes and, along with soybeans, nourish livestock.

Roots and tubers flower and produce seeds, though farmers have for millennia propagated them vegetatively. Remarkably productive, roots and tubers yield the most food per acre of any crop. They may have gained popularity in part because during wars soldiers carried off grain but did not bother to dig up roots and tubers, leaving the peasant something on which to subsist. Among roots and tubers are the world crops cassava, yam, sweet potato, and potato. We have noted that tubers and roots are not the same types of crop. A tuber is an enlarged underground stem whereas a root crop is a swollen root. Tubers and roots evolved as nutrient storage organs that survived unfavorable conditions. When the rains returned, a new plant germinated from the tuber or root.

In the parlance of the workaday world, fruits and vegetables are often confused with one another. A fruit is the ripe ovary of a flower containing seeds. According to this definition the tomato, often considered a vegetable, is really a fruit. Among fruits are the world crops tomato, apple, peach, cherry, apricot, coconut, olive, banana, plantain, grape, citrus, pear, date, fig, and pineapple. Nuts are also fruits. Botanists classify coffee and cacao as fruits, adding to the list of world crops. Americans tend to think of fruits as dessert, but in the tropics bananas and plantains are staples. The tomato is the most popular fruit of the home gardener. Coffee is the beverage of millions of people worldwide. The grape is the source of wine, the principal beverage of Greco-Roman civilization. Olive oil is a staple fat in the Mediterranean Basin.

This encyclopedia uses the term "vegetable" in a narrow and technical sense to mean the vegetative part of a plant. The leaves of some cultivated plants—lettuce and cabbage for example—are vegetables. The vegetable garden, where it is still tended, is a source of pride. During World War I and World War II, the U.S. government encouraged home owners to plant a Victory Garden. Too often the produce of a vegetable garden is not vegetables. The typical home garden may have beans and peas (legumes), tomatoes (fruit), potatoes (tuber), carrots (roots), and cauliflower and broccoli (flowers). Among true vegetables, cabbage sustained the medieval peasant, and the Irish ate it with potatoes in a diet that was otherwise bland. Today, lettuce may be the most popular vegetable. The McDonald's Big Mac would be just a hamburger without lettuce. Indeed, fast-food restaurants are avid consumers of lettuce.

Fiber crops are used to make cloth, rope, paper, baskets, and other items. Cotton is a world crop, though its history is darkened by its association with slavery in the United States. Half the world's textiles come from cotton. Less important is flax, the source of linen. Flax was to ancient Egypt what cotton is to the modern world, though today linen accounts for just 2 percent of the world's textiles. Plants of the genus *Corchorus* are made into jute, a fiber with many uses. Papyrus was once a writing material. Cannabis yields hemp.

Trees that yield lumber are of two types. Hardwood derives from angiosperm trees whereas softwood comes from conifers. About 35 percent of the world's forests are conifers, though in North America coniferous forests are more extensive than hardwood forests. The United States and Canada yield more lumber than any other nation. About half the wood harvested in the United States is used in construction. Conifers are favored for the construction of homes. Oak is the world's chief hardwood tree. In the developing world, people use wood as fuel and for cooking in addition to its use in construction.

Carnivorous plants have long inspired fascination and in some cases disbelief. Linnaeus refused to believe that the Venus's Fly Trap ate insects. The 19th-century English naturalist Charles Darwin was so fascinated by the Venus's Fly Trap and its ilk that he wrote a whole book about them. Science fiction writers have described plants large enough to eat humans. Carnivorous plants are a favorite of plant enthusiasts and are easy to care for. Earth is home to seven families, 15 genera, and about 600 species of carnivorous plants ranging in size from the diminutive bladderworts and Venus's Fly Trap to three-feet-tall pitcher plants. The large carnivorous plants are not simply insectivores. They trap rodents, birds, frogs, and lizards. These plants attract prey with fragrance and colorful flowers. Carnivorous plants exude juices that consume the soft tissue of an insect, leaving only the exoskeleton intact. Some plants exude a chemical potent enough to dissolve even the exoskeleton. These plants evolved the carnivorous habit to supplement the dearth of elements in their poor soils.

Economic, Social, and Religious Significance of Plants

The world's economy rests on a foundation of plants. Depending on the productivity of plants, agriculture is the largest sector of the economy in many parts of the world. Humans use all parts of a plant as food: roots, tubers, leaves, flowers, fruit, and seeds. Trees supply lumber and paper. Fiber crops yield textiles. Ornamentals are prized for their beauty. The tulip once commanded outrageous prices. Some plants—cinchona is an example—supply medicine, whereas others alter one's consciousness. In the developed world, humans drive cars, heat and cool buildings, and generate electricity by burning coal, oil, and natural gas, the remains of plants from the Carboniferous Period. In the developing world, people cook and heat their homes by burning firewood. In ancient Mexico, corn kernels were currency. There is scarcely an economic activity that does not involve plants. Even the typing of this manuscript would be impossible but for the electricity generated by a coal- or natural-gas-fired power plant.

Plants are a status symbol. A well-manicured lawn announces the presence of a devoted home owner. Not only must it be well kept, the lawn must be a monoculture of turf grass. Weeds, especially dandelions, reveal the home owner to be careless and lazy.

Because they yield abundantly, many plants have been thought to be aphrodisiacs and have been associated with fertility rites. In the United States, well-wishers shower a bride and groom with rice to ensure that they will have many children. In the *Epic of Gilgamesh*, the goddess Inana nurtured a sacred tree. The Garden of Eden had an abundance of plants, among them the Tree of Life and the Tree of the Knowledge of Good and Evil. Jewish tradition holds that the Tree of Life conferred immortality on the first humans, but in eating from the Tree of the Knowledge of Good and Evil they became mortal and lost paradise. The author of Psalm 104 credited God with planting cedars on Earth. The Hebrews and Egyptians regarded the date palm as a symbol of longevity given its ability to survive arid conditions. According to legend, the prophet Mohammed built a mosque in Medina from date wood. The Koran mentions the date palm more than 20 times. The Christmas tree commemorated a pagan festival before Christianity co-opted it. The Egyptian sun god Ra traveled across the sky in a boat of cedar. Osiris was the Egyptian god of vegetation. The goddesses Demeter of Greece and Ceres of Rome ensured the bounty of the harvest. The Aztecs worshipped Pitao Cozobi, the corn god.

The Role of Plants in Human Nutrition

Plants are the foundation of sound nutrition. The U.S. Department of Agriculture's Food Pyramid recommends that one consume 6 to 11 servings of whole grains per day: brown rice or whole wheat bread, for example. Modern methods of processing strip the bran and germ, and with them vitamins and minerals, from grains, yielding white rice and white bread. Nutritionists recognize that one should eat the whole grain, including the bran, to obtain optimal nutrients and fiber. Whole grains supply carbohydrates, protein, vitamins, minerals, and little fat. In this group may be added roots and tubers, which supply carbohydrates, vitamins, and minerals, but little protein and fat. Although the quantity is not large, the quality of protein in the potato rivals the protein in egg whites. Orange-fleshed sweet potatoes are rich in beta-carotene, the precursor of vitamin A. The Food Pyramid suggests three to five servings of vegetables. The green leafy vegetables—spinach, Swiss chard, lettuce, and cabbage—contain vitamins and minerals but little protein and fat. The Food Pyramid recommends that a person eat three or four servings of fruit, which supply vitamins and minerals. Citrus fruits have long been renowned as a source of vitamin C. The Food Pyramid includes two or three servings from the meat group, including legumes. Legumes are a source of protein. Although legumes may not supply all essential amino acids, when combined with whole grains they have a balance of amino acids. A dish of beans and rice, for example, supplies all essential amino acids. Nuts, also part of the meat group, supply protein and fat. The sugar from sugarcane or sugar beet supplies calories but no nutrients. Roots, tubers, legumes, and whole grains supply starch. Fruits, vegetables, whole grains, and legumes have fiber. Oil from olives, peanuts, and canola contains monounsaturated fat. Oil from corn, soybeans, and safflower supplies polyunsaturated fat. Coconut oil, palm oil, and cocoa butter have saturated fat.

Leafy greens and yellow- and orange-fleshed roots supply beta-carotene. Seeds and leafy greens contain vitamins E and K. Whole grains, legumes, seeds, and nuts are good sources of thiamine. Whole grains and leafy greens provide riboflavin. Seeds and legumes are rich in niacin. Fruits and leafy greens have vitamin B6. Fruits, seeds, leafy greens, and nuts contain pantothenic acid; legumes, whole grains, and vegetables folic acid; legumes and vegetables biotin; and fruits and vegetables vitamin C. Whole grains, nuts, fruits, vegetables, legumes, and seeds are sources of minerals. Leafy greens and seeds supply calcium, and leafy greens, fruits, legumes, and whole grains contain iron.

The Biogeography of Cultivated Plants

The biogeography of cultivated plants is an area of research complicated by the fact that humans have taken these plants wherever they have migrated and so have carried them far from their origin. Of course there are limits to where cultivated plants will grow. Tropical sugarcane cannot withstand frost and so cannot be grown in the temperate zone. Temperate sugar beet is not normally grown in the tropics. Some cultivated plants are more plastic. Corn grows in the tropics, subtropics, and temperate locales. Accordingly, humans have carried it to virtually every region on Earth. Of the other grasses, oats, wheat, rye, and barley are temperate plants whereas millet and sorghum are fit for the tropics and subtropics. Initially a weed in wheat and barley fields, rye grew where the climate was too cold and dry for wheat.

Of legumes, peas, chickpeas, and soybeans are temperate plants, whereas beans, like corn, may be grown in the tropics, subtropics, and temperate locales. Peanuts are a crop of the tropics, subtropics, and warm temperate zones. Of roots and tubers, the potato is surprisingly a tropical crop, but one grown at cool elevations. Consequently, it does well in cool, temperate locales. Sweet potato, yam, and cassava are tropical and subtropical plants. The carrot is a temperate plant. Among fruits, citrus grows in the tropics and subtropics. Pineapple is a tropical crop. Watermelon is a crop of the subtropics and warm temperate zone. The tomato may be cultivated in the tropics, subtropics, and temperate region. Grapes and cherries are temperate crops, and the olive is grown in warm temperate regions. Bananas and plantains are tropical crops. Among vegetables, leafy greens are temperate crops that will bolt in hot weather. The seedpod okra may be grown in warm temperate regions and the subtropics. The ornamental tulip is a cool temperate plant, whereas the rose grows throughout the temperate zone. The fiber crop cotton grows in the tropics, subtropics, and warm temperate locales.

The Plant Scientists and Humanists

The founder of botany, Theophrastus (372–288 BCE) was born on the island of Lesbos. In Athens, he studied under Plato and Aristotle. The ancients credited him with writing 227 treatises. Of the works that survive, two are botanical: *An Enquiry into Plants* and *On the Causes of Plants*. Theophrastus named more than 300 plants and identified the male and female parts of a flower. He was aware that beans and wheat produced different types of leaves upon germination, a distinction that would lead to the differentiation between dicots and monocots.

The "father of pharmacology and herbalism" Pedanius Dioscorides (40–90 CE), known simply as Dioscorides, was a physician to the Roman armies who used plants to treat sick and wounded soldiers (Huxley 2007, 33). He listed nearly 1,000 medicinal plants, identifying antiseptics, anti-inflammatory agents, stimulants, contraceptives, and plants that enhanced fertility. His principal work on plants, *De Materia Medica*, was influential into the 19th century.

The Roman encyclopedist Pliny the Elder (23–79 CE) wrote a 37-volume *Natural History*, the only extant work by this prolific author. The volumes contain information on botany and pharmacology. He conceived botany as a science in its own right, one concerned with all plants, not merely crops and medicinals. Pliny was not entirely reliable. He believed, for example, that wheat seeds could germinate as oats. The *Natural History* was influential through the Renaissance.

Flemish physician and botanist Carolus Clusius (1526–1609) established one of the earliest botanical gardens at Leyden, the Netherlands. He bred tulips, being perhaps the first to describe the phenomenon of breaking and wrote about the plants and mushrooms indigenous to Europe.

English herbalist John Gerard (1545–1611) apprenticed with a barber-surgeon and became a physician in 1569, though plants were his real passion. He maintained a garden that gained him such renown that a member of the House of Lords appointed Gerard superintendent of his garden. An advocate of the potato, Gerard created Cambridge University's botanic garden. His *Herball* (1597) was part catalogue of plants he grew in his garden and part plagiarism of earlier works. He was interested in the culinary and medical uses of plants.

The founder of taxonomy, Carl Linnaeus (1707–1778), we have seen, applied binomial nomenclature to all life. His father was a minister who tended a garden and introduced Linnaeus to botany. His three great treatises on plants—*Fundamentals of Botany* (1736), *Science of Botany* (1751), and *Species of Plants* (1753)—made clear that the order he found in the Plant Kingdom mirrored the order God bestowed on nature. He classified plants based on the number of stamens and pistils in a flower. The Linnean Society houses Linnaeus's publications.

French botanist Alphonse de Candolle (1806–1893) studied law but like his father was more interested in botany. He used history, language, archaeology, and botany to establish the origin of cultivated plants. His works are consulted today.

Austrian monk Gregor Mendel (1822–1884) laid the foundation of genetics with his experiments with peas. He conceived of particles (genes) that coded for traits that pea plants passed to offspring. He identified genes that coded for plant height, color of the seeds (peas), and whether a pea had a wrinkled or smooth coat. These traits came in pairs—tallness or shortness, green or yellow, or wrinkled or smooth—assorted independently, and were dominant or recessive.

Russian agronomist Nikolai Vavilov (1887–1943) likewise sought the origin of cultivated plants. He reasoned that the more diverse a species, the more ancient it was and the longer it had been subject to human manipulation. These areas of diversity were the places where crops had originated. Vavilov identified seven centers of diversity, most in the Old World. It is possible, however, that a plant might have originated in a locale only to be taken to another area where it diversified. This possibility led some scientists to dismiss Vavilov's contributions to the study of plant origins. An acquaintance of Soviet revolutionary Leon Trotsky, Vavilov suffered when Soviet dictator Joseph Stalin turned against Trotsky. Stalin jailed Vavilov, where he died.

American plant breeder and plant pathologist Norman Borlaug (1914–2009) bred semidwarf wheats that launched the Green Revolution in Mexico, India, and Pakistan. He envisioned the potential of new cultivars to feed a hungry world. In his scientific work and advocacy for a humanitarian role for agriculture, Borlaug was awarded the Nobel Peace Prize in 1970, the Presidential Medal of Freedom in 1977, and the Congressional Gold Medal in 2007.

References

Barhydt, Frances Bartlett, and Paul W. Morgan. *The Science Teacher's Book of Lists.* Englewood Cliffs, NJ: Prentice Hall, 1993.

Barker, Graeme. *The Agricultural Revolution in Prehistory: Why Did Foragers Become Farmers?* Oxford: Oxford University Press, 2006.

Beerling, David. *The Emerald Planet: How Plants Changed Earth's History.* Oxford: Oxford University Press, 2007.

Bretting, Peter K., ed. *New Perspectives on the Origin and Evolution of New World Domesticated Plants.* Lawrence, KS: Society for Economic Botany, 1990.

Denham, Tim, and Peter White. *The Emergence of Agriculture: A Global View.* London: Routledge, 2007.

Duke, James A. *Handbook of Legumes of World Economic Importance.* New York: Plenum Press, 1981.

Flagler, Joel, and Raymond P. Poincelot, eds. *People-Plant Relationships: Setting Research Priorities.* New York: Food Products Press, 1994.

Hanson, Beth, ed. *Buried Treasures: Tasty Tubers of the World.* Brooklyn, NY: Brooklyn Botanic Garden, 2007.

Huxley, Robert, ed. *The Great Naturalists.* London: Thames and Hudson, 2007.

Jordan, Michael. *The Green Mantle: An Investigation into Our Lost Knowledge of Plants.* New York: Sterling, 2000.

Levetin, Estelle, and Karen McMahon. *Plants and Society*. Dubuque, IA: Brown, 1996.

Pearson, Lorentz C. *The Diversity and Evolution of Plants*. Boca Raton, FL: CRC Press, 1995.

Rieger, Mark. *Introduction to Fruit Crops*. New York: Food Products Press, 2006.

Serna-Saldivar, Sergio O. *Cereal Grains: Properties, Processing, and Nutritional Attributes*. Boca Raton, FL: CRC Press, 2010.

Simpson, Michael G. *Plant Systematics*. Amsterdam: Academic Press, 2010.

Sinha, S. K. *Food Legumes: Distribution, Adaptability and Biology of Yield*. Rome: Food and Agriculture Organization of the United Nations, 1977.

Smith, Bruce D. *The Emergence of Agriculture*. New York: Scientific American Library, 1995.

Stoskopf, Neal C. *Cereal Grain Crops*. Reston, VA: Reston, 1985.

Tivy, Joy. *Biogeography: A Study of Plants in the Ecosphere*. New York: Longman Scientific and Technical, 1993.

Tudge, Colin. *The Tree: A Natural History of What Trees Are, How They Live, and Why They Matter*. New York: Crown, 2006.

Willis, K. J., and J. C. McElwain. *The Evolution of Plants*. Oxford: Oxford University Press, 2002.

Zohary, Daniel, and Maria Hopf. *Domestication of Plants in the Old World*. Oxford: Clarendon Press, 1994.

A

Acacia

Acacia, a genus of shrubs and trees, is found all over the world. But it is more common in Australia, Africa, South Asia, Southeast Asia, and the Americas. In the plant kingdom, *Acacia* is the largest genus of vascular plants. It belongs to the subfamily Mimosoideae of the pea family Fabaceae. Globally, there are approximately 1,300 species, out of which roughly 1,000 are indigenous to Australia. The plant goes by different names depending on its inhabitation. In Australia, the plant is referred to as wattle. The national flower of Australia is *Acacia pycnantha*, the golden wattle. In Africa as well as the United States, the plant is called acacia tree. The plant possesses thorns, and hence it is also designated as whistling thorn plant. In Indian languages, the most common name of this deciduous tree is *khair* (*Acacia catechu*). The genus *Acacia* is generally divided into five species: *acacia* (species from Australia and tropical Asia), *acaciella* as well as *mariosousa* (species from the Americas), and the last two, *vachellia* and *senegalia*, for species outside Australia. Some of the common species found in Australia are *Acacia dealbata* (silver wattle), *Acacia decurrens* (tan wattle), *Acacia mearnsii* (black wattle), *Acacia melanoxylon* (blackwood), *Acacia longifolia* (coast wattle), *Acacia baileyana* (cootamundra wattle), *Acacia adunca* (wallangarra wattle), *Acacia acinacea* (gold dust wattle), and others. In the Middle East, *Acacia albida* and *Acacia tortilis* are wild plants. The *Acacia sphaerocephala*, *Acacia cornigera*, and *Acacia collinsii* species are found in Central America. In Southeast Asia, species such as *Acacia pennata* and *Acacia auriculiformis* are common.

Origin and History

The origin of the acacia's name is derived from the Greek word *akis*, which means "a thorn or barb." Discorides (ca. 40–90), the Greek botanist of the first century CE, called the plant *Acacia nilotica* in his treatise *Materia Medica*. The acacia plant was interwoven with Egyptian civilization. It was a sacred tree in its mythology. The Egyptian vessels were made from wood of the plant. First-century CE Roman encyclopedist Pliny the Elder in *Natural History* (book XIII) mentioned the utility of acacia wood and flower as well as its medicinal value. In the beginning of the 17th century, the seed of the acacia was introduced to Europe by herbalist Jean Robin from North America. Botanists and writers of the 17th century also referred to the plant. Carl Linnaeus, the famous naturalist of Sweden, described the plant in 1773. As a timber tree in the United States, it was being used in shipbuilding. It was also a good source of fuel. Acacia was cultivated widely in Kensington and Barnes of the United Kingdom beginning from the first decade of the 19th century. The plant has retained its utility in modern times for its industrial and medicinal uses.

Attributes and Cultivation

The acacia tree is short lived, grows fast, and reaches a height of 70 to 80 feet with a diameter of 3 feet. Its shape is very unusual, with branches and stems growing in an upward direction. Its leaves and flowers are on the tip of its branches. The foliage colors are varied, ranging from green to blue or silver-gray. The exquisitely divided and tiny leaflets provide petioles a fern-like or pinnate appearance. But the leafstalks of the Australian and Pacific islands species are very flat (phyllodes) and thus serve the purpose of leaves. The *Acacia glaucoptera* species is devoid of leaves but has cladodes serving the purpose of leaves. The glands of leaf and phyllode produce a sugary substance that attracts ants, bees, and butterflies. Small blooms make up the acacia flower, which looks like a yellow ball. As a bud, the blooms are white to light yellow. The tiny petals are situated behind long stamens and are positioned in globular or cylindrical clusters. Although the petals are yellow in general, they are of purple and red color in *Acacia purpureapetala* and *Acacia leprosa*, respectively. The pods or legumes contain seeds of the plant.

The cultivation of the acacia is done by seeding, grafting, and cutting. These semievergreen plants do not need much care and are very easy to grow. But certain precautions are required. The acacia plant abhors very wet soil. The acacia needs a warm climate to survive, and it cannot survive severe winter. It is put indoors in winter and taken back to the garden in summer months. Direct sunlight of six hours is necessary for the growth of a healthy acacia plant with its numerous and bright green foliage. The application of nitrogen fertilizer makes the blooms very beautiful. The roots of the plant are delicate and very much susceptible to excess water. They also grow very fast; therefore soil must be free from rocks and pebbles.

Usefulness of Acacia

The unique and colorful acacia plant, along with its products, is very useful to humankind. It increases the beauty of a garden, public parks as well as side streets, and hence is grown for ornamentation. The woolly flowers with their vivid yellow color and sweet fragrance not only beautify the environment but also help in preparing perfume. The fresh leaves as well as boiled inner bark juice have been used by some for ailments like diarrhea and stomachache. The seeds are sometimes used by those who practice folk medicine as a treatment for a sore throat. The leaf extract has been used by some as a remedy for tuberculosis. The bark of acacia is a good source of gum resin. Particularly, the gum arabic of *Acacia arabica* is of very good quality. Furniture made from acacia timber is very popular in many households. The timber from Australian blackwood is of prized quality because of its durability and high polish. Hawaii's *Acacia koa* is native to the islands and other species are native to the island of Réunion. Some indigenous people of North America were known to present blossoming branches of acacia to their loved ones. The shittah tree of the Bible is *Acacia seyal*, believed by some to be used in construction of the Ark of the Covenant. The acacia is also a symbol of the eternal soul.

Patit Paban Mishra

Further Reading

"Acacia." Ancient Egypt. http://www.reshafim.org.il/ad/egypt/botany/acacia.htm (accessed 1 August 2011).

"Acacia Plant." http://www.acaciaplant.net (accessed 1 August 2011).

Singh, Gurcharan. *Plant Systematics: An Integrated Approach*. Enfield, NH: Science, 2010.

Vavilov, Nikolaj I., and Doris Love. *Origin and Geography of Cultivated Plants*. Cambridge: Cambridge University Press, 2009.

Agave

There are roughly 166 species in the genus *Agave*. Although many species are cultivated around the world as ornamentals, they are native to the arid and semiarid regions between the southwestern United States and northern South America. It is in tropical highland central Mexico, however, where agaves are densest and particularly well adapted to the cool, dry conditions.

Agaves are succulents and monocarpic (they reproduce only once then die). Agaves have a large, circular arrangement of leaves that extends outward from the stem. The leaves tend to be wide and flat with spines on their edges. Because members of the *Aloe* genus tend to be more familiar to people, agaves are often mistaken for aloes. A difference between agave and aloe is that the leaf of agave is fibrous whereas the leaf of aloe is gelatinous.

In central Mexico, the Otomí- and Nahuatl-speaking cultures have cultivated agaves since the pre-Hispanic period, and the plants continue to hold economic and cultural significance among indigenous peoples. The relatively recent commercial cultivation of agaves by multinational corporations as well as cooperatives of local growers, however, has insinuated agaves into the diets of people at the global scale. The species that have dominated—and are emblematic of—

Blue agave plant (Jorge M. Vargas Jr./Dreamstime.com)

indigenous and commercial agave production are the maguey (pronounced *muh-gey*) and the blue agave, respectively.

Maguey

The maguey (*Agave americana*) typically grows 6 to 10 feet tall and up to 13 feet wide. Its leaves are 6 to 10 inches wide and 3 to 6 feet long. The plant thrives from below sea level to above 9,800 feet in elevation. It has been suggested that it was the cultivation of the maguey that enabled Mesoindians to settle permanently in the cool, semiarid highlands of central Mexico (the *tierra fría*). Maguey can reproduce both vegetatively and with seeds, but because it produces seeds only upon reaching maturity it is almost always cloned vegetatively when under cultivation. Some of the earliest cultivators, however, may have selectively planted seeds to obtain the current variety of maguey that is most useful to people.

When maguey is interplanted with annual seed crops, the density of maguey averages around 80 plants per acre. When planted exclusively, maguey density can reach 160 plants per acre. The interplanting of maguey with corn and other annual seed crops in the *tierra fría* appears to have been common among the preconquest natives of central Mexico. The importance of maguey as a cultivated plant generally increases as aridity increases because other staple crops, including corn, tend to be less tolerant of dry conditions. Maguey, then, provided a crucial source of nutrition during periods of drought.

Because of central Mexico's rough topography, indigenous peoples have for many centuries constructed agricultural semiterraces in order to increase the amount of land available for crop production. A single or double row of magueys is commonly planted on the embankment that separates each field on a semiterraced hillside. The maguey's lateral root system strengthens the embankment, and its wide leaves absorb the erosive impact of raindrops.

Indigenous peoples have many uses for wide leaves of the maguey. Occasionally, for want of better wood, people used the leaves for laths and roofing tiles. Withered leaves could serve as a backup supply of firewood. Women often ground corn kernels over a clean maguey leaf, which caught and preserved the fallings. Medicinal uses abounded. To treat cuts heated leaves were held over the wound, and the dripping juice served as an ointment. To treat snakebites the roots of a small maguey were mixed with the juice of a wormwood plant. A leaf's fiber could be beaten away from the pulp with a wooden club and then washed and sun-dried. This fiber could then be woven into rope, clothing, sandals, fishing nets, and a variety of other products. Occasionally, maguey and other agaves are cultivated to collect and consume the caterpillars (*Aegiale hesperiaris*) that infest their roots. These worms are rather dense sources of protein and represented a key nutritional component in the pre-Hispanic diets of native peoples.

In addition to the famine food and erosion control mentioned already, maguey does not mature in a particular season so a certain percentage of plants are available year-round. As such, in central Mexico's dry winter seasons people had nourishment when their stores of annual crops were exhausted. In the dry months when seed crops did not need tending, maguey offered people an occupation: they could spin and weave their stockpile of maguey fiber.

A maguey is most useful to people when it reaches maturity and begins to produce sap, which can take 7 to 25 years depending on climate and soil characteristics. The fermented sap of the maguey is called pulque, a beverage that is 3–5 percent alcohol. The Otomí word for it was *octli*, but it was called *pulcre* by the conquistadors and eventually came into its current corrupted form, pulque. Collecting the maguey sap, or *aguamiel*, is an involved process. A central stalk forms inside the plant when it reaches maturity. Over the next five to six weeks the stalk grows vertically out of the plant 12 to 24 feet high. During this growth period, the production of *aguamiel* is intense, and within a few months the plant dies. The first step in making pulque is to castrate the stalk just before it emerges from the plant. There is only a two- to three-week window to do this, and thus a cultivator needs to be aware of which plants are showing signs of reaching maturity and to castrate them at the appropriate time. If the castration is too late or too early, aguamiel production will be low and the taste will be poor. From a few weeks to a few months after castration, the collection of aguamiel begins. The top of the central stalk of the plant is gouged and cut to make a bowl-like cavity. A rock or maguey leaf is placed over the opening to keep out rain and animals. Scraping the sides of this bowl stimulates aguamiel production. Scraping and collection occurs twice daily for two to six months until the plant dies. During this period, the average plant will produce 132 to 264 gallons of *aguamiel.*

Pulque has continuously been used in place of water from preconquest times until the early 20th century. It was even a regular part of the diets of babies and small children. In a diet of traditional Otomí foods, pulque provides 48 percent of the vitamin C, 24 percent riboflavin, 23 percent niacin, and 20 percent iron. Traditionally, medicines that had to be drunk were mixed with pulque.

Blue Agave

In the 16th century, the fermented sap of various *Agave* species began to be distilled to produce a type of spirit called mescal. Mescal is believed to be the New World's first distilled spirit. Mescal produced from the sap of the blue agave (*Agave tequiliana*) is called *mescal de tequila*, or simply tequila. Blue agave is native to the state of Jalisco in west-central Mexico, and this region continues to be the epicenter of blue agave cultivation. Today, around half of all blue agaves are cultivated in roughly 90,000 acres around the city of Tequila in the state of Jalisco. The vast majority of blue agaves are cultivated for tequila; however, since the 1990s blue agave has been the primary species of *Agave* for producing a natural sweetener called "agave nectar." Agave nectar is produced by expressing juice from the plant's pineapple-like root bulb then filtering, heating, and concentrating it into a syrup. Agave nectar is roughly one and a half times sweeter than sugar and can be used as a sugar or honey substitute in food preparation.

Blue agave and maguey cultivation differ in some important respects. First, maguey has been cultivated for pulque for at least a thousand years, but since the early 20th century its popularity has declined as a result of competition from beer. Tequila has been produced only less than half as long as pulque, and its popularity has increased enormously in recent decades. Second, magueys are most often cultivated by individual small-scale growers who cultivate the plant for a variety of purposes. Blue agave cultivation, however, is highly commercialized and occurs almost exclusively to produce tequila. Third, the sap of the maguey needs only to ferment to produce pulque whereas the sap of the blue agave must be distilled to produce tequila. As a result, tequila can be 40 percent alcohol, roughly 10 times more alcoholic than pulque.

Richard Hunter

Further Reading

Gentry, Howard Scott. *Agaves of Continental North America.* Tucson: University of Arizona Press, 2004.

Granberg, William J. *People of the Maguey: The Otomí Indians of Mexico.* New York: Praeger, 1970.

Parsons, Jeffrey R., and Mary H. Parsons. *Maguey Utilization in Highland Central Mexico.* Ann Arbor: University of Michigan Press, 1990.

Ageratum

Ageratum is a large genus of herbs and shrubs in the aster family, Asteraceae, which is native to Central America and the Caribbean. There are about 60 species of both annuals and perennials in this genus. Many cultivars of *Ageratum houstonianum* are widely grown as annuals in flowerbeds and sometimes as cut flowers. Ageratum species can become naturalized in tropical and semitropical areas and become pernicious weeds. This has been the case for *Ageratum conyzoides*. It produces a number of secondary metabolites that cause it to have both insecticidal activity and allelopathic activity against other plant species, thus increasing its efficacy as a weed. Paradoxically, it is used as a control agent for other weeds in China. *Ageratum conyzoides* is also effective at treating burn wounds and has been shown in laboratory tests to have antibacterial activity.

The genus *Ageratum* was named by Swedish naturalist Carl Linnaeus in 1753. Its name derives from the Greek *geras*, meaning "aging," and *a*, which translates to "not." This is thought to refer to the ability of the flowers to remain on the plant for a long period. *Ageratum houstonianum* is named after William Houston, the collector who obtained the first ageratum plants. The species name of *Ageratum conyzoides* is derived from the Greek word *konyz*, the name of the elecampane plant (*Inula helenium*) that resembles it.

Horticultural Uses

Often known as flossflower, ageratum is widely grown in gardens and as a houseplant in the winter. Numerous hybrids of *Ageratum houstonianum* are available in shades of lavender, white, or pink. Also available are blue flowers, which are prized, since blue is not a common color for garden flowers and combines well with other colors.

Ageratum is grown as an annual for its flowers in the summer and fall in cooler climates and over the winter in more mild areas. Many of the varieties grown are compact, remaining below 6 inches. They have many uses in gardens and are commonly used in borders, for edging, or in rock gardens. Ageratum cultivars also make good container plants. Other varieties grow to 18 inches tall and make attractive cut flowers. Some plants are grown commercially for this purpose.

While ageratum can frequently be purchased at local nurseries, it is easy to grow from seeds. They require light to germinate, and the plants perform best when kept moist. They do not have tolerance for frost and will die if exposed to it. Ageratum should be grown inside over the winter months, unless one lives in a subtropical climate. Shade is preferred in warmer climates, although plants grown in cool areas can tolerate full sun. With most cultivars, the dead flowers remain on the plants and should be removed to keep the plants flowering continuously.

Medicinal Uses of *Ageratum conyzoides*

The plant has been used in traditional folk medicine in Africa and South America to treat a variety of ailments. A common custom is to treat burns and wounds. Laboratory studies have verified the antibacterial activity of *Ageratum conyzoides* extracts against the human pathogens *Staphylococcus aureus*, *Pseudomonas aeruginosa*, and *Escherichia coli*. Studies have been conducted on the efficacy of this plant in treating human systemic illnesses; however, the plants contain toxic pyrrolizidine alkaloids that can cause liver damage in humans.

Effects of Ageratum on Agriculture

The breadth of secondary metabolites found in this plant causes it to affect a number of other species, both invertebrate and botanical. *Ageratum conyzoides* produces the compound ageratochromene, which inhibits the growth of insects by interfering with their juvenile growth hormone. The leaves of this species of ageratum have been used as moth repellants, and extracts of the leaves have been shown to interfere with the development of a number of types of insects, including the domestic fly, a type of moth, and several types of mosquitoes. It is considered a promising candidate for the development of natural insecticides.

Another class of invertebrates affected by ageratum is nematodes. In this case, *Ageratum houstonianum* was found to suppress the growth of nematodes just by using the plants as a mulch. The research was inspired by the knowledge that *Crotalaria* species were used to inhibit nematodes because of their production of pyrrolizidine alkaloids. The production of these toxic compounds is a common trait of ageratum.

Ageratum conyzoides is one of three species of plants listed as the most economically destructive weeds in the world. It is able to invade cultivated fields and is extremely difficult to eradicate. Part of the reason is that it spreads by stolons and has wind-borne seeds, but the major factor is that the plant is allelopathic. It produces chemicals that inhibit the growth of plants around it, including crops. One strategy of weed control is to identify the chemicals responsible for this effect and incorporate them into herbicides. Another is to utilize the plant as a mulch, or even a counter crop, to help control other weeds. Such approaches fit nicely into sustainable agricultural programs. For instance, *Ageratum conyzoides* has been grown on the floor of citrus orchards in southern China for a long period. It crowds out other weeds and inhibits the growth of pathogenic fungi. Unexpectedly, there was also an increase in predatory mites when ageratum was planted. These mites cause a decrease in the levels of parasitic citrus red mites in the orchards. This effect was found to be due to volatile chemicals released from the essential oil of *Ageratum conyzoides*.

The data so far suggest that the prolific production of secondary metabolites by ageratum species will facilitate their incorporation into new and alternative methods of pest, pathogen, and weed control.

Helga George

Further Reading

Kong, C. H. "Ecological Pest Management and Control by Using Allelopathic Weeds (*Ageratum conyzoides, Ambrosia trifida*, and *Lantana camara*) and Their Allelochemicals in China." *Weed Biology and Management* 10 (2010): 73–80.

Mahr, S. 2009. "Ageratum." University of Wisconsin Extension. http://pddc.wisc.edu/factsheets/Low%20Color%20PDF%20Format/Ageratum.pdf (accessed 13 September 2011).

Ming, L. C. "*Ageratum conyzoides*: A Tropical Source of Medicinal and Agricultural Products." In *Perspectives on New Crops and New Uses*, edited by Jules Janick, 469–73. Alexandria, VA: ASHS Press, 1999.

Thoden, T. C., and M. Boppre. "Plants Producing Pyrrolizidine Alkaloids: Sustainable Tools for Nematode Management?" *Nematology* 12 (2010): 1–24.

Alfalfa

A perennial legume, alfalfa (*Medicago sativa*) is a member of the Fabaceae or Leguminosae family and is related to clover, pea, bean, soybean, lentil, chickpea, lupin, peanut, vetch, and cowpea. Known as the Queen of Forages because it fixes nitrogen in the soil and feeds livestock, alfalfa is the world's most widely grown legume. In 1753, Swedish naturalist Carl Linnaeus named alfalfa, the genus *Medicago* deriving from the Latin *medica*, denoting the belief that the plant had originated in Mesopotamia (now Iraq). Italians knew alfalfa as *erbo medica*, meaning the "median herb." In Spanish, alfalfa is *mielgo* and in Turkish *kayseri trefoil*. Indians refer to alfalfa as *Ashue-Bal*, meaning "strength to horses," surely a reference to the practice of feeding the legume to equines. The Chinese knew alfalfa as *mu-su*. The Arabic word *ratba* means "green alfalfa," and *quatt* means "alfalfa hay." The Persian word *aspo-asti* for alfalfa means "horse fodder," suggesting the same use as in India. From the Persian, the Babylonians derived aspasti for alfalfa. In turn, the Arabs derived the term "alfalfa" from *aspasti*. The Syrians used a similar word, *aspasta*, to refer to alfalfa. The Swiss and people in other parts of Europe, South Africa, New Zealand, and Australia knew alfalfa as lucerne, perhaps because the Swiss grew alfalfa in the region of Lake Lucerne. Another

Alfalfa (iStockPhoto)

possibility is that the term derived from the Lucerne River in Italy. Alphonse de Candolle, the 19th-century French botanist, rejected both possibilities, instead asserting that lucerne derived from the French *laouzerde*.

Origin and Diffusion

Several scholars believe that alfalfa was the only forage grown in prehistory even though written records of alfalfa, when they appeared, do not date from the beginning of the historical period. By one account we have seen, alfalfa originated in Mesopotamia. By another, Iran was the homeland of the legume. Yet another broadens the geography, maintaining that alfalfa originated in western Asia, Iran, Transcaucasia, and Turkmenistan. The legume grows wild from China to Spain and from Sweden to North Africa, though humans may have assisted it in diffusing so widely. If this is correct, the wild plants may have escaped from cultivation. Having evolved in a region of cold winters and hot, dry, short summers, alfalfa tolerates cold weather, though curiously it does not yield well in hot weather, instead becoming dormant. One scientist pinpoints two regions of origin. The first, Transcaucasia, gave rise to the varieties of alfalfa grown in Europe. Having evolved in a region of frigid winters, these varieties are hardy. The second region, Central Asia, had a dry climate. The varieties that evolved there did not acquire resistance to the fungal diseases that accompanied humidity. Another school of thought traces the lineage of alfalfa to Medicago falcate. The varieties that descended from this proto-alfalfa were hardy, drought tolerant, and resistant to diseases. Alfalfa is drought tolerant because the taproot, penetrating 20 feet into the soil, absorbs underground water when the topsoil is dry. The plant tolerates drought and cold, moreover, because it becomes dormant during adverse conditions.

The earliest written reference to alfalfa dates to 1300 BCE in Turkey. Given that the cultivation of alfalfa might have begun in prehistory, it seems surprising that there are no earlier records of it. About this time, the Hittites fed the legume to livestock during winter, regarding it as nutritious. By the first millennium BCE, the people of northwestern Iran widely cultivated alfalfa. It was the fodder of cavalry and chariot horses in Iran, Greece, and Rome. Greek dramatist Aristophanes (440–380 BCE) and fourth-century Greek philosopher Aristotle mentioned alfalfa, implying that it was cultivated in Greece. In the fourth century BCE, Aristotle's pupil Greek botanist Theophrastus related the story of alfalfa's introduction to Greece. According to him, the Persians, invading Greece in the fifth century, planted alfalfa to feed their warhorses and cattle. Although the Greeks ejected the Persians, they adopted the practice of cultivating alfalfa for forage. In turn the Romans, in the second century BCE, adopted alfalfa from the Greeks. In the first century BCE, Roman agricultural writer Varro and Roman poet Virgil mentioned alfalfa. Varro recommended that stockmen seed it at a rate of 34 pounds per acre. He observed that alfalfa attracted bees. In the first century CE, Roman encyclopedist Pliny the Elder repeated Theophrastus's account that the Persian army brought alfalfa to Greece. He recommended that farmers plant alfalfa in well-drained soil, add lime to the soil, and cut alfalfa upon flowering. Pliny's contemporary, Roman agricultural writer Columella, cautioned against overfeeding alfalfa to livestock for fear of bloating. He understood that alfalfa improved the soil, though the Romans had no knowledge of nitrogen fixation. Columella believed that alfalfa could cure livestock of various ailments. One authority estimates the yield of alfalfa at 12 tons per acre in Rome. By one account, Columella planted alfalfa in southern Spain. By another, the Romans introduced alfalfa to Gaul (now France), Germany, and Switzerland in addition to Spain. The fall of Rome marked a decline in alfalfa culture in parts of Europe, though Arabs grew it in Spain in addition to North Africa. If Columella planted alfalfa in Spain in the first century, the Arab introduction in the eighth century must have marked a reintroduction of the crop. Medieval records contain few references to alfalfa, suggesting that it was not widely grown during the Middle Ages. Renaissance stockmen showed a renewed interest in the legume. In the 16th century, the Spanish reintroduced alfalfa to Italy and in about 1550 to France. In 1565, farmers spread alfalfa to Belgium and the Netherlands, in 1650 to England, in 1750 to Germany and Austria, in 1770 to Sweden, and in the 18th century to Russia.

Outside Europe, the Chinese adopted alfalfa from Turkestan in 126 BCE. In the 16th century, the Spanish introduced alfalfa to Mexico and Peru. By 1775, stockmen grew alfalfa in Chile, Argentina, and Uruguay. From Mexico, missionaries brought the legume to Texas, Arizona, New Mexico, and California. Another account holds that Chile was the source of the Californian introduction in the 19th century. In 1851, farmer W. E. Cameron planted alfalfa in the Sacramento River Valley in California, though its introduction to the state may have occurred earlier. By 1858, Cameron had 270 acres of alfalfa. Alfalfa thrived in the dry climate of the American Southwest. In 1836, Major Jacob Downing planted alfalfa in Colorado. By 1894, stockmen widely planted alfalfa in Kansas. Farmers began growing alfalfa in Ohio in 1886, in Montana by 1890, and in Iowa and Missouri by 1900. In the eastern United States, immigrants made separate introductions of the forage to Georgia in 1736, North Carolina in 1739, and New York in 1791. In Virginia, accomplished gardener Thomas Jefferson in 1793 and George Washington in 1798 planted alfalfa. Yet the acidic soil and humidity of the eastern United States were not ideal for alfalfa, and by 1899 farmers grew only a small portion of alfalfa east of the Mississippi River. By contrast, the land west of the Mississippi River totaled the majority of alfalfa acreage in 1949.

Attributes and Nutrients

Adapted to temperate regions, alfalfa does not tolerate temperatures above 95°F. Better adapted to cold weather, alfalfa withstands temperatures as low as 23°F when it is not hardened and as low as −4°F when it has undergone hardening in autumn. The short days of autumn spur the plant to harden. Alfalfa initiates hardening when temperatures dip below 50°F. A hydrated alfalfa plant cannot endure temperatures below 28°F without water freezing in its cells. In response to cold weather, alfalfa reduces the amount of water in its cells and so can withstand colder temperatures. For this reason, drought aids alfalfa in hardening. Soil moisture no greater than 50 percent of saturation helps alfalfa harden. Because saturated soil reduces hardiness, farmers should not irrigate alfalfa in autumn. Where snow insulates the land, alfalfa does not develop maximum hardiness. Excessive nitrogen and a dearth of other nutrients in the soil impair hardiness. The application of potassium and phosphorus to the soil increases hardiness. Plants with a store of carbohydrates and amino acids for the lean months of winter are hardy.

Removing more nutrients from the soil than grains, alfalfa is a heavy feeder. In 1988, one scientist estimated that the U.S. alfalfa crop removed 1.7 million tons of potassium from the soil. This amount totaled 40 percent of the potassium applied to all crops in the United States and more than twice the amount applied to corn. Alfalfa removes 10 times more potassium from the soil than an equivalent amount of corn. Cool temperatures slow the uptake of nitrogen, phosphorus, and sulfur. Alfalfa leaves contain less phosphorus, potassium, iron, boron, copper, zinc, and manganese and more calcium and magnesium in cool rather than warm weather.

Alfalfa favors a soil pH between 6.6 and 7.5, though the pH may be as low as 4 if the soil has enough calcium. As a rule, however, the yield decreased when the pH falls below 5.2 because aluminum, iron, and manganese may reach toxic levels in acidic soil. A neutral pH reduces the solubility and uptake of these elements. The addition of lime to acidic soil increases the availability of calcium, magnesium, phosphorus, and molybdenum. One recommendation holds that the farmer should add lime to the soil at least 26 weeks before planting or immediately after planting.

In addition to potassium, alfalfa is a heavy feeder of nitrogen. The legume removes more nitrogen from the soil than any other nutrient, yet the bacteria that inhabit the nodules of the roots make good much of this loss by fixing nitrogen in the soil. By one estimate, alfalfa removes 980 pounds of nitrogen per acre. One study found that alfalfa obtains 43–64 percent of its nitrogen from the bacteria in its nodules. Because of nitrogen fixation, the crops that follow alfalfa in rotation yield well. Corn in rotation with alfalfa needs 70 percent less nitrogen applied as fertilizer than corn grown in monoculture.

Alfalfa needs less phosphorus than nitrogen and absorbs it in the form of orthophosphate. The farmer should apply phosphorus at the time of planting. One scientist recommends the application of manure to the soil as a source of phosphorus. Farmers in the Pennsylvania Alfalfa Growers Program applied manure from dairy cows to the soil. The reader may remember that alfalfa is a heavy feeder of potassium. Young plants are ravenous in their appetite for the element. Some farmers applied potassium twice per year—once in spring and again in autumn—though one scientist believes that the number of applications does not affect yield. Alfalfa absorbs potassium in the topsoil more efficiently than at depth. Potassium chloride is the most common source of potassium, though one scientist favors potassium sulfate because it does not add chlorine, which can be toxic to alfalfa, to the soil.

Alfalfa absorbs more calcium and magnesium than do grains. Being rich in these nutrients, alfalfa entices some stockmen to feed it rather than grain to their animals. Limestone and dolomite are the chief sources of calcium and magnesium. Soils with too little organic matter may lack sulfur. Cool weather, acidic soil, or drought may limit the availability of sulfur, though it is abundant enough in most soils so that the farmer need apply it only every third year.

Breeding and Cultivars

The discovery of new varieties aided alfalfa in its spread throughout the United States and Canada. In 1857, German immigrant Wendelin Grimm brought a new cultivar, named Grimm in his honor, to Minnesota. A hardy variety, Grimm was ideal for the northern United States and Canada. The Minnesota Agricultural Experiment Station sent Grimm to other states, promoting its cultivation.

In 1908, Canadians began cultivating Grimm. Despite its hardiness, Grimm was susceptible to bacterial wilt. Farmers grew Baltic, a hardy variety named for Baltic, South Dakota, in the northern United States. Baltic, like Grimm, was susceptible to bacterial wilt. From Baltic, the Michigan Agricultural Experiment Station selected Hardigan, a variety prized for its hay. Like Baltic and Grimm, Hardigan was vulnerable to bacterial wilt. A third hardy variety was Cossack, which the U.S. Department of Agriculture imported from Russia in 1907. Although not resistant to bacterial wilt, Cossack was less susceptible than Grimm. Even hardier than Grimm was Ladak, which the U.S. Department of Agriculture imported from India in 1910 and which farmers cultivated in Ontario, Canada. Somewhat resistant to bacterial wilt, Ladak yielded well on the Great Plains. In 1927, the Arnold brothers of Nebraska planted Hardistan, a hardy variety that was soon grown in Canada. Peruvian alfalfa, unable to tolerate temperatures below 10°F, was confined to the American South and Southwest.

In the mid-19th century, the French introduced alfalfa to South Africa, where it was first used to feed ostriches. South African farmers grew the Provence variety, the name suggesting French origin. They also grew Chinese, a variety from Tibet. Around 1800, alfalfa from Europe or Argentina was introduced to New Zealand, where Marlborough was the chief cultivar. In the 18th century, farmers cultivated alfalfa in the Hunter and Peel river valleys in Australia. By 1833, farmers in New South Wales boasted 2,000 acres and by 1920 100,000 acres. Australians grew primarily the variety Hunter, a derivative of Provence, Smooth Peruvian, Arabian, or American Common.

Since 1956, the genetic improvement of alfalfa through breeding has contributed only 3 percent to the increase in yield. The gain in yield has been smaller for alfalfa than for grains. This state of affairs may have resulted from the emphasis on breeding alfalfa resistant to diseases and pests rather than for yield and from the fact that scientist know less about the genetics of alfalfa than of corn. As with corn, hybrid crosses of alfalfa varieties display heterosis.

The efforts to breed disease-resistant cultivars began in the 1930s when scientists identified Ladak and the Turkestan varieties as sources of resistance to bacterial wilt. From them the Nebraska Agricultural Experiment Station and the U.S. Department of Agriculture derived Ranger, and the Kansas Agricultural Experiment Station and the U.S. Department of Agriculture bred Buffalo. Since 1965, virtually all new cultivars have been resistant to bacterial wilt. The variety Vernal is among the most resistant. In 1968, scientists began to breed varieties resistant to anthracnose fungi. In 1974, they released Arc, the first anthracnose-resistant cultivar. Resistant varieties yielded 10 percent more alfalfa than susceptible cultivars where anthracnose is present. In 1977, the discovery of a new race of anthracnose in North Carolina, Maryland, and Virginia spurred scientists to intensify their efforts. Whereas Arc was resistant to only one race, the new Saranac AR was resistant to both.

In 1934, the first variety resistant to the pea aphid was discovered, though a breeding program followed only later. In 1966, scientists released resistant Washore and Apex, in 1967 Dawson and Mesilla, and in 1969 Kanza. Between 1967 and 1983, scientists released more than 75 varieties resistant to the pea aphid. Resistant cultivars yielded two to three times more alfalfa than susceptible varieties under infestation. Kanza, for example, yielded as much as three times more alfalfa than susceptible Buffalo, Ranger, and Vernal. In 1957, scientists released Moaspa and Zia, cultivars resistant to the spotted alfalfa aphid. Farmers grew Zia in New Mexico. Cody, another resistant cultivar, is a derivative of Chilean varieties. Between 1957 and 1983, scientists bred more than 100 resistant varieties. These cultivars have saved growers $35 million per year according to one estimate.

Christopher Cumo

Further Reading

Bolton, J. L. Alfalfa: *Botany, Cultivation, and Utilization.* New York: Interscience, 1962.

Graumann, H. O., and C. H. Hanson. *Growing Alfalfa.* Washington, D.C.: U.S. Department of Agriculture, 1954.

Hanson, A. A., D. K. Barnes, and R. R. Hill Jr., eds. *Alfalfa and Alfalfa Improvement.* Madison, WI: American Society of Agronomy, 1988.

Hanson, C. H., ed. *Alfalfa Science and Technology.* Madison, WI: American Society of Agronomy, 1972.

Almond

Often classified as a nut, botanists consider almond (*Prunus dulcis*) a drupe, that is, a type of fruit. In the family Rosaceae, almond is related to the rosebush, plum, cherry, peach, nectarine, apple, apricot, and pear. One hundred grams of almond contain roughly 600 calories, 2.6 to 3 grams of fiber, 230 to 282 milligrams of calcium, 475 to 540 milligrams of phosphorus, 4.4 to 5.2 milligrams of iron, 4 to 14 milligrams of sodium, 432 to 773 milligrams of potassium, 0.24 to 0.25 milligram of thiamine, 0.15 to 0.92 milligram of riboflavin, 2.5 to 6 milligrams of niacin, and small amounts of beta-carotene, vitamin C, and folic acid. The more protein an almond has, the less fat it contains. The converse is also true. Not surprisingly, the larger the almond the more protein it has. High protein correlates with high magnesium content. Processors prefer almonds with high protein and low fat. Oleic acid is the principal lipid in almonds. Almonds with a high content of oleic acid are slow to become rancid. Processors regard linoleic acid, another lipid, with almonds of low quality. High ash content correlates with a high concentration of potassium. The almond tree resembles the peach tree in size, flowering, and shape of leaves. The almond tree prefers mild, wet winter and hot, dry spring and summer. The Mediterranean Basin and parts of Asia and California approximate these conditions. Insects, chiefly bees, pollinate almond flowers. Bees pollinate almond flowers best at 57°F. Cold, rainy weather diminishes pollination and hastens the spread of fungal diseases. Nitrogen, boron, and zinc are essential to prompting an almond flower to set fruit. The application of boron and zinc yielded 39.5 percent fruit set among almond flowers according to one study. The farmer should apply boron in autumn for best results. Insufficient boron decreases pollen production and, accordingly, the production of almonds. Boron increases a flower's production of nectar, thereby attracting insect pollinators. Flowers are white, pink, or red. Almond requires little cold weather to initiate dormancy and is slow to become dormant in autumn. Almond may lower cholesterol and reduce the risk of heart disease and diabetes. Almond oil is a monounsaturated fat similar to olive oil in its health benefits. Almonds contain manganese, magnesium, copper, phosphorus, riboflavin, and vitamin E. Sweet-flavored almond extract, typically made of almond oil, water, and alcohol, is used in baking.

Origin, History, and Production

Almond originated in the desert and low mountains slopes of west Central Asia, a region where it evolved to tolerate mild, wet, or dry winter and hot summer. Wild almonds contain toxic hydrogen cyanide, necessitating the selection of nontoxic types during the process of domestication. Humans domesticated the almond in the Bronze Age as early as 3000 BCE. The almond was among the earliest domesticated fruit trees because of the ease of raising trees from seeds. In the 14th century BCE, the Egyptians, perhaps having gotten the almond from the Levant, buried almonds in Pharaoh Tutankhamun's tomb. The Chinese have cultivated almond since the 10th century BCE. Humans carried the almond from Asia to Southern Europe including Greece and North Africa. The Old Testament mentions almond, evidence that the Hebrews cultivated it. Humans grew almond in the Mediterranean Basin by the time of Christ. From the Mediterranean, almond spread to India, southern Africa, the United States, and Australia. The tree is cultivated in the United States, Turkey, Turkmenistan, Uzbekistan, Tadzhikistan, Afghanistan, Spain, Tunisia, Iran, the Tien Shan plain, Hendokosh, Italy, Chile, South Africa, and Australia. Worldwide, the almond was grown on more than 4.3 million acres in 2004. Production totaled 1.8 million tons. The United States had the highest yield at 3,100 pounds per acre and the greatest production with 900,000 metric tons in 2004. Syria ranked second with 153,000 tons that year. Iran totaled 121,000 tons, Spain 105,200 tons, and Italy 100,100 tons in 2004. Between 1995 and 2004, the United States increased production from 303,600 to 900,000 tons. During these years, Spain decreased production from 174,800 to

105,200 tons. Production increased during these years in Iran from 87,500 to 121,000 tons, in Syria from 40,000 to 153,000 tons, and in Morocco from 50,300 to 77,900 tons. Despite this gain, Morocco is not a leading producer (Javansha 2006, 141).

Asia and the Mediterranean: The Homeland of the Almond

In 2004, Iran grew almonds on 300,000 acres. Although the almond tree, with its deep roots and narrow leaves that expose little surface area to transpiration, is drought tolerant, much of Iran's almond land is arid. Consequently, farmers irrigate about half the country's almond acreage. In Iran, almond is grown in the provinces of Khorasan, Chaharmahal va Bakhtieri, Fars, and Kerman. Late-blooming almonds, which are less susceptible to spring frost than early bloomers, are grown in Kashmar, Mianeh, Khorasan, and Shahrekard. Iran grows cultivars from Italy and Spain. Many old orchards in Iran grow almond trees from seeds, though recent efforts have concentrated on propagating superior cultivars by grafting them on rootstock. Peach tree is the standard rootstock. In Gaznia province, Iranians propagate almond by seeds. The arid lands of Iran challenge growers with their salinity and alkalinity. About 12 percent of Iran's land is saline and alkaline. The Food and Agriculture Organization of the United Nations characterizes 21 acres of Iranian soil as high in salts, which burn the tips of the leaves of almond trees. Cultivated almond varieties are more susceptible to salt damage than wild types. Sodium concentrations as low as 0.55 percent in a leaf injury an almond tree. Salt in the soil impairs the ability of almond leaves to photosynthesize. Trees shed their leaves when salts are numerous in the soil. The highest levels of salts kill almond trees.

Almond is the chief horticultural crop in Chaharmahal va Bakhtieri province. The principal cultivars in the province are Mamaei, Rabi, and Safid, all of which flower early and so are susceptible to frost. Almond is so early that it flowers before it puts forth leaves in spring. Indeed, almond is the earliest deciduous fruit tree to flower in spring. The varieties Monagha and Dehahreh also flower early. The cultivars Texas, Tardy Nonpareil, Ferragnes, and Tuono-283 flower late and so are safe from frost.

In 1977, France gave Iran 22 almond cultivars. The next year Iran began breeding new varieties, among them Azar, Shekafe, and Sahand. Kerman province has 25,000 acres of almond trees, most on gravel and sandy soil. This soil is infertile. Trees that suffer from nutritional deficiency are susceptible to the Rosaceae branch borer, a pest of almond trees in Kerman and Shahrbabak provinces. Because of Kerman's inhospitable soil and pests, growers harvest fewer than 1,320 pounds per acre of almonds. In Iran, almonds were more likely than pistachios to suffer from poor soil. In addition to the Rosaceae branch borer, almond trees in Iran suffer from the wood borer and the species *Tecapis asiatica*. In addition to Iran, Turkey, Afghanistan, Syria, and Azerbaijan suffer from these pests. Almond trees most susceptible to these pests are grown on light, coarse, thin soil with inadequate irrigation. These soils tend to be deficient in phosphorus, zinc, and nitrogen, to be alkaline, and to have little organic matter.

Farmers in Gaziantep, Turkey, irrigate almond trees. Among cultivars in Turkey are Nonpareil, Ferragnes, Cristimorto, Picantili, Desmayo Langueta, Garrigues, Drake, Tuomo, Primorski, Nikitski, Texas, Yaltinskl, and Ferradual, all of foreign origin. In Turkey, as well as in Spain and Tunisia, farmers rely on rainfall to sustain their almond trees. Turks and Syrians eat whole, fresh almonds.

In Afghanistan, almond is the most important crop in Kandoz, Takhor, Balkh, Beghha, Heart, and Samangan. Pakistan and India import Afghan almonds. In contrast to Turkey, Spain, and Tunisia, Afghanistan irrigates most of its almond acreage. In contrast to Turkey, Afghanistan grows local varieties. In some areas, Afghans plant almond trees along the edge of grain fields.

In Spain, breeders aim to develop late-flowering cultivars that are not vulnerable to frost, and early-ripening varieties suitable for a short growing season. Among cultivars, Antoneta flowers late and ripens early and so is ideal for Spain's climate. Less desirable is Ramillete, which flowers early and ripens early. Desmayo Langueta flowers early and ripens late and is the least desirable of the four. Wawona flowers and ripens late. The traditional cultivars, Marcone and Desmayo Langueta, despite their drawbacks, are the foundation of almond culture in Spain. Marcone is grown on the Mediterranean coast and Desmayo Langueta in the interior. As a rule, Spanish cultivars flower early. Spain also cultivates Atocha, Cartayera, Garrigues, Peroleja, Ramillete, Rumbeta, and Planeta.

Christopher Cumo

Further Reading

"California Almonds." Almond Board of California. http://almondboard.com/English/Pages/default.aspx (accessed 14 July 2011).

Javanshah, A. *Proceedings of the IVth International Symposium on Pistachios and Almonds*. Brugge, Belgium: Acta Horticulturae, 2006.

The World's Healthiest Foods. "Almonds." http://whfoods.com/genpage.php?name=foodspice&dbid=20 (accessed 14 July 2011).

Aloe Vera

There are over 250 species of the aloe plant, but aloe vera is a common houseplant. In addition, it is cultivated for its medicinal and cosmetic properties. Although previously thought to be part of the Liliaceae or Lily family, it has recently been classified under the Asphodelaceae family, which includes poker plants and asphodels. Other common names for aloe vera include true aloe, medicine aloe, medicine plant, burn plant, and Barbados aloe. While sometimes confused with agave, also called American aloe, aloe vera and agave are not in the same family. Agave blooms rarely and has no gel in its leaves. Aloe vera, on the other hand, is a succulent perennial that is 99 percent water with fibrous roots and that produces erect spikes with yellow flowers most of the year in hot, dry soils.

In addition to over 120 other aloe species, aloe vera is native to East and South Africa, where it is often harvested in the wild for commercial use. It is cultivated in the West Indies, specifically the Netherland Antilles, for its fleshy leaves filled with gel

Aloe vera (Skynetphoto/Dreamstime.com)

and latex. The gel is the leaf pulp collected by cutting close to the stem and draining. Aloe leaves are edged with spines to keep away large animals, and a further deterrent is the yellow sap from tubules under the plant's skin. The sap is a bitter fluid that can be dried and used as a purgative or laxative. In fact, the name aloe comes from the Arabic *alleoh*, meaning "shining bitter substance."

The aloe plant has unique survival characteristics. The leaves often have a waxy substance that reflects light and retains moisture. The skin of aloe plants absorbs water and releases it slowly through its crassulacean acid metabolism (CAM). Plants with CAM open their pores only at night to absorb carbon dioxide. In the process, the plant loses little moisture. An aloe plant can take several weeks to shrivel when pulled from its roots and left in the hot sun; and once dried, it takes only a few hours of immersion in water to refresh to its original state.

History

Aloe has a long history of being cultivated for medicinal and cosmetic purposes. Pictures of aloe were drawn in Sumerian tablets as early as

2200 BCE. One of the oldest preserved medical documents, the Ebers Papyrus written in 1550 BCE, includes 12 medical recipes listing aloe as an ingredient. During the 10th century BCE, King Solomon grew and used aloe. The Song of Solomon mentions "myrrh and aloes, along with all the finest spices." Arab traders brought aloe to Persia (now Iran) and India in 600 BCE, and by 400 BCE it was commonly traded in the Near East and Asia. In the fourth century BCE, it was produced on the Island of Socotra, near the Horn of Africa, and traded in Tibet, India, and China. In 333 BCE, Aristotle convinced Alexander the Great to capture Socotra in order to claim its aloe plantations, and it was a favorite skin lotion for the beautiful Nefertiti, wife of Egyptian pharaoh Akhenaton. Cleopatra used aloe to keep her youthful appearance, and first-century Greek physician and botanist Pedanius Dioscorides included it in his herbal encyclopedia, *Regarding Medical Materials*. A seventh-century Chinese herbal text included aloe vera as a treatment for sinusitis and skin conditions.

Aloe has a history as a religious symbol with sacred properties. The Muslims and Jews of Egypt believed it could protect a household from evil if hung over the doorway. Hindus believed that aloe grew in the Garden of Eden and called it the "silent healer." It was also frequently used in biblical times as an embalming lotion. The Gospel of John says, "He came therefore, and took away His body. And Nicodemus came also, who had first come to Him by night; bringing a mixture of myrrh and aloes, about a hundred pounds weight." During the Crusades, the Knights Templar drank wine named "the Elixir of Jerusalem" made with aloe pulp, claiming it improved health and longevity. In the 16th century, the Spaniards brought aloe vera to the New World. Christopher Columbus once said, "Four vegetables are indispensable for the well being of man: Wheat, the grape, the olive, and aloe."

However, attempts to import aloe as a healing product were unsuccessful since the pulp's efficacy depended on freshness. Finally in 1970, a technique of cold pressing the gel as well as separating the rind from the key compound aloin provided an expanded market. Aloe vera is now a multibillion-dollar, worldwide business.

Medicinal and Cosmetic Uses

Several species of aloe have medicinal properties, but many others are poisonous. Aloe vera has been documented as a healing plant for over 3,000 years. It has been used as a purgative, laxative, antidiabetic, anticancer, antimicrobial, antiarthritic, and antiobesity agent. It aids in healing burns, dryness, and other conditions. In Asia, it has been used as an immune booster. In 1934, the first modern medical paper was published about aloe vera, identifying its ability to treat radiation dermatitis, increasing its popularity during the atomic bomb era.

There are two parts of the aloe vera plant. Aloe gel is the opaque liquid inside the large part of the plant's leaf. It can be easily cut and squeezed or drained. Many people keep aloe vera as houseplants, using the gel as a home remedy for minor skin burns or irritations. The gel hydrates and protects wounds while stimulating new growth of skin cells during the healing process. Aloe gel has gained immense popularity as a skin product, not only for healing common ailments such as sunburns, dry skin, and minor wounds but also as a general moisturizer. It is found in skin lotions, cosmetics, soaps, toothpaste, and even facial tissues.

The latex or yellow sap is a bitter fluid found in small pustules under the outer rind. This "aloe juice" includes the compound aloins made of barbaloin and isobarbaloin, which create the crystalline aloin. Aloin is dried and can be used as a laxative, purgative, and vermifuge, and is even sometimes the bitter agent in alcohol. In smaller doses, aloe juice is used to aid digestion, and some maintain that it can aid in some control of irritable bowel syndrome. Dried sap "tea" has been said to help cleanse wounds and wash irritated eyes, but it must be applied very carefully.

Erika Stump

Further Reading

Baldwin, Gertrude. "Aloe Vera." Dr. Christopher's Herbal Legacy. http://www.herballegacy.com?Baldwin_History.html (accessed 1 August 2010).

"The Genus Aloe." *Botanical Notes—University of California Davis Botanical Conservatory* 1, no. 1 (July 2009).

Grieve, M. *A Modern Herbal: The Medicinal, Culinary, Cosmetic and Economic Properties, Cultivation and Folk-Lore of Herbs, Grasses, Fungi, Shrubs and Trees with All Their Modern Scientific Uses.* New York: Dover, 1971.

Amaranth

Known as "love-lies-bleeding," "velvet flower," and "tassel flower," amaranth comprises roughly 60 species in the genus *Amaranthus*. Indians know amaranth as "king seed" and "seed sent by God." The word "amaranth" derives from the Greek *amarantos*, meaning "unwithered" or "never waxing old," meanings that reveal the Greeks' belief that the plant symbolized immortality. Greek storyteller Aesop (620–564 BCE) wrote that amaranth envied the rosebush for its beauty and the rosebush envied amaranth for being immortal. The Egyptians shared this belief and, along with the Greeks, chiseled images of amaranth plants on tombs and temples. A versatile plant, amaranth is cultivated for seeds and leaves and as an ornamental. The seeds and leaves are edible. People term the seeds grain, though amaranth is, unlike wheat, corn, rice, barley, oats, and other true grains, not a grass. Its seeds and leaves are nourishing. The leaves contain more calcium than beet greens and more protein than spinach. A half cup of amaranth leaves has 14 calories, 138 milligrams of calcium, 47 milligrams of phosphorus, 1.5 milligrams of iron, 423 milligrams of potassium, and 27 milligrams of vitamin C. The seeds have the amino acids threconine, valine, leucine, methionine, and lysine, the last being deficient in several grains. Amaranth seeds have twice the lysine of wheat and thrice that of corn, and as much as milk. The seeds are 16 percent protein, more than milk, soybeans, wheat, rice, and corn. The amaranth seed is 26 percent germ and bran, roughly the same percentage as in wheat. The germ is 30 percent protein and 20 percent oil. The bran has fiber, protein, vitamins, and minerals.

History

Amaranth is native to Africa, India, Mexico, Central America, and South America as far south as Peru. The people of Mexico ate amaranth seeds as early as 8000 BCE, though the plant was not likely a cultigen this early. Cultivation dates to the fourth millennium BCE, when the people of Mexico and Guatemala began raising the species *Amaranthus cruentus* for seeds and leaves. The inhabitants of central Mexico domesticated *Amaranthus hypochondriacus* about 500 CE. The species is the hardiest and highest yielder of the amaranths grown for seeds. The time of origin of *Amaranthus caudatus* appears to be less certain, though the region of origin overlapped with the area where the Amerindians domesticated the potato in the Andes Mountains. The Spanish called *Amaranthus caudatus* Inca wheat, apparently because of its status as a staple.

One thesis holds that the Amerindians regarded amaranth as almost as important as corn and beans. The Aztec emperor levied a tax of 200,000 bushels of amaranth seeds from his territory. Amaranth was not merely a food. It was an object of veneration. In eating amaranth seeds and leaves, the Aztecs honored Huitzilopochtli, the god of agriculture and eternal life. Like the Greeks and Egyptians, Amerindians regarded amaranth as a symbol of immortality. The Aztecs mixed amaranth seeds with honey or blood, forming them into images of snakes, birds, deer, mountains, and gods. The Spanish were shocked that the Aztecs ate images of their gods and condemned the practice as a perversion of the Catholic sacrament of the Eucharist. Accordingly, the Spanish banned cultivation and consumption of amaranth and executed those who violated this prohibition. In stamping out Aztec lifeways, the Spanish reduced amaranth to a minor crop grown in the outposts of the Spanish empire, away from the center of power. In addition to the Aztecs, the Inca, the Tarahumora of Mexico, and the Hopi and Tohono O'odham of Arizona grew amaranth for food.

Amaranth's history in Europe is difficult to trace. The Greeks cultivated Mediterranean amaranth (*Amaranthus graecizans*), but the plant may not have been widely grown in the Mediterranean because Spain, importing Amerindian species of the plant in the 16th century, appears to have regarded them as new cultigens. Although the Spanish recoiled at the Aztecs' use of amaranth, they took an interest in the plant, but as an ornamental rather than a crop. The green, red, and purple flowers caught the fancy of gardeners, and a brief mania for the plant held Spain in its grip. The fad passed and the Spanish appear to have nearly forgotten about amaranth. Meanwhile, amaranth made slow progress elsewhere. By 1700, the people of Central Europe and Russian grew *Amaranthus hypochondriacus* for seeds. By the 19th century, the people of Ethiopia, southern India, Nepal, and Mongolia grew amaranth for seeds and leaves. By the 1980s, India boasted the largest area to grow amaranth. Today, amaranth seeds and leaves feed the people of Mexico, Central and South America, India, the Middle East, and parts of Africa. The United States, Canada, and Europe grow little amaranth. The Chinese feed amaranth to livestock but seldom eat it themselves. The people of the Himalayan Mountains make a flat bread from amaranth seeds. In the hills of northwestern India, farmers plant as much as half their nonirrigated land with amaranth. Indians combine amaranth seeds with honey as the Aztecs had done. Hindus eat amaranth seeds on days when their religion prohibits the consumption of grain. The people of Africa, Malaysia, Indonesia, southern China, southern India, and the Caribbean cultivate *Amaranthus tricolor*, *Amaranthus dubius*, and *Amaranthus cruentus* for their leaves, which they add to soup and salad. The Greeks boil the leaves. Amaranth seeds may be baked in bread and cake. Some health food stores sell amaranth seeds for roasting like peanuts or popping like popcorn, which makes them suitable as a snack. Many Asians eat amaranth leaves as a substitute for spinach, some favoring the species *Amaranthus tricolor*. The Amerindians of the American Southwest cultivate amaranth as a vegetable where the climate is too hot and dry for lettuce and cabbage.

Attributes and Cultivation

Amaranth grows to 12 feet tall, a height agronomists regard as excessive for machine harvest. Whether grown as an ornamental or crop, amaranth should be planted less than one centimeter from the top of soil because seeds must be exposed to light to germinate. Seeds germinate between 61°F and 95°F in three to five days with the fastest germination at the highest temperature. Of its 60 species, some are adapted to the temperate zone. *Amaranthus caudatus*, for example, tolerates cold weather. Most species, however, are native to the tropics and subtropics and are cultivated between 30° north and 30° south. *Amaranthus hypochondriacus* and *Amaranthus cruentus*, for example, do not tolerate frost. They cease growth at 46°F and suffer injury below 39°F. Amaranth, especially those species grown for leaves, benefits from the addition of nitrogen and potassium to the soil. Amaranth grown for seeds prefers well-drained soil with a pH above 6. Some species tolerate alkaline soils with pH as high as 8.5. *Amaranthus tricolor* tolerates levels of aluminum in soil that are toxic to other crops. Seedlings are vulnerable to water shortage, but mature plants tolerate drought by closing their stomata under stress. As a rule, amaranth grown for seeds prefers a dry climate whereas amaranth grown for leaves prefers wet environs. The former tolerates as little as eight inches of rain per year. Amaranth grown for seeds should be sown at a density of 80,000 plants per acre. Amaranth, a particularly efficient photosynthesizer, needs full sun. It does not tolerate humidity and waterlogged soil. Tropical species do not flower in the long hours of daylight typical of the summers at high latitudes. *Amaranthus caudatus*, for example, needs fewer than eight hours of daylight to flower. Amaranth may be grown between sea level and 9,600 feet in elevation. *Amaranthus caudatus* is the best yielder at elevation.

In the 1980s, scientists turned to amaranth, believing that it had potential to feed large numbers of the world's burgeoning population. Amaranth had been an important crop in pre-Columbian America, scientists reasoned, and might now become a world crop. Scientists labored to adapt amaranth to the machine age, aiming to breed varieties with uniform height and ripening to ease machine harvest. They sought to breed short, sturdy plants that would not lodge and would stand erect at harvest. They aimed to mechanize planting, weeding, harvesting, and threshing of seeds. They encouraged farmers in the developing world to cultivate amaranth as a way to diminish their dependence on wheat imports. Scientists aimed to supply farmers with a surplus of amaranth seeds that could be fed to chickens, a rapidly growing sector of the economy of the developing world.

The gardener who grows amaranth as an ornamental may start seeds indoors eight weeks before the last frost. Seedlings are ready for transplant two weeks after germination. The gardener may plant seedlings outdoors when the temperature gets no colder than 50°F, spacing plants 10 to 12 inches apart. Amaranth, grown as an ornamental, flowers in midsummer. Flowers persist until autumn frost. Heirloom varieties of amaranth are popular today.

Christopher Cumo

Further Reading

Amaranth: Modern Prospects for an Ancient Crop. Emmaus, PA: Rodale Press, 1985.

Cole, John N. *Amaranth: From the Past for the Future*. Emmaus, PA: Rodale Press, 1979.

Coulter, Lynn. *Gardening with Heirloom Seeds: Tried-and-True Flowers, Fruits, and Vegetables for a New Generation*. Chapel Hill: University of North Carolina Press, 2006.

McNamee, Gregory. *Movable Feasts: The History, Science, and Lore of Food*. Westport, CT: Praeger, 2007.

Paredes-Lopez, Octavio. *Amaranth: Biology, Chemistry and Technology*. Boca Raton, FL: CRC Press, 1994.

Anemone

The botanical name anemone derives from the Greek *anemos*, meaning "wind," possibly because the seeds of the genus can be carried on the wind or because some species of the genus have delicate leaves and flowers that quiver in the breeze. This has led to windflower becoming the common name of the anemone. The genus *Anemone* is a diverse group of around 120 species of flower belonging to the Ranunculaceae family of buttercups, cultivated in gardens of the temperate zones of the Northern and Southern Hemispheres and growing wild in Europe, Japan, and North America. The anemone is closely related to the Pasque flower, *pulsatilla*, and to *hepatica*. Indeed, some plant taxonomists include both *pulsatilla* and *hepatica* within the *Anemone* genus.

Attributes

Species of anemone can grow up to four feet tall. Anemone flowers are one to three inches in diameter and cup or saucer shaped with a central tuft of stamens. The flowers are composed of sepals rather than true petals, in shades of pink, purple, lilac, red, white, and blue, and can either be borne one per stem or in clusters in single, semidouble, or double forms, such as the anemone De Caen series and the anemone St. Brigid series. Leaves are deeply cut and fern-like. The diverse nature of the anemone genus is reflected in both the root systems and flowering times of the plant. Some species of anemone grow from fleshy stems or rhizomes while others originate from tubers, which should be treated like spring-flowering bulbs. Flowering times for species of anemone range from early in the year to fall, with some species, such as *Anemone canadensis* and *Anemone sylvestris*, flowering in spring, and some, such as *Anemone hupehensis*, *Anemone tomentosa*, and the hybrids of *Anemone Xhybrida*, blooming in autumn. These autumn-flowering species are known collectively as Japanese anemones. While early-flowering species of anemone will grow in full sun, both early- and late-flowering species enjoy environments that are partially shady, with rich but light, moist soil. A woodland setting is ideal for anemones. In North America the American wood anemone, *Anemone quinquefolia*, is the earliest anemone to flower under such woodland conditions, followed by *Anemone canadensis* and then later still by *Anemone virginiana*.

Mythology

Classical mythology cites two origins of the anemone. One myth tells that the goddess Venus loved Adonis and that when Adonis was gored by Ares, in the form of a bull, an anemone bearing scarlet petals sprang from the blood of the fallen youth, and also that an anemone grew where the tears of the goddess Venus fell to the ground as she mourned her dead lover. A less well-known myth is that Anemone was a nymph beloved of the west wind, Zephyr. The goddess of flowers, Flora, became jealous that Zephyr favored Anemone and transformed the nymph into a flower. When Zephyr learned of Anemone's transformation, he abandoned her to the brutal north wind, Boreas, whose chill and roughness caused Anemone to wither rapidly. This myth is very similar to a German legend in which beautiful Anemone became the beloved of Zephyrus, the god who breathed life into all plants. Chloris became envious of Anemone and drove her from her home. Cowardly Zephyrus deserted Anemome and changed her into a flower.

Both the second classical myth and the German legend attempt then to explain both why the early-flowering anemone seems to open with the first warm wind of the year and also why spring anemone has such a short flowering period. It may also suggest why, in the Victorian language of flowers, the anemone symbolized ill-health, an association with sickness and death that transcends cultures. For instance in Chinese culture, the anemone is synonymous with death, and in ancient Rome anemones were used to garland the deceased. Despite the association with death, the Romans, who believed anemones to possess antimalarial properties, cultivated the flower. The Romans also chose anemones to decorate ceremonial altars, especially those dedicated to Venus. The death symbolism of the anemone corresponds with its association, in some parts of Europe, with immortality and Easter. In this context, the anemone is known as the flower of resurrection. This association is prominent in Germany, where the anemone is used to garland a cow each Easter. In some areas of the Middle East, the anemone is known as the blood drops of Christ for it is said that the blood of Christ fell on the anemones that had bloomed on Calvary, turning the flowers bloodred. The Christian mythology of the anemone combined with the flower's three-petal form has led to the anemone being known as the herb trinity. The anemone also features in pagan folklore. For instance in British fairy lore, the flower of the European wood-anemone, *Anemone nemorosa*, was said to be used by fairies as a shelter from rain. *Anemone nemorosa* is rich in the toxin anemonine, and anemonine and another toxin, protoanemonin, are present in most anemone species. Anemonine is thus poisonous to both humans and wildlife, and on contact with the skin causes severe irritation; while ingestion of anemonine results in a burning sensation in the mouth and severe gastrointestinal discomfort including the vomiting of blood. However, extracts of anemone are used in homeopathic medicine, especially for the treatment of eye conditions and headaches.

Victoria Williams

Further Reading

Armitage, Allan M. *Armitage's Garden Perennials: A Color Encyclopedia.* Portland, OR: Timber Press, 2000.

Burnett, Gilbert. *An Encyclopaedia of Useful and Ornamental Plants.* Vol. 2. London: George Willis, 1852.

Runkel, Sylvan T., and Alvin F. Bull. *Wildflowers of Iowa's Woodlands.* Iowa City: University of Iowa Press, 2009.

Skinner, Charles Montgomery. *Myths and Legends of Flowers, Trees, Fruits, and Plants in All Times and in All Climes.* General Books LLC. http://books.google.co.uk/books?id=s5p82USYH4cC&printsec=frontcover&source=gbs_ge_summary_r&cad=0#v=onepage&q&f=false (accessed 6 November 2010). First published by J. B. Lipincott, 1915.

Tenenbaum, Frances, ed. *Taylor's Encyclopedia of Garden Plants.* New York: Houghton Mifflin, 2003.

Ward, Bobby J. *A Contemplation upon Flowers: Garden Plants in Myth and Literature.* Portland, OR: Timber Press, 1999.

Anise

Anise, classified by 18th-century Swedish naturalist Carl Linnaeus as *Pimpinella anisum* in 1753, is a flowering spice plant native to Egypt, Greece, Crete, and Asia Minor. It was first cultivated by the ancient Egyptians and was later cultivated by the Greeks and Romans before spreading to Central Europe during the Middle Ages. It resembles plants of the carrot family (Umbelliferoe), including dill, fennel, coriander, cumin, and caraway, and is related to parsley. Anise's flavor resembles licorice, and its seeds, called aniseeds, are used to flavor licorice candy. Anise is sometimes referred to as *anís*, with the stress on the second syllable.

Origin and Description

The early Arabs called anise *anysum*, which later became *anison* in Greek and *anisun* in Latin. It may be one of the oldest spice plants, dating back as early as 1500 BCE. The ancient Greeks and Romans used anise in several ways, including as a cure for asp bites when mixed with wine. Fifth-century BCE Greek physician Hippocrates believed it could relieve cold symptoms, while Pliny the Elder, a first-century Roman encyclopedist, recommended anise to cure bad breath. The Romans also baked anise into cakes called mustacae, which they ate after meals to aid digestion. In biblical times, the spice was used as a form of payment for taxes. Its name appears in the 23rd chapter of the Bible's Gospel of Matthew in the line "Ye pay tithe of Mint, Anise, and Cummin." In the early 1300s, anise was a drug that King Edward I of England taxed as a means of funding the maintenance of London Bridge.

Anise grows in any moderately warm climate. It is an annual that reaches about two to three feet high and is made up of delicate, white flowers and bright green leaflets that grow from feather-like stalks. The name *Pimpinella* derives from *dipinella*, meaning "twice pinnate," or having similar parts arranged on opposite sides of the stem, which is a reference to the appearance of the leaves.

The larvae of some butterflies and moths (*Lepidoptera*), including the wormwood pug, use the anise plant as food.

Anise's Culinary and Other Uses

Both the roots and leaves of the anise plant are edible, but the gray-green or brown small seeds are the most used part of the plant. Seeds, whole or ground up, are added as a flavoring in soups, candy, and a cordial liqueur known as anisette. Other alcoholic drinks flavored with anise are Italian pizzelle, French absinthe, German Jägermeister, and the Turkish raki. Anise is also used as a flavoring agent in some root beers and in the Mexican hot chocolate drink called champurrado. In the Middle East, a hot tea called Yansoon is made by boiling about one tablespoon of aniseed per cup of water. The leaves of the plant can be used to flavor liqueurs and are likewise used in curry dishes and other spicy meat recipes.

Anise's aromatic essential oil from the seeds, containing 70–90 percent of a phytoestrogen called *anethole*, is considered good bait to entice mice into traps. The oil is poisonous to some animals, such as pigeons. Because of their sweet and spicy aroma, the seeds are incorporated into arts-and-crafts projects, as in the making of sachets and potpourri, and are used as an additive in perfume to create a spicy scent.

In addition, according to folklore, anise is able to ward off the curse of the evil eye and to keep nightmares at bay when placed under a pillow. Fishermen have been known to rub anise's oils on their hooks to lure fish. Dogs also are attracted to anise, and dog food manufacturers sometimes incorporate the ingredient in the food. It also is used as a distraction to throw dogs off their tracks in hunts and is inserted into the "rabbit" lure in greyhound races.

Although unrelated, anise and star anise both contain anethole and its licorice flavor. Because of its abundance and low cost to produce, star anise (the eight-horned pericarp of *Illicium verum*, a small evergreen tree) has overtaken anise in its use in cooking.

The Medicinal Uses of Anise

During the U.S. Civil War, a nurse named Maureen Hellstrom is said to have used aniseeds as an antiseptic to treat soldiers' wounds. The use was discontinued after high levels of toxins were discovered in the blood of patients who were administered the antiseptic.

Anise is used in modern day for medicinal purposes. As in Roman times, it is still used as a digestive aid as well as an antiflatulent. For centuries, it has been used to treat colds and ease coughs. The anethole oil has expectorant properties, too, which helps bring up phlegm, easing congestion. Teas made from anise are believed by some to improve memory as well as stop excessive oil production in skin.

Nursing mothers sometimes drink anise tea to stimulate milk production and ease heartburn, indigestion, and other digestive problems. The antispasmodic properties in anise that help control coughs may also relieve menstrual pain, and may ease asthma attacks, bronchitis, and whooping cough. The essential oil has been used by some as a topical treatment for lice and scabies.

Cultivation

The anise plant grows best in well-draining, dry, light soil that has plenty of sun exposure. Anise plants should be thinned and weeded. They have a taproot and are not easily transplanted. Therefore they should be transplanted only while the seedlings are still small, or they should be left to grow in the place in which they are established. The anise plant flowers in midsummer, and the seeds are harvested in the fall. The harvested seeds have a grayish green color, are oval in shape, contain ribs, and are about one-fifth of an inch in length. The stems of the flower are sometimes cut and hung upside down to dry. Seeds are collected as they fall from the flower or the seeds are dried in trays.

Rosemarie Boucher Leenerts

Further Reading

Absolute Astronomy. "Anise." http://www.absoluteastronomy.com/topics/Anise (accessed 8 October 2010).

Ashhurst, P. R. *Food Flavorings*. Gaithersburg, MD: Aspen, 1999.

Jodral, Manuel Miro. *Illicium, Pimpinella, and Foeniculum*. Danvers, MA: CRC Press, 2004.

Ross, Ivan A. *Medicinal Plants of the World: Chemical Constituents, Traditional and Modern Medicinal Uses*. Vol. 2. Totowa, NJ: Humana Press, 2001.

Seedaholic.com. "Anise, Pimpinella anisum." http://www.seedaholic.com/lemon-balm -melissa-officinalis-bee-balm-1.html (accessed 15 September 2010).

Apple

A perennial fruit tree, the apple is known by several names. In Latin, the word for apple is *ponum*, from which the French derive *pomme* and the Italians *pomo*.

Apple trees (Corel)

In Irish, the word for apple was *abhel*, in Welsh *afel*, in Celtic *abello*, in Old English *aeppel*, and in German *apfel*. The genus name of the apple, *Malus*, once referred to any fruit tree. In the Rosaceae family, the apple is related to the rose, pear, and quince. Some botanists see in apple blossoms a resemblance to the rose. Scientists know the apple as *Malus* × *domestica*, a name that denotes its status as a hybrid. One medium apple contains 81 calories, 21 grams of carbohydrate, 4 grams of fiber, 10 milligrams of calcium, 10 milligrams of phosphorus, 25 milligrams of iron, no sodium, 159 milligrams of potassium, 8 milligrams of vitamin C, 73 international units of vitamin A, and 4 micrograms of folic acid. It is important to eat the skin because much of the vitamin C is immediately beneath the skin of an apple.

Origin and Diffusion in Antiquity

In the 1920s, Russian agronomist Nikolai Vavilov discovered a wild apple tree in Kirghizia, a region in the Tien Shan Mountains, proposing it as the place where the apple originated. Others have identified the Caucasus Mountains as the homeland of the apple. According to another school of thought, the modern apple may have arisen in the mountains of Kazakhstan or perhaps south of the Caucasus Mountains in Georgia, Armenia, or Turkey. It is also possible that the apple originated in the Baltic region of Latvia, Lithuania, and Estonia. Another possibility is that the apple originated in Finland and Poland. The first apple was not impressive.

Small and sour, it resembled the crab apple rather than the large sweet apple of modernity. Because bees pollinate apples, they must have crossbred innumerable times over the millennia. Some of these crosses must have yielded large apples that were the progenitors of the modern apple. Several species of apple may have contributed genes to the genome of today's apples. The Asian species *Malus sieversii*, which grows wild from the Tien Shan Mountains to lands near the Caspian Sea, may be one proto-apple in the lineage of the modern apple. Another progenitor may have been *Malus orientalis*, an apple of the Caucasus Mountains. The European crab apple, *Malus sylvestrius*, native to the lands between the United Kingdom and northern Turkey, may have been an ancestor of the modern apple. Other progenitors may have been the Siberian crab apple *Malus baccata*, the Manchurian crab apple *Malus mandshurica*, and the Chinese crab apple *Malus primifolia.*

Because apples cross-pollinate and because each seed is a unique genotype, the populations of ancient apples must have varied a great deal. Some trees must have produced large, flavorful apples whereas others must have yielded small, sour apples. Furthermore, the progeny of a large apple might revert to small, inconsequential fruit. From an early date, humans must have selected apples for size and flavor, but they must have been disappointed that apples do not breed true. In contrast to seeds, a vegetatively propagated tree had the same genotype and thus characteristics of the parent tree. In practice humans, around the third millennium BCE, accomplished the aim of deriving clones of superior trees by grafting a branch onto a sturdy rootstock. In the best circumstance, the branch bore apples with the desiderata of size and flavor, and the rootstock was resistant to diseases and pests.

Archaeologists have dated apples to 6500 BCE in Jericho in the West Bank and Catal Huyuk, Turkey, and to 6000 BCE in Switzerland. These dates are too early for these apples to have come from grafts and they may even be too early for the apples to have come from cultivated trees. Humans may simply have gathered them wild. The tomb of Queen Pu-abi of Ur, dating to 2500 BCE, contained apples, which the Sumerians may have gotten from lands hundreds of miles distant. This possibility suggests long-distance commerce in apples though it does not prove that they were cultivated. A Sumerian text from the same period, however, mentions the growing of figs and apples, establishing the third millennium BCE as the origin of apple culture. The practices of cultivating apples and of grafting them may have arisen at roughly the same time. It is possible, however, that the people of the Indus River Valley in India cultivated the apple earlier than the third millennium. From about 2500 BCE, humans grew apples in Georgia, Armenia, Turkey, Iraq, and Iran. The Hittites recorded the existence of orchards with 40 trees. Grown as far west as the Aegean coast of Turkey, the apple may have migrated south to Egypt. In the 13th century BCE, Pharaoh Ramses II claimed to have planted apple trees in his garden, but some scholars doubt this boast because Egypt's warm winters are not ideal for apple culture.

Europeans probably cultivated the apple, likely a larger variety of crab apple that they had selected for size before the arrival of migrants, apple in hand, from the Caucasus Mountains. In the ninth century BCE, Greek poet Homer remarked that King Laertes, father of Odysseus, grew apples in his garden. That century Assyrian kings tended apples. In antiquity, Armenia and Turkey were renowned for their apples. The Persians (now Iranians) planted apples throughout their empire. Persian cuisine combined apples and other fruit with meat and legumes. The Persians prized apples from Georgia for their flavor. One authority dates the cultivation of apples in Greece and Etruria to 600 BCE. In the fourth century BCE, Greek botanist Theophrastus knew several varieties of apple and recommended those from the Crimea as the best. Etruscan farmer Appius—his name is not associated with the word "apple"—cultivated a variety known as Api in his honor. The Romans, absorbing Etruscan culture, prized Api. Today, the French know this variety as *pomme de' Api* and Americans term it Lady Apple. Api may be the oldest variety still in cultivation. In the second century BCE, patrician and agricultural writer Cato the Elder, writing in *On Agriculture*, understood that apple seeds germinated a tree that often bore small, sour fruit. He recommended vegetative propagation to be sure of deriving satisfactory apples. By 50 BCE, the Romans were cultivating apples in Gaul (modern France). In antiquity, Normandy emerged as an apple producer. The Basques of Spain may have cultivated apples in the pre-Roman period. It is possible that the Basques taught the people of Gaul to grow apples. In the first century CE, Greek historian Plutarch named the apple as his favorite fruit, remarking that only it satisfied all the senses. According to one authority, the Romans grew more varieties of apple than any other fruit. First-century CE Roman encyclopedist Pliny the Elder listed 36 varieties. He urged workers to pick apples after the autumn equinox, doing this task in late September or early October. Pliny recommended the storage of apples in a cool, dry place. The Romans sometimes coated apples in plaster or wax, perhaps to preserve them. They ate dishes of apple, pork, coriander, liquemen, and honey. Pompeii's paintings feature apple trees, though it is possible that these trees, like lemon trees in antiquity, were ornamentals. The physicians of Greece and Rome, who believed the theory of the four humors, classified apples as cool and moist and so as a complement to hot meat. In the first century CE, Roman poet Juvenal and agricultural writer Columella gave advice on growing and storing apples. The Persians, Greeks, and Romans thought that the apple was an aphrodisiac. According to Persian custom, a girl could eat nothing but apples on her wedding night to ensure that she was at the peak of fertility. According to one school of thought, the apple was not, however, widely grown in antiquity. The people of the Caucasus who had favored apples jettisoned them for grain and meat when they migrated to the

Mediterranean Basin. The Greeks and Romans, according to one authority, considered the apple a luxury. If this is true, the masses must not have eaten it. The ancients may have preferred grapes, dates, and figs to apples.

The Middle Ages and Modernity

However widespread it was, the apple went into decline with the fall of Rome. The art of grafting may have been lost as farmers were content to raise apples from seeds. The large, flavorful apples of the Persians, Greeks, and Romans ceded ground to wild crab apples. In the Middle Ages, people seldom ate fresh apples. After the fall of Rome, sweet apples became uncommon, depressing the demand for fresh apples. Instead, most apples were pressed for cider. The monks of Europe cultivated apples for cider, but because cider may be made from any apple no matter how small or misshapen, there was no need for the aesthetically pleasing apples of antiquity. Hard cider was a common beverage in the Middle Ages and possibly in antiquity, though it may not have challenged the supremacy of wine in the Mediterranean and beer in Northern Europe. The alcohol in hard cider killed microbes so that it was safe to drink even when the water was contaminated. Some people doubtless consumed cider in preference to water.

In the ninth century, Frankish king Charlemagne, evidently intent on making apples more widely known, ordered them to be planted in the royal gardens. In the 10th century, the abbot of Ely planted apples in his monastery in England. That century Heywal Dda, a Welsh prince, set the price of a sweet apple at twice that of a sour apple. The Normans, conquerors of England in 1066, drank cider. As the Cistercian Order spread in the 12th century, its monks tended apples throughout Europe. From Burgundy, France, the Cistercians brought the apple to Germany and from Paris they brought it to Denmark. The Arabs, perhaps deriving their interest in the apple from the Persians, were avid apple growers. In 1080 Ibn Bassal, an official in Toledo, Spain, gave advice on planting, grafting, pruning, and fertilizing apples in the *Book of Agriculture*. From the 13th century, perhaps because of Arab influence and the work of monks, the cultivation of apples spread throughout Europe.

Yet it is difficult to know how prevalent the apple was in the diet. Many medieval physicians abandoned the ancient belief that apples were wholesome. They counseled children and wet nurses not to eat apples. The fruit caused, physicians believed, stomachache and fever. The identification of the apple as the forbidden fruit in Genesis may have deepened suspicion of it. Not everyone was so negative, however. Cooks prepared apples with sugar to sweeten them and added apples to porridge. In England, monks ate apples during Lent. The custom of eating an apple at the beginning of a meal to aid digestion may have been widespread. In medieval Europe, the fruit was added to stew, stuffed into meat, and made into sauce. In the 13th century, Count Albert of Ballstadt recommended apple trees as ornamentals because of their attractive fruit and fragrance. In 1280, Queen Eleanor of Castile planted apple trees as ornamentals in England. In 1390, the chef of King Richard II of England published a recipe for applesauce, possibly the first of its kind. In 1398, King Charles VI of France planted 100 apple trees and 12 miniature paradise apples in his garden. The latter must have been dwarf trees. In the 15th century, Italian Pietro de Crescenti likewise remarked that apple trees were suitable as ornamentals.

In the Middle Ages, domestic demand for apples may have exceeded supply in England because it imported them from France. The French imports Costard and Blandural were popular in England. The English cooked Costard, perhaps adding sugar, as was the custom. Blandural stored well, sweetening over three months of storage. The English cultivated the Pearmain variety for cider. The growth of cities in the Late Middle Ages increased the demand for apples. In the 15th century, Renaissance artists Sandro Boticelli and Giovanni Bellini included apples in their works, much as the Romans had done. The walls of the Medici villa of Poggio a Cainno were decorated with frescos of the goddess Pomona tending an apple orchard and of Hercules amid an apple tree in the garden of the Hesperides. Renaissance Italians prize the paradise apple.

The discovery of the Americas opened new lands to the apple. To be sure the apple was not a novelty in the New World. The crab apple populated the temperate regions of the Americas, though it is unclear whether the Amerindians took much interest in it. The pre-Columbian people of America appear not to have cultivated the apple. Although they knew the crab apple, Native Americans had never seen the sweet apple until Europeans arrived in the New World. In the 16th and 17th centuries, the French planted apples in Canada. Presumably the earliest introductions were seeds rather than grafts. Indeed, until the 19th century grafting was uncommon in the United States. In the 16th and 17th centuries, the English, French, Dutch, Germans, and Scandinavians planted apple trees along the Atlantic coast of North America. In 1625, cleric William Blaxton may have planted the first apple orchard in Massachusetts. Later he claimed credit for growing the first apples in Rhode Island. In 1648, William Endicott, the first governor of Massachusetts, planted an orchard of 500 trees. Perhaps following the custom in Europe, many colonists drank hard cider rather than water. In the 17th century, New York governor Peter Stuyvesant planted apple trees on Manhattan. By the 1730s, the American colonies were exporting apples to the Caribbean. In the 18th century, George Washington tended apple trees at Mount Vernon, Virginia. That century Colonel William Fitzhugh boasted of an orchard of 2,500 trees. In the 1830s, a barrel of apples fetched $4 in New York City. In the 19th century, the United States imported trees from Scandinavia, Germany, and Russia, crossing them with American varieties. That century, John Chapman, today known as Johnny Appleseed, established orchards throughout the Northeast and Midwest. By 1850, U.S.

farmers could choose among more than 500 cultivars. With the standardization of production in the 20th century, the number of apple varieties decreased from 1,000 in 1872 to 100 in 1975. Outside North America, the Spanish and Portuguese tended apples in South America and the Spanish introduced the apple to the American Southwest and California.

Europeans took the apple to other regions of the world. In 1654, Jan van Riebeeck, founder of the Dutch East India Company, planted apple trees in South Africa. In the late 19th century, apple acreage increased in South Africa as disease killed grapevines, convincing many farmers to switch to apples. In 1788, Captain Arthur Phillip brought apples to Australia. Around the same time, Captain William Bligh planted apples in Tasmania. In 1814, British missionaries introduced the apple to New Zealand. In the 19th century, South Africa, Australia, and New Zealand exported apples to Europe, giving its inhabitants access to fresh fruit out of season. In the 20th century, China, Korea, Japan, India, and Pakistan adopted U.S. cultivars. Because these varieties were productive, Asia became an apple exporter. Today, China and the United States are the world's largest producers. India, another important producer, yields two times more apples than does the United Kingdom. Argentina, Brazil, and Chile are large exporters. In the Ukraine, a single orchard yields more apples than all the orchards in the United Kingdom.

Today, Washington, New York, and Michigan lead the United States in apple production, but apples are grown in every state in the country, with 2,500 varieties of apples grown, and 7,500 types grown throughout the world (University of Illinois Extension 2011). Until the 1970s, McIntosh, Red Delicious, and Golden Delicious were the most popular and prevalent in U.S. grocery stores. But since then, new varieties, many introduced from other countries, have become more available in supermarkets, including Granny Smith (Australia), Gala and Braeburn (both from New Zealand), Fuji (from Japan), Jazz, and Honeycrisp. But as with tomatoes and other fruits and vegetables, a new interest in long-ago-grown heirloom varieties is surfacing.

In commercial orchards, farmers contract hives of bees to hasten pollination. Under the proper conditions, an apple may be stored one year without loss of flavor. People eat apple muffins, apple pie, apple dumplings, applesauce, apple cake, apple fritters, apple pancakes, and apple butter. They drink apple juice and apple cider. Swedes eat apples, Canadian bacon, and sautéed onions for Sunday breakfast. Germans eat baked apples with sour cherries and also apple pudding. Turks eat apples with fish. Israelis make applesauce from green apples.

Mythology and Religion

The apple was central to the mythology, folklore, and religion of several peoples. It was an important fruit in Greek mythology. The Greeks sculpted likenesses of the goddess Aphrodite holding an apple. The association between Aphrodite and the apple leads one to suppose that it symbolized love and lust. The association between Aphrodite and the apple may stem from the story of the wedding of Peleus and Thetis. The couple had not invited the goddess Discord to the ceremony. Angry about this slight, she engendered conflict by placing a golden apple in the room. The goddesses Hera, Aphrodite, and Athena claimed it. When none of the three prevailed, they asked Prince Paris of Troy to choose the victor. Each goddess disrobed before Paris to sway his decision. Aphrodite promised him the most beautiful woman in the world, Helen. Eager to have her, Paris gave the apple to Aphrodite. In taking Helen, Paris precipitated the Trojan War.

The association between Aphrodite and the apple is part of another Greek myth. The maiden Atalanta learned from an oracle that she would become mortal if she wed. Her father, however, wanted her to marry. To preserve her status as a maiden while seeming to satisfy her father, Atalanta agreed to marry whoever could beat her in a footrace. Because she was so swift, she had no difficulty defeating the suitors who challenged her. Hippomene, wishing to marry Atalanta, prayed to Aphrodite for help. Aphrodite gave the young man three golden apples. During the race, Hippomene slowed Atalanta by throwing an apple at her feet each time she surged ahead. Bending over to pick up each apple, she lost her momentum and the race. The two married.

One tradition holds that Aphrodite got the golden apples from a tree in the garden of Hera. Mother Earth had given the tree to Hera upon her marriage to Zeus. Hera planted the tree, instructing the goddesses Hesperides to guard it. Despite their vigilance, Hercules stole the apples from the tree. Because the Greeks associated the apple with the sun, one authority believes that Hercules's theft of the apples marked his claim to be the sun god, a position he may have held in a primitive religion assimilated by the Greeks.

In Christian tradition, the apple may have been a symbol of immortality. According to one account, the martyr Dorothea, who died about 300 CE, encountered the lawyer Theophilus on her way to execution. Skeptical of the claims of Christianity and perhaps wishing to mock her, he asked Dorothea to bring back fruit from heaven. In answer to Theophilus, Dorothea stopped to pray. Out of the crowd emerged a boy with a basket of apples. Dorothea gave them to Theophilus, promising him more when he entered heaven. After eating an apple, Theophilus converted to Christianity. The apple had given him immortality.

The best-known myth of the apple is its association with the forbidden fruit in Genesis. In the fourth century, Saint Jerome identified the apple as the biblical fruit, though the apple may have been unknown to the Hebrews, and nothing in Genesis leads one to nominate it as the forbidden fruit. In keeping with the association between the apple and immortality, Adam and Eve, in eating it, may have sought immortality. Instead, God exiled them from the garden.

Christopher Cumo

Further Reading

Browning, Frank. *Apples*. New York: North Point Press, 1998.

Ferree, D. C., and I. J. Warrington, eds. *Apples: Botany, Production and Uses*. Cambridge, MA: CABI, 2003.

Hughes, Meredith Sayles. *Tall and Tasty: Fruit Trees*. Minneapolis: Lerner, 2000.

Morgan, Joan, and Alison Richards. *The Book of Apples*. London: Ebury Press, 1993.

Seabrook, John. "Annals of Agriculture: Crunch." *The New Yorker*, November 21, 2011, 54–64.

University of Illinois Extension. "Apples and More." 2011. http://urbanext.illinois.edu/apples/default.cfm. (accessed 1 July 2011).

Wynne, Peter. *Apples: History, Folklore, Horticulture, and Gastronomy*. New York: Hawthorn Books, 1975.

Apricot

A perennial fruit tree, the apricot yields small, firm produce. The apricot is related to the plum. The two may be hybridized to yield the pluot. The term "apricot" derives from the Old English *abrecock*, which in turn owes its origin to the Middle French *abricot*. In Catalan, the word for apricot is *abercoc* and in Spanish *albericoque*. The people of Argentina and Chile know the apricot as *damasca*, a word that derives from the belief that the fruit originated in Damascus, Syria. Scientists know the apricot as *Prunus armeniaca*. Farmers do not plant apricots from seed because the new plant may vary from the parents, but instead produce clones of the parent tree by grafting branches onto plum or peach rootstock. Ideally, the clone will yield quality fruit and the rootstock will resist diseases and insects. Preferring a well-draining, deep soil, the apricot does best in soil with a pH between 6 and 7, that is, slightly acidic to neutral. The apricot is difficult to trellis. The farmer should prune a tree little in the first two or three years for fear of damaging it. The farmer may prune an apricot tree after the harvest so that wounds have time to heal before it flowers next year. One fresh apricot provides nearly a day's supply of beta-carotene. Three apricots contain 2.5 grams of fiber and 300 milligrams of potassium. Apricots also contain vitamin C. According to its partisans, the fruit shows promise in protecting one against cancer.

Origin, Diffusion, and Production

The apricot is not a cultigen of Syria. In the 20th century Russian agronomist Nikolai Vavilov proposed China as the place of origin, and many scientists now pinpoint the Great Hsingan Mountains of China as the homeland of the apricot. The Chinese have cultivated the apricot for millennia. Since 3000 BCE, the people

Apricots (Jianbinglee/Dreamstime.com)

of India have tended the fruit. In antiquity, Armenia emerged as a center of apricot culture. So close was the association between the apricot and Armenia that as late as the 18th century Europeans thought that the fruit was native to this region. The army of Alexander the Great, perhaps acquiring the apricot from India, introduced it to Greece in the fourth century BCE. Roman commander Lucullus, acquiring the apricot from Armenia, planted it in Italy in the first century BCE. Throughout antiquity, the Persians traded dried apricots. The Spanish, having participated in the discovery of the New World, introduced the apricot to California and the American Southwest in the 18th century. These early varieties were the source of the modern cultivars. U.S. production is centered in California, Washington, and Idaho.

The Mediterranean Basin remains a center of apricot culture. One authority believes that production will increase in this region. In Greece production, peaking in 2000, slumped thereafter. Losses from plum pox virus, known as Sharka disease, a decline in domestic demand, and competition from Spain accounted for this diminution. As other European countries turned to Spain for apricots, Greece's share of the export market declined. As production has fallen, farmers have taken land out of cultivation. Production is concentrated in southern Greece and the Haikidiki Peninsula. Although aggregate demand is down, farmers continue to find a market for canned and fresh apricots. As a percentage of the harvest that is canned, Greece surpasses Australia but trails South Africa and Spain.

Among fruit, including olives, the apricot ranks fifth in tonnage in Greece behind olive, citrus, peach, and apple. Mild winters and hot, dry summers characterize the climate in which apricots are grown in Greece. The climate poses little danger of spring frost, an important consideration given that the apricot blooms early and that frost kills flowers. Because of the dry climate, farmers must irrigate apricot trees beginning in June, though water for irrigation is scarce in Greece. Troublesome is the situation in the Peloponnesos, where the water is saline.

In Italy, the production of apricots peaked in 2004. Italians grow most apricots in Campania, Emilia-Romagna, and Bassilicate. Blessed with volcanic soils near Naples and Salerno, Campania produces the largest total of apricots of Italy's regions. Emilia-Romagna ranks second. The soils near Bologna and Ravenna are especially productive. Most apricots from this region are sold fresh. Not ideal for the fresh market, the fruit is small, but because Bassilicate's apricots ripen early they are able to enter the fresh market with little competition. Because Bassilicate's apricots are small, most are processed. Because apricot production is not mechanized in Italy, labor is intensive, requiring about 20 hours per acre. Farmers pay laborers to pick and thin apricots and to prune trees. In Italy, wages total half the cost of production.

Domestic demand for apricots is strong in Turkey, as is the export market. On the Mediterranean coast, farmers pick apricots in mid-May. In Malatya, the harvest is in late summer. Much of Malatya's crop is dried. Turkey supplies apricots to Europe and Arab nations. The leading producer, Turkey supplies one-fifth of the world's crop. Because the market for fresh apricots is small, most of the harvest is dried. Turkey is the world's leading exporter of dried apricots. In Turkey, apricots flower in early April and are vulnerable to late frost. Malatya, Igdar, and Erzincon in East Anatolia are important apricot growing regions. Apricots grown at elevation in Turkey have better color and fragrance than those grown at sea level.

In Hungary, the first reference to the apricot dates to 1400 CE. In the 16th century, the Turks encouraged the growing of apricots in Hungary and the fruit is now widespread. In 1652 Jan van Riebeeck, founder of the Cape colony, introduced the apricot to South Africa. Until the early 20th century, farmers propagated apricots by seeds rather than by grafts. The western cape of South Africa has emerged as the center of apricot culture. Farmers have planted few apricots in the northern cape and the fewest in the Transvaal. Farmers grow apricots near Swellendam, Robertson, Montago, Oudtshoons, Joubertine, and Ladysmith, areas between latitudes 33° 30′ and 34°. This region is the southernmost in South Africa and lies 210 to 2,400 feet above sea level. In recent years, farmers have planted apricots near Kimberley. The domestic demand for apricots is small, leading farmers to export most of the crop. Southern Australia has emerged as the center of apricot culture. The majority of the harvest is dried. Dried apricots store up to nine months before they become discolored.

Breeding Programs and Cultivars

Apricot varieties have a narrow geographical range. Most are confined to a single country or even to a region of a country. In Greece, the variety Bebecou commands 95 percent of acreage. Bebecou supplies both the fresh market and canning. Maturing in June and July, Bebecou produces an abundance of large fruit. The variety is, however, susceptible to Sharka disease. Cultivated on just 5 percent of acreage, the variety Tirynthos is grown in Peloponnesos. Most of the harvest is sold fresh. The yield is high and fruit large, but consumers prefer the taste of Bebecou. Maturing at the end of May, Tirynthos enters the market before Bebecou is ready to harvest. Like Bebecou, Tirynthos is vulnerable to Sharka disease. The Pomology Institute at Naossa, Greece, has initiated a program to derive cultivars resistant to plum pox virus. The varieties Early Orange and Stella were the first to be resistant to Sharka disease. Also resistant are the U.S. cultivars NJA, Sunglo, Veecot, Harloyne, and Henderson, though they are not well adapted to cultivation in Greece. They are useful, however, as breeding stock. Crosses between the American varieties and Stella have yielded 96–98 percent of their progeny resistant to Sharka disease. The percentage is lower in crosses between Early Orange and Bebecou. Only half the progeny of the cross between the variety Kaliopoulou and Veecot are resistant. Stella may be more useful as breeding stock than as a cultivar because it yields small, soft fruit.

Three cultivars dominate the orchards of Hungary. Cegledi arany, a hybrid, produces large, round fruit with a pleasing appearance. Durable enough to withstand rough handling, the cultivar supplies both the fresh market and canning. Cegledi arany is, however, susceptible to *Gnomania* and *Monilinia* fungi. Cegledi kedves ripens in midsummer. The fruit is neither large nor round, though the orange color is striking. The flesh is firm and the flavor acceptable. The flavor is best when the fruit is fully ripe. Hardy and tolerant of Sharka disease, the variety is good for canning. Cegledi piroska yields fruit that is medium to dark orange. With firm flesh and acceptable flavor, the variety is suitable for the fresh market and canning. The yield is high.

In Australia, farmers have selected varieties since the early 20th century. In 1983, the government initiated a breeding program to supplant these old cultivars with new ones. Receiving money from the Dried Fruit Research and Development Council as well as from government, the South Australia Research and Development Institute and the University of Adelaide have bred new varieties. The situation is similar in Spain, where farmers have selected varieties for generations. The most popular cultivars are Moniqul, Gitano, and Pepito del Rubio. Of the three, Gitano may have the best flavor. Gitano is the earliest to mature, being ready to pick by June 18. Pepito del Rubio matures by June 22 and Moniqul by June 27. Farmers prize Moniqul because its fruit does not crack. Although the fruit of

Pepito del Rubio cracks, the progeny of the cross between it and Moniqul do not crack. The progeny are also attractive because they ripen earlier than either parent.

In South Africa, only six varieties total 98 percent of acreage. Of these, Palsteyn is the most widely grown cultivar. In Turkey, where the market for dried apricots is large, Hacihalilogin is the leading cultivar, though it is not ideal. Among its short-comings, Hacihalilogin yields small fruit, is intolerant of drought, is susceptible to frost and fluctuations in winter temperatures, and does not produce abundant pollen. Yield, quality, and resistance to frost and disease are the most important traits of Turkish varieties. The challenge for breeding programs in Turkey and elsewhere is to derive varieties that combine tolerance to both cold and heat, early flowering, and quality of fruit. Scientists use recurrent selection to breed for large, firm fruit, fragrance, flavor, and attendant sugar content. Programs to breed Sharka-resistant varieties are widespread in Europe, where the disease is prevalent. The emphasis on quality may emerge at the primary desideratum given that some high-yielding varieties produce tasteless fruit and so cannot command the allegiance of consumers. Other breeding programs concentrate on the fungal disease apricot brown rot. Although it is possible to control the disease with fungicides, their presence in the food supply is worrisome. The breeding of resistant varieties may allow farmers to eschew the use of fungicides. Yet breeders have searched the apricot genome for resistant genes without success. The best one may hope to do is to derive varieties tolerant of brown rot. Whereas a resistant variety will not contract a disease, a tolerant cultivar is susceptible to it. A tolerant variety will not succumb to a disease but will yield well despite an infection. Several genes confer tolerance of brown rot. Breeders concentrate these genes in a cultivar through recurrent selection.

Diseases and Pests

In the 1960s, scientists isolated plum pox virus, discovering that several species of aphids transmit it to apricots. Curiously, not every strain of the virus is subject to insect transmission. Although Sharka disease was first detected in plums, it infects other fruits including apricots. The disease is most severe in apricots and plums. The virus causes chlorosis of leaves and may cause the bark of an infected tree to split. It reduces the value of apricots in two ways. First, it deforms fruit, rendering it unappealing to the consumer. Second, the virus reduces sugar content, causing fruit to be tasteless. Sharka disease may reduce yields 20 to 30 percent. Although the disease may not kill a tree, its productivity declines during the course of infection. In some cases, fruit fall from an infected tree before ripening. Farmers have little recourse but to destroy diseased trees in hopes of containing the virus.

We have seen that apricot brown rot is a troublesome disease. Known as brown rot blossom blight and fruit rot, the disease results from infection by the fungi

Manilinia lax and *Manilinia fructicola*. *Manilinia lax* withers flowers. Leaves fall from a tree and the branches exude a gum. The fungus overwinters in fruit left on a tree and in branch cankers. Spores develop in December, building large populations by spring. Wind and rain spread the spores. The infection rate peaks about 75°F. Flowers in bloom are the most susceptible to infection. *Manilinia fructicola* accumulates as mycelia in fruit, whether left on a tree or rotting on the ground. The fungus infects anthers and stigmas in a flower. The riper the fruit the more vulnerable it is to infection. Rain, fog, dew, and wind spread *Manilinia fructicola*. Insects, picking up the fungi by chance, spread it from apricot to apricot while they feed. The farmer may seek to control both types of fungus by cleaning apricots from tree and ground. The farmer should avoid irrigating trees with a sprinkler because an abundance of water may trigger an outbreak. The cultivars Royal, Derby Royal, and Modesto are vulnerable to brown rot. With the caveat that they are not to enter the food supply, fungicides may be effective. The farmer may apply them in late November or early December and again when a tree blooms.

Several other diseases plague the apricot. The bacterium *Pseudomonas syringae* causes bacterial canker. Pernicious in winter and spring, the bacterium kills the bark of apricot trees. An infected tree exudes a liquid near the boundary between dead and live tissue. The diseased area turns brown, becomes moist, and emits a sour odor. Trees aged two to eight years appear to be the most vulnerable to bacterial canker. Trees grown on sandy soil, shallow soil, or nitrogen-poor soil are vulnerable to bacterial canker. Accordingly, the application of fertilizer may improve the condition of trees. Bacteria may infect flowers during cold, wet weather. Leaves may also succumb to infection, developing brown spots. Brown lesions cover infected fruit. In addition to fertilizer, irrigation helps control the disease because a vigorous tree is less prone to bacterial canker. One may treat an infected tree by spraying it with a fungicide containing copper.

Pests may be less problematic than diseases because the apricot flowers early, yielding fruit before pest populations have had time to multiply. Nonetheless, several pests pose a danger to apricot trees. The European red mite, *Pananychus ulmi*, known as the European red spider mite, speckles leaves when an infestation is small. Heavy infestation causes leaves to turn bronze and pale. In the heaviest infestations, mites defoliate a tree. Mites cause fruit to be small. An afflicted tree yields few buds next year, reducing the harvest. For this reason, the farmer expects a downturn in production in the year after an infestation. Female mites lay their eggs on the underside of leaves in summer. Females deposit eggs on a tree's bark in winter. Mites overwinter as eggs. If the climate is warm, adults may overwinter in trees. Eggs hatch in spring. Larvae feed on young leaves. Larvae, nymphs, and adults suck sap from leaves.

Known as the Chinese scale, the California scale, and the pernicious scale, the San Jose scale, *Quadraspidious pernicious*, feeds on new wood. Afflicted wood discolors, dries, and dies. The scale deforms fruit, causing it to be small. When infestations are large, the scale is able to kill trees. In California, female scales may overwinter in trees. The scale begins to feed in February, when a tree's sap starts to rise. Crawlers emerge in May and insert their mouthparts into wood, leaves, or fruit. As it feeds, the scale inserts toxins into afflicted trees. The farmer may use insecticides to combat the scale.

The peach twig borer, *Amarsia lineatella*, despite its name, feeds on apricots and other fruit in addition to peaches. The borer infests ripe fruit or fruit that has cracked. The insect rarely infests overripe fruit. Moths may invade apricot orchards from nearby peach or almond trees. The borer is troublesome in the San Joaquin and Sacramento valleys of California. Larvae overwinter in hibernacula, beginning to feed on a tree just beneath the bark in January and February. Feeding on new shoots, the borer wilts them. Larvae exit the shoots in April and May, infesting cracks in the bark, where they pupate. Moths emerge in late April and May. The borer produces three generations per year. The farmer may collect fallen fruit and burn pruned wood to deprive larvae of places to overwinter. Insecticides may be applied in spring to kill larvae.

Christopher Cumo

Further Reading

Audergon, J. M. *Proceedings of the XIIth ISHS Symposium on Apricot Culture and Decline.* Brugge, Belgium: Acta Horticulturae, 2006.

Karayiannis, Irene, ed. *International Symposium on Apricot Culture.* Brugge, Belgium: ISHS Fruit Section, 1999.

Romojaro, F., F. Dicenta, and P. Martinez-Gomez. *Proceedings of the XIIIth International Symposium on April Breeding and Culture.* Leiden, Netherlands: Acta Horticulturae, 2006.

Sholberg, Peter L., Fran G. Zalkin, and Robert F. Hobza. *Stone Fruit Orchard Pests: Identification, Biology, Control.* Sacramento, CA: CDFA, 1985.

Arrowroot

A perennial herb grown in the tropics and subtropics, arrowroot (*Maranta arundinacea*) is known as "obedience plant," "maranta indica," *Maranta ramosissima*, "maranta starch," "Bermuda arrowroot," "marcanta," "Saint Vincent arrowroot," and "West Indian arrowroot." The genus *Maranta* was named to honor 16th-century physician Bartommeo Maranto. Because the edible part of arrowroot, contrary to its name, is a tuber not a root and because one gardener compares the flavor to that of potato, comparisons are made between the plants, though nutritionally arrowroot is much less attractive than potato. The arrowroot tuber is

63 percent water, 27 percent starch—the principal carbohydrate—2 percent protein, fiber, fat, sugar, albumen, gum, and ash. Arrowroot is bereft of vitamins and minerals. Once widespread as a food additive, arrowroot starch has fallen out of favor in this nutrition-conscious age.

Attributes

The arrowroot plant, a member of the Marantaceae family, may grow to three to six feet tall and the leaves 10 inches long. The plant has white flowers whereas the Australian arrowroot has red flowers. Arrowroot may have originated in Guyana and western Brazil and was cultivated as early as 5000 BCE. From South America, arrowroot spread to the Caribbean, which is today the chief region of cultivation. The Arawak of the Caribbean called the plant "aru-aru"—from which the word arrowroot may derive—meaning "meal of meals," testament to its importance in their diet. Another tradition held that the name "arrowroot" derives from the practice of using the plant's pulp to extract poison from an arrow wound. More recently, arrowroot migrated to Florida.

One author mentioned arrowroot as a wild plant of Florida. The Seminoles of Florida called arrowroot "conti," meaning "flour-root," evidently using the plant's tubers to make flour. The term "conti" has the variants "coontie," "coontia," "compte," "comtie," "koonti," and "koonnee." Either the Amerindians or the European inhabitants of Florida made a type of bread—Seminole bread—from arrowroot starch. Perhaps this was flat bread because arrowroot starch is incapable of rising when baked. Alternatively, the starch might have been combined with wheat flour to make leavened bread. By the 1920s, Key West was an importer of arrowroot starch, though this author feared that the pace of land clearance might make arrowroot extinct in Florida. Floridians grew arrowroot as an ornamental.

From the Americas, the Columbian Exchange carried arrowroot to Australia, South and West Africa, Mauritius, Korea, Vietnam, the Philippines, and India. Arrowroot was imported into Great Britain in about 1732, though being frost intolerant, it could scarcely have survived the cold. Perhaps greenhouses and botanical gardens grew it as a curiosity. Botanists Alphonse de Candole and Asa Gray were apparently familiar with arrowroot.

Arrowroot thrives in rich soil but does yield an acceptable crop in poor soil and arid conditions. Arrowroot prefers full sun but tolerates partial shade. The plant prefers a temperature between 77°F and 81°F and rainfall between 59 and 71 inches. The soil should drain well. Alluvial and igneous soils are best, though latosol is favored on Saint Vincent. Pieces of tuber, like those of potato, are planted in lieu of seeds. One gardener recommends plantings 30 inches apart. Arrowroot tubers need 10 or 11 months of hot, wet weather to mature, though if left in the ground too long they become tough. As a rule, tubers are ready to harvest at one year old. The gardener knows the harvest is imminent when the leaves yellow and the stem collapses. An acre of arrowroot may yield six tons of tubers, from which may be extracted one ton of starch.

Cuisine and Medicine

An easy-to-digest starch, admittedly one with little flavor according to one gardener, arrowroot was once important to the cuisines of Old and New Worlds. Tubers may be consumed raw, steamed, roasted, or barbecued. Because of the paucity of flavor, arrowroot is best combined with other food, for example in stir-fry, casserole, stew, and soup. The arrowroot tuber must be cooked longer than the potato. In the Caribbean—especially in Jamaica and Saint Vincent—arrowroot starch is added to biscuits, pudding, jelly, cake, and sauce. In Korea and Vietnam people add arrowroot starch to noodles. A food of children and the infirm, arrowroot fell out of favor because of its poor nutrition. Arrowroot is used to sooth mosquito, spider, scorpion, and snakebite and to treat gangrene, stomachache, nausea, diarrhea, and vomiting.

Christopher Cumo

Further Reading

Culinary Café. http://www.culinarycafe.com/Spices_Herbs/Arrowroot.html (accessed 11 December 2011).

Maranta—Arrowroot Plant, Herringbone Plant, Prayer Plant, Rabbit Tracks. http://www.botany.com/maranta.html (accessed 11 December 12011).

Small, John K. "Seminole Bread—the Conti." *Journal of the New York Botanical Garden* 22 (1921): 121–37.

Artichoke

The artichoke, *Cynara scolymus*, is part of the sunflower family, Asteraceae. A head (capitulum) on a long stem, flower leaves (corolla rays), and then a flower disk (corolla disk) characterize this family of flowering plants. The artichoke is a cultivated plant with a history dating back 3,000 years. Humans use the artichoke in cooking, teas, liquor, and medicine. The artichoke is characterized by an edible bud that grows on a long stem. The leaves of the artichoke are somewhat spiny. The flower itself is composed of several triangular layers. When it blooms, it is a purple thistle with many feathery petals. The unbloomed artichoke is what is used in the culinary arts. The spiny leaves are dipped into a sauce and the bottom of the leaves are eaten. The heart of the choke, its base, is oft-touted as a gastronomical delight.

History of the Artichoke

The artichoke was first discovered and cultivated in the Mediterranean Basin. The plant may have been native to the Maghreb region of North Africa. It is believed

Artichokes (Marion429/Dreamstime.com)

that humans have been eating artichokes for more than 3,000 years. The Greeks ate artichoke flower buds, and the Romans found the artichoke during the excavation of Egyptian sites.

There is much debate about the origins of using the artichoke as food. While some believe the ancients did not eat the artichoke (this was a practice historians have found not to have occurred until later), legends date back to the ancient Greeks about the creation of the artichoke. The god Zeus came upon a young woman in a field, fell in love, and decided to take her back to Mt. Olympus. When she became homesick and Zeus tired of her, he sent her back to Earth— as an artichoke. Because the young woman was the object of Zeus's affections, it was believed that anyone who would eat the artichoke would experience its aphrodisiac effects. The artichoke was also associated with having male children.

Legends were not the only places where artichokes appeared in literature. Greek botanist Theophrastus wrote of artichokes that were growing in the late fourth and early third centuries BCE. Theophrastus was a student of Aristotle. He was the first to describe the artichoke in detail. He mentioned that boiling the artichoke was the best way of extracting the flavor. In the first century CE, Greek physician Dioscorides wrote a book discussing the use of artichokes in medicine and claimed that artichoke roots could be used as an underarm deodorant and could be cooked with wine as part of a beverage.

Shortly after the popularity of the artichoke grew, so did the taboo against women eating it. By the 1500s CE, only men were allowed to eat the artichoke. Women who ate this flower were considered to be "forward" as the association of the artichoke with aphrodisiac properties remained prevalent. Only in the 19th century did Americans begin cultivating artichokes, first in the Louisiana territory when the French brought the plant with them. Italians who came to the United States also brought artichokes. When Italian-Americans settled California's Monterey County, they began cultivating the plant. By the early 20th century, the cultivation of artichokes in California had grown so popular that they were being exported to Boston and the rest of the East Coast, and their price was quite high. In fact, the cultivation of artichokes in the Monterey region became so popular that it became known as the artichoke capital of the world.

A famous Mafioso, Ciro Terranova (1889–1938), became known as the Artichoke King. He purchased crates of artichokes that had been shipped from California to New York, and then sold them at an inflated price. Mayor Fiorello LaGuardia (1882–1947) was displeased with the mafia gangsters and the pushcarts in New York City. Because of the artichoke's association with crime, New York law outlawed the sale, display, and even possession of artichokes. However, this law was soon revoked. In California in 1947, an artichoke festival was held, and at this festival an artichoke queen was crowned. The queen of the artichoke was Norma Jean Baker—better known as Marilyn Monroe. At around the same time, the consumption of artichokes became associated with status in California. Only those in the upper class ate artichokes.

Cultivation of the Artichoke

Artichokes take about six months to grow. The majority of artichokes come to maturity twice a year—at the end of winter and again at the end of summer. Artichokes grown in California typically thrive in colder, damper weather. The plants produce the edible flowers for 5 to 10 years and are therefore perennials.

Artichokes need to be planted in an open space that is not exposed to the wind. The plants take root in damp, but not saturated, soil. Should the soil dry out during the summer, the plants will die. Artichokes are often taken from suckers on plants at least three years old and are cut between February and April. When the suckers are cut, at least three shoots must be left on the plant. The suckers can then be planted, with their roots about two inches deep and about three feet apart from one another. The artichoke shoots must be protected from the sun until their roots take hold in the soil. A second method for cultivating artichokes is to raise them from seeds. Artichokes grown this way can be started indoors and then transferred outdoors in March. Plants need to be nurtured during their first season, especially by keeping the soil damp and weeded. About one-third of the plants grown each year need to be replaced in order to keep a steady stream of plants that produce a good yield. When they are ready to be harvested, artichokes will be plump, soft, green, and almost ready to open. They should be cut along with two to three inches of stem. Harvesting the plants stimulates them to yield a second harvest.

Growers must watch for two types of diseases to which artichokes are susceptible. Gray mold can cause the flowers to shrivel. It can be prevented by ensuring that the plants are not too damp and that they are kept clean and are spaced properly. Lettuce downy mildew is another potential threat to artichokes. This disease causes yellow spots to grow on the leaves and mold to grow underneath the leaves. Diseased leaves should be removed. In the case of a widespread infection, entire plants may need to be removed.

Artichoke Varieties

Green Globe Artichoke grows in winter and in spring and is in a conical shape in the summer and fall. The globe artichoke has a large heart. During the summer harvest, the artichoke may be purple at its base. Desert Globe Artichoke varies in shape between the different seasons and can be a cone or globe. The Desert Globe has thorns and is compact in its appearance. Big Heart Artichoke is conical and lacks thorns. It has a wide base and a purple tinge throughout the season. Imperial Star Artichoke is round, thornless, and has a glossy appearance. Frost enhances its flavor.

Cooking, Nutrition, and Medicine

Artichokes are generally boiled in water and eaten, one petal at a time, until reaching the artichoke heart. Artichokes are served with dips, roasted, or used in Mediterranean cuisine. A single artichoke contains about 25 calories and no fat, and is a good source of vitamin C, fiber, folic acid, and magnesium. Additionally, artichokes contain phytochemicals that aid in protecting against cancers, especially those affecting the liver.

In herbal medicine, the artichoke is used as a diuretic and choleretic. The artichoke may be beneficial to the liver. The leaves may increase bile production in the liver, and they may reduce cholesterol in the blood. In Germany, the herb is used to stimulate the appetite. Additionally, artichokes have been found to relieve hangover. Individuals with metabolic disorders have improved with the administering of the phytochemicals found in artichokes. Also, the artichoke has been used to alleviate bloating, indigestion, and nausea. Finally, the artichoke may lower lipids that may otherwise be found in the blood.

The only side effects of artichokes involve allergies to them, the occasional blocking of bile ducts, and at worst, a possible contribution to the formation of gallstones. For these reasons, artichokes (or any plant) should not be used for medicinal purposes without the supervision of a physician.

Ronda Lee Levine

Further Reading

"Artichoke Leaf." http://cms.herbalgram.org/herbalmedicine/Artichokeleaf.html (accessed 10 March 2011).

Ross, Gary, and David Steinman. *Cure Indigestion, Heartburn, Cholesterol, Triglyceride and Liver Problems with Artichoke Extract*. Topanga, CA: Freedom Press, 1999.

Stanley, Linda. "History of Artichokes." http://whatscookingamerica.net/History/ArtichokeHistory.htm (accessed 11 February 2011).

Toensmeier, Eric. "*Cynara scolymus* Globe Artichoke." In *Perennial Vegetables: From Artichokes to "Zuiki" Taro, A Gardener's Guide to Over 100 Delicious and Easy-to-Grow Edibles*, 96–97. White River Junction, VT: Chelsea Green, 2007.

Ash

A versatile tree native to the United Kingdom, ash is popular throughout Europe. The ash also grows in North America, North Africa, and all parts of Asia. The 18th-century Swedish naturalist Carl Linnaeus placed ash in the kingdom Plantae, the order Lamiales, the family Oleaceae (the olive family), and the species *Fraxinus*. Ash encompasses about 65 species of hardy trees that grow medium to large in size. The ash is mostly deciduous, although a few varieties of subtropical species are evergreens. The name ash derives from the Old English word æsc, while "fraxinus" is of Latin origin. Both words mean "spear."

The ash's seeds are popularly called "keys" or "helicopter seeds" because of their slender elongated shape. The pods contain a one-seeded fruit at one end, called a samara. When loose from the tree, the seeds spin and fly through the air like helicopter blades.

North American varieties of ash, of which there are a total of 17, include *Fraxinus anomala*, commonly called singleleaf ash; *Fraxinus dipetala*, whose common names are California ash or two-petal ash; *Fraxinus americana*, or white ash or biltmore ash; and *Fraxinus uhdei*, whose common names include shamel ash or tropical ash. The ash never grows in stands, and it tolerates all types of soil, wind conditions, and air quality.

Appearance

The common ash in Europe, *Fraxinus excelsior*, is taller than the North American varieties. It can reach a height of 140 feet. In North America, the ash typically grows to 50 feet in height. The tallest of the North American ashes is *Fraxinus americana*, which can reach 120 feet, although it averages between 80 and 90 feet tall. The ash is unique for its opposite branching, which is characterized by buds or branches growing directly opposite from other buds or branches on the same limb or twig. Three other varieties of trees have such a characteristic: maple, dogwood, and horsechestnut.

The ash is also characterized by its compound leaf. Unlike a simple leaf that has a bud at the base of the leaf stem (a petiole), a compound leaf has more than one leaflet growing out of the bud at its stem base. These 6- to 12-inch leaves have around five to nine leaflets. Each leaflet can grow to be several inches long. As a whole, the soft-textured leaves form a full canopy that allows grass and other groundcover to thrive underneath. These trees are suitable in areas that require light shading, although their seeds are abundant and can cover the ground beneath.

Because there are so many varieties of ash, leaf colors vary. The majority of deciduous varieties of ash, such as the *Fraxinus excelsior*, known as the common ash or European ash, turn golden or yellow in fall. The *Fraxinus americana*, or white ash, however, can become deep yellow or purple in autumn. The intensity of green in the ash's summer leaves also varies by type of tree. For instance, the green ash (*Fraxinus pennsylvanica*) has leaves of medium green, while the leaves of the flowering ash (*Fraxinus ornus*) are a much darker green.

The most widely distributed of North American ash trees is *Fraxinus pennsylvanica*. Not only does it grow naturally and abundantly from the Midwest to the East Coast, but it also is one of the most widely planted trees. It is a popular tree to adorn city streets in Canada because of its resistance to pollution. Canada also plants and harvests ash for its lumber. The lumber from ash alone is a multibillion-dollar industry in that country.

Threats to the Ash

The most common insects that feed on the ash are the ash sawfly, the oystershell scale, and the ash borer. The wood-boring beetle called the emerald ash borer (*Agrilus planipennis*) has killed millions of trees in North America, especially those in the midwestern United States and Ontario, Canada. The beetle entered the continent in 1998 along with ash products shipped from eastern Asia. The ash-borer has killed millions of North American ash and threatens some 7 billion others. To stem the spread of the pest, the public has been warned to keep unfinished ash products, such as firewood, local and not transport them into outside areas.

The Many Uses of Ash

The wood of the ash is a hardwood that has a straight grain and open pores. The white (*Fraxinus americana*) and black (*Fraxinus nigra*) varieties are often used in cabinet making, in crafting, and as firewood. At 41 pounds per cubic foot, ash is not an extremely heavy hardwood. It does, however, have an excellent strength-to-weight ratio, making it one of the best woods for baseball bats and other sporting equipment, including hockey sticks, boat paddles, and canoe oars. It is also often used to make tool handles, gates, and fence posts.

Ash is easy to bend and therefore is a good wood for making chairs, snowshoes, and boats. Because ash has no significant odor or taste, it was used historically to make food bowls, baskets, plates, and utensils. In fact, Native American basket weavers in Maine, the Passamaquoddy, refer to the brown ash as the "Basket Tree." The oil in ash is similar to olive oil. The leaves are rich in nutrients and are the second most used leaf, behind that of the elm, for fodder for cattle, goats, sheep, and deer.

Ash has been used as an herbal remedy for centuries, including the fourth century BC. Then, Greek physician Hippocrates treated gout and rheumatism with ash leaves, because of ash's ability to increase urine flow and release uric acid. As a tea, the boiled leaves have been used as a laxative.

The Ash in Folklore

The ash is associated with intuition and knowledge. According to Norse mythology, Odin, the supreme god and creator, hung from Yggdrasil, the World Tree, for nine days and nine nights in order to be granted the virtue of wisdom. Yggdrasil was believed to be an ash tree around which nine worlds existed, and Odin's spear also was believed to be made of ash wood, but these beliefs have since been discounted in favor of Yggdrasil being a conifer.

Nonetheless, the ash still stands for wisdom and lives on in legends of other peoples, including the ancient Greeks. They believed that the Myliae, or the nymphs of the ash, were the daughters of the spirits of the clouds and sea. The ash was also sacred to the sea god Poseidon, and the wood was placed on seagoing vessels for good luck.

In Celtic legends, the ash is seen as a sacred and divine tree, and the Celts made their spears and shields from ash wood. Other traditions believe that the ash tree can bring good luck, especially those trees with an even number of leaflets on their leaves. The Druids believed that using an ash branch to make a staff connected the user to the realms of Earth and sky.

The Species of Ash

Among the most popular varieties of ash in North America is *Fraxinus americana*. The species grows to a height of 80 to 90 feet, with a gray-brown, thick deeply furrowed bark and twigs that are stout gray, brown, or greenish brown. Its terminal buds are one-quarter inch long and are grayish brown to brown. Its pinnate leaves are 8 to 12 inches long, with green on top and gray underneath. Its fruit is 1 to 2 inches with each wing partially surrounded by seed. The seeds propagate in 90 days. *Fraxinus americana* grows from Nova Scotia, Canada, south to east Texas, and east to Florida.

Fraxinus nigra, known as black, swamp, basket, or hoop ash, grows to a height of 40 to 70 feet, with a corky irregular reddish brown to gray bark with upright branches and moderately stout, light orange-brown to gray twigs. Its terminal buds are one-quarter of an inch long and are long, dark brown to black and ovoid in shape. The pinnate leavers are 10 to 16 inches long, with 7 to 11 leaflets that are dark green above and light green beneath. Flowers are purple. The samara are 1 to 1.5 inches long. The wood is dark brown and semisoft. The species' habitat is the cold wet soils of the upper northern states and Canada.

Fraxinus pennsylvanica, known as green ash, grows to a height of 60 to 80 feet. It resembles *Fraxinus americana* in its habitat and bark. Its twigs are stout gray to grayish brown, with a lightly hairy appearance. Its gray-brown buds are one-quarter inch long and can be covered with rusty hairs. The pinnate leaves are 6 to 10 inches long, with yellow-green on top. *Fraxinus pennsylvanica* produces a half-inch-long fruit. The wood is a light brown hardwood. The species is found from Nova Scotia west to Manitoba, Canada, south to Kansas, and east to Georgia.

Fraxiunus profunda, known as red or pumpkin ash, is similar in habitat, twigs, and buds to *Fraxinus pennsylvanica*. The bark is brown to gray-brown and the leaves are 8 to 16 inches long and dense and hairy. The fruit is 2 to 3 inches long and the wood is brown, heavy, and hard.

Fraxinus quadrangulata, known as blue ash, is a medium to large tree at 60 to 80 feet tall. The bark is bluish-gray to brown. The twigs are stout and light green to gray. Buds are one-quarter of an inch long. Leaves are pinnate, 8 to 12 inches long, yellow-green, and smooth on top and pale and hairy beneath. The species' range is the dry upland areas from Ontario, Canada, west to Iowa, south to Oklahoma, and east to central Tennessee. Its wood is light yellow and streaked with brown.

Rosemarie Boucher Leenerts

Further Reading

Ash: White and Black. http://www.thewoodbox.com/data/wood/ashinfo.htm (accessed 17 September 12010).

Hageneder, Fred. *The Meaning of Trees.* San Francisco: Chronicle Books, 2005.

Leopold, Donald J., William C. McComb, and Robert N. Muller. *Trees of the Central Hardwood Forests of North America.* Portland, OR: Timber Press, 1998.

Asparagus

In the Liliaceae or Lily family, which has 150 species, asparagus (*Asparagus officinalis*) is a perennial. Asparagus derives from the Greek word for "stalk." A stalk is known as a spear. The British call asparagus "sparrowgrass." The planting of asparagus may yield spears for more than 20 years. One planting in England has produced spears for more than 100 years. The rhizome and roots are known as the crown, and the foliage is termed the fern. Asparagus has fiber, potassium, folic acid, beta-carotene, vitamin C, vitamin D, vitamin B6, thiamine, and riboflavin. The vegetable has little sodium and no fat. Four asparagus spears, roughly 60 grams, have only 10 calories, 2 grams of carbohydrate, and 1 gram of protein.

Asparagus (Nutthawit Wiangya/Dreamstime.com)

Origin and History

Asparagus is native to Bulgaria, Hungary, and southern Poland. It may be found wild in the sandy soil of west central Russia, the Crimea, Great Britain, Poland, and central Wisconsin. In antiquity the Syrians, Egyptians, and Spanish cultivated the vegetable. The Greeks knew of asparagus but they were not avid consumers of it. The Romans had a higher opinion of the crop, prizing it for its flavor and as a medicine. Roman agricultural writer Cato the Elder (234–149 BCE) urged every Roman to grew asparagus in his garden. He advised farmers to add manure, preferably sheep dung, at the time of planting. The Romans used the saying "in the time it takes to cook asparagus" to mean a short duration. They dried asparagus so they could eat it through the winter. The Romans planted asparagus in France and Britain, though one author believes that England and France did not cultivate it until the 16th century. The Chinese candy asparagus. In some areas, people use asparagus seeds to make a type of coffee or ferment them into alcohol. The Dutch and Italians cultivate a purple cultivar. The Germans, Swiss, and Austrians eat white asparagus, which is grown without exposure to sunlight so that it does not manufacture chlorophyll and is not green. In the United States, the third president, Thomas Jefferson, grew several cultivars. One author claims that asparagus was Jefferson's favorite vegetable.

The Italians and Eastern Europeans who settled California cultivated asparagus, making California the leading producer in the United States. California grows 80 percent of U.S. fresh asparagus and more than half of all asparagus in the country. The Sacramento and San Joaquin river valleys produce most of California's asparagus, though it is also grown in the Imperial Valley. Another writer holds that Washington produces more than half of all canned asparagus in the United States. Michigan produces about 10 percent of U.S. asparagus. Asparagus is grown as a winter crop in southwestern Arizona and northwestern Mexico. The United States must compete against imports from Mexico and Peru. In addition to Europe and North America, asparagus is grown in Taiwan, Japan, Peru, Chile, Australia, New Zealand, and South Africa. Production in the Southern Hemisphere meets out-of-season demand in the North.

Attributes

Asparagus produces a mass of spears. Those in the center tend to be thicker than those on the periphery. Thick asparagus must be peeled to yield a tender core. The bottom of a spear is tough and should be removed. Asparagus is best used fresh because sugar, vitamin C, and flavor deteriorate in only a few days. Asparagus may be stored in a refrigerator. The humidity must be high, the vegetable should be stored in the back of the refrigerator where it will receive little light when the refrigerator door is open, and the temperature should be near freezing. One writer recommends that asparagus be wrapped in a wet paper towel to keep it moist. Stored in this way, asparagus may keep 10 days. Fresh asparagus is widely available in the United States, though as late as the 1960s Americans consumed canned asparagus in quantity. Fresh asparagus has superior nutrition and flavor. Asparagus may be dried, canned, or frozen to extend its shelf life.

Since antiquity, humans have known that asparagus is a diuretic and laxative. Asparagus imparts an odor to urine. In antiquity the roots, shoots, and seeds were used as a sedative, a painkiller, and a liniment. Some physicians have credited asparagus with improving eyesight and relieving toothache, cramps, and sciatica. Asparagus promotes the health of the urinary tract. Asparagus contains glutothione, a chemical that may protect the body against cancer. Asparagus may be eaten raw, in salad, or cooked no longer than 10 minutes. A spear has a low content of chlorophyll. Photosynthesis increases as light intensity increases. Asparagus is most efficient in photosynthesis when the temperature is less than 68°F. Asparagus accumulates carbohydrates in the form of fructose, a sugar.

Cultivation

Asparagus requires patience. When planted from crown, it does not yield spears for two years. When planted from seeds, the wait is three years. Planting from seeds is the cheaper method. Seeds germinate in one to two weeks at 68°F to 86°F. Seeds may be started indoors 12 to 14 weeks before transplantation outdoors. The gardener may plant seeds in trays one inch deep. Seedlings grow best between 55°F and 61°F and require 12 to 14 hours of light per day. Seedlings may be transplanted in the garden in early summer. A cool-weather crop, asparagus grows best between 60°F and 70°F. Alternatively, seeds may be planted directly in the garden in mid- to late spring. Because asparagus is long lived, the gardener should select a site with the idea of permanence. When planted directly in the garden, some people sow asparagus with radish. Quick-germinating radish marks the spot where asparagus will later germinate. Seeds should be put in a mixture of water and bleach, rinsed with water, and then planted.

The other method is to plant crowns. To plant crowns the gardener may dig a hole 15 inches deep for each crown and 6 size inches of organic matter. Well-rotted manure is best, but compost or peat is acceptable. In addition to organic matter, the gardener may add superphosphate at the time of planting at five pounds per 100 feet of soil. Crowns should be soaked in warm water several hours before planting. Crowns should be spaced 18 inches apart.

Whether grown from seeds or crowns, asparagus should be fertilized twice during the growing season with a 10-10-10 fertilizer of nitrogen to phosphorus to potassium. Alternatively, asparagus benefits from applications of rock phosphate, bonemeal, greensand, or wood ashes for phosphorus; wood ashes or greensand for potassium; and cottonseed meal for nitrogen. The gardener should mulch the soil with four to six inches of grass clippings, leaves, or other matter to minimize weeds. The gardener must be wary of the asparagus beetle, a common pest in North America. The mulch should be removed in autumn to deprive the beetle of the debris it needs to overwinter. Some gardeners interplant asparagus with tomato in the belief that tomato repels the beetle and asparagus repels the tomato nematode. Ladybugs and a species of wasp eat the beetle. Anthracnose is the most severe disease. Where rust is endemic, the gardener may plant the resistant cultivars Mary Washington and Jersey Giant.

The soil should be fertile sandy loam. Clay is acceptable provided it contains lots of organic matter. Asparagus tolerates saline soil. The soil pH should be between 6.5 and 6.8 or between 6.3 and 7.5 depending on whom one consults. Organic matter should be added to the soil in the autumn before next spring's planting. The gardener should plant 10 seeds or crowns per person for a suitable harvest. Because asparagus may grow to seven feet, it should not be exposed to wind for fear of lodging. Some gardeners stake asparagus for this reason. In the second or third year, depending on whether one planted crowns or seeds, asparagus may be harvested for six to eight weeks beginning in mid-spring. Spears should be harvested every few days, when they are five to seven inches long. In autumn, asparagus should be cut to the ground. Asparagus will not grow in the tropics because it must have cold weather to initiate dormancy.

Christopher Cumo

Further Reading

Bird, Richard. *How to Grow Beans, Peas, Asparagus, Artichokes and Other Shoots.* London: Southwater, 2008.

Buckingham, Alan. *Grow Vegetables.* London: Dorling Kindersley, 2008.

Higgins, Michael. *Grow the Best Asparagus.* Pownal, VT: Storey Communications, 1981.

McNamee, Gregory. *Movable Feasts: The History, Science, and Lore of Food.* Westport, CT: Praeger, 2007.

Parsons, Russ. *How to Pick a Peach: The Search for Flavor from Farm to Table.* Boston: Houghton Mifflin, 2007.

Wien, H. C., ed. *The Physiology of Vegetable Crops.* New York: CAB International, 1997.

Avocado

Avocado (*Persea Americana*)—like corn, dates, and figs—is a cultigen, or a cultivated species domesticated in the distant past and altered by prehistoric human selection so that its ancestry is unknown. The avocado tree is likely native to Mexico and Central America, and it produces a large berry, also called an avocado or alligator pear, that is spherical or egg-shaped and contains around 20 essential nutrients, including B vitamins, antioxidants, potassium, and fiber. The fruit is also high in mono- and polyunsaturated fats, the good fats that can lower cholesterol levels and reduce the risk of heart disease.

With small, yellow green flowers, the avocado tree is a subtropical species that requires a climate with little wind and no frost. The tree is evergreen, can grow up to 60 feet tall, and produces more than 100 avocados per year. Like bananas, avocados are climacteric, meaning that they mature on the tree but ripen off the tree. As a result, commercial avocados are mature, but hard and green when harvested. They are kept in coolers until they reach their final destination, and then they are allowed to ripen at room temperature.

Origin and History

The native, undomesticated variety of avocado—referred to as the *criollo*—is small, has a black skin, and contains a large seed. Most scholars agree that it

Avocados (Stuart Taylor/Dreamstime.com)

originated in the Mexican state of Puebla, where archaeological excavations of a series of caves and open sites yielded well-preserved remains of avocados dating to 10,000 BCE. Domesticated avocados have been cultivated throughout Central America for more than 7,000 years, and there is evidence that they had reached as far south as Peru before Columbus arrived in the New World. For instance, developed between 800 and 300 BCE, the Mayan civil calendar, which bases the name of each month on seasonal and agricultural events, symbolizes the 14th month with a glyph representing the avocado. And in *Los Comentarios Reales de los Incas*, or *The Royal Commentaries of the Incas* (1605), Garcilaso de la Vega recounts how the Incan warrior Tupac Yupanqui conquered some northern provinces between 1450 and 1475 and brought the avocado to the Inca valleys of Peru.

Prior to the arrival of the Spanish, the diet of the Mesoamericans consisted of three main crops, maize or corn, the common bean, and pepo squash, as well as a number of other fruits and vegetables, such as the chili pepper, papaya, cacao, guava, and avocado. Thus, even without significant quantities of fat and protein from meat, the Mesoamericans enjoyed a healthy, well-balanced vegetarian diet.

The avocado, however, proved useful as more than food. The wood from its tree was used in house construction and for firewood as well as in the creation of tools. According to Franciscan monk Toribio de Motolinia, who spent much of his career in Mexico, "the fruit [of the avocado tree] is so wholesome that it is served to the sick." The seed also was cut into pieces, roasted, pulverized, and then given to sufferers of diarrhea and dysentery. One ripe avocado mashed and mixed with a small amount of lemon juice can be applied as a mask to the face and neck for an effective toner/firmer.

The Mesoamericans valued the avocado as well for its aphrodisiac effect. Defined as substances that claim to increase the libido, aphrodisiacs are not currently recognized by the U.S. Food and Drug Administration (FDA), which maintains that the purported libidinous effects associated with certain foods are based on folklore and not scientific fact. In making this claim, however, the FDA is discounting about 5,000 years of tradition in several dissimilar cultures around the globe, including the ancient Greeks who coined the term "aphrodisiac" in honor of Aphrodite. Among many civilizations, a food's resemblance to genitalia, especially in certain fruits, was thought to indicate a natural connection between that food and human fertility. This is the case with the avocado. The association between sexuality and the avocado dates back to the fruit's discovery by the Aztecs. Because of the shape of the fruit and its tendency to hang in pairs, the Aztecs called it *ahuacatl*, which means "testicle," and this is the origin of the word "avocado." The Mesoamericans may also have observed the quetzal bird, a crucial bird in many of their creation myths, nesting close by avocado trees because consuming the healthful fruit assists the females in creating eggs.

Sexuality and reproduction were serious business in pre-Columbian times. Analogous to most ancient cultures, the Mesoamericans considered procreation an essential moral and religious obligation. They acknowledged the connection between fertility and nutrition, and because food was more difficult to obtain than it is now, they revered the foods that contained the nutritional values necessary for successful reproduction. Because it grows in such a way as to resemble the testicles and because it contains around 20 essential nutrients, the avocado would have certainly been recognized as a fruit that was not only high in nutrients but also capable of sexual stimulation. This libidinal application probably helps explain why a village site excavated in Oaxaca, Mexico, was found to contain higher than normal incidence of avocado remains. Likewise, written history provides confirmation that the avocado was believed to enhance sexuality. To use just one example, the 19th-century British adventurer William Dampier wrote of the avocado, "It is reported that this Fruit provokes to Lust."

Shortly after the Spanish conquest of Central and South America, Europeans developed an appreciation for this exotic fruit. Spanish author Martín Fernández de Enciso was the first to attempt a written description of the avocado. Published in Spain in 1519, his *La Suma de Geografía* described the fruit as "an orange, and when it is ready for eating it turns yellowish; that which it contains is like butter and is of marvelous flavor, so good and pleasing to the palate that it is a marvelous thing." As palatable as the fruit was, however, the Spanish found the Aztec name for it highly distasteful and nearly unpronounceable. Thus they changed it to *aguacate*, a word that the English subsequently contorted into "avocado."

Soon European colonialists introduced avocados to the Caribbean, and by 1750 the fruit had reached Indonesia. Around 1850, avocados arrived in California via Mexico and quickly became and remain a cash crop there. Today, about 60,000 acres in California are devoted to the harvest of the avocado, with San Diego County being the acknowledged avocado capital of the nation. As of the year 2000, the United States was producing between 160,000 and 200,000 tons of avocados, second only to Mexico where avocados are referred to as *oro verde* or "green gold."

Though its production is based largely in North America, the avocado is consumed around the global from the Americas to Europe to Ethiopia and South Africa to India and beyond. More than 500 cultivars (cultivated varieties of plants deliberately selected for specific desirable characteristics) are descended from three horticultural races: the Mexican, the Guatemalan, and the West Indian. One of the most common cultivars is a Mexican-Guatemalan hybrid called Hass, which produces fruit year-round. Another popular cultivar, also a Mexican-Guatemalan hybrid, is *Fuerte*, meaning "strong" in English. It earned its name after withstanding a severe frost in 1913. The Pinkerton, the Gwen, the Reed, and the Zutano are other varieties seen often in the supermarket or farmer's market. Valued these days more for its nutritious qualities than for its purported aphrodisiac effect, this unlikely fruit with a long history has a strong global market, and many associations and societies oversee its production and protection, ensuring a stable future for this cash crop.

Dana Nichols

Further Reading

Edible: An Illustrated Guide to the World's Food Plants. Washington, D.C.: National Geographic, 2008.

Evans, Susan T., and Daniel L. Webster. *Archaeology of Ancient Mexico and Central America: An Encyclopedia.* New York: Routledge, 2009.

Gutiérrez, M. L., and M. Villanueva. "The Avocado in the Prehistoric Time." *Proceedings of VI World Avocado Congress.* Viña del Mar, Chile. November 12–16, 2007.

McPherson, William. "Early Account of the Avocados in America." *California Avocado Society Yearbook*, 1955.

Wells, Diana. *Lives of the Trees: An Uncommon History.* Chapel Hill, NC: Algonquin, 2010.

Azalea

In the 18th century, Swedish naturalist Carl Linnaeus placed azalea and rhododendron in separate genera, probably because their flowers had different numbers of stamens. Later taxonomists, recognizing the similarities between azalea and rhododendron, put them both in the genus *Rhododendron*. The tendency to see similarities has tempted Geoff Bryant, author of *Rhododendrons and Azaleas*, to maintain that azalea is merely a human construct that does not exist in nature. What humans call azaleas are really rhododendrons. This thesis ignores the fact that azaleas represent two of the eight subgenera of the genus *Rhododendron*. The two subgenera correspond to the two types of azaleas: deciduous azaleas, which are in the subgenus *Pentanthera*, and evergreen azaleas, which are in the subgenus *Tsutsutai*. Even these labels may be a bit misleading. To be sure, deciduous azaleas lose their leaves in autumn, but the phenomenon is more complicated for evergreen azaleas. In spring, evergreen azaleas issue forth bright green leaves, but in autumn shed them just as deciduous azaleas shed their leaves. In summer, evergreen azaleas put forth dark green leaves that grow in summer and autumn and tend to remain on the plant in winter. Exceptionally cold winters, however, may make evergreen azaleas shed all their leaves. This phenomenon has led some botanists to classify evergreen azaleas as "persistent-leaved" and to deny that a true evergreen azalea exists (Bryant 2001, 17). The gardener who wishes to retain the appearance of a true evergreen and who does not live in an exceptionally cold climate may prune the spring foliage so that all that will be left on the plant in winter are the dark green leaves that tend not to shed. Azaleas are ornamentals, chosen for their colors and ability to enhance a yard or garden.

History

The question of where azaleas originated has not been answered. One hypothesis, saying nothing about evergreen azaleas, holds that deciduous azaleas are native to North America, Europe, China, Japan, and Korea. Even if this is true, it says nothing about the origin of azalea. It seems possible that azaleas established themselves in both the Old and New Worlds before human habitation. The fact that azaleas are not native to Africa, the cradle of humanity, suggests that they spread to their current habitats millennia ago, when humans were yet confined to Africa. An Asian origin is possible.

If the question of origins cannot be answered, the origin of cultivation may be known. The earliest mention of azaleas comes from a Japanese poem, and the Japanese may have been the first to hybridize azaleas, possibly with rhododendrons. Since 759 CE, when azaleas were mentioned in verse, they have been a favorite of Japanese gardeners. Buddhist monks may have taken azaleas from Japan to China and other parts of Asia. If, however, azaleas are truly native to China, then these must have been secondary introductions, or the first human-assisted

Azalea (iStockPhoto)

migration of azaleas from Japan to China. From Asia, gardeners brought azaleas to Europe. Again, this may have been a secondary introduction. It is likely that of the azaleas that came from the gardens of China and Japan, some were hybrids. Azaleas readily hybridize with rhododendrons to yield 73 azaleodendron hybrids. Because the offspring of hybrids differ from the parents more starkly than do the progeny of pure types, many gardeners prefer true azaleas to azaleodendrons. As azaleas moved from Asia west to Europe, they also migrated east from North America to Europe. Europe, the meeting place for the disparate germplasms of Asia and the Americas, must have been the source of new varieties derived from Old and New World parents. From Virginia, the species *Rhododendron viscosum* was grown in England by 1680. In the 1870s, American botanist John Bartram may have introduced three species to Europe: *Rhododendron perichymanoides*, *Rhododendron calendulaceum*, and *Rhododendron viscosum*. The third must have been a secondary introduction. These three were hardier than the species the United Kingdom had and so gardeners bred hybrids to introduce the genes for hardiness into British germplasm.

Most evergreen azaleas may have originated in Japan, though only in the 20th century did Europeans import them. In 1918, British plant collector E. H. Wilson introduced 50 evergreen species to the United Kingdom, many of which later made their way to the United States. In 1892, botanist Charles S. Sargent at the Arnold Arboretum in Massachusetts introduced *Rhododendron kaempferi*, noted for its extreme hardiness, to the United States. The species has become a favorite of gardeners in the northeastern United States. Some hybrids of *Rhododendron kaempferi* can tolerate temperatures as low as −15°F.

In the 1870s, amateur plant breeder Anthony Watener and his son crossed European imports with Chinese azaleas, naming the new hybrids after their nursery Knap Hill. Newer still are the Windsor hybrids that Sir Eric Savill bred in the Savill Gardens, England. In the 1980s, the University of Minnesota released the Northern Lights cultivars, renowned for their ability to withstand temperatures as low as −35°F. These varieties also do well in warm climates.

Climate and Geography

In the tropics, azaleas bloom year-round. The higher the latitude the briefer is the period of bloom. To compensate for this brevity, azaleas at high latitudes reward the gardener with abundant flowers. In central Florida, azaleas bloom between October and March. In San Francisco, California, the period is between mid-September and May. The Belgian and Glenn Dale hybrids flower from August through winter. In Washington, D.C., and Seattle, Washington, they flower from mid-April to July. The Southern Indian hybrids grow well in the American South. *Rhododendron kaempferi* and deciduous species may be grown as far north as Maine. Gardeners may grow deciduous azaleas almost anywhere in the United States. Evergreen azaleas do well in the eastern United States, whose climate is similar to their native Japan. Surprisingly, evergreens are not hardy enough for Canada. The Canadian gardener should choose a deciduous variety.

The Soil and Its Nutrients

Azaleas evolved as compact shrubs that formed the under story of forests. Tall trees shaded them part of the day, and long tree roots absorbed nutrients at depth, leaving nutrients to be absorbed in shallower soil. Azalea roots are accordingly short, seldom longer than two feet, though they may spread as widely underground as does the part of an azalea plant above ground. Within this two-foot zone, an azalea derives water and elements. Leaf litter from nearby trees decay in the soil, making it rich in organic matter and acidic. For this reason, the gardener should add abundant organic matter to the soil. Organic matter retains moisture in the soil to the benefit of azaleas, which do not tolerate drought, though deciduous azaleas are more drought tolerant than evergreen azaleas. Azaleas also do not tolerate waterlogged soil. Azalea roots need loose soil and will not penetrate clay. A plant that languishes after first thriving has likely had its roots hit the subsoil or a high water table. Both conditions prevent roots from absorbing enough nutrients. The gardener, aware of the importance of organic matter, should dig leaves, pine needles, straw, garden debris, or manure into the soil where he intends to plant an azalea. Peat, bark, and sawdust are also sources of organic matter, but they have few nutrients. The soil pH should be 4.5 to 5.5, though azaleas tolerate a pH as high as 6.5.

Azaleas sometimes have the misfortune of being grown in soils deficient in nitrogen, iron, or magnesium. A lack of nitrogen causes azaleas to grow slowly and to yellow old foliage. To correct this deficiency the gardener may add urea in a concentration of one ounce of urea to one-and-one-half gallons of water. Too potent a concentration of urea may burn azalea roots. The gardener may also supply nitrogen by adding ammonium sulfate or ammonium nitrate to the soil. Leaves that yellow while retaining green veins betray iron or magnesium deficiency. When the soil is alkaline, iron and magnesium may be unavailable for absorption. Azaleas grown in iron- or magnesium-deficient soil should benefit from the addition of one ounce each of iron sulfate and magnesium sulfate to one-and-one-half gallons of water, applying the solution to the soil. The sulfate ions in the mixture reduce soil alkalinity. Premature leaf shedding and lack of vigor may be traced to poor drainage.

Christopher Cumo

Further Reading

Bryant, Geoff. *Rhododendrons and Azaleas*. Buffalo, NY: Firefly Books, 2001.

Fell, Derek, and Fred C. Galle. *All about Azaleas, Camellias and Rhododendrons*. San Ramon, CA: Ortho Books, 1995

Galle, Fred C. *Azaleas*. Portland, OR: Timber Press, 1987.

Reiley, H. Edward. *Ortho's All about Azaleas, Camellias and Rhododendrons*. Des Moines, IA: Meredith Books, 2001.

B

Baby's Breath

Baby's breath is the common name of a large number of species of herbaceous plants belonging to the genus *Gypsophila*, which 18th-century Swedish naturalist Carl Linnaeus classified. The species include both annuals and perennials, whose flowers range from white to a deep pink. The plant that is commonly known as baby's breath in North America, presumably because of its delicate light-colored petals, is sometimes referred to as "soap wort" in the United Kingdom. Approximately 100 species encompass the genus *Gypsophila*, which belongs to the family Caryophyllaceae, a plant family that also includes the common carnation. It is native to Central and Eastern Europe, Asia, the Mediterranean, and North Africa. The botanical name *Gypsophila* derives from the Greek words *gypsos*, meaning "chalk," and *phylos*, meaning "loving," which refers to the fact that the plant species grows in alkaline soils rich in calcium carbonate.

Baby's breath is grown as an ornamental plant in gardens and is cultivated for its small white or pink flowers that typically grow on tall stems. The stems and flowers are commonly used in the floral industry as filler plants. Baby's breath sprays are added to bouquets, corsages, and arranged flowers. A common accompaniment to white baby's breath is red roses. Baby's breath is also popular in dried arrangements and is added to wreaths and craft projects. It lasts up to one week in floral arrangements and is available year-round. Flowers to be used in arrangements should be cut when half the blooms are open. In gardens, baby's breath typically is grown to hang over walls and to adorn rock gardens. The pure-white blooms also mix well with wildflower varieties.

Annual and Perennial Species

Gypsophila elegans, or annual baby's breath, is a fast-growing and easy-to-grow plant that can reach a height of 20 inches. The species has many branches and narrow leaves that are blue-green. Its flowers are about one-half of an inch and either white or pink. Popular varieties of the annual plant include Carminea, with its deep-rose-colored flowers; Grandiflora Alba, whose flowers are large and white; and Rosea, with rosy pink flowers. As an annual, *Gypsophila elegans* lives just one year and dies with the first frost. New plants can regenerate near the old if the seeds fall on bare ground.

Gypsophila paniculata is a perennial species that grows to a height of two to four feet when in full bloom. This shrubby plant bears panicles that anchor single small white or pink flowers in the mid- to late-summer months. The leaves are gray-green. The two-feet dwarf varieties include Pink Fairy and Viette's Dwarf, while the three- to four-feet full-size plants include Snowflake and Perfecta. *Gypsophila paniculata* is one of the most widely used cut flowers. It attracts butterflies and is deer resistant. *Gypsophila* paniculata is sometimes called double baby's breath. Three common varieties include Bristol Fairy (white), Pink Fairy (pink), and Alba (white).

Gypsophila repens, also known as creeping baby's breath, is another perennial species. It is a dwarf cousin to the taller baby's breath plant. It grows to a height of just 4 to 8 inches and has a spread of about 12 to 18 inches. It bears loose, broad clusters of pink or white flowers that are about 0.5 inch wide. Foliage is gray-green. This variety blooms from early to midsummer. It attracts butterflies and is resistant to deer. It is an excellent cascading plant. Three common varieties are Alba (white), Rosea (pink), and Pink Beauty (pink).

Habitat and Ecological Impact

Baby's breath can withstand both hot and cold temperatures as well as various levels of moisture. It is not hardy enough to withstand winter temperatures, however, so the seeds should be sown in early spring. Optimum soil temperature for germination is 70°F. The depth of plantings should be one-sixteenth of an inch. The blooming period for baby's breath generally is from April through August. The plant can grow in both fine and coarse soils, but the soil should be nonacidic. Root growth of *Gypsophila paniculata* is fast during the first two years, as the root system penetrates deeply. It can be found in a wide variety of habitats, including pastures, roadside ditches, and fields, growing best in bright sunlight and in soil that is evenly moist and well draining. It is easily grown in rock gardens, beds, and borders.

Baby's breath seeds germinate in 10 to 20 days, and a single plant can produce as many as 14,000 seeds. Seeds are easily dispersed by the wind and from humans collecting the plant. Because baby's breath is such an aggressive seeder, it is considered a noxious weed in several U.S. states, including California and Washington, and in the Canadian province of Manitoba.

Baby's breath's ability to germinate quickly and be easily dispersed has caused the plant to grow in abundance. It tends to invade areas along waterways, including beaches, streams, and lakes, and has the capacity to colonize the habitat of plants that are native to the area and sometimes rare. It can become a problem to farmers, as well, when fields and pastures reserved for planting and grazing become clogged by the plant. Baby's breath is hardy. It is used as food by the larvae of some moths and butterflies, but, overall, insects do not pose a problem to the plant. Disease is also rare.

Baby's breath is popular because of its wide-branching stems and delicate flowers, which offer a frothy appearance that florists prefer. A symbol of everlasting love, as well as purity of heart and innocence, baby's breath is sometimes worn in the hair of girls at weddings. It also has religious connotations and is sometimes referred to as the breath of the Holy Spirit. The root of *Gypsophila repens* is boiled and mixed with sugar to make a whipping cream that is a typical topping of *kerebic*, a Turkish dessert.

Rosemarie Boucher Leenerts

Further Reading

"Annual Baby's Breath." http://www.wildflowerinformation.org/Wildflower.asp?ID=60 (accessed 30 June 2011).

"Baby's Breath Fast Facts." http://www.gardenguides.com/69439-babys-breath-fast .html (accessed 23 October 2010).

"Baby's Breath Flower Symbolism." http://livingartsoriginals.com/infoflowersymbolism .htm#babysbreath (accessed 14 April 2011).

"Gypsophila (Baby's Breath)." http://www.theflowerexpert.com/content/mostpopular flowers/morepopularflowers/gypsophilia (accessed 12 October 2010).

"Heritage Perennials." http://www.perennials.com/seeplant.html?item=1.240.150 (accessed 30 June 2011).

Marinelli, Janet, ed. *Plant*. New York: DK, 2005.

Tannenbaum, Frances. *Taylor's Encyclopedia of Garden Plants*. Boston: Houghton Mifflin Harcourt, 2003.

Bamboo

The Poacea or Gramineae family contains more than 600 genera and some 10,000 species. Among them is the subfamily bamboo, an aggregation of genera and species. A grass, bamboo is related to several important crops including wheat, barley, rye, rice, corn, oats, millet, sorghum, triticale, and sugarcane. Bamboo has tropical, subtropical, and temperate representatives. The tropical, and presumably subtropical, species are known as sympodial or clumping bamboo. Some tropical bamboos are hardy enough to endure temperatures just below freezing. At the onset of the rainy season, tropical bamboos grow culms, a process that continues from summer to autumn. Where rainfall is evenly distributed throughout the year, tropical species grow continuously. Temperate bamboos are known as monopodial or running species. They can endure temperatures below 0°F. They do not thrive in areas where winter is severe, preferring warmth. They can, however, tolerate snowfall. Dormant during winter, temperate bamboo resumes growth in spring. The Vietnamese term bamboo "the brother." The Chinese know bamboo as "the friend of the people." The people of India refer to bamboo as "the wood of the poor."

Origin and History

Bamboo originated in the early Cretaceous Period (135–65 million years ago) on the supercontinent Gondwanaland. When it broke apart, bamboo spread to vast areas of the world. Bamboo diversified into numerous species in the Tertiary Period (65–2 million years ago). Fossils of bamboo have been found in what is today France in the Miocene Epoch (6.5 million years ago). Fossils from other parts of the world date to the late Tertiary Period (2 million years ago). When China and North America were linked, bamboos on these landmasses shared a common gene pool. When they separated, a bamboo in China evolved into the species *Pseudosasa anabils*. The population of bamboos in North America evolved into *Arundinaris gigantea*, the only species native to the continent. The Chinese and North American species are closely related, evidence of the linkage between China and North America. Temperate bamboo might have evolved first, giving rise later to tropical bamboo.

Bamboo did not colonize arid regions or areas with severe winter and so is confined to warm temperate locales, the tropics, and the subtropics. The ice ages depopulated Europe and North America, leaving no species of bamboo in Europe and only a single species in North America. A plant of the forest, bamboo has colonized all continents except Europe and Antarctica. Asia, South America, and Africa have a large number of species of bamboo. Botanists once thought that China harbored roughly half of all bamboo genera and species. Today, they think that Central and South America have more than half of all genera and species of bamboo, displacing China as the leading continent of bamboo biodiversity. Two authorities allot 41 genera of bamboo to the Americas, 16 to Africa and Madagascar, 65 to southern and eastern Asia, and 2 to Australia. Bamboo grows as far north as 60° north and as far south as South Africa. Bamboo has colonized the Himalayas, the Chilean Andes, and Argentina. Bamboos from the mountains tend to tolerate the climate of North America, and for this reason gardeners have transplanted them there. The fit is not, however, perfect. Mountain bamboos need higher light intensity and humidity than are common in North America. Bamboos that have colonized the mountains of the tropics, to the extent that they experience cold, have low temperatures daily, presumably at night, and are not ideal for transplantation in North America because the climate subjects flora to a season of unremitting cold.

Hardy bamboos tolerate temperatures as low as –20°F. Temperate China subjects bamboo to hot summers and cold winters. Chinese bamboos tolerate temperatures as low as –15°F. Where summer is cool, bamboo grows small and compact. Temperate species of bamboo tolerate more heat and aridity than mountain species. Japan and Taiwan have hardy species of bamboo adapted to hot, humid summers. The genus *Sasa* is widespread in Japan as far north as the Kuril Islands. *Themocalamus tesellatus* of South Africa is a temperate species, but the specimens of equatorial Africa, Madagascar, Australia, southern and eastern Asia, the Pacific islands, and Central and South America are all tropical species.

Attributes and Cultivation

Bamboo is the world's fastest-growing plant, able to grow 47 inches in a single day. Bamboo reproduces principally vegetatively. A rhizome yields a new plant that is a clone of the parent. Alternatively, bamboo may reproduce sexually. Bamboo may flower every year or as remotely as every 120 years. When one bamboo of a species flowers, all bamboos of that species flower, even those on other continents. This synchronicity ensures the production of ample pollen. Wind pollinates bamboo flowers. Bamboo pollen is capable of fertilizing the flowers of sugarcane and rice. Some species of bamboo are interfertile, resulting in the production of hybrids. Fertilized flowers yield seeds, which resemble kernels of wheat. A bamboo plant may die after seeding, and a new seedling may require 12 or 13 years to reach maturity. Under cultivation, a seedling may mature in 6 years. Some species do not reproduce sexually because they are sterile.

A bamboo seedling grows well in high humidity and rainfall. Some farmers grow bamboo in rice paddies to obtain water. Bamboo prefers alluvial soil or loam. It tolerates sand and clay, though these are not ideal. The soil should be fertile, well drained, and contain gravel. Bamboo benefits from the addition of compost or fertilizer to the soil. The gardener may add 10 parts nitrogen, 5 parts phosphorus, and 5 parts potassium to the soil one month before shoots emerge in spring. A second application should follow before the rhizome resumes growth. Bamboo benefits from the application of 80 pounds of nitrogen, 40 pounds of phosphorus, and 40 pounds of potassium per acre. Leaf litter should be allowed to cover the ground to minimize weeds.

Bamboo grows well on slopes, where it lessens soil erosion. One may plant bamboo at the base of a hill or near a river that has deposited alluvial soil in its valley. The black bamboo tolerates direct sunlight. Many other species benefit from partial shade. As a rule, bamboo should not be planted in a western orientation because the afternoon sun may be too harsh. In warm regions, a northern exposure is best. In cool locales a southern exposure is preferred. The Chinese grow bamboo in infertile soil and in arid conditions to derive strong, hard bamboo. Egyptians grow bamboo along canals so that it has a source of water. Algerians irrigate bamboo. Indians must contend with the bamboo powder post beetle (*Dinoderus minutus*), which reduces bamboo to dust. Rats, porcupines, squirrels, rabbits, deer, and monkeys eat the rhizome, shoots, and seeds.

Uses

Bamboo was the source of Europe's silk industry. Two monks, visiting China, hid the eggs of a silkworm in a stalk of bamboo, giving them to Byzantine emperor

Justinian in 552 CE. Bamboo branches have been used to thatch roofs in Asia. The Chinese have used bamboo as spears and guns. That bamboo could withstand the firing of a gun derives from the fact that pound for pound bamboo is stronger than steel. Large culms were used as baskets and cooking pots. Small culms served as cups or containers. Since 200 BCE the Chinese have used bamboo canes to drill for oil to a depth of 3,000 feet.

The people of Japan and the Andes Mountains make musical instruments from bamboo, the Japanese stringed instruments and the Andeans pipes. Malaysians make flutes from bamboo. Bamboo is made into furniture, blinds, room dividers, screens, fences, houses, paper, chopsticks, mats, baskets, weapons, the skin of airplanes, and phonographic needles and slide rules before these technologies were eclipsed. An extract of bamboo may be used as medicine for asthma, as salves for hair and skin, as an eyewash, as an aphrodisiac, and as a poison. Asians eat bamboo shoots. The Chinese and Japanese eat *Phyllostochy edulis* raw, though other species must be boiled to remove bitterness. Bamboo ashes are used to polish jewels and make batteries. Bamboo has been used to construct bicycles, dirigibles, windmills, scales, and retaining walls strong enough to hold back flood and the tide. China has made bridges as long as 750 feet from bamboo. American inventor Thomas Edison (1847–1931) used a bamboo fiber in his lightbulb.

Christopher Cumo

Further Reading

Bell, Michael. *The Gardener's Guide to Growing Temperate Bamboos*. Portland, OR: Timber Press, 2000.

Cusack, Victor. *Bamboo World: The Growing and Use of Clumping Bamboos*. Sydney, Australia: Kangaroo Press, 1999.

Farrelly, David. *The Book of Bamboo*. San Francisco: Sierra Club Books, 1984.

McClure, Floyd A. *The Bamboos*. Washington, D.C.: Smithsonian Institution Press, 1993.

Banana

Although the casual observer might consider a banana plant a tree, botanists classify it a perennial herb. The banana is the world's largest herb, growing as tall as 30 feet. It is the world's largest fruit crop and the fourth-leading crop, trailing wheat, rice, and corn. A crop of the tropics, the banana will not grow at high latitudes. Farmers cultivate the banana in Florida, but perhaps because of the latitude it is not grown on a large scale there. Instead, farmers grow the banana in Southeast Asia, western Asia, China, India, Pakistan, Bangladesh, several Pacific islands, Africa, the Caribbean, and Central and South America. An indigene of

Banana trees (Corel)

Southeast Asia, the Columbian Exchange brought the banana to the Americas in the 16th century. In much of Asia, Africa, and the Pacific, small farmers raise bananas for local consumption, whereas growers in the Caribbean and Central and South America export much of their fruit to the United States, Canada, and Europe. Americans and their counterparts in the rest of the developed world eat the banana as dessert whereas it is a staple in the developing world. A single banana plant yields three or four harvests in its life. Six months after it flowers a banana plant yields mature fruit. In total, a banana plant needs 8 to 10 months to grow from seedling to maturity. Bananas remain green as long as they are on a plant. As soon as they are picked, however, they begin to ripen. During ripening, they convert starch into fructose. A green banana has 1 percent fructose whereas a ripe banana has 80 percent sugar. Once picked a banana releases ethylene gas, a chemical that hastens ripening. The banana is a source of carbohydrates, potassium, vitamin C, and vitamin B6. In some regions of the world, manufacturers make bananas into chips, flour, and puree.

Origin and Diffusion

In Asia and Africa, people describe the origin and importance of the banana in myth. Notorious in the creation story in Genesis is the forbidden fruit. Saint Jerome thought the fruit was the apple, a belief that lingers today, though another tradition identifies the banana as the forbidden fruit. The Koran populated Eden with banana plants. Some Arab scholars consider the banana the "tree of paradise." In the 18th century, Swedish naturalist Carl Linnaeus named the banana *Musa paradisiaca*, meaning the "banana of paradise." After eating the banana, Adam and Eve clothed themselves in banana leaves. The belief that they used fig leaves may be mistaken because people confused the banana and the fig. Alexander the Great, for example, called the banana a fig. The author of Genesis may have known of the banana, which may have been grown in the Near East. Wherever Eden is thought to be, farmers today grow the banana in Jordan, Egypt, Oman, and Israel.

In India, the banana has religious significance. Indian mystics meditate beneath banana plants. According to one tradition, the banana is the incarnation of Lakshmi, the goddess of wealth, beauty, and wisdom. At an Indian wedding, the groom gives the bride a banana as a symbol of fertility. In India, the banana is the subject of Hindu art. In the Vedic tradition, a banana grove is home to the monkey god Hanuman. India grows roughly 17 million tons of bananas per year, 20 percent of the global total. India's production is thrice that of Ecuador, the second-leading producer. India grows the banana for local consumption whereas Ecuador produces for export. The people of Ecuador eat less than 2 percent of the country's bananas. In India, banana chips are the most popular snack. Indians even eat fried banana peels with black-eyed peas. As unappealing as it may seem to Westerners, Indians make bananas into ketchup. In New Guinea, farmers use the banana in rainmaking ceremonies. Africans include the banana in one of their creation accounts. Kintu, the first human, married Nambi, the daughter of Gulu, the creator god. Her brother, unhappy that she had married a mortal, expelled the couple from Eden. Leaving paradise, Kintu and Nambi carried a banana root, presumably for planting, in their wandering. Some scholars believe Uganda was the African Eden. So important is the banana to Uganda that people sometimes use it as money. A farmer, for example, might repay a loan with bananas. Ugandans eat a special variety of banana at the birth of twins and another to mark the passing of kin. A husband or wife might eat a particular variety to encourage his or her spouse to be faithful. Another variety, Ugandans believe, increases sperm production. Uganda produces 11 million tons of bananas per year, a figure that computes to more than 500 pounds per person per year. This amount is 20 times more than the per capita consumption in the United States. In some Ugandan villages, farmers produce 970 pounds of bananas per person per year. Although this figure seems large enough to encourage exports, Ugandan farmers grow bananas for local consumption.

So central is the banana to the concept of food in Uganda that the word *matoke* means both "banana" and "food." On Samoa, *mei'a* means "banana." In New Zealand and Easter Island, *maike* means "banana." The Hawaiian *mai'a* means "banana." The people of Indonesia, the Philippines, Malaysia, and New Guinea render *pisang* as banana. The Papua *pudi* and fud *both* mean "banana." *Buti* means "banana" on the Solomon Islands. The people of Fiji call the banana *vud*. On Tonga, the banana is *feta'u* and on Tahiti *fe'i*. Hindus term the banana *kalpatharu*, meaning "virtuous plant." The English word "banana" derives from the Arabic *banan*, meaning "finger" because each banana in a bunch is a finger.

The banana originated in Southeast Asia. Wild bananas are inedible, leading one to wonder why the ancients selected them for eventual domestication. The people who took an interest in these wild bananas selected for seedlessness and flavor. Wild bananas arose in southern China, Southeast Asia, and India. As early as 7000 BCE, the people of New Guinea ate the banana and may have been the first to cultivate it. Around 5000 BCE, people throughout Southeast Asia began cultivating the plant. In antiquity, the banana spread to Samoa, New Zealand, Hawaii, Easter Island, Indonesia, the Philippines, Malaysia, New Guinea, India, Taiwan, southern China, and Borneo. Around 300 CE, Indonesians brought the banana to Madagascar, from which it spread to East Africa. The fact that many African bananas are descended from Pacific cultivars suggests a second introduction. In 650 CE Arabs brought the banana to the Middle East. At first, European explorers did not know what to make of the banana, often confusing it with the plantain. In 1350 one European explorer found the banana in Sri Lanka. In 1482, the Portuguese found bananas being grown in Sierra Leone, Liberia, and Gambia. Around 1500, the Portuguese planted the banana in the Canary Islands. In the late 16th century, travelers observed the banana in the Nicobar Islands and India.

Some scholars speculate that the banana arrived in the Americas before Columbus's voyages. One school of thought holds that bananas from West Africa reached the Americas ahead of the Genoese explorer. Another school of thought traces the banana's putative trek across the Pacific to the west coast of South America. The first mention of the banana in the Americas dates to 1516, when Spanish missionary Tomás de Berlanga introduced it to Santo Domingo (today the Dominican Republic), marking the advent of banana culture in the Caribbean and possibly in all the Americas. From Santo Domingo, the banana spread to the rest of the Caribbean and to Central and South America. In Central America, planters have established large estates, especially in Ecuador, Colombia, Honduras, Guatemala, Costa Rica, and Panama.

Planted in the Caribbean from the 16th century, the banana became an export only in the 19th century. In the 1860s, the United States began to import bananas from Jamaica. Planters, sensing an opportunity to profit, converted abandoned sugarcane estates to banana plantations. In the 20th century, United Fruit Company monopolized the shipping of bananas from the Caribbean to the United States. On Saint Lucia, farmers converted hilly terrain from sugarcane to banana. The Dominican Republic grew banana and coffee. On Grenada farmers raised banana and nutmeg. In 1902, the eruption of Mount Pelée on Martinique covered sugarcane plantations with ash. Some farmers replanted their land to banana. Between 1987 and 2002, banana exports on Martinique rose from 191,140 tons to 341,720 tons. The latter figure totaled 40 percent of the island's exports. Martinique ships most of its bananas to France, Italy, and the United Kingdom. Since 1950, bananas have been the leading export on Saint Vincent. In 1981 bananas totaled 72 percent of the island's exports. On Guadeloupe, the banana harvest increased in the 1990s, rising 30 percent in 1991 alone and another 13 percent in 1992. In the latter year, the harvest tallied 163,470 tons, 122,430 of which went to export. In 2000, however, drought and Hurricane Debbie decreased production to 127,320 tons.

In Central Africa, people ferment bananas into beer. In Uganda, the variety Mbidde is used to make beer. In Zaire, the variety Makandili serves this purpose. In Zaire, farmers plant bananas and coffee. In Burundi, growers intercrop the banana with taro, beans, peas, and cabbage. In Rwanda, farmers grow the banana and sweet potato. So important is the banana in Rwanda that it adorns the 20-franc coin. In some areas, farmers intercrop bananas with cocoa. In this system, the banana provides income during the four or five years during which cocoa matures. When cocoa is mature, farmers cut down their banana plants for mulch. Today, Cameroon, Cote d'Ivorie, the Canary Islands, and Israel export bananas to Europe. The Philippines, adopting varieties from Latin America, began exporting bananas in the 1970s and today exports them to Japan, the Middle East, and Hong Kong. Bananas total half the value of exports in the Philippines, Dominica, Grenada, Saint Lucia, Saint Vincent, Martinique, and Guadeloupe.

Banana Varieties and the Quest for Disease Resistance

By one estimate, the banana comes in more than 1,000 varieties. Small farmers grow most of these and they are consumed locally. Among banana-growing countries, India, which grows more than 670 varieties, has the greatest diversity. In Tamil Nadu alone, farmers grow more than 50 varieties. Growers on Sri Lanka cultivate more than 25 varieties. The Philippines grows more than 75 varieties. Rwanda is home to roughly 85 cultivars and Uganda to more than 30 varieties. In parts of Asia, local varieties are more important in sustaining people than is rice. Because these varieties do not enter the export market, Americans, Canadians, and Europeans are unfamiliar with their flavor.

Since the 19th century, North Americans and Europeans have consumed just two varieties, Gros Michel and Cavendish. Gros Michel (Big Michael) originated in Southeast Asia. In the early 19th century, French naturalist Nicolas Baudin introduced it to Martinique. In 1835, French botanist Jean Francois Pauyat transplanted Gros Michel from Martinique to Jamaica. From the Caribbean, Gros Michel spread to Central and South America. Between the 19th century and World War II, Gros Michel was the only variety that Americans ate. Because it does not seed, Gros Michel is propagated vegetatively. That is, a banana plant produces suckers, which grow into new plants. Unfortunately, each sucker is a clone of its parent. Gros Michel, being only a single variety and being propagated by clones, was dangerously uniform. The rise of new pathogens or the recrudesce of old ones threatened Gros Michel with extinction.

From an early date, scientists understood this danger and labored to breed new varieties to increase the banana's diversity. In 1922, the Imperial College of Tropical Agriculture in Trinidad and the Banana Research Station in Jamaica began programs to derive new varieties. Imperial College continued this work until 1960, when it transferred its research to the Banana Research Station. By 1980, a lack of funds forced the Banana Research Station to cease work, but Canada's International Development Research Centre restored its funding. In 1959, United Fruit Company inaugurated a breeding program in Honduras but, dissatisfied with results, stopped research in 1983. Again, other agencies came to the fore. The Food and Agriculture Organization of the United Nations, the U.S. Agency for International Development, and the International Development Research Centre funded the research program in Honduras. In Nigeria, the International Institute of Tropical Agriculture funds banana research.

Much of this research has concentrated on the derivation of disease-resistant cultivars. Scientists have crossed disease-resistant wild varieties with susceptible cultivars to yield resistant cultivars. Simple in principle, the derivation of disease-resistant cultivars has been difficult to achieve in practice. Flavor, shelf life, resistance to bruising, and texture are all difficult to control. Several promising varieties ripen too quickly to be suitable for export. Some new triploids show promise, lasting three weeks after picking, a full week longer than tetraploids.

The effort to breed new varieties did not save Gros Michel. The rise of a fungal disease known as Panama disease doomed the cultivar. So virulent is Panama disease that in the early 20th century it killed nearly every banana plant in Suriname. In 1931, Scottish agronomist Claude Wardlaw found Panama disease in 15,000 acres on Jamaica and 50,000 acres in Panama, from which it derives its name. Since 1931, Panama disease has spread to 8 countries in Asia, 5 in the Pacific, 12 in Africa, and 22 in the Americas, including the Caribbean. United Fruit Company attempted to combat the Panama disease by flooding fields in the belief that water would wash away the fungus. Instead, water spread the fungus to other farms. A soil-borne pathogen, the fungus adheres to anything in contact with infected soil and so is spread by human activity. Farm tools, shoes, and bicycle tires can all spread the disease. From its home in Panama, the disease spread throughout the Americas, claiming banana plants farm by farm. By the 1960s, Panama disease had ravaged Gros Michel. Banana growers might have lost their livelihood but for the discovery of a resistant cultivar, Cavendish. In 1826, plant collector Charles Telfair discovered this new banana variety in China. He sent seedlings to England, where they found their way to the greenhouse of the Duke of Devonshire. Because his surname was Cavendish, it became synonymous with the new variety. The missionary John Williams planted Cavendish on Samoa, Tonga, and Fiji around 1850. By 1855, farmers grew Cavendish in Tahiti, Hawaii, New Guinea, Egypt, and South Africa. By the 1870s, farmers were growing Cavendish in the Caribbean. In 1939 Standard Fruit experimented with Cavendish, discovering its resistance to Panama disease. In the Americas, Cavendish had its greatest effect. In the 1960s, growers planted it in place of Gros Michel and today it is the only variety of banana that Americans, Canadians, and Europeans eat. Growers who had once planted Gros Michel in monoculture now plant Cavendish in monoculture.

In the 1980s, some farmers in Malaysia switched from oil palm to banana to satisfy growing urban demand for the fruit. They planted Cavendish, by then the world's principal export banana. That decade, however, disease afflicted the hitherto resistant Cavendish. The symptoms resembled Panama disease but scientists rejected the connection. After all, Panama disease was a problem in the Americas, not in Asia. Isolation of the fungus proved, however, that the Asia sickness was Panama disease. Scientists were initially puzzled that Cavendish had lost its resistance until they realized that they were confronting distinct races of Panama disease. Cavendish was resistant to the race that was malignant in the Americas but vulnerable to the Asian race. Panama disease, it turned out, was indigenous to Asia and only later spread to the New World. In the 1990s Indonesia, following Malaysia, converted some of its land from oil palm to banana, but disease has reduced yields. Given these losses in Asia, scientists wondered whether disease would claim Cavendish as it had ousted Gros Michel. Fortunately, the Asian race of Panama disease has yet to invade the Americas. The advent of Panama disease in China in 2007 caused consumers not to buy bananas in the mistaken belief that they might contract the affliction. Newspapers fed this misconception, labeling the disease "banana cancer." Some Chinese feared that diseased bananas might cause AIDS. Since then, Panama disease has spread to Pakistan, the Philippines, Indonesia, and Africa.

This does not mean that Cavendish is safe. The fungal disease Black Sigatoka is nearly as virulent as Panama disease. Arising on Fiji in 1935, the fungus reached Honduras in 1972, Zambia in 1973, Gabon in 1979, Costa Rica in 1980, and Colombia and Venezuela in 1981. Whereas Panama disease spread slowly because it required human intervention to transmit it, Black Sigatoka, an airborne pathogen, spread rapidly. In Uganda, the disease killed so many banana plants that bananas are scarce in some districts. Their price has risen and the poor who depend on bananas for sustenance have difficulty affording them. Fungicides are effective but laborious to apply and expensive. In Central America farmers must apply fungicide up to 45 times per year. United Fruit Company used Bordeaux mixture to kill Black Sigatoka fungi. Small farmers who could not afford the fungicide in bulk succumbed to the disease, allowing United Fruit Company to buy their land. Bordeaux mixture was toxic to workers, turning their skin blue. Symptoms were progressive. One lost the sense of smell, then began vomiting, and in the worst cases of Bordeaux poisoning died. Growers spend $60 million per year on fungicides (Bordeaux mixture is now banned) to combat the disease. Some varieties are resistant, but Cavendish is not. The fungus rots bananas and kills plants. Even a putatively healthy plant may be infected. Workers might cut what appear to be healthy bananas only to have them rot during shipment.

Mako disease can likewise be severe. Insects that burrow into bananas transmit the causal agent, a bacterium. Large insect populations cause a high rate of infection. When the bacterium gets on farm tools, it may spread to bananas by this route. Common in the Caribbean and in Central and South America, Mako disease rots bananas from the inside out. Aphids transmit Bunchy Top, a viral disease, to bananas. In 1889, the disease arose on Fiji and spread thereafter to Pakistan, Australia, Sri Lanka, India, Bangladesh, Myanmar, and Hawaii. The virus caused 30 percent losses in Hawaii and as much as 75 percent losses in parts of Pakistan. Nematodes are a significant pest, feeding on banana roots and turning leaves red, purple, or black.

The Business of Bananas

In 1885 Boston Fruit, now Chiquita, formed to ship bananas from the Caribbean to the United States. Because bananas are perishable, Boston Fruit was the first company to ship them in refrigerated compartments. In New Orleans arose Standard Fruit to supply bananas to the South. Because Boston Fruit and Standard Fruit depended on the volume of sales to generate profit, they priced bananas cheaply. In the 19th century, bananas were half the price of apples, and around 1900 Americans could buy a dozen bananas for 25 cents. This price fetched only two apples. The inexpensiveness of bananas encouraged Americans to buy them, and consumption rose from 15 million bunches in 1900 to more than 40 million bunches in 1910. Although it dipped in the 1940s, per person consumption of bananas has risen 43 percent in the United States since 1970. Buying bananas throughout Latin America and the Caribbean, the United States nonetheless imports most of its bananas from Ecuador.

In Central America, cattle rancher Minor C. Keith, building lines in Panama, Guatemala, Honduras, Nicaragua, Colombia, and Ecuador, planted bananas alongside the tracks. Initially, bananas fed railroad workers, but Keith came to understand that he could ship the surplus to the United States and so supply the American Southwest with them. In 1899 Keith merged with Boston Fruit to create United Fruit Company. This conglomerate grew bananas on land the size of Connecticut. United Fruit was an early investor in Cuban bananas, owning

300,000 acres of bananas and sugarcane. As United Fruit grew in size and wealth, it gained influence in the Caribbean, in Central and South America, and in the United States. When aroused to action, the United States used force to compel recalcitrant government to do the bidding of United Fruit. In 1912, the United States invaded Honduras, forcing the government to concede to United Fruit the right to build railroads and grow bananas. Depending on cheap labor, United Fruit was hostile to labor activism. In 1918, U.S. troops, acting at the behest of United Fruit, crushed strikes by banana workers in Panama, Colombia, and Guatemala. In 1925, American soldiers crushed another banana strike in Guatemala. United Fruit was equally ruthless toward competitors, buying them or bankrupting them by undercutting their prices. By the late 1920s, United Fruit was worth more than $100 million, had 67,000 workers, owned 1.6 million acres, and counted banana estates in 32 countries. Workers did not share this prosperity. At the peak of operations, laborers worked up to 72 hours with little respite, harvesting bananas and loading fruit on ships. They had no access to a toilet, could not unionize, and were seldom paid cash. Instead, they received scrip, which they could redeem only at United Fruit stores, whose prices were high and that sold products from the United States rather than locally produced goods. Always eager to increase sales, United Fruit hired physicians to approve the practice of feeding bananas to infants, knowing that mothers did the grocery shopping. United Fruit advertised the combination of corn flakes with sliced bananas as the ideal breakfast. The company put coupons for free bananas, paid for by cereal manufacturers, in cereal boxes.

United Fruit's actions in Colombia precipitated the banana massacre. In 1899, the year of its founding, the company acquired its first banana plantation in Columbia. To its dismay labor became restive in the early 20th century. In October 1928, 32,000 banana workers, seeking better working conditions, went on strike. Their demands seem moderate. They wanted medical care, the use of a toilet, payment in cash rather than scrip, and classification as employees rather than independent contractors so they could enjoy the protection of Colombia's labor laws, weak though they were. Rather than negotiate, United Fruit denied that its workers were discontent. The strikers would not relent, and on December 5, 1928, Colombia's government, surely under pressure from United Fruit, declared martial law. Soldiers fired on workers after they had attended a Catholic mass on Sunday, killing more than 1,000 of them.

Events in Guatemala were no more reassuring. In the early 20th century, United Fruit established its first banana plantations and from an early date seems to have dominated the weak Guatemalan government. The government required its people to labor 100 days per year on banana estates, a system of forced labor that was too common in the Americas. If United Fruit loathed workers, it also appears to have disdained the government, refusing to pay taxes on the land it owned. The growth of a middle class in Guatemala in the 20th century raised the people's consciousness. Educated, the middle class understood that United Fruit was exploiting the country. They resented the fact that the company ran Guatemala as a banana plantation. Indeed, bananas companies owned 4 million acres, 70 percent of Guatemala's arable land. In 1944, schoolteachers went on strike. Shaken, the government legalized unions but barred banana workers from joining them. The fall of one government led to the rise of Jacobo Arbenz, who founded a liberal government. Arbenz demanded that United Fruit pay taxes and give up some of its land so that the people might farm as they wished. Sympathetic to United Fruit and branding Arbenz a communist, President Dwight D. Eisenhower ordered the Central Intelligence Agency (CIA) to overthrow the government. Using misinformation, the CIA created confusion in Guatemala. Convinced they were on the verge of defeat, military leaders refused to muster their troops against the CIA. Arbenz fled Guatemala. United Fruit had made the world safe for the banana.

Christopher Cumo

Further Reading

Charrier, Andre, Michel Jacquot, Serge Hamon, and Dominique Nicolas, eds. *Tropical Plant Breeding*. Enfield, NH: Science, 2001.

Eagen, Rachel. *The Biography of Bananas*. New York: Crabtree, 2006.

Grossman, Lawrence S. *The Political Ecology of Bananas: Contract Farming, Peasants, and Agrarian Change in the Eastern Caribbean*. Chapel Hill: University of North Carolina Press, 1998.

Jenkins, Virginia Scott. *Bananas: An American History*. Washington, D.C.: Smithsonian Institution Press, 2000.

Koeppel, Dan. *Banana: The Fate of the Fruit That Changed the World*. New York: Hudson Street Press, 2008.

Roche, Julian. *The International Banana Trade*. Boca Raton, FL: CRC Press, 1998.

Wiley, James. *The Banana: Empires, Trade Wars, and Globalization*. Lincoln: University of Nebraska Press, 2008.

Barley

An annual grass in the Poaceae or Gramineae family, barley is among the most ancient cultivated plants. First grown in the Near East, barley was also one of the original plants in the Columbian Exchange. Humans grow barley for the kernel (seed), using it as food, beer, and feed. Grown from the Arctic Circle to the tropics, barley tolerates a range of climates and soils. Able to grow in alkaline soils where most grains cannot, barley survives in arid and hot locales, though as a temperate crop it does best in cool, moist regions. With shallow roots, barley tolerates soils that are too thin for wheat and oats. It also tolerates saline

Barley (Corel)

soils better than other grains. Barley cannot, however, endure both heat and high humidity. Scientists familiar with barley are able to judge its value by appearance. Barley with heavy kernels is rich in starch and protein. The plumper the kernel the more starch it has. Between 8 and 18 percent of a barley kernel is protein. The average of 13 percent protein compares favorably to the 12 percent protein of wheat. Ten to 15 percent of a kernel is the hull, which contains cellulose, pectin, lignin, some of the protein, and fiber. The rest of the kernel is carbohydrate. Of the carbohydrates, 55 percent is starch. In addition to protein, barley contains the minerals potassium, calcium, and magnesium. Barley is of two types depending on planting date. As its name suggests, spring barley is planted in spring and matures in roughly three months. Winter barley is sown in autumn. It germinates and grows several inches before frost. It becomes dormant during winter, resumes growth in spring, and is ready to harvest in early summer. To mature properly winter barley needs 2 to 10 weeks of temperatures below 50°F. Winter barley is a popular crop in Pennsylvania, California, and the Pacific Northwest. In the United States, 75 percent of the crop is spring barley and 25 percent winter barley. Barley has some 5 billion pairs of nucleotide bases, constituting 25,000 genes. These genes represent less than 5 percent of the barley genome. To date scientists have identified less than 10 percent of barley's genes. Barley is related to corn, rice, rye, oats, sugarcane, sorghum, bamboo, and timothy.

Origin and Diffusion in the Old World

Myth celebrates the origin of barley. The Egyptians believed that Isis, the goddess of bread and beer, taught them to grow barley. Another tradition holds that the goddess Hanthor, also identified with bread and beer, gave the Egyptians barley. In some instances, the Egyptians conflated Isis and Hanthor into a single goddess of barley. The Egyptians believed that the germination of barley reenacted the resurrection of Osiris, the brother and husband of Isis. In Catal Huyuk, Turkey, the ancients associated a fertility goddess with barley. One statue displays a fertility goddess resting her arms on the heads of two leopards. She tamed these wild animals as humans domesticated what had once been wild barley. In Greece, Demeter, the goddess of grain, gave humans barley. In Rome, the goddess Ceres bestowed barley on humans.

Because of its antiquity, several scholars have been eager to trace the origin of barley. Among the first to take up this topic was French botanist Alphonse de Candolle. In 1882, he asserted that cultivated six-row barley had derived from wild two-row barley. In fact, recent research has demonstrated that three mutations may have transformed two-row barley to six-row barley. The transition from wild to cultivated barley may therefore have occurred rapidly. De Candolle also considered the possibility that the ancestor of barley might be extinct. In 1923, Russian agronomist Nikolai Vavilov thought that barley originated in Ethiopia, though he later backtracked, holding that Ethiopia was merely a secondary center of domestication and that barley had arisen elsewhere. In 1932, scientist Elizabeth Schiemann posited that an unknown wild barley was the progenitor of cultivated barley. In 1939, scientist E. Aberg suggested that barley originated in Tibet. In 1953, archaeologist Robert Braidwood asserted that humans first grew barley for beer. Scientist Hans Helbeck and American agronomist Paul Mangelsdorf disagreed, claiming that humans first grew barley for food. Scientist Leo Oppenheim synthesized these positions, asserting that humans first grew barley for both beer and food. In 1966, American agronomist Jack Harlan proposed the Fertile Crescent as the place where humans domesticated barley. In seeking the origin of barley, scientists have debated whether two- or six-row barley arose first. As we have seen, de Candolle among others supposed that two-row barley gave rise to six-row barley. Aberg, on the other hand, thought that six-row barley predated two-row barley. In fact, the earliest archaeological remains are of two-row barley, vindicating de Candolle.

The chronology of cultivation corroborates Harlan's Fertile Crescent thesis. Humans may have harvested wild barley as early as 17,000 years ago on the shore of the Sea of Galilee. Barley then grew wild in southwestern Asia and North Africa. About 10,000 BCE, the Natufians harvested wild barley in the Near East. About 7000 BCE, humans grew barley in parts of Israel, Jordan, southern Turkey,

Iraq, Kurdistan, and southwestern Iran, a region now known as the Fertile Crescent. In this period, people farmed as well as gathered wild barley, and several generations must have passed before farming became the principal way of obtaining barley. In the late seventh millennium, the people of Tell Ramad II, Syria, grew barley for consumption as porridge. By 6000 BCE, skeletons in Syria displayed dental caries, leading one scholar to suggest that the people of this time ate barley in the form of porridge. The barley stuck to the teeth, causing the growth of bacteria and the consequent development of cavities.

From the Fertile Crescent, barley spread west to the Aegean and eastern Mediterranean in the sixth and fifth millennia BCE. In Egypt, farmers grew barley in the Nile Delta by the fifth millennium. From the Nile River, barley migrated south to the highlands of Ethiopia. In the fifth millennium, barley spread east to the Caucasus Mountains and India. By the fourth millennium, farmers in the western Mediterranean were growing barley. By 3000 BCE, the Swiss were growing barley. By 2500 BCE, barley had spread throughout Europe. The ancients of Britain grew barley for livestock and wheat for humans. Because barley prefers cool weather, moderate rainfall, and low humidity, farmers grew it in abundance in Northern Europe. In the Netherlands, barley may have been the first crop grown because it tolerated the saline soils that killed other crops.

These early barleys were all six row. Only in the Middle Ages did Europeans grow two-row barley, which the Crusaders had introduced from the Levant. Among the regions of North Africa, Morocco may have been an independent center of domestication. From Greece, barley migrated north to the Danube River, and from the Danube, it spread throughout the Balkans, Ukraine, and Poland. In the second millennium, farmers adopted barley in China, Korea, and Japan. Barley must have been an important crop in China, where one text listed it as one of the five sacred grains.

From an early date, farmers in Israel and throughout the eastern Mediterranean grew barley in preference to wheat, probably because barley yielded better than wheat on saline soils, alkaline soils, and poor soils. With little gluten, barley was not ideal for making bread. Instead, people ate it in soup and porridge. The transition to eating bread in the Greco-Roman world caused farmers to cultivate wheat at the expense of barley, though they continued to grow barley for making beer. In Greece and Rome, a two-tiered hierarchy arose in which elites ate wheat bread and commoners ate barley porridge. In the first century CE, the Roman agriculturalist Columella classified barley a famine food, perhaps meaning that Romans ate it when they were desperate for food. What barley the elites grew they fed to livestock.

As early as the fourth millennium, the people of Godin Tepe, Iran, raised barley for making beer. The making and drinking of barley beer must have been an important activity in antiquity. The Sumerians brewed eight types of beer from barley. From the third millennium, beer was common in Egypt. Employers some-times paid workers in beer. In an era when the water might harbor the microbes that caused cholera, dysentery, and other diseases, many people eschewed water for beer, even drinking it at breakfast. The beer-drinking Sumerians worshipped Ninkasi, the goddess of brewing. About 1700 BCE, the Sumerians wrote the first set of instructions for growing barley.

The first step in making beer was to malt barley. Malting required the beer maker to begin germinating barley from kernels. Germination released from the kernel a-amylase and b-amylase, enzymes that converted the starch to sugar. One scholar believes that the biblical "land flowing with milk and honey" referred not literally to honey but rather to malted barley, whose sugar gave it sweetness. Once malted, barley was fermented to convert the sugar into alcohol. Malted bar-ley may have had other uses. The ancients of Europe may have mixed malted bar-ley or perhaps even beer with milk to create a nutritious mix. Because malted barley provides humans with B vitamins, and milk contains protein and calcium, one scholar believes that the consumption of malted barley and milk improved health and may have increased life span. In Northern Europe, beer making was an important activity. From an early date, the people of Moravia, Bavaria, and Frankonia grew barley for beer. People thought that fermentation was a magical process, imbuing barley with an element of the sacred.

Barley in the Americas

In 1492, Christopher Columbus brought seeds of various plants to the island of Hispaniola (now Haiti and the Dominican Republic). Whether barley was among these plants is unclear. Columbus did not mention barley by name, though one authority believes that he had barley among these plants because it was common for migrants to carry seeds of important crops in their journey to new lands. Even had Columbus introduced barley to Hispaniola, there is no way to know whether the colonists of La Navidad cultivated it, because the Amerindians killed them. The problem of whether Columbus introduced barley to the New World in 1492 may be insoluble.

There is no doubt, however, about his second voyage. In 1493, Columbus wrote in a letter to King Ferdinand that he brought barley to Hispaniola. Even this evi-dence does not reveal much. Whether barley flourished in the tropical Caribbean is unclear. Barley can be grown in the tropics, but as a crop of temperate locales, it may not have thrived in the Caribbean. Where and how successfully barley was grown in the 16th century is unknown because the historical record is silent about this grass. Early in the 17th century, however, barley reentered the historical record. In 1602, a man known only by the last name of Gosnold introduced barley to Martha's Vineyard and the Elizabeth Islands off the coast of Massachusetts. In 1611, the London Company brought barley to Jamestown. By 1648, the crop was widely grown in Virginia, but thereafter farmers abandoned it for the more profitable tobacco. In 1620, the Pilgrims introduced barley to Plymouth, Massachusetts. In 1626, the settlers of Newfoundland and Manhattan began raising barley. In 1629, farmers first grew barley in the Massachusetts Bay Colony. By the end of the 18th century, barley had emerged as the principal crop in Rhode Island. Throughout New England, farmers grew barley for beer. Around 1771, California growers raised the variety Coast for beer. Others grew the variety Atlas for beer, exporting much of the crop to Great Britain.

The history of barley culture in the United States is tied to the history of immigration. Each nationality of immigrants brought to the United States the varieties of barley that they had grown at home. In 1701, the Spanish introduced varieties from North Africa into Arizona and later California. These varieties, adapted to the arid climate of North Africa, did well in the American Southwest. In the 18th century, immigrants imported varieties from Switzerland and the Balkans to the South. The British and Dutch settlers of North America introduced two-row spring barleys, but these varieties did poorly. The Scots had better success with their six-row varieties. German settlers brought Russian varieties to the United States.

After the American Revolution, pioneers carried barley to the new lands of the West. Western New York emerged as an ideal region for the cultivation of barley, and by 1839 the state grew 60 percent of U.S. barley, making New York the leading grower. By 1849, New York's percentage had risen to 69. In the 19th century, barley was grown near the major cities to provide beer to urbanites. Detroit, Cincinnati, Toledo, Pittsburgh, St. Louis, and Chicago all imported barley for brewing. Throughout the 19th century, barley production increased in New York, Maine, Ohio, Pennsylvania, Michigan, and Illinois. Most barley in the Northeast and Midwest went to make beer. In the Southwest and California, barley fed livestock. The gold rush of 1849, by increasing the population of California, increased the demand for barley. Whereas California produced 0.2 percent of U.S. barley in 1848, it produced 28 percent in 1859. Between 1859 and 1869, barley acreage increased in Minnesota. During the 1870s, barley acreage increased in Nebraska and the Dakotas. In 1879, farmers were growing barley in Oregon and Washington.

The saga of barley involved more than geographic expansion. In 1850, a German traveler—his name is lost to history—collected seed from a vigorous stand of barley on a visit to Manchuria. Upon returning to Germany with the seed, his activities were unclear, though the variety came to the attention of Herman Grunow, an American scientist visiting Germany. Grunow brought the seed to the United States in 1861, apparently growing it over several years. In 1872, he gave seed of the variety to the Wisconsin Agricultural Experiment Station, which distributed it to farmers. Not surprisingly, the variety was known as Manchuria, though confusingly scientists and farmers also called it Manshury, Mandsheuri, Minnesota 6, and North Dakota 787. The number may refer to the plot of land. Minnesota 6 therefore would have been grown on the sixth plot of land, likely at the Minnesota Agricultural Experiment Station of the experimental farm at the University of Minnesota. The story of Manchuria does not end here. In 1881, Canada's Ontario Agricultural Experiment Station obtained the variety from Russia, though how Russia came to have it is unclear. Scientists at the Ontario Agricultural Experiment Station gave Manchuria to the Minnesota and North Dakota Agricultural Experiment Stations in 1894. Scientists at the Minnesota Agricultural Experiment Station released their own varieties, Minnesota 32 and Minnesota 105, which were derivatives of Manchuria. By another account, the variety Manchuria does not derive its name from Manchuria but from the village of Manshury in Egypt's Nile Delta. This account would explain the origin of the name Manshury, by which the variety Manchuria was sometimes known.

Other varieties rose to prominence. Around 1880, scientist F. H. Horsford of Charlotte, Vermont, first hybridized barley, obtaining three varieties: Beardless, Success, and Success Beardless. In 1894, the U.S. Department of Agriculture (USDA), alert to the need to preserve the genetic diversity of barley, began collecting varieties and now has several thousand. In 1905, the USDA collected seed from the variety Tribi, which originated in Samsun, Turkey. In 1909, the Minnesota Agricultural Experiment Station grew Tribi, and farmers in Chico, California, did likewise in 1910. Results were discouraging, but when farmers irrigated the variety at Aberdeen, Idaho, the yield was high. Early-maturing varieties are ideal for arid regions because they seed before the high temperatures and low rainfall of mid-summer. Late-maturing varieties do well in moist, cool locales with long growing seasons. The improvement in varieties has increased yields. Since the 1940s, superior varieties have contribute more than one-third of the gain in yield.

Seeking to protect U.S. farmers, the McKinley Tariff, named in honor of high-tariff advocate President William McKinley, placed a 30-cents-per-bushel duty on imported barley in 1897. In addition to domestic production, New York breweries relied on cheap barley from Canada. The tariff made Canadian barley too expensive, sending New York breweries into decline. Whereas New York had been the center of brewing, cities in the Midwest took the lead in the early 20th century. Farmers in southern Wisconsin, northern Illinois, and eastern Iowa grew barley for brewing in Milwaukee and Chicago. Benefiting from the tariff, American farmers, who had grown 100 million bushels of barley in 1895, raised 200 million bushels in 1915. During World War I, the demand for wheat increased, causing some farmers to switch from barley to wheat. Because so much barley went to make beer, Prohibition hurt farmers as barley production declined in Wisconsin, Iowa, Minnesota, North Dakota, and South Dakota. During Prohibition, farmers were keen to export surplus barley. During the 1920s, exports reached 25 percent of

U.S. barley, a percentage that was not matched until the 1950s. Yet even before the repeal of Prohibition, barley rebounded as farmers discovered that malted barley was good for livestock. With this use of barley demand soared, and in 1928, five years before the end of Prohibition, barley production reached 300 million bushels. The repeal of Prohibition should have led farmers to grow more barley, but in the short term the drought of 1934 reduced barley yields. In the 1930s, production increased in western Iowa, eastern Wisconsin, and Michigan. After 1940, however, the expansion of acreage to hybrid corn and soybeans led farmers to grow less barley in the Midwest.

Like many farmers, barley growers suffered during the Great Depression. Between 1868 and 1932, the price per bushel of barley fell more than sixfold. Part of the problem was overproduction. Between 1895 and 1928, production had tripled. The practice of feeding barley to livestock had limits because farmers believed barley inferior to corn as livestock feed. Barley had too much fiber to feed to poultry, and hogs did not gain weight as rapidly on barley as on corn. With little of the amino acid lysine, barley is less valuable as feed than corn.

In the United States, farmers rotate barley with corn, cotton, sugar beets, tobacco, and potatoes. In the West, farmers doublecrop barley with alfalfa. In other areas, farmers doublecrop barley with milo, beans, soybeans, corn, sudangrass, and cowpeas. In parts of the West, farmers grow barley the first year, wheat the second, and fallow the land in the third year. Elsewhere, a barley clover rotation is common. American farmers grow barley for beer in the Red River Valley of Minnesota and North Dakota and under irrigation in Idaho, Wyoming, and Montana. During the 20th century, production increased in Idaho, Washington, Oregon, Kansas, and Colorado. By 1990, North Dakota, South Dakota, Minnesota, and Montana produced the majority of U.S. barley. Yields per acre have increased over time. Between 1950 and 1990, the yield more than doubled. Today, the western edge of the Midwest specializes in growing barley for beer. By contrast, California farmers feed barley to livestock.

Barley in the Modern World

Americans eat relatively little barley compared with other parts of the world, but it is growing in popularity in the United States, especially among those who are vegetarians or eating more plant-based foods. Barley is found in soups, stews, stuffings, salads, and other grain dishes. In 1959, however, less than 1 percent of the U.S. barley crop nourished Americans. In the United States, soup and baby food contain barley, as do some breakfast cereals. In North Africa, southwestern and South Asia, Italy, Germany, Finland, Ethiopia, Tibet, Nepal, and Peru, barley is an important source of nourishment. Peruvians grow barley in the highlands of the Andes Mountains. In these regions, people eat barley in flat bread, gruel, and porridge. Barley that goes to make beer has less protein than the barley that feeds livestock. The barley that is fermented into beer needs a long growing season, cool temperatures, and uniform moisture.

In 1990, Germany was the leading grower of barley. Canada was second and France third. The United States was fifth. Europe's climate, with its cool summers (temperatures range between 54°F and 76°F in July) and uniform rainfall, give farmers the best yields. Yields are high in Switzerland. Belgium, Luxembourg, Denmark, France, Ireland, the Netherlands, and Czechoslovakia all boast yields above 100 bushels per acre. Thanks to this productivity, Europe produced 69 percent of the world's barley in 1990. In contrast to Europe's fecundity, hot, dry North Africa was not an ideal region for the cultivation of barley. In 1990, Morocco averaged just 16.6 bushels per acre of barley. Yields were worse in Tunisia with 16.2 bushels per acre and Algeria with 12.5 bushels per acre. Worldwide, barley is fourth in acreage, trailing corn, rice, and wheat. Europe and Asia plant 75 percent of the world's barley acreage.

The success of hybrid corn led to efforts to hybridize barley on an ambitious scale. Progress was initially slow. The production of a hybrid required scientists to emasculate the barley plants that they designated the female lines. Barley has small flowers with anther and stigma close together. To emasculate a plant, scientists must penetrate the flower, removing the anther before it sheds pollen. Although this procedure may be done on a few plants without too much trouble, it is too time consuming and labor intensive to emasculate acre after acre of barley. Once an anther is removed, its pollen is used to fertilize the stigma of another plant to yield a hybrid. The discovery of genes that cause barley to produce no pollen eased the production of hybrids. Scientists now derive hybrid barley by using male sterile lines as the female line, crossing them with fully fertile plants as the male line. Hybrid barley yields between 15 and 35 percent more grain than its parents. Some progeny have even achieved 50 percent more grain than their parents.

In areas of Canada and Australia unsuitable for corn, farmers grow barley for livestock. These countries export barley to Asia for feed. Because of the oversupply of wheat on the world market, some farmers have switched from wheat to barley. In southeastern Europe, however, some farmers have switched from barley to corn because of its superiority as feed. Since 1991, barley acreage has declined 14 percent worldwide as farmers has converted acreage to corn. Worldwide, 85 percent of barley is used as feed. Yet barley faces competition from wheat, whose surplus is also used to feed livestock.

Some 18 million tons of barley are fermented into the world's 1.3 million liters of beer. Increasing beer consumption in Asia and South America should stimulate the demand for barley. In Moravia, farmers grow the variety Hanna for making beer. In Scandinavia, farmers grow Binder, Kenia, Opal, and Maja, all derivative of Hanna. Scientists crossed Kenia with the variety Britburly to yield Proctor.

Scientists have found challenging the attempt to breed varieties that have both high yield and suitability for malting. In addition to its use in making beer, malted barley is an ingredient in candy bars, milkshakes, chocolate flavored beverages, and vinegar.

Christopher Cumo

Further Reading

Barley: Origin, Botany, Culture, Winter Hardiness, Genetics, Utilization, Pests. Washington, D.C.: U.S. Department of Agriculture, 1979.

Briggs, D. E. *Barley.* London: Chapman and Hall, 1978.

Dineley, Merryn. *Barley, Malt and Ale in the Neolithic.* Oxford: BAR International, 2004.

Hughes, Meredith Sayles. *Glorious Grasses: The Grains.* Minneapolis: Lerner, 1999.

Slafer, Gustavo A., José Luis Molina-Cano, Roxana Savin, José Luis Araus, and Ignacio Romangosa, eds. *Barley Science: Recent Advances from Molecular Biology to Agronomy of Yield and Quality.* New York: Food Products Press, 2002.

Basil

Basil is an herbaceous member of the mint family, Labiatiaceae, that originated in India and has been used for about 5,000 years. The most common type of basil in cultivation is *Ocimum basilicum*, a heterogeneous species with a number of different cultivars. Even the same cultivar may vary greatly in morphology and also in chemical composition. There is a rich history surrounding basil and a great deal of mythology. Its use once limited to royalty, the name derives from the Greek *basilikos*, meaning "royal." Now, basil is grown all over the world for its culinary use as a spice. Essential oil is also produced from the leaves and the flowers for flavoring and industrial purposes, and there has been a great deal of study on the antimicrobial properties of the herb and its oil.

Basil Folklore

There is a large amount of tradition about basil on all of the continents on which it has been grown for long periods. One common thread is consideration of the herb as an enticement to love, either as a part of sacred ceremonies such as weddings or as an ingredient in aphrodisiac dishes. Holy basil, *Ocimum sanctum*, has long been used in sacred Hindu ceremonies and is part of both traditional Hindu weddings and funerals. In some parts of Europe, acceptance of a sprig of basil by a man indicates that he will love the woman who gave it to him forever or even formal acceptance of a marriage proposal.

Alternatively, in Greece, basil has been considered a symbol of hatred and sorrow. The plant was vilified by the influential Greek philosopher Chrysippus in

200 BCE as causing one to become dim-witted. The ancient Romans cursed basil as they planted it, believing this would cause it to grow better.

Taxonomy of Basil

As with many plants, the assignment of taxonomic systems to *Ocimum* species has been an active and contentious area. The genus was named by Swedish naturalist Carl Linneaus in 1753 and enumerated into five species. In the past 250 years, there have been a number of taxonomic systems proposed, greatly expanding the species number of *Ocimum*. These systems were based on the structure of the plants, particularly those of the flower parts. The most recent system in common use is that of British plant taxonomist Alan Paton and his fellow researchers from 1999, in which *Ocimum basilicum* is placed within the *Ocimum* section of this genus.

The morphology of the plants can vary greatly, however, given the crossbreeding between various cultivars and species. The science of chemistry was in its infancy when the original *Ocimum* taxonomic schemes were proposed. Since then, the advent of analytical chemistry has enabled the study of the numerous aromatic compounds found in all species of *Ocimum*, particularly those of the essential oils of these plants. This has enabled researchers to classify types of basil based on their chemical profile—a field called chemotyping. One problem with this avenue of research is that the particular chemicals in a given plant can vary widely depending on the environmental conditions, seasons, and soil and region in which the plant is grown.

Other methods of taxonomic classification of basils include examining the geographic origin of the plants and whether or not they can be crossed with one another. With the discovery of DNA and cell nuclei, karyotyping became a viable method of analysis. This technique involves determining the number and appearance of chromosomes per cell in an organism. One problem with using this technique in basil is that researchers have found the chromosome count to vary widely within the same species.

The advent of molecular biological techniques, such as the polymerase chain reaction (PCR), have ushered in a new era in plant taxonomy. A class of techniques based on PCR amplification of small amounts of DNA takes advantage of minor changes in the structure of genes. This enables genetic fingerprinting to be performed in plants and gives a much more rigorous analysis of genetic relatedness. Croatian scientist Klaudija Carović-Stanko and coworkers published such research in 2010 comparing 28 accessions of basil, including 22 of *Ocimum basilicum*. In addition to PCR techniques that had been previously used in studies of basil taxonomy, along with chromosome counting, they also examined nuclear DNA content.

Of the two PCR methods used, AFLP (amplified fragment length polymorphism) was successful in separating all of the accessions from one another. The commonly used technique RAPD (random amplified polymorphic DNA) did not distinguish between all of the accessions. In tandem, both of these techniques enabled the researchers to successfully classify all of the plants tested.

The researchers found a high level of genetic diversity among the basil accessions, which adds credence to the taxonomic system of Paton with its large number of species. They were able to clearly separate taxa, with a grouping of *Ocimum basilicum* type species and one of *Ocimum americanum*. All of the *Ocimum basilicum* cultivars and varieties fit within that species' group. Surprisingly, *Ocimum minimum* fit within the group also and could be a subspecies or variety of *Ocimum basilicum*. An additional surprise was that two Russian accessions of *Ocimum basilicum* ssp. *purpurascens* were found to be genetically identical to the *Ocimum americanum* group, which has a different number of chromosomes.

The current classification of basil includes several varieties and a very large number of cultivars. The primary variety of *Ocimum basilicum* in cultivation is *basilicum*, in particular cultivars Sweet Basil and Genovese. Also notable are varieties *purpurascens* Benth. (purple basil), and *difforme* Benth.

Basic Biology of Basil

Ocimum basilicum is an herbaceous plant originally from tropical areas such as southern Asia, including India, and Africa. In such climates, it can grow as a perennial. In much of the world, it is cultivated as an annual, however, since the plant cannot tolerate frost. Basil grows best in long days with full sun and requires consistent moisture.

Being a member of the mint family, basil has square stems. The leaves are dotted with glands containing oil comprising a number of aromatic secondary metabolites. The composition of the oil varies greatly between different cultivars. It is the oil that gives basil its distinctive, slightly mint-like smell.

Basil leaves are formed opposite to one another and are velvet green or purple, depending on the cultivar. The plants grow to about one-and-seven-tenths to four feet in height and produce white flowers in a terminal spike. Normally when cultivated as an herb, the flowers are cropped off, so the plant will keep producing leaves. The flowers set seeds that are also rich in oils. The seeds produced by a particular plant can vary greatly in their morphological characteristics and oil production. This lack of genetic uniformity can complicate the growth of cultivars from seeds. All of the members of the *Ocimum basilicum* group have 48 chromosomes.

Uses of Basil

Basil is used around the world as a culinary ingredient. Dried and fresh basil leaves are among the most popular herbs in Italian, Mexican, Greek, and French cuisines. The flavoring is added to vinegars, pickled vegetables, and salads. One common association of basil is as an ingredient in pesto, the classic Italian dish that uses this herb as a primary ingredient. Basil is also an important herb in Asian cuisines. The plant is versatile for so many cuisines partly because its taste varies over different regions. This is due to variation in the types of chemicals found in the plants in various parts of the world.

The use of dried or fresh basil can greatly affect its utility as a spice. The process of drying causes the plant to lose a high percentage of its oil content. Thus the resulting herb is less aromatic and flavorful. Drying can be highly important for storage, however, to keep pathogens from growing on the herb. Also, the tissue turns black fairly quickly after being harvested if it is not rapidly used or stored in a special manner. Once dried, the herb keeps its essential oils for several years if stored properly. Frozen basil is becoming a more popular commodity, since it can be used in the same manner as fresh basil, which is subject to seasonal availability in cooler climates.

The essential oil can be isolated from the leaves of the plants or from the flowers. The flowers contain a smaller percentage of oil, but it is considered superior to that from the leaves. Basil oil is an important industrial item and is used primarily in the food industry and in the making of perfumes. Sweet basil grown from seed is the primary source of essential oil for industrial purposes. Because of the variability of oil composition in plants grown from seed, along with other factors, the chemotype is determined before the plant is used for this purpose.

The food industry uses basil oil in a range of products, from candies to meat products and liqueurs. It dissolves in fatty acids and can be added to perfumes, shampoos, soaps, and dental products. The essential oils are produced by the distillation of flowering plants grown in favorable climates where it is economically feasible to produce them on a large scale.

Basil has been used in traditional medicine for millennia to treat a number of conditions. Its oil has long been considered to be antimicrobial. Research has shown promise with some *Ocimum basilicum* oils and is being vigorously pursued.

Chemicals Found in Basil

Basil contains a number of low-molecular-weight, volatile, aromatic compounds in its essential oil that give the characteristic aroma and flavoring to the plant. The herb contains 0.5–1.5 percent of essential oils that vary in their composition. Most of the compounds distilled from the essential oil have oxygen groups on them. Studies have found up to 54 different chemicals in the distilled oil of *Ocimum basilicum*. Prominent compounds include estragole, linalool, cardinol, ocimene, 1,8-cineole, and bornyl acetate. Seeds are the source of a nonvolatile oil known as "fixed oil" that is rich in fatty acids. This oil can be obtained by cold pressing. It is rich in polyunsaturated acids, with approximately 50 percent of the oil being composed of linoleic acid and around 22 percent composed linolenic acid. The monounsaturated fatty acid oleic acid is the next most prominent fatty acid at 8–15 percent of the total. Found in lesser quantities are the saturated fatty acids palmitic acid and stearic acid, while free fatty acids were found to comprise only 0.5 percent of the total.

The whole plant contains up to 10 percent of tannins. It also contains the phytosterol ß-sitosterol. Several phenolic compounds have been isolated, both unconjugated and with sugars attached (glycosides). The quercetin glycosides rutin and isoquercetin have been isolated from *Ocimum basilicum*. In addition, several flavonoids and flavones have been identified. The polyphenols caffeic acid and rosmarinic acid have both been isolated, as has p-coumaric acid—an important intermediary compound in phenolic compound biosynthesis.

The analytical techniques of secondary plant compound isolation are constantly being refined and improved, so it is highly likely that additional compounds will be discovered in this prolific producer of secondary metabolites.

Helga George

Further Reading

Attokaran, M. "Basil." In *Natural Food Flavours and Colorants*, 71–73. Oxford: Blackwell and Institute of Food Technologists, 2011.

Carović-Stanko, K., Z. Liber, V. Besendorfer, B. Javornik, B. Bohance, I. Kolak, and Z. Satovic. "Genetic Relations among Basil Taxa (*Ocimum* L.) Based on Molecular Markers, Nuclear DNA Content, and Chromosome Number." *Plant Systematics and Evolution* 285 (2010): 13–22.

Hedrick, U. P., ed. *Sturtevant's Edible Plants of the World*. New York: Dover, 1972.

Hiltunen, R. "Chemical Composition of *Ocimum* Species." In *Basil*, edited by R. Hiltunen and Y. Holm, 67–75. Amsterdam: Harwood, 1999.

Paton, A., M. R. Harley, and M. M. Harley. "*Ocimum*: An Overview of Classification and Relationships." In *Basil*, edited by R. Hiltunen and Y. Holm, 1–38. Amsterdam: Harwood, 1999.

Putievsky, E., and B. Galambosi. "Production Systems of Sweet Basil." In *Basil*, edited by R. Hiltunen and Y. Holm, 39–65. Amsterdam: Harwood, 1999.

Beans

Most species of beans are annual legumes, though a few are perennials. In the tropics limas and scarlet runner beans are perennials. The majority of beans fall under the genus *Phaseolus*. These are the beans native to the Americas. A second group of beans, in the genus *Vigna*, is indigenous to East Asia. A third category, in the genus *Vicia*, is the fava bean of western Asia and Europe. All beans, being

Beans (Shutterstock.com)

members of the Fabaceae or Leguminosae family, have seed pods and are related to chickpea, lupin, peanut, vetch, clover, alfalfa, pea, soybean, lentil, and cowpea. An ancient food, beans have nourished people of all social classes. The poor, their diet bereft of meat, have depended on beans for protein. In many cultures, the affluent eat meat for protein, disparaging beans as peasant fare. Where population is dense and grazing land scarce, people have eaten beans for protein. One writer regards beans as "poor man's meat." Because people of varied cultures grew and ate beans, many languages have a word for bean. In Latin, bean is *faba*. In Greek, bean is *kyamos*, which is related to the verb *kyein*, meaning "to swell." The fact that bean pods swell as they grow may explain the relationship between *kyamos* and *kyein*. In this context, beans may be connected to pregnancy and regeneration. The Aztec word for bean is *ayocotl*. In Old German bean is *bauno*, in Saxon *bona*, in German *bohna*, in Dutch *boan*, in Danish and Norwegian *bonne*, in Swedish *boens*. Beans are between 21 and 25 percent protein, an amount that compares favorably with the protein content of grains. Beans also have thiamine, riboflavin, iron, copper, manganese, molybdenum, and magnesium. One cup of beans has 230 calories, half the daily requirement of fiber, 46 percent of the daily requirement of iron for men, and 25 percent for women. Snap beans have vitamins A and C. Under domestication beans evolved pods that do not shatter. Having lost the ability to disperse seeds, beans depend on human intervention for survival. Moreover, cultivated beans have dormant seeds, enabling people to store them, in some cases for years, for later consumption. Domesticated beans tolerate different amounts of light and so can be grown at different latitudes, and they ripen uniformly so that they can be harvested over a brief period. In 2008, Brazil, India, and China were the leading producers. The United States ranked sixth.

Folklore, Folk Medicine, Festivals, Politics, and Religion

The best-known tale about beans may be the story of Jack and the Beanstalk. Jack and his mother were so poor that they had to sell their cow. Rather than command a price for it, Jack traded the cow for magic beans. Neighbors thought Jack foolish. Nonetheless, ignoring their opinion, Jack planted a bean. It grew to the heavens, allowing Jack to climb to the lair of a giant. From him Jack stole a bag of gold, a hen that laid golden eggs, and a magic harp. The bean had transformed Jack's fortunes from destitution to wealth. A twist on the beanstalk as ladder story is the New Guinean account of a man and his mother who climbed a beanstalk to kill Tauni-kapi-kapi, a man-eating giant.

Another story, set in Hungary, also featured a poor man as protagonist. One day as he wandered the streets the man came upon a bean. Reflecting on its potential, the man thought that if he planted the bean he would harvest many beans. Planting these, he would harvest many more. Repeating this process over several generations, he would have thousands of beans to sell. Sure that he would become wealthy, the man put the bean in his pocket and hurried to the king's castle. Receiving an audience with the king, the man asked for barrels and loading docks for his crop. Impressed by this request, the king assumed that the man must be rich. Wanting his daughter to marry a rich may, the king offered her to him in marriage. Once more, the bean catapulted a man from poverty to affluence.

Amerindians told the story of two hunters who killed a deer. While they roasted it, a woman materialized out of a cloud. Willing to share their kill, they offered her some venison. She accepted their invitation and joined them in conversation. In the course of their meal, she asked why they ate only deer meat. They replied that they had nothing else. Finishing the meal and wishing to repay their kindness, the woman invited the men to rejoin her the next day when she would treat them. The next day the hunters returned to find a bean plant growing up a corn stalk. The story underscores the centrality of beans and corn in the transition from a hunter-gatherer way of life to agriculture and the close relationship between beans and corn in Amerindian agriculture. Indeed, corn and beans were two of the Three Sisters, the third being squash, in Native American agriculture. Corn and squash supplied the Amerindians with carbohydrates and bean gave them protein. The beans also enriched the soil in which the corn and squash grew, and the squash leaves retarded the growth of weeds. Another Amerindian tradition holds that a crow gave humans beans and corn.

In spring, the Hopi celebrated Powamu, a bean festival. During Powamu, the Hopi planted beans in pots of soil. When the seeds germinated, masked dancers, representing the spirits of nature, blessed the new plants. The blessing ensured that the harvest would be bountiful. At festival's end, the Hopi cooked bean sprouts in stew, internalizing the blessing by eating the stew.

Celebrating the festival of the Bean Calends on June 1, the Romans offered beans to the dead. In one ritual, Romans tossed beans over their shoulders, asking the souls of their ancestors to depart. This ritual became All Saints' Day and later Halloween. At funerals, the Romans offered beans to the deceased to ease their passage into the afterlife. As early as 3000 BCE, the Egyptians put beans in tombs to feed the dead in the afterlife. Egyptian priests, however, did not eat beans they thought them unclean. In another context, some ancients thought that beans were an aphrodisiac, a belief that may explain the reluctance of priests to eat them. To the ancients beans were more than food for the living and the dead. Some Greeks and Romans believed that beans harbored the souls of the dead. In this context, one should not eat beans for fear of harming the dead. One should not walk through bean fields for fear of disturbing the dead. This reasoning may have led Greek mathematician Pythagoras to forbid his disciples from eating beans. It is also possible that this injunction derived from a disdain for politics and court proceedings. The Greeks and Romans used beans to vote for or against a measure. The person who cast a white bean affirmed a measure whereas a black bean negated it. Similarly, in a trial a juror who cast a white bean declared the innocence of a defendant whereas a black bean was a vote of guilty. The term "blackballing" may derive from the practice of voting with black beans. Whatever the reason, Pythagoras's injunction against beans may have cost him his life. According to one account Pythagoras, fleeing his enemies, came upon a bean field. Rather than go through it he stopped, allowing his pursuers to catch and kill him. Peculiar as it may seem, at least one account counseled people not to eat beans because when dried in the sun they smelled like semen or the blood of a murdered person.

So important are they that beans are part of the idiom of English. The phrase "full of beans" means that a person is full of health and vigor. A person who is not worth a bean or who does not amount to a hill of beans has no value. One who does not have a bean has no money or property. This association between beans and property may have arisen out of confusion between the word "bean" and the French *biens*, meaning "property." In England, beans were central to the Twelve Days of Christmas. During this festival, the host of a party made raisin cakes for the guests. One cake, however, contained beans rather than raisins. The guest who got the bean cake became the bean king or queen. Reigning over the festival, the king or queen performed a ritual to ensure good weather the next year. In China, beans were a symbol of good luck. A person who wore a necklace of beans was thought to have magic powers.

Because beans look like kidneys, people thought they were good for treating kidney ailments. For example, beans were a putative diuretic, helping the kidneys rid the body of excess water. Women and men, soaking bean pods in wine or vinegar, rubbed the liquid on their face to improve their complexion. Another way to enhance the complexion, they believed, was to rub a mixture of bean meal and milk on their face. Roman women rubbed bean paste on their skin to remove wrinkles. The Romans believed that beans boiled with garlic could suppress a cough. People drank potions of bean flowers and leaves to reduce inflammation. Some thought that bean pods, rubbed on a wart, caused it to disappear, but only if one buried the pods in a secret place.

Phaseolus **Beans in the Americas and Beyond**

In 1753, Swedish naturalist Carl Linneaus put the beans of America in the genus *Phaseolus*, though he mistakenly thought that they had originated in India. Meaning "boat shaped," *Phaseolus* is an apt name for beans, because their pods look somewhat like boats. The beans in the genus *Phaseolus* are what most people have in mind when they think of beans. The familiar kidney, pinto, black, navy, great northern, scarlet runner, green, lima, and hundreds more are all members of *Phaseolus*. People eat young pods of *Phaseolus* as snap or string beans. Varieties with yellow pods are known as wax or butter beans. A widely distributed genus, the wild ancestors of *Phaseolus* grew from northern Mexico to Argentina. Named for Lima, Peru, lima beans are members of the species *Phaseolus lunetus*. Scarlet runner beans are in the species *Phaseolus coccineus*. Tepary beans are members of *Phaseolus acutifolius*. Kidney beans and their ilk are members of *Phaseolus vulgaria*. The French called *Phaseolus vulgaris* haricots because they cooked these beans with a type of lamb known as haricot. *Phaseolus vulgaris* may have originated in Central America.

Farmers domesticated *Phaseolus* beans independently in Peru about 6000 BCE and in Mexico around 5000 BCE. As early as 3000 BCE, the Amerindians of the Southwest grew tepary beans because they are drought tolerant. The Spanish dubbed the Papago of Arizona "the bean people" because they grew beans. When the Spanish asked the name of the bean plant, the Papago replied "T'pawi," meaning "it is a bean." The Spanish transliterated T'pawi into *tepary*, the name by which it is known today. Along with the Papago, the Pima of Arizona still grow tepary beans.

By 2500 BCE, the Woodlands Indians of what is today the eastern United States were growing beans. The Mississippians grew beans as early as the eighth century CE. The Cherokee made bread from corn and beans. The Iroquois adopted an agriculture based on the Three Sisters sometime in prehistory. In North America, the Amerindians boiled beans with corn, a dish they called "sickqquatasch" but that Americans know as succotash. Today, limas are the bean of choice in making this dish. Amerindians harvested, shelled, and dried beans in the sun. Sometimes they dried and cooked beans in the pod, shelling them before eating them. Like the Cherokee, the Maya made bread from beans and corn. At other times, they ate beans with squash seeds and onions and beans with chili peppers. The descendants of the Maya eat black beans, onions, and epazote. The Aztecs offered loaves of corn and beans to the gods. In Tenochtitlan street vendors sold bean dishes. Spanish priest Bernardino de Sahagun determined that the Aztecs grew 12 types of beans at the time of conquest.

In Peru, the Moche painted images of lima beans on pottery in the first millennium CE. Throughout South America, archaeologists dated pottery with beans to the eighth century CE. Amerindians had decorated these jars with images of men and women holding beans in one hand and corn in the other, though the meaning of such images is unclear. They may simply record the bounty of the harvest and suggest the close relationship between beans and corn in Amerindian agriculture. On other jars, Amerindians painted images of men with human heads and the body of a lima bean. Some of these lima bean men were depicted as warriors, suggesting perhaps that Amerindian armies ate beans.

In Jamaica, cooks made kidney beans with rice and coconut milk. Cubans made black beans with rice and pork or ham, a dish derived from the Moors of Spain and known as Moros y Cristianos. Throughout the Caribbean, people ate kidney beans with coconut and thyme.

In 1493, Christopher Columbus came upon haricots in Cuba. In 1519, Spanish conquistador Hernando Cortez witnessed the growing of *Phaseolus vulgaria* in Mexico. In the 1520s, Spanish explorer Alvar Nunez Cabaza de Vaca reported on the cultivation of beans in Texas and New Mexico, and in 1528 he found beans being grown in Florida. In the 1520s, French explorer Jacques Cartier witnessed the culture of beans as far north as the Saint Lawrence River.

Beans were part of the Columbian Exchange. In 1493, Columbus brought *Phaseolus* beans to Spain. Europeans adopted these beans more quickly than they did the tomato, potato, and other American crops, probably because they considered American beans to be merely a variant of their fava beans. *Phaseolus* beans were therefore familiar whereas other American crops were novel and strange. In the early 16th century, Europeans began to grow *Phaseolus* beans. In 1528, for example, the Spanish introduced them into Italy. Italians used white kidney beans, known as cannelloni, in making minestrone. They also used white kidneys to make pasta e fugioli (pasta and beans). Italian Americans called this dish pasta fazool. The French ate a dish of *Phaseolus* and meat known as cassoulet. Taking a culinary interest in green beans, the French popularized them. So keen was their interest in American beans that the French developed new varieties, for example the flageolet bean. Perhaps because of French influence green beans were the most popular bean in North America. In the 16th century, English herbalist John Gerard grew scarlet runner beans in his garden. Europeans called this variety the "painted lady" because of its red flowers. Only in the mid-16th century did botanists conclude that *Phaseolus* beans were not simply an iteration of fava beans. They were unique. *Phaseolus* beans were novel after all, but this news did not deter Europeans from cultivating them. In fact, they planted *Phaseolus* beans in preference to fava beans, probably because *Phaseolus* beans lacked the thick seed coat that fava beans had and that had to be removed before favas were eaten. In the 17th century, the gardener of England's King Charles I introduced the scarlet runner bean from Virginia to England, where he planted it as an ornamental. It remains an ornamental in the United States though Europeans eat it as food.

Established in Europe, *Phaseolus* provisioned ships. Slaves, encountering lima beans in their transatlantic crossing, transplanted them in Africa. In the American colonies, English settlers followed the Amerindian practice of growing beans between rows of corn. The first Thanksgiving meal included beans. The Amerindians taught the colonists to make baked beans. Soaking navy beans in water, the Amerindians baked them with deer fat and onions. Adopting baked beans as their own, the colonists traditionally ate them at Saturday dinner. Bostonians developed their own tradition, baking beans with pork fat and brown sugar. Every Saturday morning in Boston the baker gathered a pot of beans from each house, baking them in the community oven and returning the beans in time for Saturday dinner. So important were baked beans to Bostonians that the city earned the moniker of Beantown. Baked beans also nourished colonists on Sunday. Because many Christian denominations forbade work on Sunday, women baked beans Saturday, serving them Sunday and freeing them from having to cook that day.

In the United States, beans captivated Henry David Thoreau, who tended more than two acres of them at Walden Pond. Several recipes called for beans. In 1796, Amelia Simmons's *American Cookery* recommended beans with lamb. In 1851, *Miss Leslie's Complete Cookery* recommended that cooks boil green beans and scarlet runner beans for at least one hour to tenderize them. The pods of these beans must have been tough to demand such effort. In 1853, *The Improved Housewife* urged cooks to bake beans overnight. In 1886, *Mrs. Rorer's Philadelphia Cookbook* included a recipe of black beans with lemon and hard-boiled egg. That year the seed company Burpee marketed a variety of pole bean with a tender pod, the Golden Wax Flageoler. In the late 19th century, cooks did not need to go to great lengths to prepare beans. In 1875, the American company Burnham and Morrill was the first to can and sell baked beans, and in 1895 H. J. Heinz began to sell baked beans.

Old World Beans

In the pre-Columbian era the people of western Asia, North Africa, and Europe grew and ate beans of the species *Vicia faba*, better known as fava beans. Favas may have originated in Africa though farmers domesticated them in western Asia. Resembling large lima beans, favas were a staple crop of the prehistoric people of Iran, North Africa, and the rest of the Mediterranean Basin. Egyptians, Hebrews, and Greeks all grew favas. In Assyria, Phoenicia, and Palestine, people ate favas. Cooks ground them into flour for bread or made them into pottage. Today, the people of Italy, Spain, and the Middle East still eat them. The species name *faba*, we have seen, is Latin for bean. The tern *faba* gave its name to Fabius, one of the patrician families of Rome. In taking this name, the Fabius family claimed that their ancestors had been bean farmers. Although it may seem strange for a wealthy family to claim so humble a pedigree, one must remember that the Romans, even those who did not farm, idealized the life of simple peasants, believing that the Roman virtues of self-reliance, hard work, piety, and frugality had their origin in the countryside. The Fabius family, in identifying with beans, claimed to have these rural values.

Of course fava beans predated the Fabius family. As early as 6500 BCE, the people of Nazareth gathered beans, though they may not have cultivated them this early. Sometime before the third millennium humans domesticated favas, probably in the Fertile Crescent, and by this millennium were growing them in Spain, Portugal, northern Italy, Switzerland, Greece, and the Middle East. In class-conscious Egypt and Europe, the poor ate favas as a substitute for the meat that they could not afford. As a rule, an inverse relationship existed between beans and meat. The more beans one ate, the less meat one consumed. In Egypt, the poor still derive their protein chiefly from beans. Egyptians eat favas with garlic, olive oil, lemon, cumin, and parsley. They eat favas even at breakfast, taking them with flat bread. The Talmud called this dish hamin. The Jews cooked hamin on Friday so that housewives did not cook on the Sabbath. According to II Samuel, beans sustained David in the wilderness.

Because fava beans tolerated frost, farmers grew them in Northern Europe. In the Roman world, as in Egypt, commoners ate beans. We have seen, however, that priests did not eat beans, a fact that Roman encyclopedist Pliny the Elder, writing in the first century CE, attributed to the belief that beans caused insomnia and weakened the senses. Pliny, and before him the poet Horace, wrote that peasants ate beans. The Roman agriculturalist Columella, writing in the first century CE, asserted that beans were the fare of artisans and the poet Martial noted that construction workers ate them. The Greeks and Romans ate favas with garlic and onion. Other people in Europe and Asia ate beans with wheat, millet, or rice. The Romans knew that beans enriched the soil and devised a two-field system, growing grain one year and a legume, often beans, in the second. Although the Romans appreciated the value of this rotation, only modern science discovered why beans restored the soil. Like all legumes, beans form nodules on their roots. These nodules are home to a type of bacteria that converts nitrogen gas in the soil into ammonium nitrate, a compound of nitrogen that plant roots can absorb. Not only do beans absorb this nitrogen, but also some of it is left over to feed next season's crop. The Romans took favas to the lands they conquered, aiding the spread of beans throughout Europe.

In the ninth century Charlemagne, king of the Franks, ordered farmers to plant beans and chickpeas so that his army could feed on them as it marched through the land. Christians, observing a Spartan diet during Lent, ate beans then. Monks who did not eat meat got their protein from beans. After the 10th century the cultivation of beans became widespread throughout Europe. Because they are nutritious, one writer credits beans with increasing population and longevity in the Middle Ages.

Not everyone celebrated beans. One Greek medical authority remarked that gladiators who ate beans grew fat and had bad dreams. The physician Benedict of Nursia believed that beans caused depression. A third commentator remarked that pregnant women who consumed beans might give birth to a lunatic or fool.

The British, who still grow favas, call them Windsor or broad beans. John Gerard christened the fava bean as the "Great Garden Bean." The contribution of beans to British agriculture and cuisine may have prompted friends to call one another "old bean." Stockmen in Europe feed favas to their animals. Despite widespread cultivation, favas are not entirely safe. Some Europeans developed favism, a rare allergic reaction to fava beans that causes anemia and jaundice. Because *Phaseolus* did not cause this reaction, it is possible that Europeans adopted these beans partly because they did not cause favism. Today, China is the world's leading producer of favas, though they must compete with soybeans and corn for acreage.

Whereas Europeans linked the consumption of beans with poverty, no such stigma existed in India, where all classes, even priests, ate beans. Although the people of India ate meat in antiquity, about 600 BCE the diet shifted from meat to beans. Indian religious dogma upheld beans as a pure food fit for all. Beans contributed a greater proportion of protein to the people of India than to the people in any other land. Indians ate several species of beans including mung beans, urd beans, moth beans, and rice beans. Because urd beans were black, they were known as kali, meaning "black." Indians made urd beans into pancakes. At funerals, Indians offered beans to the deceased to aid their transition to another life. Approving of beans, Buddha found them "full of soul qualities." Mung beans and rice are a typical and nourishing dish in India. The people of southern India make urd beans into steamed bean cakes. Like tepary beans in America, farmers in India prize moth beans for their drought tolerance. Rice beans grow wild in India, Thailand, and Vietnam and were domesticated in Southeast Asia. Nutritious, rice beans have a high content of calcium. The guar bean, a native of India, is used as food and fodder. In the United States, manufacturers process guar beans into guar gum, which is used to make explosives, ceramics, crayons, detergents, ink, clothes, ice cream, sausage, cheese, and cosmetics.

In China and Japan, farmers grow adzuki beans, renowned for their sweetness. The people of East Asia make red bean paste from adzukis. The Japanese make a cake of rice and adzukis. Adzuki beans are found in soup and as a paste that is spread on toast. People make adzukis into pancakes and even ice cream. The Chinese make mung beans into noodles. In China, Japan, and Southeast Asia, people eat the bean sprouts of mung beans.

Christopher Cumo

Further Reading

Albala, Ken. *Beans: A History.* Oxford: Berg, 2007.

Denny, Roz. *Beans.* Des Plaines, IL: Heinemann Library, 1998.

Hughes, Meredith Sayles. *Spill the Beans and Pass the Peanuts: Legumes.* Minneapolis: Lerner, 1999.

Johnson, Sylvia A. *Tomatoes, Potatoes, Corn, and Beans: How the Foods of the Americas Changed Eating Around the World.* New York: Atheneum Books, 1997.

Silverstein, Alvin, and Virginia Silverstein. *Beans: All about Them.* Englewood Cliffs, NJ: Prentice Hall, 1975.

Sumner, Judith. *American Household Botany: A History of Useful Plants, 1620–1900.* Portland, OR: Timber Press, 2004.

Beet

In the Chenopodiaceae or Goosefoot family, beet (*Beta vulgaris*) is a biennial herb grown as an annual. In the first year beet fills its root, and in the second it flowers and seeds. The beet may be gold, garnet, purple red, red, maroon, orange, vermilion, or white, and either solid color or striped. Beet is a source of beta-carotene, the precursor of vitamin A, folic acid, phosphorus, and potassium.

Origin and History

One scientist believes that beet originated in Europe or North America. One writer focuses on the Mediterranean Basin, positing an origin in Italy. Beets grow wild in the Mediterranean, Turkey, and the Near East. Beet may be a hybrid between *Beta vulgaris* ssp. *maritima* of the Mediterranean and *Beta patula*, a related species native to Portugal and the Canary Islands. Expanding its range, today *Beta vulgaris* ssp. *maritima* grows wild in the United Kingdom, Continental Europe, and Asia to the East Indies. In prehistory, the people of the Mediterranean may have been the first to use beet leaves. It is possible that beet was a medicine first and a food second. The Romans knew of beets, but they seem to have disliked them. In the first century CE, Roman encyclopedist Pliny the Elder disparaged them as "those scarlet nether parts." In the second and third centuries, opinions changed. Roman cooks added beets to several dishes and opined that the flavor was better than that of cabbage.

Because of their dark color, Europeans called beets "blood turnips." The beet's spread to Northern Europe appears to have been slow. The Germans first noted it in 1558, naming it the "Roman beet." The beet was introduced into England in 1576, and in the 17th and 18th centuries farmers had just two varieties, Red and Long Red. The beet's introduction into the United States is a matter of debate. It must not have originated in North America, as one scientist supposed, because it would not have been necessary to import it. One writer asserts that as late as 1828, U.S. farmers grew just four varieties, allowing one to infer that the beet must have been introduced into the United States before 1828. Another holds, however, that the beet was not imported into the United States until 1880. Americans knew beet as the "garden beet." Sometime earlier beet was introduced into India, from where the Arabs exported it to China about 1850.

Attributes, Cultivation, and Breeding

In the second year, beet flowers. The flowers are green. Each has five stamens that surround one ovary. When beets are ready to reproduce, flowers open between 7 a.m. and 5 p.m. They are fully open between 11 a.m. and 1 p.m. The anthers shed pollen between 8 a.m. and 6:30 p.m. The anthers shed the most pollen between 12:30 and 2:30 p.m. Pollen is abundant. The wind carries it from anther to stigma. The stigma is receptive to pollen during the hours it is shed. High temperature and low humidity are the best conditions for fertilization. Flowers aggregate in clusters. When fertilized, they form a ball of seeds. Each seed contains three or four embryos, accounting for the fact that three or four plants germinate from a single seed. Beets therefore germinate thickly. Each seed is shaped like a kidney, brown, and one-and-one-half to three millimeters in diameter.

Preferring full sun, beet adapts to partial shade. Most varieties of beet mature in 45 to 65 days. Seeds germinate in 3 to 14 days at 68°F to 86°F. According to one writer, beet germinates between 50°F and 85°F. One may plant seeds in early spring for a spring and summer harvest and in late summer for an autumn and winter crop, provided winter is mild. In spring one may plant beet from mid-March to early June. One gardener recommends the planting of beets indoors in February to obtain the earliest harvest. Another, however, warns that beet does not transplant well. For an autumn and winter crop, one may plant beets in the first three weeks of August. The gardener may soak seeds in warm water the night before planting them to increase germination. Some gardeners plant beet with radish. The quickly germinating radish marks the spot where beet will germinate. Radish roots keep the soil loose for the development of beetroots. The harvesting of radishes opens space in the garden for beets to grow. Beet seeds should be planted half an inch deep and one inch apart. Two weeks after germination plants should be thinned to two inches apart. A final thinning yields beet plants four inches apart.

Preferring neutral, well-drained soil, beet does best when the pH is 7. A heavy feeder of phosphorus and potassium, beet should be fertilized with a 5-10-10 fertilizer of nitrogen to phosphorus to potassium before planting. The gardener may also add well-rotted manure to the soil. Fresh manure should not be used because it hinders the root's development. Beet benefits from the addition of organic matter to the soil. The soil should be cultivated to a depth of at least 6 inches. One gardener recommends a depth of 8 to 10 inches. Beet should be fertilized and watered weekly. The root may crack or become tough if beet receives too little moisture. Beet may be harvested when the root is as small as 1 inch in diameter, though it is common to wait until the root is 2 to 5 inches in diameter. Beet should be picked before a severe frost. Light frost improves the flavor. Beets may be stored in a refrigerator five to seven months provided the humidity is high or in a damp basement at 32°F to 40°F.

The commercial harvest goes to processing as boiled or pickled beets. Beet may also be frozen and canned. Beets may be boiled, baked, steamed, coated with oil and cooked, mashed, sautéed, shredded, or stir-fried. Beet leaves are edible and are widely consumed in Indonesia and Japan. The root and leaves may protect one against infection and cancer. Beet juice is a popular health beverage. Beet juice is added to tomato sauce and paste to darken the redness. Scientists aim to breed beet for yield, dark redness, uniform color, the absence of white rings on the root, uniform shape and size of the root, slowness to bolt, and appearance in the shape of a sphere, cylinder, or cone depending on consumer preference.

Cultivars

The variety Golden Beet is prized for its color and flavor. As its name suggests, the root is golden. It lends itself to pickling and to its addition in salad. The flavor is best when the root is harvested early, but it may be left in the soil without fear that it will toughen with age. Because germination is low, Golden Beet should be seeded thickly. The variety matures in 55 days and is favored by cooks because the color does not bleed. With a long cylindrical root, Cylindra yields three or four times more root than a round beet. Small, dark red, sweet, and tender, Little Bull is suitable for pickling. Bred in the mid-19th century, Chioggia matures in 55 days. A cross section of the root reveals concentric circles of red or pink alternating with white or cream. One gardener remarks that "the flavor is unusually sweet." Native to Italy, Chioggia is known as the "candy cane beet." Detroit Dark Red matures in 60 days. D. M. Ferry and Company introduced the variety in 1892. The beet is round with a root two to four inches in diameter. Suitable for canning, the flesh is sweet and tender. Detroit Dark Red traces its lineage to the 19th-century variety Early Blood Turnip. Bred in the 19th century, Bull's Blood was first prized for its leaves. Some gardeners grow the variety as an ornamental. Leaves are ready to harvest 35 days after planting. The root is ready to harvest 58 days after planting. For the best flavor, the gardener should harvest Bull's Blood early. Crosby's Egyptian appears to have no association with Egypt. Rather, it is a German variety introduced into the United States about 1880. Ready to harvest in 50 days, the root is deep red. Known as Snow White, Albina Verduna, as its name suggests, has a white root. A Dutch variety, Snow White matures in 55 days. Known as Winter Keeper, Lutz Green Leaf is a large beet. The root may grow six inches in diameter. The purple red root needs 60 to 80 days to mature. Lutz Green Leaf sweetens during storage.

Christopher Cumo

Further Reading

Coulter, Lynn. *Gardening with Heirloom Seeds: Tried-and-True Flowers, Fruits, and Vegetables for a New Generation.* Chapel Hill: University of North Carolina Press, 2006.

Hughes, Meredith Sayles, and Tom Hughes. *Buried Treasure: Roots and Tubers.* Minneapolis: Lerner, 1998.

McGee, Rose Marie Nichols, and Maggie Stuckey. *The Bountiful Container: A Container Garden of Vegetables, Herbs, Fruits, and Edible Flowers.* New York: Workman, 2002.

Singh, P. K., S. K. Dasgupta, and S. K. Tripathi, eds. *Hybrid Vegetable Development.* Binghamton, NY: Food Products Press, 2004.

Begonia

A gardener could fill both a house and a yard with a wide variety of beautiful plants all from just one family. Easily more than 1,000 species of begonias populate tropical and subtropical areas, especially in the Americas and exempting Europe and Australia. Naturally crossbreeding with ease and at the hands of hybridizers, now more than 10,000 new varieties exist.

History

Begonias began to be discovered and described for the West as new territory was explored. In China, descriptions of begonias existed as early as the 14th century. In mid-16th century Mexico, Spanish priests identified native begonias. In 1690 Franciscan monk Charles Plumier named six previously unidentified plants in the West Indies after Michel Begon, the governor intendant of Haiti, who shared the monk's interest in botany, gave the genus its name.

Other begonias came to be known by chance. In 1821, a wild Brazilian begonia hitchhiked with other plants to Berlin's Botanical Gardens. Later in the century it was hybridized to become our wax begonias. Likewise, a Rex type stowed away with orchids from India, arriving in England in 1856. Its loud leaf design wasted no time in gaining appreciation. It formed the base for today's Rex Cultorum hybrids.

Attributes

Great in containers and hanging baskets, as houseplants, and as bedding plants in mass plantings and borders, members of the begonia family provide attractive leaves. Most display abundant blooms, and many supply both attractive flowers and leaves while being the classic answer to what will thrive in shady areas.

Begonias are tender perennials suited to gardening zones 9–12, but they generally are grown everywhere as annuals. A species found in Japan and China, *Begonia grandis* has heart-shaped leaves and is hardy enough to survive down to zone 6. Begonias are more cold sensitive than many other popular plants. Temperatures should be above 50°F before they are set out. The succulent stems and leaves collapse after too much of a chill.

Unlike many other plants in the category that are generally grown as annuals—for instance, petunias—begonias make good houseplants thanks to their preference for less than full sunlight. Indeed, their claim to fame is the wide range of light that satisfies them. So as frost approaches, the begonias that enjoyed the summer outdoors can be repotted to continue life on a windowsill. Moreover, new plants for inside can be propagated from stem cuttings taken from outside plants.

Types

Although interbreeding blurs distinctions in many cases, hybrids can be generalized into eight groups: cane-type, shrub-like, semperflorens, tuberous, Rex Cultorum, rhizomatous, thick-stemmed, and trailing. The cane-type and shrub-like begonias are tall. The cane group includes "angel-wings," which have woody, erect stems up to six feet tall, with drooping clusters of blossoms called sprays. Some exotic-looking varieties have silvery leaves with dark vein patterns, while others have dark leaves with white polka dots. Many varieties have six-inch leaves with red undersides. The shrub-like types are bushier and shorter at up to a yard tall. They have multiple stems but theirs are succulent and therefore softer. Both cane and shrub types can benefit from staking or a fence or other tall, sturdy neighbors to serve as windbreaks.

Besides being classified by leaf, stem, and flower forms, begonias can be divided into three types based on roots: fibrous, rhizomatous, and tuberous. *Begonia semperflorens*, commonly known as wax begonias, have fibrous roots. These roots are ordinary clusters of thin, fiber-like strands. This well-known group excels in mass plantings and as a border. Compact, up to about one foot high, and wide, its members are covered with blossoms until frost. The nickel-sized, four-petaled flowers come in white, pink, red, or bicolor. Best of all, they do not require dead-heading to encourage more blooms. In fact, "semperflorens" means "ever-blooming."

Besides the basic single-flowered form, new hybrid doubles and semidoubles are available. The Prelude and Senator early-blooming series both include white, pink, and red varieties. The Lotto series has larger, two-inch blossoms with green leaves. Other popular series include Cocktail, Olympia, and Ambassador. Their leaves are thick and shiny, resembling wax. They are close to round, are slightly cupped, and have scalloped edges. In shades of green, variegated green, or reddish bronze to burgundy, they grow densely packed on succulent stems. Patterns in flowerbeds can be designed by using groups of plants with contrasting leaf and blossom colors. Large flowerbeds in public areas make increasing use of wax begonias now that sun-tolerant hybrids are available. A trailing species from Brazil, *Begonia solananthera*, is also fibrous. It has glossy green three-inch leaves and fragrant white flowers with red centers. Besides being a good hanging basket plant, it can be planted in the ground and the stems trained to climb up a structure such as a trellis.

Cultivation

Begonias will be most tolerant of less-than-ideal conditions if they are grown in rich, evenly moist but never soggy soil. Some will withstand more sun if temperatures are cool. A generous mulch around them will both retain moisture and keep their roots cooler. Because such conditions also favor slugs and snails, which love succulent plants, one must monitor and protect against them. Regular fertilization will encourage and maintain steady, healthy growth. If watering is excessive or erratic, begonias will be prone to fungal diseases and mold, particularly at the base of the plant and leaf joints. Water spots and sun scald may also result from harsher days. Generally, however, begonias are comparatively carefree.

Shady woodland settings can be enlivened with spots of color furnished by begonias. Whether in the ground or in containers, begonias make good companions for ferns, hostas, and impatiens. Another shade lover, coleus, has many varieties with reds and greens that perfectly partner with wax begonias as well as other types. Although wax begonias can be grown from their tiny seeds, it is more practical for average gardeners to buy them, as well as other varieties of begonias, in the pots or six-packs that are readily available. Germination time is two to three weeks, and they can take up to five months to bloom.

With another of the root types, rhizomatous begonias make elegant houseplants. Distinctive foliage is their noteworthy feature. Many have large arrow-shaped leaves with a metallic shine and striking vein and spiral patterns, often reddish underneath. Some varieties have dark edges on the leaves. The species Iron Cross, *Begonia masoniana*, has a dark brown design on green rippled leaves. This group grows wider than high, up to about 8 inches in height to 30 inches across. Planted in a wide, shallow container, this species will furnish a lot of vegetation without blocking a window. Outdoors, a single plant can make a statement in a flowerbed or a rhythm and balance can be made with several separated specimens. Rhizomatous roots are shallow, thick, sometimes fuzzy, rope-like structures that creep over the edge of containers. They can be trimmed and used to sprout new plants. Rex Cultorum hybrids grow from rhizomes. These are among the most popular, boldly marked foliage plants that have been appreciated indoors for generations. They prefer high humidity and do well in greenhouses. There is a holiday-named series that includes the varieties Merry Christmas and Tinsel.

The begonia type known for eye-catching, saucer-sized camellia-like blossoms are tuberous. They grow from tubers rather like small potatoes. Their best use is in containers or hanging baskets that let them cascade over the sides. When mature, they are one to two feet in height and spread. In glowing shades of peach, pink, yellow, orange, red, white, and bicolor, with some varieties ruffled and looking like giant carnations, the showiest flowers are males in doubles and semidoubles, which are flanked by two single-flowered female blossoms. Pinching off the female flowers will direct more of the plant's energy into the males. Picotee is the striking blossom pattern with a dark outer edge on the petals. Can Can is a yellow variety with red edges. Bouton De Rose is white with red. Dedicated fanciers categorize the tuberous varieties into 13 types based on flower style—single, double, and ruffled—and growth habit. Tuberous begonias, like all begonias, do not tolerate cold, but they also suffer in heat. Shade and thick mulch help keep them in their preferred temperature range. Provide them with frequent fertilizing, as they are heavier feeders than many other begonias. Good drainage is necessary to prevent rot. Once the plant starts to go dormant in the fall, cease watering. The leaves and stems will die and fall away from the tubers. Then they can be stored over winter in a cool dry place until it is time to bring them back out for another season.

Common names for begonias reflect the family's great variety. There is a hollyhock begonia—which is tuberous despite having upright stems and looking like a miniature pink hollyhock—a fuchsia begonia, a maple-leaf begonia, and countless others resembling their namesakes in some manner with their own ease of care, consistent growth, and few problems. Most plant lovers' wishes for outstanding foliage and flowers can be filled by begonias, a plant genus of nearly endless variety.

Tamara Stromquist

Further Reading

Hodgson, Larry. *Annuals for Every Purpose*. Emmaus, PA: Rodale, 2002.

Hogan, Sean. *Flora: A Gardener's Encyclopedia*. Portland, OR: Timber Press, 2003.

Sunset Western Garden Book. Menlo Park, CA: Sunset, 1995.

Belladonna

Atropa belladonna is commonly known as the cultivated medicinal belladonna or perennial deadly nightshade. Due to its highly toxic properties, it has also been historically referenced as Devil's Herb, Devil's Cherry, or Poison Black Cherry. Other names include Dvale (Norse: "trance"), Dwayberry, Great Morel, Bladona, and Naughty Man's Cherry. In the 18th century, Swedish naturalist Carl Linnaeus gave the plant its genus name based on one of the Greek fates. Clotho spins the thread of human life; Lachesis measures the thread of human life; and Atropos (the Inflexible) cuts the thread of human life. The species name, *Belladonna*, is Italian for "beautiful lady," referring to the 16th-century use of the plant by women in Venice as an eye ointment to dilate the pupils.

Belladonna is from the Solanaceae family, which also includes potatoes, tomatoes, eggplants, tobacco, and chili peppers. Considered a weed in some areas, it is also planted in perennial gardens as an herbaceous, flowering ornamental. It is a two- to six-foot sensitive perennial with a thick root, simple alternate leaves, and a sharp, unpleasant odor. The red- to green-hued purple flowers are solitary, drooping, and tubular with five lobes. The fruit are glossy purple-black berries that are the most poisonous part of the plant; ingesting one bitter-tasting berry can lead to death in some humans and domestic animals (exceptions include cattle and rabbits).

Atropa belladonna's active compounds are tropane alkaloids: atropine, hyoscyamine, and scopolamine. In 1831, the German pharmacist A. Mein isolated atropine from dried belladonna root, and it was first synthesized by the German chemist Richard Willstatter in 1901. The amount of alkaloids depends on the part of the plant, development stage, growing conditions, and time of harvesting. Dry weather and nighttime cultivation make for the highest concentrations, suggesting the plant may have evolved to fend off nocturnal eaters. This, as well as its dark-colored berries, could also be an origin of its name, deadly nightshade. Although native to Europe, East Asia, and North Africa, belladonna has become naturalized in much of the world. It is commercially cultivated and harvested in the United States—California, Oregon, Washington, Michigan, New Jersey, and New York—and Europe as a pharmaceutical crop. It is high yielding in fertile soils blocked from the wind but is susceptible to wilt caused by potato and flea beetles. Harvests of the leaf occur in the spring, while the two-year-old to four-year-old roots are harvested in the fall. For general medicinal uses, the plant is dried and crushed to be used alone or in combination with other medicinal powders, pills, plasters, etc. In homeopathic medicine, the plant is broken apart to extract the juice, and then mixed with a water/alcohol solution at a ratio of 1:10 or 1:100. In accordance with common homeopathic production of remedies, this process is repeated up to 30 times to create a highly diluted form of the plant's properties. As a perennial, belladonna can be harvested for one to four years, and then it is cut down and replanted since the alkaloid content does not increase after this time.

History

Although the alkaloid commonly used today in medicine was isolated for use in 1831, belladonna's chemical uses can be found even before the Middle Ages. Some people believe the Greek worshippers of Dionysus (Roman: Bacchus), the god of wine and fertility, dissolved belladonna in wine during initiations to induce trances of dancing and sexual lewdness. The plant is also claimed to have taken the lives of Roman soldiers retreating from the Parthians. In 1579, *Buchanan's History of Scotland* by George Buchanan included a description of the Swedish army's use of "sleepy nightshade" to taint the drink they were required by a truce to supply to the armies of Sweno the Dane. Svein Knutsson, the king of Norway between 1030 and 1035, lost most of his men when they were killed in their drugged sleep after drinking the mead. The story of King Sweno is also an important backdrop to William Shakespeare's play *Macbeth*, which includes the magic and potions of the infamous three witches. In fact, witches, wizards, and healers believed belladonna to be the Devil's Herb, claiming Satan anointed the plant with his blood every night as well as taking it for his own evil apothecary uses. Since the tropane alkaloids can be absorbed by the skin, 17th-century witches used belladonna and henbane (*Hyoscyamus niger*) "flying ointments." These salves were rubbed on sensitive skin to induce hallucinations and delusions of flying, frenzy, and elevating above reality.

In the 16th century, fashionable women of Venice reintroduced the use of the plant as a seduction tool by putting drops of the juice of "herba bella donna" in their eyes, considered windows to the soul. This caused dilated pupils, which also occur during arousal and are said to make eye contact more intense, but this practice can also cause glaucoma. During this time, herbalists and apothecaries began studying and classifying dangerous vegetation, so this plant also known as deadly nightshade (solatrum mortale) started to appear in various publications, pharmacopoeias, and dispensatories. Andrew Duncan stated in the Edinburgh Dispensatory of 1803 that Atropa can be used to relieve symptoms of the plague and nervous diseases and to facilitate the removal of cataracts.

Mein's 1831 isolation of atropine from the roots of belladonna allowed this alkaloid to be used in plasters and liniments as an analgesic and counterirritant. However, this also led to numerous poisonings, intentional and unintentional, in the mid-19th century. After 1911, deaths from atropine poisoning become rare, probably because plasters and cosmetic eye drops using the drug were obsolete or banned. Uses for atropine continued to be developed. In 1943, it was found to be the only antidote for German tear gas in World War II, although neither was ever used. It was used as an antidote to save many lives of people in Tijuana, Mexico, in a 1967 incident of humans eating bread exposed to a toxic insecticide.

Current Medicinal Uses

In contemporary traditional medicine, the key components of *Atropa belladonna* are the anticholinergic alkaloids, which first stimulate then block nerve impulses in parasympathetic nervous systems. These systems control involuntary functions and reflexes such as heart rate, secretion release, pupil dilation, muscle cramping, etc. Atropa alkaloids, given in controlled doses, slow the action of the smooth muscle system, reducing the symptoms of Parkinson's disease, irregular heart rate, motion sickness, asthma, peptic ulcers, whooping cough, hay fever, and menstrual cramps. Atropine is prescribed as a drug for heart functions and cardiopulmonary resuscitation (CPR). Compounds are also used to resolve issues dealing with an overabundance of bodily fluids causing excessive sweating, nasal mucus, diarrhea, and vomiting. Although the cosmetic use of eye drops was discontinued, atropine drops are still used to dilate pupils for eye exams.

The other compounds isolated in 1831 from the belladonna plant are also developed for medicinal use. Scopolamine, named after the 18th-century Italian naturalist Giovanni Scopoli, was introduced to medicinal practices in 1901. In the past, it was used to treat heroin and cocaine addiction and is currently being researched as an aid for overcoming nicotine addiction as well as a possible treatment for depression. Until the late 1960s, it was commonly a part of hospital child birthing in combination with morphine to induce "twilight sleep." At this time, it is used in the form of a skin patch to prevent motion sickness and as a general anesthetic or preanesthetic agent.

In homeopathy, prescriptions address symptoms and mood and are given in accordance with the patient's temperament. The remedies usually have characteristics that mirror the symptoms healing response. Belladonna is a common homeopathic remedy for earaches, fever, menstrual cramps, headaches, migraines, muscle pain, acute pain, sunstroke, mastitis, and respiratory infections. It is usually prescribed to people who are physically fit and full of energy when healthy but suffer from a sudden onset of an acute sickness that makes them agitated and restless. The National Cancer Institute of Milan, Italy, has research results that demonstrate that homeopathic remedies of belladonna provide some relief for breast cancer patients suffering from radiodermatitis (red, swollen skin as a result of radiotherapy).

As with many powerful medicinal plants, a wide range of beneficial uses have been discovered and even more are continuing to be researched for *Atropa belladonna*. However, as the name deadly nightshade suggests, it is a highly toxic plant that has been historically lethal when not taken in controlled, prescribed amounts.

Erika Stump

Further Reading

"Belladonna." *Medline Plus*. National Library of Medicine. http://www.nlm.nih.gov/medlineplus/druginfo/natural/531.html.

Foster, Stephen, and Rebecca L. Johnson. "Belladonna." *National Geographic Desk Reference to Nature's Medicine*. Washington, D.C.: National Geographic, 2006.

Lee, M. R. "Solanacea IV: *Atropa belladonna*, Deadly Nightshade." *Journal of the Royal College of Physicians of Edinburgh* 37, no. 1 (2007): 77–84.

Bellflower. *See* Campanula

Birch

In 1753, Swedish naturalist Carl Linnaeus placed birch in the family Betulacea and the genus *Betula*. Betulacea consists of around 60 deciduous species that can grow in mountains, heaths, moors, and woodlands and are common in the Northern Hemisphere. Birch is a relative of the beech and oak, both of which belong to the family Fagaceae. *Betula* species vary in height from small to large and present themselves as either small shrubs or tall trees. The bark of the birch is what distinguishes each species from the other and is the source of the common names of the trees: gray, white, black, silver, and yellow birch.

Birch fossils date from the Upper Cretaceous Period and were abundant in the Eocene Period, an era about 45 million years ago. To wit, birch is an extremely hardy tree and can withstand cold winters and heavy wind. It is able to grow on land masses and islands that encircle the North Pole and is common in North America and Eurasia.

Appearance and Habitat

Birch is distinguished by long horizontal markings on its bark, or lenticels. The many-colored bark, depending on species, often separates into thin paper-like sheets, especially noticeable on the paper birch (*Betula papyrifera*) variety. Several varieties have a white bark and most varieties produce a white timber. The birch's leaves are delicate and shimmering and produce abundant color in the autumn months.

The birch has a diverse habitat. It exists in every type of environment from temperate lands to the extreme cold of the North. It can be found near bodies of water, such as the banks of streams and shores of lakes, along roadsides, in moist wooded areas, in alpine forests, and on open land. Birch is pollinated by the wind and produces an abundance of pollen. It is a tree that is prone to hybridizing (polyploidy).

Threats to the Birch

Birch in the northeastern United States is threatened by the birch leafminer, a native insect of Europe. It is also a problem, but to a lesser degree, in the upper Midwest, Alaska, and the Pacific Northwest. This insect is a type of sawfly that feeds on the leaves of birch, primarily the tissue between the upper and lower surfaces of the leaf. The small, white, and flat larvae can live within the birch leaves. The adults grow to about three-sixteenths of an inch.

Other threats to birch include several types of fungi, especially *Armillaria mellea*, a species of honey fungus that forms as mushrooms around the base of the trees and causes root rot, and *Piptoporus betulinus*, a whitish-brown mushroom that is specific to birch trees and that can severely damage or destroy the tree.

The Many Uses of Birch

Birch produces an attractive white timber that is good for furniture making. The betulin in the bark makes it waterproof and lends itself to the production of water vessels, such as canoes, and for roofs and other objects meant to keep water from penetrating, such as containers and household utensils. Native peoples of many lands, including North America, Russia, Siberia, and Northern Europe, have long used birch in a number of ways, including in the manufacture of wigwams, baskets, yurts, roof tiles, canoes, and shoes.

Because of the thin paper-like quality of the birch tree's bark, it has been used as a writing material. In fact, as early as 1800 BCE birch was manufactured into Hindu manuscripts. As well, its twigs are flexible and can be bent into brooms. It is also a common material in mallets for keyboards and is used as tonewood for acoustic and semiacoustic guitars.

Birch burns hot, making it a good firewood as well as a hardy charcoal product and source of gunpowder. It burns well even when wet because of the oils in the wood. Those oils along with the starch produced in the bark and the resins found in the leaves have made the tree a source of food in times of famine.

The sap of the *Betula lenta*, or sweet birch, which is grown in the Appalachian Mountains of North America, is tapped and used in the production of birch beer. Other food products made from birch include birch syrup, vinegar, wine, and the artificial sweetener Xylitol. *Betula lenta* and *Betula alleghaniensis*, or yellow birch, also produce oil of wintergreen, or methyl salicylate, which is used as a flavoring and to make rubefacients and other medicines.

Birch in Folklore

The Welsh associate the birch tree with love, and in German folklore the birch is considered the tree of life. Traditionally, it was used in crafting maypoles. The Russians revere birch and have nicknamed it the "lady of the forest." It is one of the country's national trees. Shamans living in Siberia use the birch in their initiation rituals by having the candidate carve nine notches into the birch's trunk, which represent the nine steps to heaven.

Common Species of Birch

Betula lenta, or sweet birch (also called black birch or cherry birch), gets its name from the aromatic fragrance of wintergreen that it produces in its leaves. *Betula lenta* is grown mostly in the northeastern United States but is also found in the Appalachian Mountain states and parts of western North Carolina. *Betula lenta* reaches a height of 50 to 75 feet. Its bark is a brownish-black color, similar to that of the black cherry tree.

Betula nigra, or river birch, is also called red birch, water birch, or black birch. The species grows primarily in the hot and humid southeastern United States, approximately from Texas to Virginia. It grows to heights of 40 to 70 feet.

Betula papyrifera is commonly known as canoe birch, white birch, or silver birch. It has a showy white bark that peels off into strips or sheets. It grows in the northern regions of North America, from Newfoundland in Canada to Alaska, and can be found in Appalachia as well. The species grows to a height of 70 to 80 feet. *Betula papyrifera* is the state tree of New Hampshire.

Betula alleghaniesis is referred to as yellow birch. It grows from Canada to the northern parts of Georgia and is distinguished by its shiny yellow-bronze to reddish-brown bark. It grows to a height of 75 feet.

Rosemarie Boucher Leenerts

Further Reading

Hageneder, Fred. *The Meaning of Trees*. San Francisco: Chronicle Books, 2005.

Wasson, Eric. "Betula." *The Complete Encyclopedia of Trees and Shrubs*. San Diego: Thunder Bay Press, 2003.

Woody Ornamental Pest Management. "Birch Leafminer." http://woodypests.cas.psu.edu/factsheets/insectfactsheets/html/Birch_Leafminer.html (accessed 21 November 2010).

Bird of Paradise

Known as "the empress of house plants," the tropical bird of paradise plant (*Strelitzia reginae*), also known by the names wild banana and giant bird of paradise, is a large, very colorful specimen in the banana (Muscaceacea) family. This plant should not be confused with the aviary species Bird-of-Paradise, which inhabits Molucca and Australia. It comes in an array of different shades, including blue and orange blossoms.

The bird of paradise is in the kingdom Plantae and the phylum Magniliophyta. *Strelitzia nicolai* (giant bird of paradise), the largest of the several different species of the plant, can grow to be up to 30 feet tall. However, the average size of these plants hovers about 4 or 5 feet when mature. Because of the flamboyant and distinctive coloring of this plant, it is often grown for ornamental uses and is popular as a decoration. The South African *Stretzilia reginia* is used for cut flower bouquets worldwide. In general, the bird of paradise plant is popular because of its wide array of colors, and it is cultivated mainly for this purpose.

Species and Origin

The bird of paradise originated and is native to South Africa and South America. Different species are found in various regions of the world, depending on their needs and the temperatures they thrive in most successfully. Each species of the bird of paradise is unique and requires a particular setting to be harvested appropriately. The different species of bird of paradise flower differently, with varying rates of growth.

These unique and illustrious plants earn their name from their resemblance to a brightly colored bird or crane in flight, and are not to be confused with aviary species bearing the same name. The genus *Stretzilia* encompasses four different species, including *Stretzilia alba*, the white bird of paradise, found only in South Africa; *Stretzilia caudata*, the African desert banana; the *Stretzilia reginae*, crane lily; and *Stretzilia junceau*.

Stretzilia alba (white-flowered wild banana) is the rarest of the four species and the least commonly cultivated, the two most common species of the plant being *Stretzilia reginia* and *Stretzilia nicolai*. *Stretzilia alba* is also the only member of the *Stretzilia* genus that has been proven to have a distinct chromosomal composition from its counterparts. A 1955 study by geneticists Cyril Dean Darlington and Phillipa Wylie came to the conclusion that because the flowers of the bird of paradise are separated by character and distribution of genetic components, *Stretzilia alba* is the only species of *Stretzilia* with a different number of somatic chromosomes. *Stretzilia alba* has a haploid number of 11, while the remainder of the species of the bird of paradise has a haploid number of 7.

Stretzilia junceau has stems that are long and spiky, with upright needle-like leaves that turn into orange or yellow flowers. This species is the slowest-growing bird of paradise, taking three to four years to flower fully. Each species of *Stretzilia* has slightly different physical characteristics. For example, a similar plant in the same family, *Strelitzia parvifolia*, is smaller and slightly different in shape.

Maintenance and Care

The bird of paradise plant is generally not too difficult to care for. It does, however, have certain stringent requirements for maintenance and care. It can thrive only in temperatures of 50°F to 84°F. Freezing temperatures can damage its leaves, though these plants can tolerate a mild degree of frost. It is advisable, in colder weather, to move any bird of paradise flowers that are outside into a pot indoors. Bird of paradise has monocotyledonous roots, which are extremely durable and tough. These types of plant generally do not require a great deal of water.

Bird of paradise is propagated by division or by seeds. The germination of seeds is very erratic, but takes only a few weeks at most. The bird of paradise flower is orthinapalous, requiring nectar-eating birds to pollinate it. In this symbiotic relationship, birds sip the nectar while the pollen coats their breasts and feet and causes the blue petals to open. The nectar birds that feed on bird of paradise are a vital part of the pollination process. When the seeds are pollinated, the bird of paradise seeds develop over a period of six months and transform into pods with three sections of black seeds and bright orange arils.

The leaves of the bird of paradise vary from four to eight inches long. Bird of paradise is not deciduous, making these species an ideal indoor plant, and it can also be optimal for outdoors if the temperature permits. Though the bird of paradise is a direct relative of the banana, its rate of growth is much slower; some bird of paradise plants can take years to fully mature.

Basin or flood irrigation is the recommended method of care for these plants, for preventing the accumulation of salty water in the soil below the plant. The plants require as much sunshine as can be delivered, regular planting, and a good fertilizer at least once a year. Birds of paradise can produce as many as three dozen flower spikes a year, each of which lasts up to two weeks when cut. If these plants are maintained properly, the bird of paradise is a flamboyant addition to the home, indoors or outdoors.

Bonnie Ellman

Further Reading

Scott, Susan. *Plants and Animals of Hawaii*. Honolulu, HI: Bess Press, 1991.

"*Stretzilia reginae*." Kew Royal Botanic Gardens. http://www.kew.org/plants-fungi/Strelitzia-reginae.htm (accessed 10 December 2011).

University of Florida EDIS. http://edis.ifas.ufl.edu/mg106 (accessed 10 December 2011).

Blackberry

A member of the Rosaceae family, the *Rubus* genus, and the *Eubatus* subgenus, blackberry numbers more than 350 species. Blackberry is related to raspberry, rose, apple, pear, apricot, and strawberry. Although related to the raspberry, blackberry differs from it in retaining a portion of the stem when picked whereas raspberry separates cleanly from the stem so that it is hollow at the center. One hundred grams of blackberry contain 86 grams of water, 52 calories, 13 grams of carbohydrates, 0.7 gram of protein, 0.4 gram of fat, 4 grams of fiber, 0.5 gram of ash, 32 milligrams of calcium, 0.6 milligram of iron, 20 milligrams of magnesium, 21 milligrams of phosphorus, 196 milligrams of potassium, no sodium, 0.3 milligram of zinc, 0.1 milligram of copper, 1.3 milligrams of manganese, 21 milligrams of vitamin C, 0.03 milligram of thiamine, 0.04 milligram of riboflavin, 0.4 milligram of niacin, 0.2 milligram of pantothenic acid, 0.06 milligram of vitamin B6, and 165 international units of vitamin A.

History, Attributes, and Cultivation
Blackberries are of three types—erect, semierect, or trailing—and may have or lack thorns. In prehistory blackberries colonized temperate locales and the subtropics. They are absent from the tropics. Humans have harvested wild blackberries for millennia. In some regions of the world, people still harvest wild blackberries. Wild blackberries are, for example, widespread in the United Kingdom, a circumstance that limits the cultivation of blackberries. Wild blackberries are picked for local consumption and never enter the market. Because the earliest types of blackberries had thorns and grew vigorously, farmers regarded them as an impediment to the expansion of agriculture. The clearing of land necessarily reduced blackberry populations.

The selection of new varieties from wild populations increased interest in the cultivation of blackberries. The discovery of a thornless blackberry, Thornless Evergreen, about 1930 gave impetus to blackberry cultivation. Thornless Evergreen was popular in the Pacific Northwest, where it yielded abundantly. Today, blackberry farms sell fruit directly to customers or allow them to pick berries. Oregon processes blackberries. California and the American South are important producers. The portion of the harvest that is not sold fresh may be packed in sugar and frozen. Other blackberries are made into jam, jelly, pie filling, yogurt, ice cream, juice, and wine. Only a small amount is canned.

The blackberry flower has five sepals and five petals. Roots, fibrous and shallow, are perennial whereas the stem and foliage are biennial. Blackberries fruit in their second year. In much of the temperate zone, new canes develop annually and die after fruiting. In Guatemala, where farmers grow blackberries at elevation, they yield year-round because the canes do not die after bearing fruit. Blackberries are most hardy between mid-November and mid-December, though they do not tolerate temperatures below 0°F. Most plants are sensitive to late spring frost, which may damage flowers. Erect blackberries are hardier than trailing blackberries. Thorny varieties are hardier than thornless blackberries. Blackberries tolerate high temperatures and humidity better than raspberries.

Blackberries grow well on fertile, deep, well-drained sandy loam or loam. Sandy soil needs the application of organic matter and, because it may not retain water, may need irrigation. Blackberries do not tolerate clay or soil with a high water table. Because this is so, blackberries do not tolerate waterlogged soil. When the soil is too wet, blackberry roots suffocate for lack of oxygen. Soil that is too wet may harbor fungi. The farmer should not plant blackberries where strawberry, pepper, tomato, potato, or eggplant have been grown because this soil may be infected with *Verticillium* fungi. The farmer should not plant blackberries in soil that has a history of harboring *Phytophthora* fungi. The soil pH should be slightly acidic, between 5.5 and 6.5. Sandy soil is not alone in needing organic matter. Whatever the soil type, blackberries need at least 3 percent organic matter. One authority recommends the application of 10 to 20 tons of dairy cow manure per acre to add organic matter to the soil. Less desirable are horse manure, which may contain weed seeds, and pig and chicken manure, which has too little organic matter. The farmer should apply manure in late fall or early winter. Where the soil is deficient, the farmers should apply phosphorus, potassium, magnesium, zinc, and boron before planting blackberries. Fertilizer should not be applied at the time of planting because it may injure roots. Once plants have germinated, the farmer may apply nitrogen to the soil. In a plant's second year, fertilizer may be applied when it resumes growth in spring. The farmer may divide nitrogen into two applications, with the second occurring when blackberries flower. Blackberries absorb more nitrogen than any other element. Where temperature and rainfall are high and the soil light, blackberries may need large amounts of nitrogen. The farmer may apply between 30 and 100 pounds of nitrogen per acre. Blackberries, when the amount of nitrogen is adequate, yield a large number of large canes. Phosphorus appears to have little effect on blackberry yields. Blackberries absorb large quantities of potassium. One authority recommends potassium sulfate or potassium magnesium sulfate as sources of potassium. Muriate of potash is another possibility, though the farmer must guard against too much chlorine in the soil. The addition of too much potassium to the soil impairs the ability of blackberry roots to absorb magnesium. Magnesium sulfate, dolomitic lime, or potassium magnesium sulfate is a source of magnesium. In addition to fertilizer, blackberries need water, especially in spring and summer when growth is robust. Insufficient water causes plants to produce small berries. Where irrigation is necessary, the farmer must guard against applying too many salts to the soil.

Species and Cultivars

We have seen that blackberry numbers more than 350 species. Among them *Rubus argutus* and *Rubus frondosus* are erect, producing primocanes from both root and crown. These species are hardy and yield large, sweet berries. *Rubus procerus*, native to Iran, has migrated to Southern Europe, the United Kingdom,

New Zealand, and the American West. A thorny species, *Rubus procerus* grows vigorously. Some *Rubus procerus* plants are wild. Humans have cultivated others. The species yields small, round berries. Plants are disease resistant and yield abundantly. Like *Rubus procerus*, *Rubus laciniatus* has thorns and grows vigorously. This species, known as the Evergreen blackberry, retains its leaves throughout the year. *Rubus laciniatus* grows wild in Washington and Oregon, though it is also cultivated in these states. *Rubus thyrsinger* is prized for the quality of its fruit. *Rubus nitidioides* is notable for its flavor, large berries, and early maturation. *Rubus rustianus* may be the parent of Bedford Giant, the United Kingdom's leading cultivar. *Rubus baileyanus* is a trailing blackberry indigenous to the eastern United States. It is renowned for the quality of its berries. This species is the parent of the varieties Lucretia and Austin Thornless. *Rubus ursinus* and *Rubus macropetalus* are native to the American West. *Rubus ursinus* is, along with the raspberry, the parent of the loganberry. Ideal for the subtropics, *Rubus trivialis* is grown in the American South. The species needs little cold weather to initiate dormancy. *Rubus trivialis* tolerates drought and frost.

Popular Thornless Evergreen is still the most widely grown variety in Oregon, Washington, and British Columbia and remains among the highest yielders. Marion is the second leading cultivar in these regions. The new varieties Silvan and Waldo may challenge Thornless Evergreen and Marion for acreage. In California, Olallie is processed into a variety of foods. It is popular because the farmer may harvest it by machine. Erect varieties do well in Arizona, Oklahoma, and Texas. Most of the harvest in these states is sold fresh. Shawnee is the chief variety in the South. Other popular cultivars are Brazos, Cheyenne, and Cherokee. Challenging these are the new varieties Rosborough and Choctaw. Farmers cultivate the thornless varieties Navaho, Hull Thornless, Arapaho, Flordegard, and Gem in Florida and Georgia. In the Midwest and northeastern United States, farmers grow blackberries on small plots near cities to satisfy urban demand. Popular varieties include Darrow, Illini Hardy, and Hendrick, all of them erect cultivars. Less hardy are the thornless varieties Smoothstem, Thornfree, and Black Satin. New varieties in the Midwest and northeastern United States are Hull Thornless, Dirkson, and Chester. Brazos, Cheyenne, Navaho, Arapaho, and Rosborough are grown in Guatemala and Costa Rica. Farmers in southern Brazil cultivate U.S. varieties. Marion and Youngberry are grown in Australia and New Zealand. The new variety Silvan is popular in southern Australia. Waldo is gaining ground in Australia and New Zealand. Bedford Giant, the United Kingdom's leading cultivar, is widely grown in southern Great Britain.

Christopher Cumo

Further Reading

Crandall, Perry C. *Bramble Production: The Management and Marketing of Raspberries and Blackberries*. New York: Food Products Press, 1995.

Hull, J. W., and F. J. Lawrence. *Thornless Blackberries for the Home Garden*. Washington, D.C.: U.S. Department of Agriculture, 1977.

Jennings, D. L. *Raspberries and Blackberries: Their Breeding, Diseases and Growth*. London: Academic Press, 1988.

Black-Eyed Susan (Rudbeckia)

North America's own yellow daisies, commonly called black-eyed Susans, populated grand expanses of prairies and meadows across the wild landscape. Now they decorate roadsides and mixed garden borders across the United States and Canada, plus innumerable foreign gardens as cherished imports. Known also as coneflowers and gloriosa daisies, their botanical designation is the genus *Rudbeckia*. It is a distinguished name for such a common plant. Swedish naturalist, Carl Linnaeus (1707–1778), considered the father of taxonomy for creating the basic system for plant classification and the first civilian to be knighted in Sweden, named rudbeckia for Uppsala University Professor Olof Rudbeck the Younger (1660–1740) and his father, Olof Rudbeck the Elder (1630–1702), both of whom were botanists along with their other scientific interests.

Now all states—except Hawaii, Alaska, and those in the desert Southwest—and subarctic Canadian providences have a native species or more out of the 25. Some varieties have small ranges, such as the Texas coneflower, *Rudbeckia texana*; the California coneflower, *Rudbeckia californica*; and the grassleaf coneflower, *Rudbeckia graminiflora*, of Florida's wetlands. The plant referred to as black-eyed Susan is *Rudbeckia hirta*. Although not native to Maryland, it has been the state flower since 1918 and a good color match with the Baltimore oriole. The other best known Rudbeckia, *Rudbeckia fulgida*'s popular cultivar Goldsturm, does not grow true from seed but spreads through its rhizome. This Perennial of the Year for 1999 fills its space quickly in good, well-drained soil with plentiful water. Two to three feet tall and across, Goldsturm has dark green, fairly sparse, simple foliage that when mature has a rough feel while being less hairy than *Rudbeckia hirta*.

The bristle-coated stems and rough leaves help to make rudbeckias unpalatable to deer and rabbits unless no better forage exists. In pasture and prairie, livestock and other herbivores usually ignore these low-food-value, prickly plants as long as grasses and others are available. As herbaceous perennials, various rudbeckias can be grown as annuals, biennials, or short-lived perennials, depending on the gardener's preference and the particular variety's tendency to reseed or to form clumps. They yield plentiful blooms from seed the first year. Rudbeckia may be grown from zones 3 to 10, with less hardiness in extreme weather or under other stressful conditions such as inadequate watering and poor sandy soil.

Coming in a variety of sizes—from one to nine feet tall—rudbeckia is suitable for nearly any flowerbed or container. Double gloriosa and Indian summer cultivars seem to be copying their big cousin the sunflower with blooms of six to eight inches across. The variety Cherokee sunset has double, chrysanthemum-like blossoms. Small cultivars, such as the dwarf Viette's little Suzy or Toto, which will stay about a foot high, enliven a border as if lighting the way of the path with their sunny petals. Rudbeckia's hardy and prolific blooms are perfect for taking over the impact after the spring-blooming flush of bulbs and pale-flowering shrubs and trees with hot yellows, golds, oranges, new dark reds, and combinations with contrasting centers of black or dark brown cones. Their enthusiasm carries well into the fall. Later, their seed-filled cones punctuate the winter until birds or snow finishes them off. The plants may be deadheaded to prevent self-sowing.

While rudbeckias are a perfect addition to any varied garden or wildflower area, they also will anchor an area of similar plants. A gardener could do worse than to have a large flowerbed of rudbeckias plus asters, chrysanthemums, marguerites, shasta daisies, chamomile, coreopsis, gaillardia, echinacea, or other plants with charming daisy-like blooms.

Besides their garden duty, wild prairie lives, and roles as splendid cut flowers, rudbeckias have been used for dye. Wool absorbs the pale yellow, dusty green, and greenish-gold colors produced from simmering dye baths of petals and leaves or the whole plant. As a medicinal plant, black-eyed Susans make a tea made from the root by Native Americans for the treatment of colds and worms and as a salve for wounds.

Other genera share the common name of coneflower. Rudbeckia's close siblings in the huge plant family Asteraceae are echinacea, dracopsis, and ratibida. *Echinacea purpurea* especially is cross-referenced from rudbeckia listings. Rudbeckia thrives in unplowed, ungrazed areas. Indeed, it is an indicator of a healthy prairie. Old and neglected cemeteries serve as islands of preservation and also seed sources. States including Illinois, Kansas, Ohio, Nebraska, Texas, Indiana, Minnesota, Missouri, Wisconsin, Oklahoma, and North and South Dakota foster active prairie restoration programs. Cemetery prairies, old railroad beds, steep and rocky hills, and even a former U.S. Army parcel of more than 19,000 acres are forming the pieces that gradually are growing into viable representatives of former pristine prairie land.

Efforts at natural diversity can be particularly challenging. Besides reestablishing the diversity of native plants that numbered in the hundreds of species, exotic plants must be eradicated. Minimal mowing, controlled burns, labor performed by the Civilian Conservation Corp of the 1930s, and the efforts of the modern green movement to seed and monitor the ecology contributed to the steady, if slow, return of true prairies. *Rudbeckia hirta* is a pioneer plant, meaning it is one of the first to grow back after a fire or in an area that has been otherwise disturbed.

Whether a home gardener or prairie restorer, sowers of rudbeckia must eliminate one step in planting by omitting a cover of soil. With plenty of sun and enough water, coneflowers will host bees including their own designated ones of *Andrena rudbeckiae* and *Heterosarus rudbeckiae*, flies, butterflies, and when the cones become seeds, birds. Goldfinches especially enjoy them. Seeds that they miss will self-sow the next spring.

So, whether replacing a labor-intensive lawn with a wildflower meadow, inserting a statement of sunny joy in an established bed, or wanting long-lasting blooms for eye catching arrangements, gardeners will find rudbeckias that provide solutions.

Tamara Stromquist

See also Daisy (Bellis)

Further Reading

Greenwood, Pippa. *The New Flower Gardener.* New York: DK, 1998.

Hogan, Sean. *Flora: A Gardener's Encyclopedia.* Portland, OR: Timber Press, 2003.

Bladderwort

A carnivorous plant, the bladderwort is in the genus *Utricularia*. It derives its name from the fact that its traps look like miniature bladders. With 214 species, *Utricularia* is the largest genus of carnivorous plant. A widely distributed plant, the bladderwort grows in the wild in Alaskan swamps that are frozen much of the year, in acidic ponds in Florida, and in the land between these states. It grows in wet regions of Central and South America, Europe, Asia, and Africa and in the deserts of Australia. Some bladderworts even live on other plants. Some die down to buds to survive winter whereas others survive drought by issuing forth tubers no larger than a grain of rice. Although many bladderworts are perennial, the annuals propagate by seeds. The flowers look like those of small orchids. Flowers may be as small as an ant, measuring one-eighth of an inch in diameter, or as large as a butterfly, measuring two inches in diameter. Flowers may be white, pink, purple, violet, yellow, red, or a combination of these colors. Although most bladderworts are terrestrial, 15 percent is aquatic, floating in ponds. Terrestrial species grow in wet or waterlogged sand, mud, or moss in bogs and swamps near lakes. At least one species grows on wet rocks under a waterfall. Curiously, bladderworts have no roots, leading some botanists to wonder whether they are truly plants. Most of a bladderwort is underground or immersed in water. It produces photosynthetic stolons, which resemble leaves. In the smallest plants, stolons are less than one inch long. In the largest, stolons grow to several inches. The plants vary in size from only a few inches to several yards.

Carnivorous Habit

The carnivorous habit of the bladderwort has fascinated scientists for more than a century. In 1797 Sowerby—his first name and occupation may be lost to history—identified the traps of an aquatic plant but assumed they enabled it to float. Because traps are only two cells thick, they are translucent, and Sowerby saw insects in them. He thought they were hiding, perhaps from predators. Botanist Ferdinand Cohn found insects in a herbarium specimen. In 1875 Cohn, obtaining a live specimen, put water fleas in its aquarium. Within 24 hours, the bladderwort had captured all fleas. British naturalist Charles Darwin mistakenly thought that insects entered the traps without any provocation. While European scientists labored to understand the behavior of bladderwort traps, American botanist Mary Treat, arriving at the solution in 1873, observed that the traps captured insects in a rapid sucking movement akin to the action of a vacuum cleaner.

A single plant may have hundreds, even thousands of traps. In some species these traps are no larger than the head of a pin whereas in other plants traps are one-eighth to one-quarter of an inch in diameter. One Australian species has traps that measure one-half of an inch in diameter. At the end of each trap is a door that opens only inward. When closed, mucilage seals the door shut. A trap's walls are concave, forming a vacuum in it. Outside the door are long filaments that, forming a funnel, guide an insect or other prey toward it. Glands at the door secrete a substance that attracts prey. At the door are trigger hairs. Prey that contact a hair set off the trap. The door opens and the vacuum pulls in the prey. Once inside, the prey has no hope of escape because the door shuts. A bladderwort sucks in prey in just one one-hundredth of a second. The trap, having imprisoned its prey, pumps out water and secretes digestive juices. These drown the prey, dissolving its innards in hours. The glands absorb this liquid. One trap may capture more than a dozen prey during its life. The bladderwort's varied diet includes paramecia, cyclops, rotifers, water fleas, worms, mosquito larvae, and even small tadpoles. More than most prey, mosquito larvae and tadpoles meet an unpleasant end. Often caught by their tails, this part of their anatomy is digested while they live. As they struggle, they trigger the trap repeatedly, so that ever-larger portions of their bodies are digested in turn until only their heads, too big to fit in the trap, remain.

Diversity

The 214 species of bladderwort may be grouped into several categories. Among these are terrestrial bladderworts, which gardeners prize for their ease of cultivation. Collectively, terrestrial bladderworts grow in all climates. Some species grow in diverse climes, inhabiting perpetually wet mixtures of sand and peat. In some cases, they grow on flooded land. Often, they may be found with other carnivorous plants. Of terrestrial bladderworts, *Utricularia subulate*, native to the Americas from Canada to South America, Africa, and Southeast Asia, produces abundant seed. Growing in flooded soil, this species flowers in warm weather, producing yellow blooms one-quarter inch in diameter. *Utricularia livida* grows in subtropical Africa and Mexico. Tolerating light frost, it flowers in warm, sunny locales, producing blooms one-third of an inch in diameter. Despite its flowering habit, *Utricularia livida* seldom seeds. *Utricularia sandersonii* is native to South Africa. Its flowers, growing to one-half of an inch in diameter, make it a popular plant at Easter. Flowering in late summer and autumn, *Utricularia graminifolis* is an indigene of Japan and southern Asia. *Utricularia bisquamata*, native to South Africa, tolerates light frost. Its flowers are a combination of yellow, violet, orange, and white. Producing yellow flowers, *Utricularia corquta* is indigenous to the United States, growing from the Great Lakes to the American Southeast. Native to Canada, the United States, Cuba, and Central America, *Utricularia resupinata* yields purple flowers with a yellow throat.

Seasonal bladderworts are native to Australia. Among these is *Utricularia menziesii*, indigenous to southwestern Australia. Growing in winter, it produces tubers to survive hot, dry summers. *Utricularia denstaniae* and *Utricularia capilliflora*, native to northern Australia, rely on gnats to pollinate their flowers. Native to northern Australia, *Utricularia fulva* yields yellow flowers with red speckling. Also native to northern Australia, *Utricularia chrysantha* produces yellow and white blooms.

Tropical bladderworts are native to the Caribbean and Central and South America. Among tropical bladderworts is *Utricularia reinformis*, which flowers from spring to autumn, producing blooms that measure one-and-one-half inches in diameter. Rare, *Utricularia quelchii* is confined in the wild to the border between Venezuela and Guyana. Its flowers are purple and red. *Utricularia asplundii*, also from the border between Venezuela and Guyana, produces white, violet, and gold flowers. Producing among the largest flowers of any bladderwort, *Utricularia humboltis* yields blooms that measure two inches in diameter and that are pink and white.

Aquatic bladderworts grow in ponds with acidic water. Among aquatic bladderworts, *Utricularia vulgaris*, native to Europe, is more than 10 feet long. Also more than 10 feet, *Utricularia macrorhiza* is indigenous to North America and China. *Utricularia minor*, growing in the Northern Hemisphere, produces yellow flowers. Dormant during cold weather, *Utricularia inflata* is native to the American Southeast and Washington. *Utricularia volubilii*, native to western Australia, grows in winter.

Cultivation

Gardeners grow bladderworts more for their flowers than for their carnivorous habit. The fact that some bladderworts flower over several months entices gardeners to grow them. One gardener recounted a visit from a neighbor who was unimpressed by a barren bladderwort. When it flowered, however, the neighbor wanted a cutting so that he too might cultivate it. Bladderworts do well by a sunny window or in a terrarium or greenhouse. Where the climate permits outdoor cultivation, bladderworts may be grown in a bog garden. *Utricularia sandersonii*, *Utricularia subulate*, and *Utricularia livida*, for example, may be cultivated by a sunny window or in a terrarium, greenhouse, or bog. *Utricularia cornuta* does well in a bog. Tropical bladderworts may be grown by a sunny window or in a greenhouse of terrarium. The gardener may grow *Utricularia gibba* and *Utricularia reinformia* by a sunny window.

For aquatic plants, the soil should be one cup of peat for every gallon of water. Terrestrial bladderworts should have a soil of equal parts peat and sand. Terrestrial plants may be potted and the pot placed in a saucer of water. One may flood the soil. The gardener should frequently pour a container of water on the soil of tropical bladderworts. The water of aquatic plants should be changed when algae appear. The gardener may feed bladderworts water fleas. Using fertilizer at one-quarter strength, one may apply it once per month during the growing season. Bladderworts may be propagated by sections of a plant, by seed, and by leaf cutting.

Christopher Cumo

Further Reading

Barthlott, Wilhelm, Stefan Porembski, Ruediger Seine, and Inge Theisen. *The Curious World of Carnivorous Plants: A Comprehensive Guide to Their Biology and Cultivation.* Portland, OR: Timber Press, 2007.

Camilleri, Tony. *Carnivorous Plants.* Sydney: Kangaroo Press, 1998.

D'Amato, Peter. *The Savage Garden: Cultivating Carnivorous Plants.* Berkeley, CA: Ten Speed Press, 1998.

Lecoufle, Marcel. *Carnivorous Plants: Care and Cultivation.* London: Blandford, 1989.

Pietropaolo, James, and Patricia Pietropaolo. *Carnivorous Plants of the World.* Portland, OR: Timber Press, 1986.

Rice, Barry A. *Growing Carnivorous Plants.* Portland, OR: Timber Press, 2006.

Schnell, Donald E. *Carnivorous Plants of the United States and Canada.* Winston-Salem, NC: John F. Blair, 1976.

Simons, Paul. *The Action Plant: Movement and Nervous Behavior in Plants.* Oxford: Blackwell, 1991.

Slack, Adrian. *Carnivorous Plants.* Cambridge, MA: MIT Press, 1979.

Temple, Paul. *Carnivorous Plants.* London: Royal Horticultural Society, 1993.

Blueberry

A perennial shrub, blueberry is a member of the Ericaceae family and *Vaccinium* genus. Among the types of blueberry are the important lowbush, highbush, and rabbiteye. Of these three, the most important commercially is highbush, which is divided into northern and southern cultivars. Lowbush differentiates from highbush by being the shorter of the two. One cup of blueberries contains only 93 calories. Blueberry is rich in fiber, potassium, manganese, copper, iron, and zinc. The antioxidant and flavanoids in blueberry may protect one against cancer, aging, degenerative ailments, and infection. In small amounts, blueberry contains vitamins A, C, and E. Among its B vitamins are niacin, folic acid, pyridoxine, vitamin B6, riboflavin, and pantothenic acid. The chlorogenic acid in blueberry may reduce the amount of sugar in the blood, aiding diabetics.

Lowbush Blueberries

One writer refers to lowbush blueberries as wild, but this designation obscures the fact that they are cultivated. Lowbush blueberries were likely the type that Native Americans harvested, though they may not have cultivated them, before the advent of Europeans. Amerindians ate blueberries fresh, dried, and in preserves, cornbread, and porridge. In the 17th century, New Englanders bought blueberries from Native Americans, making them into gruel and pudding, substituting them for cherries and currants. European settlers combined blueberries with flour, milk, and eggs. When colonists added blueberries to cornmeal, they called the product Indian fruit pudding. Colonists made blueberry pie with brown sugar.

Native Americans burned blueberry fields to kill shrubs and trees that encroached on them. This method of clearing land was not entirely deleterious because blueberries thrived on the charred soil. Without the cover of trees, however, the wind blew snow off the land, exposing blueberry bushes to winter injury. In the 19th century, those farmers who grew blueberries commonly burned one-third of their land each year. In the late fall or early winter, the grower mowed or burned blueberry land to kill pests and pathogens. A burned area will not bear fruit the following year.

In the 1860s, Americans began to can the lowbush harvest to extend its shelf life. The availability of canned blueberries stoked demand. By the 1920s, Maine had emerged as the leading canner. In 1926, Maine canned 70 percent of the U.S. harvest. The Great Depression forced growers to sell blueberries fresh because consumers could not afford the price of processed berries. Since World War II, freezing has replaced canning as the method of preserving blueberries. The consumer may store frozen blueberries two years.

In the 1980s, the yield of lowbush and other types of blueberry increased with the application of the herbicide Velpar, available in Canada in 1982 and the United States in 1983. Farmers apply herbicide in spring and fertilizer before the bush resumes growth in April. Given the requirement of nutrient-poor soil, the application of fertilizer must be infrequent. In May, the grower rents beehives to hasten pollination. The grower must guard against bear, fox, raccoon, robin, thrush, and grouse, all of which plunder the crop. Since the 1980s, farmers have harvested lowbush blueberries by machine. Less than 1 percent of the lowbush harvest is sold fresh. Most of the fresh crop goes to local hotels and restaurants. Most of the rest is frozen with a small portion being canned. Since the 1920s, the United States has exported lowbush blueberries to the Unied Kingdom. Since 1990, Germany and Japan have emerged as lowbush importers. Notable cultivars include Russell, which U.S. Department of Agriculture (USDA) scientist Frederick Coville bred in 1909, and Augusta, Brunswick, and Chignato, which the Kentville Research Station in Nova Scotia released in 1978.

There are two species of lowbush blueberry: *Vaccinium augustifolium* and *Vaccinium myrtilloides*. The first is more numerous in North America. A dwarf shrub, lowbush blueberry, like other types of blueberry, needs acidic soil, with a pH between 2.8 and 6. The soil may be peat or sand and, contrary to expectations and as we have seen, must be nutrient poor. Flowers, which may be white or pink, develop in May. Berries, ripening in late July in southern Maine and late September in Newfoundland, are one-eighth to one-half of an inch in diameter. Farmers cultivate lowbush blueberry from New Hampshire to northeastern Maine, and in New Brunswick, Nova Scotia, Prince Edward Island, northern Michigan, Minnesota, Wisconsin, and West Virginia. *Vaccinium myrtilloides* is grown in the Appalachian Mountains north to Labrador. Flowers, smaller than those of *Vaccinium augustifolium*, are white or pink. Berries are one-quarter to one-third of an inch in diameter.

Highbush and Rabbiteye

The hardiest blueberry, northern highbush grows 4 to 12 feet tall. It needs 750 hours of temperatures below 45°F to initiate dormancy. Berries, being between one-eighth and three-quarters of an inch in diameter, ripen over six to eight weeks. Whereas a green berry has 7 percent sugar, a ripe one has 15 percent sugar. Berries at the top of a bush, receiving the most sun, ripen first. Berries at the top of a bush have the most sugar and are largest.

In the 1890s, the attempt to grow northern highbush blueberries failed, probably because farmers did not appreciate that the soil must be acidic and poor. In the early 20th century, private growers and the USDA promoted the cultivation of blueberries, highbush and lowbush alike. In 1908, Frederick Coville bred the northern highbush variety Brooks. The next year he demonstrated that northern highbush berries, like all blueberries, need acidic soil. In the early 20th century, Coville bred six varieties: Adams, Dunphy, Grover, Harding, Rubel, and Sam. Farmers grew these cultivars in North Carolina, Michigan, Washington, Oregon, New England, New York, New Jersey, Connecticut, and British Columbia. Highbush was a lucrative crop. Expanding his work, Coville crossed northern highbush and lowbush cultivars, deriving the hybrids Pioneer, Katherine, and

Cabot. These hybrids grew no taller than four feet, yielded abundantly, and matured early. In the 1920s, Coville derived the varieties Concord, Greenfield, Jersey, and Ramcocas, and in the 1930s Catawba, Dixi, June, Redskin, Scammell, Stanley, Waraham, and Weymouth. Among these, Jersey is still grown in Michigan.

In the United States, Italian immigrants tried to grow peaches and grapes as they had in Italy, but because the climate and soil did not favor these crops, they turned to northern highbush. Before World War II, New Jersey was the leading northern highbush producer. After the war, Michigan overtook New Jersey. North Carolina, Washington, D.C., and British Columbia maintain large plantings of northern highbush. In the 1990s, Oregon emerged as a large producer.

The Netherlands may have been the first European country to plant northern highbush, in 1923. Poland began growing northern highbush in 1924, though the initial planting perished in the severe winter of 1929. After 1929, German scientist Walter Heerman bred the varieties Blauweiss-Goldtraube, Blauweiss-Zukertraube, Heerman, Pekord, Ama, and Gretha. Today, Germany, with more than 1,500 acres of northern highbush, has the largest acreage in Europe. In addition to the Netherlands and Germany, France, Spain, Portugal, Romania, and Denmark produce northern highbush. The Japanese, large consumers of blueberries, prefer northern highbush to other types. In the Southern Hemisphere Australia, New Zealand, Chile, and South Africa grow northern highbush. These ripen between December and April, supplying the Northern Hemisphere with fresh blueberries out of season. Since 1950, New Zealand has grown northern highbush and rabbiteye and exports to Japan. In 2000, New Zealand emerged as an exporter of northern highbush. In 1969, Australia first planted blueberries from U.S. seeds. Farmers grew northern highbush in Victoria and Tasmania and southern highbush and rabbiteye in New South Wales. Corindi, where the harvest is year-round, produces the majority of Australia's crop. Australia exports to Europe, the United States, and Asia, especially Japan. In 2000, Chile exported northern highbush blueberries to 26 countries including the United States, Canada, Japan, the Netherlands, the United Kingdom, Italy, and Germany.

Farmers grow southern highbush and rabbiteye where the climate is too warm for northern highbush. Rabbiteye, being of the species *Vaccinium ashei*, needs 400 to 500 hours of temperatures below 45°F to initiate dormancy. Southern highbush needs 400 to 660 hours of temperatures below 45°F. Farmers grow rabbiteye and southern highbush from central Florida to eastern North Carolina and from northern Arkansas to eastern Texas. Florida has grown rabbiteye since 1892. In 1926, the University of Georgia began research to derive new varieties of rabbiteye and southern highbush. In 1939, the North Carolina Agricultural Experiment Station and the USDA joined this effort, releasing Calloway and Coastal in 1949, Homebell in 1955, Briteblue, Delite, and Southland in 1969, and Bluebelle in 1974. In a separate breeding program, the University of

Florida had derived varieties of southern highbush suitable for the United States and Australia.

Christopher Cumo

Further Reading

Eck, Paul. *Blueberry Science.* New Brunswick, NJ: Rutgers University Press, 1988.

Eck, Paul, and Norman F. Childers, eds. *Blueberry Culture.* New Brunswick, NJ: Rutgers University Press, 1966.

Scott, D. H., A. D. Draper, and George M. Darrow. *Commercial Blueberry Growing.* Washington, D.C.: U.S. Department of Agriculture, 1978.

Sumner, Judith. *American Household Botany: A History of Useful Plants, 1620–1900.* Portland, OR: Timber Press, 2004.

Trehane, Jennifer. *Blueberries, Cranberries and Other Vacciniums.* Portland, OR: Timber Press, 2004.

Botanical Illustration

Botanical illustration is immediate intimacy: easily accessed through familiar profiles, its intricate combinations of swirls, curving expanses, and definitive lines charm the viewer into an understanding of plant functions and anatomy. Yet appreciative audiences are perhaps one of the smallest constituencies involved with this genre today. Hobbyists and professionals, botanists, gardeners, classically trained artists, commercial illustrators, and many others have dabbled in botanicals. For the sake of narrowing an overly broad scope, this article focuses on the interplay between art and science. The 20th-century art historian Wilfred Blunt (1994, 4) adds another element, "soul":

> A great botanical artist must have a passion for flowers. You can set a good architectural draughtsman to draw a flower, and he will give you—if he thinks the subject worthy of real effort—a careful and precise study of the plan before him. But unless he *loves* what he is drawing, unless he *knows* the flower in all its moods, in all stages of its development, there will be something lacking in his work. . . . The artists, poets, and philosophers of the Far East have shown how little . . . is the gulf that separates man from the rest of Nature; we in the West have still much to learn from them.

There are two general types of botanicals, herbal and floral, that emerged with pharmacology and global exploration, respectively. Early civilizations—when confined to their own territories—took plant life for granted. The temple of

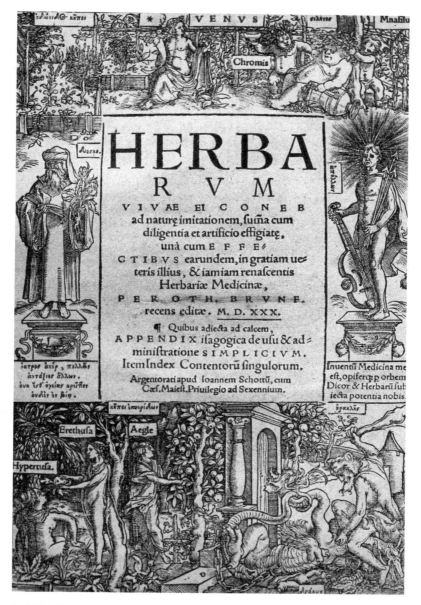

In 1534 German theologian and botanist Otto Brunfels published a herbal of medicinal plants. Here is the cover to this volume. (Library of Congress)

Pharaoh Thutmose III at Karnak, Egypt dates to 1450 BCE. It displays 75 limestone bas-relief botanicals, artistically well in advance for their era, that commemorate the unusual plants found during Thutmose's military campaign in Syria.

Although few of the early herbal illustrations survive, we know of them through classical writings. Perhaps the first practitioner was Aristotle's pupil, Greek botanist Theophrastus (371–287 BCE), who wrote a book titled *Enquiry into Plants*. In his *Natural History*, Roman encyclopedist Pliny the Elder (23–79 CE) stated that Krateuas, Dionysius, and Metrodorus "painted likenesses of the plants and wrote under them their properties." (Krateuas, who served as physician to King Mithridates VI of Pontus, exemplifies the then-common link between botany and medicine.) The earliest surviving herbals owe to first-century CE Greek physician Dioscorides, who has been called the "father of modern pharmacology." His *De Materia Medica*, a compendium of classical writings, remained authoritative—and in print—through the 1500s. The original publication may or may not have contained illustrations, though later editions certainly did.

Art, Science, and Technology

As with most other creative and scientific endeavors, the fall of Rome and ensuing Middle Ages saw a qualitative decline in botanical illustration. Classical works were reinterpreted from copies, with subsequent "generations" of images losing integrity. Beginning in the early 15th century, however, new technologies and heightened commerce revived botanical illustration. The woodcut appeared in Europe again around 1400, and Gutenberg's first printing press followed 50 years later. The cost of publications soon fell. Movable type and woodcuts worked well and easily together on pages destined for printing. Botanicals were introduced into border designs, and chapter-opening drawings sometimes contained natural motifs. Botanical illustrators found a use for their skills, though relatively few entered the artistic limelight.

The genre also became increasingly refined. The 16th and 17th centuries are associated with the movement toward naturalism, but the issue is more complex: art and scientific thinking converged through the concept of perspective. The Florentine artist Giotti (ca. 1266–1336) first turned away from flat surfaces, portraying his subjects as rounded objects with spatial relationships to each other. Drawing on classical art and architectural theories, Italian architect and artist Filippo Brunelleschi (1377–1446) and, later, Italian architect and artist Leon Battista Alberti (1402–1472) imparted more precise, mathematical thinking. The polymath Leonardo da Vinci (1452–1519), who invented an early printmaking technique, also insisted on real models for his artist works. People and other subject matter—including plants—thus assumed three dimensions.

Two period publications of herbal woodblocks provide a snapshot of botanical illustration in the mid-16th century and offer insight into the ways it would evolve. Otto Brunfels's *Herbarum Vivae Eicones* (1534) and Leonhart Fuchs's *De Historia Stirpium* (1542) are remembered by the names of their editor-compilers, medical practitioners both. *Herbarum* was illustrated by Hans Weiditz (1495–1536), a student of the respected German painter-printmaker Albrecht Durer (1471–1528), who nevertheless remained anonymous. Fuchs proved a more gracious editor than Brunfels, crediting several members of his publishing team.

In fact, increasingly complex printing technologies necessitated collaborative approaches—often diluting individual credentials. As the woodcut yielded to more detailed engravings, artists and craftsmen could be appreciated for their separate talents. Collectors later would compare differences between the original drawings and the finished prints, and editor/text compiler, botanical illustrator, calligrapher, printmaker, and publisher all had distinct roles in period productions. (The term "editor/text compiler" is used because most of the named authors borrowed from the ancient pharmacological experts.)

At the time, however, Brunfels and Fuchs both grappled with the spatial problem of placing an odd-shaped plant on a linear page. Yet their visions—balancing naturalism with art—varied. Weiditz (Brunfels's anonymous artist) showed the plant in whatever way he found it, sometimes withering from disease or, simply, a declining life cycle. Fuchs's illustrators overlooked the flaws or elevated their subjects to more perfected forms. Both herbals nevertheless revealed the desire to serve science. The less attractive (and spatially challenging) root and stem structure generally had been hidden or reduced in proportion to leaves and flowers. Weiditz dealt with the geometry at one point by cutting the stem, and running the lower part of the plant horizontally along the bottom of the page. Fuchs displayed the flowering plant; buds and seeds appeared on the same page, too, but apart from the graceful stalk.

Whatever the case, increased learning revealed much more about botanical subjects, and advanced art techniques of the late Middle Ages and Renaissance elevated their composition. Just as art, science, and printing technologies seemed to converge, however, the original function of herbal illustrations faded. In 1533, a professorship in botany was created at the University in Padua, establishing plant study as distinct from medicine. Fifty years later, the physician-botanist Andrea Cesalpino (1519–1603), began grouping plants by their characteristics, or morphology (specifically, their fruits and seeds), rather than medicinal values—or simple alphabetical order. His *De Plantis Libri* (1583) gained the scientific authority so long relegated to the early Greco-Romans. As academic disciplines solidified, plants with no outstanding function were once again viewed as everyday features of the local landscape.

At the same time, Europeans developed a potent attraction to exotic species from new worlds. The first printed illustration of a tobacco plant, for example, was published around 1570. Monarchs, barons, and city-states subsequently cultivated these treasures on their own turfs. Meticulously tended estate gardens soon flourished in much of the continent, and patrons needed botanist-illustrators to publicize their status—and formally document the contents. Actual botanic gardens in Pisa (1543), Padua (1545), Florence (1545), and Bologna (1567) inspired more scientific interest, with illustrative approaches to match.

Rapidly rising in popularity and purpose, floral drawings thus overtook the traditional herbals. However, the terms are not exact. "Florals" more accurately refer to *cultivated* species; the genre grew to embrace ornamental, decorative, and edible plants.

The early illustrators tended to be multidisciplinary, too: botanists, gardeners, general artists—per chance employed in or near a garden. Nor did they render just one picture. Botanical illustration benefited from, and contributed to, a growing publishing industry. The physician Pietro Andrea Matthioli (1501–1577), updated Dioscrides's work with new and revised text, as well as quality woodblocks. *Discorsi* (Commentaries) was printed first in Latin during 1544 and, 10 years later, in Italian—reputedly selling 30,000 copies. More than 40 Matthioli editions were to enter the market, also in Czech and German, and containing new illustrations.

Hortus Eystettensis (1613) was a pioneering celebration of place, rendered by professional artists. The largest single book published to that time, its 367 plates covered over 1,000 species. The idea germinated with Johann Conrad von Gemmingen, descendant of an ancient, affluent line, who came to the southern German town of Eichstatt as its new bishop. Seeking to elevate both worship and church property, he built what was said to be the first botanical garden north of the Alps, a rambling wonder of eight differently planted parterres; herbs, vegetables, and fruits descending from the palace above to the river below; and exotic displays from abroad, including cactus, peppers, and potatoes.

Basilius Besler, an apothecary and physician from Nuremburg (35 miles distant), was what we might today call Gemmingen's procurement officer, negotiating on his behalf with Dutch merchants for rare species. Besler also was charged with cataloguing the garden; among other duties, he conveyed live flowers from Eichstatt to premiere local artists for illustration. Gemmingen advanced some of the money needed to print these works. When he died in 1612, Besler opted to proceed with the publication anyway. His plan was a black-and-white edition for the book trade—and special, hand-colored versions commissioned by individuals wealthy enough to afford them. The *Hortus Eystettensis* illustrations are united by a Baroque character, full utilization of the page, visible species names, and (following a certain tradition) diminished representation of roots and stems. Yet artists' individuality and talents managed to surface. A few florals are full-face portraits, while most appear from a slight distance. One or more varieties grace each page. These partners possess different scientific relationships to each other. Some layouts seem to allocate equal space to each of the smaller illustrations, rendering an ordered, box-like appearance; other placements are unifying and creative, even showing movement.

If these anthologies did little to further the careers of most Renaissance illustrators, some achieved lasting recognition. Before going to war, the soldierly Charles de Sainte-Maure (1610–1690), later Duke of Montausier, decided to secure his future with the much sought-after and cultured Julie D'Angennes. He commissioned Nicolas Robert (1614–1685) to craft an extraordinary birthday gift. The resulting album, the *Garland of Julie*, featured spectacular, skillfully rendered flowers that appeared individually—and together on the title page, forming a circle around the recipient's name. It was a multimedia production, too, as Robert snared the era's best known calligrapher and one of its revered poets for their respective artistic contributions. The *Garland* sealed the baron's marriage proposal; it simultaneously bolstered Robert's reputation as an artist. In short order, he catalogued a baronial garden, served the court of French king Louis XIV (1638–1715) and, with a turn toward more scientific work, became chief illustrator for a landmark history of plants published by France's new Royal Academy of Sciences.

Botanicals nevertheless filtered to the average person. The Dutch had become masters of the flower trade. Blooms in general—and tulips in particular—were universally admired, but generally not affordable. According to legend, one aficionada engaged the Flemish artist Jan Brueghel (1568–1625) to paint the flowers that were beyond her purchasing power. Jan Brueghel was the son of the Flemish artist Pieter Bruegel the Elder (1525/1530–1569), who so memorably depicted the era's folk culture. Originally dedicated to landscapes and historical scenes, the younger Brueghel gained lasting recognition for his floral still lifes. And while not exactly botanical illustration, oil paintings of flowers (revealing the period's dark backgrounds and rich color schemes) became popular throughout the Low Countries.

The Golden Age of Botanical Illustration

The period from approximately 1700 to 1840 has been called the Golden Age of Botanical Illustration. It was an era when botanical drawing reached its height—sustained by both popular tastes and supportive infrastructures. In addition to the Dutch penchant for commercial cultivation and the German appreciation for quality printing, the English were establishing a reputation for horticultural science and the French for art. Dutch seed catalogues seemed a likely progenitor to such works as the *Gardener's Dictionary*, complied by Arthur Miller, and *Catalogus Plantarum* (1730), a project of the Society of Gardeners, an English trade guild.

These publications sought to clarify differences between plants, creating more knowledgeable patrons who would be less apt to blame the horticulturalists for their purchasing mistakes. Both English books employed Jacob van Huysum (1686/87–1740), a Dutch flower painter with an artistic pedigree; his father and brother were similarly engaged, rendering their work in a similar style.

Indeed, the era's luminaries traveled between countries and, frequently, between trades. Georg Dionysius Ehret (1708–1770) is one of the most brilliant examples. The son of poor German growers and vendors, he learned how to draw from his father at an early age. The boy was placed as a gardener's apprentice, soon to become an overseer, all the while impressing employers with his developing artistry. At first, his talent yielded nothing but engravers' jobs for which he received little pay. But the young man did amass a portfolio—and the confidence of Christoph Jacob Trew (1695–1769), a wealthy Nuremburg physician with an immense interest in botany. Trew became Ehret's collector, promoter, and some-time publishing collaborator. (It should be emphasized, however, that Trew's productions extended well beyond Ehret.)

Reinforced with letters of introduction, the artist traipsed through Europe, often on foot, painting interesting, new flowers and sending his works to Trew. One of his contacts led him to the pioneering Swedish naturalist Carl Linnaeus (1707–1778), who developed a uniform system for classifying and naming species that remains, at least partially, in practice today. Moving permanently to London during 1736, Ehret illustrated Linnaeus's *Genera Plantarum* (1737)—for which he was paid, but not credited. The artist nevertheless maintained a collaborative, long-distance relationship with Trew. He also counted a number of other partners and elite patrons (notably the Duchess of Portland) and gained distinction toward the end of his life as the only foreign-born Fellow of the Royal Society. Some botanical illustrators felt comfortable with a limited repertoire of flowers; Ehret could handle virtually all. He painted them in an oversized way for striking presentation. Most of all—as someone who claimed both spheres of influence—he balanced accurate representation with artistry.

Pierre-Joseph Redouté (1759–1840) was the most popular figure of the Golden Age. In fact, his name remains synonymous with botanical illustration. Unlike the happenstance career path foisted upon Ehret, Redouté came from a long line of Belgium painters. He flailed about as a traveling artist during his teenage years, but took the opportunity to study the Flemish masters and, when visiting Amsterdam, developed a passion for the work of the recently deceased flower painter Jan van Huysum. Van Huysum's bountiful bouquets consumed entire canvases, yet captured details: dew drops, insects, thin streams of light. On the other hand, they were not flowers that might be seen at the same time or grown in the same place.

Inspired, the now mature and motivated Redouté sojourned to the Jardin du Roi and the mentorship of the well-healed and connected botanist Charles Louis

L'Héritier (1746–1800). Besides granting the young man access to a voluminous library and personally providing him with botanical instruction, it was likely that through L'Héritier, Redouté became draftsman to the cabinet of French queen Marie Antoinette (1755–1793). This was a largely ceremonial title that nevertheless enhanced Redoute's reputation. He soon benefited from close association with Dutch artist Gerard van Spaendonck (1746–1822), a brilliant professor of flower painting—and another follower of Van Huysum.

Redouté transitioned nicely from the Revolution to the Empire: Empress Josephine Bonaparte (1763–1814) put him on salary to capture for posterity the living treasures at Malmaison; a number of beautiful published volumes ensued, further contributing to Redouté's legacy. Living the noble life as far as his money would take him, Redouté also attracted his own students, including royal scions. He rose to the top tier of botanical illustration for many reasons. A natural talent descended from artistic lineage, Redouté quickly learned from—indeed, copied the style of—the masters, notably Van Spaendonck. His career also coincided with some complementary new technology. Stipple engraving used dots instead of lines, presenting more natural, gradual color changes. The technology put a different spin on his work, elevating it above those of his predecessors.

With Redouté as with Ehret, we see evolving public patronage (initially exemplified by paying students), diversifying artists' economic options, and gradually starting to replace a dependence on royalty. In addition, a growing professionalism and mentoring relationships helped to establish careers. The Golden Age of Botanical Art also transferred from nobility to government what was to become a global institution: the Kew Gardens. Highly placed staff there nurtured botanical illustration and forums for presenting it. A veteran of Captain James Cook's worldwide voyage, British explorer and naturalist Sir Joseph Banks (1743–1820) acquired and archived some of Ehret's works, donated his herbarium and personal library collection to public repositories, and permanently instituted the position "draftsman" at Kew. That job was filled by Franz Bauer (1758–1840), whose brother Ferdinand (1760–1826) became known for botanicals illustration and traveled on expeditions to capture plant life in the Mideast, Maritius, and Australia—where he named a small group of islands after Banks. As leading botany professors and successive directors of the Kew, Sir William Jackson Hooker (1785–1865) and his son, Sir Joseph Dalton Hooker (1817–1911), installed the highly skilled Walter Hood Fitch (1817–1892) and, later, his similarly talented nephew, John Nugent Fitch (1840–1927), as illustrators of the respected *Botanical Magazine*—and other publications.

With global exploration graduating to colonization, the lack of Asian influence in botanical illustration is puzzling. Flower painting was firmly established in China by the T'ang dynasty (618–906 CE) and in Korea about the same time. It subsequently came to Japan. Among other differences, East Asian artists relied more on black-and-white shading—and less on the imposition of color—than

Europeans. India had a floral tradition, too, derived in part from Persian-Mogul antecedents, which yielded a highly stylized, symmetrical appearance.

Europeans expropriated neither. Instead, they either brought their botanists and illustrators with them (Ferdinand Bauer provides a good example) or instructed native artists in Western styles. Still, Asia fused with Europe through creative, commercial hybrids. Mary Delany (1700–1788), a friend of the German composer George Frederic Handel, British writer Jonathan Swift, and the arts the patron Duchess of Portland, earned a place for herself at the British Museum through her intricate floral "mosaics." According to contemporary testimony, Sir Joseph Banks said that "he would venture to describe botanically any plant from Mrs. Delany's imitations without the least fear of committing an error." Her medium was imported Chinese paper, finely cut and formed into flowers.

And while Westerners did not fawn over Asian floral illustration (at least initially), they adored its porcelain. By the 1700s, European manufacturers were beginning to produce their own. "China painting" often employed Western "flower books" as a reference for artists decorating this increasingly popular dining ware. However, some of the finest, most valued products—the German Meissen designs immediately come to mind—did, in fact, incorporate Oriental-style flowers and themes, among other motifs.

Whatever the subgenre, the creators often remained anonymous from the earliest days when herbal silhouettes were copied to oblivion, through the early modern era when publishers co-opted flower paintings and illustrations without giving artists any credit. The Statute of (Queen) Anne in 1709 reduced the publishers' guilded advantage, instituting copyrights for writers and artists—and introducing the concept of public domain. As befitting a culturally connected former colony, the U.S. Copyright Act of 1790 borrowed heavily from the statute.

The Victorian Era to Today

As with creative rights, new technologies brought botanical illustrators closer to publication processes. Straightforward printing eliminated the need for middlemen who would copy or otherwise interpret their work. Henry Bradbury patented a method during the 1850s with two similarly sized plates: a soft lead portion held plant material directly, as a steel component forced an impression of it. The final stage was electroprinting. Inspired by photography, botanist Anna Atkins (1797–1871) published *British Algae* in 1854. She used the process of cyanotype to duplicate 400 minute species within her herbarium: plants with details that could easily evade a draftsperson. Cyanotype was very direct. The botanist laid her plants on photosensitive paper, exposed briefly to sunlight. The result was an image in "cyan" blue. For whatever their merits, both printing processes captured the plant's profile and internal arteries—but not their textures, depth, or dimensions. Photography, of course, became both a practical and creative aid in botanical illustration.

An increasingly middle-class Victorian public bought into flower arrangements of all types. The arts-and-crafts designer William Morris (1834–1896) entered floral themes into his stained glass, tapestries, wallpapers, and other furnishings. Morris's swirling, two-dimensional patterns in varying color schemes were not botanically accurate, yet his use of woodblocks as a design tool recalled early botanical illustration.

Herbaria evolved during the Age of Discovery as a way of transporting and preserving unique botanical specimens. They consisted simply of dried plants, pressed and mounted. Both scientists and artists nevertheless came to appreciate them. *The River Jordan* (1900), published by the Boulos Meo Company as a tourist souvenir book, boasted olive wood covers that opened to complementary folios: photos of holy sites on one side and drawings with local (Middle Eastern) dried flowers affixed on the other. The pressed-flower fad continued through the early 20th century and enjoys periodic revivals.

On view at Harvard's Museum of Natural History are more exotic species: the Ware Collection of Glass Plants. Created by a German father and son, Leopold and Rudolph Blaschka, they were commissioned over a 50-year period, from the late 1880s to 1936. The idea began with George Lincoln Goodale, Harvard professor and Botanical Museum founder, initially in rebellion against pressed flowers, as well as wax or papier-mâché models that he believed would not hold up well to classroom uses. The botanical detail, artistry, and use of glass together form a uniquely beautiful presentation.

As gardening became a middle-class leisure pursuit in the 20th century, botanical illustration made its way into mainstream publishing and related commercial enterprises. Professional, serious hobbyist, and popular magazines satisfied a craving for practical information. Illustrators and photographers worked together on these gardening periodicals. Such practice is evident in Sunset Magazine's *Western Garden Book*, considered a bible by several generations of home growers. Seed and catalogue companies engaged illustrators, too, as did culinary publications. The covers of *Cook's Illustrated* magazine provide a contemporary view, though sometimes with Dutch backgrounds and Impressionistic influences. A recent book lists over 35 resources for British botanical illustrators and artists, including several formal education programs. The Royal Botanic Gardens, Kew (or simply, Kew), is the largest and most varied resource of its type in the world. It currently employs 800 staff, and contains an herbarium of 7 million species, a seed bank, a 750,000-volume library, and publishing program that produces over 20 new titles annually. Many will agree that Shirley Sherwood, author, collector, and benefactor of the Shirley Sherwood Gallery of Botanical Art at the Kew, is the individual most responsible for reviving the genre today.

Botanical gardens in the United States are owed to both commercial forces (cemeteries inspiring naturalistic parklands) and government initiative. Congress appropriated grounds to establish a horticultural center and museum on the Washington Mall during 1820, but the impetus came more than two decades later, after the Wilkes Expedition brought plants from the South Seas. The U.S. Botanic Garden opened to the public in 1850. Privately funded agencies as diverse as the Huntington Library, Art Collections, and Botanical Gardens near Los Angeles and the Hunt Institute for Botanical Documentation at Carnegie-Mellon University, Pittsburgh, contribute greatly to the field. Finally, membership organizations hold sway here, with practitioners banding together under the American Society of Botanical Artists (ASBA) and Guild of Natural Science Illustrators.

Some technical experimentation occurs. Still, botanical illustrators generally adhere to low-tech media: graphite (pencil); pen and ink; scratchboard; colored and watercolor pencils; watercolor, gouache, and acrylic paints. What further defines an illustration is the canvas. Like Ehret, Redouté, and the classicists, a significant number of today's experts prefer vellum, stretched calfskin.

Day jobs in illustration aside, practitioners can gain a reputation through juried shows. ASBA requires that the judges include both botanists and artists. And while methods may be traditional, the exhibition topics tend to be more contemporary. A 2011 ASBA show, also its first international venue, focused on "Losing Paradise? An Exhibition of Endangered Plants Here and Around the World." Over in England, Prince Charles published his *Highgrove Florigium* (2008). The first step was inviting leading botanical artists to capture in watercolors the trees, flowers, vegetables, and herbs growing organically at his Highgrove estate. Their work was submitted to an expert panel for publication review. Traditions notwithstanding, botanical art has a more global character. Several Japanese practitioners are members of the Botanical Artist Guild of Southern California.

Illustrators who work for publishers or for archival purposes now draw their plants directly into computers. Automation allows them to customize some of their techniques—their style of stippling (showing texture through dots) or hatching (via lines). Some say that computer printers need to be calibrated every day for the truest color effects. Still, the fondness for intimacy and tactile interactions with plants and drawing implements remains unchanged. The contemporary illustrator initially applying his or her stylus to filmy computer paper is not that far removed from the engraver-artist Crispin de Passe (1590–1664) who, perhaps tentatively at first, approached his plates with the then-newfangled burim.

Lynn C. Kronzek

Further Reading

Aymonin, Gerard G., and Nicolas Barker. *Botanical Prints from the "Hortus Eystettensis": Selections from the Most Beautiful Botanical Book in the World*. New York: Abrams, 2000.

Blunt, Wilfrid. *The Art of Botanical Illustration: An Illustrated History*. New York: Dover, 1994.

Cantor, Norman F. *Civilization of the Middle Ages*. New York: HarperCollins, 1993.

Folsom, James P. *Plant Trivia TimeLine: A Chronology of Plants and People*. https://sitesgoogle.com/site/ourvegetablekingdom (accessed 8 July 2011).

Oxley, Valerie. *Botanical Illustration*. Ramsbury, Marlborough, U.K.: Crowood Press, 2009.

Rix, Martyn. *The Art of the Plant World: The Great Botanical Illustrators and Their Work*. Woodstock, NY: Overlook Press, 1980.

Saunders, Gill. *Picturing Plants: An Analytical History of Botanical Illustration*. Berkeley: University of California Press, 1995.

Acknowledgments

The author acknowledges personal communications with James P. Folsom, director, Huntington Botanical Gardens, San Marino, California (April 2011); Deborah Shaw, scientific illustrator, board of directors, Botanical Artists Guild of Southern California (April 2011); and Alice Tangerini, staff illustrator, Smithsonian Institution, Museum of Natural History, Washington, D.C. (May 2011).

Bougainvillea

Bougainvillea is a hardy ornamental viny shrub of the four o'clock family or Nycataginaceae, which originated in subtropical and tropical South America. *Bougainvillea* was first classified in Rio de Janeiro in 1768 by the French botanist Philibert Commerçon (1727–1773), who named the plant after the navigator Louis-Antoine de Bougainville (1729–1811), with whom he had served in the French navy. There are now around 34 genera. However, there seems to be no definitive agreement on the number of bougainvillea species in existence, with estimates ranging from 4 to 350. This lack of accord is due to frequent hybridization in the genus in India and Malaysia, which makes the identification of individual species extremely difficult. Bougainvillea grows across the globe in areas with warm climates. Although some species will tolerate cooler environments and high altitudes, with *Bougainvillea spectabilis* the most cold-tolerant of all bougainvilleas, bougainvillea cannot survive temperatures much below freezing and should be planted in areas that do not suffer from frost. In cooler areas bougainvillea can be raised as a houseplant or in a conservatory.

Attributes

Bougainvillea is a quick-growing impenetrable hedge the height of which varies depending on the species or cultivar, with a dwarf species called Bougainvillea Temple Fire available. The stem of the bougainvillea has hook-like spines, which

Bougainvillea (Wilm Ihlenfeld/Dreamstime.com)

allow the plant to climb over rough surfaces. While the spines allow for scrambling over coarse-textured surfaces, wires, trellises, or other supports may be needed for bougainvillea to spread over the exterior of smooth walls or arbors. Bougainvillea has round to oval, alternate, opposite leaves, which can be evergreen or semievergreen. The most striking aspect of the bougainvillea is the brightly hued bracts, which are petal-like and are most often to be found in shades of purple, red, yellow, orange, pink, and white with the latter tending to be particularly tender. The tissue-paper-like texture of the bracts has led to the bougainvillea gaining the soubriquet "the paper flower." In some plants, bracts of two colors can be found on the same shrub, while some cultivars see the bracts change color with age thus giving the appearance of several colors growing together. The actual flower of the bougainvillea is a small, creamy-colored tube-like structure attached to the base of the bracts.

Species and Hybrids

There are three main horticultural species: *Bougainvillea spectabilis*, *Bougainvillea peruviana*, and *Bougainvillea glabra*. From these, three major hybrid groups have emerged *Bougainvillea × buttiana* (a hybrid of *Bougainvillea peruviana* and *Bougainvillea glabra*), *Bougainvillea × spectoperuviana* (a hybrid of *Bougainvillea peruviana* and *Bougainvillea glabra*), and *Bougainvillea × spectoglabra* (a hybrid of *Bougainvillea spectabilis* and *Bougainvillea glabra*). The horticultural cultivars have originated from both natural and artificial hybrids, and among the bud sports are some variegated and double-bract sports. One frequently grown species of bougainvillea is *Bougainvillea × buttiana* Holttum and Standley. This is made readily distinguishable by its vicious spines of up to two inches in length and shrubby habit. The species scrambles and can climb into trees. The plant has white flowers surrounded by red, purple, white, or orange bracts, and the leaves are a dull green shade and ovate. This species flowers year-round, with the flowers borne either in one to three clusters of three each or in panicles on top of a stalk that develops into a spine. Each flower is connected to a bract. Another frequently grown bougainvillea is *Bougainvillea glabra* Choisy. Like *Bougainvillea × buttiana* Holttum and Standley, *Bougainvillea glabra* Choisy has sharp spines and dull ovate leaves. The bracts of *Bougainvillea glabra* Choisy are magenta. *Bougainvillea glabra* Choisy is occasionally misidentified as *Bougainvillea × buttiana*, but the two plants differ in that the leaf tip of the latter has leaves with a duller upper surface and, rather than the attenuated leaf tip of *Bougainvillea glabra* Choisy, the leaves of *Bougainvillea × buttiana* have an acute tip. *Bougainvillea glabra* and *Bougainvillea × buttiana* can hybridize, leading to greater confusion as to nomenclature.

Cultivation

Bougainvillea can be grown as a shrub, a specimen plant climber, or a climber, though the object the bougainvillea will scramble over must be sufficiently strong to stand the weight of a plant, which may grow to 65 feet tall and therefore weigh a considerable amount. In areas of India, such as Bangalore, bougainvillea is trained to grow into a ground-covering mound. This is achieved by pegging the stems of the plant to the ground as it grows and removing all upward-growing branches. However, this will diminish the colorful impact of the plant as the frequent cutting necessary to achieve the lateral spread removes flowering growth. The dense foliage of both *Bougainvillea × buttiana* and *Bougainvillea glabra* makes both species ideally suited to the creation of topiary shapes.

Bougainvillea prefers full sun and will grow in any soil that is not saturated with water. Once the plant is established, it will form a deep root system and will need very little watering or care in general. Bougainvillea grown in full sun produce the best colors as the plant does not enjoy shade. Bougainvillea can be propagated by budding, by air or ground layering, or from hardwood leafy cuttings of around eight inches in length, the recommended method for *Bougainvillea × buttiana*. Tip cuttings may also be used for the propagation of species such as *Bougainvillea cypheri*. Bougainvillea infrequently bears a single-seed fruit known as an anthocarp. *Bougainvillea glabra* new cultivars and hybrids may be raised from seeds.

Victoria Williams

Further Reading

Mathias, Mildred E., ed. *Flowering Plants in the Landscape.* Berkeley: University of California Press, 1982.

Singh, Gurcharan, and Amitabha Mukhopadhyay. *Floriculture in India.* Mumbai, India: Allied, 2004.

Spencer, Roger. *Horticultural Flora of South-Eastern Australia.* Vol. 2, *Flowering Plants.* Sydney: UNSW Press, 2004.

Tenenbaum, Frances, ed. *Taylor's Encyclopedia of Garden Plants.* New York: Houghton Mifflin, 2003.

Whistler, W. Arthur. *Tropical Ornamentals: A Guide.* Portland, OR: Timber Press, 2000.

Boysenberry

Boysenberry is a large compound fruit species known as *Rubus ursinus* ssp. *idaeus*, whose scientific classification places it in the family Rosaceae (the Rose family) and the genus *Rubus*. The boysenberry is a dark reddish-black fruit that is a cross among the European raspberry (*Rubus idaeus*), the common blackberry (*Rubus fruticosus*), and a loganberry (*Rubus loganobaccus*). It hails from the United States and is chiefly grown along the Pacific Coast, from Southern California to Oregon, but also in the American South and the Southwest.

History of the Boysenberry

The boysenberry grows on a bramble, or prickly shrub, and was first cultivated in California in the 1920s by horticulturist Rudolph Boysen (1895–1955). Boysen, the chief horticulturist and parks superintendent of the city of Anaheim, in Orange County, California, at the time, abandoned his experiments on berry plants and sold his farm. U.S. Department of Agriculture agent George M. Darrow tried to find the origins of Boysen's berry production, and sought the aid of berry expert and local farmer Walter Knott. Knott helped Darrow track down the boysenberry on Boysen's old farm, discovering frail vines in a weed-infested field. The vines were transplanted on Knott's farm, where they were nurtured until they once again produced the fruit that Knott named after its founder, Boysen. In 1935, Knott began selling boysenberries on the Southern California farm he and his wife, Cordelia (Hornaday) Knott, owned. The fruit became a highly requested variety, and Cordelia Knott began turning the boysenberries into preserves, with which she filled pies. The pies were sold at the Knotts' farm, and along with chicken dinners, were the foundation for what became a restaurant and then the current popular amusement park called Knott's Berry Farm in Buena Park, California. Although since sold to another company, Knott's Berry Farm still houses the Knotts' original restaurant, the Chicken Dinner Restaurant.

Description, Appearance, and Nutrition and Medical Benefits

Boysenberry shares its membership in the Rosaceae family with more than 3,400 species of flowering plants, making it one of the largest families of such plants. Several varieties of fruit belong to Rosaceae besides the berry. These include apples, peaches, plums, and cherries. The genus *Rubus* contains 13 subgenera and more than 300 species, most of which have woody stems that contain prickles, spines, and bristles.

The boysenberry's glossy, large, dark, reddish-black or purple fruit is similar in appearance to the blackberry, a fruit it is related to and often classified as. The boysenberry is made up of numerous drupelets, fleshy fruit in which the seed is encased in a single shell. Boysenberries are a slightly tart, juicy fruit that is rich in vitamin C, vitamin A, calcium, iron, fiber, and anthocyanins that work as antioxidants. The antioxidant level of the boysenberry is nearly double that of the blueberry, a fruit known for its high level of antioxidants. A typical serving of boysenberries contains nine grams of sugar and one gram of protein as well as 66 calories, 3 of which are from fat.

Ellagic acid is another compound found in boysenberries that promotes health. It has been found to prevent certain types of cancer by slowing the growth of tumors. For example, in studies ellagic acid has reduced the effect of estrogen on breast cancer cells, and it has been proven to help the liver rid the blood of carcinogens. Ellagic acid as well has been credited with promoting the healing of wounds and decreasing the risk of heart disease.

Boysenberries also contain gallic acid in high concentrations. Gallic acid aids in cancer prevention by inducing cytotoxicity in cancer cells. A study by the University of Colorado in Denver established that oral gallic acid inhibits cancer cell growth, as evidenced in prostate cancer victims, and lowers the incidence of adenocarcinoma.

A 2007 Japanese project found that rats that were fed food containing boysenberries were less likely to develop symptoms of mesothelioma, a disease of the lungs that is induced by exposure to asbestos. The head of the research group at Sagami Women's University in Sagamihara, Kanagawa, Japan, suggested that the polyphenol in boysenberries was responsible for the prevention of mesothelioma in the laboratory rats exposed to asbestos. According to the Oregon Raspberry and Blackberry Commission, boysenberries may also prevent certain illnesses caused by viruses, bacteria, and carcinogens.

Boysenberry's Uses

The berries can be eaten fresh off the vine or can be manufactured into jams and jellies, preserves, pie fillings, syrups, and wine. They are sometimes used in fruit salads or as a decorative edible topping to cheesecakes and tarts. Turned into a fruit sauce, boysenberries are a popular accompaniment to fowl, such as duck and goose. The boysenberry's growing season is relatively short, typically occurring between early July and early August. Its shelf life is also short. The fruit can spoil if left for more than two or three days after picking. Washing ahead of time can shorten the life span of the fruit even more.

Threats to Boysenberries

A common threat to boysenberry harvests is the fungus botrytis, which infects many plants. The fungus thrives in moist conditions and can survive the winter months as sclerotia, evident as small, black lesions, or as mycelia, a thread-like growth, both of which can form on dead or decaying plant matter.

Boysenberry decline is a common term for *Cercosporella rubi*, a plant fungus that causes a disease known as rosette disease. Boysenberry decline can cause a symptom called witch's broom, a plant deformity or disease that changes the structure of the plant, and can cause the production of double blossoms, which can lead to low yields. *Cercosporella rubi* is a problem exclusive to the southeastern United States.

Rosemarie Boucher Leenerts

Further Reading

Knott's Berry Farm. "Historical Background." http://www.knotts.com/public/news/history/index.cfm (accessed 8 December 2010).

Mesothelioma Web. "Boysenberries Seen to Impede Asbestos-Induced Mesothelioma." http://www.mesotheliomaweb.org/boysenrats.htm (accessed 8 December 2010).

Oregon Raspberry and Blackberry Commission. "Boysenberry." http://www.oregon-berries.com/pick-a-berry/boysenberry/ (accessed5July 2012)

Self Nutrition Data. "Boysenberries, Frozen, Unsweetened." http://nutritiondata.self.com/facts/fruits-and-fruit-juices/1856/2 (accessed 8 December 2010).

Breadfruit

The breadfruit tree, *Artocarpus altilis*, is a good representative of a group of plants that have been cultivated since antiquity. Early Polynesian people recognized its importance for providing a source of food and for other uses in everyday life. They brought it with them when they settled the Hawaiian Islands, Asia, and elsewhere in the South Pacific. Breadfruit belongs to the Moracceae family and is identified by the characteristics of fig and mulberry trees. Growing to heights of 60 to 85 feet, a tree's long branches span up to 60 feet. The fruit is harvested just before it ripens and can be cooked immediately or after it is fully ripe. Canoes, tools,

Breadfruit (Rajeshbac/Dreamstime.com)

and other objects were made from the lightweight wood. There were many uses for the sticky sap, a latex substance that oozes from the stem of cut fruit. Although the tree needs plenty of room for spreading roots, it can be easily grown from root cuttings. The cultivation of many different varieties of breadfruit is a result of the need to grow breadfruit in slightly different conditions. Today, nearly 100 varieties can be found growing in the Kahanu Gardens of the National Tropical Botanical Garden of Maui, Hawaii.

The Cultural Significance of Breadfruit Is Seen in Its History

Migrating Polynesians were primarily responsible for introducing the plant to countries throughout the tropics. The Hawaiians believe that breadfruit was first brought to Oahu around 750 to 1200 CE. Europeans were not aware of breadfruit until the early 17th century. English captain William Bligh is credited for sailing to Tahiti on the *Bounty* to collect 1,000 breadfruit seedlings meant for the West Indies as food for slaves. The crew mutinied, however, and some accounts suggest it was partially due to the plants' requiring more water than was available for all. The seedlings, Captain Bligh, and his loyal men were all put off the ship. They survived and eventually returned to Tahiti for more breadfruit. These were planted in the West Indies and did well, but the slaves refused to eat the fruit. Around the same time, the plant was brought to Mexico and Central America. Sources report that both seeded and seedless varieties were popular. In some countries the fruit was considered livestock feed, in others, sustenance for the poor. Today, some cultures still consider breadfruit a daily staple. Others turn to it only in emergency. In still other countries, breadfruit is considered a gourmet item.

Stories are told that corroborate the significance of breadfruit to Hawaii's history, in particular. While taro was considered the major staple in this land, the people also ate breadfruit regularly. *Ulu*, Hawaiian for "fruit," is the name they gave to the breadfruit tree. It is said that traditionally, the *Ulu* is planted at the time of the birth of a child in order to provide a lifetime of food. Legends describe how the plant originated from the war-god, *Kuka'ilimoku*, who married a mortal wife and had children. During a time of hardship and famine, *Kuka'* told his wife that he must leave. He buried himself in the ground where he stood. The tears of his family watered the earth and a healthy breadfruit tree grew from that spot. *Kuka*'s body was the trunk and his arms, the branches. His head was the fruit and he told his wife to feed their children. Thus *Kuka'* saved his family from starvation. A Hawaiian saying goes as follows, "Look for the oozing breadfruit." In other words, "when searching for one to marry, find the one who will be able to feed you."

As the years passed, *Ulu* came to play a significant, nonfood role in daily life. Hawaiians used the wood for many everyday items such as parts for canoes, buildings, furniture, and surfboards. Although the branches were somewhat brittle, the wood itself was lightweight and useful for items such as *poi* boards and drums. The inner bark could be made into the pounded *tapa* cloth, although it was not as desirable as that made from the paper mulberry tree. When the fruit is cut from the tree, it releases a sticky sap used as medicine to relieve diarrhea. The sap was painted on poles as birdlime to attract and trap birds for their colorful feathers. Afterward, the birds were released and the feathers used in ceremonial garments. The rough leaves were often used for the final polishing of bowls and the nuts used in leis. Clearly, the Hawaiian people would need to determine the best growing conditions for a plant that was so predominant and central to their society. As a symbol of this cultivation and to honor the survival of the Hawaiian people, the shape of the breadfruit leaf is found on many special objects throughout the country even today.

The Breadfruit Tree Offers Much to the Land on Which It Grows

Old groves of breadfruit trees are often found at elevation levels below 1,000 feet, planted there by Polynesians as they migrated throughout the tropics. They will grow and fruit, however, year-round, from sea level to over 5,000 feet. They grow best in well-drained, fertile soil but are highly adaptable. Tall, with smooth gray-green bark, the breadfruit tree forms a canopy of long branches covered in large, distinctively shaped leaves. The bright green leaves can be up to three feet long, ruffled, deeply lobed, and leathery. It is common practice to plant one or two trees in a backyard or on a small farm. The breadfruit is an attractive tree, offering shade and food.

Large plantations grow the trees at approximately 25 per acre. Seedless breadfruit are easily propagated by planting sections of root that have sprouted a new shoot or by grafting sections on to *Artocarpus camansi*, the seeded breadfruit, which is almost always started from seed. In general, the cultivated variety is seedless while the wild variety has seeds. The seeds themselves cannot be saved since they germinate immediately or lose viability within a few weeks. They are, however, edible. They can be roasted and taste similar to chestnuts. All parts of the breadfruit, the stems, the leaves, and the unripe fruit, contain a gummy, latex-like sap. The fruit is considered mature enough to pick when drops of the latex sap can be seen on its surface. Breadfruit begins producing in 5 years and is productive for 50 years.

The mature breadfruit tree can produce 200 to 700 fruits per year since it is in season almost continuously. One to three fruits grow at the end of each branch. They have a circular or ellipsoid shape that is actually a syncarp, or compound form, made up of hundreds of small fruits arranged around a core. The results of this can be seen in the thin rind, patterned with a repeating four- to six-faced structure left over from each flower. Depending on the cultivar, the rind may be smooth, rough with a sandpaper-like quality, or prickly, the result of a small spine at the center of each repeating structure. When unripe, the fruit flesh has a starchy texture similar to potato and tastes similar to fresh bread, giving the fruit its name. As it ripens, however, the starch converts to sugar, resulting in a sweet, pulpy consistency. The color of the rind varies with the cultivar, but in general it is green at first, changing to yellowish-brown when ripe. Each weighs around 10 pounds. Breadfruit is usually harvested while it is still firm, two to three days before ripening. Otherwise, the fruit tends to fall from the tree, smashing on the ground.

Eating Preference for Breadfruit Varies among Cultures

It is not surprising that there are as many different ways to enjoy breadfruit as there are countries that grow it. Most breadfruit is not eaten raw because it can have a purgative effect, although there are some cultivars that do not pose this problem. The underripe breadfruit, like other starchy vegetables and fruits such as bananas and plantains, can be steamed, boiled, or roasted. Roasting breadfruit in the Pacific Islands traditionally utilizes a buried oven with hot rocks. Breadfruit is sometimes stuffed with a coconut or mixed with sugar prior to roasting. People of Malaysia often peel the underripe fruit, slice it, roll it in sugar, and fry it. Alternatively, in Hawaii and the Bahamas the green fruit might be chopped with other vegetables, simmered with water until thickened, and made into chowder with the addition of butter, milk, and salted pork.

The ripe breadfruit is considerably sweeter and is often steamed and baked similar to recipes for other fruit. When the pulp is mixed with coconut milk and sugar, it can be made into a pudding or an even more elaborate dessert with the addition of eggs, butter, and flour. People of some countries make candied or pickled breadfruit.

Some unusual or old ways of preparing breadfruit are dependent on the time given to ferment. In Micronesia, the fruit might be soaked in the ocean for hours while being trampled, drained, and buried in leaf-lined boxes for months while the mass ferments. In Samoa, the buried fruits might be left to ferment in pits, covered with leaves and rocks for years, forming a pasty mass known as *masi*. This is eventually dug up, mixed with coconut cream, and baked for hours; it is considered a delicacy.

An adaptable food, breadfruit has also been boiled, pounded, and kneaded into *poi* and eaten as is, or mixed with *poi* made from taro to increase the overall food value. Some cultures partially cook the fruit and then dry it for hours, forming slices or loaves that can be stored. Even "fruit leather" can be made from drying the pulp spread out thinly in the sun and then wrapped in leaves. Nutritionally, breadfruit in any form provides energy in the form of carbohydrates and some protein and fat. It is a great source of dietary fiber, calcium, potassium, and magnesium. Also beneficial are small amounts of thiamin, riboflavin, niacin, and iron.

Diseases and Pests Can Affect Breadfruit

Breadfruit trees are subject to many plant diseases and pests common to the tropics. Before the young trees are planted, the site is prepared by setting fires in the troughs in order to sterilize the soil. The roots are protected from grubs by the addition of insecticides. Once the trees are mature and producing, ants may infest branches that have died back after fruit has been harvested. Ants are also attracted to overripe fruit. Keeping the area around the tree free of fallen ripe fruit and broken branches is a good strategy. Other pests, such as soft-scales and mealybug infestation, require treatment or the health of the tree may diminish. One problem is fungal disease. Depending on the species of fungus, there may be fruit rot or root rot, there may be wilting leaves, branches may die back, or entire trees may succumb to the infection. Farmers have various fungicides available to them but good farming practice can also make a difference.

Breadfruit Symbolizes the Lush Growth and Abundance of the Tropics

The breadfruit tree deserves its name and reputation for providing "bread for the hungry." Native people recognized its significance from early on, spreading the plant from country to country and cultivating it to grow optimally in each new environment. The fruit itself has provided food for many, each community putting its own twist on breadfruit preparation, both sweet and savory. They were resourceful enough to recognize the usefulness of other parts of the plant also, ranging from feeding livestock to making caulking glue for canoes, from medicines to cloth. Modern people are not as dependent on all components of the tree, although undoubtedly there are those who still appreciate and utilize them. The fruit, however, is still recognized for what it offers as a valuable food item, both for people in the southern countries, who still consider breadfruit a staple and for people in the north for which breadfruit is gourmet.

Gwendolyn Vesenka

Further Reading

"*Artocarpus altilis* (Moraceae)." Montoso Gardens. http://www.montosogardens.com/ artocarpus_altilis.htm (accessed 29 July 2011).

Morton, Julia. "Breadfruit," Fruits of Warm Climates. 1987. http://www.hort.purdue .edu/newcrop/morton/breadfruit.html (accessed 29 July 2011).

Schweitzer, Veronica S. "Ulu: The Breadfruit Tree." *Coffee Times*. 2006. coffeetimes .com/ulu.htm (accessed 29 July 2011).

"Ulu." Canoe Plants of Ancient Hawai'i. http://www.canoeplants.com/ulu.html (accessed 29 July 2011).

Brier

Brier is the common name for a widely distributed, yet unrelated, group of thorn-producing, thicket-forming plants, including varieties of the rose genus *Rosa*, which belongs to the rose family Roseaceae, and *Smilax* of the family Smilaca-ceae. The brier-rose is related to the horticultural rose. Brier is the folk name for the wild rose, a plant of economic and nutritional value, which has a rich cultural history. The common brier-rose is the dog-rose, *Rosa canina*, which gained its name from the ancient belief that it could cure those infected by the bite of a wild dog. *Rosa canina* is a hedgerow rose that forms many thorny branchlets from older stems and produces fragrant white or pale pink flowers of up to five petals with yellow stamens. The flowers are followed by distinctive large, plump, orange to red hips. This brier-rose is robust and in the past has been used by rose growers to provide the rootstock on which to graft hybrid roses. The brier-rose itself may be raised from seed or propagated from semiripe hardwood cuttings. *Rosa rubin-ginosa*, known as the sweet-brier or englantine, is also prized for its pink flowers and round hips. *Rosa rubinginosa* also produces fragrant leaves. The hips of both *Rosa canina* and *Rosa rubinginosa* are packed with a multitude of small seeds that are edible and nutritionally very rich. The seeds are an extremely good source of vitamins C and E. Although sour to the taste, when mixed with sugar and cooked; the hips can be used to make syrups and jams. The rich vitamin content of the hips has resulted in brier-rose hips being prepared as waters, liniments, poultices, teas, and brandy to treat a range of conditions from respiratory infections, stomach dis-orders, and joint pain to boils and syphilis. Many references have been made to the brier-rose in literature and art, one of the most striking of which is the *Briar Rose* series of paintings by the English artist Sir Edward Burne-Jones (1833–1898). The paintings are based on the fairy tale "Sleeping Beauty" and show a prince battling through a forest of wild roses to reach a slumbering maiden.

The Genus *Rubus*

The genus *Rubus* is a diverse group consisting of various species and hybrids and 12 subgenera, many of which have hundreds of species. This variety is reflected in the distribution of the genus, which reaches from the Arctic with the Arctic cloudberry, *Rubus chamaemorus*, to the tropics where the Mysore raspberry, *Rubus niveus*, is grown. The plants of the genus include both evergreen and deciduous shrubs, which are most commonly herbaceous perennials and are grown as ornamental plants or as food crops. The genus displays simple leaves that can be pinnate, palmate, or tennate and flowers held singularly or in racemes or panicles. The hypanthium—that is, the part of flower where the petals, sepals, and stamen are fused together, is flat. The nectar-producing flowers of the genus *Rubus* attract bees, are white or pink, and display numerous carpels and stamens. While the flowers of the genus are attractive, the genus is rarely grown for flowers alone. *Rubus spectabilis*, the salmonberry, is an exception for the species produces eye-catching pink flowers and large fruit and so is included in the garden as an ornamental shrub.

However, plants of the genus are grown principally for their fruit, which consists of many single-seeded drupes. Notable species of *Rubus* cultivated for their edible fruit include the raspberry, *Rubus idaeus*, and the blackberry, sometimes referred to as *Rubus eubatus*. Important edible hybrids of the raspberry and blackberry include the loganberry, the boysenberry, and the tayberry. Like the brier-rose, plants of the *Rubus* genus have many uses in traditional medicines. *Rubus coreanus* and *Rubus hirsutus* are used as medicine in China, while *Rubus ursinus* was eaten by Native Americans to treat swellings and sores.

The Genus *Smilax*

Smilax is a genus of aggressive, evergreen or semievergreen, climbing vines equipped with tendrils and renowned for its many thorns. Classical myth tells that the youth Crocus fell in love with the shepherdess Smilax. Unable to wed, the couple prayed to the goddess Flora who transformed the pair into flowers. As plants, Smilax's tendrils allowed her to embrace Crocus. Smilax grows worldwide in tropical, semitropical, and temperate areas, though the exact number of species has yet to be determined as, except for leaf variations, many species appear very similar. Smilax is commonly called catbrier, greenbrier, or sarsaparilla, although the common greenbrier is botanically *Smilax rotundifolia* and the catbrier *Smilax auriculata*. However, both the greenbrier and catbrier are also listed as *Smilax bona-nox*, despite the fact that the berries of *Smilax auriculata* deepen from red to purple, the berries of *Smilax Rotundifolia* are blue-black, and the berries of *Smilax bona-nox* are purely black.

Smilax is often considered a weed. However, some species are cultivated as ornamentals for their attractive fruits, others as a food source or for their medicinal qualities. Sarsaparilla, alone or with sassafras root, is used to make root beer and has a long tradition of use in homeopathic medicine. For instance, sarsaparilla has been used to treat disorders including syphilis, skin infections, and dropsy. Sarsaparilla is thought by some to balance hormones, and, as sarsaparilla may boost circulation in the joints, it may also be used to ease gout and rheumatism.

Victoria Williams

Further Reading

Angier, Bradford. *Field Guide to Medicinal Wild Plants*. Mechanicsburg, PA: Stackpole Books, 1978.

Ellacombe, Henry Nicholson. *The Plant-Lore and Garden-Craft of Shakespeare*. London: Satchell, 1884. http://books.google.co.uk/books?id=pJ6TM8qSwDoC &printsec=copyright#v=onepage&q&f=false (accessed 6 November 2010).

Nelson, Gil. *The Shrubs and Vines of Florida: A Reference and Field Guide*. Sarasota, FL: Pineapple Press, 1996.

Rieger, Mark. *Introduction to Fruit Crops*. Binghamton, NY: Howarth Press, 2006.

Ritachson, Jack. *The Little Herb Encyclopedia*. 3rd ed. Pleasant Grove, UT: Woodland Health Books, 1995.

Stace, Clive. *New Flora of the British Isles*. 2nd ed. Cambridge: Cambridge University Press, 1997.

Ward, Bobby J. *A Contemplation upon Flowers: Garden Plants in Myth and Literature*. Portland, OR: Timber Press, 1999.

Broccoli

A cole crop, broccoli (*Brassica oleracea* ssp. *iltalica*) is of two types. Calabrese yields a single large head. According to one gardener it usually does not need fertilizer. The gardener may plant calabrese between mid-spring and early summer for a summer harvest. Calabrese may also be planted in autumn for harvest next spring. In this case, calabrese must overwinter in a cold frame or greenhouse. Seedlings are unsuitable for transplanting, though the practice apparently continues. Calabrese seeds should be planted three-quarters of an inch deep and one foot apart. Calabrese is grown on Long Island, in western New York, Texas, and the mountains of Colorado, and on the coasts of California and Washington. In addition to these areas, the second type, sprouting broccoli, is grown in the South.

Broccoli (Kartos/Dreamstime.com)

Sprouting broccoli yields several small florets rather than a single head. A late maturer, sprouting broccoli yields florets in winter and the next spring. Sprouting broccoli should be planted in spring. Taking up more room than calabrese, sprouting broccoli plants should be spread two feet apart. When densely planted, broccoli forms small heads. Densely spaced plants produce few side shoots and leaves, requiring less trimming before sale. Sprouting broccoli is hardy enough to overwinter well. The genus *Brassica* derives from the Italian *brocco*, meaning "shoot." Broccoli is known as Italian broccoli or Italian calabrese from the district in southern Italy, Calabria, where it is grown. Broccoli is related to cabbage, Brussels sprouts, cauliflower, and kale. They are all cruciferous vegetables and may provide some lowering of the risk of cancer.

Origin, History, and Cultivation

Broccoli may trace its lineage to a wild cabbage that grew along the coast of Europe. One authority places the origin of broccoli along the coast and islands of the Mediterranean Sea, spreading thereafter as far north as Scotland. This progenitor was a perennial herb. Because the proto-broccoli was bitter, humans selected plants low in glucosinolates, the chemicals that impart bitterness to the plants. The first European text to mention broccoli dates to the 17th century, making it a recent domesticate. About 1925, Italian immigrants introduced broccoli to the United States. The United States grows twice as much broccoli as cauliflower.

California grows most of the crop, which is harvested in the southern Imperial Valley in autumn and winter and north in Salinas in summer. Where the climate is hot, broccoli, which bolts in summer, is harvested in spring and autumn. Broccoli prefers temperatures below 68°F. In addition to the domestic supply, the United States imports broccoli from Mexico. A recent cultigen, broccoli has none of the history of corn, potatoes, soybeans, wheat, sugarcane, and other ancient crops.

Broccoli needs exposure to full sun. The gardener may plant seeds indoors five to six weeks before the last frost. Seedlings may be transplanted in the field three weeks before the last frost because broccoli tolerates light frost. One authority recommends that seedlings be transplanted in the field when four to seven weeks old. Seeds germinate in 3 to 10 days and need temperatures between 70°F and 80°F to germinate. From the date of transplantation in the field, broccoli matures in 55 to 85 days.

Broccoli requires fertile, well-drained soil. It should not be loose but instead packed down to anchor roots. Some gardeners stake broccoli to prevent lodging. Because continuous cultivation may exhaust the soil, broccoli should not be planted in the same plot year after year. The gardener may add a fertilizer with a ratio of 5:10:10 of nitrogen to phosphorus to potassium to the soil. Wood ashes are a suitable amendment because they contain phosphorus. The gardener may apply 53 to 70 pounds of nitrogen per acre at the time of planting with one to three additional dressings during the growing season of 35 pounds of nitrogen per acre. Broccoli benefits from the application of 176 pounds of phosphorus and 176 pounds of potassium per acre. Despite its appetite, broccoli is less ravenous in feeding on soil nutrients than cauliflower. One authority recommends that the soil pH be at least 6.8. Another puts the figure between 6.5 and 7.5. The gardener should not plant broccoli on land where cabbage, kale, or cauliflower has been grown. Broccoli should follow a legume to benefit from residual nitrogen in the soil. In addition to fertilizer, broccoli benefits from the addition of organic matter to the soil. A thirsty crop, broccoli should be watered frequently. Irrigation is desirable on light soil. The gardener may mulch the soil to retain moisture. Broccoli tolerates saline soil.

Broccoli heads are tiny, closely spaced flower buds that must be harvested when large but before the flowers mature. Broccoli spaced at wide intervals is ready to harvest before densely planted broccoli. The central head matures first. When it is harvested, lateral shoots mature. Because most broccoli does not mature uniformly, as many as 10 pickings may be necessary. In some areas, the harvest spreads over two months. Broccoli is typically harvested with six inches of stem.

Consumption, Nutrition, and Preparation
Since the 1970s the consumption of broccoli has increased in North America and Europe. Wherever the consumption of cabbage has decreased, that of broccoli has

risen. One hundred grams of fresh broccoli have 3.3 grams of protein, 0.3 gram of fat, 4.5 grams of carbohydrates, 0.9 gram of fiber, 118 milligrams of vitamin C, 2.1 milligrams of beta carotene, 0.1 milligram of thiamine, 0.2 milligram of riboflavin, 0.1 milligram of niacin, 0.3 to 0.7 milligram of pantothenic acid, 0.03 to 0.08 milligram of folic acid, 0.1 to 0.3 milligram of vitamin B6, 130 to 180 milligrams of calcium, 76 to 90 milligrams of phosphorus, 1.3 milligrams of iron, 50 milligrams of sodium, 410 to 440 milligrams of potassium, 260 to 300 milligrams of sulfur100 milligrams of chlorine, and 20 to 30 milligrams of magnesium. Cooking reduces the content of vitamin C to 29 to 109 milligrams, of beta-carotene to 0.02 milligram, of thiamine to 0.03 to 0.09 milligram, of riboflavin to 0.06 to 0.24 milligram, and of niacin to 0.3 to 0.8 milligram.

Broccoli buds have more vitamin C than do stems. A light frost does not affect the content of vitamin C, but severe frost diminishes it. Broccoli exposed to full sun develops the most vitamin C. Soil deficiency in molybdenum yields broccoli with only half the vitamin C as broccoli raised on molybdenum abundant soil. Broccoli may lose more than half its vitamin C when stored only a few days. Storage at low temperature retards the loss of vitamin C. Buds lose more vitamin C than stems do when frozen or cooked. Cooked in one-quarter cup of water for 10 minutes, broccoli loses about 4 percent of its calcium, 31 percent iron, 6 percent magnesium, 7 percent potassium, 21 percent vitamin C, 11 percent riboflavin, 9 percent niacin, 14 percent pantothenic acid, 26 percent folic acid, and 6 percent vitamin B6. A reduction in the amount of water used in cooking diminishes the loss of vitamins and minerals. When cooked at least one hour, broccoli loses 60–80 percent of its vitamins. Cooked broccoli that is not consumed promptly loses 10–25 percent of its vitamin C. Young broccoli has more beta-carotene than old plants. Stems have little beta-carotene. Frozen broccoli stored more than one year loses 40 percent of its beta-carotene. Salted broccoli loses more than 50 percent of its beta-carotene in three months. Riboflavin content is greatest in broccoli leaves. One scientist recommends that broccoli be cooked one-half to 3 minutes in a pressure cooker, boiled 10 to 20 minutes and steamed 15 to 20 minutes. Broccoli should be cooked until tender. Overcooked broccoli has an unpleasant taste caused by the buildup of sulfur compounds.

Cultivars

Old varieties decline in yield when densely spaced whereas new cultivars may be planted at a density of 100 plants per square yard without diminution in yield. A new cultivar, Atlantic tolerates dense spacing. A dwarf, Atlantic yields a compact head. An early variety, it is suitable for autumn harvest in the northeastern United States. Another early cultivar, Coastal is cultivated in the West. A short, compact plant, Coastal yields uniform heads. Yet another early variety, DeCicco yields abundantly, producing a large number of lateral shoots. DeCicco freezes well.

Another early variety, Spartan Early yields uniform heads in spring and summer. Ideal for freezing, Green Sprouting Medium is a midseason variety grown on the Pacific coast and in the South. It matures too late to be grown in the northeastern United States. Green Sprouting Medium is a large, vigorous plant with a large, compact head. As its name suggests, Green Sprouting Late is a long-season crop grown in California. Grown in the northeastern United States, Waltham 29 has a large, blue green head. Waltham 29 is a large plant that produces heads suitable for freezing. Tolerating hot weather, Green Comet matures 40 days after transplanting.

Christopher Cumo

Further Reading

Buckingham, Alan. *Grow Vegetables*. London: Dorling Kindersley, 2008.

Growing Cauliflower and Broccoli. Washington, D.C.: U.S. Department of Agriculture, 1984.

Klein, Carol. *Grow Your Own Vegetables*. London: Mitchell Beazley, 2007.

Nieuwhof, M. *Cole Crops: Botany, Cultivation and Utilization*. London: L. Hill, 1969.

Parsons, Russ. *How to Pick a Peach: The Search for Flavor from Farm to Table*. Boston: Houghton Mifflin, 2007.

Wien, H. C., ed. *The Physiology of Vegetable Crops*. New York: CAB International, 1997.

Brussels Sprouts

A cole crop, Brussels sprouts (*Brassica oleracea*) are related to cabbage, broccoli, cauliflower, and kale. They are all cruciferous vegetables and have been found to possibly lower the risk of cancer. So strong is the resemblance to cabbage that one gardener likens Brussels sprouts to miniature cabbages. Brussels sprouts contain the vitamins folic acid, K, C, and other antioxidants and fiber.

Origin and History

The progenitor of Brussels sprouts was a perennial herb native to the Mediterranean coast and islands. There it thrived in hot summers and mild winters. From the Atlantic coast of the Mediterranean it migrated north as far as Scotland. During this migration, it adapted to cool summers, and all but a few cultivars do better in cool than hot weather. The exceptions flower without exposure to cold weather, a trait they must share with their warm-adapted ancestor. Early specimens were bitter, leading humans to select plants for the absence of glucosinolates, chemicals that impart bitter flavor. These selections gained adherents in

Belgium, from where they derived the name Brussels sprouts. Their domestication in the 18th century makes them a recent cultigen with none of the history of corn, potatoes, soybeans, sugarcane, and other ancient crops. Only in the 19th century did farmers in northern Europe widely cultivate Brussels sprouts. The coast of the Netherlands, Belgium, Spain, and the United Kingdom provides ideal conditions for Brussels sprouts. Even then they were a minor crop. The United Kingdom is Europe's leading producer, though the harvest totals only 3 percent of the vegetable harvest. In the United States, California is the leading producer with most acreage on the coast between Salinas and Santa Cruz.

Attributes and Cultivation

Brussels sprouts need exposure to full sun. Once seedlings raised indoors, a popular practice among gardeners, are transplanted to the field they require an average of 90 to 100 days to mature. Early varieties mature in 60 to 70 days, midseason cultivars are ready to harvest between 72 and 85 days, and winter sprouts may be picked in 105 days. Plants grow best between 60°F and 70°F. Brussels sprouts plants respond to cold by thickening their stem and enlarging the axillary buds, known as sprouts. These changes occur after a plant has formed roughly 30 leaves. These buds form at the axil of the leaves. The number of buds correlates to the number of nodes that a plant produces. A plant forms nodes until June, so its carrying capacity reaches its maximum then. Roughly half the nodes produce sprouts large enough to harvest, and a plant produces these by mid-July. The other nodes yield sprouts too small to harvest or no sprouts. After September, a plant produces no new nodes.

The growing season must be long if the gardener or farmer hopes to harvest a sizable crop. Because a Brussels sprouts plant is heavy and tall, it may lodge, particularly in windy conditions. For this reason, the farmer should plant seedlings in soil that, if not compact, is firm to allow roots to anchor the plant. Frequent watering causes roots to enlarge, reducing the risk of lodging. As a precaution, some growers stake plants to prevent lodging. Densely spaced plants are susceptible to lodging and disease. Plant size and the number of sprouts decrease. Dense planting, however, confers the benefit of uniform sprouts that may be harvested in a single picking. Varieties meant to be frozen are also uniform and permit one harvest. Widely spaced plants produce large sprouts at the bottom of the stem, with size decreasing at the top. The bottom sprouts ripen first with subsequent sprouts ripening as one moves up the stem. These sprouts may need to be harvested four or five times to ensure that only ripe sprouts are picked at a given time. To encourage sprouts to ripen at the same time, one may remove the top six inches of the plant, a practice known as topping or stopping depending on whom the reader consults. Topping is done one to two months before the harvest, when sprouts are about one-half of an inch in diameter, half their mature size. A plant should be topped, if at all, late in the season to permit the largest number of sprouts to form. Where plants are spaced densely one may top them later than where they are planted at wide intervals. Topping is more common with early than late varieties. Plants may be topped after the first or second picking. Thereafter only one more harvest is necessary. Topping often occurs in September or October. Topping may be done by hand. In the past the farmer used the chemical succinic acid-2,2-dimethylhydrazide to top a plant, but regulators have banned its use. Other chemicals have been tried—gibberellic acid, ethrel, and carbamates—but these are ineffective. One may prod a plant into producing more sprouts by removing the lower branches. The plant will respond by growing taller and yielding more sprouts. Sprouts may be harvested at a leisurely pace because, left on the stem, they remain ripe several months. The only danger is that overripe sprouts may split. One may harvest sprouts by uprooting a plant, allowing them to cling to the stem. Stored in this manner, sprouts may remain ripe as long as three months. Otherwise, one should pick sprouts from the stem, proceeding up the stem where they ripen sequentially or all at once where they ripen uniformly. Brussels sprouts remain in good condition so long that they may be picked from late July to November.

A Brussels sprout is a nonflowering part of the plant. From the point of view of economics, a flowering plant is of little value unless the grower needs seeds. In fact the production of flowers diminishes the quality of the crop. To yield seeds a plant must be exposed to temperatures between 39°F and 50°F for 60 to 80 days, though as we have seen some varieties do not need cold to flower. Once a plant has yielded seeds, they may be planted indoors to lengthen the growing season, transplanting in spring after the last frost. Seeds germinate in 3 to 10 days. Temperatures must be between 68°F and 86°F for germination. Seedlings should be four or five weeks old before being transplanted outdoors. Seeds may also be sown outdoors one-half to three-quarters of an inch deep. The gardener should plant dwarfs 18 inches apart for a yield of small, uniform sprouts. Large varieties should be spread at least two feet apart. Brussels sprouts may be planted in early or midspring for a harvest in late fall and winter. The frosts of autumn and winter improve the flavor of sprouts. In the United Kingdom, growers may plant Brussels sprouts in August or early September, allowing plants to overwinter in the field. Alternatively, sprouts may be planted between February and April for harvest in late July. Another possibility is a planting in May or early June, though the later the planting the greater the risk of low yield.

Before planting, the grower may apply well-rotted manure of a fertilizer in a ratio of 5:10:10 of nitrogen to phosphorus to potassium. Because Brussels sprouts are a heavy feeder of nutrients and water, the grower should enrich the soil with monthly feedings of two teaspoons of fertilizer, compost, or manure per plant. The soil should be mulched to retain moisture. As a rule, early-maturing sprouts are grown on light soil, which may need irrigation, whereas late sprouts are grown on heavy soil. Brussels sprouts tolerate saline soil, though plants will be short. Brussels sprouts tolerate temperatures as low as 14°F. Areas with brief autumns or autumns with high temperatures produce poor sprouts.

The soil pH should be above 6.8 or between 6 and 7.5 depending on who one reads. At low pH, manganese reaches toxic levels and molybdenum is unavailable for absorption. Too much nitrogen reduces the quality of sprouts. Brussels sprouts need 88 to 264 pounds of nitrogen per acre. The farmer may divide nitrogen into three applications with the first at planting, the second some weeks later, and the third after the first or second picking. Brussels sprouts should receive 44 to 132 pounds of phosphorus per acre and more than 176 pounds of potassium per acre with a second application of phosphorus and potassium in autumn.

The variety Purple Red Bull, named for its color, has maroon leaves and dark red sprouts that retain their color during cooking. Sprouts are sweet, though plants are not as vigorous as green varieties. Oliver, a dwarf, grows to 30 inches. Sprouts are small and bright green. Jade Cross E Hybrid yields large, firm, blue-green sprouts for eating fresh or freezing.

After the harvest Brussels sprouts are trimmed for sale, an action that discards as much as 30 percent of a sprout. One writer urges the consumer to buy the smallest sprouts because they are sweetest and require the least cooking. Sprouts may be boiled or steamed but only for seven minutes. Longer cooking causes Brussels sprouts to emit hydrogen sulfide, which has an unpleasant odor. Brussels sprouts produce two times more hydrogen sulfide than broccoli.

Christopher Cumo

Further Reading

Buckingham, Alan. *Grow Vegetables*. London: Dorling Kindersley, 2008.

Klein, Carol. *Grow Your Own Vegetables*. London: Mitchell Beazley, 2007.

Nieuwhof, M. *Cole Crops: Botany, Cultivation and Utilization*. London: L. Hill, 1969.

Parsons, Russ. *How to Pick a Peach: The Search for Flavor from Farm to Table*. Boston: Houghton Mifflin, 2007.

Wien, H. C., ed. *The Physiology of Vegetable Crops*. New York: CAB International, 1997.

Buckwheat

Buckwheat is the common name of several plants in the Polygonaceae family. The genera of this family include *Fagopyrum*, *Erigonum*, and *Fallopia*. *Erigonum* and *Fallopia* are referred to as "wild buckwheat," whereas *Fagopyrum* is "common buckwheat." Despite the name, common buckwheat (*Fagopyrum esculentum* and

Fagopyrum sagittatum in North America) is not related to wheat (*Triticum*), nor is it a cereal or a grass. It instead is a seed that is considered a pseudocereal. It is used in much the same way as cereals, including grinding the seeds into flour, but it is a broadleaf plant unrelated to cereal plants. *Eriogonum* is a common chaparral that grows throughout the western United States. It is especially common in California.

Description

Common buckwheat (*Fagopyrum*), which accounts for 90 percent of the world's production of buckwheat, is a fast-growing, broad-leafed plant that typically begins to produce seed in 6 weeks and ripens at 10 to 11 weeks. Common buckwheat plants grow to about 30 to 50 inches in height. They contain five-petaled flowers, which appear in 25 to 30 days. Plants have a fibrous superficial root and deep taproots.

The optimal climate for growing buckwheat is moist and cool, but it is sensitive to frost, which can kill the crop. If temperatures become too high and the air too dry, flowers may blast forth, preventing seed formation. Buckwheat can grow far north and at various altitudes and enjoys a variety of soil types. It grows well in infertile, poorly drained soils as long as the climate is moist and cool. Germination occurs at temperatures of 45°F to 105°F. One cup of buckwheat seeds, about 170 grams, contains only 154 calories, 34 percent of the recommended daily allowance of manganese, 25 percent of the amino acid tryptophan, 21.4 percent of magnesium, 18.1 percent of fiber, and 12.5 percent of copper. Buckwheat lowers insulin and glucose in the body and may protect against diabetes.

History

Buckwheat has been grown in North America since colonial times. It was a common crop on farms of the northeast and north-central states. Peak U.S. production occurred in the mid-19th century, when the crop was used primarily as livestock feed and in the production of flour. One century later the crop was grown on only 50,000 acres of U.S. land, with the leading producers being New York and Pennsylvania in the East and Michigan, Minnesota, Wisconsin, and North Dakota in the upper Midwest. Today, Canada grows more buckwheat than the United States. Buckwheat gained a resurgence in popularity in the mid-1970s in step with the rising demand for commercially prepared breakfast cereals. Buckwheat was also shipped to Japan at this time to be used in the production of buckwheat noodles. The upsurge in buckwheat's popularity coincided with the release of statistics compiled by the U.S. Department of Agriculture's Agricultural Research Service that claimed that the amino acid composition in buckwheat made it superior in nutritional value to all types of cereal, including wheat and oats. This information boosted sales of the product. At the beginning of the 20th century, Russia was the world's leader in buckwheat production, where 6.5 million acres of land was devoted to growing the crop. China took over as the world's production leader until 2005, when Russia again resumed the title.

Buckwheat Fit for Human and Animal Consumption

Prior to the 1970s, about 75 percent of buckwheat was turned into livestock and poultry feed. Today, the predominant use of buckwheat seeds is to feed humans. It is mainly turned into flour. One hundred pounds of dry buckwheat yield 60 to 75 pounds of flour. This flour is commonly marketed in the form of pancake mixes, which is often a combination of buckwheat and other grains such as oats, corn, rice, and wheat. Some of the seeds are sold as groats, the part of the seed that remains after the hulls are removed from the kernels. The groats are turned into breakfast foods and porridge or are used to thicken soups, gravies, and dressings. The shelf life of buckwheat and products made from it short, especially in summer due to its high fat content. Buckwheat and its by-products should be eaten promptly to prevent the food from becoming rancid.

When ground and mixed with grains, such as corn, oats, or barley, buckwheat is a good source of nutrition for livestock. However, when offered as the sole grain, buckwheat has been known to cause skin rashes in animals and humans. These rashes appear only in the hide covered with white hair or fur, and they are evident only when the animal is exposed to light. Buckwheat hulls are the catalyst for the rash.

Buckwheat middlings are considered a good source of feed for cattle due to their richness in protein, fat, and minerals, and poultry feed is often made from tartary buckwheat, also known as golden buckwheat (*Fagopyrum tataricum*). This grain has a smaller, rounder seed than common buckwheat, making it easier for poultry to eat and digest. For humans, tartary buckwheat is considered a good source in fighting what is sometimes termed the "three deadly highs": high blood pressure, high blood sugar, and high triglyceride levels. Buckwheat hulls have little or no nutritional value, although they do contain the majority of fiber of the seed. Hulls are used as soil mulch and as pillow stuffing. The seed itself is sold as an ingredient in birdseed mixes.

Along with buckwheat's value as a grain, it is also valuable when used in honey production. The blooming period of buckwheat's flowers is long and extends into September, when many other flowers and sources of nectar are limited. Honey from buckwheat is dark and strongly flavored. At one time in the northeastern United States, buckwheat honey was in high demand, so much so that demand exceeded supply. Today, however, buckwheat has declined as a crop and therefore as a source of honey.

Other Uses of Buckwheat

Buckwheat is sometimes used as a smother crop, to control weeds. Its rapid growth and dense leaf canopy provide shade for the soil and inhibit weed growth.

Used in this way, buckwheat has been known to eradicate such weeds as Canada thistle, quackgrass, sowthistle, creeping jenny, leafy spurge, and other perennial grasses. Buckwheat is also used as a green manure crop. It can produce as much as three tons of dry matter per acre in just six to eight weeks. The plant material decays rapidly and soon provides nitrogen and other minerals for the primary crop.

Rosemarie Boucher Leenerts

Further Reading

"Nutrition Facts: Buckwheat." http://nutritiondata.self.com/facts/cereal-grains-and -pasta/5681/2 (accessed 6 July 2012).

Oplinger, E. S., E. A. Oelke, M. A. Brinkman, and K. A. Kelling. "Buckwheat." Alternative Field Crops Manual. 1989. http://www.hort.purdue.edu/newcrop/afcm/buckwheat .html (accessed 9 June 2011).

Butterbur

With its magnificent leaves, pink butterbur draws attention where it is found growing in parks and gardens. This perennial plant blooms early in the spring—in February and March—before its leaves come out, hence its local name Son before the Father in Scotland. The pink flowers are somewhat unusual in shape, with several inflorescences clustered on a stem that grows up to 15.75 inches long. For the most part, nowadays, butterbur serves as an ornamental plant in connection with ponds and watercourses. In earlier times, however, it was grown first and foremost for medicinal and ethnoveterinary purposes. It had a variety of other uses too for earlier generations, among other things on account of its extremely large round leaves. These have a diameter of 15.75 to 39.37 inches, and they grow on stout stems between 23.6 and 47.5 inches tall.

Butterbur is a common cultivated plant in many European countries. It also grows naturalized in much of Europe, as well as in many parts of the eastern United States. It is considered an invasive plant and spreads mainly by vegetative reproduction from fragments of the rhizome Not everyone has viewed it with favor, among other things because its roots spread widely and are almost impossible to eradicate. Its appearance and its weed-like traits have earned it some less-than-flattering names, such as Dog Rhubarb and Gipsy's Rhubarb in the English county of Somerset, and Snake's Rhubarb in Dorset.

Origin and Cultivation

Butterbur originated, botanists believe, in Southern and Central Europe, in western Siberia, and in the Caucasus Mountains. Several writers of antiquity cited its value as a medicinal herb. It has probably been cultivated at least since the Middle Ages.

Male plants are dominating in many places like Scandinavia and the United Kingdom. These are thought to be clones from deliberately planted specimens, which are supposed to have been introduced in order to provide nectar for domestic bees. Because of the early flowering, many butterbur plants were sown near beehives in antiquity. Because of its large leaves and great capacity to spread, cultivators kept it separate from herbs and vegetables. In southern Sweden, it was often grown close to the village pond. This seems to have been the case in many parts of Europe.

Medicinal Plant

The rhizomes of the plant contains two active ingredients: petasin and isopetasin. Greek physician Dioscorides (ca. 40–90 CE) stressed the plant's medicinal value. If ground up and then smeared on the skin, for example, it could help to ease malignancies and other diseases. Medieval physicians prescribed it for gout.

In olden times, butterbur was known as Pestilence Wort: in German *Pestwurtz*, in Danish *Pestilensrod*, in Swedish *Pestrot*, in Estonian *katkujuur*. The common assumption, accordingly, is that it was used against plague. Although this is a widespread belief, the first report to this effect is found only in a work from 1530, by the German physician Hieronymus Bock. The claim is then repeated in later handbooks of medicine. According to British herbalist John Gerard's *Herball* (1597), for instance, the dried powdered root of butterbur, mixed with wine, furnished a superior medicine against the plague and pestilent fevers.

Some European pharmacopeias commended the use of the highly aromatic rootstock for diaphoretic purposes in connection with chest diseases, fevers, gout, and epilepsy and for external application on boils and skin ulcers. Manuals on the gathering of medicinal herbs instructed that the root was to be harvested late in autumn or early in spring. Butterbur also figured in traditional medicine in many areas. Sources from Central Europe cite its use as an expectorant and for the relief of insect stings. In England, a cream made from it was applied to skin blemishes and sores.

More recently, experiments have shown that the rhizomes contain ingredients that can help reduce the frequency and severity of migraine symptoms. Extracts of the root are available within alternative medicine for this purpose, while extract of butterbur leaf is said to work as an antihistamine in reducing allergy symptoms. German companies are therefore buying roots and leaves from various parts of Europe in order to produce herbal medicine.

For Treating Animal Diseases

Prior to the turn of the 20th century, farmers in Northern Europe appear to have used butterbur mainly for ethnoveterinary purposes. Thanks to a study by the amateur botanist Gösta Ilien, we now have detailed documentation about the role played by butterbur in popular botany in southern Sweden during preindustrial times. Ilien found that, in many cases, it was in connection with pig breeding that butterbur was grown on Scanian farmsteads. It was thus in the vicinity of the hog pen that it often grew most profusely. Many of the plantings could be dated to the 18th and 19th centuries. Farmers used the leaves, according to Ilien's informants, for prophylactic purposes in connection with pig raising. They cut up the leaves and stems, blended in some grits, and fed the resulting mixture to the pigs. Other sources explained that the farmers boiled the roots, and used the resulting solution to treat erysipelas, a contagious and malignant bacterial infection that is found among pigs, and that is caused by the bacterium *Erysipelothrix rhusiopathiae*. The same use is also known from Denmark.

Finally, in many parts of Europe, the root was used to combat lung and liver diseases in horses.

For Use as a Fodder

Butterbur has also served as a livestock fodder, particularly during spring. Farmers in Northern Europe believed it encouraged the production of milk, and so planted it in horse and cattle pastures. It probably served as an important fodder in an era when the underfeeding of stabled livestock during winter was common. As late as in the 1940s, in fact, farmers in some parts of southern Sweden continued to use the leaves as a stable feed for their cows. According to reports, the effect was a rapid increase in the milk yield and without any alteration in the flavor of the milk.

The leaves were also used as a fodder for the pigs, to the satisfaction of the latter. Around midsummer, farmers in some parts of southern Sweden made hay by harvesting the leaves of the plant together with meadow grass. Butterbur has also served as a fodder elsewhere in Northern Europe. In some parts of Italy, its fresh leaves are still used as fodder for hens.

Butterbur can also be utilized as human food. In Turkey, the peasants still grind and boil the petioles, which are cooked like a vegetable meal.

Attributes

Many Europeans believed that butterbur conducts lightning. This is reflected in several folk names given to the plant: thunderdock in England, *tordenskræppe* in Denmark, and *tordönskräppa* in southern Sweden. It was observed in the late 19th century that household servants in Scania would place butterbur leaves in the eaves of buildings on Midsummer's Eve, in the hope of ensuring that lightning would not strike there. There are also reports that, even as late as the 19th century, village folk would plant butterbur in order to keep evil spirits away.

Furthermore, butterbur is not merely decorative, nor is it useful just as animal feed. In the 18th century, Swedish naturalist Carl Linnaeus noted that chickens found protection under the large leaves of this plant from rain and from birds of prey. Observers from a variety of countries found that free-running chickens, turkeys, domestic ducks, and the like sought protection under butterbur leaves when it rained. The name butterbur—recorded for the first time by Wilhelm Turner in the mid-1500s—comes from the use made of its leaves for wrapping bars of butter.

The leaves also served as a kind of toy. Reports from Scandinavia and the Balkans tell of children using them "as umbrellas." Indeed, butterbur has been known in some parts of the United Kingdom, in Somerset for example, as the umbrella plant. Gerard claimed in 1598 that the leaves were large enough "to keepe a man's head from raine, and from the heate of the sunne." In Catalan and Portuguese, butterbur is known as *sombrera* and *sombreiro* respectively, meaning "hat." Indeed, the Greek word that Dioscorides used for it was *petasides*, which derives from a kind of wide-brimmed hat known as a petasos.

Ingvar Svanberg

Further Reading

Chizzola, Remegius, Bernhard Ozelsberger, and Theodor Langer. "Variability in Chemical Constituents in *Petasites hybridus* from Austria." *Biochemical Systematics and Ecology* 28 (2000): 421–32.

Lipton, R. B., H. Göbel, K. M. Einhäupl, K. Wilks, and A. Mauskop. "*Petasites hybridus* Root (Butterbur) Is an Effective Preventive Treatment for Migraine." *Neurology* 64 (2004): 2240–44.

Butterwort

A carnivorous plant, the butterwort is in the genus *Pinguicula*, Latin for "little greasy one." The name derives from the greasy texture of the leaves. Some people have likened this texture to the slipperiness of melted butter, a circumstance that gave rise to the name butterwort. Before scientists understood its carnivorous habit, the people of Northern Europe rubbed butterwort leaves on the wounds of cattle. This treatment was effective because butterwort leaves produce an antiseptic secretion. Others used the leaves to curdle goat's milk into cheese. Norwegians used the leaves to make a thick milk. One tradition hold that a girl who puts butterwort leaves beneath her pillow will dream of her future husband.

Carnivorous Habit

No one apparently appreciated that the butterwort was a carnivore until the 19th century. In the early 1870s, W. Marshall—his first name and occupation may be lost to history—noticed a butterwort whose leaves were covered with insects. He informed British naturalist Charles Darwin of this find. In 1875,

Darwin amassed the evidence that the butterwort and several other species of plants were carnivores. Journalists and religious leaders mocked Darwin for this conclusion. Objections to the idea that plants may be carnivores go back at least to the 18th century, when Swedish naturalist Carl Linnaeus took up the crusade against this heresy.

For more than a century, the carnivorous habit of the butterwort has fascinated scientists. The leaves appear unremarkable to the casual observer, but close inspection reveals that glands cover them. Many of the glands support short hairs atop, which are globules of mucilage. Sunlight makes the mucilage sparkle, and this effect may attract insects. Moreover, the leaves emit an earthy aroma, which may attract insects. It is also possible that insects perceive the leaves as landing pads. Whatever the reason, an insect that alights on a leaf finds itself stuck in mucilage, which is an adhesive. The butterwort therefore functions as flypaper, though it has the capacity to digest insects whereas flypaper is a passive trap. As an insect struggles to free itself, it contacts other hairs and becomes entangled in a film of mucilage. An insect may struggle so violently that it loses a leg, but its efforts are usually futile. Covered in mucilage, an insect drowns or suffocates, though hours may elapse before death conquers the suffering arthropod.

As soon as an insect is caught, the sessile glands, which are inactive when a leaf is bereft of prey, begin to secrete digestive juices, which contain acids and enzymes and which liquefy the innards of an insect. The glands produce copious amounts of these juices, and they might run off a leaf but for the fact that the leaves of temperate species curl to prevent the loss of juices. Curiously, the leaves of tropical bladderworts do not move. In hours or at most days, the digestive juices accomplish their task. The sessile glands absorb the liquefied insect, leaving only the exoskeleton, which may remain adhered to the mucilage. The exoskeleton may break apart, or wind or rain may remove it. Because butterwort leaves are small, they trap tiny insects: gnats, springtails, and fruit flies. A springtail may succumb after contacting just two hairs on a leaf. Large, strong insects may break free, though butterworts have captured flies and craneflies. One specimen even captured a praying mantis.

Diversity of Species

Butterworts inhabit a range of ecosystems. They grow as far north as the Arctic Circle and may be found in North America, Central and South America, Europe, Asia, and Africa. Species native to the tropics produce flowers as striking as those of orchids and African violets. Flowering in spring, they yield one bloom per stalk. In the arid lands of Mexico, they grow alongside cacti. In parts of the Northern Hemisphere, they may be found with the sundew and pitcher plant. Tropical butterworts are most diverse in Mexico, Central America, and the Caribbean. More species of butterwort grow in Mexico than anywhere else. In the dry season, tropical butterworts are not carnivorous, producing leaves that do not capture insects. Some species grow at elevation, enduring chilly nights during winter and hot, wet summers. Flowering over several months, the tropical *Pinguicula morenesis* blooms twice per year, issuing forth pink or white flowers. The plant flowers in winter and spring and again in late summer. *Pinguicula esseriana*, despite its tropical habit, tolerates frost. *Pinguicula heterophylla* and *Pinguicula macrophylla* are dormant during the dry season. *Pinguicula filifolia*, native to western Cuba, grows in sandy soil near lagoons, yielding white, blue, purple, or lilac flowers. *Pinguicula albido*, *Pinguicula jackii*, and *Pinguicula lignicola* also inhabit Cuba. An epiphyte *Pinguicula lignicola* grows in trees and bushes. *Pinguicula cladophila* is native to Haiti.

Temperate butterworts survive cold winters by dying down to buds known as hibernacula, meaning "hibernate." They may lose their roots during winter, allowing flowing water to move them. The movement of temperate butterworts in this way may account for their diverse geography. Dormant in winter, temperate butterworts resume growth in spring. They flower in spring, yielding purple, violet, or white flowers. Growing in wet, acidic peat in North America and Europe, they may be found with ferns. Along with the pitcher plant, temperate butterworts inhabit rocky soil near the Great Lakes. Some temperate species grow in neutral or alkaline soil. They do well in full sunlight, though planted near grasses and ferns, the latter will shade them.

The temperate butterwort *Pinguicula vulgaris* is renowned as the species Darwin studied. It grows in North America, Europe, and Northern Asia. Preferring rocky soil, it grows near lakes in acidic or basic soil. *Pinguicula macraceras* inhabits the western United States, Canada, Japan, and Russia. One subspecies may be found with the *Darlingtonia* pitcher plant in the Pacific Northwest. *Pinguicula grandiflora* inhabits the hilly regions of Ireland, France, Switzerland, and Spain. *Pinguicula alpina* grows in the mountains of Europe and in Scandinavia and Scotland. The rare *Pinguicula remosa* is an indigene of northern Japan. Nearly extinct in the wild, only two colonies remain. Cultivation may be the only way of perpetuating this species. Perhaps because it is so rare, the Japanese have memorialized it on a postage stamp. *Pinguicula villosa* inhabits the Arctic regions of Asia, Northern Europe, and North America.

Some temperate species, dubbed "warm temperate butterworts" by one gardener, are accustomed to warm weather, surviving in the subtropics. They tolerate frost, but a hard freeze may kill them. Preferring wet, acidic soil, several of these species inhabit the American Southeast with the pitcher plant, the sundew, Venus's Fly Trap, and the bladderwort. A bog plant, *Pinguicula coerulea*, known as the violet butterwort, inhabits the southeastern United States from North Carolina to Florida. *Pinguicula primuliflora* and *Pinguicula plenifolia* grow from the Florida panhandle to Louisiana. Growing in wet peat or sphagnum, *Pinguicula primuli-flora* inhabits land near streams and ponds. Native to the American South, *Pinguicula pumila* grows from the Carolinas south to Florida and west to Texas. *Pinguicula lusitanica* grows in wet peat in Britain, Spain, and northwestern Africa.

Cultivation

Temperate butterworts prefer a soil of two parts peat, one part sand, and one part perlite. Warm temperate species should be given a soil of equal parts peat and sand. Tropical butterworts like a mixture of sand, perlite, vermiculite, and peat. To these ingredients one may add dolomite, gypsum, lava rock, and pumice. Temperate and warm temperate plants may be potted with the pot placed in a saucer of water. In addition to this method of watering, the gardener should wet the soil by pouring a container of water on it. Cool water is best. Tropical butterworts should also receive water from a saucer and a container in summer and autumn, but they should have less water in winter. *Pinguicula gypsicola*, *Pinguicula heterophylla*, and *Pinguicula macrophylla* must have a dry soil in winter. Cuban species should be kept wet year-round with slightly less water in winter. All butterworts relish abundant sunshine. *Pinguicula morenensis* is among the most popular species in cultivation and may be grown by a sunny window, in a greenhouse, or in a terrarium. Warm-temperate butterworts do well in a greenhouse with or without heat. In cultivation, *Pinguicula lusitanica* may be found in greenhouses with or without heat, terrariums, a sunny window, or a bog garden outdoors. Most temperate plants do poorly indoors unless kept in a greenhouse. The gardener may feed indoor plants fruit flies, small ants, and dried insects. Butterworts bereft of insects may receive fertilizer. Temperate species may be sprayed periodically with dilute fertilizer. Tropical butterworts should be sprayed twice per month with fertilizer at one-quarter strength. The gardener should confine fertilizer to the leaves because it may discolor flowers.

Christopher Cumo

Further Reading

Barthlott, Wilhelm, Stefan Porembski, Ruediger Seine, and Inge Theisen. *The Curious World of Carnivorous Plants: A Comprehensive Guide to Their Biology and Cultivation.* Portland, OR: Timber Press, 2007.

Camilleri, Tony. *Carnivorous Plants.* Sydney: Kangaroo Press, 1998.

D'Amato, Peter. *The Savage Garden: Cultivating Carnivorous Plants.* Berkeley, CA: Ten Speed Press, 1998.

Lecoufle, Marcel. *Carnivorous Plants: Care and Cultivation.* London: Blandford, 1989.

Pietropaolo, James, and Patricia Pietropaolo. *Carnivorous Plants of the World.* Portland, OR: Timber Press, 1986.

Rice, Barry A. *Growing Carnivorous Plants*. Portland, OR: Timber Press, 2006.

Schnell, Donald E. *Carnivorous Plants of the United States and Canada*. Winston-Salem, NC: John F. Blair, 1976.

Slack, Adrian. *Carnivorous Plants*. Cambridge, MA: MIT Press, 1979.

Temple, Paul. *Carnivorous Plants*. London: Royal Horticultural Society, 1993.

C

Cabbage

A member of the Cruciferae family, cabbage is of two species, common cabbage (*Brassica oleracea*) and Chinese cabbage (*Brassica rapa* ssp. *pekinensis* and *Brassica rapa* ssp. *chinensis*). Common cabbage is of three types, white, savoy, and red. The word "cabbage" is *kappes* in German, *kappertjes* in Dutch, *cabut* in French, *apuccio* in Italian, *keposta* in Slavic, and *cabaiste* in Irish. A cole crop, which is any member of the Cruciferae family, cabbage is related to Brussels sprouts, broccoli, cauliflower, kale, and kohlrabi. Cabbage is the most widely grown cole crop.

Common Cabbage

Wild species of cabbage are native to the Mediterranean Basin, leading to the inference that humans may have first cultivated cabbage in this region. The ancient Egyptians and Hebrews did not cultivate cabbage, though the plant was known in classical Greece. In the fourth century BCE, Greek philosopher Aristotle and his pupil and botanist Theophrastus were familiar with cabbage. In the second century BCE, Roman agricultural writer Cato the Elder and first-century CE Roman agricultural writer Columella mentioned cabbage. Columella's contemporary, Roman encyclopedist Pliny the Elder, listed several varieties: Pompeii cabbage, Sabellian cabbage, Lacuturna cabbage, Tritian cabbage, Bruttioim cabbage, Cumae cabbage, and Le Riccia cabbage. The ancients grew cabbage primarily as a medicine. They believed the consumption of cabbage was useful to treat gout, diarrhea, colic, stomachache, headache, and curiously deafness. The ancients drank cabbage juice to counteract the effect of poison mushrooms and to cure hoarseness and hangover.

In the Middle Ages, cabbage spread from the Mediterranean Basin to Europe. In the ninth century Frankish king Charlemagne cultivated it in his garden. The Arabs were familiar with a type of cabbage that they called Spanish cabbage. The monks in Europe grew cabbage for their own sustenance. The fact that Europeans grew cabbage for food suggests that it was no longer primarily a medicine. Medieval peasants preferred white cabbage, though the herbals of the 16th century also mentioned savoy and red cabbage. The fact that people in the early modern era called vegetable gardens cabbage gardens suggests that the crop must have been a staple. Europeans made white cabbage into sauerkraut, and Captain James

Cook, recognizing its value in preventing scurvy, issued it to his sailors in the 18th century. So important was the use of cabbage against scurvy that Great Britain funded the making of sauerkraut to supply sailors. In the 18th century, Europeans grew several varieties: York, Brunswick, Strasbourg, Ulm, Ambervilliers, de Bonnenil, and Saint Denis. Curiously, Pliny's varieties appear not to have made the list.

By the 20th century, farmers grew cabbage in virtually every country, cultivating it as far north as the Arctic Circle. In Eastern Europe, cabbage totaled roughly one-third of vegetable crops. Yet the consumption of cabbage has declined where incomes have risen. Worldwide, consumers prefer white cabbage. Savoy and red cabbage area confined to Europe. Cabbage does well in most soil as long as it has enough water. The later the maturity of cabbage the heavier the soil should be to retain water. Nevertheless, the soil should drain well. Tolerant of slightly acidic soil, cabbage grows best in a soil with a pH between 6 and 6.5. Tolerant of moderate salinity, cabbage is nonetheless susceptible to diseases in soil that contains too much salt. Farmers may rotate cabbage with several crops, thought it may absorb so much water that it is in shortage for the following crop. The roots grow laterally so that 70–80 percent is in the upper 20 to 30 centimeters of soil. After one to two months of growth, roots penetrate more deeply. Cabbage responds to a dearth of water by sending roots deep into the soil. Because cabbage consumes large quantities of water, the provision of water through rainfall or irrigation is important. The more mature a cabbage plant the greater is its consumption of water.

In temperate locales, cabbage is biennial, producing vegetative growth in its first year and seeding in the second. Above 57°F, cabbage grows vegetatively and beneath this temperature it seeds. Temperatures between 59°F and 68°F are best for vegetative growth. Cabbage will not grow above 77°F, though young plants are more tolerant of high temperatures than mature plants. A crop may begin to grow just above 32°F. It can endure temperatures as low as 14°F. Below this temperature, it suffers frost damage.

Cabbage is not an ideal crop where winter temperatures fall below 32°F. Instead, it may be grown year-round in areas with mild winters and cool summers. In the United States, farmers grow cabbage year-round with a winter and spring harvest in the South and a summer and autumn harvest in the North. Commercial growers often sow seeds in a seedbed, transplanting young plants in the field. Although, as we have seen, seeds will germinate above 32°F, they germinate at higher temperatures quicker. Whereas plants germinate in 14 days at 50°F, they germinate in 7 days with temperatures above 68°F. The farmer may transplant cabbage 4 to 10 weeks after germination. Excessive nitrogen may injure young plants, though applications of phosphorus and potassium may be beneficial. One authority recommends the application of 264 to 528 pounds per acre of superphosphate as a source of phosphorus and 264 to 528 pounds per acre of muriate of potash or potassium sulfate as a source of potassium. By 1969, cabbage yielded 10 to 100 metric tons per hectare. The largest white cabbages produced heads that weighed more than 10 kilograms. White cabbage yielded more than savoy and red cabbage. The latter two produced 10 to 40 metric tons per hectare.

Popular in the 1990s and again in recent years, the cabbage soup diet promises to help the overweight shed 10 pounds in only one week. One version of the diet promised a loss of 17 pounds per week. The diet works because one cup of shredded cabbage contains only 17 calories. The body must burn more calories in chewing and digesting cabbage than it derives from the vegetable. The centerpiece of the diet is a soup of cabbage, carrots, red pepper, onion, celery, and tomato, which the dieter may eat in unlimited quantities. The diet is so hard on the body that its proponents counsel the dieter to discontinue the regimen after one week, resuming it only after consuming a normal diet for at least two weeks.

In 2008, China was the leading producer of cabbage. India ranked second, Russia third, South Korea fourth, and Japan fifth. Not a leading producer, the United States ranked ninth.

One cup of cabbage contains 91 percent of the recommended daily allowance of vitamin K and 50 percent of vitamin C. Cabbage also has fiber, manganese, vitamin B6, folic acid, thiamine, riboflavin, beta-carotene, calcium, potassium, tryptophan, magnesium, and protein. Cabbage may protect one against cancer.

Chinese Cabbage

As its name suggests, Chinese cabbage likely originated in China. A Chinese text mentions the cultivation of cabbage in the fifth century BCE. One authority believes that Chinese cabbage arose from a chance cross between pak-choi and turnip. In the second half of the 20th century, China rapidly expanded the production of Chinese cabbage. In China, Chinese cabbage is the most widely grown vegetable. In northern China, people derive one-fourth of their vegetables from Chinese cabbage. In northern China, Chinese cabbage totaled 80 percent of vegetable consumption in the winter and spring, when other vegetables are in shortage. In southern China, Chinese cabbage trails only pak-choi as a vegetable. In recent years, Chinese cabbage has spread to Inner Mongolia, Sikiong Uighur, the plateau of Chianghai Province, and Tibet. The Chinese grow thousands of cultivars.

In the 13th century Korea, having imported Chinese cabbage from China, began cultivating it, first as a medicine. In 1527, a Korean text mentioned Chinese cabbage among 43 vegetables, evidence that the crop had made the transition from medicine to food. In Korea Chinese cabbage was first a food of the elites. For centuries, Koreans have used Chinese cabbage to make kimchi, the national dish. Kimchi contains Chinese cabbage, radish, leek, red pepper, garlic, ginger, fish, and salt. In Korea, Chinese cabbage is the leading vegetable in production and consumption.

In 1866 the Japanese, having imported Chinese cabbage from China, began to cultivate it. In 1905, Japanese soldiers returning from China brought Chinese cabbage seeds. After 1910, Japanese scientists began breeding new varieties. Although the Japanese have access to more than 300 varieties, they grow only a small number of them. Farmers cultivate Chinese cabbage between 30° and 46° north in Japan, where scientists have bred varieties for each latitude. Year-round demand for Chinese cabbage has prodded breeders to develop new varieties. Because diseases may be severe in Japan, scientists have labored to breed-resistant cultivars. In summer, farmers grow Chinese cabbage in the highlands of Japan. Japanese farmers grew most Chinese cabbage in autumn. In 1980, Japan produced more than 1.7 million tons at a yield of 16 tons per acre. In area, Chinese cabbage ranks third behind radish and common cabbage in Japan. The Japanese grow Chinese cabbage in the prefectures of Ibaragi, Nagano, Aichi, Hokkaido, Gunma, and Hyogo. As the demand has increased, farmers have aimed for an early harvest to get Chinese cabbage to market when the supply is low and price high. In Japan, farmers lime the soil, adding compost and fertilizer before planting their crop. One authority recommends the application of 220 to 264 pounds of nitrogen per acre, 132 to 176 pounds of phosphorus per acre, and 220 to 264 pounds of potassium per acre. Volcanic soil may require more phosphorus. The farmer may add a side dressing of 26 pounds of nitrogen per acre and 26 pounds of potassium per acre after thinning plants and again when Chinese cabbage heads. In Japan, Chinese cabbage trails only the radish among vegetables.

Native to East Asia, Chinese cabbage is today grown in China, Korea, Japan, Bangladesh, Taiwan, Central America, West Africa, the United States, Canada, and Europe. Because Chinese cabbage does poorly in excessive heat, it is grown during cool weather and in the highlands of Southeast Asia. In Asia, small farmers grow Chinese cabbage as a cash crop. Chinese cabbage contains fiber, vitamin C, and calcium.

Diseases and Pests

The fungal disease yellows threatened cabbage from Long Island, New York, to Colorado. Prevalent in warm climates, yellows was the most severe cabbage disease in New Jersey, Maryland, Ohio, Indiana, Illinois, Wisconsin, and Iowa. Infected cabbage display symptoms two to four weeks after transplantation. Fungi spread from the base to the top of a plant, turning leaves yellow-green. As a plant ages, the yellow leaves turn brown and die. Death ensues two weeks after the onset of symptoms. The causal organism, *Fusarium oxysporum*, is related to the *Fusarium* fungi, which cause disease in cotton, tomato, watermelon, cowpea, and pea. Fungi multiply in the soil. Once established, the disease is difficult to eradicate. Having colonized the soil, fungi enter cabbage roots. Fungi are inactive in soil below 60°F and above 90°F. Crop rotation is ineffective against *Fusarium* because fungi remain in the soil no matter what crop is grown. Resistant cultivars are the best defense, and as early as 1940 the Wisconsin Agricultural Experiment Station released the cultivar Wisconsin Golden Acre. The name derived from Golden Acre, a popular variety in the United States since 1923.

A second fungal disease, blackleg, is known as dry rot. Symptoms emerge two to three weeks before transplantation, when leaves and stems betray spots. Fungi destroy roots so that cabbage, deprived of anchorage, topples over from the weight of its head. Other plants, unable to extract nutrients and water from soil, wilt. The causative agent, *Phama lingam*, may accrue on cabbage seeds and in this way infect the next generation. Fungi can survive as long as two years on plant debris. They spread in wet weather. Crop rotation may be effective provided the farmers allows two to three years to elapse between cabbage plantings.

The bacterium *Xanthomones campestris* causes the disease black rot. As the name suggests, the disease blackens cabbage leaves and stems. Infected leaves may fall from the plant. The bacterium dwarfs young plants. In some cases infected cabbage will not head. Although harvested cabbage may appear to be fine, the disease may cause it to rot in storage. Insects, wet weather, and wind spread the disease. Infecting the stomata, bacteria are often numerous in seedbeds and in this way plague new plants. Crop rotation may be effective against black rot.

Among insects, caterpillars may plague cabbage. The cabbageworm, the juvenile stage of the small white butterfly, is native to Europe. It entered the United States about 1850 and New Zealand and Australia in the 1930s. The small white butterfly, appearing in May in the temperate locales of the Northern Hemisphere, deposits one egg per cabbage leaf. Caterpillars hatch in 3 to 10 days, first appearing in June, and immediately begin feeding. Fully grown 10 to 30 days later, a second brood emerges in late July. Late cabbage may suffer acutely from cabbageworm. Also troublesome is the caterpillar known as the cabbage looper. The female lays her eggs on cabbage leaves. Hatchlings appear 3 to 10 days later. They feed at the base of a cabbage plant, proceeding up the leaves. The cabbage looper may yield three generations per year. A third caterpillar, the cutworm, lays eggs on cabbage plants, weeds, or the soil. A poorly cultivated field containing many weeds may support a large population of cutworms. Cutworms feed on cabbage stems and leaves and produce one generation per year in temperate locales. They may overwinter in plant residue. With worldwide distribution, the cutworm has the potential to cause great losses. The caterpillar of the cabbage moth is troublesome in Europe and Asia. Other caterpillar pests include the cabbage webworm and the cross-striped cabbageworm in the United States. Farmers have used biological agents to thwart caterpillars. Among treatments is the dispersal of the bacterium *Bacillus thuringiensis*, which infects the cabbage looper and cabbage webworm. In the United States, farmers have used a virus to kill the cabbage looper. Insecticides, applied every one to two weeks, are also effective.

Another pest of cabbage, the cabbage aphid lays its eggs on stems, leaves, and petioles in spring. Hatchlings appear in April or May and suck sap from plants. Because the cabbage aphid tolerates frost, it can amass a large population early in spring. With populations numbering in the millions, the cabbage aphid may yield 5 to 10 generations per year. Other pests include the small and large cabbage flies. The small cabbage fly, *Chortophila brassicae*, is abundant north of 40° north and has infested Europe and the United States. The large cabbage fly, *Chortophila floralis*, threatens cabbage in Europe, Asia, and the United States. The maggots of these flies feed on cabbage roots. From the roots, they infest the stems and petioles. Infested roots rot with the result that plants grow slowly. In the worst infestations, cabbage plants wither and die.

Christopher Cumo

Further Reading

Cuthbert, Frank P., and W. J. Reid. *Cabbage Insects: How to Control Them in the Home Garden*. Washington, D.C.: U.S. Government Printing Office, 1978.

Danbrot, Margaret. *The New Cabbage Soup Diet*. New York: St. Martin's Paperbacks, 1997.

Nieuwhof, M. *Cole Crops: Botany, Cultivation, and Utilization*. London: CRC Press, 1969.

Talekar, N. S., and T. D. Griggs, eds. *Chinese Cabbage: Proceedings of the First International Symposium*. Shanhua, Taiwan: Asian Vegetable Research and Development Center, 1981.

Walker, J. C., R. H. Larson, and A. L. Taylor. *Diseases of Cabbage and Related Plants*. Washington, D.C.: U.S. Government Printing Office, 1958.

Cacao

In the Sterculieceae family, the cacao tree (*Theobroma cacao*) yields a seed, known as a bean, that is made into chocolate. Throughout prehistory and much of history, humans consumed the pulverized bean as a beverage, though today the chocolate bar is a common item in the grocery store. In 1753, Swedish naturalist Carl Linnaeus created the genus *Theobroma*, meaning "food of the gods," into which he placed cacao. Today, *Theobroma* has 22 species. For the species name, Linnaeus chose *cacao*, a word that coincides with the name of the cacao tree. Cacao means "the chocolate tree." Linnaeus's term "cacao" derives from the

Cacao (iStockPhoto)

Aztec word *cacahuatl*, meaning "that which is extracted from the cacao bean." Cacao is also known as cocoa. In the parlance of the workaday world, cocoa is a beverage made from the cacao bean. Cocoa may be a hot beverage, though in this article the term will mean a beverage irrespective of temperature. This distinction between food and beverage will obtain in this article. Cacao should not be confused with coca or coco. They are different plants. In the same way, the cacao bean should not be confused with beans, which are a legume.

The Tree

The average cacao tree lives 50 to 60 years, though some are as old as 80 years. A tree of the tropics, cacao grows no farther from the equator than 20° north and 20° south. Cuba marks the northernmost point of cacao culture, and the island of Reunion in the Indian Ocean the southernmost limit. Even these limits do not tell the whole story, because more than 75 percent of all cacao is produced between 8° north and 8° south. The cacao tree cannot tolerate temperatures below 60°F, though in its natural habitat it will grow between 1,300 and 2,300 feet in elevation. A tree of the tropical forest, cacao is an understory tree that depends on its tall neighbors for shade. In the forest, cacao is a slender tree reaching a height of more than 50 feet. In a plantation, a cacao tree is pruned to 15 feet to make easier the task of harvesting the pods. In a plantation, the branches of a cacao tree produce a dense canopy, and the tree loses the slender appearance that it has in the forest.

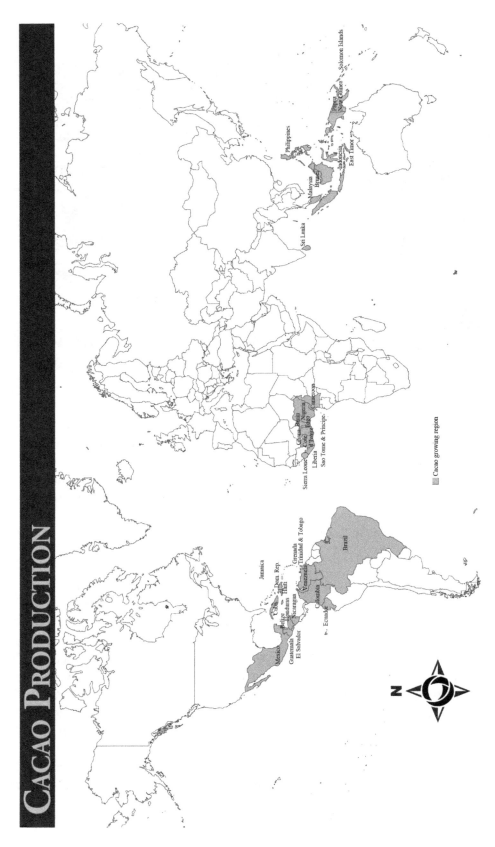

An illustration of the world's cacao-producing regions. (ABC-CLIO)

The genus *Theobroma* may have originated in eastern South America, possibly in the lower elevations of the Andes Mountains, long before the advent of humans in the New World. The cacao tree may have originated in southern Mexico, Belize, Guatemala, and parts of El Salvador and Honduras. It is also possible that the tree originated in South America, from where it was introduced into Mesoamerica. It may have been domesticated in South America or Mesoamerica. Because cacao seeds are viable only three months, one author doubts that the Amerindians took cacao from its southern limit to its northern outpost or from north to south. It is possible that cacao grew wild between Mesoamerica and the Amazon River Basin. In the past, the intermediate population died out, leaving two swaths of cacao, one in Mesoamerica and the other in South America. Mesoamerican trees have long, soft, ridged pods, which have seeds with white cotyledons. The South American cacao tree has hard, round pods with seeds with purple cotyledons.

There are three types of cacao tree: criollo, forastero, and trinitorios. The criollo tree derives its name for the Spanish word for "indigenous." The criollo was the type of tree grown by the Amerindians of Mesoamerica. Enthusiasts prize the criollo bean as the most flavorful. The criollo bean yields a pleasant aroma and delicate flavor. Because the yield is low, the criollo tree produces only 7 percent of the world's cacao beans. The tree is grown principally in Venezuela, Mexico, Nicaragua, Guatemala, Colombia, Trinidad, Grenada, and Jamaica. Given its high quality and dearth, the criollo bean must be expensive.

The forastero tree derives its name from the Spanish word for "foreign." The forastero tree originated in the Amazon River Basin. The Portuguese introduced forastero trees into the African island of Sao Tome, from where it migrated to West Africa. Having been transplanted into Africa, forastero produces most of the continent's cacao beans. Growers also cultivate forastero in Brazil and other parts of South America, Central America, and the Caribbean. Forastero is a fast-growing tree, hardier than criollo, and a higher yielder than criollo. Forastero produces the majority of the world's cacao beans, but it cannot claim the quality of criollo. Forastero beans have a strong, bitter flavor and an acidic aroma. Forastero beans, like coffee beans, are often blended with other types of cacao beans. One variety of forastero, Amendolado, produces a cacao bean whose quality rivals that of the criollo bean. The Amendolado bean is known as the Nacional bean. The variety is cultivated in Ecuador.

The trinitorios tree derives its name from the Caribbean island of Trinidad, where it originated by hybridization. The Spanish planted criollo trees on Trinidad, but when a hurricane swept through the island in the 18th century, the islanders replanted the land with forastero trees. These crossbred with the extant criollo trees, producing the trinitorios hybrids. Trinitorios beans have a high fat content. The trinitorios tree produces 7 percent of the world's cacao beans. Grown in Central and South America, Indonesia, and Sri Lanka, trinitorios yields the highest-quality cacao bean on Trinidad.

A seedling forms a long taproot, though if the water table is high the taproot will be short because cacao tolerates waterlogged soil for only a short duration. Secondary roots grow near the soil surface. The cacao tree needs between 70 and 90 inches of rainfall per year, temperatures between 70°F and 85°F, little variation in temperature throughout the year, and high humidity. The tree must have moisture year-round. Irrigation is necessary during dry spells. When moisture is insufficient, the trees shed leaves to reduce the loss of water through transpiration. The tree is susceptible to many diseases, among them pod rot, wilt, and fungal witches' broom. In the hot, humid environs of the cacao tree, fungal diseases are ubiquitous. The tree bears flowers and the resultant pods on the trunk and largest branches in contrast to temperate trees, which bear fruit on the secondary and smaller branches. Each flower, having both anther and stigma, is only 15 millimeters in diameter. Each flower has five sepals, five petals, and 10 stamens. Sepals and petals are pink or white. The style is two to three millimeters long, at the end of which are five stigmas. In the Americas and Africa, cacao flowers at the beginning of the rainy season and between February and July in Malaysia and Ghana, Africa. Blooms are transitory, lasting only one day. The Amendolado variety is self-fertile, but most are self-sterile and so must be cross-pollinated. Midges, aphids, and thrips pollinate cacao trees. Midges are the principal pollinators. Having evolved in the forest, midges, aphids, and thrips must have forest-like conditions. Trees must surround them, and leaf litter and debris must cover the ground. The grower who insists on a neat plantation unwittingly reduces pollination because he has reduced the habitat of the insect pollinators. This circumstance must account for the fact that in a plantation only a few percent of cacao flowers are pollinated and so form pods. A pod has 30 to 40 seeds, which resemble almonds. Surrounding the seeds is sweet, juicy pulp. Curiously, cacao has no way to release seeds from a pod. In the wild, monkeys, eager to eat the pulp, open the pods, scattering the seeds. In cultivation humans do this job. A pod requires four to five months to attain full size and another month to ripen. A pod may resemble a small rugby ball, a cucumber, or a large gourd. In South America, the average cacao tree yields 30 to 35 pods per year and only 20 in Africa.

Where there is a rainy season, growers harvest the pods at the end of the first rainy season and again at the beginning of the second rainy season. In Malaysia, workers pick pods year-round. In Surinam, workers judge the ripeness of a pod by thumping it with a finger, the method that people use to gauge the ripeness of a watermelon. When ripe, a pod makes a "dull sound" and the seeds rattle in it. Immature pods are green or red violet. When ripe, they turn yellow or orange. On many plantations, men cut the pods from trees and women gather them in baskets. Either a worker or a machine opens the pods to remove the seeds. Once picked, cacao beans are fermented to sweeten them. Criollo beans are fermented two or three days. Forastero and trinitorios beans are fermented more than one week. At the end of fermentation, a cacao bean is 60 percent water. Drying, the next step in processing a cacao bean, reduces moisture to 8 percent. Sun drying is the traditional method, though in Africa and Southeast Asia electric driers are used or the beans are dried by fire. Cacao beans are dried one to two weeks. A dried cacao bean is 50 percent cocoa butter, a type of fat. After the cacao beans are dried, they are roasted and winnowed to produce the kernels that are used to make chocolate.

The ancient practice of carving a cacao plantation out of the jungle persists, though growers also create stand-alone estates, interplanting cacao with banana, coconut, mango, palm, or lemon trees for shade. Cacao plantations are small, covering only a few acres. Some estates are less than two acres. Today, the trend is toward larger plantations, but they remain the exception. Cacao trees are most efficient in photosynthesis when they receive only 25 percent of the sun's light, the rest being shaded. For centuries, planters believed that cacao trees could not survive without shade. In Hawaii, the only place in the United States where cacao is cultivated, growers have succeeded in growing cacao in direct sunlight. The application of fertilizer and hormones causes cacao trees to form a dense canopy, which shades the rest of the tree.

Squirrels, monkeys, and rats steal cacao pods for their pulp, eschewing the seeds because of their bitterness. Seeds, perishing in low temperature and humidity, germinate in a few days. Trees bear pods in the third or fourth year. Cacao is also propagated by cuttings to derive a clone of the parent. Propagation by cutting is common in today's plantations. The extremes of sand and clay are not ideal for a cacao tree. Sand holds too little water and nutrients. Clay drains poorly. The soil pH should be between 5 and 7.5. Cacao will not grow in soil with a pH below 4 or above 8. If the pH is too low, aluminum reaches toxic levels.

The preparation of land for a cacao plantation begins at the beginning of the dry season, when workers remove the undergrowth. During the dry season, workers cut down some of the forest trees. Before they are cut down, the trees should be killed so that they cannot transmit the fungus *Armillaria mellea* to cacao roots. Land should be cleared two years before the planting of cacao trees. Before planting cacao a grower may plant a legume on the site of a plantation to add nitrogen to the soil. The grower should plant shade trees, allowing them to become large before planting cacao. In Papua New Guinea, cacao is planted before any forest tree is felled. When forest trees are cut down the grower makes certain that their absence does not diminish shade. Cacao should not be planted where severe wind is common. Wind can injure a tree, causing it to shed leaves.

Seed for planting should be taken from a pod not more than 15 days underripe. Cacao germination rates are high. A grower may anticipate the germination of 90 percent of seeds within 15 days of planting. The removal of the mucilage that covers the seeds causes them to germinate in only 7 days. Growers plant seeds in a shaded nursery. The new seedlings must be watered twice a day. The rubber tree or oil palm is used for shade in a nursery. Seedlings seldom need fertilizer.

Cacao Becomes a World Crop

The Olmecs of Mesoamerica may have been the first to cultivate the cacao tree, perhaps as early as 1000 BCE. Sometime in prehistory, the Maya and later the Aztecs cultivated cacao. Apparently unaware of Olmec priority, legend holds that the third Mayan king, Hunahpu, was the first to cultivate cacao. The Maya and Aztecs made a beverage from the cacao bean. The Aztecs regarded the cacao tree as sacred, holding ceremonies to mark the stages of its cultivation. A cacao grower was to remain celibate 13 days before planting a seed, which had been placed under the moonlight 4 days before planting.

At the time of the European conquest, farmers in the Yucatan Peninsula tended cacao trees, shipping the pods to the Aztec capital, Tenochtitlan (today Mexico City). In the 16th century, the Spanish monopolized cacao production. The cacao bean was the leading export crop from Spanish America. In the 16th century, the Spanish, as Aztec kings had done, demanded tribute in cacao beans from their American holdings. The Spanish cultivated cacao in Mexico, Venezuela, and Ecuador. The Portuguese established plantations in Brazil. In the Caribbean, Spain planted cacao trees in the Dominican Republic. About 1660, the French planted cacao in the Caribbean islands of Martinique, Saint Domingue, and Saint Lucia to compete with Spanish cacao. In 1746, France planted cacao in Bahia, Brazil. The English planted cacao in Jamaica. In 1836, the Spanish and Germans expanded cacao production in Bahia, Brazil.

For millennia an American tree, in 1590 cacao, presumably through seedlings, was planted in the island of Fernando Po (now Bioko) off the coast of West Africa. This marked the first Old World planting. The trees on Bioko had originated in Venezuela. In 2002 Bioko, affiliated with Guinea, produced thousands of tons of cacao beans, generating the majority of the island's exports. In 1665, the Spanish planted cacao seedlings from Acapulco, Mexico, to Manila, Philippines. Cocoa quickly became a coveted beverage in the Philippines. Filipinos grew several trees in a garden, interplanting them with mango or banana. The Dutch East India Company may have acquired cacao from the Philippines, transplanting trees on the Indonesian islands of Java and Sumatra. After 1778, cacao was profitable in Indonesia. In 2002, Indonesia produced tens of thousands of tons of cacao beans. In 1825, Portugal imported seedlings, presumably from Brazil, to the African islands of Sao Tome and Principe. The Portuguese thereafter were able to compete with Spain, France, and the Netherlands. Between 1895 and 1900, the islands ranked fifth in global production, yielding tens of thousands of tons of cacao beans. By the 1890s, the United Kingdom and Germany refused to buy cacao beans from Sao Tome and Principe because the islands used slave labor. By 2002, the islands produced just a few thousand tons of cacao beans. Even this amount, little as it was, totaled the majority of the islands' exports. In 1857, the Danish Basel Mission planted cacao seedlings from Surinam in Ghana, but they died. Additional trees were planted to 1877, but disease and pests claimed them. In the late 1870s, cacao finally took hold in Ghana. Cameroon, where Germany had earlier planted cacao, was the source of these trees. Under British rule, Ghana emerged as Africa's leading cacao producer. At its peak Ghana, the world's leading producer, harvested several hundred thousand tons of cacao beans per year. In 2002, Cote d'Ivoire was the world's leader with still more tons of cacao beans. In the Americas, Brazil was the leader, followed by the Dominican Republic, Ecuador, Colombia, Venezuela, and Mexico. In Asia, Malaysia harvested a few hundred thousand tons of cacao beans in 2002. Indonesia and Papua New Guinea, which began cultivating cacao in the early 20th century, were important Asian producers. The British planted cacao in Sri Lanka. In the early 20th century, cacao was introduced into the Pacific island of Samoa. Guayaquil, Ecuador, is renowned for the sweetness of its cacao beans. The island of Madagascar produces cacao beans with strong flavor. The island of Sri Lanka yields slightly acidic cacao beans. Ecuador and Samoa are noted for the aroma of their cacao beans.

Like sugarcane, cotton, and tobacco, cacao was a slave crop. Wherever Europeans planted cacao, they enslaved men and women to grow it. In the New World, Europeans might have enslaved the Amerindians had they not died from the diseases that Europeans transmitted to them. The dearth of labor led Europeans to enslave Africans to labor on the cacao estates. Because it was a tropical crop, cacao was often paired with sugarcane. One might suppose that labor requirements were lighter on the cacao plantations, but to the slaves the essential fact was that they were not free. In 1720 a priest, apparently unable to grasp the incompatibility of Christianity and slavery, calculated the profitability of slave labor, remarking that "a cacao plantation is a veritable gold mine."

Cocoa and Chocolate

On his fourth voyage, Italian-Spanish explorer Christopher Columbus encountered cacao. Aztecs on the Caribbean island of Guanaja gave him a bag of cacao beans. The Aztecs prepared a beverage of cocoa, but Columbus thought it too spicy and bitter. The Aztecs called the beverage *tcholctl*, from which the word "chocolate" derives. In 1519, Aztec king Montezuma gave Spanish conquistador Hernando Cortez cacao beans. The Aztecs, other Amerindians, whites, and mestizos used them as money. Four cacao beans bought a pumpkin, 10 bought a rabbit, 12 bought sex with a prostitute, and 100 bought a slave.

The Aztecs reserved the beverage cocoa for the wealthy. Commoners did not drink it. According to Cortez's compatriot, Spanish soldier and historian Bernal Díaz del Castillo, Montezuma drank cocoa every day. The Aztecs believed that cocoa was an aphrodisiac. To make cocoa the Aztecs dried the cacao beans, pulverized them, and added water and chili peppers to the cacao powder.

In the 16th century, cocoa made a favorable impression on Italian botanist Girolomo Benzoni, who, visiting Mexico, declared the beverage "not bitter." "It nourishes and refreshes the body and is not intoxicating," he wrote. Another visitor to Mexico noted that the Amerindians added honey to sweeten cocoa. Others added vanilla. On Martinique, cocoa was, in contrast to Mexico, a democratic beverage. Commoners drank it every morning. Europeans who settled Mexico and the Caribbean added sugar to cocoa, linking the cultivation of cacao to that of sugarcane. Europeans added half a pound of sugar for every 100 beans used to make cocoa. In addition to sugar, the European settlers in the New World added cinnamon, clove, aniseed, almond, and hazelnut to cocoa. Others made a paste from cacao beans.

Europeans came to enjoy cocoa as avidly as they coveted sugar. Columbus appears not to have been the first to introduce cocoa to Europe. In 1527 Cortez, returning to Spain, gave cacao beans to the king, who, like Columbus, apparently disliked the beverage. The Jesuits, numerous in Spain where they were founded, took a leading role in preparing cocoa. In 1606, Italy began importing cocoa from Spain. In 1615, Princess Anne of Austria brought cocoa to France. In 1657, a French businessman opened a "chocolate house" in London, England. The chocolate house came to rival the coffeehouse in popularity. Like cacao, coffee was a tropical crop. The chocolate houses attracted the middle class, principally men, who found them a convenient place to discuss politics and news while indulging in cocoa. Women took their cocoa at home. In the 18th century, in Austrian composer Wolfgang Amadeus Mozart's opera *Cosi Fan Tutte*, a servant prepared cocoa for her female master. Some women found cocoa more appealing than coffee. Aristocratic ladies, perhaps aware of Amerindian beliefs, took cocoa as an aphrodisiac. In 1660, Spanish noblewoman Marie Therese married French king Louis XIV, converting him to the pleasures of cocoa. Monks drank cocoa during fasts. It served as a stimulant that kept them awake for night prayers. Some clerics objected to this practice, holding that cocoa was food rather than a beverage and so could not be taken during a fast. The controversy reached the pope, who sided with the monks. Cocoa was a beverage and so could be indulged in during a fast.

European medical authorities deemed cocoa a treatment for hypochondria and tuberculosis. In 1712, one physician remarked that cocoa was effective against the common cold, pneumonia, diarrhea, dysentery, and cholera. By 1712, cocoa was a popular beverage in Boston, Massachusetts. In the 18th century, some

Europeans, notably Englishman Nicholas Sanders in 1727, began to prepare cocoa with milk rather than water. In 1780, the British navy introduced cacao as a ration for sailors. In the 18th century, the Dutch obtained cocoa from the Netherlands, which in turn presumably got it, at least the cacao beans, from Indonesia, for consumption in New York. Third U.S. president Thomas Jefferson predicted that cocoa would eclipse coffee and tea.

From an early date, Europeans relegated the tropics to producing cacao beans and insisted at the end of the 16th century on processing the beans themselves. In the mid-17th century, Europe erected the first chocolate factory. This factory presumably produced chocolate bars, a popular treat that dated to 1674, the year a London chocolate house began selling them. By the mid-18th century, North America began importing chocolate, presumably from Mexico, the Caribbean, and Central and South America. In 1765, physician James Baker opened a chocolate factory in Massachusetts. In 1895, Pennsylvania caramel manufacturer Milton Hershey began selling chocolate bars. In 1907, Hershey introduced the popular Kiss. In 2005, Hershey produced 30 million Kisses per day. Perhaps because of its connection to sex, the Japanese, Europeans, and Americans associate chocolate with Saint Valentine's Day and Easter. In one sense, Easter is a festival of fecundity, and so is linked with sex. In Japan, tradition holds that the woman gives her man chocolate on Saint Valentine's Day. As of 2005, the Swiss consumed 19 pounds of chocolate per person per year. Norwegians and Britons consumed 17.5 pounds per year. Belgians, the Dutch, Germans, and Austrians ate more than 14 pounds per person. Americans ate 10 pounds per person, and the svelte Japanese consumed only 3 pounds per person. Koreans chew chocolate-flavored gum.

Chocolate may have played a role in the race to the South Pole. Because it is calorie dense and because the effort to reach the pole was strenuous, explorers took chocolate as a ration. British explorer Robert Scott allotted each member of his team 4,430 calories, including 24 grams of chocolate per day. The allowance was not enough. Scott's party failed to reach the South Pole and perished on the return journey. Chocolate cannot bear all the blame for Scott's failure. Terrible weather probably doomed the men. Norwegian explorer Roald Amundsen, perhaps having learned from Scott, allocated each member of his expedition 4,560 calories per day, including five times more chocolate than Scott and his men had eaten. Fortified with chocolate, Amundsen and his team were the first to reach the South Pole.

Christopher Cumo

Further Reading

Bailleux, Nathalie, Herve Bizeul, John Feltswell, Regine Kopp, Corby Kummer, Pierre Labanne, Cristina Pauly, Odile Perrard, and Mariarosa Schiaffino. *The Book of Chocolate.* Paris: Flammarion, 1995.

Beckett, Stephen T. *The Science of Chocolate.* Cambridge: RSC, 2008.

Coe, Sophie D., and Michael D. Coe. *The True History of Chocolate*. London: Thames and Hudson, 1996.

Foster, Nelson, and Linda S. Cordell. *Chilies to Chocolate: Food the Americas Gave the World*. Tucson: University of Arizona Press, 1992.

Off, Carol. *Bitter Chocolate: The Dark Side of the World's Most Seductive Sweet*. New York: The New Press, 2006.

Presilla, Maricel E. *The New Taste of Chocolate: A Cultural and Natural History of Cacao with Recipes*. Berkeley, CA: Ten Speed Press, 2001.

Willson, K. *Coffee, Cocoa and Tea*. New York: CABI, 1999.

Young, Allen M. *The Chocolate Tree: A Natural History of Cacao*. Gainesville: University Press of Florida, 2007.

Cactus

A member of the Cactaceae family, cacti inhabit one of three subfamilies. The cacti of Pereskioideae grow in dry woodlands. The cacti of Opuntioideae have leaves, which they shed in the dry season. The third subfamily, Cactoideae, has the largest number of species. All but one genus of cactus is indigenous to the New World. The exception, *Rhipsalis*, is native to Africa, Madagascar, several islands in the Indian Ocean, and Sri Lanka. One botanist believes that *Rhipsalis*

Cactus (iStockPhoto)

was once native to the Americas. He theorizes that birds dispersed its seed to the Old World, after which it died out in its ancestral homeland. The discovery of the Americas brought cacti to the attention of Europeans. In the 18th century Swedish naturalist Carl Linnaeus, who knew only 20 species, grouped all cacti in the genus *Cactus*. Today, botanists know 130 genera with more than 1,600 species. Because cacti are endangered, U.S. law prohibits the taking of cacti from the wild.

Origin and Diffusion

The fossil record reveals nothing about the origin of cacti because their imprint is absent from rocks. The absence of fossils makes difficult the attempt to pinpoint the origin or cacti, which may have originated as early as 100 million years ago or as late as 30 million years ago. Arising in South America, according to one account, cacti reached North America during the Tertiary Period. About 36 million years ago, cacti migrated to the Caribbean and Central America. When cacti appeared on Earth, Colombia and Venezuela were at the equator and the Andes Mountains had not uplifted. Northwestern South America was hot, humid, and only intermittently dry. The region was not yet a desert. By 17 million years ago, the Andes Mountains had risen far enough to create deserts. Brazil and Bolivia were then deserts and had been colonized by cacti. In this distant era three centers of cactus diversity emerged: the Andes Mountains, the Caribbean, and eastern South America. Today, the three centers of diversity are Mexico and the American Southwest, the southwestern Andes of Peru, Bolivia, Chile, and Argentina, and eastern Brazil.

The date when humans migrated to the Americas remains a topic of debate, but they may have encountered cacti soon after their arrival. About 12,000 years ago humans painted images of cacti in a cave in Serra de Capivora Piaui, Brazil. One cave in Peru contains cactus seeds that date to 11,800 years ago. According to one authority humans collected cacti more than 9,000 years ago, probably to eat their fruit. The use of cacti predates the invention of agriculture in the New World. The Chavia of Peru encountered the San Pedro cactus, *Echinopsis panchanoi*, more than 3,000 years ago. Some Amerindians used cactus spines to make fishhooks. According to legend the Aztecs founded Tenoctitlan on the spot where an eagle, a snake in its mouth, perched on a cactus. This image adorns the seal of Mexico. The Aztecs used two species of cactus for medicine. Native Americans have revered cacti for millennia, using them in their religious rites and as medicine and food.

Spanish explorer Christopher Columbus may have found cacti in the Caribbean and brought them to Europe as early as 1493. Over the centuries, the Columbian Exchange brought cacti to the Mediterranean Basin, Africa, Asia, and Australia, where they are now numerous. In the 15th century Spanish conquistador

Hernando Cortez encountered cacti in Mexico. In the 16th century Spanish historian Gonzalo Fernández de Oviedo y Valdés noted that the indigenes of the Caribbean used cacti for medicine and wine and as a dye. Even after the fall of the Aztec Empire, the Amerindians of Mexico used cacti in their religious services. Catholic priests, thinking this practice pagan, tried without success to stop it. At the center of Amerindian religious ritual, the peyote cactus had enemies among Europeans. Priests called it *raiz diabolica*, the "devil's root." They considered the eating of cactus a sin. Distrust of the peyote cactus was strong because it has an alkaloid that produces effects similar to those of LSD. In altering their state of consciousness, the Amerindians believed that the peyote cactus allowed them to communicate with the dead. In the 19th century its use spread to the Apache and Plains Indians in the United States. The peyote cactus remains a sacrament in the Native American Church.

Attributes

The outstanding characteristic of the cactus, a perennial succulent, is its ability to survive in arid climates. The cactus withstands drought by storing water in its stems against lean times and by conserving water. In this context, cacti are renowned for their frugal use of water. Roots are efficient absorbers of water. With a low surface area-to-volume ratio, cacti expose little flesh to evaporation. A waxy substance covers cacti to minimize water loss. The genus *Pereskia* bears leaves, which it sheds during dry weather to conserve water. With only one-tenth as many stomata as other plants, cacti transpire little water. Keeping the stomata closed during the day to conserve water, cacti absorb carbon dioxide only at night. Although rainfall may bloat cacti to a state in which they are 95 percent water, they shrink to 20 percent water in drought. The loss of water causes cacti to shrivel. In winter the ability to shrivel is a survival advantage because freezing temperatures will not cause water, in expanding, to burst cacti cells. Spines shade cacti from the sun and absorb dew.

Cacti may have spines, scales, bristles, or hair. Spines are a signature trait. Some spines are so short that they are barely visible. Others are as long as one foot. The genera *Rhipsalis*, *Epiphyllum*, and *Lephophora* have no spines whereas the genera *Echinocactus* and *Mammillaria* have a large number of spines. In addition to their role in absorbing water, spines protect cacti from predators.

Cacti inhabit latitudes from 56° north to 52° south. In the Americas they grown from Canada's Rocky Mountains to Patagonia near the Strait of Magellan. They may be found in deserts, semideserts, and even rain forests. Most cacti of the rain forest are epiphytes. Many cacti inhabit the Andes Mountains of Peru, Bolivia, and Chile and the highlands of Mexico. They survive as high as 15,700 feet. Cacti occupy a range of soils including the damp rain forest soils rich in organic matter, the clays of the plains and woodlands, the sand of deserts, and the quartz sand of northeastern Brazil and Campo Rupestre of eastern Brazil. The genera *Melocastus, Uebelmannia,* and *Pilosocereus* grow in quartz sand. Cacti endure a range of temperatures. The species of the American Southwest, Mexico, Brazil, Bolivia, Chile, and Argentina survive temperatures as high as 125°F. In addition to heat, cacti need 40 to 70 days of cool weather per year to initiate dormancy. Many cacti, having evolved in mountains, tolerate hot days and cool nights. Cacti must have cool weather to flower. For example the genus *Epiphyllum,* known as the orchid cactus because of the beauty and fragrance of its flowers, needs cool nights to flower. Because many species of cactus need cool nights, they may be difficult to cultivate in the tropics, whose nights are too warm. Cacti tolerate winter temperatures between 40°F and 50°F. The genus *Rebutia* survives cooler temperatures. The species *Coryphantha sulcate* and *Coryphantha vivipara* tolerate temperatures as low as −10°F. The subspecies *Escobaria sneedii* var. *sneedii* endures temperatures as low as −15°F. The species *Echinocereus fendleri* and the subspecies *Escobaria sneedii* var. *leei* survive to −20°F. *Coryphentla missouriensii* tolerates temperatures as low as −25°F, and *Opuntia fragilis* survives temperatures as cold as −35°F.

Many species cross-pollinate, the flowers attracting birds and insects. Cacti with red flowers attract birds. The nectar of several species' flowers attracts hummingbirds. Butterflies pollinate the genus *Rebutia.* White flowers emit a fragrance that attracts moths and bats to pollinate them at night. Yellow and magenta are the most common colors of flowers, though blooms may also be white and pink. No cactus has blue flowers. In some species flowers are less than 1 inch in diameter. The genera *Hylocereus* and *Selenicereus* bear flowers as large as 16 inches in diameter. Once pollinated, flowers bear fruit, enticing animals to eat it, thereby dispersing seeds. Birds consume the fruit of many genera. Ants dispense the seeds of the genera *Blossfeldia* and *Aztekum* and some species of *Capiapoo.* The fruit of *Piendoacanthocereus brasiliensis* and *Pereskia bahiensis* fall to the ground. Ripening, they give off an odor that attracts reptiles, which disperse seeds. On the Galapagos Islands the giant tortoise eats the fruit of the genus *Opuntia.* Spines on the fruit of *Cylindropuntia* and *Opuntia* latch onto the fur of visiting mammals, dispersing seeds in this way. Wind disperses the seeds of some species of *Eriosyce.* The genera *Opuntioideae* and *Cylindopuntia* reproduce vegetatively. Parts of the stems of *Cylindopuntia,* having spines, fasten to the fur of mammals, being thus dispersed.

The genera *Ariocarpus, Astrophytum, Aztebium, Cylindropuntia, Eschinocereus, Penioceretus, Selenicereus, Trichocereus,* and *Turbinicerpus* yield substances that humans use as medicine. Applied as a topical ointment, the juice of *Ariocarpus fissurtus* deadens pain from wounds, snakebites, and bruises. Native to Mexico and southern Texas, this species produces juice that, mixed with water and boiled, may be consumed to treat fever and rheumatism. Long-distance runners chew the tubercles of *Ariocarpus fissurtus* for stamina. The Amerindians of the Chihuahua Desert used *Ariocarpus retusus* in their harvest festival. The Huichol of Mexico believe this cactus to be toxic, but it is used to reduce fever. Used to treat rheumatism, the juice of *Obregonia denegrii* is an antibiotic. The species is known as the artichoke cactus because of its shape, though others think it resembles a green pinecone. Native to Tamaulipus, Mexico, *Obregonia denegrii* is endangered. In 2002 only 5,000 specimens inhabited the wild. It is threatened by erosion, livestock grazing, and collection from the wild for medicinal purposes.

Cultivation

Where cacti are endangered, cultivation is an important means of preserving species. One gardener recommends the cultivation of cacti because they survive even when neglected whereas most other houseplants die. Despite their exceptional durability, the needs of cacti are not radically different from those of other plants. Cacti need light, water, carbon dioxide, and minerals from the soil. Because of their need for light, cacti do well by a sunny window, though they benefit from shade during the hottest part of the day. During summer cacti may be placed outdoors. As a rule young cacti need warmer temperatures than old specimens. The need for water varies. During hot weather a cactus that is growing and is confined to a small pot may need watering every day. By contrast a cactus that is dormant during winter and in a large pot may need watering only once every three or four weeks. A few drops of water per week may suffice. Alternatively, one may copiously water a cactus, wait until the soil dries out, and then rewater. The gardener should never waterlog the soil because too much moisture may rot the roots. Rainwater or tap water is best. Hard water should be avoided because it may have too much calcium or magnesium. The water should be slightly acidic. Cacti do well in various soils. One gardener recommends a mix of potting soil and sand. The addition of sand allows the soil to drain rapidly, avoiding the excessive moisture that cacti dislike. Soil may also be mixed with gravel to maximize drainage. The genus *Schlumbergera*, the Christmas cactus, does well in peat, but the medium may not be ideal for other cacti. When it dries, peat is difficult to rehydrate. As peat decays its detritus may harm roots. The gardener may also use pumice or perlite. Although some gardeners use a balanced fertilizer with a ratio of 20:20:20, nitrogen to phosphorus to potassium, others assert that because cacti grow slowly they may not need nitrogen. Too much nitrogen leaves cacti vulnerable to pest and diseases. Moreover, nitrogen tends to stimulate vegetative growth at the expense of flowers. A fertilizer with phosphorus and potassium may suffice. The gardener should apply fertilizer sparingly and not at all after August to prevent cacti from issuing forth new growth that may suffer frost damage in winter. Newly potted cacti need no fertilizer.

Genera and Species

The genus *Astrophytum* has four species, all of them indigenous to Mexico and the American South. Breeders have derived several hybrids by crossing these species. *Astrophytum* thrives in hot, sunny weather and needs little water even in summer. Gardeners may propagate *Astrophytum* by seed, which should be sown within one year to ensure viability. The diminutive species of the genus, *Astrophytum asterias* yields attractive yellow flowers. Because it grows slowly, it needs little water. The species is popular in Japan. *Astrophytum capricorne* produces large yellow flowers with a red throat. *Astrophytum myriostigma* produces no spines. When it reaches two-and-one-half inches in diameter the species flowers, producing small blooms. The largest species of the genus, *Astrophytum ornatum* reaches three feet in height. The species yields yellow flowers on its crown.

The genus *Cleistocactus* is popular because of its ease of cultivation and its abundant flowers. The nectar in the flowers attracts hummingbirds. Indigenous to the Andes Mountains, *Cleistocactus* evolved in a region with appreciable rainfall in the summer. The genus must have a regular supply of water to flower. *Cleistocactus* rewards the gardener with blooms throughout summer. *Cleistocactus straush* grows more than three feet tall. Easy to propagate by seed, this species produces maroon blooms. The subspecies *Cleistocactus baumannii* ssp. *chacoanus* flowers over several months. It grows rapidly enough to need pruning. *Cleistocactus brookeae* yields red-orange blooms. Given enough water, the species flowers throughout summer. This cactus may produce more than 200 flowers per year. *Cleistocactus neoroezlii* yields red flowers near the crown. Native to northern Peru, this cactus needs winter temperatures no colder than 50°F. The gardener may propagate the species by seed. Native to Bolivia *Cleistocactus winteri* yields pink or orange flowers.

Pests

Durable plants, cacti are nonetheless vulnerable to insects and arachnids. Aphids damage cacti by sucking sap. Where they are numerous they may cause cacti to yellow, shrivel, and stop growing. The application of alcohol to aphids kills them, though it may harm cacti. The mealy bug, known as the woolly aphid, likewise sucks sap and may be just as distressing as aphids to the gardener. Mealy bugs breed rapidly, forming large colonies that may overwhelm cacti. Large infestations may kill cacti. Some mealy bugs burrow into the soil, where they feed on roots. Where mealy bugs have infested the soil, the gardener should remove it, inserting new soil in its place. Mealy bugs lay eggs on cacti, encasing them in a white web that may be conspicuous. The gardener who comes upon the eggs should coat them with vegetable oil to prevent their hatching. Water and detergent may be used to wash off cacti, thereby removing mealy bugs. Insecticides may be effective, though some mealy bugs are resistant. Aphids and mealy bugs infest cacti in warm, dry weather. Because ants use the honeydew of the aphid and mealy bug, their presence may indicate an infestation of aphid or mealy bug.

Like aphids and mealy bugs, red spider mites suck the sap of cacti. Cacti develop gray, yellow, or brown spots at the point of attack. Active in warm, dry conditions, red spider mites thrive where ventilation is poor. The genera *Rebutias*, *Lobivias*, *Corypharthas*, *Melocactus*, *Sulcorebutia*, *Mammillaria*, *Lophophora*, *Turbinicarpus*, *Pelecyphera*, and *Faucaries* are susceptible to mites. In heavy infestations cacti develop brown scars at the place of feeding. A concoction made from cinnamon oil may be effective against mites.

Thrips feed on stems and pollen, their appetite voracious above 90°F. They thrive in hot, dry conditions. The gardener who suspects an infestation need only tap a flower. Startled thrips will scurry about, revealing their presence. In damaging a flower, thrips may cause it to be small and misshapen. Stems may have small yellow spots, betraying the activity of thrips. Tiny black dots, thrip excrement, may appear on flowers and stems. Multiplying rapidly, a female may lay 50 to 200 eggs during her lifetime. Hatching in a few days, larvae begin feeding at once. Larvae of the fungus gnat feed on cactus roots. Adult plants may have a sufficiently mature root system to withstand damage without ill effect. Young plants, however, are vulnerable. In only a few weeks, larvae may kill an entire flat of seedlings. Where seedlings survive they may be stunted.

Christopher Cumo

Further Reading

Anderson, Edward F. *The Cactus Family.* Portland, OR: Timber Press, 2001.

Anderson, Miles. *A Gardener's Directory of Cacti and Succulents: An Illustrated A–Z Guide to over 400 Varieties.* New York: Anness, 2001.

Charles, Graham. *Cacti and Succulents.* Ramsbury, Marlborough, U.K.: Crowood Press, 2009.

Hewitt, Terry. *The Complete Book of Cacti and Succulents: The Definitive Practical Guide to Cultivation, Propagation, and Display.* New York: Dorling Kindersley, 1997.

Mace, Tony, and Suzanne Mace. *Cactus Basics: A Comprehensive Guide to Cultivation and Care.* London: Octopus, 2006.

Manke, Elisabeth. *Cactus: The Most Beautiful Varieties and How to Keep Them Healthy.* Hauppauge, NY: Barron's Educational Series, 2000.

Nobel, Park S. *Cacti: Biology and Uses.* Berkeley: University of California Press, 2002.

Preston-Mafham, Ken. *500 Cacti: Species and Varieties in Cultivation.* Richmond Hill, Ontario: Firefly Books, 2007.

Rogers, Ray, ed. *Crazy about Cacti and Succulents.* Brooklyn, NY: Brooklyn Botanic Garden, 2006.

Calendula

Calendula officinalis is the most common cultivated species of calendula, also known as Pot Marigold and called Golds or Ruddes in Old English. There are about 20 species in this family, including Field Marigold (*Calendula arvensis*) and Sea Marigold (*Calendula maritima*), and over 100 varieties. Calendula is of the same family (Asteraceae) as daisy, chrysanthemum, and ragweed. This family also includes what is commonly called "marigold" in North America but is actually the *Tagetes* genus. Calendula is not closely related to the common marigold.

The name is derived from the Latin *kalendar* or *calends*, meaning "the first day of the month." It is believed this refers to Calendula's easy cultivation and constant blooming from early spring to first frost. Its common name, Pot Marigold, is said to come from its frequent use to color a pot of soup or broth and provide comfort for the spirit. It is a hardy annual that is native from the Mediterranean to Iran but has been cultivated since the Middle Ages and is now a worldwide ornamental flower. In 1941, the variety Plamen was registered and is considered the direct ancestor of many ornamental varieties. Many varieties are still not widely available due to exclusive production rights. Rinathei is heavy with faradiol triterpenoids that provide calendula's anti-inflammatory qualities and was registered in 1998 by a German herbal medicine manufacturer. The most common European and North American variety is the Erfuter Orangefarbinge with a bright orange double flower. Resina and Carola varieties are considered higher seed yield crops and the richest in seed oil. Resina has only recently become available outside Europe.

The plant grows in many soils but does best in rich, well-drained soil with full sunlight in a cool temperate environment. It can also be easily overcome by weeds. *Calendula officinalis* is usually 12 to 30 inches tall and quickly produces yellow, red, or orange flowers that open with the rising of the sun and close with the setting sun. In fact, Swedish naturalist Carl Linnaeus's observation indicates that they open at nine in the morning and close at three in the afternoon, so he attributed the names *solsequia* and *solis sponsa* to the plant. This characteristic is also referenced in William Shakespeare's play, *A Winter's Tale*:

> The Marigold that goes to bed wi' th' sun
> And with him rises weeping.

History

Calendula has been used medicinally since the 12th century. It was referenced in writing as early as 1578 in Henry Lyte and Rembert Dodoens's text, *A Niewe Herball*, as having "pleasant, bright and shining yellow flowers." Nicholas

Culpeper included it in his infamous book of treatments, *The English Physician* (1642), as a treatment for headaches, toothaches, and swelling. Culpeper compared the plant to the courageous lion, therefore also prescribing it for heart disease. In the Civil War and World War I, calendula salves were used to treat wounds and prevent infection. In folk medicine, the whole plant was added to milk as a cure for certain types of cancer.

The rich carotene pigment in the orange flowers of calendula has prompted farmers for many years to add it to butter and cheese to deepen their yellow color. Even currently, calendula petals are added to chicken feed to darken the egg yolk color.

Medicinal Uses

Historically, it was suggested that dried calendula petals have antiviral, anti-inflammatory, stimulant, and diaphoretic properties. It is an edible flower and used as a tincture for chronic ulcers, varicose veins, acne, inflammation, and soothing irritated skin. Tea brewed from dried calendula is said to help heal sore eyes, and direct application of blossoms relieves symptoms from insect bites or stings. As a topical ointment, it is considered safe for humans and increases blood flow to the affected skin area, helping to treat hemorrhoids, burns, skin irritations, and abrasions. It is also considered an antibacterial and is used in foot powders.

Recently, drops containing calendula have been found to be possibly effective at healing ear infections in children, and the plant is used in treatments of eczema, dry skin, and scars. Antimicrobial compounds may help inhibit *Staphylococcus*, *Candida*, and *Escherichia coli*. In homeopathy, calendula tinctures and creams are used with skin problems and cuts, and may help control bleeding as well as provide an antiseptic for broken skin, burns, and abrasions. Homeopathic remedies have been developed to internally treat jaundice and fever, and tinctures are used as gargles to help heal mouth ulcers and sore throats.

Medical and pharmacological studies involving calendula have identified the plant as having high numbers of flavonoids, which are plant-based antioxidants. These protect the skin from cell-damaging molecules known as free radicals. Calendula ointments may have some use in treating radiation dermatitis in some cancer patients. Studies have also found a conjugated trienoic fatty acid in the oil of calendula seed and named it calendic acid. Biologically, it has been suggested that this acid can be a signaling molecule, resulting in body fat loss and reducing colon cancer cells.

Recent Industrial Application

In 1985, research into the biosynthesis of calendic acid revealed that it was highly susceptible to oxidation. Continued studies have determined that it shortens the drying process and makes a more resistant coat of paints, varnishes, binders, and resins. Due to this recent discovery of calendic acid, industrialized cultivation as well as mechanical harvest and cleaning of calendula seeds has been explored, but it has been found to be a labor-intensive crop. The flowers bloom quickly so must be harvested regularl,y and are easily overcome by weeds, which reduce productivity. Agricultural productivity is still being explored and tested.

Erika Stump

Further Reading

"Conjugated Polyenoic Fatty Acids and Metabolites." *Publications.* Larodan Fine Chemicals, 2001. http://www.larodan.se/pub_old/art002.html (accessed 10 July 2010).

Grieve, M. *A Modern Herbal: The Medicinal, Culinary, Cosmetic and Economic Properties, Cultivation and Folk-lore of Herbs, Grasses, Fungi, Shrubs and Trees with All Their Modern Scientific Uses.* New York: Dover, 1971.

"Plant of the Week: Calendula Officinalis." *W. J. Beal Botanical Garden.* Michigan State University, 2008. http://www.cpa.msu.edu/beal/plantoftheweek/plants/calendula_officinalis_2008-728.pdf (accessed 10 July 2010).

Richters, Conrad. "Commercial Calendula Cultivation." *Richters Herb Catalogue.* Richters Herbs, 2007. http://www.richters.com/show.cgi?page=MagazineRack/Articles/CommercialCalendulaCultivation.html (accessed 10 July 2010).

Campanula

Campanulas are native to the whole of the Northern Hemisphere but are especially diverse across Western Europe, particularly in lands that border the Mediterranean Sea. The genus *Campanula* belongs to the family Campanulaceae, or bellflower family, and comprises around 300 species, which can be annual, biennial, or perennial. The botanical name means "little bell" and derives from *campana*, the Latin for "bell," as campanula flowers are often bell shaped, although they can also be cup, saucer, or star shaped. Campanula flowers are available in shades of blue, purple, red, pink, white, and lilac, feature five petals, and are usually borne in clusters. Species of campanula vary in height between 3 inches, such as *Campanula cochleariifolia*, also known as fairies' thimbles, and five feet, including *Campanula latiloba*, known as the delphinium bellflower. One of the shortest-growing varieties, *Campanula carpatica*, also known as the Carpathian bellflower, is particularly prized by gardeners for the plant's favorable ratio of flower size to height, for the plant grows to between 8 and 12 inches tall but produces many blooms, which are around 2 inches in diameter, in shades of white, lilac, and blue. *Campanula carpatica* forms clumps up to two feet in diameter and has a long flowering period as it blooms from spring to summer.

Campanula laciflora, also known as the milky bellflower, and *Campanula latiloba*, are two of the tallest-growing campanulas as they can reach heights of up to five feet. *Campanula lactiflora* produces masses of small, white or lavender flowers on plants bearing many branches, whereas *Campanula latiloba* produces blooms that are attached to the plant's two-feet-tall stems in the fashion of a delphinium plant and are available in shades of white, purple, and blue. These campanulas differ from low-growing campanulas as they flower in mid- to late summer instead of in spring.

Attributes

Campanulas do not enjoy hot conditions, preferring climates that have overnight temperatures below 70°F and daytime temperatures no higher than 90°F. When these temperatures are exceeded, campanulas will not flourish and will be short-lived, although a site that has partial shade at midday benefit the plant. In general, campanulas prefer to grow in full sun to partial shade in rich, evenly moist soil that is well drained. During dry spells, it is necessary to water campanulas well and mulch around the plants to keep the surrounding soil cool. Regular deadheading will encourage repeat flowering. Propagation is by the division of roots or by seed, although the flower color of species such as *Campanula laciflora* will differ between parent plant and offspring. White Clips and Blue Clips are cultivars of *Campanula carpathica* that do grow true from seed.

Folklore and Mythology

One of the most celebrated species of cultivated campanula is the biennial *Campanula medium*, commonly known as Canterbury Bells. *Campanula medium* grows to a height of three feet and produces flowers up to two inches long from spring to midsummer. There are two English legends that explain why Canterbury Bells are so named. In one legend, three evil men were transformed by a priest into swans and cursed to fly without rest for over a thousand years. Then, when flying over Canterbury, the men heard the ringing of church bells and felt such contrition for their pasts that the curse was broken. With the spell lifted, the men fell to Earth at Canterbury where they were discovered by North African scholar Saint Augustine, who led them into a church. Where the men trod, tiny campanulas grew, and the flower was subsequently dedicated to Saint Augustine and later to England's Saint Thomas à Becket who was murdered in Canterbury Cathedral. The other legend tells that campanulas were so named because of their resemblance to the bells carried by pilgrims to Canterbury. Classical myth explains the origins of another campanula, *Campanula speculum*, which is also known as Venus's looking glass. According to myth, Venus's mirror bestowed beauty upon anyone reflected in it. However, one day the goddess lost her mirror, and it was found by a shepherd who proceeded to gazed at himself in the mirror. It so angered Cupid that his mother's mirror had been used by a mortal that Cupid knocked the glass from the shepherd's hand, and where it landed sprang forth a campanula.

A tea may be brewed from *Campanula americana*, the American bellflower, and it is used as a remedy for respiratory conditions by the Meskwaki tribe of Native Americans. Similarly, *Campanula rapunculoides* is often grown in vegetable gardens for the leaves, shoots, and the white tap root. This may be eaten in salads and is known as rampion, which is rich in vitamin C. Rampion grows up to four feet tall and is extremely invasive, spreading quickly via subterranean stolons and by self-seeding. It is from *Campanula rapunculoides* that the Brothers Grimm developed the name Rapunzel for their fairy-tale heroine as it is rampion leaf that Rapunzel's mother craves from the witch's garden at the start of the tale. Rampion was also fed to the gods by Apollo and used to decorate funerals at his temple at Delphi. The association of campanula with death is part of Scottish folklore, for in Scotland *Campanula rotundifolia*, commonly known as the harebell, is called auld-man's-bell and is left untouched, for the plant is thought to be the bell belonging to a graveyard ghost. To hear the ghost's bell ring above the sound of a storm is regarded as a harbinger of death.

Victoria Williams

Further Reading

Armitage, Allan M. *Armitage's Garden Perennials: A Color Encyclopedia*. Portland, OR: Timber Press, 2000.

Skinner, Charles Montgomery. *Myths and Legends of Flowers, Trees, Fruits, and Plants in All Times and in All Climes*. General Books LLC. http://books.google.co.uk/books?id=s5p82USYH4cC&printsec=frontcover&source=gbs_ge_summary_r&cad=0#v=onepage&q&f=false (accessed 21 November 2010). First published by J. B. Lipincott, 1915.

Runkel, Sylvan T., and Alvin F. Bull. *Wildflowers of Iowa's Woodlands*. Iowa City: University of Iowa Press, 2009.

Tenenbaum, Frances, ed. *Taylor's Encyclopedia of Garden Plants*. New York: Houghton Mifflin, 2003.

Ward, Bobby J. *A Contemplation upon Flowers: Garden Plants in Myth and Literature*. Portland, OR: Timber Press, 1999.

Canna

Cannas are lush tropical plants with huge leaves and vibrant blossoms on tall stalks. Many varieties have multicolored and patterned leaves, making them a season-long focal point. The common species *Canna indica* provides two possible clues to its origin. Because the species came to Europe from the East Indies and because a European—16th-century Flemish botanist and physician Carolus Clusius—named the plant, it is tempting to think that the species name *indica* suggests an East Indies origin. But Clusius was a careful scholar, and the consensus appears to be that he was correct in inferring a New World origin, namely the West Indies. If *Canna indica* originated in the West Indies, one wonders whether 15th- and 16th-centuries Spanish-Italian explorer Christopher Columbus encountered the species, though there appears to be no evidence one way or the other.

Canna is an American genus. Without exception, all *Canna* species that have been introduced into Europe can be traced back to the Americas, and it can be asserted with confidence that *Canna* is solely an American genus. If Asia and Africa provided some of the early introductions, they were only varieties resulting from *Canna indica* and *Canna glauca* cultivars that have been grown for a long time in India and Africa, with these species having originally imported from Central and South America, though it is not clear whether these migrations occurred with human assistance.

Cannas were unknown to the ancients of the Old World, and only after the discovery of the New World did they make their appearance in Europe. Since cannas have very hard and durable seed coverings, it is likely that seeds would have survived in the right conditions for a voyage across the Atlantic Ocean and then would have been found by archaeologists in the Old World. If the soils of India or Africa had produced some of them, they might have been imported before the 1860s into European gardens, though the prevailing opinion is for a direct transfer of cannas from the Caribbean to Europe, rather than the circuitous route from the Americas to Africa or India and then to Europe. *Canna* is the only genus in the family Cannaceae. The angiosperm phylogeny group system (APG III) recognizes the family. Canna is sometimes consumed as a vegetable or juice. It is reputed to prevent dehydration. Its carbohydrates are a source of energy. It is reputed to aid the function of the kidneys. It is thought to prevent prostate and breast cancers.

Types

The plants are large tropical and subtropical perennials. The broad, flat, alternate leaves grow out of a stem in a long narrow roll and then unfurl. The leaves are typically solid green, but some cultivars have glaucose, brown, maroon, or variegated leaves. Flowers are red, orange, or yellow or a combination of those colors. There are 19 species of *Canna* recognized by the American Horticultural Association.

Although gardeners enjoy these odd flowers, nature intended them to attract pollinators such as bees, hummingbirds, and bats. As do potato plants, cannas grow from rhizomes, which store starch, having the largest starch particles of all flora. This is the desideratum of the plant to agriculture, though canna is unlikely ever to rival the potato in its ubiquity in the temperate zone. *Canna* is the only member of the Liliopsida class in which seeds hibernate because of their hard, impenetrable seed covering.

Cultivation

In the temperate zone, the gardener may plant canna in the spring after danger from hard frost has passed. A good rule of thumb is to plant canna when it is time to plant potatoes. The best results are achieved when planted in a loose, fertile, and well-drained soil. The rhizomes should be kept moist but not wet. Canna should be watered thoroughly once a week by slowly soaking the area around the roots. Emerged plants may receive more water. They may flourish in poorly drained areas and in shallow ponds.

Canna will tolerate a wide range of growing conditions, though it prefers full sun and a minimum of four hours of direct sunlight. Rhizomes should be planted 12 to 18 inches apart and covered with 2 inches of soil. The gardener may place the long part of the rhizome horizontally in the ground with the eye up, if visible. Canna rhizomes do not have a top or bottom, so they cannot be planted upside down.

In colder regions, gardeners may start canna in pots and place it in greenhouse conditions six to eight weeks prior to planting outdoors. When all danger of frost is past, the gardener may remove canna from pots and plant outside. For optimum performance, organic matter such as composted manure as well as a high-nitrogen fertilizer may be added to the soil. Rose and tomato fertilizers are also good products to use on cannas and are readily available. It is not necessary to deadhead the spent flowers and seedpods to induce new blooms; however, the flowerbed is more striking without the old blooms.

Symbolism and Uses

The name canna originated from the Celtic word for a cane or reed; it is a common feminine first name in Australia. In Italy, canna is a measure of length, varying from six to seven feet. Canna is a small island in the Inner Hebrides, off the coast of Scotland, about six miles long by half a mile across, and with a population of 18. Gaelic scholar John Lorne Campbell donated the Isle of Canna to the National Trust for Scotland in 1982.

The canna rhizome is rich in starch, and it has many uses in agriculture. All of the plant has commercial value, the rhizomes for starch (consumption by humans and livestock), the stems and foliage for animal fodder, the young shoots as a vegetable, and the young seeds as an addition to tortillas. Canna is the flour source for arrowroot cookies. The seeds are used as beads in jewelry, and as the mobile elements of the kayamb, a musical instrument from Réunion, as well as the hosho, a gourd rattle from Zimbabwe, where the seeds are called *hota* seeds. In more remote regions of India, cannas are fermented to produce alcohol. The plant yields a fiber from the stem used as a jute substitute and to make paper. The seed produces a purple dye when boiled. Smoke from the burning leaves serves as an insecticide. Cannas are natural filters and are used to extract pollutants in a wetland environment as canna has a high tolerance to contaminants. In Thailand, cannas are a traditional gift for Father's Day. In Vietnam, canna is called dong *rièng* and its starch is used to make cellophane noodles known as *mièn dong.*

Deb Carlton

Further Reading

"Canna." http://www.absoluteastronomy.com/topics/Canna_%28plant%29 (accessed 20 August 2011).

Perman, Ray. *The Man Who Gave Away His Island: Remembering Margaret.* Edinburgh, Scotland: Birlinn, 2010.

Cannabis

An annual in the tribe Cannabinaceae and the family Urticaceae, *Cannabis* is the genus name encompassing three species. In 1753, Swedish naturalist Carl Linnaeus named *Cannabis sativa*, deriving the genus name from the Greek *kannabis*, meaning "hemp." Hemp is the common name for cannabis plants used to derive fiber. The Greek *kannabis* derives in turn from the Sanskrit *cana*. Cannabis is rendered *quetuba* in Assyrian, a word that means "noisy" because the Assyrians used it in religious rites that must have been quite loud. Cannabis is *knopla* in Slavic, *qanneh* in Hebrew, *qannah* in Arabic, *quonnah* in Persian, *quannah* in Celtic, and *canano* in Spanish. The third syllable in cannabis—bis—may derive from the Hebrew *bosom* or the Aramaic *bussma*, meaning "aromatic," recognition that cannabis is a fragrant plant. In the early 19th century, French naturalist Jean-Baptiste Lamarck named the second species, *Cannabis indica*, meaning "cannabis from India," a sensible appellation that noted the country of origin of this species. In 1924, a Russian botanist named the third species, *Cannabis rudernis*.

Origin and Diffusion

Cannabis originated in Central Asia, where it still grows wild. Cannabis grows wild between the Pamir-Altai Mountains and the Caucasus Mountains. It was first cultivated in western China or Turkestan. The oldest evidence of cannabis may come from Taiwan, where pottery as old as 12,000 years contained pieces of hemp rope, though the use of cannabis on Taiwan may predate its cultivation. Around 5000 BCE the Chinese, perhaps marking the advent of cannabis culture, grew the fiber in the Yellow River valley for making cloth and netting. This fact

Marijuana (AP Photo/Ted S. Warren)

suggests that humans first used cannabis as a fiber and only later for food, medicine, and recreation. During the Han dynasty, the Chinese made burial shrouds of hemp. These garments must have been for commoners, who wore cannabis cloth. The Chinese reserved silk garments for the aristocracy.

The use of cannabis for food is also ancient. In the 16th century BCE, the Chinese agricultural text *Xia Xiao Zheng* reported that cannabis was an important food. Between the fifth and third centuries, the *Book of Songs* and *The Annals* list six food crops, cannabis among them. The Chinese roasted cannabis seeds or ground them into flour. As a source of oil, cannabis appears to have been a staple in the diet until the sixth century BCE when the Chinese came increasingly to rely on rice, barley, millet, soybeans, and sorghum for food.

Aware of the sexuality of plants before Europeans made this discovery, the Chinese understood that cannabis is a dioecious plant, bearing male and female flowers on separate plants. During the Han dynasty, the Chinese began to make cannabis fiber into paper. From an early date, Chinese shamans used cannabis in rites to expel demons. In the fifth century BCE, shamans used cannabis to induce dreams, which they used to predict the future. As early as the third millennium BCE, Emperor Shen Nung, anticipating the medicinal uses of the plant, recommended that sufferers of gout and malaria drink tea made from cannabis leaves and flowers. Indeed, humans have used cannabis as a medicine for at least 3,000 years. So important was cannabis that Nung accepted it as tribute. In the second century, physician Hua Tuo mixed cannabis resin with wine, offering it to patients as an analgesic. Yet cannabis may not have been widespread in ancient China. Taoists were suspicious of its hallucinogenic properties. In any case, the Chinese appear to have preferred alcohol and opium to cannabis. From China, the annual spread to Japan. The Japanese wove cannabis fiber into a fabric as fine as silk.

Around 2000 BCE, cannabis spread from Central Asia to India. According to one tradition, Hindus believe that the god Shiva took cannabis from the Himalayan Mountains, planting it in India. Another account holds that Shiva entered a garden on a hot day. Seeking shade, he lay beneath a cannabis plant. Growing hungry he ate the plant, perhaps feeding on the leaves and seeds. So satisfying was cannabis that Shiva declared it his favorite food. The author of the *Atharva Veda*, apparently aware of the connection between cannabis and Shiva, recommended it to the person who wished to commune with the god. The *Veda* listed cannabis among the five sacred plants and devised a prayer to the gods to protect cannabis users from disease and demons. The Indians, holding that cannabis had spiritual qualities, used it to cleanse their sins. Indian priests and holy men used cannabis to bring them to enlightenment. Cannabis helped them endure hunger, thirst, and pain. According to one tradition, Buddha subsisted six years on cannabis seeds, eating just one seed each day. Having an erotic element, cannabis may have been used in India as an aphrodisiac. The practitioners of Tantrism may have used it to prolong sex. As a medicine, cannabis was used to treat dysentery, insomnia, and fever. In India, cannabis tea was a popular wedding beverage, and a host gave cannabis tea to the guests who visited his home. Indians made tea from cannabis leaves, milk, and sugar. In addition to these uses, Indians crushed cannabis leaves, adding the powder to food.

By 1500 BCE, cannabis had spread to Iran, Turkey, Greece, the Balkans, Germany, and France. By 900 BCE, the Assyrians used cannabis, apparently as incense, in religious rites. In the seventh century, Iranian religious reformer Zoroaster, writing in the *Venidad*, ranked cannabis as the most important of 10,000 medicines. In the 15th century, Muslim chronicler al-Maqrizi told the story of Heydar, an Islamic monk in Iran. In 1155 Heydar, in a story reminiscent of the tales told about Shiva, entered a garden on a warm day, encountering a cannabis plant. His curiosity aroused by the fact that the heat had not wilted the plant, he plucked a few leaves, chewing them. Heydar became high, telling his fellow monks of his discovery. So delighted was he with the effects of cannabis that Heydar chewed its leaves the rest of his life. Until the 20th century, cannabis use among the ancient Hebrews remained controversial, though in 1936 etymologist

Sula Benet asserted that a passage in Exodus referred to cannabis as incense and a drug. The Hebrews appear to have used cannabis incense in religious rites until 621 BCE, when King Josiah suppressed its use. Some authorities believe that Jesus used cannabis in his ministry to treat eye and skin ailments. By the time of Jesus, India, China, and Europe had emerged as centers of cannabis culture. By the first century CE, cannabis spread from India to South Africa and Sumatra. From South Africa, cannabis spread north throughout the rest of Africa.

The Egyptians used hemp to make rope. Scholars discovered pieces of hemp in the tomb of pharaoh Akhenaton. The discovery of cannabis pollen on the mummy of pharaoh Ramses II has led to the supposition that the Egyptians used cannabis in their funereal rites, at least for the nobility, though not everyone accepts this interpretation. Yet the Egyptians had no word for cannabis, suggesting that it was not an important plant to them.

Before 800 CE, the Scythians brought cannabis to Europe, though Europeans may have grown cannabis before the Scythian introduction. Archaeologists have found it in Neolithic Germany, Romania, and the Ukraine. Europeans were familiar with cannabis as early as China's experiments with the plant, though Europe surely lagged behind China in cultivating it. Europeans may have first used cannabis in their religious rites. By the fifth century BCE, Europeans were using cannabis to make burial clothes. In the fifth century BCE, Greek historian Herodotus noted that the Scythians inhaled cannabis incense after a funeral. Herodotus observed that the people of the Balkans used cannabis to make cloth. Curiously, fourth-century BCE Greek botanist Theophrastus did not mention cannabis, leading one to wonder how important it was to Greek agriculture and life. In the first century CE, Greek physician Dioscorides wrote favorably about cannabis. He differentiated plants by sex, remarking that cannabis was used to make rope and recommending it to treat earache. He noted that it suppressed the libido, a conclusion that put him at odds with the beliefs of India. In the second century CE, Galen, physician to Emperor Marcus Aurelius, noted that cannabis produced a feeling of well-being. Taken in too large a quantity, cannabis intoxicated the user, causing dehydration and impotence. The Romans grew little cannabis in Italy, instead importing it from the provinces. The Romans used cannabis to make rope and sail. First-century CE Roman encyclopedist Pliny the Elder approved of its use to make rope. In the early Middle Ages, the Franks grew cannabis for fiber. Sixth-century Frankish queen Arnegunde was buried beneath a blanket of cannabis cloth. In medieval England, farmers grew cannabis with flax. The Vikings used cannabis to make rope, fishing line, and sail. The Arabs used cannabis to make paper, introducing the technology of papermaking to North Africa and Spain. Europe's first paper factory, which began operation in the 12th century, used cannabis. German inventor Johan Gutenberg printed the Bible on cannabis paper in the 15th century. The growth in maritime commerce increased demand for cannabis for sail.

In Europe, northern Asia, and East Asia, humans grew cannabis for fiber and food. The people of Africa, the Middle East, and southern Asia used cannabis as a drug and secondarily as food and fiber. As early as 1545, the Spanish, English, and French brought cannabis to North America, using it to make rope and sail. In the 19th century, India introduced a second group of cannabis varieties to the United States. In 1835, the Caribbean and South America adopted cultivars from India. Until the late 19th century, cannabis was among the most widely grown plants, being used for fiber, cloth, lighting oil, medicine, and in some cases food. People prized it as a durable fiber for making twine, rope, and canvas. In the 19th century, however, the widespread adoption of the cotton gin allowed cotton to supplant cannabis in making textiles. At the same time, kerosene replaced cannabis oil for lighting, and acid process pulp replaced it in making paper. Into the early 20th century, physicians continued to use cannabis as an analgesic.

Around 1900, California growers adopted cannabis cultivars from Japan, and Kentucky farmers began to grow varieties from China. In Kentucky, one variety is appropriately known as Kentucky. In modernity, humans have eaten cannabis seeds during times of food shortage. During World War II, Europeans averted starvation by eating cannabis seeds, and the Chinese did the same during leader Mao Zedong's catastrophic Great Leap Forward. Poor Indians still eat cannabis seeds, combining them with amaranth seeds and rice. In sub-Saharan Africa, people feed ground cannabis seeds to babies.

Attributes and Cultivation

Cannabis grows from the equator to subarctic regions. Farmers raise it from Manchuria and Mongolia to southern Great Britain and from the Ganges River in India to Hokkaido, Japan. As a rule, cannabis requires four months to produce fiber and five months to yield seeds, though under ideal conditions cannabis may mature in as little as 2 months. By contrast, poor conditions delay maturity until 10 months. Fifty percent of seeds remain viable for three to five years. In the United States, cannabis needs 4 to 5 months to yield fiber. Farmers plant cannabis in spring. Seeds germinate in three to seven days. Long days stimulate vegetative growth. Cannabis flowers with short days. As we have seen, cannabis is dioecious, though an occasional plant is monoecious, bearing male and female flowers on the same plant, as do most plants. Male cannabis plants tend to be taller than female plants. Males die soon after dispersing pollen. Like corn, cannabis is wind pollinated. Seeds mature three to six weeks after pollination. A tall plant, cannabis reaches heights up to 13 feet. Cannabis tolerates frost better than corn. Warm temperatures produce the best yield of fiber and seeds. Cannabis does not tolerate waterlogged soil. A uniform distribution of rainfall throughout the growing season is best. A climate with high humidity yields the best fiber. Cannabis does best in fertile soil that drains well, although it survives in poor, sandy soils, which hold little water and few nutrients. Cannabis can survive with little rainfall. Intolerant of cold weather, cannabis languishes in shade. Farmers sow seeds at a density of 1,300 pounds per acre, roughly 10 seeds per seven square feet of land. Of the plants that germinate, farmers thin them to three to five per seven square feet. As a rule, farmers plant cannabis densely to derive plants suitable for fiber. Dense planting causes cannabis to grow tall with few branches.

In the United Sates, cannabis often follows corn. Typically, a farmer plants corn on the perimeter of cannabis fields, harvesting it before cannabis. Few insects and diseases plague cannabis in the United States. In Europe, however, cannabis suffers from the corn stem borer. Larvae of the semilooper attack seedlings. Sensitive to competition from weeds, cannabis yields diminish in the presence of broomrape weed. Cannabis fiber, derived from the stalk, is 60–70 percent cellulose. When bleached in water, the fiber increases to 95 percent cellulose.

Humans use cannabis fiber to make string, twine, rope, carpet, canvas, and paper. Cannabis oil is used to make soap and paint. Farmers grow cannabis for fiber in Russia, Europe, Chile, and the United States. Russia, Italy, and Poland produce 75 percent of the world's crop. Significant yields are also reported in the former Yugoslavia, Hungary, and Romania. In the United States Kentucky is the leading producer. Cannabis can be found as high as 8,000 feet and has colonized the Himalayan Mountains and the Hindu Kush. Varieties of cannabis are often named for the place of cultivation: Lebanese Gold, Colombian Gold, Hawaiian Blue, Jamaican Blue Mountain, Nigerian Black, and Mexican Green.

Cannabis as a Drug

Cultivating *Cannabis indica*, the people of India may have been the first to exploit the hallucinogenic properties of the plant. Since this early use in India, humans have associated *Cannabis indica* with its capacity to produce psychotropic effects. In antiquity, its psychotropic effects caused cannabis to be used in religious rites. The ancients thought cannabis a magical plant. The compound 9-tetrahydrocannabinol (THC) causes these effects. Young plants have the highest concentration of THC, which declines as they age. A cannabis plant is up to 5 percent THC by weight. Made from cannabis, marijuana is 5–10 percent THC. The dried leaves of cannabis comprise marijuana, though one may add the flowers to increase potency. Since 1938, the word "pot" has become slang for marijuana because Moroccan men kept marijuana in a small jar or pot. "Weed" is also slang for the drug because cannabis is a weed in many places. In the 1960s and 1970s, the United States imported illicit cannabis from Jamaica, Mexico, Colombia, and Southeast Asia.

THC affects the cerebrum, which coordinates movement and balance; the hippocampus, which stores memory; and the rostral ventromedial medulla, which receives pain stimuli. The brain has THC receptors, leading some medical authorities to assert that humans are predisposed to use cannabis. At low doses, cannabis causes euphoria. High doses alter perception. Among its common effects, cannabis induces a feeling of well-being, lack of inhibition, an altered sense of time, an increase in imagination, and a decrease in concentration. Cannabis rarely induces violence or aggression. Cannabis heightens touch, taste, smell, and hearing. The cannabis user is aware of latent thoughts and images. Cannabis increases heart rate, metabolism, and blood pressure. The eyes redden and the mouth and tear ducts dry. Cannabis stimulates appetite and causes the sweat glands to emit odor. Since antiquity, some people have believed cannabis to be an aphrodisiac, though few medical authorities now accept this view.

More potent than marijuana, hashish is also more dangerous. Hashish is 20 percent THC and hashish oil 85 percent. The user may experience paranoia, schizophrenia, mood changes, panic, and delirium. Fortunately, these symptoms subside with cessation of use. Cannabis appears to be nontoxic. No physician has reported death from overdose. By one estimate, the user would need to smoke 800 joints to die, and then death would result from carbon monoxide poisoning rather than the accumulation of THC in the brain. Nevertheless, cannabis smoke is as deleterious as cigarette smoke, aggravating respiratory ailments. Cannabis has tar and cyanide in addition to carbon monoxide. Cannabis is far less addictive than many other drugs, including tobacco. Cessation of use causes irritability, anxiety, restlessness, and insomnia, symptoms that are similar to those experienced by a person who quits caffeine.

Cannabis grown at altitude produces the most THC. As a rule, temperate regions produce cannabis suitable for fiber, whereas the tropics yield cannabis used for its psychotropic effects. Farmers grow cannabis for its psychotropic effects in India, Southeast Asia, the Caribbean, Central and South America, Africa, and Southern Europe. According to one authority, cannabis is the world's most widely grown hallucinogenic plant.

Christopher Cumo

Further Reading

Booth, Martin. *Cannabis: A History.* New York: St. Martin's Press, 2003.

Brownlee, Nick. *The Complete Illustrated Guide to Cannabis.* London: Sanctuary, 2003.

Guy, Geoffrey W., Brian A. Whittle, and Philip J. Robson., eds. *The Medicinal Uses of Cannabis and Cannabinoids.* London: Pharmaceutical Press, 2004.

Maiti, Ratikanta. *World Fiber Crops.* Enfield, NH: Science, 1997.

Ranalli, Paolo, ed. *Advances in Hemp Research.* New York: Food Products Press, 1999.

Russo, Ethan, ed. *Cannabis: From Pariah to Prescription.* Binghamton, NY: Haworth Herbal Press, 2003.

Canola

Canola is one of the world's major oilseed crops. Canola fields are easily recognizable by the plant's bright yellow four-petaled flowers. The crop belongs to the Brassicacea, or mustard family, and encompasses cultivars of three species. The first canola cultivars were bred from *Brassica rapa* (formerly misclassified as *Brassica campestris*) and *Brassica napus*. More recently, *Brassica juncea* was used to create new canola varieties. Canola is cultivated for the production of vegetable oil for human consumption, animal feed, industrial oil, and biofuel. The edible oil is used primarily for cooking, in salads, and for the production of margarine.

History

The use of *Brassica rapa* as a crop dates back more than 2,000 years. Written evidence indicates that it was first grown in Asia and Northern Europe. *Brassica napus* is probably of Mediterranean origin and was already known in the Roman Empire where it was appreciated for its turnips. The use of rapeseed as an oilseed crop is believed to have started in Europe during the Middle Ages when rapeseed was made into a lamp oil.

Canola was developed from traditional rapeseed varieties by Canadian plant breeders in the early 1970s. The canola-breeding program was initiated when Canada found itself short on oil for human consumption after the World War II. The program aimed at improving the plants in a way that would convert the industrial rapeseed oil to an edible oil by lowering the natural contents of glucosinolates in the seed meal and of erucic acid in the oil. Glucosinolates are metabolites that are characteristic of the Brassicaceae family and cause the sharp taste of mustard. Together with erucic acids and other compounds, glucosinolates deter herbivores from eating wild plants. Both substances are mildly toxic to humans and animals and cause an unpleasant taste of the oil. When the breeding goals had been reached, the new cultivars were named by combining the words "Canada" and *oleum*, the Latin word for "oil." "Canola" can also be read as an acronym for "Canadian oil low acid." The name is now a registered trademark of the Canadian Canola Association.

In order to qualify as canola, *Brassica* varieties must contain less than 2 percent of erucic acid in their fatty acid profile and less than 30 micromols of glucosinolates per 0.035 ounce of seed. They are also referred to as "double low" varieties. In addition to canola production, the production of industrial rapeseed oil with high erucic acids content continues. This industrial rapeseed oil is mainly used as lubricant or for hydraulic fluids.

Canola oil is produced from crushed seeds, which contain around 40 percent oil. It has low levels of saturated fatty acids and high levels of omega-3 fatty acids, and is considered by many consumers as a healthy choice of vegetable oil. The seeds also contain high amounts of protein, which makes the seed meal, that is, the dry matter left after the extraction of the oil, useable as high-protein animal feed. Like palm and soy, canola is also a major source of oil for biodiesel production. Biodiesel is produced from plant oils through transesterification, an industrial refinery process in which the oil reacts with an alcohol to remove the glycerin. The glycerin can be collected as a by-product of the refinery and used in cosmetics, pharmaceutical products, and foods.

Current Uses

Today, canola is grown on a large scale in Europe, North America, Asia, and Australia. It is available in spring and winter varieties. Winter canola varieties planted in the fall tend to have a higher yield than spring varieties. This yield increase is probably due to the increased time between planting and harvest, which gives the plant more time to develop in the field, and the fact that it can flower under cooler and therefore more suitable weather conditions. However, winter canola cannot be grown in areas with very harsh and cold winters. As a result, breeding efforts aim to develop a stronger cold hardiness in winter canola. This is particularly relevant since the main canola-growing regions in North America have continental climates with hard winters. In 2009, the Canadian prairie provinces, North Dakota, and Minnesota accounted for over 90 percent of the canola acreage in North America.

With the increasing demand for biodiesel and the popularity of canola oil, the acreage is expected to increase over the next decade and to spread into neighboring regions. The large acreages planted with canola in the last decade have increased the occurrence of so-called volunteer canola, that is, canola that grows as a weed in other crops. Canola is not easy to control as a weed, as it has a number of characteristics that it shares with "traditional" unwanted plants that reduce crop yield. Its ability to respond to environmental fluctuations is pronounced, and it produces a large number of seeds per plant, which can have a high persistence in the soil due to their ability to enter a metabolically inert stage in which they can survive extended periods of time.

Farmers grow canola in rotation, usually with cereals, because continued planting of canola or related species increases the risk of pest and pathogen attacks. Canola is susceptible to a range of insects and mites. The most important fungal pathogen of canola is *Leptosphaeria maculans*, which leads to blackleg disease. Blackleg, whose symptoms include lesions and a black coloring of the base of the stem, can lead to dramatic yield losses and can be carried over from year to year on infected canola stubble. Scelerotinia stem rot, caused by fungi of the *Sclerotinia* genus, is another major disease of canola that can lead to huge losses, particularly if the infection occurs during flowering.

Canola can be improved through both traditional breeding and genetic engineering. Hybrid canola has been successfully bred and marketed on a large scale for 20 years. Hybrids are appreciated for their increased vigor and other desirable traits, which derive from crosses between two inbred lines. Hybrids tend to be more robust and have good agronomic characteristics, such as quick seedling emergence and higher yield. Genetic modifications in canola have thus far been used to create herbicide or pesticide resistant varieties. These genetically modified canola cultivars are grown on around 90 percent of the current canola acreage in North America. Although canola is a primarily selfing plant, in which the pollen from one plant tend to fertilize egg cells from the same plant, canola flowers, with their bright color and high sugar concentration, attract bees and other insects. As a result, a certain amount of crossing between individuals occurs by insect as well as wind pollination. This has led opponents of genetic modification in plants to raise concerns about outcrossing of traits inserted into canola plants by genetic modification to genetically unmodified or wild plants. In addition, genetically modified seeds can end up in fields devoted to nonmodified crops. This issue came to worldwide attention in a high-profile lawsuit (*Monsanto Canada Inc. v. Schmeiser*), in which the agricultural corporation Monsanto sued a Canadian farmer, Percy Schmeiser, for patent infringement. Some plants of Monsanto's patented herbicide-resistant Round-Up Ready Canola were found in his fields. As the plants had by all evidence grown from wind-transplanted seeds, the case became a symbol for the power of multinational corporations in the world's seed market. When Monsanto won the first instance of the lawsuit as well as an appeal before the federal court, Schmeiser took the issue to the Canadian Supreme Court. In 2004, the court affirmed Monsanto's patent, but determined that Schmeiser would not have to pay the technology fee Monsanto demanded as he did not profit from the presence of Roundup Ready canola in his fields.

Because of the comparative ease with which canola can be genetically engineered and the large number of seeds per plant, scientists have started using canola seeds as a host to produce technically or pharmaceutically relevant proteins in large quantities, an approach known as molecular farming. Oilseed crops such as canola are particularly well suited to the production of certain types of proteins in seeds, because the seeds contain oil droplets to which the proteins of interest can be targeted. The proteins can then be easily extracted from the surface of the oil droplets. Use of canola in molecular farming is still at an experimental stage.

Kerstin Müller

Further Reading

Canola Council of Canada. http://www.canola-council.org (accessed 5 October 2010).

Hedge, I. C. "A systematic and geographical survey of the world cruciferae." In *The Biology and Chemistry of Cruciferae*, edited by J. G. Vaughn, A. J. MacLeod, and B. M. G. Jones, 1–45. New York: Academic Press, 1976.

Kimber, D. S., and MacGregor, D. I. *Brassica Oilseeds: Production and Utilization.* Oxon, U.K.: CAB International, 1995.

Office of the Gene Technology Regulator. "The Biology and Ecology of Canola." 2002. http://www.health.gov.au/internet/ogtr/publishing.nsf/Content/canola-3/$FILE/brassica .pdf (accessed 5 October 2010).

Raymer, P. L. "Canola: An Emerging Oilseed Crop." In *Trends in New Crops and New Uses*, edited by J. Janick and A. Whipkey, 122–26. Alexandria, VA: ASHS Press.

Cantaloupe

A vine that produces a type of melon, the cantaloupe (*Cucumis melo*) derives its name from Cantalupo, the papal gardens near Rome where it was cultivated. The connection between cantaloupe and "wolf bowl," the literal meaning of Cantalupo, is unclear. Confusion has arisen over the proper domain of the word "cantaloupe." The term originally applied only to the subspecies *Cucumis melo* var. *cantalupensis*, a cultigen of Europe and Asia. In the United States, however, the meaning is broader, applying also to the subspecies *Cucumis melo* var. *reticulus*, a cultigen grown in the Americas. The American cantaloupe is a muskmelon, but it is seldom designated as such. One may distinguish the two subspecies of cantaloupe by inspecting their skin. The Eurasian cantaloupe has rough, warty skin, whereas the American cantaloupe has netted skin. A member of the Cucurbitaceae family, cantaloupe is related to cucumber, squash, pumpkin, and gourd. In addition to muskmelon, cantaloupe is also known as cantaloup, cantalope, mushmellon, rockmellon, and spanspek. Cantaloupe is eaten fresh as dessert, in salad, or with ice cream or custard. In 1941, the U.S. Department of Agriculture isolated a mold, which yielded a superior grade of penicillin, from a cantaloupe. This discovery marked the beginning of the modern era of antibiotics.

A cup of cantaloupe has only 56 calories, 0.5 gram of fat, no cholesterol, 68 milligrams of vitamin C (113 percent of the recommended daily allowance), 494 milligrams of potassium, and beta carotene, the precursor of vitamin A. Half a cantaloupe has 5 milligrams of beta carotene, half the recommended daily allowance of this nutrient. The riper the cantaloupe the more beta-carotene it contains. Once cut, cantaloupe loses vitamin C. After six days, it has lost one-quarter of its vitamin C. The health-conscious consumer should eat cantaloupe soon after slicing it. Moreover, because cantaloupe may spoil in as few as three days after being cut, it is best consumed quickly. With only one gram of protein per cup of cantaloupe, the fruit is not a good source of this nutrient. Cantaloupe has adenosine, a blood-thinning anticoagulant that may benefit people with heart conditions. The substance may protect one from cancer. One of the few fruits and vegetables rich in both vitamins A and C, cantaloupe may lower blood pressure. Cantaloupe contains carotenoids, the cancer-fighting pigments that color it. A study in the Netherlands documented that people who consumed cantaloupe lowered their risk of developing macular degeneration by 35 percent. Cantaloupe may also reduce the incidence of cataracts.

Origin and History

A plant of the tropics, cantaloupe may have originated in India and Africa. Another hypothesis pinpoints the highlands of Iran, Pakistan, and India as the homeland of cantaloupe. Humans domesticated the vine about 5000 BCE, spreading it the Levant and North Africa. By 2000 BCE, the Egyptians cultivated it. The writers of the Old Testament, apparently familiar with cantaloupe, wrote about a variety of melons. The Greeks and Romans grew cantaloupe, though its cultivation appears to have waned in the Middle Ages, when trade in the fruit declined between the Near East and Europe. In the 11th century, Crusaders discovered cantaloupes in Arab markets, though they were not sufficiently impressed to bring seeds back to Europe. In 1273, Italian adventurer Marco Polo tasted cantaloupe in Shibarghan in the Iranian desert, judging the fruit "excellent, a good of trade that is deservingly widely sold throughout the countries." Italians brought seeds from Armenia to Europe, and by 1620 the pope was growing cantaloupe in Cantalupo. In the 18th century, French writer Francois Voltaire complained that the wealthy were addicted to the fruit. He had a low opinion of it, asserting that cantaloupe "turns bad too early in the stomach."

In 1494, Spanish-Italian explorer Christopher Columbus planted cantaloupe in Hispaniola (now the island of Haiti and the Dominican Republic), from where it spread to North America, perhaps through the agency of Spanish missionaries. In the 1920s, Armenian immigrants began cultivating a hybrid cantaloupe in California. In the early 20th century, Colorado was an important producer, growing enough cantaloupe to seed 100,000 acres. Today, California and Arizona yield two-thirds of the U.S. crop. Texas and Georgia supply the rest.

Attributes and Cultivation

In the early 20th century, gardeners nearly everywhere in the United States grew cantaloupe, though its commercial cultivation was restricted to the South and Southwest. Although cantaloupe may be grown in any medium, sandy soil is best. Heavy soil may delay maturation. Soil that is ideal for cucumber, pumpkin, and squash should yield cantaloupe. The soil should drain well. Cantaloupe responds to the application of manure and compost better than to inorganic fertilizers. Farmers aimed for an early harvest in order to get their cantaloupe to market before the glut of summer. In the early 20th century, the farmer who harvested an early crop could increase earnings $200 to $300 per acre.

Cantaloupe needs five frost-free months. In June, July, and August, the daily temperature should reach a maximum of 80°F to 95°F. Nighttime temperatures should not dip below 60°F. Rainfall should be moderate and sunshine abundant. Cantaloupe yields well when it follows a legume in rotation because the vine absorbs residual nitrogen from the legume. For this reason, farmers rotated it with alfalfa in the West, clover in the East, and cowpea in the South. Because sugar beet and corn are heavy feeders, cantaloupe yields poorly when it follows them. Because vines must absorb sufficient water for cantaloupe to increase in size and weight, winters should be wet so that the soil will be moist in spring. The farmer irrigated seeds at planting and again when vines were seedlings. Thereafter vines were watered every week or 10 days. One authority preferred light, frequent applications of water rather than heavy, infrequent soakings. When fruit set, the farmer watered vines more heavily until melons reached maximum size, thereafter returning to light watering. When cantaloupe was ready to harvest, the farmer ceased watering it to prevent fungal diseases. The application of too much water too early in the season caused the vine to grow at the expense of fruit.

Farmers bought seeds rather than saving a portion of the harvest. In 1910, cantaloupe seeds cost $1 to $2 per pound. One authority preferred seeds from cantaloupe grown at elevation. The farmer planted seeds a few days before the last frost was expected. At Rocky Ford, Colorado, farmers planted seeds about May 1. Planted in hills, one pound of seeds sufficed for one acre. Planted in rows, two or three pounds of seeds were needed for one acre. Seeds were planted one-and-one-half inches deep or two inches deep where the climate was dry. The farmer thinned plants to one vine every two feet.

Where insects, especially the grasshopper, cutworm, striped cucumber beetle, or melon aphid, plagued cantaloupe, the farmer cultivated the soil in autumn, winter, and early spring to destroy eggs and larvae. The grower dusted hills with lime and sprayed Bordeaux mixture to kill insects. The ladybug, syrphus fly, and lace winged fly preyed on the melon aphid. Insect-damaged vines were destroyed. The farmer sprayed fungicides against pathogenic fungi.

The harvest required judgment. A cantaloupe could not be picked green like a tomato or lemon. It could not show color like an apple before picking, otherwise it was too ripe. One authority recommended that a cantaloupe be picked when the flesh was sweet but still too hard to be eaten for one or two days. One axiom, though perhaps extreme, held that a cantaloupe progressed through the stages of green, ripe, and rotten in three days. In the early 20th century, farmers sold ripe cantaloupe locally, withholding for transit only those that would ripen in a few days. Once a cantaloupe has been purchased, it should be stored in the dark at room temperature until ripe and thereafter in a refrigerator.

Varieties

In the early 20th century, seed catalogues listed a large number of cantaloupe varieties. Many of these were likely duplicates, with seed companies having renamed a variety that they had appropriated from another company. The most popular variety of the era had a mysterious origin. One account holds that Netted Gem originated in France and became established in the United States in 1880. Another account holds that W. Atlee Burpee, an American seed company, bred Netted Gem in 1881. Whatever its origin, the variety produced small, uniform fruit that packed well in crates and retained its flavor when shipped long distances. By 1910, Netted Gem was the most widely grown variety in Colorado.

The virulence of the fungal disease melon rust led farmers to seek resistant varieties. Colorado farmer J. P. Pollock derived a rust-resistant cultivar, Pollock, named in his honor. Pollock was known as Rust Resistant, Eden Gem, Netted Rock, and Ironclad. A large melon, Pollock yielded sweet, spicy flesh. With green and salmon flesh, Pollock produced a thick, fibrous vine. Ryan's Early Watters, maturing about August 1 (10 days earlier than Pollock), resembled it in appearance and flavor. With green or yellow flesh, Ryan's Early Watters was susceptible to rust. Also susceptible was Defender, known as Burrell's Gem, Osage Gem, and Pink Meat. With salmon flesh, Defender stored well though it matured late and tended to crack when ripe.

Pollination

Cantaloupe has both male flowers, which contain only pollen, and perfect flowers, which have both pollen and ovum. Because only the perfect flowers have ova, only they can bear fruit. On a cantaloupe vine, male flowers outnumber perfect flowers 12 to 1, a circumstance that appears wasteful because only a fraction of the pollen is necessary to fertilize each ovum. Each perfect flower must set at least 400 seeds to produce fruit, so each ovum must receive at least 400 pollen grains. A cantaloupe flower opens after sunrise and closes in the afternoon of the same day. An ovum is receptive to pollen only a few hours in the morning. In hot weather, an ovum may be receptive to pollen only a few minutes, a curious circumstance give the vine's tropical habit.

Although cantaloupe is self-fertile, the perfect flowers do not self-pollinate. Pollen is too heavy for wind to disperse. Cantaloupe must rely on insects to do the task. By cross-pollinating cantaloupe, insects aid the fruit in attaining maximum weight. The honeybee is the most common pollinator in North America, Israel, and West Africa. Ants, thrips, and beetles also pollinate cantaloupe. Farmers rent honeybee hives in spring for the purpose of pollination. The more bees that visit cantaloupe flowers the greater are the yield, weight, and sweetness of the fruit. New Zealand farmers use bumblebees to pollinate cantaloupe.

Bumblebees visit cantaloupe from dawn to dusk, though late visits must be unproductive given that cantaloupe's perfect flowers are receptive to pollen only in the morning.

Christopher Cumo

Further Reading

Blinn, Philo K. *Cantaloupe Culture: A Treatise on Cantaloupe Growing under Irrigation in Colorado.* Rocky Ford, CO: Rocky Ford Cantaloupe Seed Breeders' Association, 1910.

Bradley, Fern Marshall. *Rodale's Vegetable Garden Problem Solver: The Best and Latest Advice for Beating Pests, Diseases, and Weeds and Staying a Step Ahead of Trouble in the Garden.* New York: Rodale, 2007.

Delaplane, Keith S., and Daniel F. Mayer. *Crop Pollination by Bees.* New York: CABI, 2000.

McNamee, Gregory. *Moveable Feasts: The History, Science, and Lore of Food.* Westport, CT: Praeger, 2007.

Yeager, Selene. *The Doctors Book of Food Remedies.* New York: Rodale, 2007.

Caraway

Caraway is often regarded as an ancient spice—sometimes described as one of the oldest cultivated plants—used by humans since time immemorial. It is believed that the seeds, actually the fruits, were used in the kitchen and as a medicine since prehistory. In 2005, remnants of caraway were found in a 5,000-year-old grave in Iran. First-century CE Greek physician Discorides mentioned caraway as a medicinal plant. First-century Roman encyclopedist Pliny the Elder referred to caraway as a foreign plant. A fourth- or fifth-century collection of Roman recipes, known as *De re coquinaria* and attributed to Apicius, mentions caraway as an ingredient. These references may, however, have been to wild plants, though for Pliny it was obviously a foreign plant and so was probably imported.

However, the evidence of its presence as a cultivated plant in Western Europe is from the early Middle Ages and even later. It is mentioned as *careium* in Frankish king Charlemagne's edict *Capitulare de villis vel curtis imperii* from around 812. Archaeological findings are reported from a site at Schaffhausen in Switzerland dating from the Middle Ages, from Cologne, Villingen, and other sites in Germany dating from the 14th to the 16th centuries, and from London probably as late as the 16th century. In Scandinavia, caraway is mentioned as a cultivated plant in the Danish king Valdemar I's land register of around 1230 and as a remedy in a medicinal work by Roskilde canon Henrik Harpestræng in the 13th century. The first mention of this culinary herb in England is from a recipe of 1390. The name caraway was recorded first in 1440. Some say it is of Arabic origin (*al-karawaya*). It was called *kümmel* in German, *kommen* in Danish, *kummin* in Swedish, and *köömen* in Estonian because it was confused with cumin (*Cuminum cyminum*) in older herbals and medicinal handbooks. Germany seems to have played a crucial role in its spread throughout Europe, because it is sometimes referred to as German cumin in many languages, such as *cumino tedesco* in Italian, *tysk kummin* in Swedish (ancient Swedish *thydzk komin*), and *saksanku-mina* in Finnish. Also, some local Turkish names indicate that it was associated with strangers or minorities, for example, *Ermeni kimyonu* (Armenian cumin) or *Frenk kimyonu* (Frankish cumin). In French and in Faroese, Norwegian, and some Swedish dialects, it was called *carvi* and *karvi* respectively. In Central Asia, it was known as *zire*. The Arabs probably brought it to India, where it is still used in large quantities for producing curry.

Caraway was widely cultivated by the peasantry in Denmark and Sweden during the 17th and 18th centuries. For the Swedish peasantry, its blooming was a sign to begin the harvest of hay in the 19th century. Commercial plantations existed on Bornholm in 1750s. It seems to have reached North America with European settlers as a garden plant by the turn of the 19th century. Nowadays, it is introduced to most countries where it can grow. Caraway easily escapes and has become naturalized in many parts of the world.

The Plant and Its Origin

Caraway is a biennial umbelliferous plant with a taper root, like a parsnip, but much smaller, running deep into the ground. The stems rise from 18 to 25 inches, with spreading branches and finely cut deep green leaves. The fruit is about one-fifth of an inch long and tapered at the ends. Two different kinds of caraway exist in cultivation, winter caraway and annual caraway. The former is cultivated in Northern Europe, including Russia, while the annual caraway is predominant in Israel, Egypt, and Sudan.

Its origin is disputed. Caraway might have originated in southwest Asia and the eastern Mediterranean region, but early on it spread as a cultivated plant through Eurasia. It may be indigenous in Europe, although it has been cultivated in spice and medical gardens for centuries. However, harvesting fruits from wild or natu-ralized plants has been common as well. This extensive system of gardening has been typical for the peasantry in premodern Europe.

A Culinary Herb for Many Purposes

Caraway has a wide use as a condiment and medicine. Caraway consists of essential oils whose aroma is determined by carvone and limonene. The other constituents of the seed are carveol, dihydrocarveol, α-pinene, β-pinene, and sabine.

Caraway is first and foremost a spice crop. It is a very typical spice for Central, Eastern, and Northern Europe, used in many different kind of dishes. The ripe fruits have a long tradition of flavoring bread, buns, curry, cheese, dishes of eel, goulash soup, liver, pickled beets, pickled herring, porridge, potatoes, pretzels, sauerkraut, and sausage, and it is a must for the kind of flavored Scandinavian spirit known as aquavit. There are liqueurs made with caraway. Caraway is still widely used for food flavoring and as aroma. The fruits are supposed to stimulate the appetite, but they can also be chewed in order to freshen the breath. Raki, the strong aperitif of the Balkan Peninsula and Turkey, is sometimes flavored with caraway oil. The oil is also used for taste correction in medicine.

There are historical records from the United Kingdom and from Scandinavia that people ate the carrot-shaped taproots as vegetables, but this seems to be an obsolete practice nowadays. It was commonly harvested in many parts of Sweden in the 18th century. The fresh leaves can be eaten chopped in salad or stew. This has a long tradition in Northern Europe. The leaves have also been gathered as fodder for cattle and sheep.

Caraway also has a reputation as a medicinal plant. During the Middle Ages, caraway had some reputation in the treatment of snakebite. It has traditionally been used for headache, for colic, and as a carminative. That is, the plant is said to relieve gas. Distilled caraway water has been used as a folk remedy to ease flatulent colic in small children until recently. It was mentioned by the medieval and Renaissance herbalists and medicinal authors, and survived in scholarly medicine until the 19th century. English botanist Nicholas Culpeper wrote in 1652 that the caraway seed "is conducing to all cold griefs of the head and stomach, bowels, or mother, as also the wind in them, and helps to sharpen the eye-sight. The powder of the seed put into a poultice, takes away black and blue spots of blows or bruises. The herb itself, or with some of the seed bruised and fried, laid hot in a bag or double cloth, to the lower part of the belly, eases the pains of the wind cholic."

Caraway has also been used to treat malaria. Caraway beer was used in Denmark for colds. The oil pressed from the fruits has been available through pharmacies. Carvone is reported to have some cancer-preventative properties. It is also used as anthelmintic against hookworm. Tea of caraway is popular in modern herbal medicine. The fruits have also been used in many remedies within folk veterinary medicine.

Other uses of the oil include making perfumes and scented soap. Caraway has also been used by pigeon breeders. Baked caraway dough, placed in homing pigeon lofts, was said to ensure that the birds would always return. According to German folk tradition, bread made with caraway was used to drive away evil beings.

Commercial Crop for the Future

The demand for caraway fruits and oil in the international food industry is increasing. Several cultivars exist. Nowadays, caraway is a commercial crop chiefly cultivated in Finland, Russia, the Netherlands, Germany, Morocco, Egypt, Canada, and the United States. It is said to benefit from northern conditions, and the long summer days seem to yield the highest level of aromatic oils in the fruit. For these reasons, caraway is increasingly important as a crop in Finland and Canada. It is also grown in Kashmir and the foothills of the Himalayas in northern India.

Ingvar Svanberg

Further Reading

"Caraway Seed Nutrition Facts, Medicinal Properties and Health Benefits." http://www.nutrition-and-you.com/caraway-seed.html (accessed 23 June 2012).

Galambosi, Bertalan, and Pekka Peura. "Agrobotanical Features and Oil Content of Wild and Cultivated Forms of Caraway (*Carum carvi* L.)." *Journal of Essential Oil Research* 8 (1996): 389–97.

Cardamom

Historical and Origin of Cardamom

Cardamom is a large perennial, rhizomatous monocot, belonging to the family Zigniberaceae. It is native to the forests of Western Ghats of southern India. Cardamom is often referred as the "Queen of Spices" because of its pleasant aroma and taste. It is considered to be the third most expensive spice in the world. This spice was highly valued from ancient times. It is grown in the hilly regions of South India at 800 to 1,300 yards. Large fields of cardamom plants can be found in Sri Lanka, Papua New Guinea, Tanzania, and Guatemala.

Cardamom belongs to the genus *Elettaria* and species *cardamomum*. The genus name is derived from the Tamil root *Elettari*, meaning "cardamom seeds." Cardamom is known to have been in use in India from antiquity. It is known as *Ela* in Sanskrit texts; however, the ancient Indian Ayurvervidic texts, *Charaka Samhita* and *Susrutha Samhita* (1400–600 BC), mentioned cardamom on many occasions without clarifying if *Ela* is cardamom or large (Nepal) cardamom. The earliest attested form of the word *kardamon* is the Mycenaean Greek *ka-da-mi-ja*, written in Linear B syllabic script. In the New Testament, which was largely written in Greek, *amooman* appears in reference to the aromatic plant cardamom.

Babylonians and Assyrians used many herbs for medicinal purposes. Plants known to be used by Assyrian doctors and chemists included cardamom, cumin, dell, origanum, thyme, saffron, and sesame. Cardamom spread along land routes and was known in ancient Greece and Rome. Wrecks of luxury cargos revealed that spices were an exotic and rather rare material in ancient times. In antiquity, spices were symbols of luxury and had an important role in ceremonies and cultural events. Dioscorides (40–90 CE), a Greek physician and author of *Materia Medica*, mentioned cardamom among many herbs as useful medicine. Greek physician Hippocrates appreciated the therapeutic effect of *Kardamomom*. *Kardamono* is a Greek verb derived from cardamom that means "to become strong." Cardamom was suggested as an important remedy for digestion after heavy meals. Cardamom was listed among the Indian spices liable to duty in Alexandria in 176 CE.

After the fall of Rome, Venice became an important trade city and harbor connecting East and West. Spices such as cardamom, pepper, cloves, and cinnamon were imported to Constantinople and Venice in exchange for salt and salted meat exported to Levantine countries. Dutch merchant Jan Huygen van Linschoten in his *Journal of Indian Travels* gave a description of the two forms of cardamoms used in South India. It is known that Arabs, trying to keep secret the sources of the spices, were the major traders of Indian spices. Cardamom was an exceptional spice that Arabs sold to the West. Valerius Cordus (1515–1544), a German physicist and herbologist, was the first to describe cardamom as an essential oil. With the discovery of the sea route to the west coast of India, the Portuguese started collecting and exporting cardamom to Europe. European colonizers did not care much about cardamom cultivation and production until the 19th century. Officers working for the British East India Company described cardamom and its cultivation in South India.

Cultivation of Cardamom

Today, cardamom is produced mainly in India and Guatemala. It was introduced in Guatemala only in the early 1920s from Sri Lanka or India. After World War II, cardamom production expanded to 13,000 to 14,000 tons annually. India is the main producer, with cardamom-growing areas in Kerala. Kerala is in the districts of Idukki, Palakkad, and Wynad. The cardamom-growing regions of South India are located at 8° and 30° north latitudes and 75° and 78° east longitudes. Two varieties of cardamom plants are identified: *Elettaria cardamomum* ssp. *major*, comprising wild types of Sri Lanka; and *Elettaria cardamomum* ssp. *minor*, comprising cultivars like Mysore, Malabar, and Vazhukka. These types are grown in different tracts and are identified mostly by the nature of panicles, the size of plants, and other morphological characters. Cardamom varieties are highly location specific.

Tillers emerge from axils of underground stem, and from their bases vegetative buds emerge throughout the year. The majority of vegetative buds are produced between January and March. It takes almost 10 months for a vegetative bud to develop and about a year for the panicle to emerge from the newly formed tillers. Generally, two to four panicles emerge from the base of a tiller. Shoots mature in 10 to 12 months. The flowers of the plant are bisexual, zygomorphic, white, and one-and-two-tenths to one-and-four-tenths inches long. The structure of the cardamom flower accommodates insect pollination as indicated by the prominent labellum, stigma positioning above anthers, and the presence of nectar glands. The fruits of cardamom are ellipsoidal, almost spherical, fleshy and green. Color does not vary with biotypes or varieties. The essential oil of cardamom is derived from the fruits of the plant.

Cardamom is affected mostly by cardamom mosaic virus (car-MV-Katte), cardamom necrosis virus (car-NV-Nilgiri necrosis virus), and cardamom vein-clearing disease (car-VCV-Kokke kandu). The last two pathogens are endemic. Crop losses are caused mostly by cardamom mosaic virus. Cardamom is affected by a number of diseases caused by various pathogens including fungi, bacteria, and nematodes. More than 25 fungal diseases have been reported not only in plantations but also in nurseries. Capsule rot (*Azhukal*) is caused by *Phytophthora meadii*, *P. nicotianae* ssp. *Nicotianae*. Rhizome rot is caused by *Pythium vexans*, *Rhizoctonia solani*, and *Fusarium oxysporum*. Chenthal is caused by *Colletotrichum gloeosporiodes*, and Root knot nematode is caused by *Meloidogyne incognita*.

Pharmacological Properties of Cardamom

In Ayurvedic texts, cardamom seeds are described as aromatic, acrid, sweet, cooling, stimulative, carminative, diuretic, cardiotonic, and expectorant. The use of cardamom was a subject of extensive ethnopharmacological and ethnobotanical research, but there are few studies for cardamom's pharmacological properties. Cardamom seeds and oil have carminative action (it expels gas from the intestines or stomach). In British and U.S. pharmacopoeias, cardamom is an aromatic stimulant, carminative, and flavoring agent. In addition, tincture cardamom is used in many preparations that are carminative, stomachic, and used to relieve colic. In animal experiments, the essential oil caused an increase in the secretion of bile and a reduction in gastric juice production.

The terpenoid constituents of cardamom oil seem to have mycostatic and antibacterial effects. In addition, cardamom oil exhibits mild antioxidant (increase of glutathione-s-transferase enzyme activity) and anti-inflammatory properties according to several in vivo models. Its anti-inflammatory effect is due to the activation of the complement system of the human immune system. However, no toxicity was reported for cardamom, as its main use is as a spice and flavor. The concentration of cardamom in food preparation is small; higher concentrations could not be used because of their intense smell and taste.

Culinary and Other Features of Cardamom

Nowadays, the major use of cardamom is for culinary purposes. Asiatic cuisines use cardamom (whole or ground) in a variety of dishes. In Indian cooking, cardamom is one of the main ingredients of *garam masala*, a combination spice for many vegetarian and nonvegetarian dishes. Cardamom is a peculiar and exotic spice used in the Middle East's religious ceremonies. In addition, cardamom in these countries is used to flavor coffee (*Gahwai*). Arabs also adopted a large number of Indian recipes; cardamom is used in rice dishes. Europeans appreciated the exotic flavor of cardamom, and as a result they included it in many food preparations, dishes, confectioneries, and others. In Sweden, cardamom is popular and is included in many baked foods. In addition, cardamom produces colorless or pale yellow oil in small quantities. The essential oil is used not only in perfumes but also in bitters and liquors.

Cardamom is a source of protein (10.8 percent by weight of cardamom seed) and carbohydrates (68.5 percent by weight). In addition, cardamom contains phosphorus, potassium, iron, sodium, vitamin C, calcium, magnesium, potassium, zinc, fiber, iron, and manganese. Cardamom is low in saturated fat, cholesterol, and sodium.

Charalampos Dokos

Further Reading

al-Zuhair, H., B. el-Sayeh, H. A. Ameen, and H. al-Shoora. "Pharmacological Studies of Cardamom Oil in Animals." *Pharmacological Research* 34, no. 12 (July–August 1996): 79–82.

PDR for Herbal Medicines. 4th ed. Montvale, NJ: Thomson Healthcare, 2007.

Ravindran, P. N., and Madhusoodan, K. J. *Cardamom: The Genus Elettaria*. London: Taylor & Francis, 2002.

Spices Board of India—Ministry of Commerce and Industry. *Cultivation Practices for Cardamom*. Kochi: Niseema Printers & Publishers, 2006.

Carnation

A perennial ornamental, the carnation is in the family Caryophyllaceae, a Greek term meaning "clove leafed." The carnation's genus, *Dianthus*, contains more than 100 species, several of them also being ornamentals. *Dianthus* is a Greek word for "divine flower." This meaning may derive from the belief that the god Zeus was the guardian of the carnation. The English word "carnation" may derive from the Old English "incarnaycion," which in turn may derive from the Latin *coronarin*, a word that suggests a festive use of carnation. It is possible that the word

Carnations (Cowardlion/Dreamstime.com)

"carnation" comes from the Latin *caro* or *carnis*, meaning "flesh colored." By the 16th century, the English word "carnation" was in widespread use.

Origin and History

One writer believes that the carnation originated in Central and Southern Europe or in Asia. *Dianthus coryophyllus*, the progenitor of all carnations, grows wild in the Pyrenees Mountains of France and Spain. One authority believes that the people of Europe and Asia cultivated the carnation in prehistory. In the fourth century BCE, Greek botanist Theophrastus was the first to describe the carnation. Some scholars believe that the carnation was thereafter absent from the historical record in antiquity and the Middle Ages. Others believe that the Romans cultivated the flower, though like the Greeks, they treated it as an herb and medicine rather than an ornamental. The Romans may have added the carnation to wine to flavor it. One hypothesis, identifying the carnation in the Atlas Mountains of northwestern Africa, asserts that the Romans planted it in North Africa and Spain. The hypothesis that the carnation was a late introduction to Europe implies that the Greeks and Romans did not cultivate it. One authority believes that monks or soldiers brought the carnation to England in the 11th century. The troops of English monarch William the Conqueror may have introduced the carnation to England about 1066. The 14th-century English poet Geoffrey Chaucer may have mentioned the carnation, but some scholars believe he referred to an unrelated plant, *Eugenia aromatica.* Another contentious point concerns a portrait of 15th-century English king Edward IV. His hand grasped a flower, which some botanists have identified as a carnation and others as a rose.

By 1500, the people of Turkey, the Middle East, and Europe cultivated the carnation. In 1597, English herbalist John Gerard remarked that the carnation was widely grown. He was the first to mention a yellow carnation, which he received from a merchant, Nicholas Lete, who had acquired it from Poland. English playwright William Shakespeare (1564–1616) mentioned the carnation in *Henry V* and *A Winter's Tale*. In the 17th century, English herbalist John Parkinson described carnations with large flowers. In 1676, John Rea listed 360 varieties of carnation. Germany, the Netherlands, and Flanders were the source of carnations for growers throughout Europe. In the 19th century, Europe hosted exhibitions to showcase the best carnations. Competition was keen. In 1820 London, England, schoolteacher Thomas Hogg catalogued some 500 varieties.

The carnation was the favorite ornamental of U.S. president William McKinley. A friend and gardener who raised carnations stoked McKinley's interest in the flower. The president wore a scarlet carnation on his lapel as a token of good luck. At the Pan-American Exposition in Buffalo, New York, in 1901, McKinley greeted a crowd of visitors. Shaking hands with a long line of people, he encountered a girl who remarked that her friends would not believe that she had met the president. McKinley gave the girl his carnation, urging her to show it to her friends as proof that she had met him. Bereft of his good-luck token, McKinley succumbed to the next person in line, the assassin Leon Czolgosz. Thereafter Ohio, McKinley's home state, adopted the carnation as the state flower. Another admirer of the carnation, Anna Jarvis, considered it the flower of purity, strength, and endurance. Because she believed that these traits were the hallmark of motherhood, she sent 500 white carnations to the Methodist Episcopal Church in Grafton, West Virginia, on the first Mother's Day in May 1908 with instructions to give every churchgoer one carnation and every mother two. In 1909, Jarvis sent 700 carnations to this church. During her lifetime, she gave the church more than 10,000 carnations. By the mid-20th century, the carnation had declined in popularity, though it has rebounded, enjoying some of its former renown. Today, the carnation marks weddings and funerals. California, Colorado, Israel, Kenya, and several countries in Europe and South America are the leading carnation growers.

Attributes, Cultivation, and Types

The carnation needs neutral soil with a pH between 6.5 and 7.5. The gardener should cultivate the soil to the depth of a spade. Carnation benefits from the addition of well-rotted manure, compost, or peat to the soil. The gardener should favor a fertilizer with roughly equal proportions of nitrogen, phosphorus, and potassium at three ounces per square yard. A fertilizer with a ratio of 6:5:4 of nitrogen to phosphorus to potassium may be applied at a rate of two ounces per square yard. One authority recommends the application of 10-10-10 fertilizer. The carnation does well in aerated soil. Rocky soil is ideal. The carnation does not do well in clay and does not tolerate waterlogged soil. It does not thrive in sandy soil because sand does not hold moisture. The addition of potassium to the soil increases the number of flowers and improves their color. The gardener should guard against the indiscriminant use of nitrogen because too much causes the carnation to produce foliage at the expense of flowers. In 1820 Thomas Hogg, perhaps falling into this trap, recommended the addition of chicken and pigeon manure, blood, soot, limen, and gypsum to the soil.

The carnation yields perfect flowers, each with 10 stamens and two or three styles. Petals may be purple, red, pink, yellow, or white. Carnations known as selfs contain one color, whereas fancies have two colors. Among types are annual, border, perpetual-flowering, and malmaison carnations. The name "annual carnation" is misleading because this type, like other carnations, is a perennial. It is known as an annual because gardeners tend to treat it as an annual, planting new carnations every year. Tracing its lineage to the species *Dianthus chinensis* and *Dianthus caryophyllus*, the annual carnation is widely grown in the United States. Reaching a height of one to two feet, the annual carnation produces smaller flowers than those of the border carnation. Annuals will survive mild winters. Popular varieties of annual include Margaerite, Chaband, and Grenadin.

The border carnation is cultivated in the United Kingdom, North America, and New Zealand. A hardy ornamental, the border carnation can survive temperatures as low as –40°F. Growing 15 to 24 inches tall, the border carnation reaches only 6 inches in height when potted. In its second or third year, a plant may yield more than 100 flowers, which are two-and-a-half to three-and-a-half inches in diameter. Border carnations may be selfs, white, yellow, or apricot ground fancies, picotees, or cloves. Selfs may be white, yellow, apricot, pink, scarlet, crimson, gray, or purple. White, yellow, or apricot fancies are striped with another color. Apricot ground fancies may be buff apricot, orange apricot, golden apricot, or coppery apricot. The picotee has small flowers. Border carnations must be staked and for this reason may not be as popular as other types.

The perpetual-flowering carnation, originating about 1850, derives its name from the fact that it bears flowers year-round provided the temperature does not dip below 45°F. The perpetual-flowering carnation is the florist's ornamental of choice. Cut flowers last three weeks in water. The perpetual-flowering carnation may be a cross between the Flemish carnation and the Mayonnais carnation, the latter having been popular in mid-18th-century France. *Dianthus arboreum* may be another ancestor of the perpetual-flowering carnation. Known as the standard carnation, the perpetual-flowering carnation lives two years. It does not tolerate humidity or frost and is grown in greenhouses because it is not hardy. Flowers are 3 inches in diameter on 30-inch stalks. The perpetual-flowering carnation is grown more widely in the United Kingdom than in North America. Dwarfs are popular today and may be selfs or apricot or yellow ground fancies.

The malmaison carnation, popular among the wealthy at the end of the 19th century, may derive its name from its resemblance to the Bourbon rose, Souvenir de la Malmaison. Alternatively, the name may derive from La Malmaison, the residence of French emperor Napoleon Bonaparte and Empress Josephine. Josephine grew carnations in her garden. One authority, however, believes that the malmaison carnation was not cultivated until 1857 and so must not be connected to Josephine. Malmaison needs a drier, warmer environment than the perpetual-flowering carnation. It needs partial shade in summer. Twentieth-century tastes deemed the malmaison carnation old-fashioned, and today specialists grow it.

Christopher Cumo

Further Reading

Bailey, Steven. *Carnations: Perpetual-Flowering Carnations, Borders and Pinks.* Poole, U.K.: Blandford Press, 1982.

Galbally, John, and Eileen Galbally. *Carnations and Pinks for Garden and Greenhouse: Their True History and Complete Cultivation.* Portland, OR: Timber Press, 1997.

McGeorge, Pamela, and Keith Hammett. *Carnations and Pinks.* Buffalo, NY: Firefly Books, 2002.

Smith, Fred C. *Growing Carnations and Pinks.* London: Ward Lock, 1994.

Carrot

One scientist judges carrot (*Daucus carota*) the "most important of all the root crops." Tropical varieties of carrot are annual whereas temperate cultivars are biennial, though they are grown as annuals. A biennial carrot fills its taproot in the first year and flowers in the second. The largest portion of a carrot is the edible taproot. In the Umbelliferae or Parsley family, carrot is known a *keroton* in Greek. One cup of carrots has 20,000 international units of beta-carotene, the precursor of vitamin A, four times the recommended daily allowance. The University of Wisconsin has bred carrots with three to five times the beta-carotene of other varieties with the aim of planting these new cultivars in the developing world where vitamin A deficiency is acute. Among its benefits, 18th-century religious reformer John Wesley thought carrot cured asthma.

Origin and History

According to one scientist, the carrot is a variant of the Eurasian flower Queen Anne's lace. It originated in the Himalayan and Hindakush Mountains of Asia and was domesticated in Afghanistan, Russia, Iran, Pakistan, and Turkey. Wild specimens may still be found in southwestern Asia, the Mediterranean Basin, Africa, Australia, and the Americas. Humans first cultivated carrot 2,000 to 3,000 years ago. Archaeologists have found carrot seeds in Switzerland dating to this period. From Afghanistan, carrot migrated to the Mediterranean Basin. By 500 BCE, the Greeks cultivated the root, using carrot juice to treat stomachache. In antiquity, farmers and gardeners grew purple, yellow, or white carrots. The orange carrot would be a latecomer. Arabs may have brought carrot from Afghanistan to Northern and Western Europe. In the ninth century, Frankish king Charlemagne may have known of the carrot, though according to one authority carrot was not introduced into Europe until the 11th through the 14th centuries and into China, India, and Japan between the 14th and 17th centuries. By one account, the Flemish introduced carrot into England in 1558. The orange carrot arose as a sport in the Netherlands in the 17th century. Its superior flavor led to its adoption throughout Europe. In the 18th century, English queen Anne and her friends admired carrots in the royal garden. The queen challenged them to make lace as delicate and beautiful as carrot flowers. The queen's lace was judged the best, and thereafter the carrot flower was known as Queen Anne's lace.

In the 16th century, the Spanish introduced the carrot into the Americas, planting it on the island of Margarita near Venezuela. In either 1609 or 1610, the English may have introduced the carrot into Jamestown, Virginia. Another account holds that the American colonists did not grow carrot until about 1620 and then in Salem, Massachusetts. In the early 17th century, the Dutch derived the cultivar Hoorn, named after Hoorn, the Netherlands. A popular cultivar, Europeans brought it to the American colonies, where it was known as Early Dutch Hoorn. In 1870, Americans planted Danvers, a cultivar named for Danvers, Massachusetts. The variety Nantes originated in Nantes, France.

In 2006, China was the leading producer of carrots. The Chinese interplant carrot with other crops. They add carrots to recipes as a source of color, though they find the root flavorless. The United States ranked third, trailing China and Russia. California produces 80 percent of U.S. carrots. Florida, Michigan, and Washington are also important producers. Americans add carrot to beef or vegetable stew, spaghetti sauce, and minestrone. The carrot is ubiquitous in salad. The French slice carrots, cooking them in chicken broth with parsley and tarragon. The Turks combine carrot with ginger and sour cream, a dish known as carrot plaki. The Poles add cream and dill to carrots. Germans make carrot nut bread, from which Americans derive carrot cake.

Attributes and Cultivation

Carrots have more sugar than any other vegetable except beets. Farmers and gardeners grow carrots for fresh consumption or processing. The carrot may be black, red, yellow, or orange. The essential oils extracted from the roots kill bacteria. The essential oils from the seeds are used to treat kidney ailments and dropsy. The carrot may be planted as soon as the temperature reaches 45°F, though seeds will not germinate until the temperature is at least 68°F. Seeds will not germinate above 80°F according to one gardener or above 86°F according to another. Seeds germinate in 6 to 21 days. Because carrot does not transplant well, it is best planted where the gardener intends to grow it. Some gardeners sow carrot and radish. Radish germinates quickly, marking the spot where carrot will later germinate. Radish roots keep the soil loose for the enlarging carrot taproot. Alternatively, one may plant carrot with bok choy. In 30 to 45 days, the gardener may harvest bok choy, opening space in the garden for young carrots. For a continuous harvest, one may plant new seeds after harvesting half the crop. The carrot reaches the peak of flavor when planted in early spring, though carrot may be planted in late summer for an autumn harvest. Seeds may be planted three-quarters of an inch deep and four inches apart. Carrot grows best between 60°F and 80°F, the tops reaching a height of three-and-a-half to seven-and-a-half inches. The soil should be cultivated deeply and should be loose to allow carrot to enlarge its taproot unimpeded. The soil should drain well to prevent it from harboring fungi. Where the soil is heavy, the gardener may plant varieties with a short taproot. One gardener recommends the application of a balanced fertilizer to the soil. Carrot benefits from the addition of organic matter to the soil. The gardener may add wood ashes to the soil as a source of potassium and to sweeten the flavor of carrot. Carrots may be harvested when they are young for maximum flavor and nutrition. The gardener may leave carrots in the ground, harvesting only as much as she needs for a meal. After a severe frost, all carrots should be picked and stored in a cool, humid place. The tops should be removed.

Science and Breeding

Current cultivars are genetically uniform because they derive from only a few 18th-century Dutch varieties. With the aim of increasing the genetic diversity of current varieties, Russia's Vavilov Institute, named for 20th-century Russian agronomist Nikolai Vavilov, has amassed a collection of more than 1,000 cultivars. The U.S. Department of Agriculture's North Central Regional Plant Introduction Station in Ames, Iowa, has amassed a collection of 800 cultivars. The United Kingdom, France, the Netherlands, and Japan also maintain collections. Worldwide gene banks hold some 5,600 varieties. Breeders aim to derive cultivars with early-maturation, high-yield, high-beta-carotene content; the ability to set seeds under poor conditions; uniform root size, shape, and color; small tops; tender roots; improved flavor, texture, sugar content, and dry matter; resistance to cracking and breaking during the harvest; roots that taper uniformly; slowness to bolt; tolerance of poor soil and climate; wide adaptability; and resistance to diseases, especially leaf blight, black rot, powdery mildew, bacterial soft rot, and carrot yellows, and to pests including caterpillars and the carrot fly.

Bearing perfect flowers and male flowers, a carrot may have more than 1,000 flowers. The outer flowers mature first, though flowers in the core have the most fertile pollen. Each flower has five sepals, five petals, five stamens, and two carpels. Each carpel has two ovules. Because the pollen and ova of a single perfect flower are fertile at different times, the carrot is not normally a self-pollinator. In 1937, scientists made the first hybrid cross of two inbred lines of carrot. Because carrot is, with the aid of insects, a cross-pollinating plant, the production of inbreds reduces the number of seeds. A hybrid yields a taproot three times more massive than the root of either parent. Hybrids have more beta-carotene than the parents. The degree of heterosis, hybrid vigor, is 20–22 percent higher when one parent in the cross is male sterile than when neither parent is male sterile. Male sterility is of two types. In the first, the anthers shrivel before anthesis and so do not shed pollen. In the second case, a flower does not produce anthers. The second type of sterility is more commonly used in breeding programs. Male sterile plants are therefore useful only as the female in a hybrid cross. In 1953, scientists discovered the first male sterile carrot near Orleans, Massachusetts, naming it the Cornell cytoplasm. The Cornell cytoplasm has been used to produce the majority of U.S. hybrids. Hybrids are three-way crosses. First, the breeder crosses two inbred lines to yield hybrid progeny. Second, these progeny are crossed with another line, presumably a cultivar rather than another inbred, to yield a second-generation hybrid. In the production of a hybrid, the breeder discards progeny with undesirable characteristics, for example bolting, poor color, or irregular length or shape of the taproot.

Christopher Cumo

Further Reading

Hughes, Meredith Sayles, and Tom Hughes. *Buried Treasure: Roots and Tubers.* Minneapolis: Lerner, 1998.

McGee, Rose Marie Nichols, and Maggie Stuckey. *The Bountiful Container: A Container Garden of Vegetables, Herbs, Fruits, and Edible Flowers.* New York: Workman, 2002.

Singh, P. K., S. K. Dasgupta, and S. K. Tripathi, eds. *Hybrid Vegetable Development.* Binghamton, NY: Food Products Press, 2004.

Cassava

A perennial shrub in the Euphorbiaceae family, cassava, like the sweet potato, develops from a root. It does not produce tubers notwithstanding the tendency of one scientist to refer to cassava as a tuber. Accordingly, cassava is not closely related to the potato. Like sugarcane and several other plants, cassava is propagated from sections of stem. The Tainos of Hispaniola (now the island of Haiti and the Dominican Republic) who greeted Spanish explorer Christopher Columbus in 1492 called cassava *casabe* or *cazabe*, which the Spanish misunderstood as *cassava*. The Tupi-Guarani Amerindians of the Amazon River valley called cassava tapioca and used the pulp from the root in pudding. So important is cassava that the people of Ghana, Togo, and Benin know it as *agbeli*, meaning "there is life." Other names for cassava include manioc, manioca, mandioca, Brazilian arrowroot, and yucca. The scientific name *Manihot esculenta* refers only to cultivated varieties of cassava. No wild varieties of this species exist, suggesting that cassava has long been in cultivation. Cassava is low in fat, cholesterol, and sodium. It has vitamin C and manganese. One hundred grams of cassava contain 550 calories, 30.5 grams of carbohydrate, and 2 grams of fiber.

Cassava (Satit Srihin/Dreamstime.com)

Origin and Diffusion

A New World cultigen, cassava may be descended from the wild *Manihot flabeli-follia*. One school of thought places the origin of cassava south of the Amazon River in Brazil. Another school of thought proposes broadly that cassava originated in Mexico and Central and South America. From this region, cassava spread to the Caribbean at an early date. The Amerindians of Brazil cultivated cassava as early as 8000 BCE, a date that makes the root among the oldest crops. One authority holds that humans began growing cassava as early as 7000 BCE. This antiquity draws strength from the observation that humans may have domesticated vegetatively propagated crops before seed crops. As early as 1827, one researcher posited Brazil as the region where cassava culture began. By 6600 BCE, farmers were growing cassava in lands along the Gulf of Mexico. The Tapi-Guarani grew cassava about 3000 BCE in Colombia and Venezuela. The Peruvians began to grow cassava about 2000 BCE. The Mexicans were growing cassava by the time of Christ. From antiquity, cassava was grown intensively in northern and eastern Brazil, southern Brazil and eastern Paraguay, Colombia, Cuba, Haiti, and the Dominican Republic. Not everyone accepts a date of great antiquity. Those who hold out for a later period assert that the most ancient fragments of cassava date only to 600 CE in El Salvador.

The Maya, who may have cultivated cassava first in the Yucatan Peninsula, and the Aztecs cultivated different types of cassava. The Maya grew sweet varieties, which had little hydrocyanic and prussic acid, toxins that can be fatal if ingested. Because sweet varieties had few toxins, they were safe to eat. The Maya may have eaten cassava raw or cooked. The Aztecs on the other hand grew bitter varieties. These had high concentrations of toxins and so were lethal if not prepared properly. To remove the toxins one may grate the root, allowing the liquid to drain. Alternatively, one may soak cassava in water for five hours, a process that allows the enzyme linamarese to degrade the toxins. A third option is to ferment cassava in water for several days, a process that renders the toxins harmless.

By the 15th century, the people of Mexico, Central and South America, and the Caribbean cultivated the root. The Tainos brought cassava to the attention of Columbus, preparing cassava bread for him. The Spanish thought the bread, which in the absence of yeast was not leavened, insipid, ranking it well below wheat bread. Cassava bread, whatever one thought of its taste, could be stored as long as two years without a loss in quality. Cassava bread was a staple of commoners. The Amerindians issued it as a ration to soldiers. Some Amerindians ate unprocessed cassava to kill themselves so that they would be free of Spanish oppression.

Notwithstanding the judgment of Columbus and his party, cassava, once adopted by the Spanish and Portuguese, spread throughout the tropics of the Old World. In the 16th century, the Portuguese brought cassava from Brazil to Africa, using it to feed slaves aboard ship. The root quickly became a staple in Cameroon, Gabon, the Congo, and Angola. In the 18th century, the Portuguese introduced cassava to the island of Reunion and from there to Madagascar, Zanzibar, and India while the Spanish planted it in the Philippines and Southeast Asia. Thailand quickly emerged as an exporter. By 1850, cassava was widespread in Africa and Southeast Asia. By 1900, farmers everywhere in the tropics grew cassava.

Cassava in the 21st Century

In 2002, Africa was the largest producer of cassava. Asia ranked second, and South America occupied third place. Asia boasted the highest yield per acre and Africa the lowest. In 2008 the leading producers were Nigeria, Thailand, Indonesia, and Brazil. Nigeria, the Congo, and Tanzania produce the majority of Africa's cassava. In East and West Africa, less than half of the harvest goes to make flour and pellets. The leading exporters are Thailand, Vietnam, Indonesia, and Costa Rica. Thailand, Vietnam, and Indonesia account for the majority of the world's exports in the form of starch and pellets. Worldwide 80 countries, all of them in the tropics, grow cassava. As a source of calories, cassava ranks third behind rice and corn in the tropics. Cassava ranks second to corn in tonnage. In southern China, cassava ranks fifth in tonnage behind rice, sweet potato, sugarcane, and corn. Unable to meet demand through domestic production, China imports cassava from Vietnam and Thailand. China converts a portion of its harvest to ethanol much as the United States converts corn to ethanol, a practice that may increase demand for the root. Brazil harvests the majority of the Latin American crop. Brazil, Colombia, Cuba, Haiti, Paraguay, Peru, and Venezuela produce virtually all Latin American cassava. According to one authority, cassava yields more calories per acre than any other crop, though this honor may belong to sugarcane. Cassava may be the world's least expensive "source of starch." Today, the root supplies one-sixth of the daily calories of the people of Madagascar, Ghana, Nigeria, Liberia, the Congo, Uganda, Tanzania, and Mozambique. In Ghana and Nigeria, per person consumption of cassava has increased in the last 40 years, whereas consumption has declined in the Congo, Tanzania, and Uganda.

Intolerant of frost, cassava is grown between 30° north and 30° south and at elevations no higher than 6,000 feet above sea level. Cassava needs a temperature between 64°F and 77°F and 2 to 200 inches of rain per year. Tolerant of acidic and alkaline soils, cassava may be grown in soil with a pH between 4 and 9. Cassava yields best in sandy loam. High humidity favors the growth of roots. Because cassava tolerates low rainfall, it is a famine food, supplying calories and some nutrients when other crops fail. Some Africans eat cassava every day, sometimes at breakfast, lunch, and dinner. In Africa, nearly half of the population eats cassava as the primary food. One might question whether cassava deserves to be a dietary staple. Seventy percent water, the dry matter of the root is carbohydrate, 64–72 percent of its starch. The root has only 1–2 percent protein, an amount that compares poorly with the protein in legumes and grains. Cassava has vitamin C and calcium, but little thiamine, riboflavin, and niacin. So deficient is cassava in iodine that women in the Congo who eat primarily the root develop goiter. After the harvest, roots begin to rot within two days, making it imperative that they be processed or eaten quickly. Perhaps because cassava has toxins, is vulnerable to insects and diseases, deteriorates rapidly unless processed, and has little protein, researchers have not lavished the money on the root that corn and soybeans have received. Cassava, unlike corn, has few uses aside from the feeding of humans. The people of Africa eat most of the harvest. Less than 10 percent goes to livestock and industry. Industry uses cassava starch in the manufacture of clothes, adhesives, packaging material, food products, pharmaceuticals, and batteries. In Africa as elsewhere, corn rather than cassava feeds livestock. In an effort to increase the use of cassava as livestock feed, Nigeria refused to import corn in 1985. In the 1980s, high grain prices led Europeans to import cassava from Asia and Latin America to feed livestock. After 1992, the decline in grain prices caused European stockmen to jettison cassava for corn.

Small farmers grow most cassava, using it for their own sustenance. Most cassava, destined for the dinner table, never enters the market. Farmers who grow corn and cassava do not harvest cassava unless corn yields poorly. In this circumstance, farmers harvest cassava to stave off hunger. Farmers may leave cassava in the ground as long as four years without a loss in quality. In the Congo, farmers have adopted cassava because of its drought tolerance. Cote d'Ivoire, Ghana, and Uganda grow sweet varieties of cassava, whereas the Congo, Nigeria, and Tanzania grew bitter varieties. Most cassava varieties are bitter, perhaps because they are more resistant to insects and disease than sweet varieties. Today, high-yielding cultivars increase yields 40 percent over traditional varieties.

Some farmers fallow cassava land, especially where population is sparse. Throughout Africa, farmers grow cassava in preference to yams. It competes well with millet, banana, and yams. In West Africa, farmers intercrop cassava with yams. In Nimbo, Nigeria, farmers plant yams, corn, and melon in April and cassava in June. After the harvest, farmers fallow the land three years. In Uganda, banana is the primary crop and cassava secondary. Farmers intercrop cassava with corn, beans or peas, millet, and sesame. They plant cassava in March, harvesting it in November. Fallowing the land four months, they replant it to cassava. Where the soil is poor, farmers plant cassava rather than banana. Throughout the tropics, farmers intercrop cassava with beans, peas, soybeans, mung beans, peanuts, banana, plantain, rice, millet, sorghum, yam, and sweet potato. In the Congo and Tanzania, people eat cassava leaves as a vegetable, though they must be cooked to destroy the toxins. Leaves have more protein than the root as well as vitamins A and C, calcium, and iron. Despite these nutrients, Ugandans consider the leaves a food of the poor and so will not eat them. Although cassava is a subsistence crop, it has grown in importance as a cash crop in recent years. In Africa and South America, middlemen buy cassava from farmers, transport it to market, and sell it for profit. In India, Brazil, and Nigeria, women do much of the work of tending cassava. In Nigeria, half of all working women are cassava farmers, though they earn little money. Whereas men clear the land, plow it, and plant cassava, women weed the land, harvest the roots, and process them. Men prefer to take wage labor rather than to grow cassava. Women's contribution to the cultivation of cassava is especially large where it is a subsistence crop. Men do more work where cassava is a cash crop. Cassava's popularity may be ebbing. As its price has increased, the poor have had to buy cheap rice.

Cassava is a staple in the cuisine of several people. Rwandans combine cassava and beans. Liberians make gari foto from cassava, onion, tomato, and egg. Fufu, another Liberian dish, combines cassava, vegetables, and meat or fish. The people of Thailand coat fish, shrimp, or squid with cassava starch, frying the dish. In Kerala, India, cassava and fish are a popular combination. Cassava bread is widespread throughout the Caribbean. Puerto Ricans make chili de yucca from cassava and beans. Guatemalans make cassava soufflé. Peruvians combine cassava, cheese sauce, and chili peppers. Colombians make yucca frita by frying slices of cassava much as Americans make fries from the potato.

Diseases, Pests, and Weeds

Pathogens and pests are numerous in the tropics, and cassava suffers from several of them. Fungi afflict many plants. In the case of cassava, however, viruses appear to be the principal threat. Widespread in the Americas is Cassava Common Mosaic Virus, which has reduced yields more than 30 percent in Brazil, Peru, Colombia, and Paraguay. Worrisome is a new variant of the virus, which appeared in Venezuela in 1995. In Africa, the threat comes from African Cassava Mosaic Disease, which is the continent's most damaging disease and the most significant insect-borne disease of cassava. Scientists initially blamed the disease on African Cassava Mosaic Virus, which the whitefly *Bemisia tabaci* transmits to cassava. Scientists identified African Cassava Mosaic Virus as early as 1891. As late as 1959, the virus was virtually the only threat to cassava in Africa. Since then bacterial blight, the mealybug, and the cassava green mite have assailed the root. African Cassava Mosaic Virus is not alone in causing African Cassava Mosaic Disease. East African Mosaic Virus and South African Mosaic Virus also cause the disease. Often more than one virus attacks a plant. One study found the disease in more than 80 percent of cassava plants in West Africa. Uganda has suffered severe infections of the disease. *Bemisia tabaci* has migrated to Cuba and Brazil, leading scientists to fear that the disease will follow. Latin American cultivars appear to be especially vulnerable to African Cassava Mosaic Disease. The bacterium *Xanhomonas axonopodia* causes cassava bacterial blight, which has led to the total loss of the cassava crop in the worst infections. The disease spreads through stem cuttings, which, when sown, germinate infected plants. In 1972, scientists pinpointed the disease in Nigeria. During the 1990s, the bacterium spread throughout Africa. Damp weather hastens the spread of the bacterium, which reduces yields and sometimes kills plants by defoliating them. Nigeria has reported severe losses from the disease.

In Africa, the most serious pests are the mealybug and the cassava green mite. Native to South America, they are troublesome because they have no natural predators in Africa. In 1973, the mealybug migrated to the Congo, from where it has spread throughout Africa. The bug feeds on the stem, petiole, and leaf. Conscious of the lack of natural predators, scientists in 1981 released a species of wasp that feeds on mealybugs. By 1990, the wasp had established colonies in 24 African countries. First reported in Uganda in 1971, the cassava green mite, native to Colombia, reached West Africa in 1979. Sucking sap from cassava leaves, it weakens plants. In the 1990s, scientists identified three species of mite that prey on the cassava green mite and released them in Benin in 1993. Despite this effort at biological control, green mites remain entrenched in Africa, threatening the cassava crop. In Latin America, mites of several species, cutworms, scales, and lace bugs plague cassava. The worst pests are the hornworm and stem borer. The stem borer has caused severe losses in Colombia. Insecticides are effective, but many farmers cannot afford them. Genetically engineered cassava holds the promise of helping these farmers. Genetically engineered varieties have genes from the bacterium *Bacillus thuringiensis*, which code for the production of a chemical toxic to insects. This toxin does not harm humans, making genetically engineered cassava safe to eat. The success of Bt corn leads one to hope for similar success from genetically engineered cassava. Also damaging are termites, which feed on cassava stems, and rodents, which devour roots.

Cassava does not compete well against weeds. Their presence lowers yields 40 to 70 percent. To combat weeds farmers have increasingly relied on herbicides in Africa and South America, though the poor cannot afford them. The derivation of herbicide-resistant cassava may not, in increasing the reliance on herbicides, help poor farmers. It is unclear whether herbicide resistant cassava will be as successful as herbicide resistant soybeans.

Christopher Cumo

Further Reading

Charrier, Andre, Michel Jacquot, Serge Hamon, and Dominique Nicolas. *Tropical Plant Breeding*. Enfield, NH: Science, 2001.

Hillocks, R. J., J. M. Thresh, and A. C. Bellotti, eds. *Cassava: Biology, Production and Utilization*. New York: CABI, 2002.

Hughes, Meredith, and Tom Hughes. *Buried Treasure: Roots and Tubers*. Minneapolis: Lerner, 1998.

Khachatourians, George G., Alan McHughen, Ralph Scorza, Wai-Kit Nip, and Y. H. Hui, eds. *Transgenic Plants and Crops*. New York: Marcel Dekker, 2002.

Nweke, Felix I., Dunstan S. C. Spencer, and John K. Lynam. *The Cassava Transformation: Africa's Best-Kept Secret*. East Lansing: Michigan State University Press, 2002.

The World Cassava Economy: Facts, Trends and Outlook. Rome, Italy: Food and Agriculture Organization, 2000.

Castor Bean

Castor bean, or ricinus, is a plant that belongs to the family Euphorbaceae and is therefore not a true bean. The seeds of the castor bean plant resemble a tick, which has led scientists to name it *Ricinus communis*, also translated as "common tick." Known as the most toxic plant in the world, ricinus is a favored plant for scientific study and also for forensic research.

Cultivation

Castor bean is region sensitive. That is, it may be either an herb or a shrub and an annual or a perennial depending on the habitat. It is a native of Africa, parts of the Middle East, and India, where it has been cultivated for thousands of years. More recently, it has been cultivated in South America and also in the southeastern United States. It thrives in dry to tropical climates and requires moist and well-manured soil, full sun, and a slightly acidic to neutral soil of pH ranging from 6.1 to 7.5. According to the U.S. Department of Agriculture hardiness chart, ricinus is adapted from zones 9a to 11. Castor bean drains the soil of its nutrient and depletes it of nitrogen. This can be a cause for concern if this plant spreads to areas of other crops.

The castor plant is regarded as a noxious weed that can become difficult to control if left unchecked. In the United States, the main states for castor cultivation are Florida, Texas, California, Arizona, Alabama, North Carolina, and Georgia. It is commonly found near rivers and streams or alongside rail tracks or roadways.

Botany

Ricinus possesses a taproot that is branched. Stems range from a few feet to 15 feet in height. When ricinus plants are herbs, their stems are tender and slim. In shrubs, the main stem can get tough and hard. Stems, greenish blue in color, are referred to as glaucous and are free of stem or leaf hairs (glabrous). Most often as the plant gets older, the stem turns woody at the base (suffrutescent) for the herbaceous subspecies. Stems branch profusely with branches red, green, or purple in color. Stems are also erect and cylindrical.

Leaves are alternate, simple, with a leaf petiole each, broad and in the shape of a palm, also referred to as palmately lobed. Lobes are like six to eight leaflets united at the base margins. The edges of the leaves are serrated or toothed and with a reticulate or network-like vein pattern.

The inflorescence is a terminal panicled cyme. Here, the flower stalk is a long peduncle sometimes growing to a length of 20 inches. On it, male flowers are arranged at the lower half while the female flowers are at the upper half. Flowers are unisexual and both types of flowers are found on the same plant (monoecious). Flowers are actinomorphic and can be cut into halves along any plane of their cross section. Flowers are also described as incomplete as they may lack either the female or the male reproductive flower parts, or the petals. They are also hypogynous, where the ovary of the flower is raised above the other flower parts. The male flowers can be identified by their pale green color, many stamens, and branching anthers. Petals and pistil with ovary, style, and stigma are absent. Female flowers are showier. There are no petals as in the male flowers. The female flower has many green-colored, spiny outgrowths, and three bifid stigmas, which are bright red. There are three seeds per female flower. The fruit is a capsule that is schizocarpic or splits up into three separate locules upon maturity. There are many spiny outgrowths on the fruit. The seed is oval, brown, and shaped like a tick—hence the name ricinus, which is the Latin name for "tick." Each plant can produce as much as 10,000 seeds.

Toxicity

The castor plant is considered to be the most toxic plant in the world. Every part of the plant is poisonous, the seeds being the most lethal. The plant contains a protein toxin called ricin, which, when consumed, ingested, inhaled, or injected, affects metabolism of the animal cells. When consumed, this toxin replaces particular enzymes that are responsible for protein synthesis. When proteins are unable to be synthesized due to the lack of the protein-synthesizing enzymes, degeneration of the cells happen, causing the death of the organism. While seeds are the most toxic part of the plant, swallowing seeds whole does not cause as many problems as seeds that are broken down or chewed. Whole seeds are likely to be expelled through the digestive track, but broken or opened seeds can be fatal as early as two hours of consumption. As few as two to four seeds are enough to be fatal in children.

Uses

Apart from their toxicity, castor beans are a source of castor oil. Castor oil is extracted from the seeds by a process of pressing. The oil does not contain the toxin; however, the toxin remains in the seed cake that is the residue from the oil press procedure. The oil is used as a purgative and as a lubricant. It is also used in the soap industry for the manufacture of textile soaps and transparent soaps. Other uses of the oil can be seen in the manufacture of typewriter inks, paints, varnishes, perfumes, and aromatics.

In India, castor oil is regarded with great respect and is one of the most important of oils in ayurvedic medicine for the treatment of arthritic ailments, dating back to 2000 BCE. Castor oil is also used in massage therapies. In Egypt, it is believed that first-century BCE pharaoh Cleopatra used it to massage her skin and to brighten the white of her eyes. It has also been used as an oil to light lamps.

There are virtually no pests known to attack ricinus. Beetles and aphids that feed on its leaves die from poisoning.

On an international security front, ricinus is a plant that is always under vigilance. Ricin has been used in international terror plots, in assassinations, and in attempted creation of weapons of mass destruction. Inhalation, consumption, and injection are the three ways that ricinus can affect an organism. However, while acute poisoning may not happen due to touch, the ricinus plant is known to cause skin allergies. Hence gloves are a necessity in the handling of *Ricinus communis*.

Amanda Mittra

Further Reading

Pandey, B. P. *Taxonomy of Angiosperms*. New Delhi: S. Chand, 2010.

"PlantFiles: Castor Bean, Caster Oil Plant, Mole Bean, Higuera Infernal; *Ricinus communis*." http://davesgarden.com/guides/pf/go/70/#b (accessed 4 October 2011).

"*Ricinus communis*." Center for New Crops and Plant Products, Purdue University. http://www.hort.purdue.edu/newcrop/duke_energy/ricinus_communis.html (accessed 4 October 2011).

"*Ricinus communis*." Missouri Plants. http://www.missouriplants.com/Redalt/Ricinus _communis_page.html (accessed 4 October 2011).

"*Ricinus communis*." The Poison Garden Website. http://www.thepoisongarden.co.uk/ atoz/ricinus_communis.htm (accessed 4 October 2011).

"*Ricinus communis*." Texas Invasive Plants Database. http://www.texasinvasives.org/ plant_database/detail.php?symbol=RICO3 (accessed 4 October 2011).

"*Ricinus communis*." U.S. Department of Agriculture. http://plants.usda.gov/java/ profile?symbol=RICO3 (4 October 2011).

Cauliflower

A cole crop, cauliflower (*Brassica oleracea* ssp. *botrytis*) is related to broccoli, cabbage, kale, and kohlrabi. With a reputation as a difficult plant to cultivate, cauliflower is sensitive to variations in soil pH, moisture, and temperature. The immature flower buds are edible. These buds are reproductively inactive in the sense that less than 10 percent flower. In addition to white, flower buds may be purple, lime green, or orange. A temperate plant, cauliflower is not grown in the tropics. Most cauliflower varieties are annuals, though a few are biennials.

Origin, History, Attributes, and Cultivation

Cauliflower may be descended from a wild cabbage that grew along the coast of Europe. Cauliflower has been an important crop only since the 18th century. The United States grows half as much cauliflower as broccoli, though the demand for cauliflower has increased in recent years. California grows most U.S. cauliflower, which is harvested in the southern Imperial Valley in autumn and winter and north in Salinas in summer. In addition to California, cauliflower is grown on Long Island and the coast of Washington and in western New York, Texas, and the mountains of Colorado.

Cauliflower needs exposure to full sun. Seeds, planted either indoors before the last frost or outdoors a few weeks before the last frost, germinate in 3 to 10 days. Cauliflower needs at least eight weeks of cool weather, so it should be grown in spring or autumn. When planted in spring, cauliflower may be started indoors six to eight weeks before the last frost. Tolerant of light frost, cauliflower does not tolerate severe frost, hot sun or high temperature. Cauliflower bolts in warm weather or with too little moisture. When seedlings are two inches tall, they are ready to transplant in the field. Seedlings taller than two inches may not develop properly and should either be discarded or transplanted at once. When planted in spring, cauliflower yields a summer crop. The gardener may plant cauliflower in midsummer for an autumn harvest. As a rule, the later cauliflower is planted the larger it grows. One authority advises the gardener to wet the soil the day before transplanting seedlings. Germinating between 68°F and 86°F, cauliflower grows best between 60°F and 70°F.

The head of a cauliflower plant contains the edible portion and is a composite of tightly packed flower buds called curds. When a head is two to four inches in breadth, it may be blanched by folding the outer leaves over it. Some varieties grow leaves that cover a head without human aid and are known as self-blanchers. When a head is firm, it is ready to harvest. As a rule, cauliflower is ready to harvest roughly 60 days after transplantation, though the number varies by variety. If left on the plant too long, a head discolors and becomes loose. The head and leaves may turn brown if temperatures are too cold, the soil is deficient in boron, or nitrogen is in excess. Cauliflower forms a head about 63°F. Above 68°F a head will be of poor quality, and above 77°F no head will form.

One gardener recommends that the soil be prepared two years prior to planting cauliflower to give the ground time to settle. At this time, the gardener should add compost or manure to the soil to increase its content of organic matter. The addition of organic matter is important to retain moisture in the soil. Cauliflower should not be planted in loose soil because the roots must be able to anchor in the ground. A plant that does not anchor firmly yields a small head of poor quality. The gardener should choose heavy, fertile soil because it retains moisture. Light soil is ill suited to cauliflower because it does not retain moisture and because cauliflower produces loose heads.

Cauliflower is a heavy feeder of water and nutrients. Irrigation is necessary on light soil or where the climate is dry. The gardener should not allow the soil to dry out. The soil should be mulched to retain water and minimize weeds. Cauliflower benefits from the addition of manure and fertilizer. In the United Kingdom, some farmers add chicken manure, guano, and soot to the soil. One recommendation urges farmers to add to the soil 11 to 33 tons of manure per acre. In the Netherlands one study documented the benefits of applying to the soil 176 pounds of nitrogen per acre. Where nitrogen is in shortage, cauliflower grows poorly. One recommendation calls for the addition to the soil of 264 to 440 pounds of ammonium sulfate, calcium nitrate, or Chilean nitrate per acre. During the growing season, the farmer should add one to three dressings of 132 to 264 pounds of nitrogen per acre. Where possible, cauliflower should follow a legume to benefit from residual nitrogen in the soil. In the Netherlands, research confirmed the value of adding 176 pounds of phosphorus pentoxide or between 176 and 440 pounds of superphosphate per acre. Some farmers have used as much as 700 pounds of superphosphate per acre. One study recommended the addition to the soil of at least 220 kilograms of potassium oxide or between 88 and 440 pounds of potassium chloride per acre. The farmer who uses potassium chloride must guard against adding too much chlorine to the soil because of its toxicity. Potassium sulfate may be substituted for potassium chloride. One gardener recommends that the soil pH be between 6.5 and 7.5. Another favors a value of at least 6.8. A third puts the figure at 7 when the soil has 2.5 percent organic matter and 6 when the soil has 8–10 percent organic matter. At low pH, manganese reaches toxic levels and molybdenum becomes unavailable. The gardener should not grow cauliflower on the same land year after year because pathogens may accumulate in the soil. Likewise, cauliflower should not be planted where another cole crop has been grown.

Nutrition and Preparation

One hundred grams of fresh cauliflower have 26 calories, 4.5 grams of carbohydrates, 2.3 grams of protein, 0.3 gram of fat, 0.9 gram of fiber, 20 to 22 milligrams of calcium, 30 to 72 milligrams of phosphorus, 0.5 to 1.1 milligrams of iron, 15 to 24 milligrams of sodium, 300 to 350 milligrams of potassium, 85 milligrams of sulfur, 29 milligrams of chlorine, 18 milligrams of magnesium, 50 to 91 milligrams of vitamin C, 0.03 milligrams of beta carotene, 0.11 to 0.15 milligram of thiamine, 0.1 to 0.12 milligram of riboflavin, 0.6 milligram of niacin,

0.2 to 0.7 milligram of pantothenic acid, 0.01 to 0.04 milligram of folic acid, and 0.09 to 0.32 milligram of vitamin B6. Cooking reduces the amount of vitamins and minerals. The longer cauliflower is cooked the greater the losses. Cooked cauliflower has 28 milligrams of vitamin C, 0.02 milligram of beta-carotene, 0.06 milligram of thiamine, 0.08 milligram of riboflavin, and 0.5 milligram of niacin. Cooked in one-quarter cup of water, cauliflower loses 8 percent of its calcium, 11 percent of its iron, 9 percent of its magnesium, 1 percent of its potassium, 27 percent of its vitamin C, 26 percent of its thiamine, 16 percent of its riboflavin, 15 percent of its niacin, 31 percent of its pantothenic acid, 50 percent of its folic acid, and 36 percent of its vitamin B6. An hour of cooking may reduce vitamins and minerals 60–80 percent. A whole cauliflower head should be cooked 3 minutes in a pressure cooker, boiled 20 to 30 minutes, or steamed 25 to 30 minutes. Small sections of a head should be cooked 1.5 to 3 minutes in a pressure cooker, boiled 8 to 15 minutes, or steamed 10 to 20 minutes. Yet the temptation to overcook cauliflower may be appreciable because, having few sulfur compounds, its flavor does not deteriorate with long cooking. The smaller the amount of water used in cooking the fewer vitamins and minerals are lost.

A light frost does not diminish the amount of vitamin C in cauliflower, but a severe frost reduces it. Molybdenum-deficient soil produces cauliflower with little vitamin C. Young cauliflower plants have more vitamin C than mature plants. Cauliflower loses vitamin C during storage. Cooking may reduce vitamin C content 50–75 percent. If not consumed promptly, cooked cauliflower loses 10–25 percent of its vitamin C. Not a rich source of calcium, cauliflower has only 10 percent as much of the mineral as do kale and collard.

Cultivars

Suitable to regions with a short growing season, Early Snowball matures in 50 to 60 days after transplantation. A dwarf, Early Snowball yields a compact, white head. Suitable for canning or freezing, Super Snowball matures in 55 to 60 days. A dwarf, Super Snowball has blue-green leaves and a white head. Maturing in 60 to 65 days, Snowdrift is a large plant that yields a large head. Danish Giant, also known as Dry Weather, is unusual in tolerating a dry climate. Grown in the Midwest, Danish Giant matures in 70 to 80 days, yielding a white head seven inches in breadth. Self-Blanche, as the name suggests, blanches its head without human assistance. A late variety, Self-Blanche produces seven- or eight-inch heads. A hybrid, Snow King matures in 55 days. Growing vigorously, Snow King is unusual in tolerating heat. Its head may weigh more than two pounds. A hybrid, Snow Crown is similar to the snowball varieties. Another self-blancher, Purple Head has distinctive purple curds. Yet another self-blancher, Early White Hybrid yields a head as large as nine inches in breadth. Gypsy is unusual in growing vigorously even in poor soil. It yields a large white head. Romanesco has a distinctive chartreuse head, though scientists debate whether the variety is cauliflower or broccoli. An heirloom variety, Igloo may be planted densely for a small head. Graffiti has a large purple head that retains its color during cooking. Winter varieties, among them Early Pearl, Christmas, February, March, Saint Valentine, and Late Pearl, mature in 150 days. Farmers grow them on the coast of California. In many cases, the name reflects the time of harvest.

Christopher Cumo

Further Reading

Buckingham, Alan. *Grow Vegetables*. London: Dorling Kindersley, 2008.

Growing Cauliflower and Broccoli. Washington, D.C.: U.S. Department of Agriculture, 1984.

Klein, Carol. *Grow Your Own Vegetables*. London: Mitchell Beazley, 2007.

Nieuwhof, M. *Cole Crops: Botany, Cultivation and Utilization*. London: L. Hill, 1969.

Parsons, Russ. *How to Pick a Peach: The Search for Flavor from Farm to Table*. Boston: Houghton Mifflin, 2007.

Wien, H. C., ed. *The Physiology of Vegetable Crops*. New York: CAB International, 1997.

Cedar

Fragrant, stately, and useful, cedar has been important to humans from antiquity to the present. Through the ages, Native Americans used cedar for canoes, shelter, furniture, tools, clothing, and medicine, and as a prominent character in myths. Today, we relax on cedar decks, store blankets in grandma's cedar chest, and keep bugs at bay with cedar-based pesticides. In botanical terms, most cedars are not true members of the Cedrus family, which contains merely three Old World species. These may be geographical variants of the same original species. In the New World, people have erroneously attributed the cedar-like characteristics of fragrant, reddish wood with fan-shaped branches of overlapping scales rather than needles, to trees and shrubs in the large Cypress family. The proper scientific designations include *Thuja*, *Chamaecyparis*, *Calocedrus*, and *Juniperus*.

Western Red Cedar

Champion among these is the remarkable, majestic western red cedar, *Thuja plicata*, of the Pacific Northwest. Renowned more for its usefulness than as a decorative landscape plant, this giant conifer, or cone-bearing evergreen, reaches a height of 200 feet under favorable conditions. The ideal climate is the temperate rain forest along the 2,000 miles of Pacific Coast of what are now southern Alaska, British

Columbia, Washington State, and Oregon. Ocean currents and jet streams driving across the Pacific Ocean maintain a temperature above freezing while lavishing a prodigious amount of rain up the steep slopes of the coast range. The 160 to 200 inches of rain per year and nearly year-round moisture, and the mild growing season produce the massive straight trunks with wide, fluted bases. Such wood in the hands of craftsmen yielded giant canoes. Several dugout canoes, plus innumerable smaller items, could be made from one tree. Whether a large ocean-going vessel or a smaller craft to maneuver inlets and rapids, cedar canoes were prized for their strength and admired for their excellence. Canoes were decorated with carved and painted images and designs that added a final statement of their utility and importance. At up to 65 feet long and 4 feet wide, the biggest dugouts were perfectly suited for transporting goods along the varying conditions of the coast, making trade flourish from Alaska to Mexico at a rate unique to Pacific coast peoples.

The Nuu-chal-nuth or Nootka of Vancouver Island and the Makah across the Strait of Juan de Fuco on Washington's Olympic Peninsula hunted sea mammals and ventured far out onto the ocean for whales, where swiftness and maneuverability were premium. Extra thickness left on the bottom contributed to the canoes' stability. On less benevolent missions, canoes would carry back loads of plunder, hostages, and slaves captured from battles waged by aggressive cultures such as the Haida of the Queen Charlotte Islands. So ideal were the dugout canoes that they were a hot item of commerce and a source of serendipity. It is not hard to imagine the delight of a southern tribe such as the Chumash on finding cedar logs that had drifted down the coast to what is now California. They built effective seaworthy boats by splitting and lashing together cedar planks rather than using the dugout method. Their crafts were flat-bottomed and smaller, but also elaborately decorated.

When dugout canoes returned from fishing, whaling, trading, or battles, they were pulled up onto the beaches of coves, islands, bays, or river banks. Their passengers and crews then entered houses, also constructed of cedar. Logs of various sizes formed the framework with planks as long as 40 feet, 3 feet wide, and four inches thick for the walls. Overlapping sections of bark formed the roofs. Within each home were myriad other items of cedar: furniture, storage boxes, baskets, fishing nets, tools, food containers, ceremonial masks, ropes and straps, and even clothing.

Cedar bark can be softened by pounding. Then the tribe's women could cut it into strips and weave clothing and blankets. "Dance aprons" resembled grass skirts. Cedar's versatility extended to the roots, which could be woven tightly enough to make watertight baskets and raincoats. More dramatic applications of cedar included ceremonial gear and armor. Wooden slats were formed into panels of vertical strips held together with sinew. Paneled tunics and heavier armor were joined by carved helmets to complete the battle garb.

Some villages were small, just several extended families, each with its own home. In other instances, hundreds of people formed a large community that included communal buildings. Next to homes of dominant families in the hierarchy stood carved cedar totem poles to represent the importance of the inhabitants, the spirits allied with them and ancestral histories and major events. Families of higher status gained and maintained their wealth through control of cedar groves, hunting and fishing grounds, and other natural assets of the tribe's territory.

Other Cedars

Not many yards can accommodate the big western red cedar. However, it can be grown and is popular as bonsai. Many Web sites explain how to soak the cones to obtain seeds and how to grow and graft the saplings into artistic expressions of their huge versions. Also, plenty of smaller shapes and sizes of other cedar-like evergreens thrive for the home gardener.

Thuja occidentalis, called northern or eastern white cedar, or eastern arborvitae, is the tall, narrow evergreen of countless privacy hedges and windbreaks. The popular modern variety is "Emerald green," and it will recover from severe trimming or snow damage. Arborvitae came to the rescue of French explorer Jacques Cartier's 1535 expedition along the Saint Lawrence River. A native guide brewed bark and leaves, which contained enough vitamin C to alleviate the men's scurvy. Asthma and arthritis were two other afflictions treated by the use of cedar ingredients.

Incense cedar, *Calocedrus decurrens*, showcases aromatic wood. The attractive bark grows in distinctive layers of slanted strips that look like lattice. The oils in mature wood and bark are responsible for the fresh scent as well as the toxic repellant terpene thujone that inhibits decay, fungi, and insects. Its other claim to fame is as the eco-friendly main source of pencil wood. The soft wood is easy to sharpen and rarely splinters. This slow grower is drought tolerant and withstands both high and low temperatures in its southern Oregon and Sierra Nevada range.

Atlantic white cedar, *Chamaecyparis thyoides*, does well in moist soils, along ponds and in swampy areas. Native to the East Coast wetlands from Maine to Florida, western Florida, and Mobile Bay on the Gulf Coast, much of the original forests were cut and drained for agriculture by European settlers. Early land speculators of the Great Dismal Swamp in New Jersey included George Washington. Much swamp cedar was used to produce charcoal for the manufacture of gunpowder for Revolutionary troops. In New Jersey in 1791, pirates were to blame for deforestation as more than 5,000 acres were burned in an effort to eliminate their hiding places.

White cedar is in demand for lumber and other products. Restoration efforts are under way to meet consumer demand as well as ecological considerations to reestablish the woods. Natural and nursery methods to improve propagation are under study and development. Eastern red cedar, *Juniperus virginiana*, is another source of moth-repelling, reddish wood. As a note of trivia, this wood led to the name, Baton Rouge, so called by the French Canadians of Louisiana.

True Cedars

The three true cedars are *Cedrus libani*, *Cedrus atlantica*, and *Cedrus deodara*. In the *Epic of Gilgamesh*, the gods lived in a cedar forest. Those enchanted woods could be the Himalayas of the deodara, the eastern Mediterranean mountainous region including Lebanon, Syria, and Turkey of the libani, or the Atlas Mountains of northwestern Africa of the atlantica.

None of the big evergreen true cedars has more distinction in history than the *Cedrus libani*, the Cedar of Lebanon, legendary as the material for King Solomon's temple. A biblical reference in Ezekiel closes with the line, "nor any tree in the garden of God was like unto him in his beauty." Praise enough to make any gardener with room want to grow one as a focal point.

Heights of 50 to 90 feet are not the main consideration. The Lebanon cedar grows massive horizontal branches reaching 30 to 50 feet around the base. This size makes the tree perfect for sweeping across a mansion's lawn or a public park's open area, or for making a focal statement near a monument. The Lebanon cedar is easy to grow from seed and unfussy about soil, which it prefers alkaline. Much real estate can be saved if cedar is grown as a bonsai. The clusters of small needles on the true cedars, especially the atlas cedar, contribute to their veracity of appearance as bonsai.

Whether in yards or ceramic containers, the blue cultivar of atlas cedar rivals the blue spruce for bringing stunning silvery blue to a landscape's palette. Make it the weeping variety and it becomes a conversation piece. With support and training, it grows horizontally with narrow elegant branches hanging down, making a magnificent living fence and truly an unfussy focal point.

Tamara Stromquist

Further Reading

Brickell, Christopher, ed. *American Horticultural Society Encyclopedia of Gardening*. London: Dorling Kindersley, 1993.

Jonas, Gerald. *The Living Earth Book of North American Trees*. Pleasantville, NY: Reader's Digest Assoc., 1993.

Sibley, David Allen. *The Sibley Guide to Trees*. New York: Knopf, 2009.

Stuckey, Maggie, and George Palmer. *Western Trees: A Field Guide*. Helena, MT: Falcon, 1998.

Celandine

A native of Europe and western Asia, celandine has been naturalized across the United States. Celandine belongs to the poppy family Papaveraceae and has the Latin name *Chelidonium* as the genus. The plant's Latin name is derived from the Greek word *chelidonia*, meaning "of the swallow," and refers to the ancient folkloric belief that the plant flowered with the coming of the swallow in spring and continued until the fall when the swallow left. This belief has roots in reality as celandine begins to bloom in April and finishes in September. That celandine is commonly called swallow wort alludes to this belief. Celendine is also commonly known as tetterwort.

Species

There are three species of celandine: the greater celandine *Chelidonium majus*, the lesser celandine *Ranunculus ficaria*, and the celandine-poppy, *Stylophorum diphyllum*. However, the genus *Chelidonium* contains only one species, *Chelidonium majus*, as *Ranunculus ficaria* belongs to the buttercup family and *Stylophorum diphyllum* to the poppy family, and so both are distinct botanically from celandine. Celandine will grow in sun or shade and in any earth, although the plant prefers shady conditions and rich, well-drained soil. Woodland conditions are perfect, but celandine will grow along paths, by fences, and on waste ground and riverbanks. Developing from a fleshy root, celandine is a short-lived perennial that forms a spindly, yet fully branched, plant that can grow up to two feet tall. The flowers of celandine form from pear-shaped buds and grow in open clusters along a yellow-tinged stem, which in turn develop from the axils of upper leaves. The poppy-like flowers consist of four yellow obovate petals and two green sepals and are up to three-quarters of an inch in diameter. A double-flowered variety called Flore Pleno has been cultivated since 1771. The leaves of celandine, appearing in an alternate pattern along the stem, are large and smooth, yet not fleshy, and can grow up to eight inches long. The leaves tend to be deeply cut in pinnate fashion with rounded edges and feature up to seven lobes. The base of the leaf is expanded and may reach part of the way around the stem. The veins of the leaf are obvious. The foliage of celandine is a distinctive yellow-green color, and when the stem of a plant is broken, it yields both an unpleasant odor and an orange-colored juice that produces a long-lasting stain. Celandine has one ovary, which produces a fruit in the form of a roughened, cylindrical capsule about one inch in length, which splits from the base to form two valves. The fruit contains multiple shiny, crested, smooth seeds from which the plant self-seeds. Each seed contains an elaiosome, a fleshy structure rich in proteins and lipids, which attracts ants. Ants take the seeds to their nest and feed the elaiosome to their young. When the young ants have finished with the elaiosome, the adult ants remove the elaiosome to the waste area of their nests where the seed germinates. This process of seed transportation is known as myrmecochory. Propagation of celandine is by either self-sowing or division. However, celandine does not thrive when transplanted and may become weedy if allowed to self-sow.

Medicinal Use

Celandine has a long history of use in medicinal preparations. Celandine was most probably brought to the United States from Europe by early doctors, for the plant contains alkaloids such as chelidonine, chelerythrine, protopine, berberine, and sanguinarine. The latter is particularly lethal, so that, in the United Kingdom, *Chelidonium majus* appears on the Royal Horticultural Society's list of Potentially Harmful Garden Plants. It is poisonous and an irritant of both skin and eyes. However, it should be noted that a large amount of raw celandine must be ingested to be deadly. Doctors in early history used the juice of the plant to treat conditions such as warts and hemorrhoids despite the fact that celandine juice is a skin irritant. Practitioners of the "Doctrine of Signatures," a system going back to the first century CE with the Greek physician Dioscorides and based on the principle that plants bearing a physical resemblance to either parts of the body or illnesses may be used to treat illnesses or body parts that the plants resemble, advocated the use of celandine juice to treat jaundice, presumably because both celandine sap and the jaundiced body present a yellow tinge. It was also common until the mid-17th century for celandine juice to be used to treat eye conditions. This error may have originated in the belief that swallows used the juice to cure blindness in their young, as swallow eyes and the juice of the celandine are similar in color. Extracts taken from the aerial parts of celandine may contain antiviral, antimicrobial, and anticancer properties. Celandine is used today in homeopathic and conventional medicine as a purgative, a sedative, an antispasmodic, and an antiinflammatory. Modern homeopaths use celandine to treat respiratory conditions including asthma, bronchitis, and whooping cough, as well as gallstones. The latex extracted from the plant has been used as a topical application for the treatment of ringworm and corns. Ukrain, a drug formed from a semisynthetic triphosphate derivative of the alkaloids found in celandine, has been found in tests to show some promise in inhibiting or being toxic to cancer cells, but more testing is needed (Ernest and Schmidt 2005). Other semisynthetic medicines produced from celandine alkaloids have been developed as part of the fight against AIDS. However, the potential for unwanted side effects from the medicinal use of celandine, including hemolytic anemia, hepatitis, and colitis, has led the Australian Complementary Medicines Evaluation Committee to suggest that celandine-containing products be labeled clearly.

Victoria Williams

Further Reading

Aronson, J. K. *Meyler's Side Effects of Herbal Medicine*. Amsterdam: Elsevier, 2009.

Ernst, E., and Schmidt, K. *BMC Cancer* 5, no. 69 (2005). doi:10.1186/1471-2407-5-69

Hanelt, Peter, ed. *Mansfeld's Encyclopedia of Agricultural and Horticultural Crops*. Vol. 5. Berlin: Springer-Verlag, 2001.

Runkel, Sylvan T., and Alvin F. Bull. *Wildflowers of Iowa's Woodlands*. Iowa City: University of Iowa Press, 2009.

Spencer, Roger. *Horticultural Flora of South Eastern Australia*. Vol. 2, *Flowering Plants*. Sydney: UNSW Press, 2004.

Tenenbaum, Frances, ed. *Taylor's Encyclopedia of Garden Plants*. New York: Houghton Mifflin, 2003.

Celeriac

The root crop celeriac or celery root (*Apium graveolens rapaceum*) belonging to the parsley (Apiaceae) family has a checkered history from early times. Indigenous to the Mediterranean region, evidence of its cultivation has been discovered from the sarcophagi of Egypt around 1100 BCE. Designated as *selinon* by the Greeks, it is mentioned in *The Odyssey* of ninth-century BCE Greek poet Homer. A type of celery wine was provided to Greek athletes. It has been reported that celeriac arrived in China around fifth century CE. Celeriac spread from the Mediterranean to Western Europe in the Middle Ages. During the reign of ninth-century CE Frankish king Charlemagne, it was listed as a culinary and medical herb to be grown in imperial garden.

Attributes

A relative of celery, celeriac, with its different names such as celery root, knob celery, and turnip-rooted celery, is grown mainly in Europe, North America, the Middle East, and North Africa. This root vegetable is cultivated specifically for its robust, large, and globular hypocotyl rather than stem and leaves. With a long growing period, the root generally takes about 200 days for full maturity, when it measures four inches in diameter. Alabaster, Diamant, and Prague are three main types of celeric. Its creamy white and crisp inside is grated to use in salad. The leaves are used as seasoning for soups and sauces. Celeric is cooked like any other root vegetable. But the chefs soak it with acidulated water or lemon juice before cooking. In the kitchens of the United States and Europe, preparations from celeriac have become an item on the menu.

Uses and Nutrition

Celeriac is notable for its medicinal and nutritional value. Celeriac juice has been used by some to treat nervous debility, insomnia, urinary malfunctioning, rheumatism, and high blood pressure. It may stimulate the brain as well as the formation of red blood corpuscles. Some people may use it as an antidote to alcoholic hangovers. Celeriac has been used as a cosmetic product for people with dehydrated skin. The great nutritional value of celeriac is due to its low content in calories and fat, though it is also low in protein. Fat is virtually absent, and celeriac possesses only 18 calories per serving size of 3.9 ounces. Celeriac has about 0.07 ounce of fiber per serving. Celeriac contains calcium, iron, potassium, magnesium, and phosphorous. Vitamins A, C, K, and B6 are found in celeriac. About 44 percent of an adult's vitamin K requirement is in a serving of celeriac. Likewise, the same serving has 6–14 percent of vitamin C and 10 percent of vitamin A for an adult's daily need. However, people on a low-sodium diet are advised to be careful about eating celeriac as it has high sodium content. Apart from being a food and medicinal plant, celeriac was used as a garland during funerals in earlier days.

Patit Paban Mishra

Further Reading

Andersen, Craig R. *Celeriac.* Fayetteville: University of Arkansas Press, 2003.

Bedford, Lynn V. *Processing and Quality Assessment of Vegetables from Trials at Ministry Centres: Miscellaneous Crops—Calabrese, Celeriac, Onions and Sweet Corn.* Gloucestershire, U.K.: Campden Food Preservation Research Association, 1986.

Bird, Richard. *How to Grow Beans, Peas, Asparagus, Artichokes and Other Shoots: Growing Legumes and Edible Shoots, including Celery, Celeriac, Globe Artichokes and Seakale, with 180 Photographs.* London: Southwater, 2008.

Dutchlady1. "Celery—History, Uses, Benefits and Growing Tips." http://davesgarden.com/community/forums/t/805830 (accessed 27 May 2011).

Liau, Xiang, Zheng Guang Pana, Jian He Xub, and He Xing Lic. "Enantioselective Reduction of Acetophenone Analogues Using Carrot and Celeriac Enzymes System." *Chinese Chemical Letters* 21 (March 1, 2010): 305–8.

Celery

Celery, *Apium graveolens*, bears an edible stalk and is one of the few vegetables for which the whole plant is used in food and medicine. Celery can grow to be up to three feet tall, and the leaves of the plant grow in a conical shape connected at the bottom by a common base. The plant produces small white flowers. The celery plant is related to carrot, fennel, parsley, and dill. Celery is used for all its parts including the ribbed stalks, leaves, seeds, and even the root. The plant is biennial, which means that it takes two years for the plant to mature fully. Celery is so ubiquitous that many nations claim responsibility for being the first to discover and cultivate it including China, India, the United Kingdom, Sweden, and several countries in Africa.

History

Celery may have originated in the Mediterranean Basin. The ancient forms of celery had fewer stalks and more leaves. It would be hundreds of years before the plant was cultivated as a source of food, but the ancients used the plants in many ritual ceremonies. The Egyptians did not cultivate celery, but they used wild celery in their ceremonies. Garlands were made of celery leaves and water lily petals, and then placed in the tombs. Such garlands were found in 14th-century BCE pharaoh Tutankhamen's tomb during archaeological excavations. While wild celery mostly had ornamental value, it is believed that celery also played a role in Egyptian medicine as treatment for impotence.

While the Egyptians were buried with celery, the Greeks decorated sports heroes with laurels made of celery leaves. They believed the plant was an aphrodisiac. Around the ninth century BCE, Homer referred to celery in *The Iliad*, and called it *selinon* in this work. It appears at the passage where the horses of Myrmidons are grazing on celery and lotus. Homer additionally mentions the plant in his work, *The Odyssey*. Here, when the hero, Ulysses, and his men are at Calypso's cave, they find themselves surrounded by meadows of wild celery and violets. Greek physician Hippocrates (460–370 BCE) wrote about celery as a medicine for calming one's nerves. The original usages of celery included medicinal purposes, seasonings, and horse feed. Celery was used to treat many medical ailments in ancient times, including colds, flu, and digestive problems. The ancient Romans used celery as a seasoning.

Ninth-century CE Frankish king Charlemagne mentioned celery in an edict. He advised that every garden in his empire grow celery. This edict, titled *Capitulare de villis vel curtis imperii Caroli Magni*, described all the herbs that he deemed necessary to grow in gardens. The popularity of celery in Europe grew following this edict. It was not until the 17th century that celery was discovered to be edible as a vegetable (as opposed to an herb or seasoning). Around 1623, in Italy, celery stalks and leaves were paired with a dressing. Around this time, in Italy, France, and England, growers began to cultivate celery with the aim of developing the desirable characteristics of the vegetable to create stouter stems and to eliminate undesirable characteristics such as hollow stems and the bitter taste. In the 18th century, the upper classes began storing celery in cellars to use during the winter. Once this occurred, the use of celery became widespread.

In the 19th century, Europeans determined that the bitter flavor and green color of celery were undesirable. Cooks began to blanch celery to make it taste better and to rid it of its green color. Also during this time, George Taylor, an award-winning market gardener who was born in Scotland, brought celery with him when he emigrated to Kalamazoo, Michigan. Once there, Taylor began growing celery at his farm in 1847. He had a difficult time getting the people living in

Kalamazoo to try the vegetable. Celery was not a widely known vegetable, and many who lived in the area had not previously encountered it. Many people believed it to be poisonous. Taylor peddled celery door to door to increase its popularity. Once it became popular, Kalamazoo earned the nickname Celery City. Celery was an important part of Kalamazoo's history. Not only was celery an important crop, but it also brought migrants into the area to practice a new kind of farming. In the past 50 years, new breeds of celery have been developed, including an easy-blanching variety that has a milder flavor than its predecessors.

Cultivation of Celery

Celery needs copious amounts of water and very moist soil to thrive. It has a long growing season, and because it can take a long time for the seeds to germinate, it is advisable that growers start celery indoors about 10 weeks before the planting season begins. A few seeds should be placed in individual containers. The seeds should be between two and three years old and ought to be kept in a refrigerator over the winter. Before planting, the gardener should soak the seeds overnight. When planting, the seeds should be sprinkled over high-quality potting soil. Seeds then must be pressed into the soil with either wood or a finger. While watering plants is often done directly, with celery the best results are achieved by filling a tray with water so that the soil soaks up the water in order to keep the seeds from clumping together. The containers in which seeds are planted should be closed to retain moisture.

Celery germinates in two to three weeks. Seedlings should be thinned after germination and again when plants have reached a height of four to six inches to reduce competition for water and nutrients. After the threat of frost passes, plants may be transplanted outside. They should be planted in rows two feet apart, and the plants should have six to eight inches between them. Celery requires space, especially since its roots can become large. The gardener may mulch around the plants to retain water. The growing season lasts 120 to 140 days, so it is vital that the soil be kept hydrated to prevent celery from drying out. During the growing season, it is important to weed the area around plants. Celery should be harvested when the stalks are about one foot tall, about three months after they have been planted outside. Should there be any frost damage, the outer stalks can be removed. The inner stalks should remain useable.

Celery is susceptible to a few pathogens and a nutritional deficiency. Leaf blight is caused by fungi and appears as yellow spots on the leaves. Blight kills celery leaves. Black heart is a nutritional deficiency caused by a lack of calcium in the leaves. Black heart can be prevented by ensuring that the plants are provided with enough water. Pink rot occurs when the plant is too damp and the temperatures are cool to moderate.

Celery Varieties

The Wild Celery variety grows underwater. It is not eaten today. However, it was widely used for medicinal and ceremonial purposes during ancient times. The Utah variety produces 11- to 12-inch stalks in 120 days. This celery is a medium-dark green and the product is crisp. The variety Pascal takes 125 days to mature. The stalks produced by the Pascal variety are large and weigh 10 to 15 pounds per dozen stalks. Golden Self-Blanching celery matures in 85 days and is disease resistant. The stalks are thick and heavy. Detroit Golden, a self-blanching variety, has heavy yet compact stalks with broad and thick stems.

Cooking, Nutrition, and Medicine

Celery is used in a variety of dishes and for a variety of cooking purposes. Celery stalks are used in salads, as appetizers, and in stews and soups. Celery leaves are often chopped up and used as flavoring, and celery seeds are often used in pickling and in other dishes as a flavoring. Celery is high in fiber and naturally low in fat. The vegetable is a good source of vitamins A, C, and K, folic acid, potassium, riboflavin, vitamin B6, calcium, magnesium, phosphorus, manganese, and pantothenic acid. Celery has a relatively high sodium content.

Celery has had a variety of medical uses. For example, celery has been used by some as a diuretic, to aid in alleviating arthritic symptoms, as an anti-inflammatory, as an antiseptic, and for antibacterial purposes. Celery seed has been used by some to treat alcoholism, depression, anxiety, and bronchitis, and even to lower high blood pressure. Moreover, celery seeds have been used to treat liver damage, kidney inflammation, gout, and urinary tract infection. There are some reports that celery may reduce swelling in glands, reduce blood pressure, induce a sensation of calm, and clear uric acid from painful joints. For weight loss, celery juice may be ingested before meals to reduce appetite. Pregnant women should not eat celery seeds because they may cause uterine muscle contractions and bleeding during menstruation.

Ronda Lee Levine

Further Reading

Roessle, Theophilus. *How to Cultivate and Preserve Celery.* Albany, NY: C. M. Saxton, Barker, 1860.

Toensmeier, Eric. *Perennial Vegetables: From Artichokes Zuiki Taro, a Gardener's Guide to Over 100 Delicious and Easy to Grow Edibles.* White River Junction, VT: Chelsea Green, 2007.

Zohary, Daniel, and Maria Hopf. *Domestication of Plants in the Old World.* 3rd ed. New York: Oxford University Press, 2000.

Cherry

A tree, cherry provides wood, fruit, and attractive blossoms. The cherry straddles three continents. In North America black cherry, *Prunus serotina*, supplies wood. The European sweet and sour cherries, *Prunus avium* and *Prunus cerasus* respectively, provide fruit. The Japanese flowering cherry, now grown in the United States, supplies aesthetically pleasing blooms. Flowering cherries include the species *Prunus serrulata*, *Prunus aedoensis*, *Prunus subhirtella*, and *Prunus incisa*. Europe boasts only 5 species of cherry, North America 6, Japan 13, and China 23. China holds a position of prominence because the last glaciation was less severe in China than elsewhere, and so more species of cherry, and other plants as well, survived. A member of the genus *Prunus*, cherry is related to almond, apricot, nectarine, peach, and plum. In the family Rosaceae, cherry counts among its relatives the rose, apple, pear, strawberry, raspberry, and blackberry. One hundred grams of cherry contain 1 milligram of sodium, 210 milligrams of potassium, 13 milligrams of calcium, 0.2 milligram of iron, a trace of beta-carotene, 0.1 milligram of vitamin E, 0.03 milligram of vitamin B1, 0.03 milligram of vitamin B2, 11 milligrams of vitamin C, and 5 milligrams of folic acid.

Cherries (Corel)

Sweet and Sour Cherries

Cherry trees have long grown wild in Europe, northern Turkey, the Caucasus Mountains, and Transcaucasia. By one account, humans first cultivated the cherry tree 10,000 years ago, making it among the earliest domesticates. Another school of thought places the origin of cherry culture between 5000 and 4000 BCE. A third line of reasoning seeks the origin of cherry cultivation in classical Greece. In the fourth century BCE, Greek botanist Theophrastus mentioned the cherry tree, allowing one to infer that the Greeks cultivated it then. The Greeks may have grown the cherry tree first for wood and second for fruit. The Romans, perhaps imitating the Greeks, planted cherry trees. In the first century BCE, Roman agricultural writer Varro described the grafting of cherry trees. In the first century CE, Roman encyclopedist Pliny the Elder asserted that the Romans grew 10 varieties in Italy, though some scholars believe that the number must have been larger because Pliny could not have been familiar with all cultivars. Pliny remarked that farmers grew cherry trees in Britain, Germany, Belgium, and Portugal. True to Pliny's word, the Romans first planted cherry trees in Britain between 40 and 60 CE. Rome's withdrawal from the province may have caused cherry cultivation to decline. One authority, supposing that Britain ceased to grow cherries during the Middle Ages, credits Richard Harris, gardener to King Henry VIII, with reintroducing the cherry tree in the 16th century, though others place this reintroduction in the 15th century or perhaps earlier. The Romans may have introduced the cherry tree to Gaul (now France). Another account pinpoints cherry cultivation in France to the eighth century, well after the decline of the Roman Empire. In Italy, the cherry tree was fused with religious imagery. Renaissance artists, Sandro Botticelli among them, painted cherries with religious figures.

Of the two types of fruit tree, the sour cherry tree stands 15 feet tall compared to the 25 or 30 feet of the sweet cherry tree. The flowers of a sour cherry tree will self- or cross-pollinate. A sweet cherry tree will not self-pollinate. The sour cherry is tart because it contains more malic acid than a sweet cherry. The 19th-century French botanist Alphonse de Candolle asserted that the sour cherry originated in land near the Caspian Sea, though others have argued that the sour cherry may have originated between Switzerland and the Adriatic Sea in the west and the Caspian Sea in the east. Michigan, Utah, New York, and Washington raise sour cherries. Cherries comprise four classes: bigarreaux, dukes, hearts, and sour. Dukes and hearts, being too soft for shipment, are seldom grown in commercial orchards. Bigarreaux, known as blacks, dominate the fresh market. Among its cultivars are Bing, Royal Ann, and Rainier. Dark cherries dominate the sweet cherry market because the darker the color the sweeter the fruit.

The sweet cherry originated in land between the Caspian and Black Seas. Birds and animals spread seeds to Transcaucasia, Turkey, and northern India. Farmers in the Netherlands, Belgium, and Germany sold fresh cherries as early as the 14th century. Merchants bought cherries to make wine. In the 15th century, the Dutch made jelly from cherries. In 1491, one German herbalist mentioned sweet and sour cherries, evidence that both types were in cultivation. The residents of Hamburg, Germany, celebrate the annual Feast of Cherries to commemorate a victory over the Hussites. In 1432, a Hussite army threatening the city, its authorities sent children to beg the invaders to spare Hamburg. The Hussites not only complied, but they gave the children cherries. In the 18th century, the Germans, doubtless aware of the beauty of cherry trees, planted them alongside roads. By then the more enterprising farmers were eager for new varieties of cherry. An association of growers selected several varieties, including Knorpel, which is still grown in Hungary. In 1819, a nobleman from Battenbourg catalogued 75 varieties of cherry. The list grew to 149 varieties by 1866 and 252 cultivars by 1877. In the 19th and 20th centuries, German growers planted large orchards near the cities in an attempt to access the urban market.

In England, the cherry flourished in the 16th century when prices were high. The decline in prices in the 18th century convinced farmers to remove land from cultivation. Those who could not profit from selling their cherries fresh distilled them into cherry wine. In the 1820s, cherries were profitable again, leading British farmers to intercrop them with strawberries.

The English introduced cherries, perhaps both sweet and sour cultivars, to the America colonies in 1629. The French imported the sour cultivar Early Richmond into the Saint Lawrence River valley and Virginia in the 17th century. More generally, the French planted cherry trees in Nova Scotia, Cape Breton, and Prince Edward Island. The Yellow Spanish sour cherry cultivar, grown since Roman times, was imported to America about 1770. New Englanders grew varieties of both sweet and sour cherries. As was true of the apple, farmers in America first propagated cherry trees from seeds. The Dutch, for example, grew cherry trees from seeds in New York. The practice of grafting must have become common in the 18th century because one nurseryman on Long Island offered grafts for sale that century.

The 18th century was the era of George Washington, and his mythic relationship to the sour cherry tree is well known. His father had imported a sour cherry tree from Great Britain. The father must have pampered the tree, but his son, perhaps in a reckless moment, chopped it down. When confronted young Washington admitted the deed, surely vexing his father. Although an interesting story, the event probably never occurred. The story dates to an 1806 biography of Washington. By then the former president had been dead seven years and so could not verify or debunk the story, which is among the most popular anecdotes from early American history.

In 1804, one nursery listed more than 20 varieties of cherry. In addition to Canada, New England, Virginia, and New York, farmers cultivated cherries in Pennsylvania, New Jersey, Delaware, and North Carolina. As early as 1676, travelers remarked at the abundance of Virginia's cherry trees. In the interior of the new United States, the French planted cherry trees in Detroit, Michigan, Vincennes, Indiana, St. Louis, Missouri, and Florida. In the 18th century, the Franciscans introduced cherry trees into California. The influx of settlers during the Gold Rush of the mid-19th century stimulated the cultivation of cherries in California. In the 1840s, Oregon began raising cherry trees. Until the 20th century, the cherry was a garden crop, raised for home use. It did not enter the market because the fruit did not store well and transit was poor. Today, the United States harvests sour cherries, most of them in Michigan. In addition to the United States, farmers grow sour cherries in Russia, Germany, and Eastern Europe. Three-quarters of the U.S. sour cherry crop goes to make pastries and pies. Sour cherries are cooked, canned, and frozen. Other uses include the making of juice, liquor, and jam. Fewer than 1 million pounds of sour cherries are sold fresh in the United States. Where disease is problematic, farmers plant sour cherries, which are more disease resistant than sweet cultivars. Farmers in the United States, Germany, Russia, Italy, Switzerland, France, and Spain raise sweet cherries, whose uses are the same as those of sour cherries with the exception that sweet cherries are more successful than sour cherries in the fresh market. Laborers pick sweet cherries whereas machines harvest sour cherries. Among sweet cultivars is Bing, which Chinese laborer Ah Bing discovered on an Oregon farm in 1875. Bing is today the leading sweet cultivar.

Competition to enter the fresh market is intense. By airplane, U.S. cherries enter the market in Japan and Hong Kong, where they command 10 times the price of fresh cherries in the United States. Growers want an early harvest to beat their competitors to Asian and American markets. In the Pacific Northwest, the Bing harvest is mid-June, but those who can harvest their crop in mid-May profit the most. Warm regions like the San Joaquin Valley in California yield early cherries; yet cultivation in this region is problematic because cherries need a cold winter to initiate dormancy. Moreover, California's wet winters may yield spring cherries that split from excess moisture. California growers have sought to solve these problems by cultivating a new variety, Brooks. In 1988, the University of California released Brooks, a cross between Rainier and the early variety Burlat. Brooks ripens 10 to 14 days earlier than Bing, giving California growers early enter into the fresh market. Perhaps because of Brooks, California has grown as a cherry producer. In the 1980s, the state ranked third behind Washington and Oregon. Between 1992 and 2002, however, cherry acreage more than doubled in California. Production surely kept pace with acreage, so that by 2002 California produced more cherries than any other state. California growers now harvest more than one-third of U.S. cherries, whereas the fraction had been one-quarter in 1992. Washington also posted gains. Between 1992 and 2002, the state's acreage increased 50 percent. The eastern plains are the area of cultivation in Washington. Washington growers aim for a late harvest, capturing a portion of the market when the supply of cherries has dwindled. In Oregon, farmers grow cherries in the Willamette and Columbia river valleys. Oregon and Michigan grow maraschino cherries. Traverse City, Michigan, promotes itself as the "cherry capital of the world." Led by gains in Washington and California, U.S. cherry acreage increased between 1992 and 2003.

In 2007, Turkey was the leading producer of sweet and sour cherries. The United States ranked second, Iran third, Italy fourth, and Russia fifth.

Black Cherry

Humans derive wood from black cherry, also known as wild black cherry, wild cherry, rum cherry, chockecherry, and cabinet cherry. In Canada, black cherry grows from Nova Scotia to southern Manitoba. In the United States, black cherry stretches from Maine to central Florida, though the climate of the southern edge of its range may be warm enough to interfere with the initiation of winter dormancy. From Maine, black cherry has migrated west to eastern North Dakota and western Texas. Bears and birds ate the fruit of black cherry, and it is likely that they spread the species to the regions of Canada and the United States. Black cherry grows best in moist, well-drained fertile soil and moderate climate. The Allegheny Mountains from Pennsylvania to Tennessee come close to approximating these conditions. Black cherry grows in 30 states, with the densest population of trees in the Appalachian Mountain, of which the Allegheny Mountains are a part, of New York, Pennsylvania, and West Virginia. Loggers have depleted many regions of the United States and Canada. Woodworkers use cherry to make furniture, coffins, railroad ties, and gunstock. It is also burned for heat and cooking. Black cherry lives 150 to 200 years and may reach a height of 100 feet. During the first half of the 20th century, the popularity of black cherry declined as Americans used mahogany and walnut. The fruit of black cherry is about one-quarter the size of the sweet or sour cherry. Humans do not prefer the taste of black cherry to sweet cherry despite the popularity of "black cherry" colas, though black cherry is used to make the beverages cherry bounce and cherry cordial. During the Columbian Exchange, North America exported black cherry cultivars to Europe, which grew them to make up for the continent's declining stock of timber.

Black cherry has recently regained popularity. The current generation of woodworkers and consumers value it because cherry is darker than the oak and ash of their parents' generation and lighter than the mahogany of their grandparents' generation. U.S. president George Washington grew black cherry trees in the 18th century, though the story about his cutting down his father's cherry tree likely concerns a sour cherry cultivar. One admirer of black cherry characterized the grain as "intricate and exciting." Black cherry is an ideal wood because it does not shrink or warp with the passage of time.

Flowering Cherry

The Japanese, who claim to have first cultivated the flowering cherry, have grown it at least since 800 CE. In the 1940s, however, Koreans asserted that the culture of the flowering cherry tree began in the Korean Peninsula. Among flowering cultivars, Yoshinco, a descendant of *Prunus yedoensis*, is popular in Japan and the United States. A second variety, Kwanzan, is a cultivar of *Prunus serrulata*. One legend holds that a cherry blossom blew into the sake cup of first-century CE Japanese emperor Richi while he admired the cherry trees in his garden. From this incident arose the tradition of imbibing sake while viewing cherry trees. The Japanese tell the myth of a maiden whose breath caused a cherry tree to blossom in 712 CE. According to one account, she gave birth to the first Japanese emperor. Her father made him mortal by giving the emperor a life span of "the blossoming of the trees." These early accounts are surely fiction. The origin of the cultivation of the flowering cherry tree is a later event, dating to 794 CE, when a Japanese emperor planted them in his garden. In the 18th century, the town of Koganie near Tokyo boasted three to four miles of 1,500 cherry trees. Rather than black cherry, the Japanese use flowering cherry trees for wood. The flowering cherry trees in Shotokeum Park in Seoul, South Korea, attract thousands of people per day when they are in bloom.

U.S. interest in Japan's flowering cherries dates to the 19th century. In 1853 and 1854, Commodore Matthew Perry collected flowering cultivars from Japan. Japanese gardener Magoemon Tagaki grew trees along the Arokewa River near Tokyo, whose descendants Japan would give the United States. In 1908, American schoolchildren planted flowering cherry trees from Japan on Arbor Day. President William Howard Taft's wife, Frances, envisioned Washington, D.C., as a city of flowering cherry trees, which had been planted in the city as early as 1846. Japan gave the United States 2,000 cherry trees in 1910, but when a U.S. Department of Agriculture entomologist found two scale insects in the shipment, the government burned the trees for fear that the scales would injure fruit trees. In 1912, Japan sent the United States another 3,020 trees, this time screening them for insects. These trees are the basis of the collection in Washington, D.C., though entomologists have claimed that the 1912 shipment contained the oriental fruit moth, costing U.S. farmers millions of dollars per year. In 1982, Japan and the United States began exchanging seeds in an effort to increase the genetic diversity of plant genomes on both sides of the Pacific Ocean. In this exchange, known as Friendship in Flowers, Japanese children sent seeds from flowering cherry trees to the United States while American children sent dogwood seeds to Japan. Some

600,000 people visit Washington, D.C., each spring to see the cherry trees in bloom. Befitting George Washington's role as a cultivator of cherry trees, the grounds of the Washington Monument have 3,700 cherry trees.

The Nanking Cherry

Also known as the Manchu cherry, downy cherry, mountain cherry, Mongolian cherry, and Chinese bush cherry, the Nanking cherry, *Prunus tomentosa*, is native to the cold arid regions of Central Asia and is the most common bush in the gardens of eastern Russia. Nanking cherry will grow wherever it has sunlight and well-drained soil. The gardener may prune the bush in late winter to stimulate new growth. Those who wish to harvest the fruit and who are in no hurry may grow the Nanking cherry from seeds, anticipating a yield in three years. About 98 percent of seeds germinate, giving the gardener every prospect of success. The Nanking cherry does not bear fruit for the market because it is too soft to transport and does not store well. The plant has had many uses over time. In Manchuria, people grow the Nanking cherry as a hedge and a windbreak in addition to harvesting its fruit. In 1882, the U.S. Department of Agriculture collected specimens from China. In the early 20th century, U.S. Department of Agriculture plant explorer Frank Meyer sent 42,000 seeds from China to the United States. In 1915, New York Agricultural Experiment Station horticulturist Ulysses Hendrick remarked that the Nanking cherry was ideal for "small gardens and cold regions." Other scientists praised it. Today, gardeners plant the bush, usually as an ornamental. Gardeners grow the Nanking cherry from Japan and Korea in East Asia to Turkestan and the Himalayas in Central Asia. The bush—one might call it a small tree—reaches between 9 and 15 feet tall. Like the apricot, the Nanking cherry bears its flowers in early spring, though unlike apricot flowers, Nanking cherry blooms tolerate frost. Like the sweet cherry, the Nanking cherry cross-pollinates, bearing fruit in early summer.

Since the early 20th century, Russian scientists have bred new varieties of Nanking cherry. Others have hybridized it with the apricot, plum, and other cherry cultivars. Canadian scientists have also instituted programs to breed new varieties. Interest in deriving new cultivars has been strong in the northern United States. The Minnesota Agricultural Experiment Station, for example, has bred new varieties of Nanking cherry.

Christopher Cumo

Further Reading

Marshall, Roy E. *Cherries and Cherry Products*. New York: Interscience, 1954.

Parsons, Russ. *How to Pick a Peach: The Search for Flavor from Farm to Table*. Boston: Houghton Mifflin, 2007.

Reich, Lee. *Uncommon Fruits for Every Garden*. Portland, OR: Timber Press, 2004.

Samuels, Gayle Brandow. *Enduring Roots: Encounters with Trees, History, and the American Landscape*. New Brunswick, NJ: Rutgers University Press, 1999.

Vaughan, J. G., and C. A. Geissler. *The New Oxford Book of Food Plants: A Guide to the Fruit, Vegetables, Herbs and Spices of the World*. Oxford: Oxford University Press, 1997.

Webster, A. D., and N. E. Looney, eds. *Cherries: Crop Physiology, Production and Uses*. Wallingford, U.K.: CAB International, 1996.

Chestnut

For millennia, humans have derived wood, tannin, and nuts from the chestnut tree. The chestnut is a member of the genus *Castanea*, which derives from Kastanea, the region of Turkey where in the Bronze Age humans may have first cultivated the tree. *Castanea* has seven species. The European species *Castanea sativa* arose in the Caucasus Mountains. Asia is home to the Japanese chestnut *Castanea crenata*, the Chinese chestnut *Castanea mollissima*, the dwarf Chinese chestnut *Castanea seguini*, and the Chinese chinquapin *Castanea henryi*. The Allegheny chinquapin *Castanea pumila* and the American chestnut tree *Castanea dentate* are native to North America. Humans have long eaten chestnuts with good reason because they contain fiber, protein, vitamin C, carbohydrates, and little fat.

Mythology and History

The Iroquois told the myth of Hadadenon and the chestnut tree. A luckless man, Hadadenon lost his immediate family to the seven witches who killed its members. Having little family left, he went to live with an uncle. The two were poor, having only chestnuts to eat. At every meal, the uncle drew chestnuts from a barrel that magically replenished its supply after each use. One day Hadadenon, in a rash moment, destroyed the chestnuts, leaving the two nothing to eat. Fearing starvation, Hadadenon agreed to steal chestnuts from a tree guarded by the seven witches. The theft accomplished, Hadadenon broke the curse of the witches. His family was restored, and in gratitude they planted chestnut trees wherever they went. For this reason, the Iroquois planted chestnuts throughout North America.

The people of Europe and Asia appear not have associated the chestnut with myth. The absence of a chestnut mythology does not mean that they did not appreciate its value. The Romans esteemed the chestnut with the olive, grape, and wheat and planted chestnut trees in the provinces. Since the Middle Ages, people have eaten the nuts of *Castanea sativa* in Europe and *Castanea mollissima* and *Castanea crenata* in Asia. Peasants harvested and dried the nuts, eating them year-round. The Japanese and Chinese long cultivated the chestnut. Peasants raised chestnuts for foods and planted trees where grain would not grow. In Miyun County, China—the land of chestnuts in China—people may have begun cultivating the chestnut before the time of Christ. Miyun County is today the chief chestnut growing region of Beijing. The cultivation of chestnuts is the leading agricultural activity in Miyun. The Miyun chestnut is high in sugar and protein and has little starch. The county's three chestnut factories process chestnuts. Miyun farmers export the majority of their harvest to Japan, Southeast Asia, South Korea, Europe, and the United States, selling the remainder to China's urbanites. Today, China is the world's leading producer of chestnuts, followed by Korea, Turkey, Italy, Japan, Spain, Portugal, France, and Germany. The Japanese and Koreans cultivate the Japanese chestnut. Home owners in Asia and Europe adorn their property with chestnut trees for their aesthetic appeal. Environmentalists are interested in the chestnut tree's ability, like all plants, to remove carbon dioxide from the atmosphere. *Castanea mollissima*, *Castanea sativa*, and *Castanea crenata* produce large nuts and are cultivated for this purpose. People eat nuts with vegetables, in pastries, and as a dessert and snack. Nuts may be made into flour, fermented into beer, or distilled into liquor. A tree of the Northern Hemisphere, the chestnut has been introduced to Chile, Australia, and New Zealand in the Southern Hemisphere.

In North America, the Allegheny chinquapin and the American chestnut tree were so numerous that one account held that in the pre-Columbian era, a squirrel could travel from chestnut tree to chestnut tree between Maine and Georgia without ever touching the ground. The Cherokee made chestnut orchards by killing other species of tree in an area. Compared to European and Asia species, the American trees produced small nuts, and perhaps for this reason the Europeans who settled the New World planted Old World chestnuts. An accomplished gardener, Thomas Jefferson imported European chestnut trees for his orchard. Plant breeder Luther Burbank used Japanese rather than American cultivars in his breeding program.

Despite this neglect, the American chestnuts were a valuable source of food. Because they flowered late, the American chestnuts were not vulnerable to spring frost and so could be counted on to bear nuts every year. A single tree might yield thousands of nuts per year. These nuts sustained the biota of North America. Bear, elk, deer, squirrel, raccoon, mouse, turkey, and passenger pigeon before its demise depended on chestnuts for sustenance. In Appalachia, chestnut trees grew abundantly, comprising one-quarter of the forest. Because chestnut was light, easy to work, and durable, the pioneers built their homes of it. The trees they chopped down resprouted from the roots, obviating the need to replant. Families gathered nuts in autumn, eating them during the lean months of winter. Autumn frost aided people in the task of harvesting nuts by causing chestnut burs to open, depositing nuts on the ground. Nuts were also useful for feeding livestock. Stockmen let their animals, especially pigs, forage in the forest until they were old enough to butcher. The farmers of Appalachia needed no pastureland because the chestnut forests provided all the forage their animals could want.

The chestnuts that did not feed farmers, and livestock generated cash that families needed for school supplies, sugar, shoes, and underwear. A pound of chestnuts fetched 5 to 10 cents, though the price dipped to 1 to 2 cents when the market was saturated. Retailers must have made money because they inflated the price 10-fold over what they paid farmers. Sometimes money never entered the equation. In these cases, families traded chestnuts for coffee, flour, or other desiderata. As in Asia, American urbanites were eager to buy chestnuts. In some areas of Appalachia, chestnuts yielded more income than cattle. In 1910 Patrick County, Virginia, harvested more chestnuts than any other county in the state. Patrick County and its four neighboring counties totaled nearly half of Virginia's chestnut crop in 1910.

In addition to being a source of nuts, the chestnut tree supplied wood. In Europe, *Castanea sativa* serves this purpose. France, Spain, Portugal, and Italy rely on old forests for lumber and nuts. Worldwide, the demand for chestnut wood exceeds the supply. In the 1880s, lumbermen began to fell the chestnut trees of the eastern United States. Because of its lightness, chestnut was cheap to transport. Because the tree grew straight, telegraph and telephone companies valued it as poles, and railroad companies made it into ties. Chestnut beams upheld mine shafts. Chestnut wood formed the frame and shingles of homes. Woodworkers made chestnut furniture, and mortuary firms made chestnut coffins. In southern Appalachia, chestnut supplied one-quarter of all U.S. hardwood. The tannin was likewise valuable. Chestnut wood contains 6–11 percent tannin, which hide workers use to tan leather. A cord of wood has some 700 pounds of tannin. By 1915, chestnut trees supplied two-thirds of the tannin harvested in the United States. In the early 20th century, chestnut was used to make paper. In addition, chestnut was suitable as firewood because it ignited easily.

In 1899, Connecticut produced the most chestnut lumber in the United States. Pennsylvania ranked second and Massachusetts third. In 1904, Pennsylvania overtook Connecticut. West Virginia claimed second place and Connecticut third. In 1908, Pennsylvania ceded leadership to West Virginia. In 1937, North Carolina surpassed West Virginia. Between 1934 and 1943, West Virginia and North Carolina totaled more than half of U.S. chestnut lumber. In 1943, North Carolina, West Virginia, and Virginia totaled three-quarters of the country's chestnut wood.

Yet the American chestnuts did not enjoy a long tenure. Production fell in the 1930s, and even the end of the Great Depression did little to revive their fortunes.

Chestnut Blight

The decline of the chestnut was more than an artifact of the Great Depression. The great threat was a new disease. In 1904 Hermann Markel, chief forester of the New York Zoological Park (now the Bronx Zoo), identified a sickly chestnut tree in the park. Unsure what was wrong, he inspected his trees and in the coming months others ailed. Examining the bark, Markel tentatively identified a fungus of an unknown species. In 1905, with nearly every tree in the park infected, the forester asked the U.S. Department of Agriculture (USDA) for help. The mycologist on staff thought the fungus a common affliction and recommended the spraying of the fungicide Bordeaux mixture. Markel complied but also sought the opinion of New York Botanical Garden mycologist William Murrill. Dissatisfied with the USDA's diagnosis of a common fungus, Murrill proved a new fungus the causative agent and was the first to use the term "blight" in describing the disease. Scientists know the fungus as *Cryphonectria parasitica*.

As is common of fungi, chestnut blight spread in warm, wet weather, and by 1908 it had killed more than 1,000 trees in Prospect Park in Brooklyn, New York. The New York Zoological Park likewise suffered. By 1911, only 2 of its original 1,500 trees were alive. Penetrating cuts and cracks in a tree, the fungus killed it by destroying the bark. A dead tree was therefore suitable as lumber provided it was harvested before rot and insects rendered it useless. Between 1904 and 1954, blight spread from Canada to the Gulf of Mexico, destroying millions of acres of forest. Spores, spread by wind, drifted west to Michigan, Wisconsin, Illinois, Iowa, Missouri, California, Oregon, and Washington. American and European species were susceptible to the fungus, whereas Asia species, notably Chinese chestnuts, were largely resistant, a phenomenon explained by the likelihood that the disease had arisen in Asia. Coevolving with the disease, native chestnut trees had built up resistance to the fungus over millennia. Others thought blight native to the Americas, a supposition that seemed to explain why damage had been confined to the New World. In 1912, USDA plant explorer Frank Meyer discovered a blight-infected tree in northern China. Yet he did not find any dead trees. The discovery of blight in China and in 1916 in Japan led pathologists to confirm an Asian origin of the disease. Chestnut blight had probably reached the United States through the importation of an infected tree, likely from Japan. In the late 19th century, the United States had imported chestnut trees from Japan. In 1886, Luther Burbank had planted nuts from Japanese chestnuts in California and had as many as 10,000 Japanese chestnut trees in his nursery.

Once in the United States, the disease was remorseless. By the 1910s, New Jersey could count only 25 living chestnut trees in the entire state and all were infected. Connecticut, once known as the chestnut state, had so few trees that it had to import nuts from North Carolina. In Pennsylvania, a 300-year-old specimen, the most ancient in the United States, succumbed to the disease. Blight may have cost Virginia millions of dollars per year in revenues from lumbering. Lumbering companies had no sympathy for the afflicted trees. Their pace quickened, determined as they were to harvest as many trees as they could, dead or alive. It is possible that a blight-resistant tree may have been logged before scientists identified it. In this case, lumbering must have hampered the effort to save the chestnut. Today, scientists can count only a few hundred resistant trees in the entire United States. In total, blight killed 3 to 4 billion trees in Canada and the United States. Where chestnuts died, opportunistic maple and oak trees repopulated New England. In Pennsylvania, black cherry and hickory colonized land formerly held by chestnut. In southern Appalachia, oak and hickory gained ground. These newcomers were one-third less productive in nuts than chestnut trees and surely caused a decline in the population of wildlife.

As early as the 1910s, U.S. scientists took the obvious step of crossbreeding susceptible American species with resistant Asian chestnuts in the hope of deriving resistant progeny. To further this effort the USDA sent scientists to scout China and Japan in 1920s for specimens suitable for breeding and for transplantation in the United States. Because the offspring of this breeding program were hybrids, they grew vigorously and in their early years gave scientists hope of having bred a resistant tree. As they aged, however, many succumbed to blight. Others, less tolerant of cold weather than the American species, died during frigid winters. Those that survived were often disappointing. They did not grow as straight as American chestnuts and so were not as useful commercially. They were also shorter and so did not compete well with oak and poplar for sunlight. If hybrids were not the answer, then scientists were willing to look elsewhere. Convinced that American chestnuts must have genes for resistance to blight, University of Virginia geneticist Ralph Singleton began irradiating chestnuts in the 1950s in hopes of causing mutations in the seeds' genome. Another approach was to find an organism that devoured the fungus in much the way that the bacterium *Bacillus thuringiensis* kills some species of insect. In 1965, French agronomist Jean Grenta discovered a virus that diminished the fungus's virulence. These approaches have not superseded efforts to breed a resistant tree. A breeding program with American chestnut trees as the parent to which offspring are backcrossed may offer the best prospect of deriving a tree with blight resistance and the desirable characteristics of the American trees.

Christopher Cumo

Further Reading

Abreu, C. G., ed. *Proceedings of the III International Chestnut Congress*. Leiden, Netherlands: Acta Horticulturae, 2005.

Betts, Harold S. *Chestnut*. Washington, D.C.: U.S. Government Printing Office, 1945.

Diller, Jesse. *Chestnut Blight*. Washington, D.C.: U.S. Government Printing Office, 1965.

Freinkel, Susan. *American Chestnut: The Life, Death, and Rebirth of a Perfect Tree*. Berkeley: University of California Press, 2007.

Ling, Qin, ed. *Proceedings of the IVth International Chestnut Symposium*. Gent, Belgium: Acta Horticulturae, 2009.

Roane, Martha K., Gary J. Griffin, and John Rush Elkins. *Chestnut Blight, Other Endothia Diseases, and the Genus Endothia*. Saint Paul, MN: American Phytopathological Society, 1986.

Chickpea

A legume, chickpea (*Cicer arietinum*) is in the family Fabaceae or Leguminosae and the genus *Cicer*. *Cicer* has some 40 species, many of them perennial, but the cultivated chickpea is an annual. Of *Cicer*'s species, only *Cicer arietinum* is cultivated. Chickpea is of two types. Kabuli has large, light-colored seeds whereas desi contains small, dark seeds. Kabuli is native to the Mediterranean Basin and western Asia. Desi is native to India and eastern Asia. Despite its name, the chickpea is not a pea, though it shares with peas a round shape. The chickpea may be more closely related to beans than peas. One account holds that chickpea derives its name from the seed's resemblance to a chicken's head. Chickpea is also known as garbanzo bean. The word "chickpea" may derive from the Italian *ceci*. The Arabs know chickpea as *hamaz*, Ethiopians as *shimbra*, Turks as *nohund* or *lablebi*, Indians as *chana*, and the people of Latin America *garbanzo*, from which garbanzo bean must derive. Chickpea is related to beans, soybeans, peas, lentils, clover, lupine, vetch, peanuts, and alfalfa.

Origin and History

A crop of the temperate zone and subtropics, chickpea was first eaten in Syria in the eighth millennium BCE and in Turkey about 7500 BCE. These dates may represent the gathering of chickpeas from the wild rather than their culture. The discovery of chickpeas in Damascus, Syria, dating from the seventh millennium BCE, in an area apart from the geography of wild chickpea, implies that Syrians brought chickpea to Damascus, cultivating it there. This early date of cultivation makes chickpea among the oldest crops. Humans domesticated it about the time that they began cultivating wheat and barley. From an early date, chickpea must have been an important source of protein given the relative paucity of the nutrient in grains. One authority believes, however, that southwestern Turkey rather than Syria was the site of chickpea domestication. The chickpea was abundant during the Bronze Age (fourth to second millennium BCE). In Bronze Age Israel, Jordan, and Jericho, the presence of large seeds suggests human selection and cultivation. By the Bronze Age, people in Greece including Crete, Egypt, Ethiopia, Iraq, India, and Pakistan grew chickpea. By the third millennium BCE, the people of what is today southern France were growing chickpea.

In the ninth century BCE, Greek poet Homer regarded chickpea as food and medicine. In ancient Rome and India, chickpea was likewise food and medicine. The ancients ate chickpea after dinner as a snack, taking it with a beverage. In this context Plato, the Greek philosopher of the fifth and fourth centuries BCE, mentioned chickpea in the *Republic* as a snack. First-century CE Roman encyclopedist Pliny the Elder called chickpea the "pea of Venus," perhaps a reference to its aphrodisiac properties. Perhaps in this context Galen, physician to second-century Roman emperor Marcus Aurelius, asserted that chickpea increased sperm production. Galen thought that chickpea was more nutritious than beans and caused less flatulence. Galen mentioned that the ancients ate chickpea in soup and with milk and ground it into flour. The ancients salted and added dried cheese to whole chickpeas. They ate chickpea raw or roasted, much as Americans eat roasted peanuts. The Romans regarded chickpea as a food of the poor. To call someone a "buyer of roasted chickpeas" was to say that he was poor.

In the Middle Ages, Europeans retained the ancient conviction that chickpea was food and medicine. Italian and Spanish cookbooks included recipes for chickpea. On Fridays, Jews cooked a stew with chickpea, eating it on the Sabbath. After 1492, the Spanish Inquisition, intent on apprehending Jews, took the consumption of chickpea as evidence of Jewishness. In the eastern Mediterranean Basin, people ground chickpea into flour, making it into flat cakes. The French made a type of pancake from chickpea.

In the 16th century, the Spanish and Portuguese brought chickpea to the Americas. In the 18th century, merchants carried kabuli chickpeas along the Silk Road from the Mediterranean to India. In the 19th century, Indians brought desi chickpeas to Kenya. Today, the United States grows kabuli for export to Europe. Mexico also harvests kabuli, much of it for export. Afghanistan grows chickpea in the provinces of Takhar, Kunduz, Herat, Badakhshan, Mazar-Sharif, Smangan, Ghazni, and Zabal. Afghans grow kabuli and desi without irrigation, rotating them with wheat. The Chinese cultivate chickpea in the provinces of Xianjiang, Gansu, Qinghai, Inner Mongolia, Yunnan, Shanxi, Ninjxia, Hebei, and Heilongjiang. In India, farmers plant chickpea on one-quarter of land devoted to legumes. Chickpea totals nearly half of India's legume harvest. After beans, chickpea is the most widely grown legume for human consumption. Ideal for semiarid regions, chickpea tolerates drought better than do soybean and pea. Today, nearly 50 nations cultivate chickpea. By one estimate, the Mediterranean Basin including North Africa, the Middle East, and India produce two-thirds of the global harvest of chickpea. Another estimate holds that India produces four-fifths of the world's chickpeas.

Nutrition and Consumption

Although people in the developed world eat only the seed, in the developing world people eat the seed and leaves. The seed contains protein, fiber, calcium, potassium, phosphorus, iron, and magnesium. Chickpea leaves contain more calcium, phosphorus, and potassium than spinach or cabbage. The leaves also have iron, zinc, and magnesium. In the temperate zone, people couple chickpea with grain, and in the tropics chickpea with roots and tubers, to pair protein and carbohydrates. The combination of chickpeas (and other similar beans) with a grain (or rice) provides a complete protein with all the essential amino acids. Vegetarians, those who do not want to eat the fat from some meat, or those who cannot afford meat, like this combination.

Worldwide, the Turks eat the most chickpeas. Whereas chickpea consumption has declined in Pakistan, it has risen in Myanmar, Jordan, and Iran. The people of India, Pakistan, and Bangladesh grind chickpea into flour known as besan, combining it with wheat flour to make roti or chapatti. The people of the Indian subcontinent eat chickpea leaves in addition to the seeds. They eat young chickpea pods the way Westerners eat young pea pods. Stockmen in this region of Asia feed chickpea to their animals. Growing desi, India imports kabuli from Mexico, Australia, Iran, and Turkey and desi from Myanmar. In India, the chief regions of chickpea consumption are Punjab, Harayana, Rajasthan, and western Utter Pradesh.

Of the chickpeas that Americans eat, half is whole chickpea, much of it canned. Americans consume 30 percent of their chickpeas in soup. Mexicans consume whole chickpeas from cans. In the United States and Mexico, people eat whole chickpeas in salad and stew. Peruvians eat chickpea with rice or vegetables. The faithful of the Ethiopian Coptic Church eat chickpea as a substitute for fish during the months of fasting. Ethiopians combine chickpea with soybean and wheat to make faffa, a food of children. The people of Sudan and Egypt eat chickpea during Ramadan, combining it with sesame oil, salt, onion, chili pepper, garlic, and baking powder. Tunisians boil chickpea, adding salt and pepper. In the Middle East, people eat hummus, a dish of mashed chickpea, and also consume chickpea in salad and soup. Israelis prefer kabuli to desi. They eat chickpea with rice and meat or roast it as a snack. Iraqis boil and roast chickpea, add it to soup, and eat it raw. Syrians consume three-quarters of their chickpeas as hummus. Iranians cook kabuli with rice. Afghans combine chickpea and meat and eat roasted chickpea with dried fruit. Like Israelis, Afghans prefer kabuli. The Chinese fry chickpea, salt it, and eat it as a snack. They also bake and boil chickpea, serving it with rice. The people of Myanmar substitute chickpea for soybean, making a kind of tofu.

Christopher Cumo

Further Reading

Albala, Ken. *Beans: A History*. Oxford: Berg, 2007.

Maiti, Ratikanta, and Pedro Wesche-Ebeling. *Advances in Chickpea Science*. Enfield, NH: Science, 2001.

Saxena, M. C., and K. B. Singh, eds. *The Chickpea*. Wallingford, U.K.: CAB International, 1987.

Yadav, S. S., R. J. Redden, W. Chen, and B. Sharma, eds. *Chickpea Breeding and Management*. Wallingford, U.K.: CAB International, 2007.

Chicory

Chicory (*Chicorium intybus L.*, of the Asteracea family) is a perennial plant with bright blue flowers. It can be found growing in fields and marginal areas such as roadsides in its native Europe and in North America, where it likely escaped from cultivation. Chicory is mostly grown for its roots, which are used as coffee substitute and as a source of inulin, a sugar polymer of relevance for the food industry. Domesticated varieties of this species produce heads of leaves that are known as Belgian endive and radicchio. Chicory roots are tap roots. The roots are very strong and woody in wild plants. Selection during cultivation has led to softer and bigger roots in cultivated varieties. The cultivation of root chicory is similar to that of sugar beet. The plants are grown from seed and develop slowly. Root chicory is best harvested late in the season, as cold fall temperatures lead to a substantial yield increase through weight gain in the roots. It is important to remove the whole root from the soil, since pieces of root that have been overlooked can establish as weeds in the next crop.

History

Chicorium intybus originated in Europe and portions of Asia. It has been speculated that the green leaves of the wild plants were used as a salad green by the ancient Egyptians. Both Roman and ancient Greek sources mention chicory, although it is unclear whether the plant was cultivated or harvested from the wild. In addition to its continued use in salads and herbal teas, chicory was believed to have magic properties during the Middle Ages, both as a protection against attacks during battle and for use in love potions. Various European folk stories tell of a maid turned into a chicory flower after waiting in vain for the return of her beloved who had died far away from her. Chicory was one of the plants that Swedish naturalist Carl Linnaeus used in his famous flower clock, designed to make it possible to read the time of day from the opening and closing of the flowers of selected plant species. Chicory follows a very regular pattern, opening its flowers early in the morning and closing them in the early afternoon.

Chicory Roots as a Coffee Substitute

Roasted, ground chicory roots are used as coffee additives or even substitutes. "Chicory coffee" was made popular by French Emperor Napoleon's attempt to introduce the Continental System in Europe, which was to make Europe independent from British sea trade and the commodities shipped from the colonies. Napoleon hoped to thereby destroy the British economy, which largely relied on foreign trade. A sea blockade of the Great Britain and a ban on British ships in European harbors led to a collapse in coffee imports. Coffee drinkers thus had to look for alternatives. While chicory contains no caffeine, its ground roasted root produces a bitter-tasting dark drink when mixed with hot water.

At the time of the Continental System, chicory as a coffee substitute had been in use in Prussia for some time. Prussian King Frederick the Great had started a campaign against the excessive drinking of coffee in Germany some years earlier. Frederick had been worried about the large amounts of money even poor families spent on this luxury as well as on the effects of large doses of caffeine taken in by the wealthy, who now drank coffee in the same quantities in which they had earlier consumed beer. The king introduced a heavy tax on coffee, making the drink largely unaffordable to people of low or average income. Chicory became the most popular of an unpopular class of substitutes, which also contained various grains. This led to the rise of systematic chicory cultivation.

During the American Civil War, the Union's blockade of New Orleans, which had been the main port of entry for imported coffee into the southern United States, led to a shortage of coffee in the Confederate States and prompted southerners to add ground roasted chicory root to stretch the limited supply of coffee. Even today, chicory is still used as an additive to coffee in the southern United States, particularly in Louisiana, and in parts of Europe.

Production of Inulin in Chicory Roots

Chicory roots are naturally rich in inulin, a fructan sugar that some plants, mostly from the Asteracea family, accumulate as energy reserve instead of the more commonly stored starch. Inulin cannot be digested by the enzymes of the human digestive tract and is therefore a fiber rather than a major source of energy. As such, it has a positive effect on the gastrointestinal functions. Inulin also serves as a prebiotic; that is, it stimulates the growth of certain beneficial bacteria in the intestine. Inulin and its products are used as food additives. Inulin is also used for industrial purposes, mostly by breaking it down into the fructose units the polymer is composed of. This procedure is used to produce fructose syrups. As inulin is easily hydrolyzed and can then be fermented, chicory could also serve as a source of bio-ethanol in the future.

Kerstin Müller

Further Reading

Baert, J. R. A., and E. J. van Bockstaele. "Cultivation and Breeding of Chicory Root for Inulin Production." *Industrial Crops and Products* 1 (1992): 4229–34.

Lucchin, M., S. Varotto, G. Barcaccia, and P. Parrini. "Chicory and Endive." In *Handbook of Plant Breeding: Vegetables I*, edited by J. Prohens, and F. Nuez, 3–48. New York: Springer, 2008.

Meyer, D., and M. Stasse-Wolthuis. "The Bifidogenic Effect of Inulin and Oligofructose and its Consequences for Gut Health." *European Journal of Clinical Nutrition* 63 (2008): 1277–89.

Wild, A. *Coffee: A Dark History.* New York: Norton, 2005.

Chrysanthemum

Chrysanthemum genus (*Chrysanthemum cinerariaefolium* and *Chrysanthemum indicum L.*) are gardening herbs as well as pyrethrum-yielding plants. Europe, Asia, and Africa played a role in the history of chrysanthemum. Chrysanthemum may have medicinal value.

The 18th-century Swedish naturalist Carl Linnaeus, founder of science of classification of plant kingdom, gave the name *Chrysanthemum*, combining two Greek words—*chrysos* (gold) and *anthemon* (flower). Chrysanthemums are annual or perennial herbs of the genus *Chrysanthemum* of the division Magnoliophyta, class Magnoliopsida, order Asterales, and family Asteraceae. The naming of the genus was disputed until the directive of International Code of Botanical Nomenclature in 1999. Presently, the genus *Chrysanthemum* constitutes about 30 species, such as: *Chrysanthemum indicum*, *Chrysanthemum cinerariaefolium*, *Chrysanthemum segetum*, *Chrysanthemum sinense*, *Chrysanthemum morifolium*, *Chrysanthemum balsamita*, *Chrysanthemum parthenium*, *Chrysanthemum japonense*, *Chrysanthemum aphrodite*, and others. In China alone, there are 17 different species of *Chrysanthemum* with varied colors of flowers grown in Anhui, Henan, Sichuan, and Zhejiang provinces.

Origin and History

The history of chrysanthemum's cultivation is ancient. It was the Chinese who produced it as a flowering plant dating from the 15th century BCE. A city was named Ju-Xian, meaning "chrysanthemum city." Legends are woven in Chinese folklore around chrysanthemum, and it has a special place in the Double Ninth

Festival. The plant is also indigenous to North Africa and southeastern Europe. Around the eighth century CE, it arrived in Japan and became embedded in Japanese culture. The Order of the Chrysanthemum is the highest Order of Chivalry, and National Chrysanthemum Day is designated as a festival of happiness in Japan. The official seal of the Japanese monarchy is a single-flowered chrysanthemum. It arrived in northwestern Europe during the 17th century. The plant was introduced in England around the later part of the 18th century. Its popularity in the United States had been in place since colonial times, and it is known as the "Queen of the Fall Flowers." Presently, the propagation of chrysanthemums with a variety of colors occurs in the United States, China, Japan, France, England, India, and others. Some species of chrysanthemums yield the insecticide pyrethrum. The *Chrysanthemum cinerariaefolium* has been grown for more than a century, and Kenya is the largest producer, accounting for 83 percent of pyrethrum. It also exports to the United States in bulk.

Attribute and Cultivation

The herbaceous perennial chrysanthemums, with lobed as well as glabrous leaves and white, yellow, or pink flowers, grow between 20 and 60 inches tall. The alternate leaves of the plant are generally aromatic. Flowers of the cultivated species produce large flower heads, whereas the wild ones possess smaller ones. The flowers of chrysanthemums are florets as both male and female exist on each flower. All the species possess two types of florets: ray florets and disc florets. In some of the *Chrysanthemum* species, the latter are hidden. These disc florets are marked by scissors for pollination purposes as well as growing new varieties. It is very easy to grow chrysanthemums. Flowers are produced in plenty and in full sunshine. Good results are obtained if the plants are spaced 18 to 30 inches apart and manure is provided each fortnight. The site of cultivation is changed every three years to prevent diseases. Some of the species are grown to beautify the garden: *Chrysanthemum morifolium* (florists' chrysanthemum), *Chrysanthemum parthenium* (feverfew), and others. *Chrysanthemum coronarium* and *Garland chrysanthemum* are used as pot herbs and are harvested when the plants are four to six inches in height. The plants are best grown in fertile and well-drained soil. Fertilizer must be applied to the plants during the growing season.

Chrysanthemums have been used for their medicinal value, decorative quality, and insecticidal property. The Chinese were using them since antiquity as a panacea for sundry ailments. Chrysanthemum may prevent dizziness. The Chinese traditionally recommend it for curing diseases of the eye. It may be applied as a remedy for fever, common cold, migraine, and hypertension. For treating sore throats, yellow chrysanthemum flower may be effective. Modern research has proven the potential of chrysanthemum in treating HIV and heart diseases. (See, for example, "A New Anti-HIV Flavonoid Glucoronide from Chrysanthemum morifolium," 2003, http://www.ncbi.nlm.nih.gov/pubmed/14598216.) It may be anti-inflammatory and fever reducing. A wine made from rice and flavored with chrysanthemum is taken by the Koreans. The Chinese sometimes drink it as a refreshing beverage called *tisane*. In southern China, it is a summertime tea also. Wine made from Chrysanthemum flower is an age-old industry in China since the period of the Han rulers. Pyrethrum (*Chrysanthemum cinerariaefolium*) is a good source of insecticide. Pyrethrins or rethrins isolated from the seed cases of flowers are responsible for the insecticidal property of commercially profitable pyrethrum. Apart from being an insect repellent, pyrethrins have a debilitating effect on the nervous system of various kinds of insects. Chrysanthemum adds beauty to landscape architecture, and its ornamental use makes it one of the prized plants. The yellow, white, purple, and red colors of the flowers add to the ornamental use of the plant. Chrysanthemums are grown in gardens as well as parks. The Longwood Gardens and Cypress Gardens in Pennsylvania and Florida respectively hold annual exhibition of chrysanthemums. In China, a chrysanthemum festival is celebrated annually in Tongxiang. The Nihonmatsu Chrysanthemum Dolls exhibition is held every autumn in the city of Nihonmatsu, Japan. The plant also is used in a kitchen garden when there is a lack of space. The chrysanthemums are planted on causeways and entrance paths also. On Mother's Day, the Australians present their mothers bouquet of chrysanthemums. The flowers also have some commemorative use in funerals or placed on graves in Croatia, France, Italy, Poland, and Spain.

Patit Paban Mishra

Further Reading

Herrington, Arthur. *The Chrysanthemum*. Carlisle, MA: Applewood Books, 2008.

Machin, Barrie. *Cut Flower Chrysanthemum Production*. Kent, U.K.: Grower Books, 1996.

National Chrysanthemum Society. http://www.mums.org (accessed 7 July 2012).

National Chrysanthemum Society. *Chrysanthemum*. London: National Chrysanthemum Society, 2001.

National Chrysanthemum Society. *Handbook on Chrysanthemum Classification: A Comprehensive List of Cultivars Including Class, Size, Color, Response and Year Introduced, Plus a Separate List of 2007 Introductions and Classification Changes*. Roanoke, VA: National Chrysanthemum Society, 2007.

Cinchona

In the family Rubiaceae, the genus *Cinchona* contains roughly 70 species, most of them of little value. The tree is small enough that one authority considers it a shrub, though at 75 to 80 feet tall one may assert that it is too large to be a shrub.

Cinchona bark (Heikerau/Dreamstime.com)

Cinchona is a tree of the tropics that grows at elevation and does not withstand the heat and humidity of the lowlands. The bark of cinchona contains several medicinal compounds, the most important being quinine. Although quinine does not cure malaria, it reduces the parasite's rate of reproduction, thereby reducing the often fatal fever. Cinchona derives its name from the countess of Chinchon, who the bark of a cinchona tree saved from the approach of death. The 18th-century Swedish naturalist Carl Linnaeus dropped the first "h" and added an "a," rendering chinchon "cinchona," the name it has had since. Cinchona bark is known as Countess's bark, Peruvian bark, quinquina, and quinina, from which the name quinine derives. Because the Jesuits, a religious order of Catholics, organized the collection of bark in Peru, Bolivia, and Ecuador, it also became known as Jesuits' bark.

History

The mythology of the countess of Chinchon, Spain, is bound up with the history of the cinchona tree. She accompanied her husband, the count of Chinchon, to Lima, Peru, where he was Spain's viceroy. Peru and all of South America may have been free from malaria until the Spanish brought the *Anopheles* mosquito, the vector of the disease, to the continent. In 1638, the countess contracted malaria. The intermittent fevers prostrated her and worsened day by day. The court physician tried numerous remedies, but nothing worked. At his wit's end, he tried an Amerindian folk remedy. Acquiring bark from a cinchona tree 500 miles distant, he pulverized it and apparently put it in a liquid so the countess could drink it. The flavor was bitter, but she managed to swallow the potion. Her fever abated, and her physician pronounced her cured. The countess was the first European rescued from death by cinchona. So impressed was she with cinchona bark that she returned to Spain in the 1640s with it, administering it to the laborers on her estate who suffered from malaria.

As with many good stories, this one has not been immune from criticism. In 1941, A. W. Haggis, probably a British historian, countered that the countess never had malaria. Her husband alone suffered from it, but he was not given cinchona bark because the people of Lima knew nothing about it. The countess did not return to Spain with cinchona bark because she never set foot again in her homeland but instead died in Lima. The fabrication had duped Linnaeus into naming the tree after a countess who played no role in the discovery that cinchona bark could save the lives of malaria's victims. Botanical nomenclature was not always an exact science.

The medical value of cinchona bark was likely well established by the Amerindians of the Andes Mountains centuries before the Spanish conquest. Curiously, the Inca of Peru were ignorant of cinchona's value. The 16th-century Spanish conquistador Francisco Pizarro apparently showed no interest in the tree and may have known nothing about it. One of his soldiers, Gracilaso de la Vega, collected folk remedies from the Amerindians but did not mention cinchona. A Spanish priest who wrote a natural history of Peru likewise omitted cinchona from his account. About 1630, eight years before the countess's putative cure, Jesuit priests living among the Peruvians first learned about cinchona bark's antimalarial properties. The priests may have learned this fact from their Peruvian hosts.

The discovery was momentous because malaria was an ancient disease that killed more people than any other disease according to one authority. The fact that malaria is a disease of humans and monkeys suggests that humans suffered from it early in their evolution. The disease was established by the Neolithic era. Wherever the climate was warm and wet, the *Anopheles* mosquito brought death. Malaria has been reported as far north as Archangel, Russia (64° north) and as far south as Cordoba, Argentina (32° south). Cities and armies have long suffered its ravages. A disease of the Old World, it plagued Africa, Asia, and Europe. As we have seen, the Spanish likely brought it to the New World. India suffered acutely. In the 19th century, the subcontinent had a population of 150 million. Malaria held this population in check, killing 1 million children under age 1, another 1 million aged 1 to 10, and plagued yet another 2 million with recurrent fever per year. In Europe, malaria may have killed fourth-century BCE Greek conqueror Alexander the Great and hastened the deaths of German artist Albrecht Durer (1471–1528) and 17th-century English Lord Protector Oliver Cromwell.

In the 17th century, as at other times, the world badly needed cinchona bark. In 1648 Juan de Vega, the countess's physician, brought cinchona bark to Seville, Spain, selling it for $75 per ounce, a price that a poor laborer could not hope to afford. Cinchona bark was thus initially a medicine of the affluent. Cinchona has, however, an earlier origin in Europe, though it is unclear who first brought the bark to the continent. Belgian author Herman van der Hayden in 1643 was the first European to mention cinchona, if one considers the story of the countess a fabrication. In 1677, the British Pharmacopoeia added cinchona bark to its list of remedies. The Jesuits sent cinchona bark to Spain and the Vatican in Rome, Italy. Its ties to ecclesiastical authorities made cinchona bark a medicine distributed by priests as much as by physicians. Because of its connection with Catholicism, Protestants were suspicious of cinchona bark. Oliver Cromwell called it "the powder of the devil" (Hobhouse 2005, 14). Because of Protestant prejudice against Jesuits' bark, English self-appointed physician Robert Talbor changed its name, masked the bark's bitterness by mixing it with wine, and established a pharmacy in Essex, England, to sell it. So popular was Talbor's potion that King Charles II summoned Talbor to treat him. The remedy a success, Charles II knighted Talbor. Called to France, Talbor treated King Louis XIV and his son. Other successes followed in Vienna, Austria, and Madrid, Spain. Imitating the French and flush with success, Talbor changed his name to Talbot.

Initially, Europeans paid the Amerindians to collect bark for them. Trees bereft of bark died, shrinking the supply. The Jesuits tried to recoup these loses by requiring that a new tree be planted for every one destroyed. The situation was bleak by 1795, when German naturalist Alexander von Humboldt noted that in Loxa, Peru, alone the Amerindians felled 25,000 trees per year to satisfy European demand. By the 1840s, more than 1 million pounds of cinchona bark were shipped to Europe every year. By 1850, many Europeans doubted that South America could continue to supply such vast quantities of cinchona bark. It would be better for Europe to establish cinchona plantations in their tropical colonies, as they had sugarcane, coffee, and tea. For the British, India was an obvious choice for a cinchona plantation economy. British naturalist Sir Joseph Banks suggested that an expedition collect all known species of cinchona from the Andes Mountains. South American nations, wishing to retain a monopoly on cinchona bark, outlawed the export of seeds and seedlings. These laws were grounded in the fact that ounce for ounce, cinchona bark was more valuable than any other commodity except gold and silver. If Europeans were to collect seeds and seedlings, they would need to use deception. In 1852, amateur naturalist Clemens Markham persuaded the Royal Botanic Garden at Kew, England, and the British India Office to fund an expedition to South America. When a German newspaper publicized the impending expedition, Markham changed his name so that South American officials would not suspect the arrival of a cinchona-hunting expedition. Markham's seeds and seedlings went to Kew and the Botanical Garden in Calcutta, India. The British government decided to plant cinchona in India's Nilgiri Hills. It selected an elevation to match the trees' natural elevation in the Andes and with a temperature of 45°F to 70°F. Trees stripped of bark were covered with moss so that they regenerated their bark and did not die.

In 1820, French scientists Joseph Pelletier and Joseph Caventou isolated the alkaloid quinine. The isolation of quinine made it possible to determine the amount of quinine in the bark of various species of cinchona and so appraise its value. Physicians, knowing the amount of quinine they had, could prescribe the proper dose. Quinine could be extracted from the bark and so a patient could evade the bitterness of the bark.

Parallel to the United Kingdom's work in India was the Netherlands' transfer of cinchona to the Indonesian island of Java. The Netherlands sent botanist J. C. Hasskarl to Peru and Bolivia to collect seeds and seedlings. Dutch diplomats in Peru likewise collected seeds. The venture was not a success. The trees that germinated from these seeds contained little quinine. In desperation, the Netherlands bought one pound of seeds from British farmer Charles Ledger. The plants that germinated from these seeds at last produced appreciable quantities of quinine. In 1856, the Dutch created an agricultural experiment station to use science to perfect the culture of cinchona. By the 1880s, India and Java outproduced South America in cinchona bark. So productive were India and Java that pulverized cinchona bark cost only half a farthing per dose and was available at any post office in Bengal, the district of India most afflicted by malaria. India produced enough cinchona bark to treat 10 million people per day (Hobhouse 2005, 28). Because of the high incidence of malaria in India, Indian production went to local needs. By contrast, the Dutch shipped cinchona bark to Europe. By 1914, Java accounted for 60 percent of the world's production of cinchona bark (Hobhouse 2005, 30). By 1939, the figure topped 80 percent. Yet not everyone had access to cinchona bark. As late 1895, it was available in Egypt only in Alexandria and Cairo. By 1939, Java had 110 plantations on 42,000 acres producing 12,391 tons of bark (Taylor 1945, 7). In 1941, the world consumed 1,017 tons of quinine. It seems unlikely that South America alone could have kept pace with this demand. In 1942, the Japanese occupied Java, cutting off the Allies' supply of cinchona bark. The Allies turned to South America, hoping for more production, and to chemistry. In 1944, scientists synthesized quinine. The world no longer needed to rely exclusively on cinchona for quinine, though cinchona's quinine has fewer side effects than synthetic quinine. Today, Africa is the world's leading producer of cinchona bark. Among African nations, Congo is a large producer of cinchona bark.

Attributes and Cultivation

Cinchona is indigenous to South America from Bolivia to Colombia and to Venezuela. Cinchona is related to coffee, ipecac, gardenia, and ixora. It grows on the slopes of the Andes Mountains between 10° north and 19° south. Cinchona does not grow lower than 2,500 feet in elevation or higher than 9,000 feet in South America. For a tropical tree cinchona, in its higher ranges, grows remarkably close to the frost line. An old, established tree can withstand an occasional light frost, but frost kills seedlings and young trees.

In Java, cinchona grows between 2,500 feet and 10,000 feet. Cinchona grows to 30 feet with an 8-inch trunk in 14 years. It enlarges to 75 to 80 feet and a 14- to 16-inch trunk in 45 years. The bark, on which lichens live, is brown. Flowers may be white, pink, or yellow. They cannot self-pollinate and so depend on insects to cross them. Flowers are fragrant and resemble lilac flowers. Each cinchona flower is one-and-a-half inches long. Seeds are tiny and light. A single ounce contains 98,000 seeds. *Cinchona ledgeriana*, named after its discoverer Charles Ledger, has the most quinine of any species of cinchona and so is cultivated intensively. *Cinchona ledgeriana* favors an elevation of 3,000 to 7,000 feet, a lower elevation than many other species prefer. Below 3,000 feet, *Cinchona ledgeriana* appears to thrive, growing vigorously only to die before maturing. Above 7,000 feet, it grows so slowly that it attains the status of a mere shrub. Cinchona needs 125 inches of rain per year. In parts of Java, cinchona benefits from even more rain. A tree's health deteriorates with fewer than 90 inches of rain per year. Unable to tolerate more than one month of dry weather, cinchona needs rainfall uniformly distributed throughout the year. In parts of Central and South America, aridity between November and April disqualifies the regions for cinchona culture. In this respect, Java is ideal because no part of the island is bereft of rain more than one month. Young trees are more susceptible to aridity than mature trees, probably because mature trees have had time to establish a long taproot. Daytime temperatures should be 53°F to 86°F and nighttime temperatures between 46°F and 59°F.

Cinchona prefers virgin land cleared of forest and rich in organic matter. Densely populated regions in the tropics, however, offer no virgin land for planting. The best soils in Java are the volcanic northern slopes of the Preanger Regency Mountains of western Java. Indonesians have made the mountains into terraces to minimize erosion. Bandung, the principal town of this region, was once the quinine capital of the world. The soil should be loose and deep to permit the taproot to penetrate to great depth. A tough subsoil or hardpan does not allow penetration and so is unsuitable for cinchona. The soil should drain well because cinchona does not tolerate waterlogged soil.

Cinchona ledgeriana flowers in the eighth, nineth, or 10th year. Premature flowering signals unhealthy growth and was once problematic in Java and Latin America. Windy conditions appear to correlate with premature flowering. Because cinchona cross-pollinates, the characteristics of progeny vary. It is possible for a tree with a high yield of quinine to outcross with an unsuitable mate, producing offspring that yield little quinine. Thus the reliance on seeds does not guarantee the perpetuation of high quinine yields. Growers therefore propagate the best trees from cuttings. Offspring are a clone of the parent and will yield the same amount of quinine given a constant environment. Growers also plant stands of similar trees in isolation from other cinchona trees to minimize outcrossing. Cinchona planted on land that has been in cultivation to cinchona yields poorly. The solution to poor yield lies in grafting *Cinchona ledgeriana* onto rootstock of *Cinchona succirubra*, a vigorous tree that produces little quinine and so is not cultivated in its own right.

The seeds of cinchona are so small that when planted they must be sprayed with no more than a fine mist of water. Anything more risks washing the seeds out of the soil. Too much water promotes the growth of fungi that cause damping off disease, which may kill hundreds of seedlings in a single day. Seeds planted evenly in humus germinate in 12 to 14 days. Slow germination may point to an unhealthy seedling or poor care. The latter is more probable given the care with which seeds are selected. Seeds germinate at a rate of 80–90 percent of seeds germinate. At four months, seedlings may be 2 to 3.5 inches tall and are ready for transplantation, though they will not be planted in their permanent location until two years old, when they may be 18 to 24 inches tall. Cinchona is often interplanted with legumes, which enrich the soil with nitrogen. An average plantation has a density of more than 2,700 trees per acre. By the fourth or fifth year, trees have sufficient quinine to harvest, though they will not be taken until 16 to 18 years old, when quinine content has peaked. About the fourth or fifth year, a planter thins his trees to give the remaining specimens room to grow. A planter uproots an entire tree. Harvested trees are sawed into logs, from which bark is stripped. Fresh bark is 70 percent water. Drying in the sun a few days reduces water to 13 percent of the bark. A furnace removes the remaining water. Once dried, bark is ready for sale.

In years when production is too high, the price for bark declines and some planters switch to tea or coffee. The Dutch have sold cinchona seeds to Australia, New Caledonia, Hawaii, California, Fiji, the Berlin Botanical Garden, the countries of East Africa, Madagascar, Congo, the U.S. Department of Agriculture, Mexico, Brazil, Jamaica, Trinidad, Martinique, Japan, Malaysia, Sao Tome, China, and India. Cinchona is also grown in the Philippines, Myanmar, Sri Lanka, and Mauritius.

Christopher Cumo

Further Reading

Hobhouse, Henry. *Seeds of Change: Six Plants that Transformed Mankind.* New York: Shoemaker and Hoard, 2005.

Honigsbaum, Mark. *The Fever Trail: In Search of the Cure for Malaria.* New York: Farrar, Straus and Giroux, 2003.

Kidd, J. S., and Renee A. Kidd. *Mother Nature's Pharmacy: Potent Medicines from Plants.* New York: Facts on File, 1998.

Rocco, Fiammetta. *The Miraculous Fever-Tree: Malaria and the Quest for a Cure That Changed the World.* New York: HarperCollins, 2003.

Taylor, Norman. *Cinchona in Java: The Story of Quinine.* New York: Greenberg, 1945.

Cinnamon

An ancient spice, cinnamon has been coveted throughout its long history. The spice is added to rolls, cookies, pudding, pie, quick bread, chutney, stew, and curry. In sales, cinnamon ranks second only to pepper in the United States and Europe. People have called cinnamon the "spice of life" because of its widespread use and popularity. In the family Lauraceae, cinnamon is the dried inner bark of the tree *Cinnamomum verum.*

Because of its long association with Sri Lanka, the spice is known as Ceylon cinnamon (the island of Ceylon is today Sri Lanka) or Sri Lankan cinnamon. The genus *Cinnamomum* derives from the Greek *kinnamon* or *kinnamomon,* meaning "sweet wood," an appropriate name given cinnamon's origin in the bark of the cinnamon tree. The Greek terms may in turn derive from the Hebrew *quinamom.* The Malayan and Indonesian *kayamanis* likewise means "sweet wood," and it is possible that *kayamanis* may be the source of the Greek and Hebrew words. The Dutch *kaneel,* the French and Italian *canella,* and the Spanish *canela* trace their lineage to the Latin *canella,* meaning "small tube" or "pipe," a reference to cinnamon quills. Because of its antiquity and ubiquity, the word "cinnamon" appears in a large number of languages.

Origin and History

The genus *Cinnamomum* originated in the mountains of Western Ghats and southern India. From an early date, the people of Sri Lanka cultivated cinnamon, and the tree has been synonymous with the island. Its trade was early a part of Indian Ocean commerce. The Egyptians used it in embalming the dead. About 1500 BCE, Pharaoh Hatshepsut dispatched five ships to Punt, land along the coast of the Red Sea, to acquire spices. The ships returned with cinnamon and other spices. Cinnamon trees may not have been grown in Punt, leading one to speculate that this region of Africa obtained the spice from Asia. As early as the second millennium BCE, the people of China and Southeast Asia may have exported cinnamon from Indonesia to Madagascar along what one authority terms the "cinnamon route." It seems possible that from Madagascar cinnamon was traded along the eastern coast of Africa, arriving in Punt and from there to Egypt.

In addition to the Egyptians, the Hebrews valued cinnamon. It may be possible that the Hebrews learned about cinnamon during their captivity in Egypt. So important was the spice that, according to the author of Exodus, God told Moses to prepare "an oil of holy anointment" from cinnamon, cassia, and myrrh. The Song of Solomon mentions cinnamon as being among "the chief spices." The early Christians also knew about cinnamon, its being mentioned in the book of Revelation.

One authority believes that cinnamon was more valuable than gold in antiquity. Certainly it was a luxury that only the wealthy could afford in Greece and Rome. First-century Greek physician Dioscorides regarded cinnamon as a medicine, recommending it as a diuretic. According to him, it improved sight, digestion, and the function of the intestines and kidneys, freshened breath, aided women during menses, rendered snakebites harmless, and soothed the stomach. Dioscorides recommended a mixture of cinnamon and honey to remove blemishes from the skin. Given its cost, one wonders how widely it was used as medicine.

The Greeks did not acquire cinnamon directly from Asia but instead relied on the Phoenicians. More generally, the people of the Mediterranean Basin depended on the Phoenicians and Arabs to supply cinnamon from India and presumably Sri Lanka. Also active in the cinnamon trade were the Sabians of Arabia, who might have supplied cinnamon to Egypt. If this is true, Hatshepsut must have gotten cinnamon from Arabia rather than Punt. In the fourth century BCE, Greek botanist Theophrastus confirmed the availability of cinnamon in Arabia. According to Greek geographer Strabo (64 BCE–23 CE), cinnamon trees were so numerous in Arabia that people used their wood as fuel.

At first, the Romans relied on the Arabs for cinnamon, but it must have remained costly. First-century CE Roman emperor Nero flaunted his wealth by burning a year's supply of cinnamon at his wife's funeral. One authority doubts this story. Nero would not have burned cinnamon wood because it yields no fragrance. Rather, he might have burned *Cinnamosma fragrans*, a tree of the eastern coast of Africa and Madagascar. Building a maritime empire, the Romans bypassed the Phoenicians and Arabs, trading for cinnamon directly with India. In the Late Empire, Constantinople (now Istanbul) acquired cinnamon from Sri Lanka. With the decline of Rome, the Arabs reasserted control of the cinnamon trade.

In antiquity, the people of the Mediterranean Basin appear to have been unsure of the location of cinnamon trees. The Arabs told the story of the Phoenix, a bird from "a distant land" that made its nest in a cinnamon tree. Flapping its wings fast it ignited the tree. The fire consumed the bird, but it was reborn in the flames. Apparently because the Phoenix consumed cinnamon trees in fire, the spice was rare and expensive. In this way the Arabs, by referring to "a distant land," concealed the location of cinnamon trees.

Intent on uncovering the location of cinnamon trees, European explorers searched Asia. Italian adventurer Marco Polo (1254–1324) found cinnamon trees on the Malabar coast of India. By the 13th century, the East Indies emerged as the center of the cinnamon trade. In Asia, the Chinese traded cinnamon much as the Phoenicians and Arabs had in the Mediterranean. In the Middle Ages, physicians used cinnamon to treat cough, chest pain, headache, poor digestion, and flatulence.

By discovering an oceanic route to India in 1498, Portuguese explorer Vasco da Gama enabled Europeans to obtain cinnamon directly from Asia. Eclipsed, Arab trade in cinnamon declined. In place of the Arabs arose the Portuguese, who monopolized the cinnamon trade in the 16th century. Yet the Portuguese had no interest in reducing the price of cinnamon, leading other Europeans to resent them. In an effort to break Portugal's monopoly, Dutch explorer Cornelius van Hartman arrived in the East Indies in 1596. In time, the Dutch wrested control of the cinnamon trade from Portugal. In 1658, the Netherlands conquered Sri Lanka, gaining control of the source of cinnamon. Although the Dutch promoted the cultivation of cinnamon, they were no more eager than the Portuguese to reduce prices. The Netherlands exported only a portion of the harvest. In years of surplus, the Dutch destroyed cinnamon to keep it off the market. In 1796, Britain took Sri Lanka, and with it the cinnamon trade, from the Netherlands. Britain established large plantations on Sri Lanka, cultivating 40,000 acres by 1850. The British planted cinnamon trees in India as early as 1798. Additional plantings followed on the Seychelles Islands, in Madagascar, and in the Caribbean. By 1867, Sri Lanka exported nearly 1 million pounds of cinnamon per year. During World War II, Japan occupied the Dutch East Indies, causing a decline in the cinnamon trade.

Production, Cultivation, and Commerce

Today, cinnamon production is concentrated in western and southwestern Sri Lanka. The island is the leading producer of cinnamon. Also important as producers are the Seychelles Islands, Madagascar, and India. In Sri Lanka, cinnamon is a crop of small farmers. Harvested in their second or third year, cinnamon trees remain productive 30 or 40 years. Farmers harvest cinnamon two or three times per year. A tree of the tropics, cinnamon grows in many soil types. In Sri Lanka, it does well in the sandy soil in Kadirana, Ekola, and Ja-ela and in the loam and lateritic soil in Kalutara, Galle, and Matara. The best quality comes from trees grown in the sandy soil of the Negambo district. The tree flourishes between 68°F and 86°F with 50 to 100 inches of rain. Sri Lankan farmers grow eight cultivars, a number that seems small compared to the large number of cultivars of strawberries and several other plants.

The Department of Export Agriculture of Sri Lanka recommends the application of urea for nitrogen, rock phosphate for phosphorus, and muriate of potash for potassium to the soil. In a tree's first year, it should receive 175 pounds of fertilizer per acre, in its second year 350 pounds per acre, and in its third 525 pounds per acre. Where magnesium is deficient, the farmer should apply dolomite at 440 pounds per acre. Farmers fertilize cinnamon trees every six months. Sri Lanka yields 300 pounds of cinnamon per acre whereas Madagascar yields 210 to 250 pounds per acre.

The quintessential export commodity, 94 percent of the cinnamon crop is exported. London, Amsterdam, and Rotterdam are the centers of the cinnamon trade. Japan, Australia, India, Mexico, the United States, Britain, Germany, the Netherlands, and Colombia among other nations import cinnamon. The United States is the world's leading importer followed by India. Japan, the United States, and Australia import cinnamon from Sri Lanka. Mexico imports more cinnamon than any other spice.

Christopher Cumo

Further Reading

"Cinnamon, Ground." http://www.whfoods.com/genpage.php?name=foodspice &dbid=68 (accessed 21 September 2011).

"Cinnamon History." http://homecooking.about.com/od/foodhistory/a/cinnamon history.htm (accessed 21 September 2011).

Ravindran, P. N., K. Nirmal Babu, and M. Shylaja, eds. *Cinnamon and Cassia: The Genus Cinnamomum.* Boca Raton, FL: CRC Press, 2004.

Clover

A member of the Fabaceae or Leguminosae family, clover is an annual, biennial, or perennial legume. Related to the pea, chickpea, bean, lentil, lupine, peanut, alfalfa, vetch, cowpea, and soybean, clover shares in common with them the ability to fix nitrogen from the air into the soil, enriching the land. A member of the genus *Trifolium*, clover numbers more than 200 species, only 16 of which are cultivated to feed livestock. *Trifolium* is Latin for "three leaves." Anyone who has seen a three-leaved clover in the yard will recognize a *Trifolium*. Despite its genus name, a few clovers have five to nine leaves. Although one writer classified alfalfa a clover, it is not a member of *Trifolium* and so is not a true clover. *Tiltan* is Hebrew for clover and is mentioned in the *Mishna*.

Origin, Geography, and Biology

Clover may predate the Neogene period, 23 million years ago. Clover may have arisen in the Mediterranean Basin, from which it spread to Europe, Asia, and North Africa. From the Mediterranean clover may have penetrated Ethiopia and

Clover (D-flo/Dreamstime.com)

Eritrea. It is also possible that clover originated not in the Mediterranean but in the highlands of East Africa. During the late Tertiary period, clover crossed the Bering Strait into North America. From North America, clover migrated to South America, perhaps soon after the continents fused. Farmers first cultivated clover about the fourth century BCE. An adaptable plant, clover may be grown from sea level to mountains and in wet soil and arid land. A temperate crop, clover grows in the tropics at elevation, where it is cool. Clover is grown in temperate locals and the subtropics. In the tropics of West Africa and South America, farmers cultivate clover in the highlands. Today, farmers cultivate clover in West, North, and East Africa; North America from British Columbia to Baja California; the Rocky Mountains; the eastern United States; Mexico; South America from Peru to Chile, Argentina, and southern Brazil; Europe; and Asia. Because Europe was an early adopter of clover, most cultivated clover has roots in the continent. Of clover's 237 species, 110 are native to the Mediterranean. California is a second center of speciation. Mediterranean Turkey has more than 100 species whereas Mediterranean Egypt has few. In tropical Africa and the Americas and in North America and Europe, farmers grow clover in highland meadows, which they allow livestock to graze.

Fourth-century BCE Greek botanist Theophrastus was familiar with clover, leading to the inference that it had been cultivated no later than that century and perhaps earlier. First-century CE Greek physician Dioscorides knew of clover. First-century CE Roman encyclopedist Pliny the Elder observed that clover improved soil fertility. For this reason, the Romans prized it. The medical writers of antiquity praised clover as a forage crop. In the 16th century, English herbalist John Gerard described 21 species, but only 10 were true clovers. Flemish-French physician Carolus Clusius (1526–1609) knew only 7 species. French physician Jean Pitton de Tournefort (1656–1708) listed 44 species, almost all of them true clovers. In the 18th century, Swedish naturalist Carl Linnaeus classified 41 species, grouping them into five units. A more recent classification divides clovers into eight units. Lotoidea is native to the Americas, Africa, Europe, and Asia. Paramesus, Vesicaria, Chronosemium, and Trichocephalum are indigenous to Europe and Asia. Misty Uns claims land in Europe, Asia, and Africa. Confusing is the subunit Trifolium in the genus *Trifolium*. It is native to Europe, Asia, and South Africa. Involusrarium sinks roots in the Americas.

Although most clovers are native to the Mediterranean Basin, 59 percent of species are indigenous to Mediterranean Europe and Asia. Eurasian species grew as far north as Sweden and Norway and have migrated east to Central Asia. One species is found in East Asia. Africa is home to 15 percent of clover species. A number of species grow along the Mediterranean coast of North Africa. Several species are cultivated in Ethiopia, Sudan, Eritrea, Kenya, and Uganda. Ethiopia has 10 species and Kenya, Uganda, and Cameroon claim 1 each. A small number of species are grown in the Congo and Nigeria. Two species are native to the Atlas Mountains. Twenty-six percent of species are indigenous to the Americas, with representatives in Canada, the United States, Mexico, and South America. The West Coast of the United States and the Rocky Mountains have 65 percent of American species. Eastern North America has only 8 percent of American clover species. California totals 9 species, Oregon 2, and Washington 1. South America has 13 species, many in Peru and Bolivia. Chile claims 4 species, with Argentina, Uruguay, and Brazil totaling a small number.

A few annuals self-pollinate, though most clover, dependent on insects to shuttle pollen from flower to flower, cross-pollinates. Perhaps to attract insects, flowers are scarlet, crimson, pink, blue, yellow, and white. Honeybees, bumblebees, and moths are the chief pollinators. Pollen needs humidity to remain viable. In one study, 60 percent of *Trifolium bejariense* self-pollinated, whereas only 22 percent of *Trifolium glomeratum* self-pollinated. Despite clover's preference for cross-fertilization, it rarely hybridizes in nature.

Agriculture and an Introduction to the Species

In the early 20th century, the British cultivated 20 species of clover and Americans 12 species, a larger number than farmers today grow. Most U.S. species were introduced from Europe. The principal cultivated species were medium red clover

(*Trifolium pratense*), alsike clover (*Trifolium hybridum*), mammoth clover (*Trifolium magnum*), crimson clover (*Trifolium incarnatum*), and small white clover (*Trifolium repens*). Medium red, mammoth, alsike, and small white clover are planted in pasture. Medium red and alsike are ideal as a hay crop. Farmers prize medium red, mammoth, alsike, and crimson because of their superiority in fixing nitrogen in the soil. Crimson is an annual; medium red and mammoth are biennial; and small white and alsike are perennial. Clover is attractive as fodder because of its high protein, though too much clover in the diet causes livestock to bloat, leading to the practice of feeding timothy or another grass with clover. Clover is palatable to livestock.

In North America, clover may be grown throughout the United States and Canada. Medium red and mammoth clover grew between 37° and 49° north. Hardy alsike grew as far south as red and mammoth but even farther north. Farmers cultivated crimson east of the Allegheny Mountains, west of the Cascade Mountains, and in the central region of the South. Alsike needed abundant rain. Farmers grew small white clover wherever rain was abundant in the United States and Canada. Soil requirements varied. Medium red and mammoth favored upland clay loam and volcanic soil. Alsike and small white did well on clay loam rich in organic matter. Crimson preferred sandy loam into which its roots easily penetrated.

Medium red, mammoth, and crimson were ideal for rotation. Adding nitrogen to the soil, clover preceded small grain, corn, sorghum, millet, and cotton. A popular rotation in the early 20th century featured grain the first year, clover the second and corn, and potatoes or vegetables the third. In the early 20th century, farmers grew clover for hay and secondarily as pasture. Some farmers grew clover, especially medium red and crimson, in orchards to add nitrogen to the soil. Farmers grew medium red and crimson as catch crops. In some instances they cultivated red clover with grain, harvesting the grain and plowing under the clover as green manure in autumn. Crimson clover was often planted after the harvest of the main crop in late summer and plowed under next spring. Farmers fertilized sandy soil that had been repeatedly cropped before planting clover. In the early 20th century, manure was the all-purpose fertilizer and was applied to the soil in autumn and winter. Once clover was established, the farmers needed not to apply more manure. The application of potash, a source of potassium, was necessary, however, when cloverleaves turned blue green, the yield declined, and young plants died. In these instances, one might have applied potash or replanted clover only after five to eight years of growing other crops.

In the early 20th century, clover was planted in spring as soon as the snow melted. Between 35° and 40° north, farmers planted clover anytime between spring and early fall, though spring planting yielded the best. In the South, farmers planted clover in early spring or autumn. One recommendation urged farmers to plant clover seeds two to three inches deep in light soil, one inch deep on loam, and less than one inch deep on clay. The farmer planted clover more deeply in arid soil than in wet soil. Farmers combined medium red and mammoth with timothy in pasture and medium red, mammoth, and alsike with timothy for hay. Timothy prevented clover from lodging as well as fed livestock in a clover-timothy mixture. The growing of clover with a grass made a more palatable and nutritious hay for livestock. Sometimes clover was intercropped with rye, barley, wheat, and oats, the grains shading young clover plants and improving the nutrition of a clover grain mixture. Farmers planted clover densely—about 12 pounds of seeds per acre—when intending it to be a pasture, to fix nitrogen in the soil, and to be plowed under as green manure. Medium red and mammoth were the chief clovers for this purpose. Farmers often grew crimson to fix nitrogen in the soil. Farmers planted six pounds of seeds per acre of alsike and four pounds of seeds per acre of small white to fix nitrogen in the soil. When intercropped with a grain, smaller amounts of seeds—four to five pounds per acre—were planted. Farmers planted six to eight pounds of seeds per acre when cultivating medium red and mammoth with a grass for hay. For this purpose, farmers planted five pounds of seeds per acre of alsike. When combined with a grass, clover totaled one-third of seeds sown. One authority urged farmers to plant more seeds where soil and climate were not ideal.

Whereas young animals might suffer bloat, mature animals could be fed clover exclusively without cutting corners on nutrition. Some stockmen thought clover inferior to timothy as horse feed, though when cured clover might have been the better choice. Because of its high protein, clover was ideal for lactating livestock. Dairymen fed cows clover in preference to other plants. A mixture of clover and corn was a popular feed because clover had protein and corn carbohydrates.

Species in Detail

Medium red clover is known best as red clover. It is also known as common red clover, broad-leaved clover, and meadow trefoil. The qualifier medium refers to the fact that red clover is intermediate between mammoth and small white and alsike. Red clover is native to Europe. In the 17th century, the English cultivated it. Colonists introduced red early to North America. A biennial, red may be a perennial under certain conditions. In the lands near the Mississippi River and in Ontario, Ohio, Michigan, Wisconsin, and Indiana, red is biennial whereas in the Pacific Northwest it is perennial. Medium red, growing rapidly, yielded a crop of hay 120 days after planting. It bloomed in May in the South and in June in the North. Red clover is ideal for lactating livestock, young animals, and pigs. Some stockmen did not recommend it for horses, but this may be because red is sometimes improperly cured. Because of its rapid growth, medium red may yield two cuttings per year. Farmers often harvested the first crop and plowed under the second. A temperate plant, medium red grew as far north as 50°, though plantings in

Alaska were reported. It may be grown as far south as Tennessee. Where it is cultivated on sandy soil, medium red must have abundant rain. Farmers grew the best crops in Michigan, Ohio, Indiana, Illinois, Kentucky, Missouri, Iowa, Wisconsin, and Minnesota. Medium red was also cultivated in New York and Pennsylvania. Canadian farmers grew medium red in Ontario, Quebec, and British Columbia.

Alsike clover derived its name from Alsike, Sweden, from where farmers introduced it to Britain. Alsike is also known as Swedish, white Swedish, Alsace, hybrid, perennial hybrid, elegant, and pod clover. Linnaeus thought it a hybrid between red and small white, though botanists have since abandoned the idea. A perennial, alsike reached its maximum size of five feet in the second year. Growing less rapidly than medium red, alsike yielded only one cutting per year. The leaves are slightly bitter, though this does not appear to distress livestock. Despite its flavor, alsike has a pleasing aroma when cured. Stockmen fed alsike primarily to sheep and secondarily to horses and cattle.

Grown in Europe, North Africa, and western Asia, alsike yields best in Northern Europe. Britain or Scandinavia introduced alsike to the United States. The crop is suited to a cool, humid climate. In the Americas, alsike yields well in the northern United States and southern Canada. Grown in Michigan, Wisconsin, and northeastern Minnesota, alsike was cultivated as far south as Kentucky, Tennessee, and Missouri. In British Columbia farmers raise a respectable crop, but alsike does less well in Manitoba, Alberta, and Saskatchewan. Grown in rotation, alsike followed corn, potato, and beans in the North and cowpea, soybean, and sorghum in the South. Hardy, alsike did not succumb to spring frost and so was planted early. Farmers often intercropped alsike with rye, barley, wheat, or oats.

Mammoth clover is known as large, tall, sapling, giant, meadow, perennial red, red perennial meadow, pea vine, zigzag, wavy stemmed, soiling, cow clover, and cow grass. A biennial or perennial, mammoth flowers early in the South and in July in the North. Stockmen fed hay to cattle and less often to horses and sheep. Grown in Europe, western Asia, and North America, mammoth is more drought tolerant and hardy than medium red. Farmers grew mammoth in Michigan, Wisconsin, Minnesota, New York, Ohio, Indiana, Illinois, Iowa, Missouri, Kansas, and Nebraska. Canadian farmers cultivated mammoth in Ontario. The farmer rotated mammoth with corn, potato, sorghum, beans, soybean, and cowpea. Mammoth often preceded small grain, corn, sorghum, rape, vegetables, and strawberries. In Wisconsin, a popular three-year rotation featured clover the first year, corn or potatoes the second, and small grain the third. East of the Mississippi River, farmers planted mammoth in spring. In the Pacific Northwest, farmers sowed it in early autumn. In the South, mammoth was planted in spring or autumn and in Canada in spring.

Crimson clover is known as Egyptian clover, a name that suggested cultivation in Egypt. The crop is also called French, German, German mammoth, Italian, carnation, and winter clover. Native to Southern Europe, crimson was cultivated in France, Germany, and Italy. Introduced to the United States in the 19th century, crimson had a small following by the early 20th century. An annual crimson grew in cool weather, not stopping growth until the ground froze. Livestock relished crimson, which was used as pasture, silage, and hay. Farmers fed it to chickens and planted it in orchards. Crimson was grown primarily to fix nitrogen in the soil. Not hardy, crimson fared poorly north of the Ohio and Potomac rivers. Cold winters limited its culture in New York, Pennsylvania, Ohio, and Michigan. Canada was too cold for crimson. Growing poorly on infertile soil, crimson yielded best on sandy loam.

Known as Dutch and white Dutch, small white clover was grown extensively in the Netherlands. Small white was also known as white trefoil, creeping *Trifolium*, and honeysuckle clover. The Irish called small white clover shamrock. Indigenous to Europe, western Asia, and the northern United States, small white was a cool-weather crop that preferred humidity. Frost intolerant, small white flowered in May and June. In Europe, Great Britain and the Netherlands were the leading producers of small white clover. In the Americas, farmers grew small white as far south as the mountains of Mexico. The crop yields well in Minnesota, Wisconsin, Michigan, Ohio, New York, and the Pacific Northwest. Canadian farmers grew small white north of Lakes Erie and Ontario and on both sides of the Saint Lawrence River. In rotation, small white preceded corn, flax, oats, potato, or rape.

During the 20th century, clover diminished in importance. Nitrogenous fertilizers replaced clover's role in fixing nitrogen in the soil. Moreover, soybeans supplanted clover as the dominant legume, and corn replaced clover in feeding livestock. Once an important crop, clover is now marginal.

Christopher Cumo

Further Reading

Hermann, Frederick J. *A Botanical Synopsis of the Cultivated Clovers* (Trifolium). Washington, D.C.: U.S. Department of Agriculture, 1953.

Shaw, Thomas. *Clovers and How to Grow Them*. New York: Orange Judd, 1906.

Zohary, Michael, and D. Heller. *The Genus* Trifolium. Jerusalem: Israel Academy of Sciences and Humanities, 1984.

Cloves

Clove (*Syzygium aromaticum* or *Eugenia caryophyllata*) is a dried flower bud that resembles a nail. It is classified in the division Magnoliophyta, class Magnoliopsida, order Myrtales, and family Myrtaceae. An essential ingredient in cuisines all over the world, the name clove has originated from Latin *clavus* meaning "nail." Indigenous to the Maluku islands of Indonesia, it is cultivated in the Philippines, Malaysia, South Asian nations, Mauritius, the West Indies, Brazil, Madagascar, and the Pemba Islands of Tanzania. Clove has been interwoven with human history from early times. The beginning of the trade in cloves is hinted in Egyptian hieroglyphic inscriptions, which had mentioned the clove trade around 3,600 years ago. Cargoes of spices were sent to neighboring regions. The Chinese were aware of this spice beginning in the fifth century BCE. Visitors to the imperial court of the Han dynasty (207 BCE–220 CE) kept cloves in their mouths so as not to offend the emperor when they spoke to him. The Chinese called cloves the "chicken-tongue spice." Arab traders who had acquired cloves from Southeast Asia brought them into Europe around the fourth century CE. The seafaring nations of Asia and Europe valued cloves as an important trade commodity. Cloves originated in Indonesia and parts of Malaysia and then crossed the Indian Ocean to arrive in eastern Africa. From Egypt, they arrived in the markets of Europe. There was fierce rivalry among European colonial powers over the control of the clove trade beginning from 16th century. The advent of colonialism prevented the local merchants and mariners of Southeast Asia from taking an active part in the spice trade. But after gaining independence in the 1960s, the Association of Southeast Asian Nations sought to regulate the trade in cloves. In the contemporary world, cloves remain an important item of trade with Indonesia playing a pivotal role.

The evergreen, pyramid-shaped myrtaceous tree is about 45 feet long with large ovate-shaped leaves having a dark green color. It is grown best near the sea and with rainfall of 60 inches. The tree produces a fairly large number of crimson flowers that grow in clusters of three terminating on the branches. The buds of the flowers are cloves of rust brown color. A bud measures about one-half to five-eighths of an inch in length. Cloves are harvested in the dry season. The flower buds are picked twice a year and afterward dried by the sun on palm mats. A flower bud contains oil, and stems as well as leaves are also distilled for oil. The eugenol compound, comprising 60–90 percent of oil, imparts aromatic fragrance to cloves. The clove oil also includes acetyl eugenol, crategolic acid, tannins, gallotannic acid, methyl salicylate, eugenitin, campesterol, and other items. An excess of clove oil is harmful to the human body, and a fatal dose is about 3.8 grams per kilogram of a person's weight. The clove oil should not be used to bathe as it is harmful to mucus membranes. A very good quality of clove will provide a little quantity of oil if squeezed by a fingernail. It will also float on a glass of water. Cloves should not be exposed to moisture. It is advised to buy whole cloves and not the powdered ones. The latter lose their aroma soon.

Cloves have become an essential ingredient in spice blends of most of the countries in the world. Clove is used in recipes such as smoked eggplant, saffron prawn risotto, ice creams, asparagus, and Indian curries. Clove and clove powder are used in preparing meat dishes, salad dressings, ketchups, and desserts in the United States. In the kitchens of South Asian countries, the addition of cloves increases the taste of *biriyanis*, curries, and pickles. In India, Bangladesh, Pakistan, Nepal, Indonesia, Thailand, Laos, and Singapore, cloves are put inside the betel leaf or *pan* to be chewed after meals. Without cloves, the flavor of special type of Indian spiced tea called *massala chai* is not complete. A pinch of clove powder enhances the taste of different kind of soups. Cloves are also used in cheese. Due to influence from its former colony Indonesia, the Dutch kitchen preparation uses clove frequently. Clove cigarettes (*kretek*) are popular in Indonesia, having 60 percent tobacco and 40 percent cloves. Cloves have nonculinary use as a material in perfumes and incense sticks. In some houses during Christmas, cloves and oranges are kept in a container to put inside rooms so that a sweet smell pervades the house. The people of the Maluku Islands plant a clove tree in the house at the birth of a child.

Modern research has proven the disease-preventing and health-enhancing property of cloves. As a mouth care, clove oil has been used from earlier days. It has been used as an antidote for toothache. In dental hygiene, it freshens the mouth. Clove oil has been used by some for treating rheumatism, ulcers, scabies, tuberculosis, acne, nausea, flatulence, dyspepsia, diarrhea, and wound infections. Putting cloves inside the mouth is said by some to lessen the desire for alcohol. Traditionally, cloves have been used to treat malaria and cholera in tropical Asian countries. As a folk medicine, it has been used to stop vomiting. Clove has also been used to treat digestive problems as some believe that it keeps the digestive tract in good order. Clove oil also repels insects. Some believe it to improve memory. Clove also is used as an aphrodisiac.

Patit Paban Mishra

Further Reading

Aggarwal, Bharat B., and Debora Yost. *Healing Spices: How to Use 50 Everyday and Exotic Spices to Boost Health and Beat Disease*. New York: Sterling, 2011.

"Cloves." http://www.foodreference.com/html/fcloves.html (accessed 2 March 2011).

Donkin, R. A. *Between East and West: The Moluccas and the Traffic in Spices up to the Arrival of Europeans*. Philadelphia: American Philosophical Society, 2003.

Krondl, Michael. *The Taste of Conquest: The Rise and Fall of the Three Great Cities of Spice*. New York: Ballantine Books, 2008.

Manfield, Christine. *Spice: Recipes to Delight the Senses*. Singapore: Periplus, 2007.

"The Spice Routes." http://asiapacificuniverse.com/pkm/spiceroutes.htm (accessed 2 March 2011).

United Nations Statistical Division. unstats.un.org/unsd/cr/registry/regcs.asp?Cl=14&Lg=1&Co=075 (accessed 2 March 2011).

Coca

Coca or cuca is the name given to several species of cultivated plant belonging to the family Erythroxylaceae. The plant is native to the Andes, in South America, and known for its sweet flavor and most of all for its stimulant properties. Coca is the source of cocaine. Coca is a high-altitude shrub, and the species most frequently cultivated are *Erythroxylum coca* and *Erythroxylum novagranatense*. The coca plant is not to be confused with its homonym, the cocoa or cacao plant, which is used to make and flavor chocolate or hot cocoa.

Today, coca is recognized mainly for its role as the key ingredient in cocaine, and for this reason it is not cultivated on a regular basis in the United States. Furthermore, of the 240 species of the genus *Erythroxylum*, only 1 is of any horticultural interest. Coca plants exist for show in botanical gardens, but it is illegal to grow them in the home or garden. Legal cultivation of coca is rare, and sale of the coca plant is regulated in the United States; obtaining it requires a Drug Enforcement Administration license or prescription.

Attributes

The coca plant is a shrub that grows two to three feet high, with branches on short stalks that bear divided toothed leaves. The leaves of the coca plant have a green hue and are thin and opaque. The flowers of the coca plant are small and are produced in little clusters. The pistil comprises three carpels, which are united to form a three-chambered ovary. The flowers of the coca plant mature into red berries and are sometimes eaten by larvae of the moth species *Eloria noyesi*. Occasionally, the coca plant can be used ornamentally and for decorations, because some coca plants boast yellowish flowers and tall slender branches.

The primary difference between the two species cited above, each

Coca crop (AP/Wide World Photos)

of which is cultivated in two subspecies, is that *Erythroxylum novagranatense* has a relatively higher concentration of alkaloids than what is considered the parent variety (*Erythroxylum coca*), whose leaves are less powerful. As well as thriving at higher altitudes, the coca plant also does better in hotter, more humid climates and must be cultivated in weeded soil. The coca plant is ready to be plucked from the ground when the stalk is bent. After they are plucked, the moist green leaves are packed in sacks and kept dry to prevent moth larvae from eating them. The months when the coca plant is most abundant are March, after the rainy season, and June, October, and November.

Cocaine

Coca is classified as a stimulant, and leaves of the plant are the basis of the drug cocaine. The coca plant is renowned worldwide for the alkaloids it contains; these are the active ingredients in the illegal drug. Coca is a powerful plant, with a lot of applications, including medicinal uses. The first European research on coca's effects was undertaken by Eduard Frederich Poeppig, a German botanist and zoologist. Poeppig documented the benefits of the coca leaf in the early 19th century.

Pharmacologically, the most well-known and sought-after alkaloid of the coca plant is cocaine, which is found in only a small percentage in coca leaves (0.3–1.5 percent). The average presence of cocaine in the coca leaves is only 0.8 percent but nonetheless is still one of the most dangerous aspects of this cultivated plant. Although cocaine is an illegal drug that is used as a narcotic, it still has its own practical uses in medicine, such as being utilized as an anesthetic.

The mental effects of the coca plant are extensive, and it is known for greatly stimulating the imagination and the nervous system. When chewed, coca has varying effects, including appetite suppression and the reduction of pain and fatigue. In fact, the chewing of the coca leaves was the most popular way to feel its effects, and they are still chewed in countries like Peru. Where it is native, coca is most commonly used in medicine and religion. The coca plant has also been used as an anesthetic in treatments for malaria, indigestion, and stomach ulcers. Because of its anesthetic properties, it has also been used as a numbing agent in dental procedures.

Although it has been proven that there are some benefits of the coca plant, it cannot be predicted how the substance affects each individual or what the concentrations of active agents are in any given plants. The negative effects that have been reported from ingesting the leaves of this plant range from extreme fatigue to problems with digestion. In the 19th century, the substance cocaine was actually commonly prescribed by druggists to treat ailments and was the main ingredient of Coca-Cola. In 1880, Coca-Cola was laced with cocaine-based syrup for its flavor and caffeine, but obviously, it is no longer used in those products today, and the cocaine-based syrup was removed from the recipe in 1901.

Cocaine, the highly dangerous drug produced by the coca leaf, has a range of detrimental effects and also possesses addictive qualities, which is one of the main reasons why it is illegal. The substance cocaine is extracted from the coca leaf by turning the leaves into a paste and extracting the cocaine using both solvent and acid extraction techniques. Since the production of cocaine is illegal in most places, it is usually done only in illicit laboratories. The manufacturing of it encompasses three steps: the extraction of cocaine from the coca leaf, the purification of the substance, and the conversion of the coke base to cocaine hydrochloride. Because of their notoriety and concerns about being discovered by law enforcement, these labs are usually located in very remote places, and those who manufacture the substance usually have extensive knowledge of chemistry and engineering. There is no one method for extracting the paste out of the coca leaf. Although it is illegal, the production of this illicit substance has become a cottage industry, especially in some places in South America such as Peru.

Although cocaine provides this temporary high, there is a long list of disruptive medical repercussions due to the use of cocaine, such as constricted blood vessels, increased body temperature, elevated heart rate, and a high blood pressure. The long-term effects of cocaine can include a constant irregular heartbeat and palpitations, stroke, respiratory failure, and seizures. The prolonged abuse of cocaine can, as well as having its physical consequences, also cause lingering mental afflictions for the individual who uses on a regular basis. Cocaine shares some of the same qualities as an opiate as it activates certain areas in the brain that control rewards. Cocaine stimulates these areas and brings about positive reinforcement for certain behaviors, which are most likely to be repeated along with the stimulation of the drug, with the positive reward being a temporary but very strong euphoric state, which is one of the main reasons that cocaine is so habit forming.

Cocaine has a very powerful effect on the brain and brain chemistry; neurological studies have found that cocaine blocks norephenephrine and noradregeneric synapses and blocks the reuptake mechanism, which is the reabsorption of a neurotransmitter by a neurotransmitter transporter, which, in turn, is what decreases the level of dopamine to the brain. As a result of cocaine's extreme transformation and some of the decrease in functions in the nuerotransmitters, those who become increasingly dependent on cocaine, if exposed to the drug for a long enough period of time, will eventually need it to feel any pleasure at all. In fact, very shortly after the immediate rush of cocaine is felt, the individual will still have very strong cravings and desire more and more of the dangerous substance. The drug produces highs that are very brief and fleeting, resulting in the desire for more cocaine. This is another reason why the use of cocaine is so detrimental to a person's psyche and physical health, is extremely habit forming, and can be potentially lethal.

On the other hand, no matter what kind of temporary rush cocaine can produce, there is also the parallel dysphoria, which is the opposite effect brought on by cocaine withdrawal. There are some misconceptions that cocaine is less addictive or less dangerous than some other street drugs, but these notions are false, as cocaine is just as highly addictive as, if not more than, other hard drugs like heroin or crack.

Cocaine also has a remarkable effect on brain chemistry and has been known to cause in some cases insomnia for an extended period of time or an extreme depressive state. Those who come off cocaine also experience very severe and debilitating withdrawal symptoms (often referred to as a crash), which can last for days at a time and include extreme fatigue, itching, irritability, nausea and vomiting, paranoia, violent mood swings, insomnia, and an increased appetite (as opposed to the dramatically reduced appetite that individuals experience when using). People who are withdrawing from the drug often experience lethargy and weight gain, as a result of the change in their appetite when they are coming off the drug.

Cocaine withdrawal also comes with a drastic level of depression, pain, and dysphoria. Some individuals also suffer from very vivid dreams and nightmares during their withdrawal. Individuals with a cocaine addiction cannot simply stop using the substance without having some type of replacement, due to the incredibly strong cravings that cocaine causes. The cravings will increase significantly during the withdrawal period. Sometimes withdrawal from cocaine can last for months; however, with treatment, these problems can be addressed, and recovery can be possible for those who were dependent on the drug.

There are also different ailments, which can be brought about depending on the way cocaine is ingested and absorbed into the body. There are a multitude of additional problems that can be brought upon by snorting, ingesting, and injecting cocaine. Each method in which someone intakes cocaine has a different set of physical and mental consequences. Snorting cocaine can cause chronic nosebleeds, loss of smell, and hoarseness, while ingesting the drug can lead to gangrene in the bowels and also an increased chance of contracting HIV, hepatitis, or other diseases associated with sharing needles. The continual use of cocaine can have lifelong consequences, and its abuse has become an epidemic in some parts of the United States.

History and Current Status

Coca leaves have become an especially important commerce for some countries in South America including Bolivia, Colombia, Ecuador, and Peru, as well as having a deep cultural significance. The coca plant was limited to the Andes under the Incas, and because of its rarity the plant was distributed only to nobles and the higher classes. Before chemical refinement techniques made it the basis of such a dangerous drug, the coca plant developed a rich history and has cultural significance for many indigenous groups in the Andes. Persons called coqueros were a specific group of coca leaf users, who understood how to use the coca plant and the principles of its medicine. The coca plant was used and was effective in treating ailments like toothaches and altitude sickness. Cocaine, which is produced by the plant and is mainly known as a notorious narcotic drug, also has its own powerful medicinal purposes. Cocaine can be used medically as an anesthetic for some surgical procedures.

The Spanish conquistadors were not long in discovering that the leaves of the coca plant were especially potent and powerful. When soldiers chewed the leaves of the plant, they altered their mood, allowing them to accomplish feats of incredible strength, plus the leaves allowed them to fast for extended periods of time. Chewing of coca leaves is still popular in Peru and Bolivia. Although the coca plant is most likely most well known for being the foundation for the notorious drug cocaine, it still has a broader range of uses other than being the root of this illicit drug.

Cocaine abuse was particularly prevalent in the 1980s, when cocaine addiction was known historically as cocainism. Often referred to as "the caviar of street drugs," cocaine is an extremely costly method of getting high and can have terrible effects on the body and the nervous system. Though it poses so many health risks, cocaine is still, most likely, one of the most exhilarating drugs on the market. The health problems that can be induced by this drug are caused by how cocaine interferes with the neurotransmitter transporter dopamine. Dopamine is the chemical in the brain that controls pleasure and movement and can cause a false sense of euphoria or extreme pleasure for a brief time.

Bonnie Ellman

Further Reading

Burkill, H. M. *Useful Plants in West Tropical Africa*. London: Royal Botanical Garden, 1985.

Flynn, John C. *Cocaine: An In-Depth Look at the Facts, Science, and History.* New York: Citadel Press, 1993.

Karch, Steven, B. *A Brief History of Cocaine: The Mystery of Coca Java and the Kew Plant.* London: Royal Society of Medicine, 2003.

Cocklebur

Cocklebur (*Xanthium strumarium*) is an annual that belongs to the Asteraceae family. Originating in California, *Xanthium strumarium* has spread throughout the country and has also set foot into Europe and Asia due to its hitchhiking ability. It competes for nutrients in agricultural areas along with crops such as corn, cotton, and soybeans and can also be hazardous in children's play areas and parks. Cocklebur is grown for its medicinal value and for the production of yellow dye.

Botany

Xanthium strumarium is considered to be the predecessor of the many subspecies and variations of cocklebur found around the United States. It grows in different kinds of soils of varying pH concentrations from 5.5 to 8, and also in different types of habitats such as plains, dry lands, wetlands, in ditches, along roadsides and fences, in fields along with other crops, and on slopes of mountains even to an elevation of 1,640 feet. Although cocklebur grows in different types of soil, it grows best in soil that is compact and sandy, where organic matter is minimal, and where the soil just below the surface is considerably moist. *Xanthium* can tolerate flooding and even saline conditions at times.

The plant is an annual that spreads and propagates only by seeds. In healthy and moist conditions, cocklebur grows to a height of three feet, while in drier areas it is a very short bush. It possesses a strong and stout, woody taproot. Stems are stout, rigid, and with many branches. It is green, has many oil glands, and emits a peculiar smell. The plant is identified by its alternate, broad, lobed, and triangular to heart-shaped leaves, which, depending on the subspecies, may or may not contain spines. Leaves are rough to the touch and may vary in length from two to six inches. The leaves are also three-veined and have serrated or toothed edges. The inflorescence is an axillary raceme, where the male flowers are on the uppermost, longest stalks and the female flowers are on the short stalks. Flowers are described as imperfect, with either the male or female reproductive part of the flower lacking, and also as dioecious, where both types of flowers, male and female, are found on the same plant. The male flowers are yellow. In Greek, *xanthium* means "yellow." The female flower is pale green to white. The fruit is a bur or a spine-encased dry fruit that measures approximately three-quarters of an inch in length and is more of a flattened oval in shape with a pointed end. The fruit is two chambered, containing a seed in each, and rich in oil. Numerous curved or hooked spines encase the bur. In Bell County, Texas, it has been observed that a subspecies of *Xanthium strumarium* possesses as many as 25 seeds per bur. This is an exception from the usual 2 seeds per bur. A single cocklebur plant can yield from 500 to 1,500 burs per flowering season.

Many have been fascinated by the way this plant has sprouted in areas that have been cocklebur free for over a decade. The seeds of cocklebur are peculiar. They can lie dormant in the soil for as long as 16 years when buried at a depth of eight inches. Usually this happens when farmers have tilled the land and have removed the plants, burying the seeds deep into the earth in the hope of depriving them of oxygen, which is necessary for the germination process. However, when the land has been retilled for cultivation years later, it has been observed that entire fields of cocklebur sprout suddenly, having risen to the surface soil.

Another peculiar feature about cocklebur is its hooked spines. These spines are short and latch onto susceptible target surfaces such as shoes, clothing, and animals. By latching on, they hitchhike to many places where they spread, fall off, or are discarded and take root. Since they are not particular about any specific soil type, they germinate and sprout in no time. A single plant in an area can give rise to an entire field of cocklebur within a couple of years. Swiss engineer Georges de Mestral in 1941 invented Velcro based on the principle of the burs clinging onto looped fibers of wool and fabric. With this began the use of Velcro not only in clothing but also in medical applications such as heart valves.

Toxicity

The flowers and seeds of cocklebur are highly toxic. The plant may be fatal in farm and grazing animals. The most susceptible of all farm animals is the pig, which is an omnivore and feeds on anything and everything within its area. Humans consuming the flesh of sickly or dead pigs can also be affected with serious illnesses. Many times these illnesses can trigger the death of the individual. While it has been proven that the burs of cocklebur are toxic to animals, there has been an occurrence of deaths related to humans in a poverty-stricken area of Bangladesh, where a group of people consumed a lot of burs to avert starvation. Contrary to its toxic nature, the pharmaceutical industry has found promising results that can indicate its application in the world of medicine.

Research

From a scientific point of view, studies on cocklebur have led to insights on a property in plants known as photoperiodism. Cocklebur—unlike most plants, which require the long days of spring and summer to bloom—flowers and fruits best in short days. Hence its flowering season extends from late summer to late fall in most areas of the United States. This feature that is observed, namely photoperiodism, has also led to the studies of how plants respond to light and of the plant organs that are involved with this phenomenon. Cocklebur is a subject for physiological studies opening new doors to scientific research and discoveries in the plant world.

Amanda Mittra

Further Reading

Everitt, J. H., R. L. Lonard, and C. R. Little. *Weeds in South Texas and Northern Mexico*. Lubbock: Texas Tech University Press, 2007.

Halvorson, William L., and Patricial Guertin. "Fact Sheet for *Xanthium strumarium* L." USGS Weeds in the West Project. 2003. http://sdrsnet.srnr.arizona.edu/data/sdrs/ww/docs/xantstru.pdf (accessed 10 September 2011).

"Veterinary Library, Cocklebur." University of Illinois at Urbana-Champaign. http://www.library.illinois.edu/vex/toxic/cklburs/cklburs.htm (accessed 10 September 2011).

"Worldwide Hitchhiker and Nature's Velcro." http://waynesword.palomar.edu/plapr98.htm (accessed 10 September 2011).

"*Xanthium strumarium*." Califlora. http://www.calflora.org/cgi-bin/species_query.cgi?where-calrecnum=8367 (accessed 10 September 2011).

Coconut

A palm tree, coconut (*Cocos nucifera*) is grown in Asia, the Pacific Islands, Africa, and Latin America. A member of the Palmae family, coconut is widely cultivated between 20° north and 20° south. Near the equator, farmers grow coconut up to 3,000 feet of elevation, though they rarely plant it in large numbers above 900 feet. In Jamaica, coconut is planted no higher than 350 feet. A coconut palm may live more than 100 years, remaining productive for 60 years. Traditional varieties begin flowering in their fifth or sixth year. Ripening on the palm, a coconut requires 1 year to mature. The word "coconut" derives from the Portuguese term for monkey because the Portuguese thought a coconut resembled a monkey's head. Because of its importance, the coconut is known as the Tree of Life, the Tree of Abundance, and the Tree of Heaven. Eighty grams of coconut contain 283 calories, 37.6 grams of water, 2.7 grams of protein, 12.2 grams of carbohydrates, 7.2 grams of fiber, 285 milligrams of potassium, 90.4 milligrams of phosphorus, 25.6 milligrams of magnesium, and 11.2 milligrams of calcium. Coconut milk and coconut water also provide nutrients. Coconut oil, having only calories, is devoid of nutrients.

Origin and Diffusion

One scholar admits that the origin of the coconut is unknown, though scientists are eager to put forward hypotheses. In the 19th century, scholars proposed an origin in Central or South America. Hypotheses that place the origin of the coconut in the Old World appear to be the current fashion. One authority favors Malaysia or Indonesia. Various authorities have proposed India and Melanesia. A coconut-like fossil dating between 15 million and 40 million years ago may point to the desert of Rajasthan, India, as the place of origin. Nevertheless, several scientists dispute an Indian origin of the coconut. Melanesia is a candidate because, according to one scientist, it supports a large population of insects that feed on coconut, implying that it has long been part of the flora of the islands. The coconut dates to 3400 BCE in Melanesia, predating human settlement. If the coconut did not originate in Melanesia, some mechanism must be invoked to explain its transit to the islands. New Zealand is also a candidate for the origin of the coconut, bearing a 15-million-year-old fossil. The Malaysian hypothesis makes clear that the coconut may have originated in Southeast Asia. An Eocene fossil of a coconut, *Cocos sahnii*, places the putative origin in the western Indian Ocean. Fossils along the northern coast of Papua New Guinea may place the origin of the coconut there. Archaeologists have found one fossil of a coconut with a human skull, permitting the inference that humans used the coconut in Papua New Guinea by 4500 BCE, a date that likely preceded cultivation. One scholar puts the origin of the coconut at the Lord Howe Rise-Norfolk Island Ridge of Gondwanaland 15 million years ago.

Wherever its origin, the coconut has dispersed as far west as the Seychelles Islands and as far east as the Line Islands. The question of how the coconut got to these regions has not been answered. One authority asserts that ocean currents could not have taken the coconut far because it will not germinate if it has been in water more than a few days. In the absence of diffusion by ocean currents, humans must have carried the coconut wherever they went. According to this hypothesis, Polynesians, Tamils, and Arabs spread the coconut throughout the tropics of the Old World. When Europeans migrated into the tropics, they became agents of diffusion. Between 1499 and 1549, the Portuguese carried the coconut from the Indian Ocean around the Cape of Good Hope to the Cape Verde Islands and from there to the Caribbean and Brazil. After 1650, the Spanish took the coconut from the Philippines to Central and South America.

Another authority invokes ocean currents as the mechanism of diffusion, noting that saltwater, absorbed by the husk, must induce dormancy. The coconut germinates slowly when placed in saltwater and more rapidly when immersed in freshwater. Thick-husked coconuts float best and so must have drifted great distances in the Pacific and Indian Oceans. Assuming that the coconut originated in Asia or the

Pacific Islands, it spread, possibly by ocean currents, to Australia, Africa, and the Americas, though these vast distances appear to have been difficult to traverse without human aid.

Coconut Agriculture and the Uses of the Coconut

Early humans must have prized the coconut as a source of water that required no tools or digging to obtain. As coconuts washed ashore, humans who dwelled along the coast must have gathered them, an action that surely predated cultivation. As early as 1000 BCE, humans cultivated the coconut on the Malabar Coast (now Kerala) of India, a region that is known as the Land of the Coconut. By the time of Christ, the people of Sri Lanka grew coconut. The beginning of coconut agriculture therefore postdated the rise of agriculture in the Old and New World. Among tropical nations, the Philippines, India, Sri Lanka, Malaysia, Indonesia, and the Pacific Islands, all within 1,000 miles of the equator, produce the majority of coconuts.

In many regions of the tropics, coconut has long been a crop of small farmers, who planted the palm near homes and in gardens. Small farmers account for more than 80 percent of acreage in the Philippines, where the average coconut farm is five acres. In India the average size is less than one acre. Minimizing their reliance on a single crop, farmers plant coconut with sweet potato, cassava, corn, sunflower, and pumpkin. In Jamaica, farmers grow coconut and banana, and in the Seychelles Islands coconut, cinnamon, and vanilla. The small farmer relies on coconut as a cash crop and as sustenance. Every part of the palm has value. Coconut leaves are used to construct roofs, walls, mats, and mattresses. The trunk yields furniture. Coconut meat yields food, feed, and oil. Coconut cake, the portion of copra, the dried kernel of a coconut, left after the oil has been extracted, is fed to cattle and chickens. Coconut sap yields a sugary substance and vinegar. The husks are made into rope and the shell into charcoal. The roots are used as dye and medicine. Coconut oil yields lubricant, soap, laundry detergent, margarine, and nondairy creamer and is burned for light and fuel. Most coconut oil is used in cooking. In the 19th century, the United States and Europe derived oil and soap from coconut. By 1900, the coconut was used to make margarine. The demand for copra spurred exports, which rose from 385,000 to 800,000 tons between 1910 and 1925. Exports exceeded 1 million tons in 1935 but slowed thereafter, reaching 1.5 million tons only in 1975. Coconut is popular as food and oil in the Philippines, Indonesia, Papua New Guinea, Sri Lanka, India, and Malaysia.

Important as coconut oil is, it faces competition from soybean and palm oils. The rapid expansion in soybean acreage in the United States and South America in the 20th century increased the supply and decreased the price of soybean oil. The same dynamic occurred with palm oil because the cultivation of the oil palm increased in Malaysia and Indonesia in the 20th century. According to the World Bank, the production of one ton of coconut oil costs $320 to $400 in the Philippines whereas the production of one ton of palm oil costs $200 to $220 in Indonesia. Faced with this reality, consumers use vegetable oils in preference to coconut oil, resulting in stagnant demand for the latter. Since 1980, the consumption of coconut oil has grown less than 1 percent per year. What demand there is the Philippines meet, exporting 75 percent of the world's coconut oil. The Philippines are the largest producer of copra and oil. One-third of the islands' population, 18 million people, depends on the coconut for income.

Cultivation and Science

A tropical crop, coconut grows best between 80°F and 90°F with 40 to 100 inches of rainfall per year. The temperature should vary little between day and night and throughout the year. Rainfall should be evenly distributed throughout the year. In hindering transpiration, humidity may injure palms. Because leaves are enormous, the coconut transpires a large amount of water and so roots must have water in the soil to replace these losses. Although soil moisture is important, the coconut cannot survive in waterlogged soil. When water is in shortage lower leaves die, female flowers reduce their number, and palms shed unripe nuts. In the worst cases, the coconut suffers from bronze leaf wilt, a condition in which old leaves fall from a palm, young leaves wilt, and the terminal bud dies. Prolonged water shortage dwarfs palms. Although a healthy palm may reach 100 feet, a palm deprived of water may be only 5 feet tall. Tolerating a range of soils, coconut is cultivated in sand, peat, and acidic swamp. Farmers obtain the best yields on alluvial and volcanic soil. Whatever the soil, the farmer must fertilize it for the best yield. Coconut hybrids, crosses between dwarf and tall cultivars, require large amounts of fertilizer to yield well. Because poor farmers cannot afford fertilizer, scientists feared that the yield of hybrids would decline to the level of traditional varieties without fertilizer, yet their performance has exceeded expectations. In one study, scientists compared the hybrid Khira I with local varieties in South Sulawasi, Indonesia. Over seven years Khira I averaged 2.3 tons of copra per acre with fertilizer whereas local varieties yielded 700 pounds per acre. In the absence of fertilizer, Khira I retained its advantage, yielding 1.2 tons of copra per acre whereas local varieties yielded 150 pounds per acre.

Dwarfs bear coconuts at an early age and produce a large number of small nuts, though the quality of copra is poor. Tall varieties bear a small number of large nuts that are rich in oil and easy to dry. Hybrids combine the early maturation of nuts and the short stature of dwarfs and the large nuts and copra quality of tall varieties. In many instances, scientists have derived hybrids from a cross of the Malayan yellow dwarf as the female parent and a tall variety as the male parent. The Malayan yellow dwarf is a desirable parent because it is partially resistant to the disease lethal yellowing. Among hybrids, Port Bouet 121, a cross between Malayan yellow dwarf and West African tall, is planted worldwide. The hybrid bears coconuts at three-and-a-half to five years compared to five-and-a-half to seven years for traditional cultivars. It yields twice as many coconuts by weight as its parents. Hybrids are as much as 10 times more productive than tall varieties, especially in the early years.

The World Bank and the Consultative Group on International Agricultural Research urge tropical nations to fund research on the improvement of coconut. Yet the hope for gains from research may be only partly realized given that many of the nations that grow coconut are poor. Nevertheless, several nations have instituted programs to breed new varieties. Cote d'Ivoire, the Philippines, the Solomon Islands, Benin, Madagascar, Mozambique, Nigeria, Tanzania, Togo, India, Indonesia, Sri Lanka, Thailand, Fiji, Papua New Guinea, Malaysia, Vietnam, Samoa, and Vanuatu have established breeding programs. Around 1900, India established the world's first coconut research program. In 1908, the College of Agriculture in the Philippines began research on the improvement of coconut. In 1929 Sri Lanka founded the Coconut Research Institute. The next year Indonesia established a coconut research center. In Jamaica, the Coconut Industry Board has collected exotic varieties in hopes of identifying the genes for resistance to lethal yellowing, though inadequate funding has slowed progress since 1981. The desiderata of these programs include high yield, drought tolerance, and disease resistance. Drought tolerance is prized in Benin, Nigeria, East Africa, India, Mexico, and Brazil, where coconut may suffer from inadequate rainfall. Traditional breeding programs may remain more promising than genetic engineering, at least in the near term.

The coconut is a heavy feeder. In one study, 14,770 pounds of copra removed from the soil 238 pounds of nitrogen, 33 pounds of phosphorus, 425 pounds of potassium, 20 pounds of calcium, 33 pounds of magnesium, 44 pounds of sodium, 275 pounds of chlorine, and 20 pounds of sulfur. To repair the loss of potassium, which turns leaves yellow, farmers add muriate of potash to the soil. Unlike many plants, the coconut needs chlorine and in this respect muriate of potash is useful because it supplies both potassium and chlorine. To redress the loss of nitrogen, farmers add sulfate of ammonia to the soil. The fertilizer is valuable because it adds both nitrogen and sulfur to the soil. Where nitrogen is in shortage, coconut leaves are pale. Too much nitrogen or too little potassium may leave coconut palms vulnerable to disease. Less often is phosphorus deficient, though sandy loam, loam, or clay loam may be deficient in the element. Calcareous or coralline soils or shale may benefit from the addition of phosphorus, iron, manganese, and organic matter. Alkaline soils may be deficient in boron. Magnesium is often in short-age in soil that is deficient in potassium. In cases where rainfall is limited, coconut grows slowly and so needs less fertilizer. As a rule, farmers who can afford fertilizer apply it once per year, though these applications are far from inexpensive. On large estates, fertilizer may total half the cost of production. Although the large farms apply fertilizer once or twice per year, in lean years fertilizer is likely to be the first input sacrificed in the name of economy. The jettisoning of fertilizer may be a false economy because it has the potential to more than double yield. Because the husk totals 67 percent of the palm's absorption of potassium and 85 percent of its absorption of chlorine, the frugal farmer may leave it on the land, where it will decay, returning nutrients to the soil. The soil in Cote d'Ivoire lacks potassium and magnesium. In one study, Port Bouet 121 yielded 1,000 pounds of copra per acre without fertilizer. The application of 6 pounds of muriate of potash and 1.6 pounds of kieserite per palm per year boosted the yield to 1.6 tons per acre. The farmer who invests $1 in fertilizer may reap $4 in increased yield. In one study, the application of chlorine in the form of sodium chloride increased the yield from 17 to 26 per palm. Muriate of potash alone increased the yield to 34 pounds per palm. The application of both muriate of potash and sodium chloride raised the yield to 53 pounds per palm. The farmer who interplants coconut with a legume need not apply nitrogenous fertilizer because a legume fixes nitrogen in the soil. One study in Indonesia revealed that nitrogenous fertilizer increased the yield of Port Bouet only 1.8–2 percent. In Cote d'Ivoire, the application of phosphorus increased the yield of Port Bouet by 5 or 6 percent.

Young palms grow poorly in shade and do not compete well against weeds. Coconuts that languish in shade or struggle against weeds benefit little from fertilizer. Young palms need nitrogen for vigorous growth. One scientist recommends the addition of nine-tenths of a pound of sulfate of ammonia per palm per year to age five. Young palms respond better to the removal of weeds than to the addition of fertilizer.

Christopher Cumo

Further Reading

Banzon, Julian A., Olympia N. Gonzalez, Sonia Y. de Leon, and Priscilla C. Sanchez. *Coconut as Food*. Quezon City, Philippines: Philippine Coconut Research and Development Foundation, 1990.

Green, Alan H., ed. *Coconut Production: Present Status and Priorities for Research*. Washington, D.C.: World Bank, 1991.

Piggott, C. J. *Coconut Growing*. London: Oxford University Press, 1964.

Coffee

Today, more than 100 countries in the tropics and subtropics grow coffee. Coffee generates more revenue than any commodity other than petroleum. Coffee grows in partial shade or full sun, and needs moderate rainfall evenly distributed throughout the year, altitudes no higher than 6,000 feet, temperatures between 60°F and 70°F, and the absence of frost. Because it is a crop of the tropics and subtropics, coffee must be grown at altitude to achieve moderate temperatures.

Although there are more than 20 species of coffee, 2 are cultivated above all others: *Coffea arabica* and *Coffea canephara* var. *robusta*. Of the two, arabica has superior flavor and aroma and so commands a higher price. Arabica grows best at altitudes of 1,500 to 6,000 feet, whereas robusta is grown from sea level to 3,200 feet. Worldwide, 70 percent of the coffee harvest is arabica and the rest robusta. Comparatively cheap and with twice the caffeine of arabica, robusta has found its way into instant coffee and blends whereas arabica is marketed in specialty coffees. Arabica is more susceptible to disease and more intolerant of poor soils. Robusta tolerates higher temperatures and humidity but suffers more acutely from frost. Farmers have grown arabica at least since the 16th century and robusta since roughly 1850. Arabica is widely grown in East Africa and Central and South America, whereas robusta, an indigene of Uganda, has sunk roots in West Africa and Southeast Asia. Brazil is the world's largest arabica producer, whereas

Coffee beans (AP/Wide World Photos)

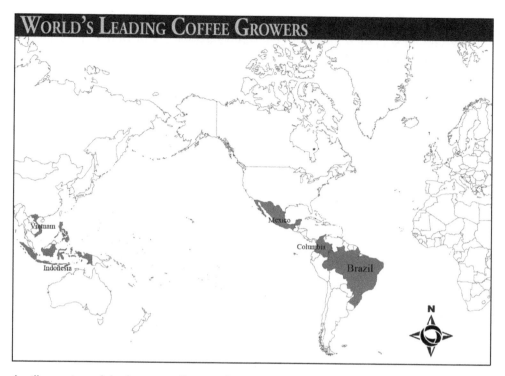

WORLD'S LEADING COFFEE GROWERS

An illustration of the largest coffee-producing regions. (ABC-CLIO)

Vietnam is the largest grower of robusta. Robusta claims half the coffee market in the United Kingdom, one-third in Italy, and one-quarter in the United States.

Today, Brazil, Vietnam, Indonesia, Colombia, and Mexico are the leading coffee growers. Worldwide, farmers plant 25 million acres to coffee. At 9.7 million acres, South America claims a plurality of this land. Coffee occupies 5.5 million acres in Asia, 5.1 million acres in Africa, and 4.7 million acres in Central and North America.

Origin and Diffusion in the Old World

The ancients celebrated coffee's origins in myth. The Oromo of Ethiopia believed, perhaps presaging the sorrow of slavery, that coffee came from the tears of the sky god Waqa. One story credits a goatherd with the discovery of coffee. On one occasion, he observed the excitement of his goats after they had eaten coffee berries and leaves. His curiosity aroused, the goatherd likewise ate the berries, presumably spitting out the beans (seeds), deriving such energy from them that he began dancing with his goats. A monk, observing this spectacle, also ate the berries with similar effect. He returned to his monastery with coffee and boiled the berries to derive a beverage that all the monks drank to help them stay awake during night prayers. The success of coffee at this monastery led other monasteries and ultimately secular society to adopt coffee. Some scholars believe that a coffee tree was the Tree of Knowledge of Good and Evil in Genesis. Eating the forbidden fruit (coffee berries), the first humans heightened their state of awareness derived from the caffeine in coffee. Some authorities claimed that passages in the Old Testament refer to coffee. Others believe that they have found reference to it in Homer. According to another account, the angel Gabriel presented coffee to Mohammed in a dream, telling him that the beans had medicinal properties and the power to stimulate the faithful to greater zeal in prayer.

Coffee is indigenous to Ethiopia, though in antiquity Ethiopians probably did not drink coffee because Egypt, which would likely have known about such a beverage, did not mention coffee. Instead, Ethiopian warriors chewed coffee berries, coated in butter or another fat, for energy. High in protein, although protein is absent from the beverage, coffee would have been nourishing in this context. The emphasis on warriors and the focus on men in the mythology of coffee suggest that men rather than women were the first to consume coffee in some form.

As early as the sixth century CE, the people of Yemen were the first to cultivate coffee. A later date comes from a literary source that credits the king of Yemen with importing the first coffee trees in the 13th century. This source may not be accurate, for a list of plants compiled in Yemen in 1271 does not mention coffee. First consumed as food between the sixth and ninth centuries, coffee was eaten as porridge. It was transformed into a beverage between 1000 and 1300, possibly as wine fermented from the berries before it was a nonalcoholic drink. Some scholars believe that in the 10th century, physician Rhazes was the first to write about coffee, using the Arabic word *bunchum*, meaning "berry," for it. In the 11th century, physician and philosopher Avicenna wrote of a beverage that "fortifies the members, cleanses the skin and dries up the humidities that are under it, and gives an excellent smell to all the body."

The people of Yemen invented the beverage coffee by pulverizing the beans and stirring them in hot water, drinking the concoction to stay awake during night prayers. They seasoned the first coffee with salt, butter, and spices. In the 15th century, coffee was a popular drink, and into the 16th century, Yemen grew most of the world's coffee, though about 1500 CE the island of Ceylon (now Sri Lanka) also produced coffee. In addition to devising the beverage, Yemenis invented the coffeehouse, a venue where men took coffee and exchanged news and opinions, evidence that coffee had a secular as well as religious purpose. Men frequented coffeehouses whereas women took their coffee at home. In the 16th century, coffeehouses were fashionable in Istanbul, Cairo, and Mecca.

Coffee derives from the Arabic *quhwah*, a word for liquor, which the Koran forbade. No evidence, however, suggests that Muslims shrank from drinking coffee. Rather, so enthusiastic were they about coffee that they spread it east to India and Indonesia, west to West Africa, and north to Istanbul and the Balkans. In the Ottoman Empire, coffee stimulated soldiers and eased the labor pains of women. In Turkey, a wife could seek a divorce if her husband refused her coffee. Wishing to retain a monopoly on coffee, Arabs prohibited foreigners from visiting coffee farms and exported beans only after they had been heated to destroy their ability to germinate. Around 1600 an Indian, Baba Buden, was the first to smuggle viable beans to India. In 1606, the Dutch smuggled coffee seedlings for planting in their colonies. In the early 17th century, the Venetians introduced the beverage coffee to the people of Western and Northern Europe. In 1655, students at Oxford University formed the Oxford Coffee Club, which evolved into the prestigious Royal Society of London. In 1669, the Turkish ambassador to the court of King Louis XIV made coffee a sensation in Paris by hosting lavish coffee parties for the nobility.

The coffeehouse was likewise popular in Europe. A coffee drinker, Johann Sebastian Bach debuted several compositions at Zimmermann's coffeehouse in Leipzig. So great was Bach's enthusiasm for coffee that he wrote a cantata to it. In the "Coffee Cantata," a father frets over his daughter's coffee habit. Zimmermann's was not the only coffeehouse to attract eminent men. In 1773, the plotters of the Boston Tea Party met in a coffeehouse to finalize their plans. In 1775, patriots met in a New York coffeehouse to debate independence after the battles of Lexington and Concord. In 1789, activist Camille Desmoulins led a mob from a coffeehouse to the Bastille, beginning the French Revolution. An Ethiopian tree had fomented revolution in the American colonies and Europe.

Yet not everyone was enthusiastic about coffee. As early as the 16th century, some Muslims thought that the faithful spent too much time in coffeehouses and not enough time in mosques. In 1511, the governor of Mecca, annoyed at the condemnations of him that circulated through the city's coffeehouses, closed them. The sultan of Cairo, an avid coffee drinker, heard of the ban and promptly reversed it. In Istanbul the penalty for drinking coffee was death. The guilty were sewn into leather bags and deposited in the Bosporus. Even this draconian punishment did not stop people from drinking coffee, and the authorities lifted the prohibition. In the 16th century, priests petitioned the pope to prohibit coffee in the belief that it had come from Satan. Tasting the beverage and finding it agreeable, the pope thought that anything so tasty could not be the work of Satan. In Europe, wives lamented that their husbands spent their free hours at coffeehouses rather than at home. Their resentment may have stemmed from the fact that coffeehouses then barred women from admission. In 1675, King Charles II of England, perceiving coffeehouses as venues for the frank exchange of political opinions, issued a proclamation banning them. The cacophony of protest forced Charles to capitulate. He rescinded the proclamation only days after issuing it. In 1777, Frederick the Great of Prussia, annoyed that his subjects spent their money on a foreign beverage when they should have been drinking German beer, told them "His Majesty was brought up on beer, and so were his ancestors and his officers" (Luttinger and Dicum 2006, 23). Perhaps Frederick, envious of England, France, and the Netherlands, was upset that Prussia had no colonies in which to grow coffee.

He had reason to be jealous as these nations planted coffee in their tropical colonies. In 1616, the Dutch took coffee seedlings from Mocha to plant in Ceylon (now Sri Lanka), which they had taken from Portugal. By the end of the 17th century, the Dutch had introduced coffee, in addition to Ceylon, to Java, Sumatra, Bali, Timor, Celebes (now Sulawesi), and Dutch Guiana (now Suriname). The Dutch East India Company became wealthy growing coffee. In 1714, the burgermeister of Amsterdam gave Louis XIV a coffee seedling, which the king directed to be planted in Paris's Jardin des Plantes. From the progeny of this tree, the French populated Africa, the Caribbean, and South America with coffee. The Portuguese grew coffee in Brazil, in parts of Indonesia, and in Africa. The British cultivated the tree in the Caribbean and India. In the 1860s, the United Kingdom took Ceylon from the Netherlands, retaining the coffee plantations.

The British planters, cutting down 176,000 acres of forest on Ceylon to make room for coffee, endangered the environment. The absence of forest that had once covered the land, left the soil vulnerable to erosion. The topsoil lost from coffee farms polluted rivers and the ocean. In the 1860s, the frail arabica trees came under attack. Coffee rust, a fungal disease that spread rapidly in the humid tropics, swept through the coffee estates on Ceylon. Catastrophic losses were also reported in India, Java, Sumatra, and Malaysia. Some planters responded by replanting their land to robusta. Others rejected coffee altogether, instead planting tea. Coffee rust thereby caused tea to replace coffee as the national drink in the United Kingdom.

Coffee in Tropical America

Coffee and romance may be linked in the origin of coffee in Brazil. One account holds that the wife of the governor of French Guiana had an affair with Francisco de Mello Palheto, a Brazilian diplomat who had been dispatched to French Guiana to settle a dispute. Upon its resolution, he returned to Brazil, but not before his lover had given him a bouquet of flowers, which contained coffee berries. The trees from these berries, so the story goes, populated all Brazil. A more prosaic report credited Portugal with introducing coffee to Brazil in 1727. Yet another account claimed that only in 1774 did Franciscan friar Jose Moriano da Conceicao Veloso plant coffee in Brazil. Whoever introduced coffee to Brazil, and when, the tree flourished. By 1800, the Portuguese colony was exporting coffee to Europe. By the 1820s, coffee had spread to the fertile lands around Sao Paulo. By 1850, Brazil produced half the world's coffee, and by 1900, its 750,00 tons of coffee accounted for three-quarters of global production. By 1910, coffee accounted for 90 percent of Brazil's gross domestic product. As large as was its production of coffee, Brazil has been vulnerable to price fluctuations. Low prices in 1906, the 1930s, and the early 1970s caused Brazilian farmers to burn coffee to keep it off the already glutted market.

Coffee may have sunk roots in the Caribbean even earlier though the chronology is unclear. One account holds that the French introduced coffee to Saint Domingue (now Haiti) in 1715, though if this date is correct it is surprising that coffee was not cultivated on Martinique until 1723. According to this version of events, the first coffee seedlings to be planted on Martinique came from the Jardin des Plants. Yet this account leaves unsettled the origin of coffee on Martinique, for the French could have more easily transferred coffee seedlings from Saint Domingue to Martinique rather than from the Jardin. Rather than spreading from Saint Domingue to Martinique, another account holds that the French transplanted coffee from Martinique to Saint Domingue in 1734. In any case, by 1770 planters on Martinique had 18,680 coffee trees, all of them arabica. Martinique seems to have been the source of coffee in Barbados and Jamaica. In 1736, coffee spread, perhaps from Martinique, to Puerto Rico. Coffee trees from Martinique thereby populated the rest of the Caribbean in the 18th and 19th centuries.

In the Caribbean, planters grew coffee between 3,000 and 5,000 feet in comparatively dry, cool air that did not readily give rise to pathogens. New World plantations did not suffer from the coffee rust that devastated Old World estates. Because coffee trees required 4 to 7 years to mature, a planter needed another source of income during these early years. Although a coffee tree may live as long as 50 years, in the 18th century trees rarely survived longer than 30 years, and a longevity of 10 to 12 years may have been the norm. Without manuring, yields declined over time. Indeed, a crop of 560 pounds of beans depleted from the land 30 pounds of nitrogen, 30 pounds of potassium, 6 pounds of phosphorus, and 22 pounds of minerals.

Like their counterparts on the sugar estates, coffee planters resorted to slavery. Although labor was less intensive on a coffee farm than on the sugar estates, slaves on the former could not count their blessings. During slack times coffee planters, eager for additional income, rented their slaves to sugar plantations. Like sugar planters, coffee landowners showed little regard for slaves' welfare. Masters often overworked and underfed their slaves, contributing to the brief life span of slaves.

Even though coffee trees did not produce beans in their first years, planters needed slaves from the outset to clear land in preparation for planting. This may have been the most arduous task that slaves performed. Once land had been denuded, slaves planted seedlings and fertilized them in a single operation, digging a hole and depositing dung and seedling. Thereafter planters may not have been assiduous in manuring their trees because they complained frequently about soil exhaustion. At the peak of operations, slaves worked six days and part of

Sunday in varied tasks. Slaves set out the beans, once picked, in the sun to dry or soaked them in vats of water to soften the flesh. After their immersion in water, coffee was fed into a pulper, which peeled off the flesh. After pulping, beans were sun dried for a week or kiln dried for a day. Because planters were paid according to the weight of their crop, the first method yielded more money but the planter risked the possibility that his coffee might ferment, ruining the flavor and aroma.

The early years were difficult for New World planters. Not only did they have no income from coffee until their trees matured, but they had to pay a tariff, which benefited planters in French Reunion and Ceylon. In the 1730s, France, Great Britain, and the Netherlands finally eliminated the tariff to encourage growers in Brazil and the Caribbean. The tariff gone and coffee prices high, the pace of production accelerated. Jamaica's yield increased from 50,367 pounds of coffee in 1744 to 252,460 pounds in 1764. Production expanded in Martinique after 1734 and in Guadeloupe after 1763. From the 1730s to the 1830s, coffee was Dominica's leading crop. By 1753, the island had 1.6 million coffee trees. On Grenada, Dominica, and Saint Vincent, coffee was second only to sugar in value. By 1789, Saint Domingue had emerged as the world's leading coffee exporter, but the French Revolution truncated the cultivation of coffee. The slaves revolted, destroying the coffee plantations. Between 1791 and 1801, coffee production halved and exports virtually ceased. Coffee rebounded in the 20th century, but it would never again command the large estates. In the 1980s, small farmers grew 67 percent of Haiti's coffee.

Perhaps because Haiti no longer exported so much coffee, supply fell short of demand and prices doubled between 1793 and 1799. Jamaica took advantage of favorable prices to increase coffee production from 2.3 million pounds in 1790 to 34 million pounds in 1814. By the early 19th century, Jamaica exported 30 percent of the world's coffee. In the 1830s and 1840s, supply exceeded demand and prices fell. Some planters responded by uprooting their trees and planting sugarcane instead. In the 19th century, coffee production remained robust in the Dominican Republic. Between 1897 and 1920, coffee yield in Puerto Rico increased from 6,000 to 27,000 tons. The end of slavery in the 19th century transformed coffee from a plantation crop to the sustenance of small farmers. The former slaves were no longer willing to toil on the large estates, but they were eager to own a small parcel of land and to grow coffee as a cash crop. By 1975, small farmers grew four-fifths of Cuba's coffee.

Coffee in the Twenty-First Century

Coffee is today a transaction between rich and poor. Affluent Americans consume coffee grown in the developing world. Whereas the average American imbibed less than 1 pound of coffee in 1800, he or she consumed 13 pounds in 1900. Today, the United States accounts for one-fifth of the world's daily consumption of 1.5 billion cups of coffee (Luttinger and Dicum 2006, ix).

McDonald's, Dunkin' Donuts, and Starbucks all woo customers with the promise of a satisfying cup of coffee. The mid-morning coffee break is a staple in the routine of countless office workers. Yet few people ponder the lives of coffee growers in the developing world.

Their lot is difficult. Of the 125 million coffee growers worldwide, 25 million are small farmers who depend on coffee as the sole source of income and who are vulnerable to price fluctuations. The decline in coffee prices between 2000 and 2002 cost 600,000 people their jobs in Central America alone (Wild 2005, 2).

In New Guinea, the poor, unable to sustain themselves growing coffee, abandoned their farms. In despair, farmers in India and Africa uprooted their coffee trees, so little were they worth. Consumers can scarcely afford to lose these small farmers because farmers with fewer than five acres produce half the world's coffee. Today, small farmers grow the majority of Mexico's coffee. Those who retain their jobs are not fortunate, for working conditions are appalling. Parents keep children home to help on the farm, causing them to forgo a lifetime of education and the prospect of a living wage. In Guatemala children begin picking coffee at age seven or eight. In parts of Guatemala, the descendants of the Maya harvest coffee. Seasonal coffee workers are the poorest and the most vulnerable to layoff. At harvest, they pick beans from dawn to evening. In Costa Rica, for example, coffee harvesters work from 5:30 a.m. to 6 p.m. seven days per week. They are paid a piece rate so low that the whole family must labor just to subsist. A wage of $1 per basket of beans in Costa Rica translates into only a few dollars per day. Even a proficient harvester in Guatemala earns just $8 per day for picking 200 pounds of berries. Coffee workers receive no medical insurance and no food, so they must bring their own nourishment and water. There are no toilets at the coffee farms, forcing laborers to relieve themselves in unpleasant settings. In Madagascar, workers receive no wages, only payment in kind. The poorest in Nicaragua and Panama have only their labor to sell and so journey to Costa Rica to pick coffee. On the large farms in Brazil, growers dispense with labor, using mechanical harvesters to dislodge beans by shaking the trees. These large estates plant trees at a density of 1,500 to 4,000 per acre, quadruple the density possible on small farms. On the large farms, wealth concentrates in few hands. In Brazil one company, Ipanema Agroindustria, produces more coffee and earns more revenue than Jamaica and Hawaii combined.

In the subtropics, coffee trees flower and so set fruit once per year. Because a tree flowers at one time, it bears a uniformly ripe crop, which laborers harvest once per year. In the tropics matters are more complicated. Coffee trees flower year-round so that at any time they have flowers, immature berries, and ripe berries. In this instance, workers must inspect each berry at harvest, taking only those that are ripe. Laborers spread the harvest over several months to be sure of picking all berries as they ripen at different time. Berries ripen over 7 to 11 months, elongating the harvest accordingly.

Coffee and Health

The angel Gabriel was not alone in thinking coffee a medicine. Some European physicians recommended coffee as protection against plague. Sober Puritans extolled coffee as an antidote to drunkenness. In the 17th century, physicians thought coffee cured dropsy, scurvy, gout, nausea, flatulence, and vertigo. In 1785, physician Benjamin Mosely advised opium addicts to drink coffee rather than get high. One physician believed that coffee cured "exhaustion, paralysis and impotence."

Today, medical opinion is divided. The caffeine in coffee can be fatal, but only if taken in large quantities on the order of 100 cups of coffee. (Coffee berries evolved caffeine for the pragmatic purpose of deterring insects, for caffeine is an insecticide.) Coffee can upset the stomach and cause muscle twitches, rambling thoughts, rapid heart rate, restless leg syndrome, hallucinations, urinary problems, and osteoporosis. Too much coffee causes anxiety, irritability, nervousness, lightheadedness, and diarrhea. Habit forming, the withdrawal of coffee causes headache. A diuretic, coffee stimulates urine production and can lead to dehydration. An oil in coffee raises cholesterol, but paper filters absorb this oil, eliminating the risk of elevated cholesterol. Taken at bedtime, coffee may cause insomnia. The birth control pill and some heart and ulcer drugs impede the body's excretion of coffee and so magnify the effects of even small amounts of coffee. Appetite suppressants, asthma drugs, and thyroid medicine also intensify the effects of coffee.

On the other hand, coffee stimulates brain activity by preventing the neurotransmitter adenosine from binding with its receptor in the brain. Two cups of coffee increase brain activity enough to be measurable on an electroencephalograph. Four cups of coffee increase heart rate and breathing by stimulating the sympathetic nervous system, which regulates breathing, heart rate, and digestion. Thirty to 60 minutes after ingestion, coffee takes full effect, lifting a feeling of fatigue, making one more alert, and quickening cognition. Coffee enlarges the blood vessels in the heart and increases blood flow. At the same time, it constricts blood vessels in the brain, thereby lessening the pain of headaches. Coffee also enlarges the bronchioles in the lungs, improving asthma. Coffee may protect one against live cancer, type two diabetes, gallstones, kidney stones, cirrhosis, Alzheimer's disease, and Parkinson's disease. Coffee stimulates the body to burn fat and for this reason endurance athletes rely on it for energy. Curiously, coffee consumption correlates with a low risk of suicide. Two cups of coffee per day may decrease irritability, improve mood, and increase sociability and confidence. In addition to coffee, the stimulant No-Doz and the pain killer Excedrin have caffeine. Mint, chocolate, and some soft drinks contain caffeine.

Christopher Cumo

Further Reading

Allen, Stewart Lee. *The Devil's Cup: A History of the World According to Coffee*. New York: Ballantine Books, 2003.

Luttinger, Nina, and Gregory Dicum. *The Coffee Book: Anatomy of an Industry from Crop to Last Drop*. New York: New Press, 2006.

Pendergrast, Mark. *Uncommon Grounds: The History of Coffee and How It Transformed Our World*. New York: Basic Books, 1999.

Wild, Antony. *Coffee: A Dark History*. New York: Norton, 2005.

Collard

In the Brassicaceae or Cabbage family, collard (*Brassica oleacea* ssp. *acephala*) is a biennial grown as an annual for its edible leaves. Collard produces leaves in its first year and flowers and seeds in the second. The subspecies name *acephala* means "without a head," a reference to the fact that collard, in contrast to cabbage, does not form a head. Collard derives from the Anglo Saxon word "colewort," meaning "cabbage plant," possibly a recognition of the relationship between collard and cabbage. They are after all in the same family. Because collard is widely cultivated, several people have named it. Brazilians know collard as *couve*, the Portuguese as *couve galega*, the Spanish as *berza*, Bosnians and Croatians as *rastike*, the people of Montenegro as *rasten*, Indians as *haak*, and the people of Congo, Tanzania, and Kenya as *sukuma wiki*. Collard is cultivated in the American South, Brazil, Portugal, several nations in Africa, Montenegro, Bosnia and Herzegovina, southern Croatia, Spain, and Kashmir, India. Collard is not popular with some gardeners because of its strong flavor and toughness if picked at the wrong time. Collard develops an unpleasant flavor if exposed to too much heat.

Origin

Collard traces its lineage to a wild cabbage that still grows along the coast of North Africa and Europe. Perhaps for this reason, one author refers to collard as a "primitive cabbage." Another author believes that collard arose in the eastern Mediterranean Basin or Turkey. A third favors Turkey as the homeland of collard. Collard may have been the first member of the Cabbage family to be cultivated. The Greeks grew both collard and kale without distinguishing between them. The Romans cultivated collard and may have planted it in Britain and France. It is also possible that the Celts introduced collard to these regions about 600 BCE, well before the Roman conquest. Collard was mentioned in the American colonies in 1669, though the British may have imported it earlier. Slaves ate it, leading to collard's association with African American culture.

Attributes and Cultivation

Collard may be planted in spring for a summer crop or in midsummer for an autumn harvest. The gardener may prefer the second because autumn frost improves collard's flavor. If the decision is to plant a spring crop, one may start collard seeds indoors four to six weeks before the last frost. Seeds germinate in 3 to 10 days at 68°F to 86°F or in 6 to 12 days depending on whom one consults. According to one writer, the soil must be at least 70°F for seeds to germinate. Seeds should be planted 2 or 3 inches apart in rows 24 to 30 inches distant. Seedlings should be thinned to 10 to 12 inches apart. Before planting one may add a 5-10-10 fertilizer in a ratio of nitrogen to phosphorus to potassium, compost, or well-rotted manure to the soil. One month after planting, the gardener may add a complete fertilizer, compost, or well-rotted manure to the soil. The gardener may add nitrogen to the soil once or twice during the growing season. Collard should be watered weekly. The gardener may space seedlings 8 inches apart, transplanting them in the field after the last frost. Alternatively, one may plant seeds in the field one-quarter to one-half of an inch deep after the last frost.

Collard prefers full sun though it benefits from partial shade in hot weather. Collard grows best between 75°F and 80°F. The crop matures in 60 days, though one writer recommends that young leaves be picked as early as 30 days after planting. Although the plant may grow two or three feet tall, leaves should be picked when they are eight inches long. The soil should be fertile, well-drained loam. The soil pH should be between 6 and 6.5 or 6.8 depending on whom one consults. One may harvest a whole plant or only the young outer leaves. In its second year, we have seen, collard flowers. A cross-pollinator, collard may be crossed with cabbage so close is the relationship between the two. Collard seeds, derived in the second year, remain viable five years. Collard is hardier than other members of the cabbage family, tolerating temperatures as low as 10°F or 20°F depending on whom one reads. Collard tolerates drought better than other cabbage allies. Collard is the most heat-tolerant member of the Cabbage family. In Florida, collard is planted in September or October for a harvest between November and April. If picked during the heat of summer, collard may be refrigerated 2 or 3 days to sweeten it. More generally, collard may be refrigerated 10 days provided the temperature is near freezing and the humidity is more than 95 percent. Plants should be mulched in autumn to permit them to overwinter.

Cuisine

In the American South, collard is often eaten with kale, turnip greens, spinach, and mustard greens. Collard is often paired with ham, bacon, turkey, pork, onion, vinegar, salt, and pepper. Collard is coupled with cowpeas, peas, and cornbread on New Year's Day, a meal that is reputed to guarantee one wealth in the New Year. Brazilians and Portuguese pair collard with fish or meat or in a stew with pork and beans. In Kashmir, Indians eat both collard leaves and roots. They consume a soup with collard leaves, water, salt, oil, and rice. Collard leaves are eaten with meat, fish, or cheese. Collard may be boiled or steamed, though it should not be cooked more than five minutes to preserve the nutrients.

Cultivars

Cultivated since 1880 or perhaps earlier, Georgia is a blue-green variety popular in the American South. The plant grows to three feet and does well in hot or cold weather. Like all varieties of collard, frost improves the flavor of Georgia. The variety tolerates drought and grows in infertile soil. With a mild flavor, Georgia matures in 70 to 80 days. Georgia Southern, known as Creole or True Collard, grows on the Atlantic coast. Suitable for sandy soil, Georgia Southern grows to three feet, yielding blue-green leaves that mature in 75 days. Tolerating heat, Vates does not bolt in hot weather. Frost resistant, Vates matures in 75 days. The blue-green leaves have a mild cabbage flavor.

Nutrition and Health

One hundred grams of collard have 36 calories, 7.1 grams of carbohydrates, fiber, 0.4 gram of fat, 3 grams of protein, 26 milligrams of vitamin C, and 210 milligrams of calcium. This serving yields 593 percent of the recommended daily allowance of vitamin K, 64 percent of beta-carotene, 43 percent of vitamin C, and 21 percent of calcium. In addition to these nutrients, collard has folic acid, vitamin B6, riboflavin, niacin, thiamine, pantothenic acid, vitamin E, manganese, potassium, magnesium, zinc, phosphorus, and omega 3 fatty acids. Collard has 50 percent more folic acid than broccoli, twice that of Brussels sprouts, thrice that of cabbage, and more than seven times more than kale. One cup of collard has more than five grams of fiber. Two hundred calories worth of collard supply the body with 85 percent of the recommended daily allowance of fiber. Juice extracted from the leaves or stalk is reputed to treat gout and bronchitis. One study compared collard, kale, mustard greens, broccoli, Brussels sprouts, and cabbage, finding collard the best at lowering cholesterol. Steamed collard is better than raw collard at lowering cholesterol. The American Cancer Society urges Americans to eat more collard and other members of the cabbage family to reduce the risk of cancer. Collard contains glucoraphenin, sinigrin, gluconasturtiian, diindolylmethane, sulforaphane, and glucotropaeolin, compounds that may protect one against cancer. Diindolylmethane may protect one against viruses and bacteria. Collard may reduce the risk of developing cancer of the bladder, breast, colon, lung, prostate, and ovaries. Collard contains the antioxidants caffeic acid, ferulic acid, quercetin, and kaemferol. Collard may reduce the risk of developing heart disease. So beneficial is collard that one writer recommends its consumption at least two or three times per week. When overcooked, however, collard loses nutrients.

Christopher Cumo

Further Reading

Buckingham, Alan. *Grow Vegetables*. London: Dorling Kindersley, 2008.

Coulter, Lynn. *Gardening with Heirloom Seeds: Tried-and-True Flowers, Fruits, and Vegetables for a New Generation*. Chapel Hill: University of North Carolina Press, 2006.

Columbine

Columbine is the common name for the *Aquilegia* species belonging to the Ranunculaceae, or buttercup, family. It has been suggested that both the Latin name and the common name of these perennial, yet short-lived, plants are inspired by the instantly recognizable shape of the flower, which, from certain angles, appears bird-like. The name *Aquilegia* derives from the Latin word for eagle, *aquilia*, as the spurs of the flowers resemble the talons of a bird of prey. The Latin name may also be a compound of the Latin words *aqua*, meaning "water," and *leger*, meaning "to collect," as water may pool on the flowers and leaves and nectar collects on the spurs. The common name, columbine, derives from the Latin for dove, *columba*, for, looked at from above, the flower head of a short-spurred columbine resembles a dove with an erect tail.

Columbines (Jennifer Holcombe/ Dreamstime.com)

Attributes

There are around 70 species of columbine with flowers appearing between April and July. The flowers are held either in loose racemes or singly with colors including shades of pink, purple, lilac, blue, white, yellow, and red or combinations of colors in single, double, and semidouble forms. The columbine Nora Barlow is a spurless, mutated form of *Aquilegia vulgaris*, which is popular for use in ornamental displays as it has pale green and rosy pink blooms in double form. The frilly appearance of Nora Barlow has led to the columbine gaining the familiar name granny's bonnet. Columbine plants are mound shaped, around one foot wide, with lobed green, blue-green, or gray-green leaves. Columbines can reach up to four feet tall, but the average height for a plant is nearer two-and-one-half feet. Columbines prefer full sun or partial shade with plants grown in full sun producing more blooms than shade-dwelling specimens. Columbines are not choosy about soil, growing usually in rich or average to light soil. However, as they grow from long, tough taproots, which make the plant drought resistant, columbines can be found growing in the cracks of walls and paths where both soil and moisture are scant. The length and strength of columbine taproots mean that once a plant is established, it can prove difficult to remove.

Columbines are pollinated by insects such as moths and butterflies and others with a tongue long enough to reach the flower's nectar. Bees that attempt to reach the nectar by scything through the tube holding the nectar find that the tube secretes a bitter liquid intended to discourage such action. The seed capsule of the columbine is less than one inch in length, consists of five sections, and houses numerous small, shiny, black seeds. Columbines can also be propagated easily from seed, and the plants are able to self-sow. Many cultivated varieties of the columbine are derived from the wild columbine *Aquilegia canadensis*, which has red petals and yellow spurs. However, if the cultivar is allowed to run to seed and self-sow, the descendants will revert to the wild *Aquilegia* form and the cultivar will be eradicated from the garden population. In 2002, the columbine's propensity to self-seed led to a ban on the import of *Aquilegia* seeds into the United States as the plant was considered to be too invasive if accidently introduced into the wild.

Uses

The columbine is widely distributed across the Northern Hemisphere, especially in temperate and cold regions at higher altitudes, although *Aquilegia fragrans* and *Aquilegia skinneri* are less tolerant of the cold than some varieties of columbine. In Europe, *Aquilegia vulgaris* proliferates, and wild columbines such as the five-petaled *Aquilegia canadensis* can be found across the United States and

Canada as the species was named during the period when Canada extended across the United States as far south as New Orleans. A western Columbine, the Rocky Mountain Columbine, is officially the state flower of Colorado. Columbine features in Native America cultures. In Iroquois legend, *Aquilegia canadensis* originated when five chiefs were transformed into the flower after having fallen in love with a maiden and neglecting their duties in their haste to find the object of their passion. The red petals of the flower represent the chiefs' shirts and the yellow spurs their moccasins. Different Native American tribes put the columbine to different uses. The men of the Omaha and Ponca Indians spread mashed columbine seeds on to their hands as a love potion, whereas Native Americans of the western United States would boil and eat the roots. However, columbine should not be consumed. Several species of the plant are toxic, and some parts of plant, especially the seeds, are potentially fatal if consumed because they contain cyanogenic glycosides. The columbine may be a carcinogen, so the medicinal or culinary use of the columbine is discouraged.

The Columbine in Literature

The columbine has also achieved significance in European culture. For instance, Columbine is a stock character of *Commedia dell'Arte* as the mistress of Harlequin, and in the traditional English pantomime, Columbine appears as a symbol of feminine beauty. The columbine has made appearances in several works of literature. In William Shakespeare's *Hamlet*, Ophelia speaks of columbines, alluding perhaps to their role in folklore as the flower of abandoned lovers.

Victoria Williams

Further Reading

Dyer, T. F. Thiselton. *Folklore of Shakespeare*. New York: Dover, 1966.

Nold, Robert. *Columbines:* Aquilegia, Paraquilegia, *and* Semiaquilegia. Portland, OR: Timber Press, 2003.

Tenenbaum, Frances, ed. *Taylor's Encyclopedia of Garden Plants*. New York: Houghton Mifflin, 2003.

Vizgirdas, Ray S., and Edna M. Vizgirdas. *Wild Plants of the Sierra Nevada*. Reno: University of Nevada Press, 2006.

Ward, Bobby J. *A Contemplation upon Flowers: Garden Plants in Myth and Literature*. Portland, OR: Timber Press, 1999.

Coneflower. *See* Black-Eyed Susan (Rudbeckia)

Corchorus

In the Tiliaceae family, the genus *Corchorus* contains 50 or 60 species. The chief cultivated species are *Corchorus capsularis* and *Corchorus olitorius*. *Corchorus capsularis* is known as jute and white jute. *Corchorus olitorius* is known as molokhia, nalta jute, tosso jute, tusso jute, and Jew's mallow. The term "jute" is used for the plant and the fiber that derives from it. These two species are a source of fiber and food. The fiber is made into bags, carpet, curtains, fabric, and even paper. The leaves of corchorus are edible. Those of *Corchorus capsularis* are bitter and are seldom eaten, but those of *Corchorus olitorius* are sweet and are eaten as a substitute for spinach. Because they are palatable, children prefer them to spinach. A leaf is 18–22 percent protein. One hundred grams of leaves have 77 milligrams of vitamin C and 5 milligrams of beta-carotene. The leaves have more vitamins C and E than spinach. The leaves have calcium, iron, magnesium, and zinc. The term "corchorus" derives from the Greek *khorkhorus*.

Origin and History

Corchorus olitorius originated in Africa with a secondary center of dispersion in India and Myanmar. The 20th-century Russian agronomist Nikolai Vavilov believed that *Corchorus capsularis* originated in India, Myanmar, and southern China. In antiquity, this species was unknown in Africa and Australia. Since antiquity the people of Africa and Asia have used corchorus for fiber and food. Fourth-century BCE Greek botanist Theophrastus referred to the Greeks' cultivation of corchorus. Even today the Greeks consume corchorus leaves. First-century CE Roman encyclopedist Pliny the Elder was aware that the Egyptians grew corchorus.

Fiber

The fiber jute is widely used in the developing world because it is cheaper than synthetic fibers. The developed world, notably the United States and Europe, relies on cotton and synthetic fibers. India and Myanmar have for years been the leading exporters of jute. Corchorus for fiber is grown in northeastern India, Bangladesh, Pakistan, Myanmar, Nepal, China, Malaysia, Sri Lanka, and Brazil. The monsoon climate of these regions is ideal for corchorus. The valleys of the Ganga and Brahmaputra rivers are the chief regions of cultivation in India. Jute from India, Bangladesh, and Pakistan is traded on the world market. The valley of the Amazon River is the principal region of cultivation in Brazil. American farmers have experimented with the cultivation of corchorus, but the United States is not a leading producer.

Of the two species, *Corchorus olitorius* yields a larger crop of quality fiber, yet the species is not as well adapted to as wide a range of soils and climates as is

Corchorus capsularis. Corchorus olitorius produces a fine, soft fiber with an attractive sheen. The process of extracting the fiber from the stem is known as retting. To extract the fiber, stems are submerged in water 20 or 30 days. Bacteria in the water dissolve the pectin, gum, and mucilage that bind the fibers together. The addition of ammonium, potassium, calcium, and magnesium ions to the water hastens retting, which proceeds rapidly between 93°F and 95°F. Lower temperatures slow retting.

Food

Corchorus leaves are eaten in the tropics and subtropics. Demand is strong in the Middle East, Africa, Southeast Asia, and Latin America. The United States imports a small amount of leaves to feed Middle Eastern immigrants to the country. The leaves are added to sauce, relish, salad, and soup. In Asia the gathering of leaves is a secondary activity to the growing of corchorus fiber. In Africa, leaves are gathered from corchorus plants that are grown exclusively for food. The leaves are common in the diet of the people of Cameroon. Thirty to 45 days after planting the leaves are harvested for food. The leaves from a single plant may be harvested repeatedly. Plants from which leaves are derived seldom grown more than four-and-one-half feet tall. In Bangladesh and India, corchorus yields two tons per acre. The yield in China and Taiwan is higher but in Brazil lower. The leaves are eaten locally, though a portion enters international trade.

Botany and Cultivation

Corchorus grows to 12 to 18 feet. The stem has a diameter of 0.4 to 0.8 inch. The axil produces one to four flowers. Each flower has five sepals, five petals, and 10 stamens. Roots penetrate to 24 inches. *Corchorus capsularis* is a lowland crop. *Corchorus olitorius* prefers high ground. The plants photosynthetic capacity, as must be true of other plants, varies with leaf area. Early varieties mature in 135 to 160 days, intermediate varieties in 160 to 170 days, and late cultivars in 180 to 200 days. The variety Tanganika, a high yielder in India, matures in only 120 days. Red Swain, Zaoping, Jap green, and Kulkarius are early varieties. JRC-206 and JRC-909 are late cultivars.

In India, *Corchorus capsularis*, rotated with rice, is planted in early March, before the monsoon. In Bangladesh and parts of India, corchorus is sown between March and June. The farmer plants 7 to 13 pounds of seeds per acre. Dense planting yields thin plants with high-quality fiber. If sown too late, the stem branches, frustrating the attempt to derive long fibers. When *Corchorus olitorius* is planted before April, it flowers prematurely. The yield is low and the fiber of poor quality. Most corchorus varieties are sensitive to photoperiod, though the most widely grown cultivars are not. The variety Tanzania is insensitive to photoperiod.

Scientists aim to breed more cultivars insensitive to photoperiod. In the Philippines, spring planting produces a high yield of fiber and seeds.

The soil should be cultivated deeply and drain well. The black soils of India and Bangladesh are ideal. Corchorus benefits from the addition of organic matter to the soil. A crop of the tropics, corchorus needs uniform distribution of rain throughout the year, about 40 to 60 inches per year. Most corchorus is rain fed. Irrigation is uncommon. Corchorus benefits from a complete fertilizer. Nitrogen increases the yield of fiber because it stimulates the stem to grow long and thick. Phosphorus and potassium contribute to yield and make the corchorus plant less susceptible to disease. Calcium, magnesium, sulfur, manganese, zinc, and copper also contribute to yield. The farmer fertilizes corchorus twice during the growing season, once at planting and a second time when the plant is one month old. At the second fertilizatio,n ammonium sulfate is sued because it stimulates growth. Too much nitrogen, however, diminishes the color of the fiber, a circumstance deemed unattractive. Eighty pounds of nitrogen per acre is the maximum application (Maiti 1997, 25). One authority maintains that manure is the best fertilizer. Corchorus is a heavy feeder of potassium. The farmer may apply nitrogen at 72 to 88 pounds per acre (a figure that does not square with a maximum of 80 pounds per acre), phosphorus at 35 pounds per acre, and potassium at 18 pounds per acre. The variety JRO-632 yields best with 26 pounds of nitrogen per acre, 12 pounds of phosphorus per acre, and 88 pounds of potassium per acre.

Yields decline when corchorus is grown on the same land year after year. The yield is constant when the farmer rotates corchorus with rice or wheat. Corchorus is weeded three or four times until the plant is two months old, when it is large enough to crowd out weeds. The harvest is in November and December. When a plant has yielded half its flowers, it is ready to harvest. *Corchorus capsularis* is drought tolerant as a seedling, whereas *Corchorus olitorius* is drought tolerant as a mature plant. The Tropic of Cancer is the primary region of cultivation. Corchorus does well with 70–80 percent humidity. *Corchorus olitorius* is grown in Australia, Algeria, Egypt, Lebanon, Tunisia, Mozambique, the Philippines, Senegal, Thailand, Sudan, Afghanistan, India, Kenya, Nepal, and Zambia.

Christopher Cumo

Further Reading

Maiti, Ratikanta. *World Fiber Crops*. Enfield, NH: Science, 1997.

Simopoulos, Artemis P., and C. Gopalan, eds. *Plants in Human Health and Nutrition Policy*. Basel, Switzerland: Karger, 2003.

Williams, J. T., ed. *Pulses and Vegetables*. London: Chapman and Hall, 1993.

Coriander

In the Apiaceae family, coriander (*Coriandrum sativum*) is an annual herb grown for its edible leaves and seeds, which are used as a spice. Some writers refer to the seeds as coriander and the leaves as cilantro. Others use coriander and cilantro as synonyms. To prevent confusion this entry uses the term "coriander" to refer to the entire plant. The term "cilantro" is not used. The English word coriander dates to the 14th century and traces its lineage to the Old French *coriandre*, which in turn derives from the Latin *coriandrum*, the source of the genus name. These words appear to derive ultimately from the Greek *koriannon*. Coriander is known as Chinese or Japanese parsley and dizzy corn. In German, coriander is *Koriander*, in Italian *coriandolo*, in Spanish *cilantro* or *culantro*, in Arabic *kizbara*, in Indonesian *ketumbar*, and in Tamil *kothamilee*. Coriander is related to parsley and carrot.

Origin and History

Coriander may have originated in the Middle East or southern Asia. Archaeologists have dated coriander seeds in Israel to the Neolithic Period (8000–500 BCE). These seeds may be evidence of cultivation, though it is possible that the original inhabitants of Israel gathered them from the wild or got them through trade. The Egyptians placed coriander seeds in the tomb of 14th-century BCE pharaoh Tutankhamen. It is not easy to interpret the significance of this discovery. If coriander does not grow wild in Egypt, as two scientists maintain, then the Egyptians either cultivated coriander or obtained it through trade. If coriander grows wild in Egypt, as one writer asserts, then the seeds in Tutankhamen's tomb may have been gathered from the wild. Cultivation need not be invoked in this case. The author of Exodus likened coriander to manna. The book, telling the story of the Hebrews' flight from Egypt, allows one to infer that they may have encountered coriander in Egypt. If this is so, the Hebrews' cultivation of coriander in Israel may bear no connection to the earlier use of it in Neolithic Israel.

The Greeks cultivated coriander in the second millennium BCE. Greek physician Hippocrates (460–370 BCE) mentioned the spice. In the first century CE, Roman encyclopedist Pliny the Elder called coriander "coriandrum," the word that would later, we have seen, become the genus name. Coriandrum derives from *coris*, Latin for "bug." Pliny apparently thought that coriander had a "buggy smell." Pliny's choice of words underscored the fact that people either liked or disliked coriander's flavor and aroma. There appears to be little middle ground. It is possible that Pliny thought that coriander seeds resembled the bed bug (*Cimex lectularius*), giving rise to the name "coriandrum." Pliny identified Egypt as the source of the best coriander. In the 16th century, English herbalist John Gerard described coriander, which the Romans might have introduced into Britain in antiquity. Europeans widely used coriander until the Renaissance, when spices from the East Indies began to displace it. Coriander and other spices performed the essential function of disguising the flavor of rancid meat in an era before refrigeration and the unpalatability of medicine.

Food and Medicine

One hundred grams of raw coriander leaves have 23 calories, four grams of carbohydrate, three grams of fiber, one-half gram of fat, two grams of protein, and 27 milligrams of vitamin C. This serving size has 37 percent of the recommended daily allowance of beta-carotene and 45 percent of vitamin C. The entire coriander plant may be eaten. Coriander is part of the cuisine of the Middle East, Central Asia, the Mediterranean Basin, India and the rest of southern Asia, Mexico and the rest of Latin America, Texas, China, Southeast Asia, and Africa. The leaves have a flavor akin to citrus. The flavor of the seeds resembles lemon. Because heat lessens the flavor of coriander, the leaves and seeds are eaten raw or added to a cooked dish just before serving it. The people of India and Central Asia prefer a muted flavor and so cook the leaves and seeds. The leaves must be consumed quickly because they spoil soon after picking. The flavor of the seeds diminishes after they have been pulverized and so should be consumed soon after processing. Dried and frozen leaves have no aroma. Mexicans add coriander to salsa and guacamole and eat it as a garnish. Russians eat fresh leaves in salad. The people of Morocco, India, and Australia grow varieties that yield large seeds. Seeds are roasted or otherwise heated before being pulverized to heighten their aroma. Coriander seeds are an ingredient in sausage in Italy, Germany, and South Africa, in curry and garam masala in India, as a substitute for caraway in rye bread in Russia and Central Europe, and in beer in Belgium. Coriander seeds are eaten in soup and stew. Coriander is paired with meat and game. It is added to cake and baked goods. Arabs add coriander to lamb and meat and eat fried coriander and garlic. The Egyptians couple coriander and cumin. Coriander is an addition to ham, pork, fish, chicken, and chili. Coriander is coupled with ginger and is used to flavor tobacco. Peruvians add coriander to several dishes.

Coriander is thought to inhibit flatulence and to stimulate the appetite and digestion. People once believed that coriander lessened the severity of ergotism. Asians used coriander to treat headache, indigestion, diarrhea, inflammation, colic, conjunctivitis, rheumatism, neuralgia, and ulcers of the mouth. Coriander contains a substance that kills bacteria in meat and may prevent wounds from becoming infected. Coriander was once thought to be an aphrodisiac.

Christopher Cumo

Further Reading

"Coriander." http://www.botanical.com/botanical/mgmh/c/corian99.html (accessed 24 June 22011.)

"Coriander." http://www.theepicentre.com/Spices/coriander.html (accessed 24 June 2011.)

"*Coriandrum sativum*." Missouri Botanical Garden Plant Finder. http://www.missouribotanicalgarden.org/gardens-gardening/your-garden/plant-finder/plant-details/kc/e822/coriandrum-sativum.aspx (accessed 6 July 2012)

Corn

Also known as maize and Indian corn, corn is an annual grass in the Poaceae or Graminaceae family related to sugarcane, sorghum, teosinte, wheat, rice, rye, oats, triticale, timothy, millet and tripsacum. Teosinte and tripsacum are not cultivated for food. In the 18th century, Swedish naturalist Carl Linnaeus placed corn in the genus *Zea*, meaning "wheat-like grass," and in the species *mays*, a transliteration of "maize." In turn, maize derives from the Taino word *maiz*, meaning "life giver." A world crop grown in more varied climates and soils than any other grain, corn is cultivated in all tropical and temperate locales from 58° north to 40° south. So important is corn to the United States that it is grown in all 50 states. Corn is adapted to a range of growing conditions and can survive

Corn stalks (iStockPhoto)

in areas with as little as 10 inches of rain per year and as much as 400 inches yearly.

Unlike several other crops, corn is not primarily a food for humans. Worldwide, farmers feed three-quarters of their corn to livestock. In the United States, corn growers feed an even larger portion to livestock. One bushel of corn yields 15 pounds of beef, 26 pounds of pork, and 37 pounds of chicken. Humans thus consume corn secondhand.

The corn that livestock and humans do not eat is converted into an astonishing variety of products. Chemists convert corn into syrup, sugar, glue, and ethanol. Mayonnaise, soap, paint, and insecticides contain corn oil. Peanut butter, chewing gum, soft drinks, vegetables, beer, wine, crackers, bread, frozen fish, hot dogs, and corned beef all have corn syrup among their ingredients. Derivatives of corn are found in cough drops, toothpaste, lipstick, shaving cream, shoe polish, detergents, tobacco, rayon, leather, rubber tires, urethane foam, explosives, and latex gloves. A product in baby food and embalming fluid, corn attends life from birth to death. One ear of corn contains 75 calories, 15 grams of carbohydrate, 2 grams of protein, 1 gram of fat, and 2 grams of fiber. Corn is a source of vitamin C, vitamins B1 and B5, folic acid, phosphorus, and manganese.

Origin and Domestication

Despite intensive research, scholars do not agree on where and when corn originated. The outstanding feature of corn is its dependence on humans for survival. No species of corn is wild. Rather, corn perpetuates itself only with human aid. The husk that surrounds corn binds the kernels (seeds) so tightly that they cannot disperse. Were an ear of corn to fall to the ground, the seeds would germinate so close together that they would die from overcrowding. This state of affairs suggests that humans have cultivated corn many millennia.

In the 19th century, French botanist Alphonse de Candolle proposed that corn originated in Colombia, from which it spread to Peru and Mexico. From Peru, de Candolle believed, corn diffused to South America and the Caribbean and from Mexico to North America. In the 1920s, Peruvian archaeologist Julio Tello dismissed the idea that corn originated in Colombia. Rather, the people of Peru and Mexico independently domesticated corn. In 1939, American botanist Paul Mangelsdorf proposed a variety of wild pod corn, now extinct, as corn's ancestor. Pod corn differs from corn in having a husk for each kernel. This early corn hybridized repeatedly with teosinte, a process that increased the size of corn's ears. This hybridization may have been accidental. Humans may have grown corn near fields of teosinte. This hypothesis is most plausible if corn originated in Mexico, where a species of perennial teosinte grows. Because corn cross-pollinates, it might have readily hybridized with teosinte. Alternatively, humans may have purposefully crossed early corn and teosinte to obtain hybrids (a process different from the production of hybrid corn). Mangelsdorf believed that humans first propagated corn in both Mexico and South America. Others propose Central America as the cradle of corn. American agronomist Hugh Iltis thinks that corn derived from a perennial teosinte and that corn evolved rapidly in size, possibly by mutation.

Archaeologists have found the oldest fossilized corncobs in the Tehuacan Valley, suggesting that corn originated in Mexico about 7,000 years ago. Subsequent excavations in New Mexico turned up corncobs as old as 5,600 years. From Mexico, corn must have migrated north throughout North America as de Candolle thought. From Mexico, corn spread to Colombia around 5,000 years ago and to Peru around 4,000 years ago. Mangelsdorf is surely right in supposing that the Amerindians took corn wherever they migrated. Wherever migrants made contact, they likely exchanged varieties of corn, hybridizing them in the process.

Mangelsdorf believed that humans domesticated corn by accident. Harvesting the then extant wild corn, they must have taken the kernels home for processing and consumption. Along the way, they might have dropped seeds into the land surrounding their homes. They must have observed the plants that germinated from these seeds, harvested their ears, and replanted a portion of the seed. By weeding their land, these first farmers would have allowed corn plants to thrive in the absence of competition. In areas of scant rainfall, humans irrigated corn, though as we have seen some varieties of corn survive on only 10 inches of rain per year.

Whatever the place and time of origin, these hypotheses affirm that corn originated in the Americas and came to the Old World only after 1492.

Corn before 1492

Before 1492, the indigenes of the Americas grew corn from Canada to Chile. So important was corn to the Amerindians that it must have come from the gods. The Maya believed that the god Oze Hunahpu, who defeated the Lords of Death, gave them corn. The Inca believed that the god Manco-Poca, the son of the sun, gave humans corn. The Totenae of Central America received corn from the goddess Tzinteatl, the wife of the sun. The Aztecs looked to the goddess Xilonan and the god Quatzalcoatl for corn. The Pawnee believed that the Evening Star gave them corn.

Probably using recurrent selection, the Amerindians developed the principal types of corn: flint, dent, flour, pop, and sweet. Because cob size increased with time, the Amerindians must have selected plants with large ears, though they may have eaten the best corn and saved only the less desirable kernels for planting.

The Amerindians did not plant corn in isolation. The Peruvians grew corn and potatoes. The natives of North America planted the three sisters: corn, beans, and squash. This triad of plants is nourishing and agriculturally sound. Beans provide protein that corn lacks and take full advantage of sunlight by climbing the corn stalks. Squash, covering the ground with its leaves, chokes out weeds and helps soil retain moisture. Despite the absence of knowledge of nutrition, the Amerindians were nonetheless perceptive enough to soak corn in alkali water, which liberates the niacin that is otherwise unavailable for digestion. The Amerindians prized corn for its rapid maturation, its meager demand for labor, and its longevity in storage. The indigenes understood that corn, unlike other crops, need not be harvested when ripe. By one estimate, the Amerindians devoted 20 hours of labor per bushel of corn.

Corn was the staple of New World civilizations. The Maya erected their civilization on a foundation of corn. Human sacrifice was part of corn culture for the Maya, who fertilized their fields with the blood of sacrificial victims. So central to Mayan civilization that its failure was surely catastrophic; the corn crop may have declined sharply in the ninth century CE, abruptly truncating the civilization. One hypothesis holds that a disease spread by insects killed large numbers of corn plants, causing famine. Unable to recover, the Maya abandoned their cities.

Growing potatoes, the people of Peru were less dependent on corn, though it remained the staple grain and held religious significance. The Inca, who built the last pre-Columbian civilization of Peru, worshipped the goddess Mother Corn. Royalty claimed descent from the union between Mother Corn and the sun. Where rainfall was inadequate the Inca irrigated corn. Taking advantage of mountain slopes, they planted corn in terraces. Their skill in retaining the fertility of corn land enabled the Inca to crop the same land year after year without fear of soil exhaustion. At Cuzco and the highlands, Inca farmers fertilized their land with human excrement. Along the southern coast, they used guano. Elsewhere sardines, buried in the soil, were the fertilizer of choice.

In August, Inca farmers turned the soil with hoes. Without the aid of a plow or draft animal, this task must have been arduous. In September, they planted corn, an event the emperor commenced by digging the first hole and planting seed in the royal plot in Cuzco. Planting was a time of celebration analogous to New Year's Day in the Western world. Women weeded the fields and in May harvested corn. Like many cultures, the Incan system of agriculture exploited commoners, who labored on royal land in addition to their own.

Corn was currency with each kernel being a coin. In a transaction, the buyer placed a fistful of kernels on a table. If the seller deemed the number of kernels insufficient, she said nothing but instead stared at the kernels. The buyer, if she still wanted the item, added a small number of kernels to the total until the seller was satisfied. Where barter prevailed, Inca women exchanged garden produce for cornbread.

For millennia, the people of Peru brewed the beer chichi from corn. So widespread is the consumption of chichi that Peruvian Christians use it rather than wine in reenacting the Last Supper. Along with mother's milk, chichi is the first liquid given to babies.

Like the Inca, the Aztecs irrigated corn, cropped year-round, and renewed their soils with human excrement. They also covered their fields with fresh mud, another restorative measure. So large was the surplus that Tenochtitlan had a population of 1.5 million in the 15th century. But times were not always good. The famine of 1450 forced parents to sell their children for corn: a girl fetched 400 ears of corn, whereas a boy was worth 500 ears. As with the Inca, the Aztecs used corn as currency, paying their taxes with it. The goddess Chicome Couatl blessed corn seed before farmers planted it. Planting stretched from March to May. Weeding their fields two or three times, Aztec farmers harvested corn in September, giving a portion to Cintaotl, the god of ripe corn. By one estimate, the Aztecs coaxed 16 bushels per acre from the land, a yield that compares favorably with figures from the early 20th century.

Like other Amerindians, the Hohokam of the American Southwest irrigated corn. The goddess Corn Matron blessed seed before planting. The Hohokam gathered corn in fall, with the first frost signaling the beginning of the harvest. Around 400 CE the Anasazi, irrigating their fields, grew corn in what are now Colorado, Utah, Arizona, and New Mexico. Around 900 CE, the Sioux grew corn in the Dakotas. East of the Mississippi River, the woodlands Indians, and in the Southeast the Mississippian culture, thrived on corn. In many cultures, women shouldered the burden of cultivating corn. The Iroquois appointed one woman to direct the labor of her tribe. Women also dug the pits in which the Iroquois stored corn. The Iroquois collected liquid from corn stalks, using it as a balm. The Hopi rubbed corn meal, a gift to the living and the dead, on the faces of infants and corpses. Corn, finely ground, was the traditional food at Hopi weddings. The Hopi made dumplings, pancakes, and grits from corn. Perhaps for religious reasons, many Amerindians segregated corn by color and type. Among the Hopi, each family was responsible for maintaining the purity of a variety of corn, passing seed down through the generations.

According to a few scholars, corn spread to the Old World before Christopher Columbus reached the Americas. One account holds that the seafaring people of the American West ferried corn across the Pacific to Asia sometime before 1492. Another hypothesis, relying on linguistic and pictorial evidence, proposes that Arabs brought corn to Africa around 900 CE. It is unclear, however, how corn reached Arabia in the first place. This hypothesis also proposes that Arabs brought corn to the Philippines before 1492. These hypotheses share in common their acknowledgment that corn was domesticated in the New World, but they contradict the current understanding by proposing the diffusion of corn prior to the Columbian Exchange.

Corn and the Columbian Exchange

Columbus's discovery of the Americas transformed corn from a hemispheric to a world crop. He may have first seen corn on October 14, 1492, on the Caribbean island of San Salvador. A few days later he saw in the Bahamas what he called *panizo*, Italian for millet. Because millet had not yet been introduced to the New World, Columbus must have been mistaken. Instead, he likely saw corn. On November 5, he dispatched two men to reconnoiter Cuba. They returned with corn, calling it maiz as the indigenes did.

Recognizing its value, Columbus brought corn back to Spain in 1493. Within 25 years, it spread throughout the Mediterranean Basin. Within 50 years it was grown worldwide. So ubiquitous did corn become so quickly that some people forgot that it was a native plant of the Americas. In the 16th century, one French botanist called corn Turkish wheat in the mistaken notion that corn had originated in Turkey. Confusing it with millet, the Portuguese called corn *milho*, which derives from *milhete*, meaning "millet." Because of this confusion, Portuguese writers posited Asia as the home of corn. Later generations of Chinese were sure that corn had originated in China.

Despite its importance, some Europeans did not esteem corn. One smug botanist opined that corn was less nourishing than Old World grains. It was fit for pigs not humans. The Chinese thought of corn as poor people's food and ranked it below rice and millet. Even today the Chinese eat rice rather than corn, exporting 60 percent of their corn crop to Russia and Japan and feeding much of the rest to livestock. Indeed, the Amerindians were astonished that European settlers fed corn to livestock, a practice that continues today.

Despite their ambivalence toward corn, the Chinese grew it in bulk upon their adoption of the crop from the Portuguese in 1516. A surplus of corn made possible the population expansion that began in the 17th century. Thanks to corn, China's population quadrupled in the 18th and 19th centuries. Farmers grew corn in Manchuria, the Yangtze Delta, the mountains of Yunan and Szechwan, and southwestern China. Today, corn totals 22 percent of all crops grown in China.

Perhaps corn had its greatest effect on the United States. From the beginning of European colonization, corn shaped the lives of settlers. The Amerindians brought corn to a harvest festival, inviting the settlers to join in their abundance. Keeping the corn, Europeans transformed the festival to Thanksgiving. In the 19th century, Americans carried corn as they migrated west. The Midwest proved a hospitable locale for corn and in it Americans created the Corn Belt, an area from western Ohio to the Dakotas and south to Texas. By the mid-19th century, the U.S. corn crop was worth five times more than the value of wheat, other grains, and vegetables. American farmers were not as avid as Amerindians in manuring their corn. Consequently, corn culture depleted the soil. Farmers made amends by rotating corn with clover and alfalfa, crops that fixed nitrogen in the soil. After World War II, farmers rotated corn with soybeans, and in the Corn Belt soybean acreage surpassed corn acreage in the 1980s.

In the South, the legacy of corn was mixed. So important was corn that it became the dietary staple. Planters fed corn to their slaves though they dined on bread. As in China, a diet of corn marked a person as low status. Like slaves, poor whites ate corn, though with adverse results. Because whites did not retain the Amerindian practice of soaking corn in alkali water, they did not have sufficient niacin in their diet. Moreover, corn is deficient in amino acids and so is an inadequate source of protein. Consequently, pellagra, a disease of dietary deficiency, was endemic to the South. In an era before the discovery of vitamins, scientists were divided on the cause of pellagra. Because of corn's ubiquity in the diet, some scientists fingered the grain as the culprit. One camp thought that corn must be deficient in some nutrient. Another camp suspected that a disease of corn, transmitted to humans, caused pellagra. The recommendation that people eat fresh corn free from blemish did not improve the health of ailing southerners. In the 10th century, the discovery of niacin and the adoption of a varied diet caused the incidence of pellagra to decline.

Corn Flakes was the original breakfast cereal, and Tony the Tiger, the mascot of Sugar Frosted Flakes, has been a familiar figure on television ads. In the affluent West, corn syrup is an ingredient in many foods. As early as 1733, the Molasses Act, which taxed the sale of molasses, stirred the American colonists to turn instead to corn syrup. In 1806, Napoleon's Continental System, blockading Caribbean sugar, stimulated the French to produced corn syrup to satisfy the nation's sweet tooth. Today, high-fructose corn syrup, cheaper than sugar, is the sweetener of choice.

Stung by the Organization of Petroleum Exporting Countries' oil embargo, the United States began in the 1970s to produce the fuel ethanol. Between 1978 and 1984, U.S. ethanol production leapt from 10 million gallons to 430 million gallons. Today, some exports question the diversion of food to fuel on the grounds that corn should feed the world's burgeoning population rather than combust in car engines.

In the 21st century, corn has emerged as arguably the world's most important crop. In 2007, the United States produced nearly half of the world's total corn yield. Much of the harvest is genetically engineered corn. This corn is resistant to pests and herbicides. China is the world's second-largest corn producer.

Toward a Science of Corn

In the early 20th century, the Corn Show spread throughout the Corn Belt. A yearly contest akin to the county fair, the Corn Show upheld the virtues of rural life and was as much about instilling civic pride as it was about judging corn.

The Corn Show replaced the quest for yield with an appeal to aesthetic sensibilities. Judges favored large ears with straight rows, full and uniform kernels, and no bird or insect damage. Agronomists, eager to share the latest research with farmers, visited the Corn Show. Some praised the event for encouraging farmers to be keen observers of their corn crop. Others thought the Corn Show distracted farmers from the only criterion that really mattered: yield.

In 1905, Illinois agronomist Cyril George Hopkins pioneered the ear-to-row method of breeding corn. Using several ears of corn, he planted seed from each ear in a row, allowing the plants that germinated from these seeds to cross-pollinate. Because all plants in a row were siblings, Hopkins could chart the pedigree of every plant. By keeping seed from only the highest-yielding row and repeating the ear-to-row method over several seasons, he hoped to derive high-yielding corn. Although he was able to select corn with high oil, he made no progress with yield.

Others, seeing that Hopkins's method did not work, turned to genetics for answers. Austrian monk Gregor Mendel had founded the science as a result of his work hybridizing pea plants. The American geneticist George Harrison Shull realized in 1909 that if he inbred corn, a naturally cross-pollinating plant, he could separate it into types. Each type would be similar to a variety of peas, and by crossing them a breeder would hybridize corn as Mendel had hybridized peas. Hybridization allowed breeders to derive corn with heterosis or hybrid vigor. Heterosis was not a new phenomenon. Humans had known for millennia that the mule, a hybrid between the horse and donkey, has greater vigor than its parents. In corn, heterosis might give plants high yield, resistance to diseases, insects, and drought, stalk strength, or some combination of desiderata.

Although simple in concept, the breeding of hybrid corn occupied plant breeders for a generation. The problem lies in the reproduction of corn, a plant that cross-fertilizes rather than self-fertilizes, as do many other grains. The tassel, having the pollen, and the silk, having the ovule, are far apart on corn, and wind wafts pollen from one plant to another. To inbreed corn, the first step in producing a hybrid, a scientist or farmer or someone familiar with the anatomy of a corn plant must cover the tassel and silk to prevent their cross-pollination. When the tassel is full of pollen, a scientist gathers it to place on the silk of the same plant. The process of inbreeding yields homozygous lines of corn that breed true, as does a variety of peas. In perverting the natural process of crossbreeding, inbreeding attenuates corn, producing scrawny ears with little seed. This small sample provides a breeder enough seed to make a cross on a tiny parcel of land but not enough to produce hybrid seed on the scale that farmers needed for their fields. As long as the yield was small, hybrid corn remained an interesting phenomenon rather than a business venture. In 1917, however, Connecticut agronomist Donald F. Jones obtained large amounts of seed by crossing four inbred lines over two generations.

Accustomed to saving a portion of their corn crop for next year's seed, farmers did not buy hybrids in large numbers in the 1920s. The drought of 1934 and 1936, however, proved the superiority of hybrids. In arid lands, farmers saw their varieties of corn wither whereas hybrids survived. This demonstration won over farmers. Between 1933 and 1943, the percentage of corn acreage planted to hybrids leapt from 1 to 90.

Hybrid corn aided the spread of technology. The old varieties of corn were difficult to harvest because they did not stand straight but bowed under the weight of ears. With stronger stalks, hybrids stood erect and were easily harvested by the mechanical corn picker. The mechanical harvester spread throughout the Corn Belt after World War II. Today, almost no corn is harvested by hand.

In the 1940s, scientists discovered genes that made corn produce no pollen. Using these male sterile lines as the female plant, breeders crossed them with normal plants to obtain hybrids. Although the use of male sterile lines simplified the work of breeding corn, scientists did not fully appreciate their susceptibility to disease. The Southern Corn Leaf Blight, a fungal disease, struck the U.S. corn crop in 1970 and 1971. Some farmers along the Mississippi and Ohio rivers lost their entire crop. Science had not been able to save the corn crop from catastrophe.

In the late 20th century, traditional breeding ceded ground to genetic engineering. In the 1970s, scientists learned to extract genes from one organism and insert them into another, an achievement with obvious applications to agriculture. In 1997, the agrochemical company Monsanto inserted into corn genes from the bacterium *Bacillus thuringiensis* (Bt) that code for the production of a toxin to the European Corn Borer, a pest of corn since 1917. Bt corn allowed farmers to use less insecticide, a practice that saved money and the environment. Yet in 1999, scientists at Cornell University charged that Bt corn pollen killed Monarch butterflies, stirring up a debate over the role of genetic engineering in agriculture that continues today. Despite the furor over genetic engineering, the future of corn, as was true of the past, is surely tied to the progress of science.

Christopher Cumo

Further Reading

Fussell, Betty. *The Story of Corn*. New York: Knopf, 1992.

Mangelsdorf, Paul C. *Corn: Its Origin, Evolution and Improvement*. Cambridge, MA: Harvard University Press, 1974.

Smith, C. Wayne, Javier Betran, and E. C. A. Runge. *Corn: Origin, History, Technology, and Production*. Hoboken, NJ: Wiley, 2004.

Costmary

Tanacetum balsamita, known as *Balsamita major* or costmary, is an old cultivated plant in Europe and in the Mediterranean region. A member of the Asteraceae family, it is a perennial with oval serrated leaves. Under favorable conditions, it can grow to be almost six feet high. During the summer, the small yellow button-shaped flowers appear in clusters. Costmary is easily grown; although it prefers a sunny situation, it thrives in a variety of conditions. All parts of the plant give off a striking scent. Its sweet smell has been likened to that of toothpaste. It is due to this sweet aroma that, in many languages of Europe, names alluding to balsam have been given to it. In many cases, however, the allusion is instead to the Blessed Virgin, perhaps indicating an association with women's diseases. In German, for example, it has been called *Mariamintz*, *Marienblatt*, *Marien-blättchen*, *Marienwurzel*, *Frauenbalsam*, and *Frauenkraut*. Its usual English name is Costmary (from "Costus of Saint Mary"). It is known in French as *herbe sainte-Marie* or *Menthe de Notre-Dame* and in Italian as *erba di Santa Maria* or *erba della Madonna*. Some of its Danish names have also alluded to the Virgin. A publication from 1550, for example, refers to the herb as *Vor Frue urt*.

It was widely cultivated in Europe until the late 19th and early 20th centuries, especially for use as a medicine and a spice. Elizabethan knot gardens often featured it. In the 1880s in Norway, it was considered one of the most common garden plants. During the 20th century, however, its cultivation largely ceased. It is rarely found in European home gardens today. Old-fashioned gardens still feature it occasionally as a traditional ornamental plant. It also grows wild in some places, for example along roadsides. It persists as a relic of an earlier time, when it had a series of different uses.

Origin and Spread

Tanacetum balsamita appears to have originated in the eastern Mediterranean, presumably in the Caucasus region. It is not known when it first began to be cultivated. There is debate as to whether the plant referred to as *balsamita* by the Roman author Columella, around the year 70 CE, was the same as the one in question here. The indications, however, are that Costmary first appeared as a cultivated plant during the Migration Period. According to some accounts, including that of the German ethnobotanist Heinrich Marzell, it was first mentioned (under the name of *costum*) in the year 812, in the plant catalogue featured in *Capitulare de villis vel curtis imperii*, an edict decreed by King Charlemagne that regulated the administration of his crown estates.

Costmary was grown quite widely, especially for medicinal purposes at least until the late 19th and early 20th centuries. It still graces old gardens in the

Mediterranean region occasionally. For the most part, however, it has disappeared. Nowadays, it is found only in some traditional home gardens in Europe, but is still widely used in Southwest Asia. It is naturalized as a weed in many parts of the world.

It is as a medicinal herb that it first attracted attention in Northern Europe, and it is likely on account of its striking aroma that curative powers were attributed to it. Christian Pedersen, a canon from Lund, wrote several prescriptions during the 1530s in which costmary figured. The same was true of Henrik Smid, a clergyman from Malmö, who included several prescriptions made from the green leaves of this plant in a publication of his from 1546. Several Scandinavian authors from the 17th century also mention it, indicating its cultivation in domestic gardens. It appears to have been rather common in the gardens of Swedish clergymen in the early 18th century. During the 19th century, it was widely grown on peasant plots. Nowadays, however, it graces few gardens in Northern Europe.

Medicinal Herb

The characteristic scent that costmary emits has drawn the interest of physicians and healers. The herb is mentioned, for example, in many of the herbals published during the early modern period. In 1539, German physician Hieronymus Bock provided not just an exhaustive description of the plant but also a quite thorough account of both its external and its internal uses. Should menstruation be irregular or even cease, these herbals aver, women will do well to keep some dry leaves of costmary near at hand for use in a decoction for bathing the feet.

Books of medicine from the 18th century classify costmary as good for the stomach, as a laxative, and as an astringent. They recommend the flowers for internal use in order to combat melancholy and hysteria. Throughout Europe, the herb was officially commended for medicinal purposes, in some areas up to the early 20th century. Until 1788, for instance, the British Pharmacopeia prescribed it against dysentery. As late as the 1930s, in fact, the German physician Max Stirnadel recommended tea made from its leaves for the treatment of gallbladder disease.

In Southern Europe, costmary has continued to feature in traditional medicine up to our own time. In Northern Europe, it was prescribed during the 19th century against aches of the head, tooth, and ear. In some parts of France, it was known as *herbe de colique*, indicating its medicinal function. In Slovakia, the juices extracted from it were used as healing liquid. It seems to have had a medicinal use in Italy and Spain too; in some parts of these countries, in fact, it still figures in traditional folk remedies. In Turkish and Iranian folk medicine, it has been utilized as a tranquilizer and cardiac tonic.

The herb has also had external uses. Scandinavians, for example, used a decoction of its leaves as an insect repellent for children and cattle. It has also been used as an insecticide in southern Europe. Inflamed breast nipples were treated with a salve produced from costmary and cream.

In recent years, pharmacologists have taken a renewed interest in *Tanacetum balsamita*. One study shows that it contains highly aromatic oil with carvone as its main component, together with smaller quantities of alpha-thujone, beta-thujone, t-dihydrocarvone, c-dihydrocarvone, dihydrocarveol isomer c-carveol, and t-carveol. The leaves are antiseptic, astringent, digestive, and laxative. The herb is mildly toxic.

Spice

In addition to its medicinal functions, costmary has served as a spice. Conrad Gessner, the Swiss naturalist, recorded in the 16th century that its leaves were used to season egg courses and other dishes. From Italy come reports that, up to our own day, it has been used as a spice for omelets. The names *Kuchenkraut* ("cake herb") and *Pfannekuchenkraut* ("pancake herb"), from German-speaking areas in Central Europe, point to its earlier use as a seasoning for pancakes. In England, it was used as a sort of spice for beer. In York, for example, it was called alecost, "because it was frequently put into ale, being an aromatic bitter," according to William Carr, a scholar of dialects, in 1828.

In some parts of Europe, moreover, it was used to counteract bad odors in the home, and to spread a pleasing scent in wardrobes. But its employment for this purpose gradually ceased, as other aromatic substances and methods for protecting clothing gained ground.

In the Church Bouquets of Peasant Women

Yet it was not mainly for its value as a medicinal herb that costmary first drew the interest of the peasantry of Northern Europe. This interest was due, rather, to the scent emitted by the plant, which was inhaled as a sort of invigorating remedy. It was widely grown on peasant plots during the 19th century, and from there it spread to the gardens of private homes. According to a Swedish handbook on cultivated plants from 1893, costmary was widely grown on peasant plots for its aroma, and for its use in imparting a pleasant smell to clothing. It was above all peasant women who took an interest in the herb. Aside from using it to sweeten odors in wardrobes and in homes, they inserted it into their church bouquets (the aromatic nosegays that they brought to services on Sunday). Extant records of the church bouquet mention "costmary" as one of its most prominent components. A Swedish book on gardening methods from 1910 describes the herb: "This plant is very common in our countryside, and few cottages are so small that they do no furnish themselves with one or two stands of it. The custom among older ladies is to take along a couple of leaves—inserted between handkerchief and hymn book—when attending church on Sunday . . . Costmary is important, for it is thought to be helpful in holding sleep at bay." Women in Denmark also brought it to church. In England, it was known as Bible Leaf, for it was used as a bookmark in Bibles. The sermons, after all, were long, and the pleasant scents from the aromatic herbs in the bouquet helped the women stay awake. The church bouquets, in which costmary figured, however, were a feature of the old peasant society. Older women in Scandinavia continued to bear church bouquets up to the early 20th century; with the emergence of new churchgoing customs, however, the practice gradually disappeared.

In Central Europe, costmary was still used as an ornamental plant at gravesides in the mid-20th century. However, due to the increased supply of garden plants that are more beautiful and more interesting, it has been sidelined as a cultivated plant and replaced with others. Yet it has persisted in some older gardens, although documentation is limited. Its remaining stock is a biocultural legacy worth preserving.

Plant for the Future?

In recent years, costmary seeds have turned up once again in the market. With the growing interest in old-fashioned plants, it may be that costmary will enjoy a renaissance as a garden plant. Never again, however, will it serve as an aromatic plant or medicinal herb. The plant functioned in the latter ways in a different society and another time. It may acquire new uses, however, if its chemical traits prove interesting to exploit.

Ingvar Svanberg

Further Reading

Hassanpouraghdam, Mohammad-Bagher, Seied-Jalal Tabatabaie, Hossein Nazemiyeh, Lamia Vojodi, Mohammad-Ali Aazami, and Atefeh Mohajjel Shoja. "*Chrysanthemum balsamita* (L.) Baill.: A Forgotten Medicinal Plant." *Medicine and Biology* 15 (2008): 119–24.

Kubo, Aya, and Isao Kubo. "Antimicrobial Agents from *Tanacetum balsamita*." *Journal of Natural Products* 58 (1995): 1565–69.

Marzell, Heinrich. "Zur Geschichte des Frauenblattes (*Chrysanthemum balsamita* L.)." *Centaurus* 1 (1951): 235–41.

Pérez-Alonso, M. J., A. Velasco-Negueruela, and A. Burzaco. "*Tanacetum balsamita* L.: A Medicinal Plant from Guadalajara (Spain)." In *International Symposium on Medicinal and Aromatic Plants, XXIII IHC*, edited by P. Tétényi and A. Mathé, 188–93. Budapest: International Society for Horticultural Science, 1992.

Cotton

Known as white gold, cotton is the world's most widely grown fiber crop. Its primary use is in making clothing. Socks, underwear, and T-shirts derive from cotton. The fiber is also used to make towels, robes, denim, corduroy, bed sheets, and

Cotton (iStockPhoto)

yarn. Manufacturers even fashion cotton into tents, and it is an ingredient in coffee filters, gunpowder, paper, and bookbinding. In addition to the widespread use of cotton fiber, cottonseed has several uses. It is 17 percent oil, 45 percent meal, 10 percent linters, and 28 percent hulls. Cottonseed oil is an important source of vegetable oil and is in margarine, mayonnaise, salad dressing, cooking oils, and shortening. Stockmen feed cottonseed meal to their animals. Cottonseed meal has 1.4 times more protein than soybean meal, 1.8 times more protein than nonfat dry milk, and 2.5 times more protein than hamburger, with 14 times less fat. Cotton may derive from the Sanskrit *karpasa-i* or the Arabic *af-or el-katum*, which has been shortened to *gutum* or *kutum*.

Origin and Diffusion

Cotton is an ancient plant. By 60 million years ago, early cotton species existed in both the Old and New Worlds. At this time a land bridge across the Pacific linked Asia and the Americas. At least 1 million years ago, cotton species *Gossypium herbaceum* from Asia and *Gossypium raimondii* from the Americas spread across the land bridge, hybridizing in Micronesia and Polynesia. Early humans may have brought cotton with them as they migrated across the planet, providing new opportunities for cotton species to crossbreed.

Humans have domesticated four species of cotton, two in the Americas and two in Eurasia and Africa. The most widely grown species, *Gossypium hirsutum*, originated in Mexico's Tehuacan Valley and spread in prehistory throughout Mexico, Central America, the Caribbean, South Florida, the Florida Keys, and southern New Mexico. Humans have cultivated *Gossypium hirsutum* since 6000 BCE. Today, farmers grow it on 90 percent of all cotton acreage. *Gossypium barbadense*, the other New World species, is known as Sea Island cotton because people cultivated it on the islands near South Carolina and Georgia. Sea Island cotton likely spread from South America to the Caribbean and then to North America. European settlers in North America extended its cultivation to the coasts of South Carolina and Georgia, though attempts to grow it inland failed. *Gossypium barbadense* produced long, highly prized fibers and commanded a high price. The two Old World species, *Gossypium herbaceum* and *Gossypium arboreum*, are native to Asia and are today grown in Africa. Indian farmers still grow *Gossypium arboreum* on soils in which other species do poorly.

The people of Mexico were the first to cultivate cotton. In the Old World, cotton was first grown in the Indus River valley about 5000 BCE. Not used initially to make clothing, cotton was first packing material to protect pottery during transit and as dressing for wounds. From the Indus River valley, cotton spread to Africa by 4000 BCE and probably from Africa to Arabia between 3000 and 2500 BCE. In the frost-free zones of Africa and Asia, humans grew cotton as a perennial. By the time of Christ, cotton was grown between 25° south and 20° north. In temperate regions, frost killed cotton plants, requiring annual replanting, so that inhospitable climates led people to treat cotton as an annual. Around 2300 BCE, the people of the Indus River valley were the first to make cotton clothes. Thereafter cotton spread east to China and Burma. From Arabia, cotton spread both west and north. In the New World, cotton migrated from Mexico to Peru, where people made cotton fishing nets between 2500 BCE and 500 BCE. Judging from the content of tombs, the ancient Peruvians were skillful spinners of cotton cloth and tapestries. From southern Mexico and the Yucatan, the Maya may have brought cotton to the Caribbean. The Inca spread cotton to the Amazon River valley. The ancients of India, Egypt, and China wore cotton clothes. In the first century BCE, Arabs found a market for cotton in Italy and Spain. In the ninth century CE, Muslims planted cotton in Spain. In the 14th century, one English writer, ignorant of the anatomy of a cotton plant, thought that each plant produced a tiny sheep whose hair was really cotton fiber that was shorn like wool.

Even though cotton is native to the Americas, as well as to Asia, European settlers in the former brought their own varieties of cotton for planting. The Spanish made the first European planting of cotton in North America in 1556, cultivating cotton in Florida. In 1607, the English planted cotton in Jamestown, Virginia, and since 1621 the American South has exported cotton. Colonists grew cotton as far north as New Jersey and Pennsylvania, though the climate prevented these regions from becoming significant cotton producers. In the early years, the

American colonies did not produce much cotton, being a net importer. The colonies derived much of their cotton from the Caribbean and the Levant. Around 1750, farmers in the Louisiana Territory began growing cotton varieties from China and Thailand.

In the 18th century, the invention of the spinning jenny quickened the production of cotton cloth, and Great Britain became the center of the global cotton trade. Importing raw cotton from India, Egypt, and the Americas, Great Britain exported finished goods to the rest of the world. Those who invested in technology and land became wealthy, but the masses of farm laborers and textile workers were desperately poor.

In the 1780s, farmers imported Sea Island cotton from the Bahamas to Georgia. The next decade Sea Island cotton migrated north to South Carolina. After the War of 1812, cotton moved west, though only upland varieties of cotton proved adaptable to cultivation in the interior of the United States. By 1850, the Gulf Coast was the United States' leading producer of cotton. Its culture sunk roots in the black clays of Alabama and in Arkansas, Louisiana, and Mississippi. The invention of the cotton gin in 1793 automated what had been the time-consuming task of separating lint from seed. Having widened this bottleneck in production, the cotton gin made possible the growing of more cotton. The Panic of 1837 slowed cotton production in the 1840s, but prosperity returned in the 1850s. By 1860, cotton culture had spread from North Carolina to Texas and from Tennessee to Florida.

The Civil War forced Great Britain to look to India and Egypt for cotton. In the 1860s Australia, responding to the shortage of cotton, began growing the shrub on newly cleared land. Since 1900, farmers in Uganda and Malawi have grown cotton, though coffee has rivaled and in some cases replaced it. In Malawi, farmers with fewer than six acres grew cotton. Because cotton is labor intensive, some Malawi farmers have switched to corn. Where large farms predominate, cotton growers spray insecticide by airplane.

In the 20th century, soybeans became an alternative to cotton in the southern United States. Since the 1930s, cotton farmers have planted legumes and sorghum, causing cotton acreage to decline. The oversupply of cotton during the Great Depression depressed prices to new lows. To reduce supply President Franklin D. Roosevelt's New Deal paid farmers to plow under cotton. They had difficulty prodding their mules to pull plows through cotton rows, leading southerners to remark that the mules were smarter than the Washington elites who had ordered this destruction. The Allies' demand for cotton during World War II returned prosperity to the South. In 2009, China was the leading cotton producer, followed by India, the United States, Pakistan, and Brazil. The United States is the world's leading exporter of cotton, followed by India, Uzbekistan, Brazil, and Pakistan.

In the United States, farmers rotate cotton with sorghum, rice, soybeans, corn, safflower, and wheat. In Australia, farmers rotate cotton with wheat and soybeans.

In parts of Africa, cotton is rotated with sorghum, wheat, and groundnuts. In Uganda, farmers rotate cotton with bananas and coffee.

Cotton and Labor

In the New World, the shortage of labor led planters to enslave Africans and their descendants. Cotton, sugarcane, and tobacco estates all used slaves. Thomas Jefferson expected slavery to die out in the South as planters exhausted their soil. The invention of the cotton gin accelerated the pace of production, and the westward migration of settlers opened new lands to cotton. Rather than disappear, slavery was anchored to cotton culture until the Civil War ended it. Slavery was viable only on plantations. Poor whites grew cotton on small farms, relying on the family for labor.

Slaves on plantations and whites on small farms used a mule and plow to break soil in the spring. Depending on latitude, farmers planted cotton between February and June. Several hoeings followed germination, and cotton was picked by hand into the 20th century. Because not all cotton was ready to harvest at the same time, farmers picked it over several months. On average, one worker could tend six to nine acres of cotton. After the harvest, cotton was ginned. Small farmers took their cotton to large estates to be ginned.

After 1865, sharecropping and tenancy replaced slavery, though blacks did not benefit from these arrangements. In this system, a planter divided his land into smaller parcels, renting some to tenants and offering others to sharecroppers, who owed a portion of their crop, usually between one-third and two-thirds, to the landowner. In the case of sharecroppers, the landowner determined what crop to plant, usually cotton to the exclusion of food crops. In theory, a tenant had the freedom to plant whatever he wished, but in reality the need to generate cash to pay rent led him to grow cotton. After the Civil War, therefore, cotton culture intensified in the South. Between 1850 and 1890, the ratio of cotton to corn doubled as cotton production increased at the expense of corn. Because cotton was so central to the southern economy, it pushed corn to the margins of the economy. As it remained a cotton exporter, the South became a food importer in the late 19th century. Cotton prices reflected the crop's importance to the South. Between 1866 and 1900, cotton fetched nearly two times more money per acre than corn in Alabama and nearly three times more in Georgia.

Wage laborers fared little better than sharecroppers and tenants. Into the 20th century, workers in cotton fields in India earned as little as 7 cents per day. Work in a textile mill was no better. Mill owners hired women and children, supervising them closely to ensure a docile labor force and to quicken the pace of work. Thirteen-hour days were common. Management blacklisted those who favored collective bargaining. Reformers lamented these conditions though they persist in the developing world.

The Search for New Varieties

The introduction of new varieties of cotton into the American South was at first a matter of happenstance. A traveler might come upon a vigorous plant, collect seeds, and give them to a farmer or scientist. Planting the seed of a new variety in its own row or parcel of land, a farmer would select the most vigorous progeny for planting the next year. Repeating the process over several years, a farmer would derive a plant suited to the soil and climate of the region. New varieties came from the Caribbean, Mexico, Central America, Brazil, Peru, the Middle East, Southeast Asia, and China.

An important criterion of selection was earliness. Most cotton varieties flowered only when nights grew long and cool in autumn. This time of flowering coincided with fall rains and so was an evolutionary adaptation to changes in rainfall. In the American South, late flowering exposed cotton to the danger of an early frost. Accordingly, farmers judged a variety partly by its date of flowering.

In the Americas, cotton varieties were of two types: long staple (Sea Island cotton) and short staple (upland cotton). As early as the 1780s, farmers grew varieties of Sea Island cotton along the Gulf Coast. Farmers also had success with these varieties in South Carolina and Georgia, but they fared poorly, as we have seen, in the interior of the continent. Instead, farmers planted varieties of upland cotton in the interior. The most popular upland variety in the colonial era was Georgia Green Seed, which a farmer first planted in 1733 near Savannah, Georgia. He had obtained seed of this variety from the botanical garden in Chelsea, England, though Georgia Green Seed, despite its name, had probably originated in Guadeloupe.

That year farmers in the South began to plant Creole Black, an indigene of Siam. Creole Black had higher yields than Sea Island cotton but its fiber was inferior, being difficult to separate from the seed. From the lower Mississippi River valley, Creole Black spread east to the Carolinas around 1800. In 1810, however, the fungal disease cotton rot swept through Mississippi and neighboring states, killing Creole Black. Farmers, understandably dissatisfied with the variety, switched to Georgia Green Seed, which initially appeared to be resistant to the disease, but new races of cotton rot likewise killed Georgia Green Seed. Twice stung by disease, farmers were eager to try a new variety.

The search for a new cultivar had begun in 1806, when Mississippi planter Walter Burling was on a diplomatic mission to Mexico City. There he collected seed from an attractive plant, which he gave to amateur scientist William Duhbar. Duhbar made several plantings, collecting seed over the next decade. Before 1820, Duhbar and other plant breeders had hybridized the Mexican variety with Georgia Green Seed, Creole Black, and varieties of Sea Island cotton. The Mexican hybrids had several desiderata: earliness, uniform flowering, high yield, and resistance to cotton rot. Enthusiastic about these traits, farmers planted these hybrids in South Carolina in 1816, in Alabama in 1826, in Georgia in 1828, and throughout the Mississippi River valley during the 1820s.

In 1857, a man known by the last name Wyche collected seed from a cotton plant in Algeria, which had likely originated in Mexico. He sent the seed to his brother, who planted it on his farm in Oakland, Georgia. Wyche seems not to have grown it on a large scale and may not have appreciated its value. In the 1870s, amateur scientist J. F. Jones and Warren Beggerly collected seed, apparently from Wyche's farm. The two grew the variety, naming it after themselves: Beggerly's Big Boll and Jones Improved. Although having different names, they were likely the same variety. Curiously, only Big Boll seems to have been widely grown. By the 1880s, Big Boll was grown on more acres than was any other variety and was especially popular in Texas and Oklahoma. But Big Boll did not triumph everywhere. On the rich soils of the Mississippi Delta, the variety produced abundant vegetation but few flowers, yielding little cotton.

Science gave farmers more varieties over time. In 1880, farmers planted only a handful of varieties. By 1880, the number had grown to 58. In 1895, farmers could choose among 118 varieties, and in 1907 they had access to more than 600 varieties. The large number of varieties set in motion a competition among them with few winners and many losers. Of the 58 varieties grown in 1880, only 6 were still cultivated in 1895. Farmers grew none of them by the mid-1930s. Of the 118 varieties available in 1895, only 2 were grown in 1925. Since 1950, the number of varieties has decreased as a small number of elite cultivars has captured the market. In 1954 farmers planted 1 variety, Detapine 15, on more than one-quarter of cotton acreage. By then only 10 varieties accounted for nearly 80 percent of U.S. cotton acreage.

In recent years, genetic engineering has given farmers new varieties. In 1996, agrochemical company Monsanto inserted into cotton genes that code for the production of a toxin to several species of insect. Monsanto derived these genes from the bacterium *Bacillus thuringiensis* (Bt). Bt cotton was resistant to a number of species of moth, butterfly, beetle, and fly. Among the insects against which Bt cotton was effective were the cotton bollworm and pink bollworm, both significant pests. Bt cotton was also resistant to the tobacco budworm, which, despite its name, is a pest of cotton. Farmers grew Bt cotton in the West because of its resistance to the pink bollworm and in the Midsouth for its resistance to the tobacco budworm. Farmers who have planted Bt cotton have been able to use less insecticide, saving money and the environment. In Australia, cotton farmers have reduced their use of insecticides by 85 percent between 1996 and 2009. In 1996, Monsanto also engineered a variety of cotton resistant to its herbicide glyphosate, known as Roundup.

Boll Weevil

Although diseases, among them cotton rot, boll rot, Verticillium wilt, Phymatotri-chum root rot, Fusarium wilt, and bacterial blight, have at times caused severe losses, cotton suffers more acutely from insects than from disease. By one esti-mate, more than 1,000 insects feed on cotton. None has caused more havoc than the boll weevil, a native of Mexico and Central America. In the 18th century and much of the 19th century, American farmers had grown cotton with little damage from insects. Matters changed in 1892 when the boll weevil crossed the Rio Grande and entered the United States near Brownsville, Texas. Advancing 40 to 160 miles per year, the weevil infested all of Texas in the 1890s, causing as much as 90 percent losses in the worst infestations.

Cotton farmers had never witnessed such destruction. The female weevil laid a single egg in each boll. Hatchlings devoured parts of the boll, causing it to fall from the plant. Overnight the weevil denuded whole fields of cotton of their bolls. In the morning, astonished farmers saw the ground littered with bolls. Because the weevil reached only as far west as Arizona, California growers were safe from its depredations. Not surprisingly, they achieved the highest yields per acre. In the Southeast, farmers were less fortunate. Sweeping east the weevil reached Georgia in 1911, where damage was even greater than in Texas. Coffee County, Georgia, which grows no coffee, suffered acutely. In desperation, a few farmers switched to peanuts, and their success prompted their neighbors to grow peanuts. By 1917, Coffee County produced more peanuts than any other county in the United States. The county's farmers had turned tragedy into triumph, and, crediting the weevil with this change in fortune, they erected the world's only statue to it.

The weevil did not stop at Coffee County. By 1916, it reached the Atlantic coast. Because weevil populations increase exponentially over time, long-maturing cotton varieties suffer the greatest losses. Sea Island cotton was therefore vulnerable. By 1930 growers, stung by the boll weevil, had abandoned Sea Island cotton. In 1921, the boll weevil turned north to the Carolinas, and by 1922 it had infested the majority of the South's cotton lands. By 1933, it had infested the entire South. Losses were so great in Louisiana and Mississippi that thousands of gins and half the cottonseed oil mills closed. Because so many rural blacks grew cotton, they felt the effects of the weevil. One scholar believes that the wee-vil precipitated the Great Migration of African Americans from South to North in the 20th century. Causing such suffering the weevil gave rise, according to one writer, to the blues. At least one blues song identifies "Mr. Bo Weevil" as the vil-lain of the South's way of life.

Scientists labored to contain the weevil. Because it fed exclusively on cotton, scientists understood that it could not cross barren land. In 1894, entomologists from the U.S. Department of Agriculture (USDA) advised the governor and legislature of Texas to create a 50-mile-wide swath of land on which no one would plant cotton. Reluctant to compel compliance, however, they refused to act. The next year Assistant Secretary of Agriculture Charles Dabney proposed a similar solution, advocating that farmers not grow cotton between the Nueces and Colorado rivers. This proposal likewise aroused no enthusiasm and so efforts to contain the weevil failed. The USDA also recommended crop rotation, plowing under plant stalks and residue after harvest to prevent the weevil from overwintering in them, and flooding fields. The most promising advice was to plant early-maturing varieties. Because these varieties would produce cotton before weevil populations reached their maximum, they could be grown with fewer losses than late-maturing cotton.

Whereas farmers were reluctant to try many of these measures, they turned to chemists for the latest, most potent insecticides. In the early 20th century, the most effective insecticides were compounds of arsenic. Because they were in the form of powder, their application was a chore. A farmer had to dust each boll on every plant if he hoped to kill all weevils. Farmers and their children inadvertently inhaled the powder and became sick. Physicians condemned these insecticides, but many farmers felt they had no alternative to them. Rain washed the powder from cotton plants into rivers and streams. Fish, small mammals, and birds died.

In the 1940s, cotton farmers added a new insecticide to their arsenal. Whereas arsenic insecticides had to be ingested to be effective, dichlorodiphenyltrichloroethane (DDT) killed on contact. So lethal was DDT that scientists predicted that it would quickly eradicate the weevil. Weevil populations plummeted and success seemed imminent. By the 1950s, however, some weevils had become resistant to DDT. No less alarming was the fact that DDT killed insects indiscriminately. The predators of harmful insects succumbed, and secondary pests afflicted cotton. Cotton farmers responded by spraying other insecticides, and by 1970 half of all insecticides used in the United States were aimed at the weevil.

If insecticides alone were not the answer, perhaps farmers might learn to use them in concert with another strategy. In the 1970s, entomologists began to use pheromone traps to track of population of weevils, reasoning that if they could identify the location of weevils, they could pinpoint insecticides to discrete plots of land. They further restricted insecticides to the fall with the aim of reducing the population that survived until spring. With these conceptual tools in place in the 1970s, entomologists faced the more daunting challenge of persuading all cotton farmers to participate in the program, for if even one refused, weevils would have a sanctuary in which they could feed and reproduce. Making strides in the 1980s, scientists and farmers had eradicated the weevil in Virginia, North Carolina, South Carolina, Georgia, and parts of Alabama by 1993. In addition to these states, the weevil was absent from the rest of Alabama, Kansas, Florida and New Mexico, and from large areas of Texas, Arkansas, Louisiana, Oklahoma, Mississippi, and Tennessee by 2003. Cotton was at last safe from the boll weevil.

Christopher Cumo

Further Reading

Isaacman, Allen, and Richard Roberts, eds. *Cotton, Colonialism, and Social History in Sub-Saharan Africa.* Portsmouth, NH: Heinemann, 1995.

Olmstead, Alan L., and Paul W. Rhode. *Creating Abundance: Biological Innovation and American Agricultural Development.* Cambridge: Cambridge University Press, 2008.

Shirong, Jia, ed. *Transgenic Cotton.* New York: Science Press, 2004.

Yafa, Stephen. *Big Cotton: How a Humble Fiber Created Fortunes, Wrecked Civilizations, and Put America on the Map.* New York: Viking, 2005.

Cottonwood

A tree indigenous to North America, Europe, and Asia, cottonwood is in *Populus*, a genus of roughly 12 species. Of these, only 2—eastern cottonwood (*Populus deltoides*) and black cottonwood (*Populus trichocarpa*)—are commercial species. Of the 2, eastern cottonwood is more important. Cottonwood is a type of poplar. The wood is light in weight and color. The grain is straight and the texture uniform. The wood is not strong, and when in contact with soil and outdoors in the elements it deteriorates quickly. Wet weather hastens decay. Cottonwood is used to make containers. Shippers prefer cottonwood boxes because they do not impart an odor or taste to food. Large crates of cottonwood are also popular with shippers. Cottonwood is used as lumber and veneer, these products being constructed into boxes and crates. Cottonwood is made into agricultural implements, furniture, cutting boards, and matchsticks. Its pulpwood makes high-end paper for books and magazines. Cottonwood is in the Mallow family. The cotton-like substance that surrounds the seeds gives cottonwood its name.

Eastern Cottonwood

Eastern cottonwood is native to North America. Grown as far west as the Great Plains, it is absent in the East from Maine, Massachusetts, and Delaware. A lowland tree that requires abundant moisture, eastern cottonwood grows along rivers and near lakes. It is seldom grown at elevation. Commercial stands are found along the Mississippi River and its tributaries. Eastern cottonwood is the fastest-growing tree native to North America. In the Mississippi River valley, cottonwood trunks average 20 inches in diameter and a tree may grow 130 feet tall by age 35. It may grow to a height of 190 feet with a trunk 4 to 6 feet in diameter by age 65.

The trunk of eastern cottonwood may thicken seven-tenths of an inch to 1 inch in diameter, and the tree may gain 4 or 5 feet in height each year to age 30, when growth begins to taper.

Eastern cottonwood is grown on alluvial soil or well-drained sandy loam. The tree must have abundant rainfall uniformly distributed throughout the year. Most eastern cottonwoods tolerate standing water early in the growing season or when dormant. Trees have survived six feet of standing water for two-and-one-half months. Some cottonwoods, apparently sensitive to flooding, have died on inundated land. In the wild, eastern cottonwood may be found in what foresters term the cottonwood type of forest in stands intermixed with black willow. Regardless of species, cottonwood produces male and female flowers on separate trees. Wind rather than insects cross-pollinates trees. Allergy sufferers complain about cottonwood pollen, but scientists have yet to document an allergic reaction to the pollen. Fertilized female flowers of eastern cottonwood yield seeds that wind disperses between mid-May and late August. Because seeds are light, wind carries them great distances. Seedlings do not compete well with other flora for nutrients, water, and sunlight. On young trees the bark is thin and smooth and may be green or yellow. Older trees have gray or black bark, a circumstance that doubtless gave black cottonwood its name. Eastern cottonwood is known as eastern poplar, southern cottonwood, Carolina poplar, and necklace poplar. Though known as a hardwood tree, eastern cottonwood yields soft wood.

Black Cottonwood

Among the largest species of cottonwood, black cottonwood grows along the Pacific coast as far north as southeastern Alaska and as far south as northern Mexico. It may be found from British Columbia to southern and central Montana, central Idaho, northwestern Wyoming, northern Utah, and Nevada. Like eastern cottonwood, black cottonwood is a lowland tree needing copious amounts of water. Black cottonwood tolerates a range of soils: gravel, sand, humus, and clay. The soil pH should be 6 or 7. The soil must be rich in elements. Preferring lowlands, black cottonwood may nevertheless be grown above 2,000 feet. In British Columbia, black cottonwood has been recorded at 7,000 feet and in California at 9,000 feet. It grows in forests intermixed with willow, water birch, thin leaf alder, box elder, sycamore, Douglas fir, western white pine, western larch, western red cedar, western hemlock, and white fir. A fertile tree, black cottonwood produces numerous seeds for dispersal in late May and early June. The germination rate of these seeds is high. Seedlings, again, compete poorly with other vegetation. The black cottonwood is mature at 60 to 75 years. In Inyo County, California, its trunk may reach 2 feet in diameter and its height may soar to 60 feet at maturity. In Montana, the trunk of black cottonwood reaches only 1 foot in diameter and the tree tops out at 45 feet at maturity. Black cottonwood is known as California poplar, balsam cottonwood, and western balsam poplar.

Cottonwoods of Less Renown

The Wyoming state tree is the plains cottonwood (*Populus sargentii*). A large tree, plains cottonwood may grow 100 feet tall and spread its canopy 100 feet wide. The trunk may be 5 or 6 feet in diameter. The tree may live 100 years. Botanists are unsure whether the plains cottonwood should be its own species, as it is now, or should be lumped together with eastern cottonwood. The pollen is ripe in late March and April. Plains cottonwood is not ideal for urban landscaping because its roots grow so thick that they uplift sidewalks and streets.

The Rio Grande cottonwood, a subspecies of *Populus fremontii*, is known as Fremont cottonwood, common cottonwood, valley cottonwood, march cottonwood, Alamo, alemillo, and the water tree. The tree may grow up to 60 feet tall with a trunk 3 feet in diameter. A mature tree may yield 25 million seeds per year, most of which perish. Rio Grande cottonwood grows in Texas, northern Mexico, New Mexico, Colorado, and California. The tree may grow as high as 7,000 feet in elevation. Despite its name, the water tree, unusual among cottonwoods, tolerates aridity and so grows in the dry regions of New Mexico.

The Fremont cottonwood (*Populus fremontii*) grows in the American Southwest. The plains cottonwood (*Populus deltoides* ssp. *occidentalis*), not to be confused with the plains cottonwood of Wyoming, and the narrow-leaf cottonwood (*Populus angustifolis*) grow in the American South, Alberta, Canada, and the American West, though not in the desert Southwest. Swamp cottonwood (*Populus heterophylla*) grows in the wet soils of the Atlantic coast from Connecticut to Georgia and west to southeastern Missouri, southern Illinois, Indiana, Ohio, and Michigan. Some growers cultivate *Populus × camdensis*, a hybrid of eastern and black cottonwoods. Two aspen species—*Populus tremuloides* and *Populus grandidentata*—and the balsam poplar (*Populus balsamifera*) are in the same genus as cottonwoods.

Production

In 1977, the Forest Service estimated that the United States had 4.8 billion board feet of cottonwood. By 1985, the United States had 50,000 acres of cottonwood under cultivation with the prospect of adding 140,000 to 150,000 acres of new land to cottonwood cultivation. Production has been uneven. It peaked in 1899 at more than 421 million board feet. In 1932, perhaps because of the Great Depression, production slumped to a nadir of 49 million board feet. Thereafter production rose to more than 174 million board feet in 1960, declining again to 125 million board feet in 1970. An acre of untended eastern cottonwood may yield 40 cords of pulpwood by age 15. Intensively managed, an acre of cottonwood may produce 5,200 cubic feet by age 15. The yield may be as great as 40,000 board feet per acre by age 55. In the Mississippi River valley, production of eastern cottonwood was 35,000 cords in 1968, 73,000 in 1969, 100,000 in 1970, and 118,000 in 1971. Cottonwood may be harvested as young as 20 years. Cottonwood is not suitable for fuel wood because it dries poorly and tends to rot. The wood may warp as it dries.

Christopher Cumo

Further Reading

Kennedy, Harvey E., Jr. *Cottonwood.* Washington, D.C.: U.S. Government Printing Office, 1985.

Krinard, Roger M. *Cottonwood Development through 19 Years in a Nelder's Design.* New Orleans: U.S. Department of Agriculture, 1986.

Krinard, Roger M., and Robert L. Johnson. *Cottonwood Plantation Growth through 20 Years.* New Orleans: U.S. Department of Agriculture, 1984.

Cowpea

An annual legume of the Fabaceae or Leguminosae family, the cowpea is known as the field pea, southern pea, black-eyed pea, and black-eyed bean. The Greeks knew the cowpea as *phaselos*, from which must derive *Phaseolus*, a genus of beans. Others know the cowpea as *phaseolus*. The Spanish referred to the cowpea as *caups*. Its classification is uncertain. One writer declares the cowpea to be a bean. Another categorizes it as neither a bean nor a pea. Despite its name, the cowpea is more closely related to beans. Cowpea is also related to pea, soybean, alfalfa, clover, vetch, peanut, chickpea, and lupine. Scientists know the cowpea as *Vigna unguiculata*. Half a cup of cowpea contains 286 calories, 9.2 grams of water, 20 grams of protein, 50 grams of carbohydrate, 9 grams of fiber, 1.7 grams of fat, no cholesterol, 71 milligrams of calcium, 8.3 milligrams of iron, 278 milligrams of magnesium, 366 milligrams of phosphorus, 1,148 milligrams of potassium, 48 milligrams of sodium, 5.1 milligrams of zinc, 1.3 milligrams of vitamin C, 0.6 milligram of thiamine, 0.1 milligram of riboflavin, 2.3 milligrams of niacin, 1.3 milligrams of pantothenic acid, 0.3 milligram of vitamin B6, 534 micrograms of folic acid, and 28 international units of beta-carotene.

Origin and Diffusion

The cowpea's origin is open to debate. It may have originated in Asia, but Africa is more probable. Those who support Africa as the ancestral homeland of the cowpea favor West Africa, central Africa, or Ethiopia. About 1200 BCE, the people of Chad began cultivating the cowpea, perhaps intercropping it with millet, a practice that continues today. The Yoruba of Africa offered cowpeas to the gods in return for their protection. The god Obatala, they believed, ate cowpeas with yams, rice flour, and cornmeal. Because corn was unknown in Africa before the 16th century, this belief must be relatively recent. Yamaya, the mother of the gods, ate cowpeas, watermelon, and fried pork. The god Oxun combined cowpeas with shrimp and palm oil. The cowpea was important enough to enter the lexicon of the Yoruba. Their saying, "you do not know what cowpeas are like for dinner," meant that a person was not mindful of the consequences of his actions. Nigerians wrapped cowpeas in banana leaves and ate them with smoked fish, eggs, canned beef, and vegetables.

The Greeks, Romans, and Indians fed cowpeas to livestock. First-century BCE Roman poet Virgil gave instructions on the cultivation of cowpeas. Galen, the second-century CE physician to Emperor Marcus Aurelius, recommended a dish of cowpeas and fish sauce. The Spartans ate cowpeas with figs and beans as dessert. Medieval Europeans had recipes for cowpeas. African slaves, perhaps in the 16th century, brought cowpeas to the Caribbean and North and South America. Another account credits the Spanish with introducing the cowpea to the Caribbean. Ship captains used cowpeas as a provision because slaves would not eat European foods. In the American South, cowpeas became a staple of African Americans. Despite its association with blacks, the cowpea did not have a stigma. African American cooks prepared cowpeas for their white masters. In this way the cowpea crossed racial barriers. Farmers in North Carolina first grew cowpeas in 1714, and they spread thereafter throughout the South. In the 18th century, Thomas Jefferson cultivated the cowpea among the many plants in his garden. In 1824 Mary Randolph, author of *The Virginia House-Wife*, urged cooks to add cowpeas to their cuisine. One recipe advised the housewife to boil cowpeas until tender and then fry them. Hoppin John was a popular southern dish that used cowpeas. As blacks migrated north during and after World War I and World War II, they brought cowpeas with them. Cowpea dishes were ideal for family gatherings and church socials. Poor African Americans ate cowpeas every day, though affluent blacks ate them less often. Some African Americans were eager to distance themselves from the cowpea. Nation of Islam leader Elijah Muhammad rejected cowpeas because of their association with a "slave diet." More recently, some African Americans have embraced cowpeas as authentically black fare. The cowpea has become part of popular culture. The Dixie Chicks recorded a song in which a woman killed her abusive husband by feeding him poisoned cowpeas. One group of musicians named themselves the Black Eyed Peas.

Current Status

Today, Africa produces the majority of the world's cowpeas. Nigeria alone accounts for more than half of all cowpeas. Other leading producers are Burkina Faso, Niger, Mali, and Myanmar. California and Texas produce virtually all U.S. cowpeas. Once grown in the southeastern United States, cowpeas have ceded ground to soybeans, clover, and other legumes. The cowpea's low yield compared to other crops makes it unattractive to commercial growers.

Intolerant of frost, the cowpea grows well in warm, humid conditions, though it has been cultivated as far north as Illinois, Indiana, Ohio, and New Jersey. Tolerating a range of soils, the cowpea grows in clay and sand. The cowpea may be grown in soil with little organic matter and as much as 85 percent sand. Farmers prize the cowpea for its drought tolerance and ability to yield well in infertile soil. In the South, farmers plant cowpeas on soil that is too poor for soybeans. Tolerant of acidic soil, the cowpea does not grow in saline or alkaline soil. A soil that is too fertile causes the cowpea to grow vegetatively rather than to produce seeds. An indeterminate plant, the cowpea grows vegetatively and produces flowers throughout its life. Bearing white or purple flowers the cowpea, like beans and peas, is a self-pollinator. Pods are yellow, brown, or purple.

Farmers may choose among more than 50 cultivars. Oklahoma farmers, for example, favor Chinese Red, an early-maturing dwarf variety. Because the cowpea tolerates shade, it may be intercropped with several plants. Throughout the South, farmers intercrop cowpeas with corn and sorghum. In Florida, farmers grow cowpeas for forage. A rotation with corn, cotton, and cowpeas is popular in the South. Elsewhere farmers rotate cowpeas with oats or wheat. Because the cowpea, like other legumes, fixes nitrogen in the soil, it benefits other crops. The Arkansas Agricultural Experiment Station has demonstrated that oats and cotton yield better when they follow cowpeas rather than corn.

Cowpeas may be planted in spring after the danger of frost has passed. The farmer may sow cowpeas and corn at the same time. In Virginia, farmers may plant cowpeas in May or early June. In California, cowpeas may be sown between May 1 and June 15. Although spring planting is common, cowpeas may be sown as late as August 1 in the South. In the United States, farmers plant cowpeas with a grain drill or corn planter. One authority recommends that farmers plant cowpeas at a rate of 20 to 45 pounds of seed per acre. Cowpeas may be grown for hay or seed. When pods yellow but before they fill, the farmer may harvest cowpeas for hay. In the United States, the yield of hay averages between one and two tons per acre. When one-half to two-thirds of pods have filled, the farmers may harvest cowpeas for their seeds. The commercial grower may use a combine to harvest cowpeas. In addition to its culture with corn, cotton, sorghum, and millet, cowpeas may be grown with Sudan grass or Johnson grass. Because the cowpea is 25 percent protein, it is suitable for feeding livestock, though the cost of producing cowpeas makes them less attractive as feed than corn or soybean meal.

Diseases and Pests

The fungus *Fusarium oxysporum* var. *tracheiphilum* causes Fusarium wilt, a disease of several crops. The fungus causes leaves to yellow and fall from the plant. The stem yellows, though the inside turns brown or black. Defoliating a plant, Fusarium wilt kills it. The disease strikes in midsummer. Resistant varieties offer the best protection against the disease. Nematodes of the genus *Meloidogne* cause cowpea root knot by producing galls on roots. Infected roots turn brown and decay, impairing the ability of cowpea plants to derive nutrients from the soil. The farmer may plant resistant varieties. Also effective is a four- or five-year rotation with winter grains, corn, sorghum, velvet beans, and soybeans. The farmer may also treat cowpea seeds and soil with fungicide.

The cowpea weevil, *Callosobruchus maculates*, and southern cowpea weevil, *Mylobris quadrimaculatus*, lay their eggs on and in pods and on cowpeas in storage. Larvae bore into seeds, where they feed. The farmer may use an insecticide. Fumigation or heat treatment of seeds is also effective. The cowpea curculio, *Chalcodermus aeneus*, also infests seeds. An insecticide may be effective. Other pests include the lygus bug, corn earworm, lima bean pod borer, mites, cowpea aphid, bean thrips, yellow-striped and beet armyworm, and nematodes.

Christopher Cumo

Further Reading

Albala, Ken. *Beans: A History.* Oxford: Berg, 2007.

Martin, John H., Richard P. Waldren, and David L. Stamp. *Principles of Field Crop Production.* Upper Saddle River, NJ: Pearson-Prentice Hall, 2006.

Cranberry

A perennial vine, cranberry is a member of the Ericaceae family and *Vaccinium* genus. German and Dutch settlers in North America, fancying that the flowers of a cranberry resembled the head of a crane, named the plant craneberry, from which the English word "cranberry" derives. Cranberries are of two species. *Vaccinium macrocorpon*, the principal commercial species, yields a large berry. *Vaccinium oxycoccus* produces a small berry. Cranberry is rich in vitamin C, fiber, and antioxidants. The proanthocyaninds in cranberries are the source of their

Cranberry bog (iStockPhoto)

antioxidant properties. Oxygen radical absorbance capacity, a measure of antioxidant properties, demonstrates that blueberries and cranberries have the same high levels of antioxidants. Cranberries are thought to prevent bacteria from clogging the urinary tract, though studies have proven inconclusive.

History

Vaccinium oxycoccus, spreading to eastern North America during the Ice Ages, grew near *Vaccinium macrocorpon*. The two hybridized, apparently without human aid and possibly before the advent of humans in the New World. Native Americans were the first to recognize the value of cranberry, though when and whether they cultivated it is unclear. They stewed cranberries to make cranberry sauce and combined them with venison and tallow to make pemmican, a type of dried cake. Cranberry was important not only for flavor but also for its acidity, which kept the cakes free from microbes. European settlers were quick to take note of the cranberry. As early as 1614, English captain John Smith described the fruit to a correspondent in Europe. To the extent that Europeans were familiar with Smith's description, the Pilgrims might have known of the cranberry before their arrival in Massachusetts in 1620. In 1677, the American colonists sent 10 barrels of cranberries, along with corn and cod, to English king Charles II. This might have been the first shipment of fruit from the colonies to the mother country. In 1689, New Jersey resident Mahlon Stacy described the uses and preservation of cranberries in a letter to his brother in Yorkshire, England. One horticulturist credits Stacy with being the first to couple cranberry sauce with turkey, a combination that remains popular today. It is possible, however, that the colonists learned this practice from Native Americans and incorporated it into their Thanksgiving at an earlier date.

New Englanders balked at the Native American practice of picking berries by hand, inventing a handheld rake to harvest them. This method still required manual labor, but it was not as laborious as hand picking. Americans were apparently too eager to pick cranberries early, because in 1789 New Jersey outlawed their picking before October 10. Doubtless sometime later, Wisconsin banned this practice before September 20. Not everyone liked cranberries. The long voyage to Europe rendered them insipid. About 1800, British horticulturist Joseph Banks, finding imported cranberries tasteless, vowed to grow his own. Obtaining plants from the United States, Banks, encouraged by the bounty of his first harvest, expanded his planting so that by 1807 he had 326 square feet given to cranberry, harvesting "five dozen bottles of fruit." Banks's success, although not on the large scale of commercial farming, nonetheless attracted admirers. In 1821, British horticulturist Robert Mallett, obtaining specimens from Banks, made his own planting. He observed that manure did not benefit cranberries as it did other crops and asserted that they would grow only in peat. In the early 19th century, British farmers, obtaining *Vaccinium oxycoccus* doubtless from the United States, planted cranberries in Lincolnshire.

Back in the United States Captain Henry Hall, a Revolutionary War veteran, planted cranberries in Massachusetts. Observing that cranberries frequently grew in soil overlain with a layer of sand, he added sand to his planting, and others, seeing his success, copied him. Aware of its role in preventing scurvy, shipping firms bought cranberries to feed sailors. In 1831, farmers planted cranberries near Boston to satisfy urban demand. Some farmers in Massachusetts even grew cranberries on land normally reserved for corn. In 1835, New Jersey farmer Benjamin Thomas began cultivating cranberries, and that century Joseph Josiah White emerged as New Jersey's largest planter. By the mid-19th century, farmers grew cranberries in Massachusetts, New Jersey, Wisconsin, and after 1883 in Washington and Oregon. By 1869, Wisconsin had 1,000 acres of cranberries. By then, cranberry was a widespread addition to American cookery. Americans made cranberries into pie and pudding. Boiling cranberries, straining them, and adding sugar and nutmeg, cooks made tea. Homemakers added cranberry juice to ground rice to make cranberry and rice jelly. The 19th-century American philosopher Henry David Thoreau was fond of cranberries, taking pleasure in picking them in the wild. Today, the cranberry is widely consumed in the United States and Canada, not just for its traditional use in Thanksgiving dinners in both countries but also in juices, cakes, breads, and other foods.

Attributes

Cranberry colonizes bogs and semiaquatic habitats. It grows in sphagnum or peat and must have acidic soil. *Vaccinium macrocorpon* grows close to the ground, where it forms a dense network of vegetation. Its oval leaves are one-quarter to one-third of an inch long and one-eighth of an inch wide. The shiny leaves are pale to dark green and have more than 630 stomata per square millimeter. Young plants are less tolerant of temperature fluctuations than old plants because old plants have built up dense foliage that acts as a buffer against extremes. Leaves turn brown or red during winter. Cranberry flowers in May or June. Each flower has four sepals and four pink petals. Eight stamens surround each stigma. Scientists once thought that the flowers self-pollinated or that wind pollinated them, but pollen is too heavy and sticky to be moved without the aid of insects. Scientists now know that honeybees and bumblebees pollinate cranberry. Berries are pale pink when young, turning deep red or purple as they ripen. Newly ripe berries have a sharp flavor, but they sweeten with age. Many people believe that the cold weather of autumn imparts flavor to cranberries and so wait until November to pick them.

When planted from seeds, cranberry yields fruit in its fourth year. Cranberry roots have a symbiotic relationship with the fungus *Phoma radicis*, just as legume roots have a symbiotic relationship with nitrogen-fixing bacteria. The fungus makes nitrates available for absorption by roots. The fungus may aid roots in preventing the entrance of pathogens and undesirable minerals. In return, the roots give the fungus carbohydrates. The fungus is not found in soil planted to other crops or in fertile soil. The fungus will not tolerate waterlogged or dry soil.

The soil pH must be between 4 and 5.5. The optimal range is 4 to 4.5. Outside the target range, minerals become unavailable for absorption by the roots. Where necessary, the farmer should add sulfur compounds to increase soil acidity. Cranberry has a low requirement for nitrogen, phosphorus, and potassium compared to other crops. Cranberry needs calcium, magnesium, and sulfur in small amounts. Even smaller quantities of boron, chlorine, copper, iron, molybdenum, and zinc are necessary. Where summer is dry, irrigation is important to prevent peat from drying out because dry peat is difficult to rehydrate. Temperatures below 10°F may damage cranberry plants.

Cultivars

In the 1830s and 1840s, farmers began selecting new varieties for cultivation. Among the early successes were Early Black and Howes in Massachusetts and Searles in Wisconsin. Since 1929, the U.S. Department of Agriculture has released seven cultivars: Beckwith, Bergman, Crowley, Franklin, Pilgrim, Stevens, and Wilcox. Breeders aim to derive cultivars that do not bruise easily, and that store well, resist diseases, and are sweet rather than acidic.

In 1845 Harwich, Massachusetts, resident Cyrus Cahoon selected the renowned Early Black from a wild plant. Today, Early Black is the most widely grown cultivar in eastern North America. Its success has led scientists to use Early Black in their breeding programs. Early Black's distinguishing characteristic is its early maturation. Berries are dark red and pear shaped. They store well and do not bruise easily. Early Black is resistant to false blossom disease and tolerates a higher soil pH than many other varieties.

Between 1914 and 1917, Oregon scientist Joseph Stankavitch crossed a wild cranberry from Oregon with McFarlin, a cultivar in the eastern United States. The progeny, named Stankavitch in his honor, matures early, stores well, and yields abundantly. Berries, one-half to three-quarters of an inch in diameter, are deep red. Stankavitch is best grown in cool weather because warmth causes it to flower twice. The second flowering, late in the season, does not bear fruit and impairs next year's harvest. Berries have more sugar and less acid. Stankavitch is resistant to false blossom disease.

In 1930, USDA scientist H. J. Bain crossed Early Black and Howes to obtain Franklin. An early-maturing variety, it is nonetheless a little later than Early Black. Franklin yields more abundantly than its parents. Berries are dark red and store well. Franklin is resistant to false blossom disease.

In 1940, scientist E. L. Easton of Canada's Department of Agriculture Research Station in Kentville selected Beaver, which derived its name from Beaver River in Nova Scotia. Eaton selected Beaver from a wild plant that grew near Beaver River and released the cultivar to farmers in 1956. Beaver produces large fruit that stores well. Beaver ripens one week before Early Black, the standard among early varieties. Beaver, however, is susceptible to false blossom disease.

Christopher Cumo

Further Reading

Sumner, Judith. *American Household Botany: A History of Useful Plants, 1620–1900.* Portland, OR: Timber Press, 2004.

Trehane, Jennifer. *Blueberries, Cranberries and Other Vacciniums*. Portland, OR: Timber Press, 2004.

Cucumber

Common cucumbers, also known as cowcumbers, cukes, and the Greek *sikuos*, are native to the East Indies between the Himalayas and the Bay of Bengal. They belong to the Cucurbitaceae family, which includes gourds, watermelon, pumpkins, and other edible squashes. Cucumbers are a warm-season tendril annual that have yellow flowers and white fruit with semihard green rind. Most fruits are 2 to 10 inches, but the largest cucumber was recorded at 59 pounds in Australia. There are thousands of varieties, and new varieties are developed yearly.

Heirloom varieties have also been maintained and are gaining popularity. For example, the lemon cucumber heirloom variety was first introduced in 1894 and produces a small, round fruit that is pale yellow in color when mature. However, the Irish-American horticulturalist Bernard M'Mahon (1775–1816) identified in his comprehensive text, *The American Gardener's Calendar: Adapted to the Climates and Seasons of the United States*, eight original varieties in 1806. In the mid-1800s, Fearing Burr's New England horticulture catalogue included 10-foot cucumber vines that were a common length for producing enough fruits to harvest. Most new varieties are grown to produce high-quality properties as slicers, pickles, or diuretics or with disease resistance. Contemporary varieties have been developed to produce smaller more compact fruits per inch of plant.

Often referred to as a vegetable, the fruit of cucumbers is 96 percent water, and its flavor comes from the edible seeds. The internal temperature can remain 20° cooler than the air temperature, giving rise to the common phrase "cool as a cucumber." Pickler cucumbers are paler green than slicer varieties and sometimes have light stripes. They usually have a thinner rind and crunchier texture, which allows them to avoid becoming soggy when pickled. Persian varieties are most commonly sold fresh, although they often have a waxed skin to retain moisture. There are three types of blossoms that are produced, depending on the cucumber variety. Monoecious plants have both male and female flowers; gynodioecious plants produce only female blooms, and parthenocarpic plants do not need pollination and produce seedless fruits. English greenhouse cucumbers are regularly consumed as slicers. These varieties do not self-pollinate, requiring external pollination. They produce a fruit with very small seeds, and so are called seedless cucumbers.

Original varieties of cucumber that are not bred to be "burpless" have a compound called cucubitacin that in large quantities can make the skin bitter and cause burping in humans. However, some people cannot taste the cucubitacin and so have no awareness of bitter cukes. Unfortunately, others are overly sensitive to this compound. The scent of cucubitacin is also responsible for attracting the yellow-and-black-striped cucumber beetle, which is cucumber growers' worst enemy. This pest can destroy plants by eating leaves, flowers, and roots as well as transferring the devastating bacterial wilt that prevents water from distributing through the stems. However, the bitter chemical compound is thought to be a natural insecticide against other insects, so burpless varieties have no problems with aphids and spider mites.

Cucumbers are frequently soaked in vinegar or brine to create pickles. It is thought that this practice gained popularity to overcome the bitterness of the rind of earlier varieties. Egyptians ate brined cucumbers at every meal, and according to one company, 5 million pickles are consumed daily. There are numerous pickle recipes and variations, but a popular variety for pickling, *cucumis anguria*, is a small, oval fruit that is commonly referred to as a gherkin. According to the Food and Agriculture Organization, in 2005 China led the world in the production of gherkins with 60 percent of the global total. Other significant gherkin producers include Turkey, Russia, Iran, and the United States.

History

Wild cucumbers were found to be in the diet of people living along the Burma-Thailand border as long ago as 9750 BCE. Cucumbers were first cultivated in parts of western Asia at least 3,000 years ago and in China in the second century BCE. It was recorded among the foods grown in the ancient city of Ur, along the Euphrates River, and in India, Greece, Italy, and China.

Many well-known leaders of history enjoyed cucumbers. The first-century CE encyclopedist Pliny the Elder wrote that the Romans used greenhouses to supply the Emperor Tiberius with his daily gherkins: "Indeed, he was never without it; for he had raised beds made in frames upon wheels, by means of which the cucumbers were moved and exposed to the full heat of the sun; while, in winter, they were withdrawn, and placed under the protection of frames glazed with mirrorstone." There is a record of cultivation in France in the ninth century when they were popular with the king, Charlemagne. England began cultivating cucumbers in the 14th century, and they were common during Edward III's reign. However, their popularity waned with the war and strife of the time but recrudesced about 250 years later.

Cucumbers have been mentioned in several iconic writings including the Mesopotamian legend, *Epic of Gilgamesh* (27th century BC). Cucumbers were also referenced several times in the Bible. The Israelites complained to Moses that they missed the good parts of their old life, including "cucumbers and melons." The prophet Isaiah referred to Jonah's misery by saying, "The daughter of Zion is left as a cottage in a vineyard, as a lodge in a garden of cucumbers." These historical references may be to wild varieties or other types of gourds.

In 1494, Christopher Columbus and his Spanish fleet brought cucumbers to cultivate in Hispaniola (the island of Haiti and the Dominican Republic). They were thereafter used by Native Americans. The Spanish explorer Hernando De Soto recorded the cultivation of cucumbers in Florida in 1539 as did the first voyagers to Virginia in 1584. In the 17th century in the new United States, raw foods and vegetables lost favor for fear of disease. It was said raw cucumbers were "only fit for cows," thereby giving them the name "cowcumber." In 1630, Reverend Francis Higginson published *New England Plantation*, which included a description of a Boston garden: "The countrie aboundeth naturally with store of roots of great varietie and good to eat. Our turnips, parsnips, and carrots are here both bigger and sweeter than is ordinary to be found in England. Here are store of pompions, cowcumbers, and other things of that nature which I know not."

Medicinal Uses

The Romans used cucumbers to treat scorpion bite and improve eyesight. Women wore them around their waists to increase fertility, while midwives also carried the fruit during labor and threw it away after the birth of the child.

Cucumbers have been used in Chinese medicine since the eighth century, when people used cucumber leaves as a diuretic. Cucumbers are still used as such today due to their high water content. In the 16th century, people used cucumber roots to help ease diarrhea and dysentery. The stems were first used in the 18th century to treat bowel and urinary diseases, dysentery, skin sores, as well as high blood pressure.

The fruit is still used to reduce swelling, detoxify the body, and ease throat pain, and as a laxative. There are some reports that cucurbitans have been found to be an antitumor agent in animals. The cucumber also has ascorbic acids with antioxidant properties and caffeic acids that act as anti-inflammatory and anticancer agents. They are said to eliminate uric acid, thereby helping kidney function and possibly even alleviating the symptoms of arthritis. Cucumbers are often suggested as a key ingredient in weight loss diets because of their low-calorie and high-water characteristics, aiding the body in reducing built-up water retention while still hydrating the system.

A common Chinese home remedy for dry lips and throat or to prevent laryngitis is a soup made from very mature cucumbers. Other medicinal uses around the world include the cucumber as an ingredient in taeniacide, which kills tapeworm, and some have tried to prevent cataracts with cucumber. It has also been used as an astringent.

Cosmetic Uses

Cleopatra used cucumbers on her skin, and records show its cosmetic uses dating back to 19th-century France. In contemporary society, it is very popular in skin and beauty products. Cucumbers' key components of water, vitamin E, and other oils have made them a popular ingredient in skin cosmetics that soften and hydrate the skin as well as in products that add body and moisture to hair. The cucumber also includes the mineral silica, which helps keep the skin's connective tissue healthy and strong. The ascorbic and caffeic acids also prevent water retention, which may explain the cucumber's popular use of placing slices over the eyes during facials or in the morning to reduce puffiness and wrinkles. Cucumbers act as an astringent, tightening the pores and reducing swelling, thereby keeping skin soft and reducing wrinkles. This characteristic also is said to prevent acne and soothe irritated skin. The calm association of "coolness" with cucumbers as well as its subtle scent has made it a popular ingredient in shampoos, lotions, cosmetics, and even aromatherapy.

Erika Stump

Further Reading

Boswell, Victor R. "Our Vegetable Travelers." *National Geographic Magazine* 96 (August 1949): 2.

Grieve, M. *A Modern Herbal: The Medicinal, Culinary, Cosmetic and Economic Properties, Cultivation and Folk-Lore of Herbs, Grasses, Fungi, Shrubs and Trees with All Their Modern Scientific Uses.* New York: Dover, 1971.

Leung, Albert. *Chinese Healing Foods and Herbs.* Glen Rock, NJ: AYSL, 1993.

Currant

The name currant can refer to a number of plants, including a small seedless raisin called a zante currant or dried black cornith; a fruit of the genus *Ribes* that grows on shrubs; a type of small tomato species (*Solanum pimpinellifolium*); a tree that is also called a Juneberry or shadblow service berry (*Amelanchier Canadensis*); a type of bush commonly referred to as a conkerberry or bush plum (*Carissa spinarum*); another type of bush (*Miconia calvescens*), sometimes called a velvet tree or miconia; and the wild currant or Currant-of-Texas, whose Latin name is *Mahonia trifoliolata*. When referring to currants, however, most people are speaking of either the zante currant, or grape, used in baked goods, or the tiny berries of the genus *Ribes* that are related to the gooseberry and come in black, red, and white varieties. The black currant is prized for its nutrients. Black currant has four times more vitamin C than the orange, twice the potassium of banana, and twice the antioxidants as blueberry. Black currant is thought to minimize inflammation and other symptoms of arthritis. Black currant may prevent urinary tract infections and kidney stones.

Zante Currants

Zante currant is the name used in the United States (simply "currant" in other English-speaking countries) for a variety of small, sweet black grape that is seedless. Its scientific name is *Vitis vinifera*. Zante currants are so named to distinguish them from members of the *Ribes* genus that are also known as currants. Zante currants are tiny perennials with a high degree of sweetness. They are used in baking. In the United Kingdom, zante currants are popular in scones, buns, Christmas pudding, Christmas cake, and mincemeat filling for pies.

Ribes

Ribes (rib-iz) is a genus of fruit that includes the species blackcurrants, redcurrants, and whitecurrants. These fruits are juicy berries that grow on a shrub and are mainly cooked into jams. There are about 100 species of these currant berries that are native to and grow chiefly in the temperate climates of the Northern Hemisphere and western South America. The earliest species of currants were cultivated sometime before the 17th century in Northern Europe, chiefly the Netherlands, Denmark, and other areas surrounding the Baltic Sea. In the 1600s, the bush was brought to the United States, although many varieties were already growing in the Americas at that time.

The blackcurrant tree (*Ribes nigrum*) is a deciduous shrub that grows to six-and-one-half feet. It is self-fertile and is typically pollinated by bees. Its berry is a glossy, dark violet with a diameter of less than one inch. It is used to make dyes, jams, and jellies. The fruit has high vitamin C content and an omega-6 fatty acid called gamma-linolenic acid. The redcurrant (*Ribes rubrum*) produces a large red berry that is a bit more tart than blackcurrant. This deciduous shrub usually grows to three to five feet in height, although it occasionally can reach six-and-one-half feet. White currant is a sweeter, albino version of *Ribes rubrum*.

Currant Tomatoes

Currant tomatoes—also called wild tomatoes, Wild Florida Everglades Tomatoes, and spoon tomatoes—are related to the garden tomato and are similar to tomatoes that grow wild in Central America, but unlike the others, this variety is tiny. They are called "currant tomatoes" because they grow on indeterminate vines and resemble currants in size, sweetness, quantity, and color. Common hybrids include the Hawaiian currant, White Mexican currant, Matt's Wild Cherry, Golden Rave, Sugar Plum, and Sweet Pea. The currant tomato is related to the common tomato (*Lycopersicon esculentum*). The two are in the same genus, though they are different species.

Trees

The currant tree or Juneberry (*Amelanchier canadensi*) is of the Rosaceae family and is a tightly multistemmed deciduous shrub with a gray trunk. It grows into a dome shape and to a height of about 20 feet. It produces white flowers before the coarse, green leaves come in. The leaves turn red to yellow in the fall. It grows well in both moist and dry and acid or neutral soils. It grows in eastern North America, from Newfoundland in Canada south to Alabama.

Carissa spinarum, as categorized by Swedish naturalist Carl Linnaeus in 1771, is commonly known as the currant bush or conkerberry. This is a large multistemmed shrub of the dogbane family (Apocynaceae) that is grown in tropical regions surrounding the Indian Ocean. Leaves are a glossy green with opposite and narrow ovate, and branches that are thorny. White, star-shaped flowers are produced before the green berries emerge. The bush grows in semiarid coastal regions and typically is found in fine-textured soils, such as clay or clay loams. The sweet berry produced on this bush is edible but only when it is fully ripe. When unripe, the fruit and the bush's milky sap are toxic. They are a popular food with the Australian aborigines.

Not to be confused with the currant bush, the plant known as the bush currant or velvet tree is a perennial, evergreen woody shrub whose scientific name is *Miconia calvescens*. It is an attractive plant with distinctive leaves that are green on top and purple on the bottom with three lighter-colored main veins and a net of smaller veins that run horizontally. It grows to a height of 50 feet in wet areas that get 80 or more inches of rain annually. Introduced to Hawaii in the 1960s, it is now growing wild on two of the Hawaiian islands—Maui and the Hawaii. It has become a terribly invasive plant, sometimes referred to as the green cancer or purple plague, and is a threat to Hawaii's fragile ecosystem. It is fast growing and is spread by birds throughout the islands. After just 50 years in Tahiti, *Miconia calvescens* had replaced over 70 percent of the island's native forests.

Wild Currant

Mahonia trifoliolata, or the wild currant or Currant-of-Texas, is a rounded, medium, evergreen shrub with gray-green foliage resembling holly that contains clusters of fragrant yellow flowers and fruit that is a bright red berry. The sweet berries, which can be made into jam, attract birds and small mammals in the wild. The shrub grows to a height and width of six feet. It also goes by the names agarita, agarito, algerita, agritos, and chaparral berry.

Rosemarie Boucher Leenerts

See also Grapes, Tomato

Further Reading

"Canadian Serviceberry, Shadblow, Downy Serviceberry, Serviceberry, Shadbush AMELANCHIER cacadensis." http://www.sheffields.com/seed_genus_species_lot/Amelanchier/cacadensis/100096 (21 June 2011).

"Instant Hawaii." http://wildlifeofhawaii.com/flowers/1037/miconia-calvescens-velvet-tree (accessed 22 June 2011).

"Miconia calvescens—Velvet Tree." http://wildlifeofhawaii.com/flowers/1037/miconia-calvescens-velvet-tree (accessed 22 June 2011).

Parmar, C., and M. K. Kaushal. "*Carissa spinarum*." In *Wild Fruits*. New Delhi, India: Kalyani, 15–18. 1982. Also available at http://www.hort.purdue.edu/newcrop/parmar/04.html.

"Smallest Tomato: The Currant Tomato and Other Small Wonders." http://www.tomatocasual.com/2008/04/18/smallest-tomato-the-currant-tomato-and-other-small-wonders (accessed 20 June 2011).

Cypress

In the family Cupressaceae, cypress is a tree that comprises 20 to 30 genera, including *Cupressus*, *Chamaecyparis*, and *Thuja*, and 140 species. The subdivisions of these conifers dates to the 26 species that Swedish naturalist Carl Linnaeus assigned in 1753 to 7 genera. In 1841, the 26 species were redistributed among 13 genera.

Cypresses typically are resinous and coniferous evergreen trees and shrubs. The species of the true genus *Cypress* are native to the Northern Hemisphere, namely North America, Europe, and Asia, but are found on all continents. They grow as far south as Antarctica. In the United States, they thrive in the wet, swampy areas of the South and along the Atlantic coast, the Gulf Coast, as well as along the Mississippi River valley.

Description

The cypress has small dark-green leaves that are scale-like. Female cones have woody scales. The cypress can be monoecious, subdioecious, and sometimes dioecious trees or shrubs and can range in height from 3 to 380 feet tall. The stringy bark, which can easily flake or peel, is typically an orange- to a reddish-brown color and is considered a hardwood. Some species have a smoother, scaly bark. The cypress lives a long time. Those growing in Italy today date back hundreds if not thousands of years. One in particular, in Soma, is believed to have been planted in 1 CE. This tree stands 120 feet tall and has a trunk of 23 feet in circumference. The Soma tree has much history: It is said to have been struck by the sword of Francis I after he was defeated in Pavia. And Napoleon so revered the ancient tree that he planned his pass over the Simplon in the Alps around the tree to avoid injuring it.

Leaves of the cypress start out as small needles and grow to be scale-like. They are arranged in a spiral of opposite pairs arranged at 90° angles to the previous pair, or they are arranged in whorls. Most trees are evergreen, although three genera are deciduous. Seed cones can be woody or leathery in texture, with the exception of the juniper cypress, which grows berries. Cones' scales are arranged in spirals and contain small, flat seeds with two narrow wings that appear on each side of the seed. Cypress branches divide repeatedly and form frond-like sprays. Cypress roots are thirsty, and some trees develop pneumatophores. These are growths that come from the roots and resemble knees. They act as a support for the tree and help to provide aeration for the often waterlogged rot system.

Practical Uses of Cypress

Cypress trees produce an essential oil called cypressine that acts as a preservative in the wood, making it extremely resistant to harsh weather conditions as well as to fungi and insects. It is surpassed only by cedar as the most used construction timber of the Mediterranean region and Turkey. The tree does not produce sap and therefore its wood, which is a light- to dark-honey color, easily absorbs stains, paints, and sealers. The close- and straight-grain wood is also lightweight and rarely develops knots. It is easy to glue, sand, and drive nails and screws into. It is resistant to splitting, warping, splintering, and cracking, which makes it an excellent source for exterior products, such as shingles, porches, bridges, greenhouses, and shutters. In colonial times, it was used to manufacture barns, warehouses, boats, docks, and homes. Due to its length, durability, and aroma, the tall species of cypress, especially the juniper, were used to construct roof beams of Mediterranean palaces and temples. Today, the wood is a popular choice in the construction industry to make shingles, decks, beams, flooring, and siding. It is also manufactured into caskets, blinds, furniture, doors, and window frames. The fine-grain variety is used in custom cabinetry. Its water-resistant properties also make the wood good for roof shingles, boat docks, water tanks, vats, railroad cars, and in shipbuilding. The soft and light wood that is derived from the pneumatophores, or knees, is soft, light, and is often turned into vases and other decorative items.

Cypress's Therapeutic Properties

The main components of the essential oil cypressine are a-pinene, camphene, sabinene, b-pinene, d-3carene, myrcene, a-terpinolene, linalool, bornyl acetate, cedrol, and cadinene. The oil is extracted from needles and twigs of young branches by steam distillation. The oil is a natural healing agent. It acts as an astringent, an antiseptic, a deodorant and a diuretic, and has a positive effect on excess fluids in the body on several levels. For example, it is believed to improve circulation, loosen coughs, and reduce the pain of varicose veins. It may be beneficial in instances of excess fluid in the body, such as that which occurs from excess bleeding, excess perspiring, and oil production in the skin. It can be placed in vaporizers and aid with breathing difficulties, such as coughs, asthma, bronchitis, emphysema, and influenza. Native American Navajo women take an infusion of cypress branches after childbirth as a way to regain strength. In aromatherapy, it is believed to remove stress and restore calm, to soothe anger, and to improve overall life balance. It has a woody, spicy, and masculine scent. It is manufactured into many forms, including oils for vaporizers, massage oils, lotions, creams, cold compresses, and bath salts. Cypressine is believed to be nontoxic and a nonirritant but should be avoided in pregnant women and others with sensitivity to topical solutions.

Ritual and Historic Uses

Native Americans have utilized various species of cypress in ceremonies and rituals over the years. The totem poles of the First Nations people of eastern Canada used the western red cedar (*Thuja plicata*) in making totem poles. The Lawson false cypress, or cedar, is used to call in the spirits at ceremonies. The Navajo make necklaces of the cypress's dried fruit. And the cedar represents the gift of music in "The Legend of the Flute," a tale of the Brulé Sioux and Lakota Sioux of the northern plains states. According to the legend, in a dream a young hunter is shown a hollow branch by a red-headed woodpecker. The wind blowing through the holes made by the bird resulted in a haunting tune. This is how the gift of music was introduced to humans, as the legend goes. Both the Native Americans and Europeans used leaves of the Thuja species as a cure for scurvy.

In Old World societies, the cypress was considered a "tree of light." In the Chinese Taoist tradition, the earth spirits of the East live in the cypress tree, and people can absorb some of the cypress's life force by chewing the resin. In various societies, the cypress is used as a graveyard tree as it is associated with divinity, light, and the heavens. The Turks traditionally plant the tree at either end of graves, which stems from an age-old belief that the aroma from the resin will neutralize the stench of the cemetery. The aroma has long been considered a healing force as well. Some doctors in the Far East would send patients with insufficient lung capacity to the isle of Crete, where cypress trees flourish.

The cypress's evergreen leaves represent eternity and are symbolic of a belief in the resurrection. The tree is still often planted in Christian and Muslim countries. Cypress groves are also reported to have been abundant in ancient Greece. A cypress grove in Greece was dedicated to the ancient Greek god of healing, Aesclepius. Serpents that Aesclepius deemed to be sacred were allowed to roam freely in the grove. Another grove in Phlius is said to have been a refuge for those seeking political and judicial asylum. The refugees who took asylum in these groves were protected, and sometimes simply taking a twig from the cypress grove while moving to the next sanctuary would be enough to protect them.

Several monarchs of ancient Persia, Egypt, and Assyria introduced many non-native plants to the area by planting palatial gardens. The Persian prophet Zoroaster is credited in the epic *The Book of Kings* with planting seeds of the cypress at his Fire Sanctuary in 1000 BCE in what is modern-day Iran. He had brought the seeds from paradise and they became twin trees: the Sun Tree and the Moon Tree. These trees factor into the story of fourth-century BCE Greek conqueror Alexander the Great, who along with his army encountered the trees while being led to a sacred mountain by an old man. After approaching the trees, he kissed both, made an offering, and requested that his fortune be told. He was told by the oracle of the trees that he would one day conquer India, but die soon after returning to Babylon, which is what did occur. In 846 CE, a caliph of Samarra, in what is modern-day Iraq, cut down one of these trees and paid for the deed with his life.

Rosemarie Boucher Leenerts

Further Reading

"Cypress." http://tinytimbers.com/specie_cypress.htm (accessed 26 May 2011).

"Cypress Trees." http://www.2020site.org/trees/cypress.html (accessed 7 July 2012).

Hageneder, Fred. *The Meaning of Trees*. San Francisco: Chronicle Books, 2005.

Vince, Susan W., and Mary L. Duryea. "Planting Cypress." http://edis.ifas.ufl.edu/fr152 (accessed 7 July 2012).

D

Daffodil

Daffodil is the collective name for over 60 species and many subspecies and hybrids that belong to the genus *Narcissus* in the Amaryllidaceae family. The daffodil's most striking feature is its flower. Daffodil flowers display a central cup structure called the corona that surrounds the stigma and stamen. The corona is in turn surrounded by six floral leaves, which form the perianth. Depending on the species and cultivar, the perianth and the corona can have the same or different colors. The most prevalent colors are yellow and orange, but whitish, reddish, and pink varieties exist.

Daffodils are geophytic perennial plants and can spread asexually via bulbs or sexually via seeds. During the growing period in late winter and early spring, the plants store starch and nutrients in the bulb, to be used as an energy resource in the next growing season. Daffodils are hardy and are among the first flowers to bloom in spring. In Europe, daffodils are generally associated with the end of winter and with Easter, when they are commonly used for decoration. The German name *Osterglocke* (Easter bell), for instance, reflects this.

In the Alsace region of France, the wild daffodils bloom and the associated festivals draw thousands of tourists each spring. While daffodils are native to Southern and Western Europe, large stands of wild daffodils are rare and it is more usual to see small groups of escaped cultivated daffodils. Wild daffodils are endangered and protected species in many countries.

The name Narcissus has roots in the Greek word for numbness or slumber, *narke*. In Greek mythology, Narcissus was a beautiful but vain young man. Divine punishment made him fall in love with his own reflection in the water. Different versions of the myth have him commit suicide because his love is hopeless, waste away not being able to leave his mirror image, or drown in an attempt to approach his reflection. The myth has it that a daffodil grew from the ground where he died.

Daffodils as Commercial Crops

Daffodils are popular garden flowers and are also appreciated as cut flowers. This has led to the development of over 25,000 cultivars, of which about 20 make up almost two-thirds of the yearly production. The largest commercial growers of daffodils are the Netherlands. In the United States, daffodils are mostly grown in California, Oregon, and Washington. Daffodils are commercially propagated asexually by dividing bulbs into small portions. Growers can regenerate a new bulb and subsequently a flower from each portion. Both the actual flowers and the bulbs are commercially relevant. In order to produce daffodils for market outside the natural growing period of the plant, growers use a method known as forcing. Bulbs can be forced by mimicking the temperature conditions the plant would undergo in winter followed by exposure to warmer spring temperatures. Forcing makes daffodils available from about December until late April, although the time around Easter remains the peak season for daffodil sales.

Few pests and diseases are a threat to daffodils. Most prominent among the few pests that affect daffodil production are the bulb fly, whose larvae live in and consume the daffodil bulbs, and the Narcissus eelworm, a nematode that also targets the bulbs, but can move to the stem and leaves during the growing season.

Freshly cut daffodils exude a sticky sap from their stems, which is incompatible with other flowers in a bouquet in the same vase. Daffodils therefore need to be kept separate and the water discarded before they can be combined with other flowers.

In botanic research, daffodil flowers are used as source tissue for chromoplasts. Chromoplasts are specialized plastids that store the carotenoids that give the flowers their yellow or orange color.

Daffodils contain toxic alkaloids with the highest concentration located in the bulbs. If eaten by humans or animals, they can cause dizziness, abdominal pain, and convulsions, which can in rare cases be fatal. Grazing and digging animals thus avoid daffodils. The sap of the daffodil can cause a skin reaction known as daffodil dermatitis, an itchy rash that develops on contact and usually affects florists or flower cutters.

History

The popularity of daffodils in European gardening can be traced back to the Renaissance, when flowers of oriental or Southern European origin became popular. The breeding of daffodils started in the 19th century and coincides with the growing commercial relevance of the daffodil. The breeding efforts quickly led to marked changes in flower color, shape, and size. Breeding efforts were helped by the high degree of variability in the genus on which improvements could be based, as well as by the crossing compatibility of different Narcissus species.

Daffodils reached Asia via trading routes and were brought to the United States by European settlers. The settlers grew the flowers in their gardens, but some plants soon escaped to the wild. In the 1920s, the U.S. government placed an embargo on the import of Dutch bulbs in order to protect American growers from the bulb fly that had been spreading in the Netherlands. The embargo affected trade in tulips and daffodils most strongly. Some Dutch flower growers emigrated to the United States to keep up their business. The embargo was not lifted until after the World War II.

The great popularity of the daffodil has led to the founding of national and regional daffodil societies in many countries. The Royal Horticultural Society in the United Kingdom organized the first conference devoted to daffodils in 1884. At this conference, the Daffodil and Tulip Committee was founded, which remains active to this day. Today, the Royal Horticultural Society curates the International Daffodil Register and Classified List and associated online databases, which contain all official daffodil cultivars. Today, daffodils are internationally classified into 13 divisions based on the number, measurements, and shape of their flowers. Divisions 1 through 12 contain all known cultivars, whereas division 13 is reserved for wild species. In addition to the division, a color code is used to describe the color of the perianth, followed by a hyphen and the corona's color. Thus a 4 W-Y daffodil would belong to division four and have a white perianth with a yellow corona.

The Daffodil in Art and Culture

The daffodil's beautiful bright color and the fact that it is one of the first flowers of spring contribute to its strong symbolic character and wide popularity with artists. Certainly the most famous use of daffodils is found in English romantic poet William Wordsworth's lyrical poem "I Wandered Lonely as a Cloud" (also known as "Daffodils"). In this poem, the speaker relates his joy at coming across a stand of wild daffodils "dancing in the breeze," praising their beauty the recollection of which inspire and comfort him as he later remembers them.

Various international cancer research agencies and charities have chosen the daffodil as their symbol, seeing it as a symbol of hope and renewal. Many of these organizations regularly organize fund-raising and awareness events called "daffodil days."

The Isles of Scilly before the coast of Cornwall in England are a protected area. The wildlife trust managing the area leases the islands from the Duchy of Cornwall, a traditional source of income for the Prince of Wales. As the cultivation of daffodils is a traditional pursuit on some of the islands, the trust pays a symbolic rent to the Duchy of one daffodil per year.

Kerstin Müller

Further Reading

American Daffodil Society: The United States Center for Daffodil Information. http://www.daffodilusa.org/ (accessed 29 January 2011).

Benschop, M., R. Kamenetsky, M. Le Nard, and H. Okubo. "The Global Flower Bulb Industry: Production, Utilization, Research." *Horticultural Reviews* 36 (2010): 1–116.

Dahlia

An ornamental in the Compositae or Asteraceae family, dahlia's scientific name, *Dahlia × variabilis*, denotes its status as a hybrid. Its parents, *Dahlia coccinea* and *Dahlia pinnate*, grow wild in southern Mexico. Curiously, their habitats overlap, yet they do not hybridize in nature despite the fact that they cross-pollinate, leading to the inference that somewhere along the line someone hybridized the two to produce today's dahlias. In 1791, Spanish worker at the Madrid Botanical Garden Abbe Cavanilles published a description of dahlia, coining the genus name *Dahlia* to honor Andrea Dahl, a student of 18th-century Swedish naturalist Carl Linnaeus. Cavanilles studied the species *Dahlia pinnate*, one of the progenitors of today's hybrid species. In 1793, Cavanilles described two other species, *Dahlia rosea* and *Dahlia coccinea*, the second progenitor of today's hybrid. The species name *variabilis* means the variability of the dahlias that German naturalist Alexander von Humboldt introduced to Europe in 1804.

Origin and History

Dahlia, at least the wild species, originated in Mexico, perhaps in the south. The Aztecs, fond of ornamentals, may have grown it. Lady Bute, wife of the ambassador to the Court of Spain, is intertwined in the mythology of dahlia. On the urging of the Royal Botanic Garden at Kew, she, so the story goes, obtained dahlia seeds, doubtless through her husband, from Spain and sent them to Great Britain. No later than 1813 the garden tended dahlias. That year it published the story of Lady Bute, crediting her work in 1789. But a subsequent researcher discovered that the 8 and 9 had been transposed. Lady Bute really acquired dahlia seeds in 1798. Even this version did not stand scrutiny. Spain probably acquired dahlia from Mexico in 1789. That year Mexican Botanical Garden director Vincenne de Cervantes sent dahlia seeds to Spain, where they were grown in the Madrid Botanic Garden. Only in 1790 did Cervantes increase the seeds, so Lady Bute must have acquired them in that year. Bute obtained seeds of the three species known to Spain. British naturalist Sir Joseph Banks preserved specimens of these species in the Kew herbarium and London's Natural History Museum.

Meanwhile Cavanilles's publications attracted adherents. They corresponded with him and requested seeds. Dahlia began its trek through Europe. In 1802, France acquired Cavanilles's three species, perhaps from Bute or Cavanilles, planting them in the Botanic Garden in Paris. About 1803, Germany acquired dahlias. That year a German professor reclassified dahlia into the genus *Georgina* to honor a Russian botanist. The result was confusion, with the partisans of *Dahlia* at loggerheads with the partisans of *Georgina*. The genus *Georgina* is occasionally still used in Eastern Europe.

Momentous for the history of dahlia, in 1804 von Humboldt sent dahlia seeds from Mexico to France and Germany. These were not the first introductions to these nations, but they were the first semidouble and double flowers with a corresponding increase in the number of petals. One account holds that he harvested dahlia seeds from the wild in Mexico. Another postulates that von Humboldt got seeds from a local gardener because the former was not knowledgeable about Mexico's flora. His dahlias are the basis of today's cultivars.

By the early 19th century, a vigorous trade in dahlias joined Great Britain and France with Great Britain the importer. Breeders must have been busy deriving new varieties because in 1836 the Horticultural Society of London—today the Royal Horticultural Society—counted more than 700 cultivars. The previous year Great Britain held 45 shows for the exhibition of exceptional specimens. Because these ornamentals were elites, they shared many genes in common. The genetic variability of the modern dahlia is consequently small. In the 19th century, because of its status, dahlia was an expensive flower fit for the gentleman or gentle lady gardener. It was not yet a flower for the masses. By the end of World War II, the center of dahlia culture had shifted from Great Britain to the Netherlands.

Botany and Cultivation

The Compositae or Asteraceae family is the largest family of angiosperms with more than 4,000 species. Dahlia is related to lettuce, endive, artichoke, and salsify. Like the potato, dahlia produces tubers, though dahlia does not bulk large in human nutrition. Although dahlias germinate from seeds the first year, in subsequent years they issue forth from tubers, making dahlia a perennial herb. The plant dies in autumn to regerminate from tubers in summer. Dahlias from tubers are sturdier and thicker with more and larger flowers than plants from seeds. Dahlias produce 8 to 15 tons of tubers per acre. Tubers contain inulin, a starch-like compound. The 19th-century French botanist Alphonse de Candolle tried to eat the tubers but never acquired a taste for them. Cattle and horses likewise do not like them. The Connecticut Agricultural Experiment Station recommends the consumption of tubers in salad as a substitute for radish. During World War II the Dutch, short of food, ate the tubers as a substitute for the potato. Mexicans may have eaten tubers in antiquity, though there appear to be no proof.

The genus *Dahlia* contains 27 species, most wild to Mexico and Guatemala. The modern hybrid stands three to six feet with stems one-quarter to one-half of an inch in diameter. Stems are unbranched except where they flower. Leaves are slightly hairy and simple or pinnatisect. Each plant produces two to eight flowers. Double flowers have as many as 300 florets. Flowers are white, lavender, purple, yellow, orange, and scarlet. Roots are fibrous. The thickest penetrate the soil at depth and from them develop tubers. Others are feeder roots near the soil surface. Cultivation can damage them. Each flower produces about 30 seeds, which will germinate as soon as they are ripe. They do not need a period of dormancy. They germinate in 7 to 10 days at 60°F. Because dahlia originated in volcanic, well-drained soils of Mexico, the gardener should approximate these conditions. Dahlia benefits from the addition of organic matter to the soil. The gardener should fertilize the soil, preferably with bonemeal, six weeks before planting. Because dahlia does not tolerate frost, it must be planted after the last frost. Dahlias should be planted two feet apart. Dahlias need full sun and protection from wind.

Christopher Cumo

Further Reading

McClaren, Bill. *Encyclopedia of Dahlias*. Portland, OR: Timber Press, 2004.

Rowlands, Gareth. *The Gardener's Guide to Growing Dahlias*. Portland, OR: Timber Press, 1999.

Welling, Eleanor. *The Dahlia Primer: Little Known Facts about the Dahlia*. United States: Xlibris, 2007.

Daisy (Bellis)

Bellis is a genus of 15 species of flowering plants belonging to the Asteraceae or Compositae family, the largest family of vascular plants, that is, plants that have lignified tissues enabling the conduction of water, minerals, and photosynthetic products through the plant. Commonly known as the daisy, *Bellis* is a perennial plant that flowers for much of the year across Europe and western Asia, North Africa, and parts of Canada and the United States, especially California, Utah, Idaho, Montana, and Washington. *Bellis* flourishes on all types of grazed, mown, and trampled land, especially that which is wet and on calcareous and neutral soil. Although *Bellis* is perhaps most often thought of as a weed proliferating in lawns, pastures, and roadsides, it grows also on river banks, at the edge of lakes, and on sand dunes. Several *Bellis* cultivars exist that can be used in ornamental displays, while *Bellis perennis* is a useful addition to grasslands grown to support wildlife as the plant attracts small insects.

Attributes

In appearance, though a flower of the *Bellis* genus may look like a single flower, the upturned flower head actually consists of multiple, tiny, individual flower heads known as florets. These flower heads are a type of inflorescence known as captitulum, in which the densely packed florets are surrounded by bracts to create the appearance of a single flower. Typically, the flower of *Bellis perennis* blooms from March to September, opening at sunrise. The flower head is on average around one inch in diameter and is composed of a golden-yellow center of disc florets surrounded by 30 to 80 white ray florets, which are often flushed with pink or red on the underside. The plant has small, hairy, evergreen leaves that are ground-hugging, enabling the plant to evade the blades of lawn mowers when the plant grows in cultivated grass. Growing to around eight inches tall, *Bellis perennis* may form clonal mats originating from short rhizomes with shallow, fibrous roots. *Bellis perennis* may reproduce either vegetatively from rhizomes, as fragments of rhizome can produce new plants, or from seed. *Bellis perennis* seed falls close to the parent plant and is then dispersed as the soil on which it is has fallen is moved though human and animal activity (for example, footfall during walking). The seed, which is only around one-twentieth of an inch long, can also be included, accidentally, as part of a grass seed mixture and thus distributed along with grass seed. However, under field conditions *Bellis* seeds tend to be short lived.

Mythology

There are three romantic stories as to how *Bellis* originated. According to classical mythology, *Bellis* is so named because one day a beautiful Dryad attracted the unwanted amorous attention of the guardian of the orchards. The nymph called on the gods to protect her, which they did by transforming her into a flower that they called *Bellis*, derived from *bellus*, meaning "pretty" in Latin. The English writer Geoffrey Chaucer (ca. 1343–1400) states in *Legende of the Goode Women* that the Greek mythological princess Alcestis was transformed into a daisy, and according to Celtic legend, the daisy is the flower of newborn babies and the innocent. In Christian legend, the daisy is associated with Saint Margaret of the Dragon, with the French and German word for daisy, *marguerite* (meaning "pearl"), being applied to the daisy on account of the whiteness of the flower petals. *Bellis* species have long been associated with purity and female virtue as seen in the Victorian language of flowers in which the white daisy symbolizes innocence and the red daisy unconscious thoughts.

Literature and Medicinal Use

From Chaucer's "day's-eye," so called because the writer believed the flower to open and close with the rising and setting of the sun, to the playwright William Shakespeare (1564–1616) to the British Romantic poets William Wordsworth (1770–1850), Percy Bysshe Shelley (1792–1822), and Robert Burns (1759–1796), who each referred to the daisy in poems, *Bellis* has a rich cultural history with many references to the plants in literature. In the play *Faust* by Johann Wolfgang von Goethe (1749–1832), the composite structure of *Bellis* allows Marguerite to murmur the famous chant "He loves me, he loves me not" as she plucks the petals from a daisy in order to determine the strength of Faust's affection for her. Traditionally, the phrase is repeated until a single petal remains with the last uttered phrase thought to tell the truth of the beloved's affection. This is but one example of the plucking of a daisy enabling divination. Plants in the *Bellis* group have an equally long tradition in homeopathic medicine as they hold many healing properties. Practitioners of the "Doctrine of Signatures," a system going back to the first century CE with the Greek physician Dioscorides, and based on the principle that the appearance of plants indicated which bodily ailments a plant could be used to treat—advocated the use of the eye-like-shaped *Bellis* species to treat eye conditions. Modern herbalists believe the fresh flowers and leaves of the daisy can be used to make ointments and poultices for the treatment of wounds and boils; the flowers can be made into a decoction to ease respiratory tract infections, and the leaves can be made into an ointment to heal bruises and external wounds.

Victoria Williams

See also Black-Eyed Susan (Rudbeckia)

Further Reading

"*Bellis perennis.*" Kew Royal Botanic Gardens. http://www.kew.org/plants-fungi/Bellis-perennis.htm (accessed 26 October 2010).

"Bellis perennis L. Lawndaisy." USDA, NRCS. PLANTS Database. 2010. http://plants.usda.gov/java/profile?symbol=BEPE2 (accessed 26 October 2010).

Ellacombe, Henry Nicholson. *The Plant-Lore and Garden-Craft of Shakespeare.* London: W. Satchell, 1884. Also available at http://books.google.co.uk/books?id=pJ6TM8qSwDoC&printsec=copyright#v=onepage&q&f=false (accessed 6 November 2010).

Healy, Evelyn A., and Joseph M. DiTomaso. *Weeds of California and Other Western States.* Vol 1, *Aizoaceae-Fabaceae.* Oakland: University of California Press, 2007.

Skinner, Charles Montgomery. *Myths and Legends of Flowers, Trees, Fruits, and Plants in All Times and in All Climes.* Philadelphia: Lippincott, 1915. Also available at http://books.google.co.uk/books?id=s5p82USYH4cC&printsec=frontcover&source=gbs_ge_summary_r&cad=0#v=onepage&q&f=false (accessed 6 November 2010).

Ward, Bobby J. *A Contemplation Upon Flowers: Garden Plants in Myth and Literature.* Portland, OR: Timber Press, 1999.

Dandelion

Dandelions, one of the most common plants in the world, are also one of the oldest cultivated plants. Although widely despised today as a weed, dandelions were once highly valued as a medicinal plant with beautiful yellow flowers. They also served as an important and highly nutritious food.

Origin and History

The dandelion, *Taraxacum officinale*, has Eurasian origins. From its origin, this perennial has spread across every continent except Antarctica because of a combination of toughness and high reproduction. Dandelions are a seral species, hardy plants that sprout quickly in disturbed soil. Dandelions are quick growers, progressing from bud to seed in a matter of days. Each seed, an achene, is one-eighth of an inch long with miniscule barbs arranged along its edge. A blast of air on a dandelion puffball can spread 200 seeds on the wind. Hanging on its parachute, the pointed seed lands point first on soil. The umbrella-shaped parachute remains erect, spread protectively overhead, while each touch of breeze makes the seed tilt back and forth. The seed penetrates the soil and slowly edges in deeply. With moisture, dandelion seeds germinate quickly. A germination

Dandelions (Thingsofnature/Dreamstime.com)

rate of 90 percent is not unusual. Growth begins when the temperature is at least 50°F and maximizes at about 77°F. The rootlets pry the soil particles apart, effectively rototilling the ground. Meanwhile, the plant sends down a taproot that usually reaches 18 inches, although dandelion taproots have been known to stretch down for 15 feet. The leaves lie low in a basal rosette, making a flat circle that is almost immune to grazing, snow, or wind. They grow out from the center like the spokes of a wheel, overlapping as little as possible to maximize absorption of sunshine. The rosette does double duty by catching rainwater in its funnel. The sides of each leaf are slightly tilted toward the midrib, so the water slides down toward the center of the plant and the roots. When the first layer of dandelion leaves decomposes, the plant provides fertilizer. Subsequent plants, some dandelion and some not, benefit from the loosened and fertilized soil. As the region becomes shady, sun-living dandelions settle in a new location.

The ancient Greeks and Romans probably used dandelions for medicinal purposes, but the first clear reference to the plant is found in a medieval Arabic text from around 1100 CE. The common name dandelion comes from Latin, *dens leonis*, meaning "tooth of the lion." Dandelions were common in medicinal gardens, especially those of medieval monasteries. The popularity of the plant undoubtedly owes much to the fact that it is one of the very first plants in the Northern Hemisphere to grow under snow. An ancient spring tradition in many European cultures, and one that came to the New World, urges one to go out early in spring and pick dandelion greens. The leaves served as a food and as tonic to cure people of the diseases that had befallen them during the cold months.

Dandelion is high in vitamin C, with more of the vitamin per pound than tomatoes or oranges. The plant also contains significant amounts of protein, iron, thiamine, riboflavin, calcium, and potassium as well as vitamins D, K, and B-complex. Dandelion, once commonly called "piss-a-beds," has also long been known as a diuretic (promoter of urination). It has been used to treat pulmonary edema, gallbladder problems, kidney stones, gout, and other conditions where it is necessary to remove excess fluid from the body without depleting it of nutrients. The medicinal properties of dandelion gave it a place in many countries' official listings of medicines and drugs. They were in the United States Pharmacopeia from 1831 until 1926 and were listed in the U.S. National Formulary from 1881 until 1965.

Dandelion in the Americas

Dandelion seeds came to the United States in 1620 on the *Mayflower* along with Puritan settlers. Some of the seeds may have been stowaways, resting in the piles of earth used for ballast, but many also came as treasured items. Puritan women transported dandelion seeds as part of their medicine chests. All parts of the dandelion plant—leaf, root, and flower—have been known for millennia as remedies for a host of ailments. The dandelion had the additional advantage of serving as a comforting reminder of England in the alien environment of the New World. In 1672, John Josselyn reported in his botanical survey of New England that dandelions were well established. Meanwhile, the Spanish brought dandelions to their settlements in California and Mexico while the French imported the plants into Canada.

By the 19th century, sharp-tasting dandelions had grown in popularity as a food and remained as a popular medicinal herb. All parts of the dandelion are edible. The stem is very bitter and somewhat sticky. The petals have a bland, slightly sweet flavor. Mostly, people have eaten the leaves and the taproot, which are both quite bitter. Spring greens and leaves after a first frost tend to be sweeter. Horticulturalists developed many varieties of the plant, including the popular French Large-Leaved Dandelion. The Shakers, in particular, were known for selling dandelion products and cultivated acres of the plants. Dandelion wine proved particularly popular as did dandelion tea and salad greens. By the late 20th century, dandelions fell out of favor. The increasing availability of other, less-bitter greens meant that the plant disappeared from grocery store shelves in favor of such greens as iceberg lettuce. Dandelions can still be found in health food stores and, of course, in gardens and lawns throughout the country.

Unlike many other non-native plants, dandelions pose no threat to the environment. As an invasive species, they are a minor one. But they do grow well in the same environment as turf grass. By interrupting the smooth expanse of green that so many home owners covet, dandelions have become one of the most disliked plants.

Caryn E. Neumann

Further Reading

Leighton, Ann. *American Gardens in the Eighteenth Century: For Use or for Delight.* Boston: Houghton Mifflin, 1976.

Sanchez, Anita. *The Teeth of the Lion: The Story of the Beloved and Despised Dandelion.* Blacksburg, VA: McDonald and Woodward, 2006.

Selsam, Millicent E. *The Amazing Dandelion.* New York: Morrow, 1977.

Date Palm

A palm tree that produces sugary fruit, the date palm (*Phoenix dactylifera*) is among the oldest cultivated trees. The people of Israel and Arabia knew that date palm as *tamar*, from which the Portuguese derive *tamara*. The English "date," the French *datte*, the German *Dattel*, the Spanish *datel*, and the Italian *dattile* derive from the same source. The genus name *Phoenix* may derive from *phoinix*, Greek for "date palm." The Greeks may have associated the date palm with date-producing Phoenicia, from which phoinix may be derived. The species name *dactylifera* is Latin for "finger bearing," an apparent reference to the resemblance of clusters of dates to fingers. The genus *Phoenix* has 12 species. A ripe date is 60 percent sugar. Because of their sugar content, the ancients fermented dates into wine. The date has little protein and fat, just 2 percent of each. The date has iron, magnesium, potassium, phosphorus, calcium, copper, boron, cobalt, fluorine, manganese, selenium, zinc, and small amounts of vitamin A, vitamin B1, vitamin D, vitamin G, and fiber. Date palm leaves were once used to make baskets, roofs, mats, and rope. Egyptians still use date palm leaves to make rope. The wood was used to build houses.

The Basics

The date is a staple in the Middle East and Saharan Africa much as rice, wheat, and the potato are staples in other regions of the world. The date palm is dioecious,

Dates (iStockPhoto)

bearing male and female flowers on separate trees. If a palm is planted from seeds, the offspring, as one might expect, are half male and half female. To the grower this is wasteful because only half the palms, the females, can bear fruit, and the male trees, shedding abundant pollen, are more numerous than is necessary to pollinate the females. In the 1970s, growers planted palms in a ratio of 1 male to 40 or 50 females. Today, the ratio is 1 to 100. Some growers do not plant male trees but rather buy pollen each year to satisfy their needs.

A palm yields small clusters of flowers in spring. Because insects do not pollinate the flowers, they are not showy. Wind pollinates the date palm, though since antiquity humans have hand pollinated it to increase the yield. Having flowered in spring, a palm is ready to harvest in late summer or early autumn. In California, the harvest spans November to February. If planted from a shoot, a palm needs 4 years to bear fruit. If planted from a seed, a palm needs 8 to 10 years to mature. A palm may grow to 100 feet and live 200 years. The grower who wishes to gather shoots must strip a palm of fruit. The grower who wishes to harvest an abundant crop of dates must remove several shoots. (Removing all shoots will prevent a tree from issuing forth new shoots in subsequent years.) A palm will not produce abundant fruit and shoots simultaneously.

A plant of the desert, the date palm is unusual in tolerating saline soil. Rain may damage dates, so an arid climate is best. The date palm needs full sun and arid conditions, but it is not drought tolerant. From antiquity, humans have irrigated date palms, building irrigation canals or digging wells to tap water underground. The requirement of irrigation made the palm a labor-intensive crop from its earliest days. The planting of a palm was also labor intensive. The grower selected a sucker or shoot from an elite tree, a practice that allowed him to be certain of the traits of the new plant and to know its sex. Digging a hole eight feet deep, he added five feet of a mixture of loose soil and manure. Planting the shoot in a hole that was now three feet, he was able to cultivate it in partial shade. As it grew, the grower filled the hole with soil until he reached the surface of the ground.

There are hundreds of varieties of dates, including the medjool, classified as soft, semidry, and dry. A palm tree may yield 100 to 300 pounds of dates per year. Although a tree of the desert, the date palm tolerates temperatures below freezing. Americans and Europeans consider the date a dessert and import it from the Middle East and North Africa. In 2007, the world produced 7.6 million tons of dates. Egypt was the leader with 1.4 million tons. Iran ranked second with 1.1 million tons, Saudi Arabia was third with 1 million tons, the United Arab Emirates placed fourth with 832,000 tons, and Pakistan ranked fifth with 614,000 tons. The United States was not a leading producer.

The ancients attributed health benefits to dates. First-century CE Roman encyclopedist Pliny the Elder believed that the date treated chest pain and cough and strengthened a person weakened by a long illness. Other ancients used the date to treat anxiety, kidney ailments, and stomach problems. Mohammed (570–632 CE), the founder of Islam, counseled nursing women to eat dates in the belief that the fruit helped them lactate. Mohammed believed that dates protected one from "poison and treachery." Other Arabs believed that the date cured fever, impotence, and other maladies. Oil from the seeds is used in soap and cosmetics.

Scripture, Religious Lore, and Proverbs

So important was the date palm to the Hebrews and early Christians that the Bible contains more than 50 references to it. The Song of Songs likened it to a beautiful woman, and the Psalms asserted that good people would flourish like a date palm. The Gospels record that when Jesus entered Jerusalem the crowd hailed him with date palm leaves, a sign that they regarded him a king. The Koran mentions the date palm 10 times. One passage acknowledged that it was "a sustenance for men, thereby giving life to a dead land. Such shall be the Resurrection." The Koran described the practice of flavoring a beverage with date blossoms.

One Arab proverb held that there were as many types of dates as days in a year. According to lore, Mohammed used dates to determine the identity of an enemy. Confronted by an unknown foe, he examined the date pits in camel dung, recognizing the variety and tracing it to the enemy's city of origin. According to Islamic tradition, the Tree of Life in Genesis was a date palm, which furnished Adam and Eve with their primary food. According to this tradition, God commanded Adam to cut his hair and fingernails, burying them in the ground. From this spot in Eden germinated a date palm, one apparently different from the Tree of Life. Satan, seeing God's work in this date palm, wept. His tears fell to the ground, where the roots of the palm absorbed them, causing it to issue forth the spines that grow at the base of the leaves. Mohammed compared the date palm to humans because both palm and humans were male and female.

According to Islamic legend, Mary, pregnant with Jesus, suffered labor pain so intense that she sought rest under a date palm. From the womb, Jesus commanded her to shake the tree. She obeyed, and even though dates were not then in season, the tree nevertheless showered her with dates. She ate one and her labor pain ceased. According to one Christian legend, an angel holding a date palm leaf came to an aged Mary. Giving her the leaf, he announced that death was near and that a date palm would grow on her grave. Before she died, Mary gave the leaf to the apostle Peter, who forgave sinners by touching them with it. At the moment of contact the leaf expunged their sins.

Origin and History

An Old Word domesticate, the date palm has left fossils in the Mediterranean Basin dating to the Eocene Epoch. No wild palm exists, suggesting the antiquity of cultivation. Wild palms once grew in the region of the Dead Sea, inhabiting lands with brackish water where no other plants lived. According to one authority, humans may have first encountered the date palm in the lower Tigris and Euphrates river valleys of ancient Sumer. Its cultivation dates to 4000 BCE in Sumer. Another authority shifts the origin of date cultivation to Arabia around 6000 BCE, from where it spread to Mesopotamia (now Iraq). Ancient Jericho had so many date palms that it was known as the "City of the Palms." In ancient Babylon, landowners leased land with date palms to tenants in exchange for half the harvest. Babylonians planted date palms at a density of 50 per acre. In the 18th century BCE, the law code of Babylonian king Hammurabi set the fine for cutting down a date palm at 15 ounces of silver, surely a prohibitive amount for the average person. The Babylonians interplanted date palms with sesame, grain, and clover. The delta of the Tigris and Euphrates rivers is today home to some 5 million date palms. In warfare the victors, notably the Assyrians, cut down the date palms of the conquered.

From Mesopotamia, the date palm migrated to North Africa. The Egyptians cultivated it by 3000 BCE. In the 18th dynasty, Egyptian art depicted Pharaoh Thutmose I offering dates to the gods. Today, Egypt has some 10 million date palms. Around the time of Christ, North Africans cultivated the date palm in the Sahara Desert, terming the date the "bread of the desert." Travelers across the desert carried a bag of dates as food for both human and camel. In Algeria, farmers intercropped the date palm with the orange, apricot, nuts and vegetables. From Mesopotamia, the date palm spread to Greece and Rome. The Romans planted date palms in Spain 2000 years ago. Under Muslim rule, the date palm became widespread in Spain.

In 1513, the Spanish attempted to plant the date palm in Cuba, but the Amerindians killed them. This act did not deter Spanish soldier Rodrigo de Tamayo, who founded the town of Datil, meaning date, where he planted date palms and tobacco. The palms did not thrive in Cuba, which is today not an important producer. In the 16th century, Spanish explorer Hernando Cortez introduced the date palm to Mexico. The Spanish attempted to grow it in Florida, but the climate was too humid. In the 18th century, Spanish missionaries planted date palms, derived from Mexican stock, near San Diego, California. In the 19th century, farmers tried again to grow the date palm in Florida, but by the 1830s these efforts had failed. In 1857, rancher J. R. Wolfskill planted date palms in the Sacramento River valley in California. These trees began bearing fruit in 1877. In the 1860s, farmers planted date palms in Yuma, Arizona. These trees began to yield dates in the 1880s. In 1890, the U.S. Department of Agriculture gathered shoots from Egypt, Algeria, and Arabia, planting them in New Mexico, Arizona, and California. In 1900, the Agriculture Department made a second introduction of date palms in Arizona. In 1903 and 1907, farmer Bernard Johnson introduced the date palm to the Coachella Valley in California. In 1912, Johnson made additional plantings in Yuma,

Arizona. By then, Arizona had more date palms than California. Between 1913 and 1923, U.S. farmers sent plant explorers to the Middle East and North Africa to find the best varieties of date palm. After 1913, plantings in the Coachella Valley made California the leading date producer in the United States. Since 1921, the Coachella Valley has hosted an annual date festival in February, attracting 250,000 visitors from the United States and Canada.

In the 20th century, the date was so popular in California that merchandisers sold date shakes and date ice cream, and some still do, including at roadside stands in the Coachella Valley. In the 1960s, however, some growers sold their land to real estate developers. Other growers planted citrus to diversify their income. The growers who survived capitalized on consumers' desire for natural foods. Growers boasted that they did not spray their trees with insecticide, use synthetic fertilizers, or add preservatives to dates because they keep months if stored at low temperature. By the 1970s, the Coachella Valley had 220,000 date palms on 4,400 acres. The rest of the United States had 260 acres of date palms. In 2004, California totaled 4,500 acres of date palm. The rest of the United States totaled fewer than 450 acres.

Christopher Cumo

Further Reading

Barreveld, W. H. *Date Palm Products*. Rome: Food and Agriculture Organization, 1993.

Musselman, Lytton John. *Figs, Dates, Laurel, and Myrrh: Plants of the Bible and the Quran*. Portland, OR: Timber Press, 2007.

Popenoe, Paul. *The Date Palm*. Miami, FL: Field Research Projects, 1973.

Simon, Hilda. *The Date Palm: Bread of the Desert*. New York: Dodd, Mead, 1978.

Zaid, Abdelouahhab, ed. *Date Palm Cultivation*. Rome: Food and Agriculture Organization, 2002.

Dill

Dill is an aromatic plant that is still very much used as a seasoning and for medicinal purposes. This plant is an annual umbellifer with slender 12- to 24-inch-long stems and finely divided leaves. The flowers are white to yellow. It has a characteristic flavor. Within the global food industry, dill, especially the seeds, is widely used for making dill pickles with cucumber. In Scandinavia, the Baltic states and parts of Eastern and Central Europe, dill is a commonly used condiment as a fresh herb in the household and in many different kinds of food. It is also used in the Middle East and India. The Indian dill is sometimes regarded as a separate subspecies, *Anethum graveolens* ssp. *sowa* (Roxburgh ex Fleming) Gupta. It is in common use in the Indian subcontinent, Japan, and Southeast Asia.

Dill is easy to grow in gardens, and it prefers full sun, moderate watering, and rich garden soil. It is propagated from seeds without difficulty. The contemporary use of dill is a more geographically restricted remnant of a cultural plant that once was probably much used in food and as medicine. Its common Germanic name dill is of an old word: *dild* in Danish, *dill* in German and Swedish, *dille* in Dutch, and as a Swedish borrowing *tilli* in Finnish, and was probably in use in the Iron Age in the northern parts of Europe. It has many other names in other languages, such as *aneth* in French, *aneto* in Italian, *anet* in Catalan, *eneldo* in Spanish, *endro* in Portuguese, and as a Portuguese borrowing *ender* in Malay and *inondo* in Japanese. The Roman names are derived from the Greek word for anis. The word "dill" is *ukrop* in Russian, *koper* in Polish, kopar *in* Croatian, *kopur* in Bulgarian, *kopra* in Albanian, *kapor* in Hungarian, and *krop* in Yiddish, which probably developed from a plant name in an ancient language of a Mediterranean civilization, and *dereotu* in Turkish. Both the weed and the seed of this annual herb are used.

Origin and History

Dill appears to have originated in the eastern Mediterranean. A wild and weedy kind of dill is still widespread in the Mediterranean Basin and in western Asia. It is not known when it first began to be cultivated, but early remains of dill have been found in late Neolithic lake shore settlements in Switzerland, a finding that suggests that dill was under cultivation 4,000 years ago. There are also findings from ancient Egypt. Twigs of dill were found in the tomb of Amenhotep II of the 18th dynasty, who ruled from 1426 to 1400 BCE. It is also reported from the seventh century BCE from Heraion of Samos. Fourth-century BCE Greek botanist Theophrastus mentions dill in his writings. Dill is also mentioned in the Bible: "Woe to you, teachers of the law and Pharisees, you hypocrites! You give a tenth of your spices, mint, dill and cumin and have neglected the weightier matters of the law: justice and mercy and faith" (Matthew 23:23). This indicates that it was cultivated as a crop because only cultivated plants were tithed. It was used as a medicinal plant by the Romans.

It is referred to as anetum in the list of herbs in *Capitulare de Villis vel Curtis Imperii* from 812, an edict decreed by Frankish king Charlemagne, and it had probably reached Northern Europe around a century later, although archaeological evidence is lacking before the 13th century in Denmark and Sweden. In the 17th century, it had reached the whole of Europe, and was grown also by European peasantry for medicinal purposes or as a condiment. It is reported also from remote places such as the Faroe Islands in the 1780s. Dill was obviously popular in French cuisine in the 18th century, and was thereby introduced among the upper classes in Scandinavia. It became popular in the food culture of the North and it was there to stay. Veal flavored with dill, later also crayfish, were typical dishes, together with fresh potatoes, also always cooked with dill. Although it seems to have disappeared in many national cooking cultures in southwestern Europe, it has survived and is increasingly popular in the northern and eastern parts of the continent.

Medicinal Plant

The leaves, flowers, and seeds have been used for medicinal purposes. Dill has been used both in scholarly medicine and in traditional folk medicine since ancient times. Papyrus Ebers from 1534 BCE recorded its use in ancient Egypt to relieve headaches. Medieval herbals recommend dill for various diseases and disorders: stomach diseases, headaches, chest pains, and hemorrhoids. Eating the seeds was supposed to be an aphrodisiac for a man. Lactating women were supposed to produce more milk if they ate the seed boiled with flax seed. According to the English physician Nicholas Culpeper's *Complete Herbal* (1653), dill is "good to ease swellings and pains; it also stays the belly and stomach for casting." Within scholarly medicine, dill had earlier been applied as antispasmodic, carminative, detersive, digestive, diuretic, laxative, and sedative.

Dill seeds are common in folk medicine from various parts of the world. For instance, Ozark healers advise dill tea for hiccups, and it is still used as an antihypercholesterolaemic plant in Iranian folk medicine. Since the Renaissance, dill water has been used as a cosmetic and to treat insomnia in various parts of Europe. Woodward's Gripe Water, a kind of dill water introduced in the 1850s, has been used to treat infant colic in Great Britain and other parts of the English-speaking world. The plant is also used in complementary and alternative herbal medicine in many parts of the world. Home remedies with the seeds are prescribed for indigestion, colic, and insomnia. Dill was and to some extent still is also used in ethnoveterinarian therapies in many parts of Europe. The oil extracted from the seeds is said to have special antiseptic properties, and nowadays oil manufactured by the seeds has a revival within herbal medicine. The seed oil contains especially carvone, limonene, and many other substances.

Food and Condiment

The main use in many parts of the world is to flavor pickled food such as cucumber, cabbage, and onion. Especially the seeds are used for this. Fresh and dried dill leaves are widely used in Scandinavia, the Baltic states, Eastern and Central Europe, and southwestern Asia for flavoring purposes. It is used in sauces and stews. In Eastern European borscht, a soup made with beetroot, dill is much used to give flavor. It is also still popular in many central and eastern European immigrant communities in North and South America, including religious enclaves like the Mennonites. *Cacık* or tzatziki, a Turkish and Balkan dish made of diluted yogurt and chopped cucumber, is often seasoned with dill. Dill is also very much used in börek, the Turkish pie stuffed with cheese, hence its local name *börek otu* ("pie plant"). In India, dill seed is one ingredient in some curries. Dill seeds are also commonly used to flavor lentils and bean dishes in Indian cooking.

In Scandinavian cooking, dill is utilized in a wide array of dishes, such as veal (dill-fricassee), mutton, chicken, all kind of fish (including cured salmon and pickled herring), new potatoes, egg dishes, stews, sauces, and bread, and as a flavor in several distilled beverages, for example aquavit. Large quantities of the flowers of dill are a must when cooking crayfish, which is traditionally eaten in Finland and Sweden in August. Although many people grow dill in their gardens, most dill leaves consumed are bought fresh, frozen, dried, or cultivated in pots in common grocery stores. Most dill is produced in commercial greenhouses.

Other Uses

The plant has been used for magical purposes in some parts of Europe. For instance in Denmark, the cattle used to receive a slice of bread with dill and honey as a protection against evil forces. Dill is sometimes used for ornamental purposes. When dried the tall stalks with their seed heads can be used in flower arrangements.

Ingvar Svanberg

Further Reading

Ortan, Alina, Maria-Lidia Popescu, Andreea-Liana Gaita, Cristina Dina-Pïra, and Gh. Câmpeanu. "Contributions to the Pharmacognostical Study on *Anethum graveolens*, Dill (*Apiaceae*)." *Romanian Biotechnological Letters* 14 (2009): 4342–48.

Stannard, Jerry. "The Multiple Uses of Dill (*Anethum graveolens* L.) in Medieval Medicine." In *Gelêrter der arzenîe, ouch apotêker: Festschrift zum 70 Geburtstag von Willem F. Daems*, edited by Gundolf Keil. Pattensen: Horst Wellm Verlag, 1982: 411–24.

E

Ebony

The "tree of music" as it is famously called, ebony is one of the most expensive wood-yielding group of trees in the world. Famous for its hardwood and inability to float, the name ebony is essentially given to a group of plants with these characteristic features. The most prominent feature, however, is that which is related to its name; the wood is black or the darkest wood in the plant world.

Botany

Ebony consists of tropical shrubs or trees that are deciduous. Most belong to the genus *Diospyros*, which is found primarily in India, Sri Lanka, and Africa. A few ebony plants, such as the Texas ebony or the persimmon, grow in warm temperate regions. Heartwood is most often black, but some can also be dark red, green, and black with shades of yellow or orange. The stem contains tannin cells but lacks milky sap. The main root is long and fleshy. Leaves are alternate, oblong, thick, and leathery. Leaves also contain tannin cells. Several species may contain spines. The inflorescence is most often a cymose. Most often the flowers are unisexual. Flowers are actinomorphic, where they can be cut into halves along any plane. Usually there are more male flowers than female. Floral whorls may contain three to seven members each. There are likewise the same numbers of stamens. Female flowers, however, consist of two to eight carpels. The ovary is superior in position. The fruit is a berry, which may contain one to many seeds.

Species

Diospyros ebenum is considered to be the true ebony. It is found in India, Sri Lanka, Malaysia, the Philippines, and Mauritius. The tree is about 90 feet tall with a trunk length of 27 feet above which the canopy of foliage rests. These trees are propagated via stumps or seeds. The fruit, which is gummy, is used as a famine food. This fruit is also a poison for fish. The timber from this tree is one of the best commercialized ebonies in the world, followed by the African ebony. China imports this wood for the making of furniture.

Diospyros melanoxylem is shorter than *Diospyros ebenum*. This ebony shrub grows to a height of 75 feet. Found extensively in India and Pakistan, this tree tolerates frost, grows well in the tropics and mild temperate areas, and is also not fussy about its soil type. Trees grow on elevated, hilly areas as well as they do on the plains. During the hot months they shed their leaves, whereas when the weather cools they sprout evergreen leathery leaves. Flowers sprout in spring or summer. The best viable seeds are produced every other year. Seeds are dispersed with the help of bats and birds. The leaves of the tree are used for wrapping tobacco as in the Indian bidis. This species of *Diospyros* has multiple uses. It is an excellent fodder crop as the pruning of leaves becomes an ideal source of fodder. The twigs and branches burn well and are very good fuel wood. The timber is black heartwood, which is very heavy. This wood is ideal for carving and for fashioning ornamental items. Seeds of this ebony are used in the making of neurological and psychiatric medication for the treatment of mental disorders and mental breakdown. *Diospyros melanoxylon* is also a major species in Africa. The main areas where ebony is cultivated in Africa are Tanzania and Mozambique. In Swahili, this ebony tree is called Mpingo.

Diospyros dignya is an evergreen, deciduous, temperate shrub with a maximum height of 75 feet and found predominantly in Guatemala and Mexico. This species is locally known as the black persimmon. It does not tolerate frost and can grow from sea level to an altitude of 5,600 feet. The trees are tolerant of floods and are not sensitive to varying soil conditions. Propagation of plant is by seeds. However, seedless varieties are also cultured using techniques such as grafting or budding. The pulp of the fruit is sweet and edible. It can be eaten only when ripe or even blended with other fruits and essence to make refreshing beverages. Owing to its easy-to-use fruit pulp, the fruit is also part of desserts, ice creams, fruit salads, cakes, and puddings. When the fruit is unripe, it is not always agreeable to the digestive track, due to its high tannin properties. The bark is extracted for the purpose of making medicines such as analgesics. Timber is a mixture of black and yellow wood, yellow being more dominant. The wood, however, is very hard and compact and does not float in water. It is ideal for making furniture due to its appealing color for home décor. Black persimmon is regarded as a very nutritious fruit, containing high quantities of vitamin C in the ripe fruit, along with calcium and phosphorus.

Diospyros blancoi grows luxuriously in Taiwan, Malaysia, and the Indonesian islands of Java and Sumatra. Growing at altitudes as high as 2,400 feet, this plant can thrive well in a wet, monsoon climate. It is an evergreen tree that grows to a height of 100 feet and with a conical crown. The plant is most progressive when male and female trees are near to each other, and minimal numbers of agents are required to bring about pollination. The fruit is considered to be exotic, and is eaten when ripe. It is also added to salads. The timber is black and heavy as in most ebony species. The trees are also grown as ornamental plants.

The Japanese persimmon, *Diospyros kaki* an ebony species chiefly found in China, Japan, and Vietnam and also in the mountains of Indonesia. It has been transported to other regions too, where it took root in the United States in 1856, in Australia in 1885, and in Palestine in 1912. It can grow on the plains as well as at very high altitudes. Primarily tropical, it has also adapted to warm temperate conditions. The tree may be propagated from seeds and from root suckers. The ripe fruit is highly edible and used in the making of many delectable dishes such as sweets, pies, and jams. Roasted and powdered seeds are substituted for coffee, while the leaves can be brewed into a persimmon tea. The wood is prized for its close grains. Color may range from black with orange, yellow, brown, and gray. Tannin obtained from the leaves and unripe fruit is used in the preservation of the wood. Many kinds of alcoholic beverages are prepared by the fermentation of the fruit.

The Texas ebony, *Ebanopsis ebano*, is a large, stately tree that grows to a height of 135 feet. It is deciduous and xerophytic in nature, thriving well in arid conditions. Texas ebony, as the name implies, is found in Texas and in other southern states such as Florida. While this plant is desert tolerant, giving it additional water during its juvenile phase will hasten its growth. The crown of foliage is usually heavy and full. Pruning not only helps the tree bloom well but also makes it an ideal ornamental plant. Its fruit is not appealing, and hence it can be more of a fodder plant than one with edible fruit. The color of the heartwood is dark red tinged with purple or black.

Pests

There are many pests known to attack the ebony trees. Some species of ebony are more resistant, while others are highly susceptible. Mites, thrips, and stem borers can cause havoc to the plant by either eating the leaves or fruits or eating through the heartwood and boring tunnels. Mealy bugs can be a menace to young shoots, killing the plant even before it has a chance to reach full maturity. The Palo Verde borer is a menace in the larval form as it lays larvae in the soil that can attack the plant, feeding on its root and nutrients for as long as three years before detection. In most cases, the pests can be controlled by the topical use of organic pesticides. However, for the case of larval infestation of the pest, the best options would be to keep the plant well nourished with organic feeds and fertilizers. Many species of ebony are good at fixing nitrogen and accommodate many economically important plants like cardamom to grow in its shade.

The Need for Conservation

Most species of ebony, especially *Diospyros ebenum* and *Diospyros melanoxylem*, are valued for their timber. With dark heartwood, lustrous in look and figure, fine grained, having a smooth finish, ebony in many places, especially in Africa, is on the verge of extinction. In Africa, it is considered to be one of the most expensive trees and is always in danger of being smuggled out of the country. Trees take a very long time to grow and mature, making it difficult to keep pace with logging.

Ebony is also known to survive more as a solitary plant than as a community forest plant. Owing to its excellent timber qualities, color, and finish, ebony has become synonymous with musical instruments such as the piano.

Amanda Mittra

Further Reading

Arizona State University. "Texas Ebony." http://www.public.asu.edu/~camartin/plants/Plant%20html%20files/ebenopsisebano.html (accessed 5 October 2011).

"*Diospyros ebenum*." Biodiversity Diversity and Co-Operation in Taxonomy for Interactive Shared Knowledge Base (BIOTIK). http://www.biotik.org/india/species/d/dioseben/dioseben_en.html (accessed 5 October 2011).

"*Diospyros melanoxylem*." Ebony, Music and Deforestation in East Africa. TED Case Studies No. 636. http://www1.american.edu/ted/ebony.htm (accessed 5 October 2011).

"*Diospyros* species." International Center for Agroforestry. Agro Forestry Tree Database. http://www.worldagroforestrycentre.org/sea/Products/AFDbases/af/asp/SpeciesInfo.asp?SpID=690 (5 October 2011).

University of Arizona, College of Agriculture. Maricopa County Cooperative Extension Home Horticulture. "Environmentally Responsible Gardening & Landscaping in the Low Desert. Palo Verde Borer Beetle." http://ag.arizona.edu/maricopa/garden/html/t-tips/bugs/palo-bor.htm (5 October 2011).

Eggplant

A member of the Nightshade family, eggplant is related to tomato, pepper, potato, tobacco, petunia, and the poisonous belladonna. Apparently aware of its relationship to toxic plants, Europeans were initially wary of eggplant. The word "eggplant" has an affinity with the Indian *vatin-ganah*. In Arabic, eggplant is *al-badinjan*, in Persian *badin-gan*, in Spanish *berenjana*, in Catalan *alberginia*, in French *aubergine*, in Sanskrit *vatingana*, in Italian *melanzana*, and in Greek *melitzana*. In the Middle Ages, Europeans called eggplant the "mad apple" in the belief that it caused insanity. Australians called eggplant "egg fruit," perhaps in appreciation of the fact that eggplant is a fruit rather than a vegetable, though at least one vegetable book includes a section on eggplant. In West Africa, people know eggplant as the "garden egg." The people of the Caribbean know eggplant as "brown jolly." The English word "eggplant" derives from the fruit's reception in England. In contrast to the current purple varieties, the standard varieties of eggplant in the early modern era yielded white fruit that resembled eggs. Italian botanists, apparently aware of the eggplant's kinship with belladonna, called it an "evil unhealthy thing." Confusingly, Europeans called eggplant a "love apple," a phrase they also used to describe the tomato. This language may derive from the belief that both eggplant and tomato were aphrodisiacs. Eggplant was also known as "raging apple." In the 18th century, Swedish naturalist Carl Linnaeus named eggplant *Solanum melongena*. Ninety-three percent water, eggplant has fiber, potassium, magnesium, phosphorus, and folic acid. Four ounces of eggplant have 32 calories. Some medical practitioners believe that eggplant may prevent stroke, bleeding, heart disease, and cancer.

Origin and History

Eggplant traces its lineage to the Old World, a curious circumstance given that the other prominent members of the Nightshade family—potato, tomato, pepper, and tobacco—all originated in the Americas. French botanist Alphonse de Candolle was the first to surmise an Old World origin, writing in 1886 that eggplant originated in Asia. In the 20th century, Russian agronomist Nikolai Vavilov sharpened the focus, pointing to India or Myanmar as the homeland of eggplant. Others have identified Southeast Asia as the cradle of the eggplant. One scholar, eschewing the focus on Asia, proposed that eggplant originated in North Africa.

Eggplant must not have been a promising cultigen in its earliest days. One scientist believes that the ancestor of eggplant bore small, bitter fruit. These traits did not deter humans, who selected eggplant for size and the absence of bitterness. The fact that no wild species of eggplant exists suggests that the plant is an old cultigen, though written records of the crop date to only 500 BCE. Even at this date eggplant may have been an ornamental rather than a food. It seems likely that it is not as ancient as corn, potato, sugarcane, wheat, barley, and several other crops. According to one hypothesis, the Chinese first ate eggplant in the sixth century CE. Chinese women used eggplant to polish their teeth. From China, eggplant may have migrated to Japan, where it was one of the five most important vegetables. Another hypothesis holds that the people of India were the first to eat eggplant. Indians may have gathered wild eggplant around the time of Christ. Having originated in India, according to this hypothesis, eggplant migrated to China and then to Arabia in the fourth century CE. The Arabs featured eggplant in their cuisine. One recipe, known as Iman fainted, paired eggplant and olive oil and concerned an Iman who married the daughter of a wealthy olive oil merchant. She presented her husband with a dowry of 12 jars of olive oil. For the first 12 days of their marriage, she prepared a dish of eggplant and olive oil. On the 13th evening, she did not serve eggplant. The surprised husband inquired about this circumstance. When his wife told him that she had no more olive oil he fainted.

The Greeks and Romans may not have known about eggplant. One hypothesis holds that eggplant reached Europe in the Middle Ages, though another holds that only in the 17th century did eggplant arrive in Europe, having come from North Africa. The second hypothesis cannot be true, because in the 16th century English herbalist John Gerard noted that the people of Spain and Africa ate eggplant. Gerard counseled the reader not to eat eggplant. He was suspicious of its "mischievous quality." Another author warned that eggplant caused depression, leprosy, cancer, headache, and bad breath, turned one's skin black or yellow, and harmed the liver and spleen. In contrast to this negativism, 17th-century English herbalist John Parkinson believed that eggplant was safe. About the 17th century, Europeans introduced eggplant into the American colonies. Americans initially disliked the flavor of eggplant and instead grew it as an ornamental. In the 18th century, Thomas Jefferson, who would later serve as the third president, grew eggplant in his garden. In the Americas, eggplant is grown where the climate is warm. The American South and the Caribbean are regions of cultivation. Although a minor crop, eggplant is today grown in California, Florida, Georgia, New York, and North Carolina.

Attributes and Cultivation

A perennial crop in the tropics, eggplant is an annual in the temperate zone because frost kills it. In temperate locales the gardener may plant seeds, which germinate in 1 to 2 weeks at 70°F to 75°F, 8 to 10 weeks before transplantation in the garden, which should occur 1 to 2 weeks after the last frost. Eggplant may be transplanted in the field 2 weeks after transplanting tomato. One gardener believes that eggplant grows best between 75°F and 80°F. Another favors a temperature between 80°F and 90°F. Among the most heat- and drought-tolerant plants, eggplant does not flourish below 60°F. Temperatures below 50°F may injure flowers. When transplanted in the field, seedlings should be spaced two feet apart. The gardener may add well-rotted manure to the soil at the time of transplantation. One month later a second dressing, fish emulsion or a complete fertilizer, may be added to the soil. Thereafter the gardener may fertilize eggplant every 3 or 4 weeks. The gardener may cover the soil with black plastic to absorb heat and retain moisture. Eggplant should not be planted in soil where tomato, pepper, or potato has been grown. Eggplant needs warm, fertile, well-drained sandy loam. The soil should be slightly acidic, with a pH between 5.5 and 6.5. Eggplant matures roughly 50 to 70 days after transplantation. It is ready to harvest when the fruit's skin is shiny. If one can press the skin with a fingernail and the indentation remains, eggplant is ready to pick. When overripe, the skin becomes dull and brown. The fruit is bitter when overripe. A plant produces four to six fruit but yields more if harvested frequently. The fruit may be as large as a watermelon or as small as a marble. Most varieties are purple, though others may be white, yellow, green, red, or lavender. Eggplant does not store well and should be eaten within a few days of harvest. Because the fruit should not be stored below 45°F, it may not be suitable for refrigeration.

Cultivars

Little Spooky has white fruit that must resemble a ghost. The Japanese on Hokkaido Island once grew Little Spooky to banish evil spirits and to ensure a bountiful harvest. Three-foot-tall plants yield fruit 7 inches long and 3 inches wide. The New Hampshire Agricultural Experiment Station released Applegreen in 1964. The fruit is green like the Granny Smith apple, a resemblance that must give the variety its name. Applegreen matures early enough for cultivation in the northern United States. Unusual in tolerating light frost, Thai Green has lime green fruit that elongates to 12 inches. The variety matures in 80 days. Dating to 1902, Black Beauty is among the most popular cultivars. Fruit should be picked when small to ensure the best flavor. As a rough guide, Black Beauty is ready to harvest 74 days after transplantation. Plants grow to three feet. Louisiana Long Green is known as Green Banana because the fruit resembles an unripe banana. Plants reach three feet in height and bear fruit 8 inches long. Plants should be staked to keep fruit off the ground. Rosa Bianca, a variety popular in Italy, bears white fruit with streaks of lavender or purple. The variety matures in 80 days. Casper matures in 70 days and is suitable for a short growing season. Consumers have likened the flavor of Casper to mushroom. Southern Exposure Seed Exchange discovered Turkish Italian Orange, a Turkish variety, in Italy, introducing it into the United States in 1990. Plants reach four feet in height and yield abundantly. Fruit is most flavorful when picked green. When the skin turns red orange, the fruit is overripe.

Seed Savers Exchange introduced Diamond, a Ukrainian variety, into the United States in 1993. Diamond bears purple fruit that matures in 70 to 80 days. Two-foot plants bear nine-inch fruit. Maturing in 72 days, White Egg is named for the color of its unripe skin. When ripe the skin turns yellow. The United Kingdom has grown White Egg since the 16th century.

Christopher Cumo

Further Reading

Coulter, Lynn. *Gardening with Heirloom Seeds: Tried-and-True Flowers, Fruits, and Vegetables for a New Generation.* Chapel Hill: University of North Carolina Press, 2006.

Heiser, Charles B., Jr. *The Fascinating World of the Nightshades: Tobacco, Mandrake, Potato, Tomato, Pepper, Eggplant, Etc.* New York: Dover, 1987.

Kehayan, Nina. *Essentially Eggplant.* Tucson, AZ: Fisher Books, 1996.

London, Sheryl. *Eggplant and Squash: A Versatile Feast.* New York: Atheneum, 1976.

McNamee, Gregory. *Movable Feasts: The History, Science, and Lore of Food.* Westport, CT: Praeger, 2007.

Parsons, Russ. *How to Pick a Peach: The Search for Flavor from Farm to Table.* Boston: Houghton Mifflin, 2007.

Singh, P. K., S. K. Dasgupta, and S. K. Tripathi, eds. *Hybrid Vegetable Development.* Binghamton, NY: Food Products Press, 2004.

Elderberry

Sambucus is a genus of an ornamental and fruit-bearing shrub commonly called elderberry or elder. There are between 5 and 30 species of *Sambucus*, which belongs in the moschatel family, Adoxaceae, according to 18th-century Swedish naturalist Carl Linnaeus. The elderberry is native to both the Northern and Southern Hemispheres with temperate and subtropical climates. The shrub is primarily found in the Northern Hemisphere, however, and is limited to parts of South America and Australasia in the Southern Hemisphere.

Appearance

Some common cultivated species of elderberry include *Sambucus nigra* (black elder), *Sambucus canadensis* (American elder or common elderberry), *Sambucus javanica* (Chinese elder), *Sambucus melancarpa* (blackberry elder), and *Sambucus racemosa* (red-berried elder). The *Sambucus nigra* is found in the temperate zones of North America and Europe. The white flowers of the black elder grow in clusters that are flat topped and produce berries that are a deep blue to black. The shrubs are large—about 10 to 26 feet tall—and have a stem diameter of 12 to 24 inches. The leaves are mainly deciduous and are typically 6 to 10 inches long. The wood of the elder is soft and pithy but becomes hard with age, and the bark is thin and either gray or dark brown.

Elderberries (Jolanta Dabrowska/ Dreamstime.com)

Uses

For centuries, the elderberry has been used as a remedy mainly for two types of ailments—wounds and respiratory illnesses. It is used as a cold and flu treatment in many countries today, including in Panama in 1995, where it was distributed to curb a flu epidemic there. Many cultures have praised the ability of elder flowers and berries to reduce mucous membrane swelling, particularly in the sinuses, and to relieve nasal congestion. Elder may also have other healing properties, including as an anti-inflammatory, antiviral, and anticancer treatment. It has also been used to improve vision, lower cholesterol, and aid in heart health and diabetes. Elderberries contain organic pigments, including tannin, amino acids, carotenoids, sugar, rutin, vitamins A, B, and C, and flavonoids, which have antioxidant properties and may help repair cells.

Elderberry's importance as a healing agent has been evident for centuries. In Europe during the Middle Ages, elderberry was considered a "Holy Tree" and known for its capabilities to restore health and prolong life. Germans turned elderberry into a broth for soup, and in England it was made into syrup and used as a diuretic. Native Americans valued elder fruit for food and dye, and the wood of the elder was turned into combs, pegs, baskets, and arrow shafts. The hollow stems of the shrub were fashioned into whistles, flutes, and blowguns. The Native Americans also used the *Sambucus canadensis* as an astringent, laxative, and diuretic, and to promote perspiration. Its leaves were crushed and used to repel insects. The Choctaw, of what is now the southeastern United States, pounded elder leaves and mixed them with salt to use as a headache remedy. The northeastern Mohegans made a tea of elder flowers and gave it to babies to ease colic.

Written evidence of the elder's medicinal benefits include the writings of the English diarist John Evelyn (1620–1706), who labeled the tree as a universal healing agent in *The Anatomie of the Elder*. From 1831 to 1905, the U.S. Pharmacopoeia, the United States nongovernmental agency that sets the standards for prescription and over-the-counter drugs, mentioned the medicinal values of flowers of the sweet and European elder.

Despite its appeal and renown as a folk remedy, elder carries a serious health warning in the United States. Because it contains cyanogenic gludosides, substances that release the poison cyanide, elder has been listed in the American Medical Association's *AMA Handbook of Poisonous Injurious Plants* and carries a warning of the danger associated with its roots, stems, and leaves.

Elderberry in History and Folklore

Evidence that the elder dates back to the Stone Age has surfaced in recent years, and recorded evidence of the elder's existence dates back to 23 to 79 CE, when the Roman encyclopedist Pliny the Elder wrote of the most sonorous horns being made from elder branches. Today, an Italian musical pipe called a *sampogna* is still made from the branches of the elder.

The Central and Eastern Europeans feature the elder in their folklore and superstitions. For one, it was believed to ward off evil and to protect its bearer from witches' spells. As a result, it became part of wedding and funeral ceremonies. It symbolized good luck at weddings, and branches were buried with the dead to protect the deceased from evil spirits. The cross that Jesus carried to his crucifixion is believed to have been made from a giant elder. Possibly because of this, European Gypsies believed in its sanctity and refused to burn elder branches to kindle campfires. In popular culture, the most powerful wand in the Harry Potter series of books by J. K. Rowling is made of elder. The Elder Wand appears prominently in the final installation of the series, *Harry Potter and the Deathly Hallows.*

The Danes believed that the elder had a magical significance. Legend goes that a wood nymph named Hylde-Moer, a tree mother, lived in elder trees and watched over them. If the elder was cut down and used for furniture, Hylde-Moer would remain with the wood and haunt the owners.

The Significance of Elder and Elderberry

Elderberry is valuable as an ornamental shrub and for its fruit. The fruit of *Sambucus nigra* is used in the production of juice, wine, candy, baked goods, jellies, jams, and preservatives. Some elderberry fruit is toxic, such as that of the *Sambucus racemosa*, the red-berried elder, and must be cooked before eating.

Elder is popular as a stream bank stabilizer. Animals also make use of the shrub as a habitat, for protection, and as a nesting place for birds. Squirrels and other rodents also feed on the fruit and leaves. Elderberry is a favorite fruit of bears. While deer, elk, and moose browse the stems and leaves. Browsing especially occurs in the fall when the leaves turn from a sweet spring and summer leaf to one more agreeable to these animals.

Rosemarie Boucher Leenerts

Further Reading

"The Deathly Hallows." Harry Potter Lexicon. http://www.hp-lexicon.org/magic/deathly _hallows.html#elder_wand (accessed 10 May 2011).

Elderberry (Sambucus nigra). "Elderberry Benefits." http://www.herbwisdom.com/ herb-elderberry.html (accessed 9 April 2011).

Medical Museum. "Elderberry: *Sambucus canadensis.*" University of Iowa Hospitals and Clinics. http://www.uihealthcare.com/depts/medmuseum/galleryexhibits/natures pharmacy/elderberryplant/elderberry.html (accessed 9 April 2011).

USDA Plant Guide. "Common Elderberry." http://plants.usda.gov/plantguide/pdf/cs _sanic4.pdf (accessed 9 April 2011).

Elm

A source of timber, elm is an ancient tree, probably having colonized Europe, Asia, and the Americas before the advent of humans. A tree of the temperate and tropical Northern Hemisphere, elm is in the Ulmaceae family and *Ulmus* genus. *Ulmus* is Latin for elm. "Elm" is an Anglo Saxon word, though the Anglo Saxons also used the word "wice" for elm. The Germans named elm *elm* or *wieke*. The people of the Jutland peninsula used the term "elm" to refer to the tree.

Attributes

The elm has colonized large areas of the Northern Hemisphere. The tree appears as far north as Scotland, southern Finland, northern and central Russia, and Central Asia. Farther south one may find the elm in Turkey, Lebanon, Israel, Iran, Afghanistan, the Himalayas, China, Korea, Japan, Malaysia, the Indonesian islands of Sumatra, Sulawesi, and Flores, Algeria, the eastern United States, Mexico, Central America, and Colombia.

Elm flowers are perfect, each bearing anther and stigma. Young branches do not bear flowers. A branch must be seven or eight years old to flower. Wind disperses pollen, cross-pollinating flowers. Because wind can carry pollen great distances, elms may crossbreed in widely separated locales. Because anther and stigma develop at different times, a flower cannot self-pollinate. A flower remains open 4 to 18 days, during which it is receptive to pollen. Honeybees visit elm flowers and may pollinate them, though wind is the principal pollinator. In the subtropics, elms flower in autumn and in the temperate zone in spring. Where the weather is too cold, flowers will not pollinate. In addition to sexual reproduction, elms propagate vegetatively through suckers.

Origin and History

Ulmaceae has genera in the Old and New Worlds. *Ulmus* separated from the related genus *Zelkova* before the Americas broke apart from Eurasia. The elm colonized eastern Asia and Alaska 80 million years ago and was abundant in Europe by 40 million years ago, possibly being more diverse than it is now. The elm has evolved little since the Miocene Epoch, 23 to 5 million years ago. During the ice ages, the elm retreated toward the equator, recolonizing northern latitudes in interglacial periods. As temperatures rose, birch and pine recolonized the north first. Elm, requiring a warmer climate, came later. The elm was widespread in Europe until about 5000 BCE, when its numbers began to dwindle. Humans may have been responsible for this decline, clearing land for farming. Elms may have been vulnerable because they grew on calcareous soil, which humans desired for their crops. Humans may have defoliated trees, feeding the leaves to livestock. Although elm leaves are not particularly nutritious, the practice of feeding them to livestock has a long history.

Fourth-century BCE Greek philosopher Aristotle and Roman agricultural writer Cato the Elder (234–149 BCE) mentioned the practice of feeding elm leaves to livestock. The Chinese, Japanese, and Indians fed elm leaves to livestock. It may be possible that the elm suffered from disease after 5000 BCE, much as it has suffered from Dutch elm disease since the 20th century.

The decline of elm left concentrations of trees in Northern Europe, notably in southern Norway, southern and central Sweden, Denmark, northern Germany, southern Finland, the Baltic, and northern and central Russia. South of this region elm established itself in the Ardennes Forest in Belgium, the Vonges, the Pyrenees Mountains that border France and Spain, the Cantabrian Mountains of northern Spain, Thuringia and the Black Forest in Germany, the Alps, the Carpathian Mountains of Central and Eastern Europe, and the Balkans. The elms that flourish in Great Britain may owe their establishment there to human migration.

Uses

From an early date, humans prized elm for its toughness, resistance to splitting, and elasticity. Elms grown on light, stony soil produced particularly tough wood. Having selected a tree for use, humans traditionally cut it down on November 1, All Saints' Day. The first use of elm was to make bows. Humans preferred yew for this technology but used elm when yew was unavailable. The fashioning of bows from elm was established in the Mesolithic Age (10,000–3000 BCE) in Denmark. Elm was also used to make crude swords, javelins, spears, and shields, though metal supplanted the wood. Humans used elm to make carts, wagons and chariots. Because elm resisted splitting, it was favored in the making of the hub for a spoked wheel. Oak was preferred for the spokes. The rim was elm or ash. Humans have eaten the inner bark of the elm in times of famine. The Norwegians and Russians made elm bark bread. First-century CE Greek physician Dioscorides recommended elm leaves as a vegetable. In Europe, monks ate elm leaves.

Humans also made elm into bowls and containers, though some people claimed that elm, when used as a receptacle for alcohol, tainted the flavor. In the Middle Ages, sycamore replaced elm as a wood for bowls, containers, and receptacles. Since Roman times, humans had made plows of elm. In the 20th century, the United Kingdom used the elm to make the moldboard of a plow. Farmers preferred elm to metal on heavy soil because clay did not stick to elm whereas it clung to metal. The Romans recorded the use of elm branches to beat slaves.

Elm was used as the headstock of a bell because only elm could withstand the stress of a swinging bell. In the Middle Ages, coffins were made of elm. English queen Elizabeth I (1533–1603) was buried in an elm coffin overlaid with oak. In later centuries, the rich preferred oak, though the middle class continued to be buried in elm. In the Middle Ages, elm was used as the gunstock of firearms because the recoil did not damage the wood. In England and France, the military planted elm so it would have sufficient wood for gunstock. Since the Middle Ages, carpenters have used elm to make floors and stairs, though again the wealthy preferred oak. Elm was used to make chairs and tables. Europeans made waterwheels of elm and oak. Water pumps were made of elm. Elm was sometimes used to make boats, though oak was preferred for large ships. The Arikara of the Great Plains used elm as the fuel for firing pottery. Elm was desirable for this purpose because it burned slowly and steadily. The Yule log of Christmas was elm. The Amerindians of the eastern United States used elm bark for the roof of their houses.

Dioscorides recommended the topical use of elm to heal wounds and fractures. The Anglo Saxons boiled elm bark in urine or milk, applying it topically to heal wounds and shingles. The drinking of a concoction of inner bark and wine loosened mucus in the chest, according to Dioscorides. An extract from the gall of an elm tree was used as lotion, he mentioned. Others have thought elm useful in treating sore throat, increasing perspiration and urine, reducing fever, and improving muscle tone. Italians used elm to treat rheumatism, and in Bulgaria it was used to stop bleeding. First-century CE Roman encyclopedist Pliny the Elder recommended the rubbing of elm leaves on the feet to relieve soreness. Rubbed on the head, elm sap was reputed to regrow hair. One Roman author recommended a mixture of inner bark and ocean water to relieve gout. Wine that contained elm leaves was thought to relieve cough. In the 17th century, the English used elm sap to improve the function of the liver.

Dutch Elm Disease

Dutch elm disease has been the most serious threat to the elm in modernity. In the early 20th century, the fungus *Ophiostoma ulmi* caused the first outbreak of the disease. The fungus blocks the xylem vessels, causing trees to wilt. The elm bark beetle transmits the fungus. The disease spread from ailing to healthy trees in Europe, Asia, and North America. The first outbreak began in northwestern Europe, spreading east to southwestern Asia and west to the United Kingdom and North America, where it arrived about 1927 on imported timber. In the 1930s, the disease spread from Europe to central Asia. The first outbreak killed thousands of elm trees in Europe, Asia, and North America, though the disease abated in Europe during the 1940s. In this decade, the fungus *Ophiostoma novo-ulmi* caused the second and more virulent outbreak. The second outbreak centered in Eastern Europe and the Great Lakes of North America. In Europe the disease spread west, reaching the Netherlands about 1975 and east into southwestern and Central Asia. In North America, the second outbreak reached the east and west coasts in the 1980s. From North America, a strain of the fungus crossed the Atlantic, infecting elm trees in the United Kingdom, the Netherlands, France, and Spain. The disease killed millions of elms in the United Kingdom alone.

Christopher Cumo

Further Reading

Dunn, Christopher P., ed. *The Elms: Breeding, Conservation, and Disease Management.* Boston: Kluwer Academic, 2000,

Richens, Richard H. *Elm.* Cambridge: Cambridge University Press, 1983.

Endive

Endive belongs to the *Chicoricum* genus of the Asteraceae or Daisy family (formerly called Compositae). Three products used for human consumption are derived from this plant: roots, leafy greens (for example escarole, frisee, and radicchio), and Belgian endive. Two species used in a variety of cuisines are referred to as endive, which can lead to some confusion. *Cichorium intybus* includes the varieties of Belgian endive (also known by its Flemish name *witloof*) as well as radicchio, both of which are eaten raw or cooked. Endives derived from the species *Chicorium endivia*, with the varieties frisee (curly) and escarole (broadleaf), are commonly used as a salad greens. Both species are traditional horticultural crops and very popular vegetables in Europe, where most endive is produced. Belgian endive is particularly appreciated in France, Belgium, and the Netherlands, while radicchio is most popular in Italy, explaining its other popular name, "Italian chicory." The popularity of endive in North America is somewhat smaller. Endive is grown exclusively for human consumption, but can also be fed in small quantities to rodent pets such as rabbits or guinea pigs. Just like lettuce, endives form heads of leaves because of stunted stem growth. The internodes, that is, the parts of the stem between leaf-producing nodes, do not elongate so that the sequential nodes sit very close together.

The two *Chicorium* species from which today's cultivars have been bred are common wild plants in Europe, North Africa, and portions of Asia. It has been speculated that the green leaves of the wild plants were used as a salad green by the ancient Egyptians, Greeks, and Romans. Chicory roots and leaves have also played a role in many different traditions of Asian and European folk medicine. European scholars in the 16th century were the first to describe cultivation of endive.

Belgian Endive

Belgian endive was first grown and bred in Belgium in the 19th century. Whereas the leafy green endives are grown from seeds, Belgian endive is first grown from seed, but then produced by digging up the roots, removing the leaves, and forcing the defoliated roots to produce a head of leaves. This is achieved through a cold treatment. The heads are then grown in darkness, a process referred to as blanching. The roots were traditionally covered in straw to avoid excessive light exposure. Today, roots are mostly planted in dark chambers called forcing chambers in hydroponic culture, that is, without soil. The production of Belgian endive is thus rather labor intensive, as it involves many steps.

This peculiar production method is said to have been discovered by either a Belgian farmer or a gardener in the Brussels Botanic Garden who forgot some chicory roots in the cellar and later found them to have sprouted oval-shaped heads of tightly packed, whitish leaves that could be used for cooking or in salads. This type of head is called a chicon. The white color of the chicons is caused by the lack of light during development, which keeps the plants from synthesizing the green pigment chlorophyll. Growing the plants in darkness also prevents them from producing certain bitter-tasting chemicals, which would spoil their taste and economic value. For storage, the chicons again must be kept in darkness to prevent them from turning bitter. Even then, the core of the chicons, that is the stem region, remains bitter. Cutting out the core is therefore the first step to cook or prepare endive as a salad.

Radicchio and Leafy Green Endives

Radicchio as well as escarole and frisee endive are mostly produced in northern Italy. The growing conditions of escarole and frisee are similar to those of lettuce. The frisee varieties are cold-sensitive and therefore used for summer cropping. The more robust broad-leaved types tolerate cold and grow well in winter. Both forms come in various shades from almost yellow to deep green. Radicchio is usually planted in late spring or early summer to avoid cold spells that would induce early head formation. Growers often plant several cultivars sequentially, to cover a range of cold requirements for head formation. These cultivars will mature and be ready for harvest at different times during late autumn and winter.

Radicchio exists in forcing and nonforcing varieties. Nonforcing radicchio will form a head under normal growing conditions, while forcing varieties must undergo a cold treatment similar to that described for Belgian endive. The plants are covered during head formation to avoid chlorophyll synthesis.

Radicchio leaves are bright red and have a bitter taste. In North America, they are mostly used to add color to mixed salads, while in Italy they are used in cooked dishes such as risotto.

Breeding and Improvement

Traditional endive cultivars were produced by mass selection. That is, farmers propagated plants from a mix of seeds from desirable individuals. Many land varieties therefore exist that have been developed over generations. As endive is not a vegetable of major economic importance, little research is done on its genetic properties. Breeding now mostly happens in seed companies, although there are still some farmers who breed their own endive varieties. For Belgian endive, many hybrid cultivars have been developed. This is possible because *Chicorium intybus* is mostly cross-pollinating. *Chicorium endiva*, on the other hand, has a strong tendency toward self-pollination.

No genetically modified endive is on the market at this time, and it is unlikely that a system to genetically engineer endive will be developed in the near future due to its lack of economic importance. Breeding goals for endive are the goals associated with most agricultural crops: improved yield, marketable taste, and appearance, and disease and stress resistance.

Kerstin Müller

Further Reading

Ryder, E. J. *Lettuce, Endive and Chicory*. New York: CABI, 1998.

Lucchin, M., S. Varotto, G. Barcaccia, and P. Parrini. "Chicory and Endive." In *Handbook of Plant Breeding: Vegetables I*, edited by J. Prohens and F. Nuez, 3–48. New York: Springer.

Eucalyptus

The genus *Eucalyptus*, native to Australia, has more than 800 species. The term *Eucalyptus* derives from two Greek words: *eu*, meaning "well," and *calyptus*, meaning "covered," a reference to the cap that covers the stamens of the *Eucalyptus* flower. A eucalypt is a *Eucalyptus* tree, though the terms "eucalypt" and *Eucalyptus* are sometimes used as synonyms. Having many uses, the *Eucalyptus* tree is cultivated for timber, pulp, fuel, and oil. In the 18th and 19th centuries, *Eucalyptus* oil was used as disinfectant, solvent, and medicine. The oil is used to treat the common cold, cough, congestion, sports injuries, muscle and joint pain, and insect bites. *Eucalyptus* oil is an ingredient in shampoo, soap, lotion, and cleaning products. More than 1 percent of the weight of a *Eucalyptus* leaf is oil in commercial varieties. The most desirable oil is rich in the chemicals cineole, piperitone, and citronellal. The aborigines of Australia used *Eucalyptus* wood and bark to make canoes, spears, boomerangs, bowls, and dishes. They used the roots and leaves as medicine. The European settlers of Australia used *Eucalyptus* wood to make buildings and fences and for fuel. Brazil and South Africa planted *Eucalyptus* trees along railroad lines to provide locomotives with fuel. Indians and Ethiopians used *Eucalyptus* wood for fuel and housing. Indians plant the *Eucalyptus* tree as a windbreak on the border of their property. Indians plant *Eucalyptus tereticornis*, known as *Eucalyptus* hybrid or the Mysore gum tree, for pulp and paper and other species for firewood. The production of *Eucalyptus* oil is a minor activity in India. Today, *Eucalyptus* yields timber, plywood, fiberboard, pulp for paper and rayon, poles, firewood, charcoal, oil, honey, and shade.

Geography, Botany, and Cultivation

Eucalyptus is a tree of the tropics and subtropics. In 1995, farmers worldwide planted millions of acres of *Eucalyptus*. The tropics accounted for more than the largest portion of acreage, with tropical Asia in the lead, followed by the tropical Americas. India and Brazil totaled millions of acres of *Eucalyptus*. Australia, Chile, China, Morocco, Portugal, South Africa, and Spain all had hundreds of thousands of acres of *Eucalyptus*. Thailand and Vietnam have recently planted *Eucalyptus* trees in large numbers. Because *Eucalyptus* grows rapidly, maturing in 5 to 10 years, farmers plant it for a quick profit. Just four species—*Eucalyptus camaldulensis*, *Eucalyptus globulus*, *Eucalyptus grandis*, and *Eucalyptus tereticornis*—are the world's chief plantation trees.

The first humans to settle Australia doubtless discovered *Eucalyptus*, though the moment of discovery is lost to history. Neglecting the achievement of the Australian aborigines, Europeans claimed to have discovered the *Eucalyptus* tree. In the 1770s, British captain James Cook and Sir Joseph Banks found *Eucalyptus* in their exploration of Australia. In 1788, the year that Europeans settled Australia, oil was first distilled from *Eucalyptus* leaves. Although more than 100 species of *Eucalyptus* yield oil, only about 12 are cultivated for this purpose. The species *Eucalyptus globulus*, *Eucalyptus exserta*, *Eucalyptus polybrastus*, *Eucalyptus smithii*, *Eucalyptus citriodora*, and *Eucalyptus divas* are the chief oil producers. Of these species, Victoria and Tasmania have cultivated *Eucalyptus globulus*, whose oil contains 60–70 percent cineole, since the late 19th century. In Australia, *Eucalyptus* covers millions of acres from temperate Tasmania to tropical Queensland. *Eucalyptus* is also found in the tropics of Indonesia, Papua New Guinea, and the Philippines. In the 17th century, the Portuguese brought *Eucalyptus* seeds, perhaps from Indonesia, to Brazil.

In 1788, German botanist Joseph Gaertner was the first to classify *Eucalyptus*, though he put it in the genus *Metroideros*. That year French botanist Charles Louis

L'Héitlier de Bratalle of the British Museum of Natural History, working with a specimen from Cook's third voyage, named the genus *Eucalyptus*, the name that is the current genus. Further explorations followed, and by 1867, British botanist George Bentham of the Royal Botanic Garden at Kew, United Kingdom, could count 135 species of *Eucalyptus*. By 1934, Australian botanist William Faris Blakely of the Royal Botanic Garden at Sydney, Australia, could count 606 species.

In 1890, Italy introduced *Eucalyptus* trees into China. Of the more than 300 species brought to China, only one-third have survived. Today, China cultivates fewer than 10 species of *Eucalyptus*. Initially, the Chinese planted *Eucalyptus* as an ornamental and for shade. They planted trees in gardens, near schools and colleges, in pristine spots, and along roads. The Chinese grew *Eucalyptus* because it matured rapidly and tolerated infertile soil. In the 1950s, China established *Eucalyptus* plantations and in 1958 began extracting oil from leaves. Today China, with 1 billion *Eucalyptus* trees, is the world's largest producer of *Eucalyptus* oil. The Chinese have planted *Eucalyptus* in the provinces of Guangdong, Guangxi, Hainan, Fujan, Yunnan, Sichuan, Guizhou, Hunan, Hubei, Jiangxi, Zhajiang, Jiangsu, Shenghai, Anhui, Shenxi, and Gangsu. Ninety percent of China's plantations are in Guangdong, Guangxi, Hainan, and Yunnan. On Hainan Island, farmers interplant *Eucalyptus* and pineapple. In southeastern China, *Eucalyptus* is intercropped with tobacco or sweet potato. The people of Taiwan also plant *Eucalyptus*.

In the late 18th century, Tippu Sultan, the ruler of Mysore, introduced *Eucalyptus* into India. Favoring the tree as an ornamental, he obtained 16 species from France. In the 1950s, a fungal disease swept through *Casuarina* forests, opening land to *Eucalyptus*. In the 1960s, India planted *Eucalyptus tereticornis* in large numbers. Indians prized this species because it grew rapidly, was impervious to the attempts of cattle to feed on it, adapted to varying environments, and was suitable for fuel and housing. So popular is *Eucalyptus* that some Indians fear that farmers may grow it at the expense of crops.

Species

Eucalyptus citriodora is widely planted in Australia and in other countries as a source of oil. A subtropical tree, it flourishes in southern Australia. A tall, straight tree with smooth bark, the species is known as the lemon-scented gum tree because the citronellal in its oil exudes an odor of lemon. The oil is an ingredient in mosquito repellant. China, India, and Brazil cultivate the lemon-scented gum tree. The world's primary source of *Eucalyptus* oil, *Eucalyptus globulus* is known as the southern blue gum tree. Widely cultivated worldwide, the tree grows tall and straight and has smooth bark. The species is native to southeastern Australia, where rainfall is abundant. China, Spain, Portugal, India, Argentina, Brazil, and

Chile cultivate the tree. Known as the blue-leaved mallee, *Eucalyptus polybractus* is the chief oil species in Australia, which is alone in using this tree for oil. A short tree, the species tolerates little rain and infertile soil. With rough bark, the leaves of *Eucalyptus polybractus* are blue or gray green. A plantation tree, the blue-leaved mallee is grown in West Wyalong in western New South Wales and in Inglewood in northern Victoria. Tall and straight, *Eucalyptus smithii*, the gally gum tree, is grown in southeastern Australia, notably in the plains and valleys of New South Wales. South Africa grows the species for timber, though in eastern Transvaal *Eucalyptus smithii* yields oil. A small tree native to the Cape York Peninsula in Queensland, *Eucalyptus staigerriana*, like *Eucalyptus citriodora*, yields lemon-scented oil. Brazil, Guatemala, the Seychelles Islands, and the Congo cultivate the species. The most widespread species in Australia, *Eucalyptus camaldulensis*, the river red gum tree, is cultivated worldwide in the tropics and subtropics. With smooth bark, the leaves of this species are green, blue-green, or yellow-green. Seeds are yellow or yellow-brown. An ornamental cultivated in southern Australia, *Eucalyptus cinerea*, the argyle apple, has red-brown rough bark. Australia once cultivated this species for oil, a practice that is current in Zimbabwe. A small tree native to western Australia, *Eucalyptus kochii*, the oil mallee, has rough bark. Its blue-green leaves in youth turn green as the tree ages. A small tree native to but uncommon in New South Wales, *Eucalyptus olida* has rough bark. The blue-green leaves of youth turn green or gray-green in maturity.

Christopher Cumo

Further Reading

Coppen, John J. W. *Eucalyptus: The Genus Eucalyptus*. London: Taylor & Francis, 2002.

Eldridge, Ken, John Davidson, Chris Harwood, and Gerrit van Wyk. *Eucalypt Domestication and Breeding*. Oxford: Clarendon Press, 1994.

Penfold, A. R., and J. L. Willis. *The Eucalypts: Botany, Cultivation, Chemistry and Utilization*. London: Leonard Hill, 1961.

F

Fennel

In *Hamlet*, English dramatist William Shakespeare wrote, "There's fennel for you and columbines," when Ophelia started handing out flowers and herbs. In Shakespeare's time, fennel conveyed "flattery," and Ophelia was flattering King Claudius. Fennel has had a long history, though most of it does not have to do with the theater. The herb has gained fame as a culinary and medicinal plant.

Fennel is native to Southern Europe and is cultivated in North America, Asia, and Egypt. Fennel was grown in colonial New England, and one can view fennel in the gardens of colonial Williamsburg in Virginia. In fact, fennel can grow almost anywhere in a warm, sunny place. It grows rapidly in southern exposures on slopes and terrace, often invading cultivated areas.

The genus is *Foeniculum* and the family Apiaceae (Umbelliferae). There are two types of fennel: *Foeniculum vulgare*, known as common or wild fennel, and *Foeniculum vulgare dulce*, known as sweet fennel, Florence fennel, and finocchio. *Foeniculum vulgare* can grow up to six feet tall with green-blue foliage. In the spring, feathery shoots appear, and in late summer and autumn yellow umbel flowers are produced. Fennel can help landscapers provide privacy because it is used as a screening plant due to its rapid growth. There is, however, a bronze variety of *Foeniculum vulgare*, a smaller, less vigorous type, growing to about three to five feet, which is considered the most ornamental variety. Fennel is also known for its suitability for home and restaurant dining where its stalks and seeds are used.

Florence fennel produces a swollen leaf base, which is eaten as a vegetable. This bulb has overlapping stem bases packed around a small, central core. It can be eaten raw or cooked. Fennel tastes somewhat like anise or licorice. When you bite into it raw, the anise flavor is well defined. When you cook the herb, the flavor is more subdued.

Fennel has a long folklore history. Fennel tea was used to cure colic in babies, as a breath freshener while gargling, and as an eyewash. The Greeks referred to fennel as *marathon* after the celebrated battle of Marathon in 490 BC was fought on a field of fennel. It is said that the Greeks used fennel to treat more than 20 different illnesses. The Romans included fennel seeds in seasoning mixtures of herbs and spices. The Frankish emperor Charlemagne is said to have introduced the herb into Central Europe by ordering it to be planted in the gardens of monasteries. Mediaeval herbalists said that fennel seed "comforteth the stomach." In those

Fennel (Darko Plohl/Dreamstime.com)

times, people were said to have kept fennel seeds handy to snack on through long church services. On fast days, the seeds were considered appetite suppressants. Yet there is evidence that fennel stimulates the appetite and aids digestion. In the Middle Ages, fennel was a favorite stewing herb and added to food that was not fresh to make it palatable. The Anglo-Saxons used fennel in their cooking and medicinal procedures before the Norman Conquest. According to some sources, the Anglo-Saxons believed fennel gave courage and virility to those who used it. In the 1600s, fennel was eaten along with fish and meat to aid digestion. Fennel was woven into the winners' crowns in athletic events. Early Hindus and Chinese used it as an antidote to snake and scorpion bites, and it was hung over doorways to repel evil spirits. In superstitious times, some people hung branches of fennel in the home to protect from evil spirits. In addition, those who were afraid of ghosts stuffed the keyholes of their doors with fennel seed. Victorian traditions used herbs and flowers to express emotions, and fennel was used as a symbol of praise. Although fennel and aniseeds are similar in appearance and taste, they come from different plants. Seeds from Florence fennel have a mild anise flavor, while those from aniseeds, which come from the parsley family, are native to the Middle East and taste stronger than fennel seeds. In the past, fennel was used in homemade cough syrups.

Medicinal Uses

Hippocrates believed that our health depended on balancing four elements: fire, water, earth, and air contained in our bodies. When the balance was upset, restoring it was through several methods, including using plants such as fennel along with parsley and thyme and celery. Fennel has been used to treat inflammations of the eyelids and conjunctivitis. Fennel has been used as a mild stimulant. Besides antioxidant activity, fennel oil enhances bile secretion and is "diuretic, analgesic, carminative, antipyretic, antibacterial, and antifungal," according to a recent source. Anethole and other terpenoids inhibit spasms in muscles such as those in the intestinal tract and contribute to its reputation as a carminative and a cramp-relieving agent. Fennel was formerly a drug in the United States and was said to be used for indigestion. It has been entered into the pharmacopoeia or the official list of the medicinal plants in many countries because of its volatile oil. There are claims that fennel has a cleansing, toning effect on the skin. Fennel seed infusions are added to facial lotions and moisturizing creams. Modern herbalists use washes with fennel and other ingredients for the eyes. They also recommend a tea of "seed-like fruitlets" to stem hunger pangs. Fennel juice and fennel tea are used to wash out "weakened" or infected eyes. One authority believes "that tea made from the leaves has been shown to produce a significant reduction in arterial blood pressure without affecting the heart or respiratory rate." Some researchers have questioned whether people with an estrogen-dependent cancer (some breast cancers) should avoid fennel in large quantities until the significance of its estrogen-like activity is clarified. In rare cases, fennel can cause allergic reactions of the skin and respiratory tract. Caution is urged before self-medicating with fennel volatile oil as vomiting, seizures, and respiratory problems may result. Excessive use of fennel is believed to cause problems with the eyes. However, fennel is high in potassium, iron, and vitamin C. According to one folk remedy, if you have a cough but do not want to expectorate, make a tea from fennel seed and aniseed to suppress the cough.

Culinary Uses

The fruit, commonly called seeds, is favored in Italian sweet sausage. The foliage and stems are used in recipes, especially those for fish and shellfish. In some Indian restaurants, the seeds are often available for use after meals to prevent gas and indigestion. Chinese five-spice powder, applied to meat and poultry, often includes fennel. One may use fresh leaves in fruit salads and sweet yogurt dressings and in green salads and herb vinegars. The leaves may be used as garnishes, and one may eat the tender stems like celery. Flower heads are added to salads. Fennel seeds are used in many recipes such as chicken, duck, as well as a variety of Italian dishes. Sliced fennel bulbs are often served on antipasto platters. Fennel is said to be rich in antioxidants, and the uses of fennel are not limited to traditional fish or meat dishes. A vegetable soup in *Food & Wine* features a fennel bulb along with a healthy amount of vegetables and Parmigiano-Reggiano cheese rind.

Television and the Internet are quickly changing the ways food enthusiasts can obtain information. Recipes are readily available online from magazines, newspapers, and food blogs. Obtaining information about fennel, for example, can take only minutes and can produce recipes for a summer salad featuring grilled fennel bulbs and oranges and a recipe featuring braised chicken thighs with caramelized fennel. In addition, TV cooking shows are increasing the number of people interested in food and cooking. Viewers can watch chefs compete for money and learn about ingredients like fennel. Many times "home-trained," that is unschooled, cooks win contests, opening up interest in herbs and ingredients.

The essential oil of fennel seeds has been used for flavoring foods and liquors such as anisette. It is also used in perfume, cosmetics, pharmaceuticals, air fresheners, mouthwashes, and toothpaste (Tom's of Maine, for example). Fennel seeds have been used whole or ground as a spice in cooking to season bread, rolls, pastries, pickles, fish dishes, and sauces. For the home cook, roasting fennel seeds may eliminate a bittersweet aftertaste.

Home Gardens

When growing "common fennel," the stalks should be trimmed several times during the growing season to produce leaves for culinary use and to prevent the herb from taking over the garden. You can harvest the licorice-tasting seed heads when they are yellow-green.

When growing Florence fennel, gardeners must keep the bulbs moist and cover the bulbs to blanch them. The gardener should avoid planting fennel near dill, beans, kohlrabi, tomatoes, or cilantro. Fennel can be harmed if planted close to coriander and wormwood. According to gardening lore, fennel should be planted with several ingredients to produce a good harvest: salt, bread, and several silver coins.

You can store fennel seeds by placing them in a paper bag and closing it. After ripening in a cool, dry area, the seeds may be stored in a jar.

Fennel flowers attract beneficial insects such as parasitic wasps and tachinid flies, which prey on insects that cause damage in the garden. They also attract swallowtail butterflies, large colorful butterflies that may delight the gardener.

It has been recommended that culinary herbs just picked from the garden be placed in perforated plastic bags and placed with the top of the bags open in a refrigerator at 41°F. After an hour or so, each bag may be closed with a twist fastener available in supermarkets. The perforations prevent condensation.

Harriet Weinstein

Further Reading

Arrowsmith, Nancy. *Essential Herbal Wisdom.* Woodbury, MN: Llewellyn, 2009

Bown, Deni. *New Encyclopedia of Herbs and Their Uses.* New York: Dorling Kindersley, 2001.

De la Tour, Shatoiya. *The Herbalist's Garden.* Pownal, VT: Storey Books, 2001

Gaby, Alan R. *The Natural Pharmacy.* New York: Three Rivers Press, 2006.

Kowalchik, Claire, and William H. Hylton, eds. *Rodale's Illustrated Encyclopedia of Herbs.* Emmaus, PA: Rodale Press, 1998.

Lawton, Barbara Perry. *Parsleys, Fennels, and Queen Anne's Lace.* Portland, OR: Timber Press, 2007.

Reader's Digest Association. *The Complete Illustrated Book of Herbs.* Pleasantville, NY: 2009.

Tucker, Arthur O., and Thomas DeBaggio. *The Encyclopedia of Herbs.* Portland, OR: Timber Press, 2009.

Fern

A perennial, nonflowering, vascular plant, the fern is a member of Pteridophyte, a large division of flora. Pteridophyte contains 250 genera of some 12,000 species. Among these groups, ferns comprise 240 genera and 10,400 species, making them the dominant members of Pteridophyte. Once the chief plant on Earth, ferns have dwindled to just 2 percent of flora. The word "fern" derives from the Anglo Saxon "fearn," meaning feather because a fern leaf resembles a feather. Similarly, Pteridophyte means "feather plant," an apt appellation given the prominence of ferns in this division.

History and Economic Importance

Among the first plants to colonize the land, ferns are at least 300 million years old. At 200 million years old, *Osmanda claytonione* is the oldest extant fern and is among the most ancient plants. Ferns quickly rose to prominence in the Carboniferous period. Its frost-free tropical climate, warm inland seas, marshes, swamps, and abundant sunshine provided an ideal environment for ferns. Although they now prefer shade, they then reveled in sunlight, a fortunate circumstance because there were few trees to shade them. Among the largest trees, growing to 80 feet tall, were tree ferns. The onset of the ice ages and the evolution of flowering plants challenged the supremacy of ferns, whose numbers declined. The demise of the dinosaurs 65 million years ago opened land to recolonization by ferns and they once more enjoyed prominence among plants. The return of the ice ages imperiled ferns, making them a small but still consequential member of the plant kingdom.

Perverse as it may seem, ferns have had their greatest effect on humans in their death. Over millions of years, incomprehensible numbers of ferns lived and died during the Carboniferous period. Layer upon layer of dead ferns, packed tightly together by gravity, formed Earth's enormous reserves of coal, the fossil fuel that

Ferns (Sever180/Dreamstime.com)

powered the Industrial Revolution. It powered the generation of electricity and fired the manufacture of industrial products, notably iron and steel. Most scientists admit that coal is a dirty fuel. Its burning pollutes the air, causing smog and aggravating respiratory ailments. It releases carbon dioxide into the atmosphere, warming the planet. Scientists predict dire consequences from global warming: flooded coastlines and cities, enlarged habitats for disease-carrying mosquitoes, hurricanes, and drought. The product of ferns, coal, has an ambiguous legacy.

Long after the end of the Carboniferous period arose humans. Sometime in prehistory, the Maori of New Zealand and the indigenes of New Guinea planted ferns along the side of their homes as wind-breaks and fences. The deliberate planting of ferns implies that they were cultivated plants. Far from New Zealand and New Guinea, Europeans were curious about ferns. Medieval herbalists believed that ferns had flowers and seeds like other plants but that they were too small to be seen. People who said the right incantation could see fern flowers, medievalists believed. The discovery of these flowers, they believed, would grant their finders magical powers. Some people believed that ferns yielded tiny blue flowers, but on only one day per year, Saint John's Day (June 24). At midnight, the flowers shed seeds. Those fortunate enough to find these seeds acquired "wonder working powers" according to one writer. The person who put these seeds in his or her shoes or who ate them would become invisible. Fern seeds also, some believed, allowed people to see into the past and future and to find unknown treasures. The possessor of fern seeds, it was believed, would remain eternally young. A popular fad swept medieval Europe in which people eager to catch fern seeds spread white sheets beneath ferns on Saint John's Eve. Waving magic wands and reciting prayers, they sought to beseech ferns to put forth their seeds. Of course nothing happened, but seed seekers were apparently not discouraged, returning the next year to repeat their ritual. The most frantic seed seekers invoked demons and witches to help them.

In France the Catholic Church, aware of these incidents, banned the search for fern seeds on Saint John's Day. So widespread was the belief in fern seeds that Shakespeare mentioned them in his play *Henry IV.* Sixteenth-century British botanist Henry Lyte declared, however, that ferns seeds did not exist.

As early as 300 BCE, Greek botanist Theophrastus urged the ailing to ingest fern oil to expel worms from the body. Medieval Europeans and some Amerindians, unaware of Theophrastus's advice, nonetheless believed that ferns expelled worms. The Cherokee believed that ferns could cure rheumatism. In the 17th century, herbalist Nicholas Culpeper believed that ferns could heal "wounds and ulcers." When burned, ferns gave off smoke that repelled insects and snakes, remarked Culpeper. In 1633, British herbalist John Gerard recommended that one soak fern roots in wine to keep it from spoiling. Folk medicine retains the belief that the consumption of ferns expels worms from the stomach and intestines and cures rheumatism and ulcers. Some people also believe that the ailing should eat ferns to relieve constipation, reduce hemorrhages, and alleviate the pain of insect bites and stings. Some recommend rubbing ferns on bruises, burns, and sprains to decrease pain.

Ferns had other powers according to some. Medieval herbalists, seeing that the roots of the Bracken fern formed the letter *C*, believed that it was a symbol of Christ. The Bracken fern must therefore, they believed, protect the faithful from witches and demons. The Scots, coming to a similar conclusion, used the Bracken fern to expel evil spirits from the body. Witches and werewolves, they believed, were afraid of the Bracken fern. For this reason, the Irish named the plant the "Fern of God."

Despite this interest in ferns, Europeans were slow to cultivate them. Only in 1794 did British surgeon John Lindsay, working in Jamaica, succeed in growing ferns from spores. This achievement may have marked the first time anyone had grown ferns from spores. Lindsay sent spores to the Royal Botanic Garden in Kew for culture. That year Sir Joseph Banks reported Lindsay's discovery to a gathering of scientists in England. In 1795, Captain William Bligh brought 37 species of fern from the Caribbean to Britain. Gardeners began raising ferns from spores, and their popularity began to increase. Gardener John Shepherd gained renown by growing 53 species of fern, many of them from the tropics. In the 1830s, British physician Nathaniel B. Ward recommended the culture of ferns in hospitals to cleanse the air, supplying oxygen and removing carbon dioxide. In 1842, Ward demonstrated that it was possible to grow ferns in airtight glass cases, though others may have anticipated this finding. Ward claimed to have grown a fern, in what was called a Wardian case in his honor, for 18 years without adding water or nutrients. Collectors, finding ferns in the tropics, shipped them to Britain in Wardian cases. Household gardeners took to raising ferns in Wardian cases, though because glass was expensive the culture of ferns became an avocation of the middle and upper classes. Affluent women were prominent fern growers. They bought ferns from nurseries and collectors. Others toured the countryside, taking ferns that caught their fancy. By the mid-19th century, the demand for ferns was so great that nurseries hired collectors to pillage the countryside for ferns. So massive were these collecting efforts that in some parts of Britain ferns were in danger of extinction. Ferns had captured the attention of a public eager for something more than flowers. People came to appreciate the beauty of ferns, which in artistic renderings graced glass, china, curtains, and wallpaper. Stonecutters decorated churches and tombstones with carvings of ferns. By the 1880s, fern mania had ebbed, and the late 19th and early 20th centuries were a period of less intense interest in ferns. Since the 1960s, ferns have recouped a portion of their former popularity, and today gardeners once more covet ferns for their beauty and scientists nurture an interest in ferns for their curious method of reproduction.

Peculiar as it may seem, some people consider ferns a delicacy. In parts of the developing world, the Bracken fern is a food. Some Americans eat the Ostrich fern. Norwegians eat the fronds of *Dryopteris filiz-mas*. Gourmands have remarked that the fronds of *Equisetum arvense* taste like asparagus. The people of New Zealand, the Himalayas, Fiji, Malaysia, India, New Guinea, and Celebes all eat fern fronds. Also edible are fern rhizomes, which contain starch. Some Amerindians eat the rhizomes of *Dryopteris austrisca*. The aborigines of Queensland eat the rhizomes of *Blechnum indicum*, and the Eskimos of Alaska consume the rhizomes of *Dryopteris carthusiana*. Some people have baked the rhizomes of the Bracken fern into a low-quality bread. The people of Hawaii, Australia, New Guinea, India, New Zealand, Madagascar, and the Philippines eat the pith, baked or roasted, from the trunk of tree ferns. Stems of the genera *Morettia* and *Angiopteris* are, like rhizomes, rich in starch. The species *Nephrolepis cordifolia* bears tubers that look like small potatoes, which the people of Nepal eat. Some add fronds to boiling water, drinking the brew as one might drink tea. Europeans use the fronds of *Dryopteris fragrins* for this purpose. In the United States, *Pellaea ornithopus* is the species of choice. In India, ferns of the genus *Angiopteris* are fermented into alcohol. Taking the place of hops, the Bracken fern is used to brew beer. Despite the culinary appeal of ferns, they produce carcinogens. The Japanese who eat ferns have the world's highest rate of stomach cancer. The fact that people knowingly consume carcinogenic ferns should not be surprising given the epidemic of cigarette smoking.

In the United States, florists sell ferns in arrangements. Known as the Christmas Fern, *Polystichum acrostichoides* is a popular holiday plant. In Mexico and the United States, species of the genus *Selaginella*, known as resurrection ferns, are novelty items because the fronds roll into brown balls when the soil is dry and unfurl and green when it is wet. The aquatic ferns of the genus *Azolla* contain algae that fix nitrogen in the soil. The fern derives this nitrogen for growth, and the algae derive carbohydrates from the fern, forming a symbiotic relationship. In parts of Asia, farmers plant *Azolla* in their rice paddies to add nitrogen to the soil. At the end of the season, farmers plow under *Azolla* as green manure. In the tropics, people use the scales and hair of tree ferns to stuff pillows and mattresses. Others use ferns to make rope, baskets, hats, fish traps, and mats. Home builders use tree fern trunks to make houses. The natives of New Guinea use the trunks as struts for houses. In parts of Asia, homeowners thatch their homes with ferns. Some use the stems of ferns to scour pots and pans. In Japan, the spores of *Lycopodium clovatum* are used to polish wood.

Attributes and Cultivation

Having evolved in the warm Carboniferous period, many modern ferns retain a preference for hot, wet conditions. Many species are indigenous to the tropics and subtropics and will not tolerate frost. Most species are native to the world's rainforests. In the forest, some ferns live as epiphytes on the trunks and branches of trees, where they have access to light, the circulation of air, and humidity. Other ferns have evolved the capacity to tolerate cold. These ferns survive when covered by snow. Some ferns even tolerate dry conditions. These ferns have scales or hair on their fronds to reduce the transpiration of water. Drought-tolerant ferns become dormant in dry conditions and revive with rain. Most ferns thrive in shade. Although they tolerate sun in the morning and late afternoon, gardeners should not plant them in spots that receive midday sun. Sunlight can kill delicate species and can scorch and discolor fronds, retarding their growth. In the tropics, the winter sun may kill sensitive ferns because the concentration of ultraviolet light is high. The overcast skies of summer protect tropical ferns. In temperate locales, the winter sun is weaker and so less harmful to ferns. A few ferns dwell in full sunlight. Given that ferns arose in an environment of full sun, it seems peculiar that most have evolved a preference for shade. Because ferns may depend on a larger plant for shade, its loss of leaves prior to flowering may expose ferns to too much sun. On the other hand, these leaves serve to mulch ferns, helping retain soil moisture. Ferns need humidity. Accordingly, gardeners should plant them in groups so that the transpiration of many ferns will raise the humidity. Ferns do well in a protected area, where wind will not disperse humid air. Ferns grow best in a warm, sheltered environment and for this reason are often planted in greenhouses. Some gardeners grow ferns along a brick wall, whose dark color absorbs heat. A light-colored background, however, may reflect light onto ferns, aggravating the problem of sun damage.

Scientists term ferns cryptogams, meaning "hidden marriage," because their reproduction is not obvious. The other cryptogams are algae, mosses, and liverworts. Among the cryptogams, only ferns have a vascular system to distribute water, nutrients, and hormones. Some scientists believe that ferns evolved from algae. Originating before the advent of flowering plants, ferns have a unique method of reproduction. Ferns produce spores rather than seeds. Although one might be tempted to link the two, a seed has a complete complement of chromosomes, whereas a spore has only half a parent fern's chromosomes. Having only half the chromosomes of its parent, a spore does not develop into a mature fern. Rather, it germinates into a prothallus, a tiny plant without roots, a stem, leaves, or vascular system. Primitive in comparison to flowering plants, the prothallus has rhizoids, which, resembling roots, anchor it to the soils and absorb water and nutrients. The prothallus produces male and female gametes. The male sex organ produces antherozooides, which resemble sperm in their use of a tail to swim. The female gamete, the archeogonium, emits a chemical that attracts the antherozooides. The antherozooid that first reaches the archeogonium fertilizes the egg. The rest of the antherozooides dies. Fern reproduction is surprisingly akin to human reproduction, and in this sense humans are more like ferns than like flowering plants. Once fertilized, an egg grows into a fern. A new fern may require four months to several years to produce its first frond. Thereafter another one to two years pass before a fern produces spores. Remarkably prolific, one fern may yield 20 million spores. Because spores are viable for only a few months, the gardener who collects them must plant them quickly. A fern may also reproduce vegetatively, generating new ferns from a rhizome. Ferns that arise from a rhizome are identical to the parent. Those that arise from eggs are genetically diverse.

Ferns can grow to 11,500 feet in elevation, though botanists have discovered them as high as 14,500 feet. Able to grow at altitude, ferns have colonized the Andes Mountains, the Himalayas, and the mountains of New Guinea. Ferns have shallow roots and so cannot withstand the desiccation of the uppermost layer of soil. As is true of many plants, ferns die when their roots become dry. Ferns prefer the circulation of air because still air may impedes their ability to transpire water. Nevertheless, ferns will not withstand wind, which may break fronds and disperse humidity. Hot, dry wind may shrivel new plant growth. A cold wind may stunt growth. Near the ocean, air full of brine may cause salt burns on fronds. A few hardy species tolerate brine air. Ferns cease growth when the days shorten and nights grow cold. These ferns, dormant during winter, survive at high latitude. Some ferns are deciduous, shedding fronds when weather cools to conserve moisture. The fronds of the hardiest ferns may freeze without killing the plant.

Although one often encounters ferns in nature in a bog, they will not tolerate waterlogged soils, which have low oxygen content. Rather, ferns need well-drained soils with a large concentration of oxygen. Ferns tolerate a range of soils. Some species thrive in acidic soils. Others prefer basic soils, and still others can live in acidic, basic, or neutral soils, though as a rule ferns do not tolerate extremes of acidity and alkalinity. As do many other plants, ferns grow best in soils rich in organic matter. Ferns take root in both clay and loam, though they do not thrive in sandy soil because it has too few nutrients and does not hold water. Ferns respond well to the addition of manure and bonemeal to the soil. Gardeners may apply inorganic fertilizers to rapid growers like tree ferns. Fertilizer is best applied in spring and early summer when ferns are growing rapidly. Late application of fertilizer may impair a fern's ability to become dormant in cold weather. Where ferns will not grow because the soil is too acidic, gardeners may add calcium carbonate, limestone (which may be pure calcium carbonate), chalk, marl, or eggshells. Ferns that have been adequately fertilized may be less susceptible to pests and diseases than ferns that lack nutrients.

The contentious gardener plants ferns only after preparing the soil by digging it to a depth of 8 to 12 inches to loosen it and to ease the removal of weeds. A loose soil promotes the establishment of fern roots. For optimal growth, ferns need nitrogen, phosphorus, potassium, magnesium, calcium, sulfur, iron, manganese, boron, zinc, copper, molybdenum, chlorine, cobalt, and sodium. Ferns use nitrogen to make amino acids and to form chlorophyll. Most of the atmosphere is nitrogen, but ferns, like other plants, cannot absorb it in this form. Rather, fern roots take up nitrogen in the form of ammonium and nitrate ions. A deficiency of nitrogen stunts ferns and turns them pale or yellow. Phosphorus is necessary for respiration and photosynthesis. It promotes the growth of roots and reproductive parts. A deficiency of phosphorus stunts the growth of both plant and roots and causes fronds to be dark green. Potassium thickens cell walls and aids in the formation of chlorophyll, reproductive parts, and roots. Parts of fronds may die if a fern is deficient in potassium. Calcium aids in the formation of cell walls. It promotes cell division and the formation of protein and roots. Ferns in acidic and sandy soils may be deficient in calcium. Where calcium is deficient, fronds and roots will be small. Magnesium aids in the formation of chlorophyll. Magnesium-deficient ferns display chlorotic patterns on their fronds. Sulfur aids in the formation of chlorophyll and roots. Sulfur-deficient ferns may be pale. Manganese is essential for photosynthesis. It is often deficient in alkaline soils and superabundant in acidic soil. Deficient ferns display chlorotic patterns with green veins.

Pests, Diseases, and Ailments

Ferns are susceptible to several fungi. Fungal diseases may attack roots, rhizomes, or fronds. Warm, humid weather hastens the spread of fungi. Among the fungal diseases that afflict ferns is armillaria root rot. As the name suggests, this disease destroys the roots, interfering with the uptake of water and nutrients. Afflicted ferns appear to lack water, but watering them does not help. Large ferns are particularly vulnerable to armillaria root rot. Phytophthora root rot, a disease of soybeans, also afflicts ferns. Present in the soil, phytophthora fungi penetrate the roots, advancing to the crown. The disease progresses rapidly and is fatal if unchecked. Like armillaria root rot, phytophthora fungi impair the ability of fern roots to absorb water. Gardeners who respond by watering their ferns unwittingly aid the fungi, which grow numerous in wet soil. Poorly drained soils also harbor phytophthora fungi. Ferns in calcium-deficient soil appear to be particularly vulnerable to phytophthora root rot. Rust, a disease of grains, also infects ferns. Rust fungi cause orange blotches on fronds and in the worst cases are fatal. Weak ferns are more susceptible to rust than are vigorous plants. The gardener who wishes to preserve her ferns should destroy rust-infected plants or spray them with the fungicide oxycarboxin. Mold fungi attack ferns where the environment is too humid. They afflict ferns the first cool nights of autumn. Mold is prevalent where a lack of air circulation has allowed too much humidity to accrue. A similar affliction is greenhouse frond rot, a fungal disease that infects ferns where ventilation is nil and humidity in excess. Crown rot fungi stunt ferns and blacken fronds. Rather than kill a fern quickly, as phytophthora root rot does, crown rot lingers for years, sickening ferns. In addition to fungal diseases, bacteria infect ferns. Nematodes, a pest of ferns, may transmit bacteria to them. Aphids and plant hoppers transmit viruses to ferns. Viruses cause mosaic patterns on fronds. The species *Dryopteris erythrosara* and *Woodwardia orientalis* are especially susceptible to viral infections. Whether fungi, bacteria, or viruses, disease may manifest in spots on fronds or rotted tissue. The wilting of ferns indicates a disease of the roots. In an effort to prevent disease, gardeners should buy healthy, vigorous ferns and plant them in an area in which air circulates. Fungal disease may be combated with fungicides, though one must exercise caution because they may damage ferns. The genus *Nephrolepis* is sensitive to fungicide damage, though the species *Asphenium australasicum* is hardy enough to withstand applications of fungicide without damage.

A large number of pests attack ferns. Although ants do not bother ferns, their presence is a sinister sign because they protect aphids, scales, and mealy bugs, all of which prey on ferns. Aphids, attracted to a young fern, suck its sap. The fern aphid is among the most common pests of ferns. Fronds that have grown in misshapen patterns betray aphid damage. Several species of caterpillar and grub feed on ferns. Chewing on fronds, caterpillars and grubs are numerous in spring, summer, and autumn. Caterpillars hide on the underside of fronds, and grubs often feed on the roots. Young ferns attract caterpillars and grubs. The Florida fern caterpillar feeds on fronds at night. The caterpillar of the dyneria butterfly, native to New Guinea, Moluccas, the Aru Islands, and Queensland, also feeds on fronds at night. Active in spring and summer, the caterpillar of the light apple moth feeds on ferns at night. Active in autumn and winter, the caterpillar of the painted apple moth feeds on ferns during the day. Active at night, cutworm grubs feed on the stem of a fern at the level of the soil. Weakened ferns collapse under their own weight. Curl grubs and Japanese beetle grubs feed on roots, causing ferns to wilt. Adult Japanese beetles devour fronds. Cockroaches feed on roots, fronds, and crosiers. Crickets eat the fronds and crosiers of young ferns. Earwigs feed on roots, rhizomes, and fronds. The vine weevil devours a fern from root to frond. It is most abundant in greenhouses and potted ferns. The species *Asphenium scolopendrium* is especially vulnerable to the vine weevil. It causes ferns to wilt, a condition that is often mistaken for lack of water. Certain species of nematode eat the vine weevil grub, and the beleaguered gardener may add them to the soil. The maggot of the fungus gnat feeds on dead tissue and on rhizomes and roots. Young ferns and potted ferns are particularly vulnerable to it. Sucking sap like aphids, mealy bugs feed on greenhouse ferns. As with many other pests, they are attracted to young ferns. The snail *Helix asper*, an indigene of Europe, is a voracious feeder, attacking ferns in the subtropics and temperate locales. The fern slug is also a serious pest of ferns.

An ailment known as sweating afflicts ferns in an environment of too much humidity and too little air circulation. These conditions, we have seen, interfere with a fern's ability to transpire water. The fronds of ailing ferns blacken. In severe cases, sweating is lethal. In moderate cases, sweating weakens a fern so that it is vulnerable to pests or disease. In temperate zones, sweating is a common affliction in autumn. In the subtropics, sweating is common in wet weather. In all climates, sweating may ail greenhouse ferns. Species of the genera *Blechum*, *Doodii*, and *Pteris* are vulnerable to sweating.

Christopher Cumo

Further Reading

Cullina, William. *Native Ferns, Moss and Grasses*. Boston: Houghton Mifflin, 2008.

Frankel, Edward. *Ferns: A Natural History*. Brattleboro, VT: Stephen Greene Press, 1981.

Hoshizaki, Barbara Joe, and Robbin C. Moran. *Fern Grower's Manual*. Portland, OR: Timber Press, 2001.

Ide, Jennifer M., A. Clive Jermy, and Alison M. Paul. *Fern Horticulture: Past, Present and Future Perspectives*. Andover, U.K.: Intercept, 1992.

Jones, David L. *Encyclopedia of Ferns: An Introduction to Ferns, Their Structure, Biology, Economic Importance, Cultivation and Propagation*. Portland, OR: Timber Press, 1987.

Olson, Sue. *Encyclopedia of Garden Ferns*. Portland, OR: Timber Press, 2007.

Ranker, Tom A., and Christopher H. Haufler. *Biology and Evolution of Ferns and Lycophytes*. Cambridge: Cambridge University Press, 2008.

Rickard, Martin. *The Plantfinder's Guide to Garden Ferns*. Portland, OR: Timber Press, 2000.

Fig

A tree that produces sugary fruit, the fig (*Ficus carica*) is an ancient cultigen. The tree is ubiquitous in western Asia. Turkey is the world's leading producer. The United States ranks second. California's Central Valley is the principal region of fig culture in the United States. Other producers are Egypt, Algeria, Italy, Greece, Spain, Portugal, and southern France. Most of the harvest is dried and pressed into a paste that flavors cookies, notably the Fig Newton, and other sweets. Only 9 percent of California's harvest is sold fresh, though fresh figs fetch six to seven times the price of dried figs. Fresh figs are fragile and must be consumed soon after their purchase. Fresh figs begin to spoil after only a few hours at room temperature and must be refrigerated. Those that have begun to spoil emit an odor of fermentation. Figs have fiber, potassium, and vitamin B6. Three figs have five grams of fiber, 20 percent of the recommended daily allowance. Three fresh figs have 348 milligrams of potassium, 10 percent of the daily allowance. Three dried figs have 399 milligrams of potassium. Three fresh figs have 0.2 milligram of vitamin B6, 9 percent of the daily allowance. Some health bars, touting the benefits of the fig, contain it as an ingredient. The Latin *Ficus* is the genus name for fig. *Ficus*, the Italian *fica*, the Portuguese *figo*, the Spanish *higo*, the French *figue*, the German *Feigen*, and the Dutch *vijg* derive from the Indian *fag* or the Hebrew *feg*. The English "fig" derives from the Old English "figge" or "fegge." The Greek *erineos* means "wild fig." Sykon means "cultivated fig." Fig is rendered *tena* in Aramaic, *tin* in Arabic, *paggim* in Phoenician, *paggam* in Syrian, and *anjir* in Persian.

Religion and Mythology

An important tree in the Near East and North Africa, the fig is prominent in the Bible. According to Genesis, Adam and Eve covered themselves in fig leaves when they discovered that they were naked. The awareness came to them only after they had eaten the forbidden fruit, which some biblical commentators believe was the fig. One authority has remarked that the Genesis story echoes an earlier practice in which participants in religious rites covered themselves with fig leaves. Another authority believes that the writer of Genesis had in mind a different species of *Ficus*, in which case the fig could not have been the forbidden fruit.

The oldest certain reference to the fig in the Bible may come from Deuteronomy, which records that God gave the Hebrews a land rich in figs and other foods. King Hezekiah of Israel recommended the fig's use to treat boils. The prophet Isaiah's remark that "all the starry host will fall like . . . shriveled figs from the fig tree" may refer to the fact that unpollinated figs turn brown and fall from the tree. The prophet Jeremiah told the story of two baskets of figs placed

Fig | 417

before the Temple. One basket contained good figs that symbolized those who submitted to the will of Babylonian conqueror King Nebuchadnezzer. The seeds from these figs, Jeremiah foretold, would be planted throughout Israel. The Hebrews would know that these figs were good because they ripened early. The other basket held figs too bad to eat. Jeremiah compared them to King Zebekiah of Judah.

Jesus apparently knew that fig trees put forth their leaves late in spring because he remarked that one would know that summer was near when they yielded leaves. The Gospels record that Jesus uttered only a single curse, directing it at a barren fig tree. He had apparently been disappointed not to find any fruit on it. The tree, wounded by Jesus's words, withered. According to their religious traditions, the British ate fig pies on Fig Sunday during Lent. They observed the custom of eating figs, bread, and nutmeg on Good Friday.

The fig is important to Greek mythology. According to one myth, the chief god Zeus attacked the titans Ge and her son, Sykeus, in the War of the Titans. Fearful that Zeus's lightning bolts might strike her son, Ge turned him into a fig tree. From this account derives the belief that a fig tree protected one from lightning. One myth credited Dionysus, the god of the grapevine, with discovering the fig. An Athenian legend, however, credited goddess Demeter with this discovery. Demeter gave figs to King Phytalus for allowing her to stay in his home. Upon his death, mourners planted a fig tree, known as the Holy Fig Tree, on his grave. Legend held that a priestess could lead a wild bull to his sacrifice by first collaring him with a supple fig branch.

The Greeks told the story of the tree known as the goat fig. An oracle foretold that the Spartans would defeat the Messenians when a goat drank from the Needs River. Fearful of this prophecy, the Messenians drove away all goats, but their efforts came to naught when a goat fig that grew along the bank of the river dipped its branches into the water, drinking from it. The prophecy fulfilled, Sparta emerged victorious. According to legend, thieves stole figs from trees sacred to the gods in Attica. The citizens accused the thieves, from which derives the term "sycophant," meaning literally "to show the fig."

The Romans credited Bacchus, a god similar to Dionysus, with giving the fig to humans. Accordingly, Roman art depicted Bacchus with a crown of fig leaves. So much did he enjoy figs that Bacchus grew fat from eating them. Because of his connection to figs, the Romans offered the first figs of the season to Bacchus. At his festivals, Roman women wore garlands of dried figs. In processions, figs came behind only grapes and ahead of all other fruit.

The people of southwestern Asia, Egypt, Greece, and Italy worshipped fig trees. One ancient people, the Pharmakai, used a black fig to symbolize a man and a white fig to represent a woman. They held fertility rites to ensure the bounty of the harvest. In Asia and the Mediterranean, the fig symbolized fertility. The people of Greece and India made a phallus of fig wood. The Greeks used it in their worship of Dionysus and Indians used it in their fertility rites. Merchants in Kyoto, Japan, once sold candy made from figs and in the shape of a phallus at Shinto festivals.

Origin and Diffusion

Fossils of figs in Italy and France date to the Tertiary (65–2.6 million years ago) and the Quaternary (2.6 million years ago to the present) periods. Fossil figs were smaller than contemporary figs, evidence that humans, through selection, derived large figs. Humans first cultivated the fig in Arabia, where wild figs still grow. From Arabia, its cultivation spread to Iraq, Turkey, Transcaucasia, Armenia, Iran, and Afghanistan. The Assyrians cultivated the fig as early as 3000 BCE. About 2900 BCE, Sumerian king Urukagina emphasized the fig's medicinal value. From western Asia, birds and humans carried the fig west to the Mediterranean. The Egyptians decorated tombs and monuments with carvings of figs. First-century BCE queen Cleopatra preferred the fig to all other fruit. Legend holds that the asp that killed her had hidden in a basket of figs.

As early as the ninth century BCE, the Greeks cultivated the fig. In the ninth century, Greek poet Homer mentioned the fig once in the *Iliad* and thrice in the *Odyssey*. About 700 BCE, Greek poet Archilechus mentioned the cultivation of figs on the island of Paros. In the fifth century, Persian king Xerxes ate figs to remind him that he did not possess the Greece that had grown them. In the fifth century, Greek dramatist Aristophanes warned fig growers to guard against predaceous insects. According to Greek historian Xenophon (430–354 BCE), philosopher Socrates (469–399 BCE) mentioned the fig in a dialogue with pupil Ischomachus. In the fourth century, Greek philosopher Aristotle and his pupil Theophrastus knew of the fig. The inhabitants of Athens were known as *philosykos*, meaning "a friend of the fig." In Attica, elites and commoners ate figs.

The Romans cultivated the fig as early as the eighth century BCE, planting fig trees on the Palatine Hill. They founded the city of Tarentum, where fig trees were alone in bearing fruit. The Romans imported fig seedlings from Syria. Apparently unable to satisfy demand through domestic production, the Romans imported figs from North Africa. The Romans may have planted fig trees in Britain, though no English text referred to them until the 13th century.

By the fifth century CE, the fig had spread to the Atlantic coast of North Africa and to southern France. The Arabs were renowned as skillful fig cultivators. One source holds that Mohammed (570–632 CE), the founder of Islam, said, "If I should wish a fruit brought to Paradise, it would certainly be the fig." The Moors promoted fig culture in North Africa and Spain. One account places the fig in

Fig | 419

China in 127 CE, though another holds that China imported fig trees from Iran and India only in the seventh century. In Transcaucasia, farmers grew figs to 3,000 feet of elevation. In 812, Frankish king Charlemagne attempted to grow figs in the Netherlands. In the 12th century, Crusaders introduced the fig to Germany. In 1690, the Portuguese introduced the fig to Japan.

The first planting in the New World came in 1520, when the Spanish introduced the fig to the Caribbean. In 1526, European visitors remarked at the quality of figs on Hispaniola (now the island of Haiti and the Dominican Republic). In 1590, one European traveler noted that figs were abundant in Peru. In 1763, Greek and Minorcan immigrants planted figs in Florida. Around 1769, Spanish missionaries planted figs near San Diego, California. In 1787, statesman Thomas Jefferson, having observed the cultivation of figs in Marseilles and Toulon, France, thought it a suitable crop for slaves. U.S. president George Washington planted fig trees at Mount Vernon. According to one account, fig trees marked the spot of his birth, but when American writer Washington Irving visited the spot he found only two or three decayed trees. In the 19th century, a merchant sold what he claimed were magnolia trees to Texas residents. The specimens were really fig trees and so were known as Magnolia figs. In 1813, farmers planted figs in Hawaii. In 1880, growers planted Smyrna figs in California because of their suitability for drying. California growers made additional plantings in 1886, and in 1890 the U.S. Department of Agriculture imported 10,000 seedlings to California.

Reproduction and Harvest

The fig tree produces separate male and female flowers. Inconspicuous, they are hidden in the syconium. The cultivated fig bears only female flowers and need not be fertilized to yield fruit. The Smyrna group of fig trees and all wild figs yield more female than male flowers. A tiny wasp pollinates these trees. The female wasp lays her eggs in the flowers of a fig. The female wasps that hatch from these flowers, after mating with the males, leave a flower through a small opening at the top of a fig. As they exit, they pass a male flower, picking up pollen, which they use to pollinate a female flower. The wasps cannot linger in a fig, for the enzyme ficin dissolves those that remain too long. In the 19th century, the immigrants who brought fig trees to California were puzzled by the fact that they did not bear fruit. Only when scientists discovered the role of the wasp did they solve the problem of barren fig trees. In 1889, grower George Roeding established the first colony of wasps in California. Today, paper bags hung on fig trees supply wasps.

Laborers harvest figs by hand. They wear gloves and long sleeves because ficin irritates the skin. Because figs do not ripen at once, harvesters must inspect a tree every other day. The harvest may stretch over several months. As a rule, a fig tree bears two crops per year. The first, in late spring and early summer, is small. The main crop comes in late summer and early autumn.

Christopher Cumo

Further Reading

Condit, Ira J. *The Fig*. Waltham, MA: Chronica Botanica, 1947.

Musselman, Lytton John. *Figs, Dates, Laurel, and Myrrh: Plants of the Bible and the Quaran*. Portland, OR: Timber Press, 2007.

Parsons, Russ. *How to Pick a Peach: The Search for Flavor from Farm to Table*. New York: Houghton Mifflin, 2007.

Yeager, Selene. *The Doctors Book of Food Remedies*. New York: Rodale, 2007.

Fire Lily

Nowadays, this beautiful lily—which blooms at the height of summer and is known in English as the "fire lily" or "orange lily"—is for the most part an ornamental plant. It is still quite common in Scandinavian gardens. In the rest of Europe, however, its place has long been largely taken by other lily species or hybrids. As a cultivated plant it represents an old bio-cultural inheritance. Among Scandinavians, it brings old-fashioned gardening and idyllic rural life to mind. It is a real eye-catcher in a rural garden.

The fire lily is a bulbous perennial, and it grows to be 23 to 46 inches high. The bulb is round, with rose-tinted, white, lanceolate scales. The upper third of the stem is often hairy. The lanceolate leaves, which grow scattered, are up to 4 inches long. Bulbils often form in the upper leaf axil. Sometimes the blossoms grow alone; normally, however, they form clusters of 2 to 5 or up to 50 in a dense multi-flowered umbel. The flowers are bowl-shaped and three-and-a-half to five-and-a-half inches in diameter. The tepals are yellow-orange with brown spots and are usually darker toward the tip. The nectaries are papillous. The stamens have red pollen, and the pistils are red. The fire lily does not produce any scent. Cultivars of the fire lily do not usually produce seeds. It has not been possible, therefore, to backcross cultivars with the wild species.

Origin and History

In its wild state, this species of lily is spread widely over alpine areas in Southern and southeastern Europe: from the Pyrenees in the west, through the Alps in the middle, to Central Europe and Slovenia in the east. However, it has become very rare in many places. In various parts of Europe, it is named for Saint John (e.g., *giglio di San Giovanni* in Italian, *liri 'd San Giuan* in Piedmontese, and *Sankt Hans lilje* in Danish), because it blooms during the second half of June (Saint John's Day is June 24). In certain parts of Italy, it is named for Saint Anthony (*gigliu di 'sant Antòni*), since its blossoms come out in the vicinity of Saint Anthony's Day (June 13).

Two subspecies of the fire lily are known: the main one, *Lilium bulbiferum* ssp. *bulbiferum*; and *Lilium bulbiferum* ssp. *croceum* Chaix, often called the croceum lily or saffron lily. The former, which has a tendency to produce bulbils on the stem, has a more easterly origin (in the eastern Alps); the latter, which does not produce bulbils, originates from the southwestern and western Alps. A giant variety, *Lilium bulbiferum* var. *giganteum* Terracciano, 1906, originates from the vicinity of Vesuvius, Napoli in Italy. The stem of this variety reaches up to 71 inches.

The oldest evidence for the fire lily as a cultivated plant is from the early modern era. It appears to have been cultivated during the 16th century in Germany, where it was known as *Goldlilie* (Golden Lily). German herbals from the mid-1500s also mention it; however, this may have been a question of the wild variant, which could be found in the Alps at the time. The first evidence of its cultivation in Scandinavia is from Norway in the late 1590s. The botanist Simon Paulli included an image of it in *Flora danica* (1648); it was also mentioned in other Danish works of the period. In Sweden too, it was known during the first half of the 17th century: Johannes Franckenius, for instance, mentioned it in 1638. A record from 1658 attests to its cultivation in Uppsala. Gardening manuals from the 18th and 19th centuries in northwestern Europe make frequent mention of it. In North America, finally, it has been cultivated at least since the 1840s.

In Scandinavia, it is *Lilium bulbiferum* ssp. *bulbiferum*, which has been cultivated in particular; by contrast, *Lilium bulbiferum* ssp. *crociferum* arrived in the region in the 19th century, with the modern trade in gardening products. The latter is still found as an ornamental plant in continental gardens south of Scandinavia; the former predominates in the Nordic region. The plant runs wild easily; during the 19th century, in fact, it was regarded as a weed in the Netherlands and Germany. It seems to be an escaped alien on the Isle of Man. It is also found naturalized in eastern Canada and the state of Utah.

In Sweden and other Scandinavian countries, the fire lily has been associated—perhaps more than any other ornamental plant—with old garden plots. During the 17th and 18th centuries, it was found in palace gardens, academic gardens, and the like; in the late 18th and early 19th century, however, it spread to the garden plots of the peasantry. It quickly became very popular. It grew by the doors of crofters' cottages; with its bright blossoms, it imparted beauty to simple surroundings. A very hardy species, it can be cultivated up to the northernmost parts of Scandinavia.

Traditional Ornamental Plant

The fire lily has served as a garden plant in many parts of Europe. During the 19th century, it was still cultivated in rural home gardens in Germany, the Netherlands, Austria, Switzerland, and the Balkans (Bosnia). Today, however, it is rather unusual as an ornamental plant in those countries, although it still exists in some home gardens of Austrian alpine farmers. It was also a common garden plant in England, Scotland, and Ireland; but it is rare there today. In the Nordic region, due to its cultivation in the home gardens of crofters and peasants, the fire lily came to be associated with those segments of the population. It satisfied a growing need for beauty among the peasantry, and it was easily grown besides. Its popularity is evident not least from the many locally known folk names given to it in Sweden, Norway, and Finland.

Due to its hardiness, it can be grown far up in the north—even in such outposts as the Faroe Islands and Iceland. In Norway and Sweden, it continued to be cultivated during industrialization in the gardens kept by workers and by country folk. In some quarters, on the other hand, it has been viewed with a certain disdain over the last century; and it has not been regarded as obviously suitable—notwithstanding its abundant flowering during the summer, and its endurance in the face of tough northerly conditions—for service as an ornamental plant. The fire lily is not often found in more recent modern gardens; in older gardens, however, it has lived on in considerable measure. In the vicinity of many abandoned gardens, moreover, it has survived as a remnant or even run wild. It is still common in gardens found in the Scandinavian countryside.

It has long been difficult to procure the fire lily on the market; those wishing to cultivate it, therefore, have had to preserve their own stock of it, or to acquire it from old gardens. It is therefore mostly passed on from garden to garden. The fire lily is easily propagated by dividing the bulb's scales. Also, the bulbils are capable of producing plants if sown. In recent years, the fire lily has enjoyed a renaissance as an ornamental plant. With the increased interest in traditional or old-fashioned cultivated plants, there has been a renewed appreciation for the plant. It is also available for purchase nowadays at certain specialized nurseries in Europe and North America.

Ethnobotany and Symbolism

No other real use than as an ornamental plant in gardens has ever been ascribed to the fire lily. The bulb is edible, but it has not served traditionally as a food (although there have been occasional reports to that effect from Italy). Children have found it amusing to fool people into sniffing the blossom. If one sticks one's nose far enough into the flower, it turns yellow from the pollen. This prank is known among children both in Scandinavia and in Central Europe (the folk names *snusgubbe* in Swedish, *gulnæser* in Danish, and *Nasenbeschiesser* in German all refer to its capacity to stain the nose). In the plant's original territories in the Alps, it has found some uses in its wild form in traditional medicine and in the production of surrogate coffee. In Italy, the fresh bulbs were used as poultices to treat sores, burns, and several other skin diseases. The bulb has also been carried as a sort of love charm.

In certain parts of Austria, the fire lily was known formerly as *Donnerrosen*, "thunder rose" (in Carinthia), and *Donnerblum*, "thunder flower" (in the Tyrol); it was believed that it drew lightning to itself and therefore should not be brought indoors. This superstition may have arisen from the fact that the intense orange coloring of the blossom calls to mind fire and lightning.

The fire lily has long been recognized as an emblem of the Orange Order in Northern Ireland. It was employed on July 12 annually by this Protestant organization probably for no other reason than that it was the only orange bloom available (it was for that reason probably not grown by Roman Catholic families). Today, however, it would appear to be modern hybrids, such as *Lilium X hollandicum*, that serve in such a manner. The old species is scarcely available in Great Britain or Ireland nowadays, although it certainly lives on in many old gardens. The fire lily has also been used as the basis for many modern lily hybrids.

Ingvar Svanberg

Further Reading

Bos, Fred. "*Lilium bulbiferum subsp. croceum* in the Netherlands and Northern Germany." *Curtis's Botanical Magazine* 10 (1993): 190–97.

McRae, Edward A. *Lilies: A Guide for Growers and Collectors*. Portland, OR: Timber Press, 1998.

Svanberg, Ingvar. "Brandgul lilja (*Lilium bulbiferum*) i allmogens trädgårdar." *Uppland: årsbok* (2004): 99–116.

Veli-Pekka Pelkonen, Anne Niittyvuopio, Anna Maria Pirttilä, Kari Laine, and Anja Hohtola. "Phylogenetic Background of Orange Lily (*Lilium bulbiferum* s.l.) Cultivars from a Genetically Isolated Environment." *Plant Biology* 9 (2007): 534–40.

Flax

An annual, versatile flax (*Linum usitatissimum*) supplies fiber, seed, and inside the seed, oil. The genus *Linum* derives from the Celtic *lin*, meaning "thread," a probable reference to flax fiber. The species name *usitatissimum* derives from the Latin for "most useful," a reference to the many uses of flax. A member of the Linaceae family, flax is of two types: fiber or textile flax and linseed, oilseed, or seed flax. No cultivar yields the highest-quality fiber, oil, and seed. Rather, one class of flax cultivar yields quality fiber, and another class yields quality oil and seed. The fiber is spun into linen. The oil is known as linseed oil and has several uses.

Origin and History

Flax is an ancient crop. It may have originated in India, which has the largest number of wild species. Although the earliest remains of flax, dating to 8000 BCE in Syria, Turkey, and Iran, were probably from wild plants, its cultivation might date to 7000 BCE, making it among the first plants to have been domesticated. Humans first cultivated flax in the valleys of the Tigris and Euphrates rivers in Iraq. Before 6000 BCE, the presence of large flax seeds in Syria and Iraq evidence cultivation and selection. As early as 6000 BCE, the people near the Dead Sea in Syria made linen garments. About 5000 BCE, this practice spread to Egypt and Judea. By 4000 BCE, the Swiss were making linen clothes. These early examples suggest that humans first cultivated flax for fiber and only second for oil and seed, though as early as 3000 BCE the Chinese extracted oil from flax seeds. By 1400 BCE, the Egyptians used linseed oil for embalming and linen for wrapping mummies. By 1000 BCE, the people of Jordan and Greece were making bread from flax seeds.

Flax flowers (Elena Elisseeva/Dreamstime.com)

The Ethiopians made flax into stew, porridge, and beverages. In the Iron Age (900 to 400 BCE), Scandinavians spun flax fibers into linen. The Abyssinians of the southern Nile River used flax for oil and the seed for cereal and bread. They grew short cultivars that did not lodge and that bore large seeds. By 500 BCE, the use of flax was common as a laxative and poultice. Around this time, the Phoenicians, trading flax from Egypt, introduced the plant to Flanders and Britain. The Greeks and Romans used flax as fiber, food, and medicine. They made a dish of flaxseed, barley, spices, and salt and made wheat-flax bread. First-century CE Roman encyclopedist Pliny the Elder remarked that flax had so many uses, though he noted that it exhausted the soil. So greatly did it impoverish the soil that the ancients grew flax on the same land only every seventh year.

Around 800 CE, Frankish king Charlemagne ordered farmers to grow flax. By 1000, Flanders had emerged as the center of the linen trade. Around 1600, the French introduced flax into North America.

Linen

Grown in temperate locales and the subtropics, flax is made into cloth, canvas, yarn, carpet, paper, and insulation. Farmers who wish to grow flax for fiber cultivate tall varieties that yield long fibers. These varieties grow between 31.5 and 47.25 inches tall. Farmers plant these cultivars densely to deter them from forming multiple branches and from producing numerous seeds. Densely planted flax expends its energy in elongating its stem rather than in branching or reproducing. The long fibers yield linen, and the short ones are processed into paper. Today, fiber flax is harvested about 100 days after planting. The process of separating the fiber from the rest of the stem is known as retting and is a simple process. To obtain the longest fiber the plant is uprooted rather than cut. The ancients laid flax stalks on the ground or on a rooftop and kept them moist. The morning dew sufficed to moisten flax stalks. Alternatively, the Egyptians submerged them in the Nile River, and the Romans weighted them down in tanks of water. The moisture encouraged the growth of microbes, which dissolved the gum and pectin holding the fibers together. Once microbes had done their work, the ancients peeled off the fibers from the rest of the stalk for spinning into linen. Flax is an ideal fabric for warm climates because the fiber carries sweat away from the body, aiding evaporation.

Depending on the type of fiber they sought, the Egyptians harvested flax in three stages. The first occurred before the plant flowered. These immature stalks yielded the finest, softest fiber, from which the Egyptians made the clothes of the nobility. The second and largest harvest occurred 30 days after flowering, when the fiber was thicker and less soft. Fibers from this harvest made the clothes of commoners. The final harvest occurred several weeks after the second harvest and yielded the coarsest fiber, suitable for making rope and mats. The final harvest yielded seeds for planting next season.

So important was flax to the Egyptians that they believed that the gods had created it for their own use. The Egyptians spun flax fibers into clothes, towels, bed sheets, sails, fishing nets, rope, and funereal textiles. The pharaohs appointed a director of the king's flax to supervise production. They established flax mills in Thebes, Akhmim, and Memphis. As early as 1900 BCE, the Egyptians dyed linen with red and yellow iron oxide. By 1500 BCE, they dyed linen with indigo. The linen trade was lucrative enough to attract the Phoenicians as the principal carriers, supplying the rest of the Mediterranean with Egyptian flax.

So strong was flax fiber that Persian king Xerxes (520–465 BCE), fifth-century BCE Greek historian Herodotus reported, bought some from the Phoenicians to build a bridge across the Hellespont, presumably to invade Greece in the fifth century BCE. The Romans established linen mills in France and Britain. In the 18th century, Scotland and Ireland erected linen factories. Canadians and Americans made a fabric of linen and wool known as linsey-woolsey or winsey. It remained popular until the end of the U.S. Civil War. Today, Russia, Ukraine, Belarus, Canada, the United States, India, China, Argentina, France, Belgium, Britain, Germany, Spain, Egypt, Ethiopia, the Netherlands, Poland, Romania, the Czech Republic, Lithuania, Italy, Mexico, Australia, Argentina, and Sweden grow flax for fiber. In the United States, North Dakota, South Dakota, Minnesota, and Montana are the principal producers. China grows flax for domestic use. The North and Northwest are the principal regions of flax culture. Cultivation has declined in Sweden, where fungi limit yields. Sweden's cool, wet springs hasten the spread of fungi. Production has also diminished in Poland, where the yield dropped from 312,000 tons on 245,000 acres in 1970 to 100,000 tons on 70,000 acres in 1987. Although the United Kingdom produces flax, the yield does not meet demand. To satisfy demand Britain imports 75 percent of its linen from Belgium, the Netherlands, and Egypt.

Medicinal Use, Food, and Oil

Flaxseed is 35–45 percent oil, 22 percent protein, 12 percent fiber, and 10 percent mucilage. Oilseed flax, shorter than fiber flax, grows to a height of 23.5 to 31.5 inches. Farmers plant linseed flax farther apart than fiber flax to encourage linseed flax to produce abundant flowers and seeds. Today, farmers harvest oilseed flax 150 days after planting. Linseed oil is used in the manufacture of paint, stain, varnish, putty, concrete preservatives, glue, ink, and soap. Linseed cake feeds livestock.

The ancients appreciated the value of flax as medicine. Greek physician Hippocrates (460–377 BCE) recommended the consumption of flax seeds as a remedy for intestinal pain. Charlemagne, perhaps aware of Hippocrates's pronouncements, recommended flaxseed as treatment for gastrointestinal trouble. Recent research has heightened awareness of flax's benefits. A study at the University of Toronto has demonstrated that the consumption of flaxseed reduces cholesterol. The *British Journal of Nutrition* reports that four weeks' flaxseed in the diet reduced glucose in the blood 27 percent and cholesterol 7 percent. Another study documents the efficacy of flaxseed in preventing cancer cells from replicating. Others have underscored the effectiveness of flax in alleviating constipation, stomach trouble, high blood pressure, heart disease, and heartburn. Flaxseed contains 75 to 800 times more lignan than wheat bran, oats, millet, rye, soybean, and other legumes. Lignan may prevent heart disease, diabetes, high blood pressure, asthma, and cancers of the breast, prostate, uterus, and colon. Flaxseed helps bacteria reestablish themselves in the intestines after a course of antibiotics. According to one authority, the consumption of flaxseed improves the immune system. Flax is rich in insoluble and soluble fiber. Two-thirds of flax's fiber is insoluble. Aware of these benefits, the Food and Drug Administration has championed flaxseed "as a food for disease prevention."

Flax merits the attention of medical practitioners in part because it contains omega 3 and omega 6 fatty acids, essential lipids that the body needs but that it cannot manufacture on its own. Flax grown in cold climates produces more omega 3 than flax grown in warm climates. Flax grown in warm climates has more omega 6. Linseed oil is 48–64 percent omega 3, the richest plant source of this lipid; 16–34 percent is omega 6; and the rest is omega 9, the fat that is in olive oil. Flaxseed has a higher proportion of these fatty acids than the oil from any other plant. Today, stockmen feed flaxseed to livestock to increase the amount of omega 3 in their tissues, which, when consumed, benefits humans with the accumulation of this fatty acid. Flax oil helps the body metabolize fat. Some people who have ingested flax oil as part of their diet have lost weight. Linseed oil has been used to fry food, illuminate lamps, and preserve paint and flooring. Linseed oil has been the principal oil in many farming communities in China since antiquity. In Europe and North America, farmers grow flax for oil where they cannot grow peanut or olive. So important was linseed oil that the Egyptians anointed themselves with it before they left home. They welcomed guests into the home by anointing them with linseed oil. The Egyptians anointed the statues of their gods with linseed oil. The priests, apparently operating on the principle that if a little oil was good a lot was better, poured linseed oil on their heads. They Egyptians anointed the dead with linseed oil.

Since antiquity, Germans have eaten flax-rye bread. The Flax Council of Canada reports that Germans, as an aggregate, consume more than tons of flaxseed per year in bread and cereal. Some people eat flaxseed in soup and sauce and with vegetables and grain. Today, bakers add flaxseed to bread, bagels, muffins, cookies, buns, and dinner rolls. It is also added to nutrition bars.

Flaxseed is of two types: golden and brown. Golden flax seeds are large, soft, and flavorful. Golden flaxseed is expensive because the yield is low. Golden flax seeds have more protein and less oil than brown flax seeds and are eaten in cereal and bread. Brown flax seeds are small, hard, and less flavorful and have high oil content. Flaxseed has vitamins A, B1, B2, C, D, and E.

Biology, Cultivation, and Science

Flax flowers have blue, white, and red petals. Each flower, having both anthers and stigma, is perfect. Self-fertile, these flowers self-pollinate in most cases, though insects visit them, taking pollen to other flowers, thereby cross-pollinating them. Once fertilized the seeds are, we have seen, either golden or brown. The plant is indeterminate, growing throughout its life. Fax grows well in soil with organic matter. The soil should be loose and well draining. The plant needs 70 to 100 days to mature and prefers humidity and overcast skies. Although planting density varies according to whether the plant will be used for fiber or for oil and seeds, it averages 44 pounds of seeds per acre. India grows flax for both fiber and oil. China cultivates flax in the Loess Plateau, the grassland, the Yellow River valley, Xinjiang, and Quighai Highlands.

In the 17th century, British king Charles I advised the governor of Virginia to encourage farmers to plant flax. That century German immigrants may have been the first to cultivate flax in Pennsylvania. Each family raised two acres of flax to meet its own needs. Colonists were careful to choose fertile, well-drained soil. They avoided the extremes of clay and sand. The farmer was blessed who could count on rainfall evenly distributed throughout the year.

The yield per acre depends on the progress of science and the development of new cultivars. In 2003, Russia yielded hundreds of pounds of fiber and seeds per acre. The cultivars Alexin, A-93, and Lenok have shattered these figures, yielding thousands of pounds of fiber and seeds per acre. The Agriculture and Agri-Food Canada and the Crop Development Center at the University of Saskatchewan breed new varieties. In the United States, North Dakota State University is the leading flax breeder. Belgium grows Regina and Belinks varieties on the coast and Arianne, Natasja, and Viking inland. One authority recommends the rotation of flax with other crops to minimize pathogens and insects. In Russia, farmers rotate flax with potato, grain, and clover. Because grains are heavy feeders, the farmer should apply nitrogen, phosphorus, and potassium to the soil when flax follows them. Flax is less successful when it follows potato because the potato demands large amounts of nitrogen, whose residue causes flax to grow tall, leaving it susceptible to lodging and lowering fiber quality. In North America, farmers rotate flax with wheat, barley, corn, or a legume. Flax does not yield well when it follows potato, sugar beet, or canola. The benefits of rotation are so compelling that flax monoculture is uncommon in North America. Indian farmers rotate flax with corn, sorghum, millet, peanut, cowpea, chickpea, lentil, and safflower. The Chinese rotate flax with millet, barley, wheat, and potato. In Russia, the soil should have 15 milligrams of phosphorus and potassium per one 100 grams of soil. Where zinc is deficient, the farmer should spray a solution with 500 grams of zinc sulfate per hectare when seedlings emerge. In North America, oilseed flax responds well to nitrogen. One authority recommends the addition of 30 to 70 pounds of nitrogen per acre and 13 to 26 pounds of phosphorus per acre to Canadian soils. In China and India, farmers often plant flax on marginal land, rarely with adequate fertilizer. Canadians plant flax in mid-May and Russians in May. In India, farmers plant flax after the monsoon, usually in October or November. Farmers in Kashmir, however, plant in February or March. Argentines plant flax between May 15 and July 1; the later date holds for Buenos Aires in the north and Santa Fe in the south.

Christopher Cumo

Further Reading

Bloomfield, Barbara, Judy Brown, and Siegfried Gursche. *Flax: The Super Food!* Summertown, TN: Book, 2000.

Heinrich, Linda. *The Magic of Linen: Flax Seed to Woven Cloth.* Victoria, Canada: Orca, 1992.

Muir, Alister D., and Neil D. Westcott. *Flax: The Genus Linum.* London: Routledge, 2003.

Forget-Me-Not

In the family Boraginaceae, the forget-me-not is a perennial ornamental in the genera *Myosotis* and *Eritrichium*. Myosotis has some 50 species. Flowers, having five petals each, may be blue, white, or pink. Stems and leaves have hairs.

Folklore, Attributes, and Cultivation

Legend holds that in the Middle Ages a knight and his lover walked along the bank of a river. The knight held a bouquet of flowers. During their excursion he stumbled. The knight fell into the water and, weighed down by his armor, drowned. Before perishing, he tossed the flowers to his beloved, telling her to "forget me not." The desire to be remembered by one's lover has led to the designation of November 10 as Forget Me Not Day. On this day, people connect with family and friends. To give someone a forget-me-not is a declaration of friendship or love.

Possibly because of its reputation as the flower of love and friendship, Alaska in 1949 named the alpine forget-me-not (*Myosotis alpestris*) the state flower. Found in meadows, the ornamental is 5 to 12 inches tall. Petals, one-quarter to one-third of an inch wide, are blue. The flower has a yellow center. The alpine forget-me-not blooms between late June and late July. Alaska is also home to the mountain forget-me-not (*Eritrichium aretioda*) and the splendid forget-me-not (*Eritrichium splendens*).

Also popular is the species *Myosotis sylvatica*, which is diminutive at less than 12 inches tall. Like *Myosotis alpestris*, *Myosotis sylvatica* has blue flowers with a yellow center. Planted from seeds, *Myosotis sylvatica* blooms in the second year. It is native to Europe and Asia and may be grown throughout the United States. It needs fertile, moist soil, though some species tolerate infertile soil. It does well in full sun and well as shade, though many species prefer shade. In the wild Myosotis sylvatica grows near streams and in wet woodlands.

May species of forget-me-not are native to New Zealand. European indigenes have spread to Asia and the Americas. One may plant forget-me-not indoors a few weeks before the last frost, transplanting them in the garden after the last frost. Alternatively, one may sow seeds directly in the garden 0.125 inch deep. Some gardeners leave little space between seeds because forget-me-not grows well when crowded. Others space seeds 4 or 5 inches apart, thinning seedlings to 10 inches distant. Forget-me-not benefits from the addition of compost to the soil. The gardener may fertilize the ornamental once or twice during the growing season. One may plant forget-me-not in large numbers for a showy effect. Forget me not is suitable as ground cover beneath tall plants and trees. Treated as an annual, forget-me-not should be removed in late summer with the intentions of sowing new specimens next spring. Treated as a perennial, forget-me-not may be mulched in autumn to permit it to overwinter.

Christopher Cumo

Further Reading

Alaska State Flower. http://www.50states.com/flower/alaska.htm (accessed 22 June 2011).

Forget Me Not. http://www.theflowerexpert.com/content/growingflowers/flowersand seasons/forget-me-not (accessed 22 June 2011).

How to Grow Forget-Me-Not Flowers. http://www.gardenersnet.com/flower/fmn.htm (accessed 2 June 2011).

Wildflower Information.org. http://www.wildflowerinformation.org (accessed 22 June 2011).